# Office

## *Skills*

### THIRD EDITION

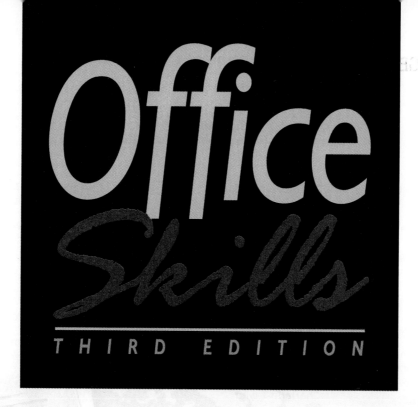

# Office Skills

## Skills

### THIRD EDITION

**Charles Barrett**
Adjunct Business Instructor
Skyline College
San Bruno, California

**Grady Kimbrell**
Educational Consultant
Santa Barbara, California

**Pattie Odgers, Ed.D.**
Coconino Community College
Flagstaff, Arizona

THOMSON
SOUTH-WESTERN

Australia · Canada · Mexico · Singapore · Spain · United Kingdom · United States

**THOMSON**

**SOUTH-WESTERN**

*Office Skills*

By Charles Barrett, Grady Kimbrell, and Pattie Odgers

**Vice President/Editor-in-Chief:**
Jack Calhoun

**Vice President/Executive Publisher:**
Dave Shaut

**Team Leader:**
Karen Schmohe

**Acquisitions Editor:**
Joseph Vocca

**Consulting Editor**
Mary Lea Ginn

**Project Manager:**
Dr. Inell Bolls

**Production Editor:**
Carol Spencer

**Production Manager:**
Tricia Boies

**Executive Marketing Manager:**
Carol Volz

**Marketing Manager:**
Mike Cloran, Nancy Long

**Marketing Coordinator:**
Cira Brown

**Manufacturing Manager:**
Charlene Taylor

**Design Project Manager:**
Stacy Jenkins Shirley

**Cover and Internal Design:**
Lou Ann Thesing

**Compositor:**
Lachina Publishing Services

**Printer:**
Quebecor World/Versailles

**Rights and Permissions Manager:**
Linda Ellis

For more information, contact South-Western
5191 Natorp Boulevard
Mason, OH 45040
Or, visit our Internet site at www.swlearning.com.

For permission to use material from this text or product, contact us by
Phone: 1-800-730-2214,
Fax: 1-800-730-2215, or
www.thomsonrights.com.

The names of all companies or products mentioned herein are used for identification purposes only and may be trademarks or registered trademarks of their respective owners. South-Western disclaims any affiliation, association, connection with, sponsorship, or endorsement by such owners.

# Expect More From South-Western... And Get It!

**Business Skills Exercises 3E** provides realistic experiences for improving the skills required for entry-level business employment. Coverage includes spelling, vocabulary, filing, telephoning, and completing forms.
Text: 0-538-69481-5

**Alphabetic Indexing 6E** features exercises and applications using ARMA filing standards, with an introduction to subject, numeric, and geographic filing methods.
Text: 0-538-66926-8

**Business Records Control 8E** introduces the comprehensive field of records management, with emphasis on ARMA alphabetic indexing rules and procedures.
Text: 0-538-69340-1

**Office Filing Procedures 8E** is an envelope simulation with 15 business record control jobs that provide hands-on activities to prepare for the world of work.
Envelope Simulation: 0-538-69330-4

**Simplifile 5E** is a self-contained box simulation that can be used to provide additional filing experience using realistic source documents.
Box Simulation: 0-538-69327-4

**Calculators—Printing and Display 3E** is designed to teach the ten-key touch method of operating print, display-print, or display calculators.
Text: 0-538-68247-7

**Calculator Simulation 5E** is an envelope simulation that covers a variety of practical uses for an electronic display calculator, printing calculator, or combination display/printing calculator.
Envelope Simulation Complete Course: 0-538-68946-3;
Envelope Simulation Short Course: 0-538-68948-X

**Calculator Applications for Business 3E** teaches how to manage time, become familiar with business forms, develop accuracy in machine operation, expand and refine math skills, and explore career opportunities.
Text: 0-538-69799-7

**Internet Office Projects** is a project-based approach to using the Internet as a research tool. Each project requires students to use the Internet to accomplish realistic tasks such as searching for jobs, planning vacation and business travel, retrieving investment and financial information, marketing a business, and designing web pages.
Text: 0-538-72186-3

**CyberStopMedia.com** is a non-software-specific integrated applications simulation. As employees of a cyber business that sells CDs and DVDs, students use intermediate to advanced word processing, voice technology, spreadsheet, database, desktop publishing, and telecommunications skills to complete their tasks.
Text/CD Package (data files on CD are Windows only): 0-538-72439-0

THOMSON
SOUTH-WESTERN

**Join us on the Internet at www.swep.com**

# Contents in Brief

# Contents

The development of *Office Skills* resulted from the experiences of one of the authors, who spent several summers as a contract employee in a wide variety of offices. These experiences, combined with consultations with many of the most knowledgeable people in office employment, showed clearly that changes in the business office curriculum were needed to prepare students for the modern office.

*Office Skills* provides practical, up-to-date information that will prepare students for working in offices. Students will study information processing, telephone procedures and filing, basic communication and math skills, and decision making and problem solving. The emphasis is on practical applications—everyday skills and knowledge needed to be successful. Topics discussed include extensive information on effective use of computers and software programs, telephone equipment, and other office technology that includes computer networking concepts and telecommunications practices.

*Office Skills* also focuses on attitudes and human relationships, emphasizing that office success depends on "people skills" as much as on functional skills. These soft skills include understanding the importance of teamwork and the value of self-confidence. Because many office workers will work for more than one boss, students are also provided information on how to prioritize their work and satisfy their bosses. Finally, career information and employability skills introduce students to the vast array of job opportunities and the most effective methods for pursuing those opportunities.

The authors have worked to make *Office Skills* interesting, as well as informative. In addition to using an easy-to-understand, lively, conversational writing style, they have developed an abundance of high-interest features to capture and hold students' attention.

- Each chapter of *Office Skills* opens with "Before You Begin" questions to help spark student interest. These questions are repeated as "Before You Leave" questions at the end of the chapter so that students can see how their knowledge and opinions have changed as a result of studying the chapter.

- Special features in each chapter, such as "Making Office Decisions," "What's Your Attitude?", "Human Relations," and "Ethics on the Job," emphasize the importance of these topics through the use of realistic scenarios.

- Perspectives of managers in major corporations are provided in the "Industry Focus" features.

- The new "Technology in the Office" feature introduces students to some of the latest technology, technology jobs, and technology-related information.

- Practical suggestions are provided in the marginal "Tips."

- In "Large Office/Small Office", the tasks and environments in large and small offices are compared, giving students help in evaluating their personal career interests and objectives.

- A comprehensive section of end-of-chapter study aids concludes each chapter.
- An ongoing "Career Portfolio" project at the end of each part of the text provides an interesting approach to word processing practice and reinforcement.
- A Reference Manual and a Glossary are included in the appendix.

The authors have also developed an extensive package of supplementary materials to help you teach with *Office Skills*.

Supplements to the text include the following:

- Instructor's Annotated Edition
- Instructor's Resource Guide
      Chapter Tests
      Transparency Masters
      Pretest and Posttest
      Final Exam
      Answers to Chapter Tests
      Answers to Student Activity Workbook
- Instructor's Resource CD:
      Computer Applications Supplement with Student Data Files
      PowerPoint® Slides
      Instructor's Manual for student text
- Student Activity Workbook
- ExamView Pro Electronic Testing Program

Office Skills contains an abundance of practical information, high-interest features and study material in both the text and the supplements. The authors believe that this approach will ensure content comprehension and thoroughly prepare students to enter the job market and advance successfully toward their ultimate career goals.

The authors extend special thanks to the following instructors/consultants for their valuable comments and suggestions throughout the development of this textbook.

**Joan Adamski**
DeSoto High School
DeSoto, Texas

**Gloria Ballard**
La Porte High School
La Porte, Indiana

**Diane Best**
North Gaston High School
Dallas, North Carolina

**Judy Bush**
North Dallas High School
Dallas, Texas

**Debbe Dubey**
Wylie Grove High School
Beverly Hills, Michigan

**Kathryn Glisson**
Harris County High School
Hamilton, Georgia

**Dawn Grooms**
Harris County High School
Hamilton, Georgia

**Cecelia Luksa Hartney**
Miami Palmetto High School
Miami, Florida

**Doris Horton**
Sterling Heights High School
Sterling Heights, Michigan

**Ronald Katzer**
Alexander Hamilton High School
Milwaukee, Wisconsin

**Joe Komaromy**
Dundee Crown High School
Carpenterville, Illinois

**Trudie A. Marks-Dooley**
Kalamazoo Central High School
Kalamazoo, Michigan

**Delores Martin**
Lakewood High School
Lakewood, Ohio

**Wendy McKeever**
Chambersburg High School
Chambersburg, Pennsylvania

**Jim McMahon**
James Madison High
School
Milwaukee, Wisconsin

**Toni Ellen Norton**
Lake Mary High School
Lake Mary, Florida

**Glenna J. Pyzik**
Morton East High School
Cicero, Illinois

**Kathryn Scott**
Nacogdoches High School
Nacogdoches, Texas

# About the Authors

**Charles Barrett** was a business teacher with the San Mateo County Schools for over thirty years. He is currently an adjunct professor at Skyline College, San Bruno, California. Through Skyline College, Mr. Barrett trains CalWorks clients in basic computer skills so that they are better equipped to make the transition from unemployment to the work world. He has been an active member of the California Business Education Association, which also includes serving as Bay Section President and statewide committee chairs, throughout his career.

In addition to his teaching experience, Mr. Barrett spent over fourteen years as a contract employee with Phase Two Strategies Public Relations firm. He has previously served as a teacher-trainer for the California State Department of Education and conducted business writing workshops for industry personnel.

Mr. Barrett earned a Bachelor of Science in Business Administration degree from Stonehill College and a Master of Business Education degree from San Francisco State University.

**Grady Kimbrell** has been involved in a business and career education more than twenty-five years. He began as a business education teacher in Kansas and California, supervising students who were part of a school-sponsored work-experience program. Later he served as District Coordinator for Work-Experience Education in Santa Barbara, California.

An interest in research and computers led to Mr. Kimbrell serving as Director of Research in Santa Barbara Schools. This experience in turn, led to a variety of consultancy opportunities, both in schools and private businesses.

Kimbrell's first business and career publications were motivated by the apparent lack of realistic goals voiced by students in California schools. Those early efforts were well received and provided encouragement for the developing new programs and more than a dozen books dealing with business and career education.

Mr. Kimbrell holds degrees in business administration, educational psychology, and business education.

**Dr. Pattie Odgers** is a product of the worlds of both business and education. She is Past President of Arizona Business Education Association (ABEA), and is a long-standing member of NBEA and WBITE. Dr. Odgers has taught a variety of courses in computer systems and applications, office and personnel management, and office skills to high school, community college, and university students in Arizona and overseas in West Berlin and Stuttgart, Germany.

Having served as Associate Dean of Instruction at Coconino Community College in Flagstaff for its first two years of operation, Dr. Odgers returned to the classroom and is currently teaching computers to nearly 150 students each semester. Her business experience has progressed through a wide range of positions, from student secretary while in college

to educational services representative and manager for IBM®, to sales representative for both IBM and Papermate/Gillette® Corporations, and now to operating a successful computer consulting and training business that serves Northern Arizona.

In addition to being a nationally recognized speaker in workplace skills and adult education, Dr. Odgers has authored seven textbooks and published numerous articles in business education journals over the years.

Dr. Odgers received her Bachelor's and Master's degrees from Arizona State University and her Doctorate from Northern Arizona University.

# PART I

# Your Place in the Modern Office

# chapter 1

## The Office Environment

### objectives

*After completing this chapter, you will be able to do the following:*

1. Describe an office environment.
2. Describe how partitions divide work areas in an office.
3. Describe an office employee's workstation.
4. List adjustments that can be made to a workstation to make it more comfortable for an employee's size.
5. List adjustments that can be made to eliminate glare on a computer screen.
6. List suggestions for relieving the stress of sitting too long at a computer.
7. Explain the flow of work in an office environment.
8. List two examples of the organizational makeup of an office environment.
9. List hazards to office safety and preventive measures for each.
10. List examples of reasonable accommodations employers have made to comply with the Americans with Disabilities Act.

### New Office Terms

- ergonomics
- modular design
- office workflow
- organizational makeup
- partitions
- safety hazard
- workstations

# before you begin...

**Answer the following questions to the best of your ability:**

**1.** How does an office environment, including an employee's workstation, look?

**2.** What are four office safety hazards? Give examples of ways to avoid them.

Anne is a student in an office careers program in the Midwest. Someday she wants to work as an office support employee for a large company. Anne understands the clerical tasks that are done in an office, but she has no knowledge of what an office looks like. Does it look like her classroom? Does it look like the school office? Does it look like the local copy center?

Anne's teacher gave her the names and telephone numbers of three former students who are currently office workers. Anne made appointments to visit each person at his or her office.

Anne visited Ivan, who works for a food processing company. Ivan gathers sales figures for the marketing department. Anne also visited Sylvia, who works in the office of a bank. Sylvia processes time sheets for the payroll department. Finally, Anne visited Darrell, who works part-time for a computer parts manufacturer. Darrell uses a PC to merge and save letters for the office services department.

©Ryan McVay/PhotoDisc

Large areas may be divided into many workstations with partitions of varying heights, depending on the need for employee interaction.

## Technology in the Office | ENCRYPTION

How private is your e-mail? When you send an e-mail message to someone at work, it is not private. It is stored on a disk, and most companies regularly back up their disks. If someone wants to read your e-mail, they may do so very easily—unless you encrypt it. Encrypting is encoding, or writing in code. Only the intended recipient will be able to read your encrypted message.

The usual rule on e-mail is to *not send anything you would not want posted by the water cooler.* However, newer e-mail systems do make use of encryption that can protect your privacy from individuals in cyberspace who would like to read your mail. The most popular programs for encrypting mail include S/MIME, PEM (privacy-enhanced mail), and PGP (pretty good privacy). PGP, at the time of this writing, is perhaps the most popular encryption software in the United States. ■

At each company, Anne was able to tour the entire facility. She realized that although the companies handled different products, the offices were similar.

# Office Design

The three offices Anne visited were all cheerfully decorated with brightly painted walls and matching carpeted floors. Soft colors and textures (wood and fabric) enhanced their tasteful quality. The office spaces appeared to be comfortable, yet efficiently planned to promote productivity.

Many executives had private offices. However, the office support employees' work areas were divided by carpeted partitions that averaged approximately five to six feet tall.

**Partitions** are panels used to separate or divide a large area into smaller work areas. Research by the National Office Products Association has shown that in some offices, how tall the partitions stand depends on the work done. For example, a marketing department may have three-foot-high partitions, a recreation area may have four-foot-high partitions, work areas of lower-level managers may have five- to six-foot-high partitions, and work areas of executives may have floor-to-ceiling partitions (walls).

In some work areas, employees share space so that they may perform as part of a team and share job functions. In these situations, partitions are low and serve merely as connections for furniture additions, not as walls separating employees. This type of design provides a more open environment for employee interaction. It also accommodates computer systems, which have become an important part of an office environment. Employees in this type of work area frequently share records, equipment, and information.

# Workstations

Years ago, office employees worked at desks, and some still do. Today, most office employees work at workstations. **Workstations** are areas that are similar to desks except that they are larger and contain more electronic

equipment. In many offices, partitions separate the workstations, providing for more privacy.

Many workstations in the offices Anne visited contained a personal computer and a multifunction telephone. They also contained shelves and storage space for paper, binders, manuals, pens, pencils, books, printouts, and computer disks. Near the workstations were computer printers that were shared by two or more employees. Anne was told that in some offices, employees also shared electronic typewriters for preparing office forms.

Workstations made from modular units may be taken apart, rearranged, and reassembled as office needs change.

**FIGURE 1.1** • Office Workstation

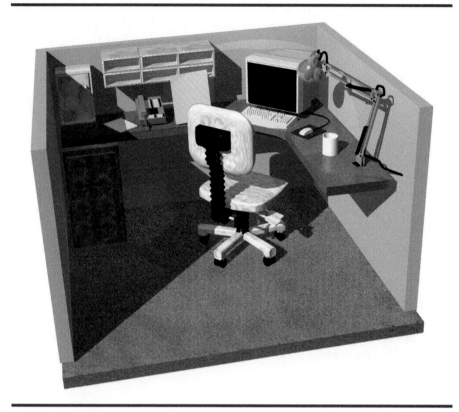

The workstation in Figure 1.1 is a **modular design**. The workstation is made of pieces that can easily be taken apart, rearranged, and put back together. The design is simple yet functional. It allows equipment to be moved anywhere on the desk with easy access to power sources. It provides storage to keep frequently used reference manuals within arm's reach, but not on the desk itself.

## Ergonomics

Have you read or heard the word *ergonomics?* **Ergonomics** is the study of the relationship between people and their work environments. It includes the study of ways to change conditions to make tasks easier and more natural. Studying ergonomics can also lead to increased productivity.

Ergonomics includes the design of the workstation because the design is critical to the physical well-being of the worker. A workstation that is proportioned for the employee's size helps the employee to be more productive and to feel less fatigue.

Figure 1.2 is an example of a well-designed workstation containing a personal computer. This workstation was designed by the National Safety Council to comply with the following guidelines: (Reprinted with permission from the National Safety Council booklet, "Video Display Terminals . . . The Human Factor," Chicago; National Safety Council.)

■ *Keyboard height.* The keyboard height should be comfortable—about 2.5 inches from the top of the table to the top surface of the space bar and bottom row of keys. At that height, the desktop can give the needed

FIGURE 1.2 • **Workstation with a PC**

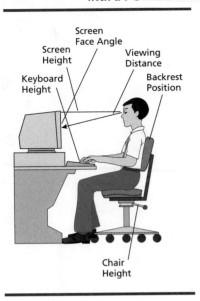

Screen Face Angle
Screen Height
Keyboard Height
Viewing Distance
Backrest Position
Chair Height

support to the operator's wrists. If the desktop is the right height, approximately 24 to 28 inches, the worker's upper arms will form a comfortable angle of approximately 90 degrees. The upper arms will then hang naturally at the sides, taking the strain off the upper back and shoulders.

■ *Screen height.* The top of the screen should be no higher than eye level to minimize eye movement.

■ *Screen face angle.* The face of the screen should be tilted back about 10 to 20 degrees for easier viewing—provided this position does not increase the glare on the screen.

■ *Viewing distance.* For comfortable viewing, the screen should be about 18 inches from the eyes.

■ *Chair height.* The chair is at a comfortable working height when the worker does not feel excessive pressure on the legs from the edge of the seat. Pressure from the seat front could make the legs go to sleep.

■ *Backrest position.* The backrest of the chair should fit comfortably at the small of the worker's back to give the back good support.

## Adjustments

Some employees may find their workstations are not ideal and do not meet the above guidelines. If so, the National Safety Council recommends making the adjustments listed in Table 1.1.

TABLE 1.1 • **Workstation Adjustments**

| Problem | Solution |
|---|---|
| **Keyboard Height** | |
| The keyboard is too high and not adjustable. | Place pads under the wrists to elevate them to a more comfortable position. |
| The keyboard is too low and not adjustable. | Set a pad of paper or a flat piece of wood under the keyboard. |
| **Screen Face Angle** | |
| The screen is too vertical and not adjustable. | Place a small wedge under the front of the monitor to tilt it back. |
| **Chair Height** | |
| You do not know what the proper height of the chair should be. | Complete the following steps:<br>1. Sit with the soles of your shoes flat on the floor. Keep your shins perpendicular to the floor and relax your thigh muscles.<br><br>2. Measure the distance from the hollow of your knees to the floor.<br><br>3. Subtract one to three inches.<br><br>The resulting measurement is the correct height for the top of the chair seat. |
| **Desk Height** | |
| The desktop is too high. | Raise the chair seat beyond the recommended height. Now your legs are dangling; use a footrest to minimize pressure from the seat front on your legs. |

*Answer the following questions:*

**1.** According to research done by the National Office Products Association, would marketing departments or lower-level managers use higher panels to divide their work areas? What height panels do executives prefer?

**2.** What five items might you find in the storage area of an office workstation?

**3.** If a workstation desktop is the right height, describe the positioning of the worker's arms while she or he keys on a computer.

**4.** How far should a computer screen be from the operator's eyes?

**5.** How does the National Safety Council recommend correcting the following problems?

    **a.** A keyboard is too high and not adjustable.

    **b.** A keyboard is too low and not adjustable.

## Other Ergonomic Concerns

Employees encounter other ergonomic concerns in the office work environment. Being aware of these problems may also lead to a more productive workplace.

### Lighting and Glare

Sometimes glare and poor lighting make reading a computer screen or copy from which an employee is working difficult. To help solve these problems, the National Safety Council suggests the following:

- Adjust the screen's brightness and contrast controls to compensate for reflections on the screen.
- Close blinds or pull shades to block daylight coming through a window from behind the terminal.
- Try to eliminate or adjust any intense light source shining directly into the eyes.
- Adjust the angle of the screen to minimize the glare.
- Place a glare filter over the monitor to cut down on glare.

### Sitting Too Long

No matter how comfortable the workstation, sitting still for long periods of time can be tiring and stressful. The following strategies are recommended:

- Stretch occasionally and look away from your work.
- Get up from your terminal and do other tasks, if possible.
- Alternate different tasks throughout the workday to vary the work rhythms. Take time out to collate papers or deliver completed work.

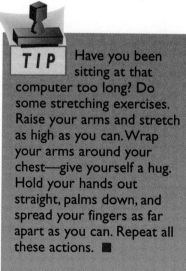

**TIP** Have you been sitting at that computer too long? Do some stretching exercises. Raise your arms and stretch as high as you can. Wrap your arms around your chest—give yourself a hug. Hold your hands out straight, palms down, and spread your fingers as far apart as you can. Repeat all these actions. ■

## Susan Schenck

*Internship Coordinator, Business Careers*
*National Aeronautics and Space Administration/Ames*

**Q.** Ms. Schenck, what is a real office environment like for a secretary?

**A.** Some secretaries have private offices and the newest in computer hardware and software. Others plead for secondhand furniture and equipment. Some secretaries can decorate their own space, putting up posters and choosing paint colors. Others work in conservative areas where the company or manager designs identical anonymous spaces.

**Q.** What are some of the excitements or pleasures gained from being an office worker?

**A.** Satisfactions include:

- Completing projects such as reports and correspondence.
- Seeing that one's work makes a difference in the function of an office.
- Learning new software and implementing new techniques.
- Getting a job in any industry or any geographic location.
- Seeing how a company works from the inside and being able to take advantage of promotion opportunities.

**Q.** Have you seen any examples of workers who have been terminated because of attitude?

**A.** Yes, mainly due to poor attitude. Poor attitude may be demonstrated through sloppy dress, poor attendance, poor interpersonal relations, and sullen facial expressions. A good attitude is a vital ingredient for success.

## Posture

Shoulder or neck pain may be caused by poor posture while working at a computer terminal. The following solutions are recommended:

- If a person must lean backward to read the screen, new eyeglasses may be necessary.
- If a person cannot read source copy that is lying flat on a table, an upright copy stand may be the solution.
- If a worker leans back too far on the chair or leans away from the chair, the chair may need adjustment.

# Federal Legislation Affects the Office Environment

The Americans with Disabilities Act (ADA) has also had an effect on the work environment. This Federal Act states, "If an individual has a disability and is qualified to perform the essential functions or duties of a job, with reasonable accommodation if necessary, that individual is protected from job discrimination by the ADA."

Since this legislation passed, employers have provided reasonable accommodations by making their workplaces readily accessible to and usable by people with disabilities. An example of reasonable accommodations would be placing grab bars in rest room stalls for individuals in wheelchairs. Other examples include: (1) devices in telephone handsets for hearing-impaired individuals, (2) page-turning devices for individuals with hand problems, (3) braille training materials for sight-impaired individuals, and (4) modified furniture for individuals with various disabilities.

Workers with disabilities who are otherwise qualified for a job are finding more acceptance in the workplace today.

# Workflow

All the office workers with whom Anne spoke talked with excitement about the jobs performed in the office section of their companies. The workers explained that their jobs were part of the **office workflow**, which is the activity that revolves around the processing of information. In the business world, information is input (gathered), processed, stored, and output (distributed) in a cycle, referred to as the information processing cycle (see Figure 1.3).

Here are examples of the information processing cycle from the companies Anne visited:

- Ivan receives input of sales figures from the marketing representatives in different states. He puts these figures into his computer, where they are processed into percentages for each district. Then they are stored on disk. Finally, they are sent by electronic mail to the regional manager.

- Sylvia receives time sheets from all employees in the bank. She verifies the time sheets and then enters the total hours into a computer. The computer processes the hours and prints paychecks. The information remains stored in the computer. The checks are given to the human resources department to be distributed to employees.

**FIGURE 1.3 • Information Processing Cycle**

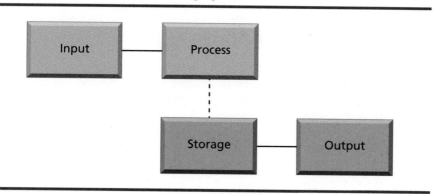

■ Darrell receives an inventory of parts from the warehouses every three months. This information is entered into his computer. The computer processes the information and prints a report that shows which parts must be reordered. The information is stored on CD-ROM. The printed report is sent to the accounting department.

The information processing cycle performed by office workers makes you realize the importance of the office operations to the entire business. Without office operations, companies would not survive. Manufacturing companies depend on office workers to keep inventory and budget figures. Law firms depend on office workers to process and store accurate legal documents. Retail stores depend on office workers to provide sales figures on a daily basis. All companies need office workers to edit and distribute correspondence, and they depend on office workers to process their payroll and keep accounting records for tax purposes.

Additional discussion about the information processing cycle and the electronic equipment that does the processing is in Chapter 5.

## Recall Time

*Answer the following questions:*

1. What are two ways to eliminate lighting glare on a computer screen?
2. What may cause shoulder pain while working at a computer?
3. Was the ADA enacted by city, county, state, or federal legislation?
4. What are the four parts of the information processing cycle?

## Organizational Makeup

When you become an employee of a company, you will be responsible for producing accurate work within an allotted time. Someone will assign you the work and see that it is completed. Depending on the company and the department, the title of this person can vary. Organizational charts illustrate companies' **organizational makeup,** or the way in which the levels of positions of authority are determined.

**FIGURE 1.4 • Organizational Chart for Company 1**

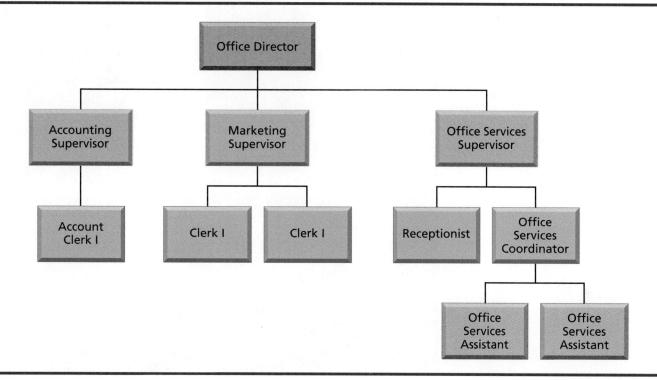

If you were an office services assistant in Company 1, to whom would you report? (See Figure 1.4.) The answer is the office services coordinator. This person would report to the office services supervisor.

Company 2 is a small company (see Figure 1.5). The administrative assistant is responsible to the office manager, who is directly responsible to the owner.

# Office Safety

Have you ever tripped over an electrical cord at home? Have you ever had the power go off because too much equipment was plugged into one electrical outlet? Have you ever banged your leg on a drawer that was left open? If not, you are extremely cautious or have been very lucky.

**FIGURE 1.5 • Organizational Chart for Company 2**

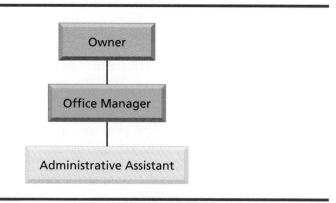

## Ethics on the Job

Erlinda is the only office employee in a small graphics company. Her boss leaves every day at 3 P.M. to make sales calls. The boss never returns until the following morning.

Erlinda would like to take a night class at a local community college, but she would have to leave early in order to get to the class on time. The boss will not know she leaves early.

*Should Erlinda ask her boss for permission to leave early, or should she just do it? The boss will probably never know.* ■

©Jim Piper/SuperStock International

Files or other items left sticking out into an aisle can pose a hazard to workers.

Many people think of work accidents as happening only in factories or at construction sites. However, some accidents also happen in an office environment. These accidents occur when workers are careless or are impatient and try to take shortcuts. Start now to build good safety habits and carry these habits over to your office job.

Office workers have indicated the items listed in Table 1.2 on page 15 are safety hazards on the job. A **safety hazard** is a danger or a chance of being injured.

# Recycling in the Business World

Anne noticed that managers in all three companies she visited were concerned with conserving natural resources. They all had recycling programs in operation. However, Darrell's company was the most impressive—it had recently won the Environment Achievement Award.

His company uses different programs to capture office paper, newsprint, magazines, bottles and cans, cardboard, and telephone books. Employees in the company even participate in Christmas tree and office equipment recycling. In addition, they use less paper by increasing electronic communications, making two-sided photocopies, and using less preprinted letterhead.

Darrell helps promote the program by doing the graphics for a newsletter on the benefits of recycling. This newsletter is distributed to all employees. The company encourages the public to learn more about these programs by visiting the company's Web site, which features an extensive environmental section.

**TABLE 1.2 • Office Safety Hazards**

| Hazard | Prevention |
|--------|-----------|
| Opening more than one file drawer at a time may cause the cabinet to fall over. | Before you open a file drawer, check to see that all other file drawers are closed. Newer file cabinets do not allow more than one drawer to open at the same time. |
| Leaving a file drawer open may cause someone to trip over it. | Keep file drawers closed when not in use or when you leave for even a short time. |
| Leaving a handbag or briefcase on the floor in a walkway may cause someone to trip. | Put purses and briefcases into a desk drawer, completely under the desk, or in a cabinet. |
| Not having enough voltage in the electrical outlet for all the equipment may cause a power shortage or a fire. | Before plugging in new equipment, check with your supervisor to be certain enough voltage is available. Have the company upgrade the electrical system when necessary. |
| Standing on a chair that is unstable may cause you to fall. | Use a step stool or a ladder to reach high places. |
| Stooping and lifting improperly may cause back injuries. | Learn the proper lifting procedures. |
| Leaving electrical cords in a walkway may cause someone to trip. | Keep electrical cords out of walkways or use rubber cord covers to prevent people from tripping. |

## Recall Time

*Answer the following questions:*

1. Refer to Figure 1.4.
   a. To whom is the Account Clerk I responsible?
   b. To whom is the marketing supervisor responsible?
   c. To whom is the office services coordinator responsible?
2. What safety hazard can cause a file cabinet to fall over? How can it be prevented?
3. What safety hazard could cause an employee to trip in an office and how can it be avoided?
4. What may cause a back injury on the job and how can it be avoided?

## Summary

Businesses may be manufacturing firms, agricultural firms, service firms, government firms, and a variety of other types of firms. Although their products and services differ, their office environments are often similar. Many companies use the same types of workstations, and their employees perform the same types of office functions.

All companies should have similar interests in ergonomics and similar concerns about the safety of their employees. The type of work may differ, but the workflow and the organizational setup are similar in most companies.

The following questions may help you decide in what office environment you want to work:

- Is the office environment cheerfully decorated?
- Are employee work areas divided to provide privacy and to allow employees to concentrate on work?
- Are areas provided for employees to work as a team and to share job functions?
- Do workstations allow for storing materials and manuals as well as for holding necessary office equipment?
- Are workstations adjustable for variations in size of employees?
- Does the lighting appear to be adequate for the total work environment?
- Does the company comply with the Americans with Disabilities Act?
- Does the organizational setup define the duties of the employees?
- Is office safety a constant concern of company managers?
- Is the company concerned with conserving natural resources?

# before you leave...

**When you have completed this chapter, answer the following questions:**

**1.** How does an office environment, including an employee's workstation, look?

**2.** What are four office safety hazards? Give examples of ways to avoid them.

# Review & Application

## Check Your Knowledge

1. Are all partitions in offices the same height?

2. Which workers usually have private offices?

3. Why might workers want to share the same work area?

4. Are workstations used only by executives?

5. Are typewriters still used in offices? If so, what kind?

6. Are all workstations made permanent so that they cannot be moved?

7. Why is being concerned with the design of a workstation important?

8. Describe how a person's arms should be held if he or she is in proper keyboarding position.

9. What is the recommended maximum height at which to place a computer screen?

10. If a person is in proper keyboarding position, where does the backrest of the chair fit?

11. How can a computer screen be tilted if it is too vertical and not adjustable?

12. What does the National Safety Council recommend doing if you do not know the proper height for your computer chair?

13. Why is a glare filter sometimes used?

14. List three ways to avoid stress from sitting too long.

15. What do the letters ADA represent?

16. Marcus gathered, processed, and distributed information for his office. What step did he omit from the information processing cycle?

17. Is each of the following an example of input or output?
    a. a movie ticket given to a customer
    b. traffic violations entered into a computer
    c. figures transferred from a CD-ROM into a computer
    d. a paycheck given to an employee
    e. a letter keyed into a personal computer
    f. a letter printed from a personal computer

18. What is an organizational chart?

19. Do accidents happen in offices?

20. What safety hazard may cause a power outage in an office?

21. What should an office worker stand on to reach high places?

## Review Your Vocabulary

On a separate piece of paper, supply the missing words by choosing from the new Office Terms listed below.

1. The study of the relationship between people and their work environments is called _____.

2. Workstations that are made of parts that can easily be taken apart, rearranged, and put back together are made by _____.

3. Some workstations are divided by _____ for privacy.

4. The _____ is the area that holds equipment and other work-related materials and is also where an employee works.

5. The _____ in an office revolves around the processing of information.

6. Employees in positions of authority are noted by the _____ of an office.

7. A chance of being injured on the job is a _____.

   a. ergonomics       e. safety hazard
   b. modular design    f. office workflow
   c. organizational     g. workstation
      makeup
   d. partitions

## Discuss and Analyze an Office Situation

Denise is an office worker for a law firm. One of her duties is directing clients to attorneys' offices. Denise is going to a party directly after work tomorrow. This party is an important one for her, and she plans to

wear nice evening clothes. She is thinking of saving time by wearing her evening clothes to work and then going directly to the party.

Should Denise dress this way at her job? Does how she dresses for work make a difference? Why or why not?

## Practice Basic Skills

### Math

1. For each item in the following purchase orders, multiply the number purchased by the price listed in the computer supply catalog below. Then add the prices for all the items in the purchase order.

   a. Purchase order 1

      8 printer stands     _____

      6 storage trays     _____

      3 computer dust covers     _____

      4 glare filters     _____

          Total     _____

   b. Purchase order 2

      4 printer mufflers     _____

      12 antistatic sprays     _____

      4 deluxe computer printers     _____

      4 modular tables     _____

          Total     _____

   c. Purchase order 3

      14 storage trays     _____

      3 printer stands     _____

      1 deluxe computer printer     _____

      1 modular table     _____

      5 computer dust covers     _____

          Total     _____

| Computer Supply Catalog | | |
| --- | --- | --- |
| | PRICE PER ITEM | |
| ITEM | If you buy 1–5: | If you buy more than 5: |
| Printer stand | $ 32.50 | $ 30.00 |
| Printer muffler | 74.00 | 70.00 |
| Storage trays | 17.75 | 14.00 |
| Antistatic spray | 8.25 | 7.00 |
| Computer dust cover | 28.50 | 25.00 |
| Deluxe computer printer | 390.00 | 370.00 |
| Glare filter | 95.50 | 90.00 |
| Modular table | 580.00 | 540.00 |

2. Garrison Contractors does not have time to do its payroll this month. It hires a computer service company to do the payroll. The computer service company charges $95 per hour. The work will take twelve hours. What is the total cost?

3. Doss Brothers Dairy needs to purchase new draperies for its office because the sun is causing problems with the computer monitors. The draperies cost $62.75 per yard. The company needs 18 yards. What is the total cost?

4. The supervisor of office services suggests to management that the company pay for eye exams for all computer operators. The eye exams cost $65 each, and the company has eight operators. What will be the total cost to the company?

### English

1. *Rule:* Most nouns form their plurals by adding *s*.
*Example:* One pencil, two pencils
*Practice Exercise:* Form the plurals for the following:

   accountant         desk

   calculator         manager

   computer         typewriter

2. *Rule:* Nouns that end in *y* with a vowel before the *y* form plurals by adding *s*.
*Example:* One key, two keys
*Practice Exercise:* Form the plurals for the following:

   attorney         day

   boy         delay

   buy         valley

3. *Rule:* Nouns that end in *y* with a consonant before the *y* form plurals by changing the *y* to *i* and adding *es*.
*Example:* One deputy, two deputies
*Practice Exercise:* Form the plurals for the following:

   agency         lady

   baby         laundry

   city         party

4. *Rule:* Nouns that end in *o* with a vowel before the *o* form the plural by adding *s*.
*Example:* One trio, two trios
*Practice Exercise:* Form the plurals for the following:

   cameo         radio

   igloo         stereo

   patio         tattoo

5. *Rule:* Nouns that end in *o* with a consonant before the *o* form the plural by adding *es*.
   *Example:* One cargo, four cargoes
   *Practice Exercise:* Form the plurals for the following:

   | | |
   |---|---|
   | echo | potato |
   | hero | tomato |

6. *Rule:* Some nouns form their plurals in different ways.
   *Example:* Foot, feet; man, men; child, children; mouse, mice; deer, deer; woman, women
   *Practice Exercise:* Form the plurals for the following:

   | | |
   |---|---|
   | goose | sheep |
   | moose | tooth |
   | ox | trout |

### Proofreading

1. Rekey the following report, correcting all errors:

   CREATING LOW-STRESS RELATIONSHIPS

   Krames Communications suggests the following ways to create low-stress relationships on the job.

   Listen Actively When you listen with sencitivity toward the speakers feelings, you are better able to understnad the speaker and can then respond by honestly expressing your own thoughs and feelings.

   Give Compliments Complimenting people lets them know you have noticed them. Give out at least one complement a day for a job well done, a suggestion at a meeting, or even a neu suit or hairstyle.

   Smile at People Smiles and courtecy keep communication open, even when you bring critisism or bad news. But while you are courteous, do not gloss over what needs to be said—express your feelings honestly.

   Admit That You Are Wrong If you honestly admit when you are wrong, coworkers will trust you more. They will know you are being honest and fare, be more willing to share information with you, and admit when they are wrong.

2. After printing the report in proofreading exercise 1, make the following changes and print a new copy:

- Use uppercase for the underlined words.
- Delete all the underlines.
- In the paragraph titled "Listen Actively," change the word *honestly* to *truly*.
- In the paragraph titled "Give Compliments," delete "a suggestion at a meeting."
- Add this paragraph to the bottom:

SHOW APPRECIATION Whether you give a coworker a gift for a job well done, write a letter of commendation, or just say thank you, showing appreciation lets others know you recognize their contributions.

## Apply Your Knowledge

1. Arrange the following words in alphabetic order. Using a personal computer or an electronic typewriter, tabulate the words into three columns.

   | | |
   |---|---|
   | time sheets | design |
   | panel | workspace |
   | privacy | functional |
   | environment | keyboard |
   | glare | guideline |
   | elevate | height |
   | stressful | posture |
   | process | cycle |
   | responsible | chart |
   | safety | outlet |
   | hazard | electrical |
   | compliment | communication |

2. Look around your classroom. Make a list of safety hazards.

3. Using the graphics or tables feature of a word processing program, prepare an organizational chart for a small company with job titles (highest to lowest) of:

   Owner
   Administrative Assistant
   Secretary
   Receptionist

## Using the Reference Manual

 Open file ch1ref.doc. Use the punctuation section of the Reference Manual at the

back of the book to help you correct comma errors. Save and print.

1. Because the project is not totally correct you will have to spend more time making it acceptable.

2. Shelves and storage space should be available for paper, binders manuals and computer disks.

3. Ergonomics the study of the relationship between people and their work environment is a topic people working in offices today cannot ignore.

4. Consequently the issue is unresolved at the moment.

5. In today's office employees frequently share records, equipment and information.

6. In the business world information is input, processed stored, and output in a cycle.

7. As a result of poor communication no one who attended the seminar was in the office.

8. Organizational makeup or the way in which employees in positions of authority are determined is illustrated on organizational charts.

9. Today most office employees work at workstations.

10. As soon as Rainey finishes the report make three copies.

# chapter 2

## Career Opportunities in the Office

### objectives

*After completing this chapter, you will be able to do the following:*

1. List the clerical job classifications that have employment opportunities through the year 2010.
2. List the types of companies that have clerical employment opportunities through the year 2010.
3. List the job duties and qualifications of an adjustment clerk.
4. List the job duties and qualifications of an order clerk.
5. List the job duties and qualifications of a general office clerk.
6. List the job duties and qualifications of a receptionist.
7. List the job duties and qualifications of a secretary.
8. List the job duties and qualifications of a medical assistant.
9. List the job duties and qualifications of a customer service representative.
10. List the soft skills.

### New Office Terms

- back-office jobs
- civil service jobs
- Employment Development Department
- full-time work schedule
- *Occupational Outlook Handbook*
- replacement needs
- service-producing industries
- temporary office workers

Answer the following questions to the best of your ability:

**1.** What is the employment outlook for clerical jobs through the year 2010?

**2.** What are the job duties and qualifications of a medical assistant?

**3.** What are the job duties and qualifications of a secretary?

**G**arrett recently completed business classes that included training in information processing, spreadsheets, and databases using a PC. He was a good student and is excited now to look for full-time work in an office. The only problem is that he does not know what jobs are available to someone with his training.

Garrett remembers that his neighbor Rochelle works for the **Employment Development Department** (EDD), a state department that handles unemployment and job placement. He makes an appointment to meet with Rochelle at her office. Garrett wants information concerning the projected employment growth of clerical jobs. He also wants information on skills required for clerical jobs, because he is not certain for which jobs he is qualified.

At the meeting, Rochelle first explains to Garrett that much of the information he wants is contained in a publication titled *The Occupational Outlook Handbook.* This handbook is published once every two years by the U.S. Department of Labor, Bureau of Labor Statistics. Using it as a reference, Rochelle shares with Garrett some information on job prospects for the future.

## Occupational Outlook

Job openings in administrative and support clerical occupations are expected to increase by more than 2 million jobs between the years 2000 and 2010. The Department of Labor predicts that because of their high number of jobs and substantial replacement needs, clerical occupations will offer abundant opportunities for qualified job seekers in the years ahead.

Garrett asks Rochelle what the handbook means by **replacement needs.** Rochelle explains that these are needs to fill job openings because people leave occupations. Some people transfer to other occupations because they wish to change careers. Others stop working to return to school, assume household responsibilities, or retire.

Most job openings that arise are the result of replacement needs. Therefore, even occupations with little or no employment growth may still offer many job openings. *Employment growth* is an increase in the number of job openings that occurs because new jobs are created in a certain occupation.

## Technology in the Office | MOUS CERTIFICATION

Microsoft® Office User Specialist (MOUS) certification is the widely accepted standard for desktop proficiency on Microsoft Office applications. More and more employers are recognizing MOUS certification as the standard for proficient employees.

You may obtain MOUS certification by choosing one of three levels of participation, then preparing for and passing an exam. The three levels are: Proficient Specialist, Expert Specialist, and Office Expert. Certification as Proficient Specialist or Expert Specialist requires passing one exam on any given Microsoft Office application (such as Word® or Excel®). Certification as an Office Expert requires passing four expert-level exams and the office integration exam. Office Expert is the highest level attainable.

MOUS exams are based on real-world assignments. All exams require no longer than one hour.

Garrett is told that advances in office technology will affect the statistics and classifications for future clerical jobs. Technological advances in mail sorting equipment, for example, will slow demand for postal service clerks. Increased use of personal computers will lead to a decline in the number of keyboarders and an increase in the need for workers with word processing skills.

Jobs that involve interaction with others (see Table 2.1, page 21) will generally grow faster than **back-office jobs,** in which employees have little or no contact with the public. The reasons for this growth are varied, but they include the following: (1) The tasks performed in the occupation require personal contact; (2) Customer service must be improved; (3) The work is not subject to significant reduction because of technological change.

Rochelle also shares information with Garrett on the types of companies that have the best outlook for employment. She states that nearly half of all job openings are projected to be in service and professional and related occupations, accounting for more than 25 million jobs. **Service-producing industries** are businesses that exist to provide service to the public.

Of the projected 20 fastest growing occupations, 9 are computer related, including the 7 fastest growing jobs. Fast-growing computer industries and the increasing importance of computers and computer networks in nearly every industry will sustain the rapid growth in these occupations through 2010.

Health care services will continue to gain jobs. Factors contributing to continued growth in this industry include the aging population, which will continue to require more services, and the increased use of innovative medical technology.

All this information concerning the outlook for clerical occupations seems to satisfy Garrett, but now he needs some information on the types of jobs for which he is qualified to apply. Rochelle encourages him to attend a job classification workshop that is being sponsored by the Employment Development Department. She says this workshop may help him answer his final questions about job classification.

**TABLE 2.1 • Projected Increase in Employment for Selected Administrative Support Occupations, 2000–2010 (numbers in thousands)**

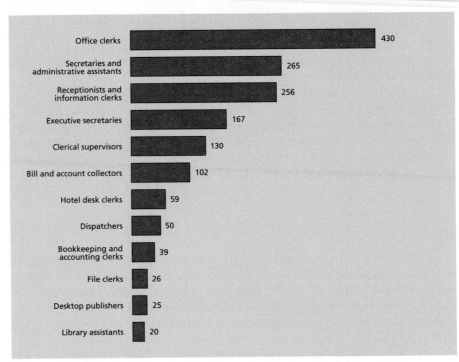

|  | |
|---|---|
| Office clerks | 430 |
| Secretaries and administrative assistants | 265 |
| Receptionists and information clerks | 256 |
| Executive secretaries | 167 |
| Clerical supervisors | 130 |
| Bill and account collectors | 102 |
| Hotel desk clerks | 59 |
| Dispatchers | 50 |
| Bookkeeping and accounting clerks | 39 |
| File clerks | 26 |
| Desktop publishers | 25 |
| Library assistants | 20 |

*Source*: Department of Labor, *Monthly Labor Review,* November, 2001.

## Recall Time

*Answer the following questions:*

**1.** Who publishes the *Occupational Outlook Handbook?*

**2.** Will the number of clerical jobs increase or decrease between the years 2000 and 2010?

**3.** Are most new jobs in the clerical area due to more work or to the replacement of workers who leave?

**4.** List three service-producing industries.

# Job Classification

The presenter at the job classification workshop that Garrett attends divides office clerical jobs into three categories. The categories include:

1. entry-level positions
2. positions requiring more than entry-level skills
3. positions requiring advanced skills

The presenter spends time discussing each category. The discussion includes job titles, typical duties, and qualifications required for the positions. The presenter refers frequently to *The Occupational Outlook Handbook* during the workshop.

Real job descriptions that have been collected from private employers and from government agencies are passed out at the workshop. The job descriptions from the government agencies were collected from federal, state, county, and city organizations. These government agency jobs are often called **civil service jobs.**

The presenter explained that most positions require a **full-time work schedule,** which usually means a 40-hour workweek. In addition, a significant number of jobs are available for individuals who wish to work as temporaries. **Temporary office workers** are employees who work for a few days or a few weeks at one company until a job is completed. They also work at various companies to replace employees on vacation or sick leave. Temporary office workers usually work through private companies known as *temporary employment services.*

Garrett was pleased that the presenter also spoke about employment for the disabled. The presenter stated that the Americans with Disabilities Act (ADA) has helped increase the number of individuals with disabilities in the workforce. Employers take a variety of measures to ensure that disabled persons are not inhibited from applying for openings and that hiring decisions are made on grounds consistent with the ADA. Employment advertisements often include a nondiscrimination statement. Have you noticed these statements in job ads in your local newspaper?

As in advertisements, employment application forms often state that disabled applicants will be given equal opportunity and reasonable accommodations. Testing of applicants should be administered in a way that allows disabled candidates to compete fairly (for example, in braille for visually challenged applicants).

# Entry-Level Positions

The following information is from the first clerical job category—entry-level positions. It includes two job classifications with a job outlook that is expected to grow faster than the average for all occupations through the year 2010.

## Adjustment Clerks

### Duties

Adjustment clerks investigate and resolve customers' complaints about merchandise, service, billing, or credit ratings. They may work for banks, department stores, utility companies, and other large organizations selling products and services to the public.

Adjustment clerks examine all pertinent information to determine the validity of a customer's complaint. After investigating and evaluating the facts, they report their findings, adjustments, and recommendations. Adjustment clerks also respond to inquiries from customers. They can frequently answer these inquiries with form letters, but at other times, they must compose letters themselves.

# Rick Stroud

*Communications Director*
*Professional Secretaries International (PSI)*

**Q.** Mr. Stroud, what is the job outlook for secretaries? What career paths are available to them?

**A.** According to the U.S. Department of Labor, the number of secretaries in the United States increased to 3,349,000 in the mid-1990s, and 265,000 new secretarial and administrative jobs will be added through the year 2010.

Now is a very exciting time for secretaries as more and more businesses are operating in a global economy. Companies are creating a multitude of career paths for persons in office professions. Secretaries have moved into training, supervision, desktop publishing, information management, and research.

**Q.** What are some of the day-to-day tasks of a secretary?

**A.**
- Information flow: Maintaining paper and electronic files and databases, as well as developing methods for organizing and retrieving information.
- Communications: Editing correspondence and overseeing office communications tools, including voice mail, fax machines, and e-mail.
- Logistics: Scheduling business travel and meetings, along with planning and developing agendas.
- Finances: Preparing vouchers and financial data.
- Customer Relations: Interacting with visitors, sales representatives, customers, and members of the community.

## Qualifications

Many employers do not require any formal education for adjustment clerk positions. Instead, they look for people who can read and write and who possess good communication and interpersonal skills. They also prefer workers who are skilled keyboarders.

## Order Clerks

### Duties

Order clerks receive and process incoming orders for such items as spare parts for machines, gas and electric power connections, consumer appliances, film rentals, and articles of clothing. Most order clerks sit at computers and receive orders directly by telephone, entering the required information as the customer places an order.

A computer provides the order clerk with ready access to information such as stock numbers, prices, and inventory. After the clerk has verified and entered the order, he or she calculates the customer's final cost and routes the order to the proper department to send out or deliver the item.

©corbisimages.com

If you order catalog items by telephone, you will probably speak with an order clerk in an office similar to this one.

## Qualifications

Most order clerk jobs are entry-level positions. Most employers require applicants to have at least a high school diploma or its equivalent and to be computer literate with good keyboarding ability.

Order clerks must be careful, orderly, and detail oriented in order to avoid making errors and to be able to recognize errors made by others. Once hired, order clerks generally receive on-the-job training to learn company procedures.

# Positions Requiring More Than Entry-Level Skills

Here is the information from the second clerical job category—positions requiring more than entry-level skills. It includes two job classifications. The job outlook for receptionists is that opportunities are expected to grow faster than the average for all occupations through the year 2010, and the outlook for general office clerks is that good job opportunities will continue to exist.

## Receptionists

### Duties

All organizations want to make a good first impression, which is the job of the receptionist, who is often the first representative of the organization that a visitor encounters. In addition to traditional duties, such as answering telephones, routing calls to the appropriate individuals, and greeting visitors, a receptionist may serve a security function—monitoring the access of visitors and determining who belongs and who does not.

### Ethics on the Job

Rosa is a part-time receptionist for a six-person, privately owned land development company. The office manager, Jennifer, is on vacation, leaving Rosa at the office with the two owners, the accountant, and the sales representative.

Because Rosa's work hours are 1 P.M. to 5 P.M., she never uses the kitchen, but she has seen Jennifer clean up frequently during the workweek. One afternoon the owner, José, left the office at 3 P.M., then popped his head back through the door and said, "Rosa, could you do the dishes before you leave?" Rosa replied, "Why should I clean up when I don't even use the kitchen?"

*What do you think of Rosa's response to José? Is cleaning the kitchen a reasonable request for José to make? How would you handle this request if you were in Rosa's position?* ■

©Duncan Smith/PhotoDisc

When you visit most businesses, the first person you are likely to see is the receptionist.

Increasingly, receptionists use multiline telephone systems, personal computers, and facsimile (fax) machines. Many receptionists take messages and may inform other employees of a visitor's arrival or cancellation of an appointment. When they are not busy with callers, receptionists may be expected to perform a variety of secretarial duties including opening and sorting mail, collecting and distributing parcels, updating appointment calendars, preparing travel vouchers, and doing simple bookkeeping, keyboarding, and filing.

## Qualifications

Skills required of receptionists include keyboarding (45 wpm), general office skills, and knowledge of word processing software. On the job, they learn how to operate the telephone system and how to greet visitors properly. However, some employers also may prefer formal office education or training.

A neat appearance, a pleasant voice, and an even disposition are important. Receptionists do not work under close supervision. Therefore, common sense and a thorough understanding of how the business is organized helps them handle various situations that arise.

## General Office Clerks

### Duties

The duties of the general office clerk are varied and diverse rather than being a single specialized task. The responsibilities of a general office clerk change with the needs of the employer. Clerks may spend some days filing or keyboarding, others entering data at a computer terminal. They may also operate photocopiers, fax machines, or other office equipment; prepare mailings; proofread copy; answer telephones; and deliver messages.

Duties also vary by level of experience. Inexperienced employees may operate calculators and record inquiries. More experienced workers may maintain financial records, verify statistical reports for accuracy and completeness, and take inventory of equipment and supplies.

### Qualifications

Employers usually require a high school diploma, keyboarding skills (40 wpm), general office skills, and computer skills. They also favor workers who are familiar with computer word processing software and applications.

Because general office clerks usually work with other office staff, they should be cooperative and willing to work as part of a team. They should be able to communicate well with people, have good organizational skills, and be detail oriented.

# Positions Requiring Advanced Skills

The following information is from the third clerical job category—positions requiring advanced skills. In this category, employment opportunities should be quite plentiful, especially for well-qualified secretaries, through the year 2010.

## Secretaries

### Duties

Secretaries, sometimes referred to as *administrative assistants*, will continue to assume new responsibilities and learn to operate different types of office equipment. In addition, secretaries will continue to perform and coordinate office activities and to ensure that information is given to staff and clients.

Secretaries are responsible for a variety of administrative and clerical duties that are necessary to run and maintain organizations efficiently. They schedule appointments, give information to callers, organize and

**TIP** Ask for extra work in slow times. ■

## Large Office/Small Office
*What's Your Preference?*

# Work Performance

Administrative assistants in large offices often work for more than one boss. In a large law office, for example, an administrative assistant may work for two attorneys. This is also true in many other businesses. Therefore, an administrative assistant must be able to schedule the work to meet the needs of all the bosses. An administrative assistant must be able to set priorities. He or she must also have the temperament to be able to take directions from more than one boss and interact with them all regularly.

In a small office, an administrative assistant usually works for and reports to only one boss. Therefore, the daily work is scheduled around only one person. Any priorities can be set with that one boss. Once a work routine is established, an administrative assistant will find working for only one boss easier than working for several.

**Both situations described above have advantages and disadvantages. Would you prefer to work as an administrative assistant in a large office or a small one? Why?** ■

A secretary's job is not only one of the most varied in the work world, but it is also constantly evolving in today's changing business environment.

©Corbis/Stock Market

maintain files, and complete forms. They may also key letters, make travel arrangements, contact clients, and operate office equipment. Secretaries increasingly use personal computers to run spreadsheet, word processing, database management, desktop publishing, and graphics programs—tasks previously performed by managers and professionals.

## Qualifications

High school graduates may qualify for secretarial positions if they have basic office skills. Secretaries should be proficient in keyboarding (55 wpm) and good at spelling, punctuation, grammar, and oral communication. Knowledge of word processing, spreadsheet programs, and database management has become increasingly important to most employers. Because secretaries must be tactful in their dealings with many different people, employers also look for good interpersonal skills. Discretion, good judgment, organizational ability, and initiative are especially valuable.

Testing and certification for entry-level office skills is available through the Office Proficiency Assessment and Certification (OPAC) program offered by Professional Secretaries International (PSI). As secretaries gain experience, they can earn the designation Certified Professional Secretary (CPS) by passing a series of exams given by the Institute for Certifying Secretaries, a department of PSI. The designation is recognized by many employers as the mark of excellence for office professionals.

**Making Office Decisions** You are the receptionist for a large law firm. Your duties include greeting new people, checking a daily sheet to see that each person is expected by someone in the firm (approved to enter), issuing the person a badge, and directing the visitor to the proper location.

A visitor arrives at your desk and says she has an appointment on the third floor with Kim Singh, the firm's computer analyst. You check your list, but the person's name is not on the list—yet she knew Kim's name, title, and location.

**Should the person be allowed to enter? How do you handle this situation?** ■

## Recall Time

*Answer the following questions:*

**1.** Employees of what category work only a few days or a few weeks at one company?

**2.** Does an order clerk have as much responsibility as a secretary?

**3.** What is the job title of an employee who may serve a security function?

**4.** What is the job title of an employee who works on a variety of tasks without concentrating in one particular area?

**5.** What does PSI represent?

# Other Areas of Employment

Garrett decided to attend a final workshop sponsored by the Employment Development Department. This workshop covers clerical jobs within specialized areas. These classifications also have a job outlook that is expected to grow faster than the average for all occupations through the year 2010.

## Medical Assistants

### Duties

Medical assistants perform routine clinical and clerical tasks to keep the offices of physicians, podiatrists, chiropractors, and optometrists running smoothly. Medical assistants perform many clerical duties. They answer telephones, greet patients, update and file patient medical records, fill out insurance forms, handle correspondence, schedule appointments, arrange for hospital admission and laboratory services, and handle billing and bookkeeping.

Medical assistants may also arrange examining room instruments and equipment, purchase and maintain supplies and equipment, and keep waiting and examining rooms neat and clean.

**TIP** Take notes on everything. Don't trust anything to memory for the first few weeks on the job. ■

©Kim Steele/PhotoDisc

Medical assistants spend much of their time dealing with people.

## Qualifications

Medical assisting is one of the few health occupations open to individuals with no formal training. Some medical assistants are trained on the job. However, some community colleges and technical colleges offer medical assisting training programs. Applicants usually need a high school diploma or the equivalent. Recommended high school courses include mathematics, health, biology, keyboarding (30 wpm), accounting, computers, and office skills. Volunteer experience in the health care field is also helpful.

Because medical assistants deal with the public, they must be neat and well groomed and have a courteous, pleasant manner. Medical assistants must be able to put patients at ease and explain physicians' instructions. They must respect the confidential nature of medical information.

# Customer Service Representatives

## Duties

Customer service representatives obtain information that organizations need to enable individuals to open bank accounts, gain admission to medical facilities, participate in consumer surveys, and apply for many other services. They solicit and verify information from people by mail, by telephone, or in person; create and update files; and perform various processing tasks. These clerks are also known as *interviewing* and *new accounts clerks*.

Customer service representatives interview people and record the data directly into a computer. They must be familiar with the products and services of the company for which they work. They also may answer telephone inquiries about policies and procedures of the company.

## Qualifications

A high school diploma or its equivalent is the most common educational requirement for a job as a customer service representative. However, more important to employers are good interpersonal skills and familiarity with computers, including good keyboarding skills.

Because many customer service representatives work with the public, a neat appearance and a pleasant personality are imperative, as are good problem-solving and communication skills. A clear speaking voice and fluency in the English language are essential because these employees frequently use the telephone.

# The Soft Skills

After the workshop, Garrett read through the job descriptions that were distributed by the presenter. He noticed that most of the job descriptions contained what employers refer to as "soft skills." *Soft skills* are nontechnical, interpersonal skills. Garrett compiled a list of the soft skills and discovered that most companies' job descriptions included the following abilities:

- Interpersonal skills
    Workers who can handle difficult people
    Workers who can work with people from different cultures
- Organizational skills
    Workers who can keep track of documents
    Workers who can prioritize

A customer service representative might work directly with the public, or by mail, telephone, and computer.

## What's Your Attitude?

Roberto has been working for five years as a general office clerk for the same family-owned company. The company has always been successful and has always hired enough office workers for the busy times.

For the last year, the company has not been doing well financially and has had to lay off employees, including office workers. At the same time, those who remain have had to take on more and more work. Roberto occasionally has to do some of the work previously done by office services assistants.

A new executive has been hired who promises to turn the company around and again make it financially successful. In the meantime, all the employees must continue to take on extra work and maintain a positive attitude that things will improve.

Roberto does continue to take on extra work and even does a little overtime without any extra pay. He believes the company has been good to him for the past five years and that he now owes it extra effort during this difficult time.

*Do you agree with Roberto's attitude? Why or why not?* ■

- Listening skills
    Workers with the ability to grasp the key points of customers' and co-workers' concerns
    Workers with the ability to take notes when necessary
- Critical thinking skills
    Workers who are able to analyze and make decisions
    Workers who are able to meet clients' needs
- Team players
    Workers who are able to work with others to achieve a goal
    Workers who are able to share ideas
- Responsibility
    Workers who can see a task through to its completion
    Workers who can deal with problems and not avoid them

## Recall Time

*Answer the following questions:*

1. Which high school courses are recommended for medical assistants?
2. Why should medical assistants be neat and well groomed?
3. What is another job title for a customer service representative?
4. Give one example of an organizational skill.
5. Give one example of a person who accepts responsibility.

# Summary

Many job openings will continue to exist in office occupations through the year 2010. Although some jobs will be available for individuals with entry-level clerical skills, most opportunities will require more than entry-level skills.

In addition to the technical knowledge and skills of personal computer operation and keyboarding, written and verbal communication skills are required for most clerical occupations. Employers prefer hiring individuals who are high school graduates. Jobs including the greatest responsibilities require the greatest abilities.

Do you qualify for any of the clerical positions discussed in this chapter? Use the following checklist to determine for which clerical level you are most qualified.

Entry-Level Clerical Skills
_____ Touch keyboarding ability
_____ Basic spelling skills
_____ Basic reading skills

More Than Entry-Level Clerical Skills
_____ Average keyboarding skills
_____ Computer literacy
_____ Knowledge of word processing
_____ Good communications skills
_____ Attention to details
_____ Willingness to be a team player

Advanced Clerical Skills
_____ Advanced keyboarding ability
_____ Proficiency in a variety of computer software applications
_____ Proficiency in oral communication
_____ Proficiency in grammar, punctuation, and spelling
_____ Aptitude for numbers
_____ Adaptability and versatility
_____ Organizational ability
_____ Initiative
_____ Office experience

## Ethics on the Job

Rita has begun a new job as a file clerk in a large software company. Her first week on the job is spent in the training department learning about the company and the details of her new job.

One of the training sessions includes a segment on "office etiquette." During this session, Rita is told to call her bosses by their last names for the first few months on the job.

Rita is offended by this requirement; she believes she is told to use this form of address because she is a file clerk. She thinks that not all new employees are told to use this procedure, only those in lower paying positions.

*Do you think Rita is correct? What do you think is best when first beginning a job, to call your bosses by first names or by their last names?* ■

# before you leave...

**When you have completed this chapter, answer the following questions:**

**1.** What is the employment outlook for clerical jobs through the year 2010?

**2.** What are the job duties and qualifications of a medical assistant?

**3.** What are the job duties and qualifications of a secretary?

# Review & Application

## Check Your Knowledge

1. By what number are job openings in administrative and support occupations expected to increase between the years 2000 and 2010?

2. List two reasons that replacement openings occur.

3. What is causing slow demand for postal service clerks?

4. Define service-producing industries.

5. List examples of service-producing industries.

6. What is the projected increase of opportunities for receptionists and information clerks through the year 2010?

7. What is meant by civil service jobs?

8. How many hours per week do full-time employees usually work?

9. What should an employment advertisement contain that indicates compliance with the ADA?

10. For what types of companies do adjustment clerks work?

11. What two types of equipment do order clerks frequently use?

12. What keyboarding ability is required of most adjustment clerks and order clerks?

13. When not busy with callers, what duties might a receptionist perform?

14. List three types of office equipment that a general office clerk might use.

15. List five types of software programs that secretaries might use.

16. What does CPS represent and how is it obtained?

17. How can individuals gain experience in the health care field?

18. Which skills do employers consider most important for customer service representatives?

19. Give one example of an interpersonal skill.

20. Give one example of a listening skill.

## Review Your Vocabulary

On a separate sheet of paper, supply the missing words by choosing from the new Office Terms listed below.

1. Banking, insurance, health care, and education are considered _____.

2. Filling job openings because people leave occupations is known as filling _____.

3. Jobs with very little or no public contact are known as _____.

4. In some states the unemployment department is known as the _____ (EDD).

5. Government jobs are also known as _____.

6. The _____ is a handbook published by the Department of Labor.

7. In most jobs, a standard 40-hour week is considered a _____.

8. Workers who work for short periods of time at various companies are _____.

   a. back-office jobs
   b. civil service jobs
   c. Employment Development Department
   d. full-time work schedule
   e. *Occupational Outlook Handbook*
   f. replacement needs
   g. service-producing industries
   h. temporary office workers

## Discuss and Analyze an Office Situation

Margarita was excited because she had two job offers. She knew she would like the work on both jobs. However, she was a little confused about which job to accept.

The first job paid $28,000 per year but offered no benefits. The second job paid $26,000 per year and included full medical benefits.

Which job should Margarita take? Why?

# Practice Basic Skills

## Math

1. Albert has had two job offers. One company pays $1,800 per month. The other company pays $20,000 per year. Which job has the highest salary?

2. Winston takes public transportation to work. He pays $1.80 one way. How much does he pay for five round-trips per week? for twenty round-trips per month?

3. Five workers go to lunch. The total bill is $56.25. How much must each person pay if the bill is split equally?

4. The following are Aurora's work expenses each day for one week. How much did she spend the entire week?

### Monday
| | |
|---|---|
| Transportation | $2.30 |
| Lunch | 5.90 |
| Breaks | 0.60 |

### Tuesday
| | |
|---|---|
| Transportation | $2.30 |
| Lunch | 6.50 |
| Breaks | 2.00 |

### Wednesday
| | |
|---|---|
| Transportation | $2.30 |
| Lunch | 12.50 |
| Breaks | 1.75 |

### Thursday
| | |
|---|---|
| Transportation | $2.30 |
| Lunch | 7.35 |
| Breaks | 0.90 |

### Friday
| | |
|---|---|
| Transportation | $2.30 |
| Lunch | 7.00 |
| Breaks | 1.25 |

5. Kurt was told he would receive a raise of $75 twice a month. How much of a raise will he receive for the year?

6. Compute the net pay (gross pay minus all deductions) for the following employees. (Note: FICA stands for Federal Insurance Contributions Act.)

| EMPLOYEE | GROSS PAY | FEDERAL TAXES | FICA TAXES | OTHER DEDUCTIONS | NET PAY |
|---|---|---|---|---|---|
| Sofia | $2,245 | $525 | $190 | $125 | $ ____ |
| Kirsten | 2,000 | 475 | 170 | 190 | ____ |
| Bon | 2,800 | 590 | 225 | 175 | ____ |
| Pablo | 1,900 | 400 | 150 | 35 | ____ |
| Marina | 2,300 | 550 | 200 | 235 | ____ |
| Walter | 2,245 | 500 | 190 | 140 | ____ |

## English

1. *Rule:* Use the pronouns *I, he, she,* and *they* as the subjects (the entities that perform the action) of a sentence.
   *Examples:* They came to class every day. He was the best student in the office skills class.
   *Practice Exercise:* Rewrite the following sentences, choosing the correct answer for each:

   a. (They, Them) were working hard.
   b. (We, Us) are learning how to use the computer.
   c. My friend and (I, me) like to study together.
   d. (He, Him) and his wife have their own business.
   e. (She and I, Her and me) were in the same class.

2. *Rule:* Use the objective form of personal pronouns—*him, her, them*—as direct objects, indirect objects, or objects of prepositions.
   *Examples:* The teacher taught them well. The interviewer asked her some hard questions. The responsibility was passed from him to her.
   *Practice Exercise:* Rewrite the following sentences, choosing the correct answer for each:

   a. The teacher recommended (she, her).
   b. The assignment gave you and (they, them) a lot of trouble.
   c. Give (we, us) the keyboarding assignment.
   d. Are you talking about (we, us)?
   e. He likes (she, her), but does not like (him, he).

## Proofreading

Rekey the following letter, correcting all errors. Also, change all contractions to full words.

Ms. Vanessa Jackson
360 Glen Springs Drive
Dallas, TX 75243
Dear Ms. Jackson:
Now's your chance, and our chance.

You've been a subscriber for the Dallas Independent for nearly a year. Now's your chance to tell us how we're doing. and her's our chance to get you to reneu.

If you like what you're getting for your investment, you'll reneu you subscription to the Dallas Independent. If you don't like what you're getting, (thousand of business leds and the latest in breaking and in-depth news on area business every week), tell us so we can do better. This reneual notice is inclosed along with a business reply envelope for you convenience. Send this right away so you can get uninterrupted delivery. Also use this opportunity to sen me your coments and suggestions so we can provide the coverage you want. Go ahead, tell us.

We're here to help your make money.

Sincerely,

James Boland, Editor

## Apply Your Knowledge

1. An order clerk's information processing cycle:

    receives order by telephone and enters it into a personal computer;

    cost is calculated by the computer;

    the total is saved in the company's computer network;

    total cost and delivery instructions are printed.

    Refer to the information processing cycle chart shown in Chapter 1, Figure 1.3, page 11. Using the graphics or tables feature of your software program, prepare a chart for the order clerk's cycle.

2. Read the job ads from a local newspaper. Choose an ad for a receptionist and list the qualifications required. Compare them with the qualifications provided in this chapter. Which qualifications are the same? Which are different?

3. Do the same for an advertisement for a secretarial position.

## Using the Reference Manual

Open file ch2ref.doc. Use the grammar section of the Reference Manual at the back of the book to help you correct the sentences. Save and print.

1. The committee meeting is on Fri., January 24.

2. The 9:30 pm showing of the play has been cancelled due to lack of ticket sales.

3. Prof. Grace Lee is a very difficult teacher.

4. Be sure to address the letter 600 Spring St. in Los Angeles.

5. The F.B.I. requires some knowledge of accounting as part of the qualifications.

6. The Made in U.S.A. tag is on most products manufactured in the United States.

7. The plural for brother-in-law is brother-in-laws.

8. The ten deputys in the Sheriff's Department received special recognition for the arrests.

9. Mister Watson is on the program to give the opening address.

10. Send the package FedEx® to 485 So. Cedar in Prescott.

# chapter 3

## Your Attitude and Work

### objectives

*After completing this chapter, you will be able to do the following:*

1. List and describe at least five reasons people work.
2. Describe the effects on others of a positive versus a negative attitude.
3. Explain how to change a negative attitude into a positive one.
4. List five attributes that all employers expect of their employees.

### New Office Terms

- esteem
- negative attitude
- positive attitude
- self-concept
- self-realization
- self-talk
- values
- work
- work ethic

**Answer the following questions to the best of your ability:**

**1.** Why do people who have no need for further income often continue to work?

**2.** What is the effect of a self-fulfilling prophecy and what is the reason for this effect?

**3.** How can your thoughts change a negative attitude into a positive one?

Your satisfaction and success in the world of work will depend to a considerable extent on your attitude toward work and toward other people in your work setting. This overall *work attitude* will, in turn, depend somewhat on your attitude and feeling about yourself—your self-concept. If you enjoy your time on the job and feel that you are doing something worthwhile, you will receive satisfaction from your work. You may actually look forward to going into the office to start a new project or to complete one on which you have been working.

If you get along well with other workers in the office, you will look forward to seeing them—and you will probably have conversations with them during breaks. You will enjoy sharing stories about how you and they spend time away from the office.

Your attitude about work will significantly affect your overall happiness even when you are not at work. In fact, your work will probably become the central activity in your life.

## What Is Work?

According to the *Random House Dictionary of the English Language,* **work** means "exertion or effort directed to produce or accomplish something; labor; toil."

Ralph Waldo Emerson, in defining the purpose of life, wrote, "The purpose of life is not to be happy. It is to be useful, to be honorable, to be compassionate, to have it make some difference that you have lived and lived well." Emerson's statement implies a choice. We choose to be purposefully engaged. We choose to work.

The dictionary definition suggests that work must be difficult; exertion and effort are a part of an activity or it is not work. On the other hand, Emerson sees the purpose of life as being or doing something useful, which is a different way of viewing work.

Do you think that what Wolfgang Mozart, Marie Curie, or Benjamin Franklin did was work? When you look at these special people and their accomplishments, you begin to see that work can have many connotations. Can you imagine any of these famous people *not* working?

Buddy Ebsen, who had several starring roles on TV, was asked during an interview when he intended to quit working. He replied that he never intended to quit. "Working is my life," he said. He was in his eighties.

Bette Davis continued making movies after she was eighty and a severe stroke had left her face partially paralyzed. In a TV interview, Barbara Walters asked Davis, "What keeps you going?" The famous actress replied,

## Technology in the Office | IMAGE EDITING SOFTWARE

In the past, office workers spent most of their time on the job keying words and calculating numeric answers. Twenty-first-century office workers deal with more than words and numbers. Photographic and graphic art images have become a significant part of how we communicate. Images are printed on everything—letterheads, correspondence content, and advertising brochures, for example. Of course, images are the major part of training videos for every type of job.

Popular word processing applications allow office workers to place photographs and graphic art into documents. Image editing is a skill used in many offices to manipulate photographs and graphic art so that images are more pleasing or have greater impact.

You will find a number of excellent image editing programs in local office supply stores. Some programs are fairly easy to use and perform many editing tasks well. The most powerful image editing programs are quite complex and require considerable time to learn to use—and they are expensive. ■

---

"Really and truly—what keeps me going is work." The driving force that kept her alive and happy was accomplishing something worthwhile.

Margaret Mead, a renowned anthropologist, said she might die some-day but she would never retire!

Work does not have to be an unpleasant activity. If you enjoy what you are doing, it can seem nearly effortless and will be an important, vital part of your life and your existence as a creative human being.

Work, then, is any useful activity or purposeful, creative endeavor.

# What Motivates People to Work?

Some jobs are not very pleasant—yet somebody has to do them. The necessities of life require that we work to earn a living. We need shelter from the elements, clothing to keep us warm, and food to keep us healthy. Generally, the way to acquire these things is to have a regular, paying job.

## Money

What do you suppose is the primary motivation for people to work? It is money, of course. Would you work if you were not receiving money for doing so?

People want money for many different reasons. Basic needs, such as food, clothing, and shelter, are obvious reasons for working. Those needs are part of a larger human need for security. Having enough money to meet your obligations brings security and independence. For example, if you do not know where the next rent payment is coming from, you can suffer enormous stress and anxiety.

Perhaps you have already had some work experience. Many young people work part-time or during the summers bagging groceries, cashiering, helping out at the neighborhood swimming pool or at a youth camp, or baby-sitting. If you have done so, you have felt the kind of independence earning your own money brings. Having money in your pocket to buy what you choose feels good.

## Ethics on the Job

You have been hired as a file clerk in a company that designs and produces sports clothing. You are very happy to have this job because you will have many opportunities to learn about the business. You hope, too, that you will meet people who will possibly help you to advance within the company.

You begin to socialize with Robert, one of the young designers. The two of you become good friends.

One evening you share some drawings of bicycle clothing that you have made. Robert is very impressed and encourages you to enroll in some clothing design classes.

At work a few weeks later you come across a series of drawings that are very similar to the ones you showed to Robert. You learn that he has submitted these drawings to his manager for consideration as part of a new line of bicycle clothing. Your discovery is affecting the way you feel about your work.

1. **Will you talk to Robert about the drawings?**

2. **Will you speak with Robert's manager about Robert's designs?** ■

Eventually, you may have the responsibility of a family. Having enough money to meet your family's expenses and obligations will make you feel secure and safe.

Most people enjoy and take pride in having a home, so they spend time and money painting and repairing their living spaces. Many people spend part of their earnings working on major home improvements and comfortable, attractive furniture.

Many people save part of their earnings for the larger expenses of educating their children, covering unforeseen medical bills, and traveling.

People also want money for leisure-time activities. Some people work even if they do not enjoy their jobs, primarily to earn money to support their hobbies. Younger people, especially, who do not have the responsibility of marriage and family, spend a large part of their earnings on consumer goods such as automobiles, TV and music equipment, and fashionable clothing. They also spend money on social and leisure activities such as parties, concerts, movies, and sports. The list of things you might buy and the ways you might spend your money are endless.

In some circles, a person's worth is gauged by how much money he or she earns. Money can bring power and influence. Some people work very hard for years to acquire things and accomplish goals that are materially based simply because it makes them feel important.

Is making a lot of money vital to you? If so, earning a lot of money will require you to spend long hours on the job instead of doing other things in your leisure time.

©Spencer Grant/PhotoEdit

Many teenagers' first work experience is cashiering in a fast-food restaurant.

## Creative Satisfaction

For Mozart, Curie, and Franklin, work satisfied a need that most people have: to be creative. Some people have very special talents and decide to follow wherever those talents take them. Writers, dancers, musicians, and artists work to utilize their special abilities. You probably have something you do especially well. For example, maybe you have a wonderful speaking voice. Even if you never become a news broadcaster, you can be a receptionist. Your good voice quality will be an asset as you greet others in person and on the telephone in an office.

Workers aware of the final result of their work take pride in knowing that a task was completed, a goal accomplished. Anything from a short report, carefully and neatly prepared, to a new automobile design can bring creative satisfaction.

## Contact with Other People

The companionship that comes from your job is an important benefit of working. While you are in school, you probably have all the friendships and social contacts you need.

When you leave school, though, work will be your primary source of social contact. You will meet people with whom you will socialize, and they will introduce you to their friends. As you broaden your circle of acquaintances, you will also broaden your life experiences by discovering new ideas and new activities.

You may find people at work whom you do not like and with whom you would rather not spend much time. These people will provide you with lessons in tolerance and teach you something about how to get along with all co-workers, whether you like them or not.

You and the people you work with will accomplish things together. Belonging to a team that sets and accomplishes important goals can be gratifying. Consider the people who work for the National Aeronautics and Space Administration (NASA) on the space shuttles. They always appear elated when one of their missions goes well. You have probably seen them on TV shaking each other's hands, clapping, patting each other on the back, and hugging. Something about this kind of working relationship is very satisfying. Accomplishing important things with people at work is a wonderful experience.

## Feeling of Importance

Influence comes, in part, from accepting responsibility. Those individuals who are most often present when the work is being done are usually also present when decisions are being made. The more you are willing to work, and the greater responsibility you are willing to take, the greater influence you will have. You are also likely to earn more money.

Some people work primarily to gain this feeling of importance and influence, and they often become leaders. They take initiative and responsibility and are most happy when doing so.

Many people, though, do not choose to accept that kind of responsibility. They do not choose to be a boss, and they do not choose to make the required investments of time. Yet they feel important because they fulfill their own particular role in a project, whatever it may be.

©Eyewire Collection

Supervisors and more experienced workers will be major sources of information to help you learn to do your job better.

Susan learned to sew when she was very young, making dresses for her dolls. As she grew up, she began to draw pictures of dresses, coats, and outfits for girls to wear. She enjoyed sewing and drawing, but she did not realize that a career might be associated with what she considered to be only a hobby.

In school, Susan learned word processing and later accepted a job as an office services assistant in a large office. She found her work interesting, but something was missing from her job. She wasn't sure why, but she knew she wasn't completely happy.

Susan's office was in a large building that also housed a dressmaking firm. The building had a cafeteria where she met and had conversations with some people who worked for the dressmaking company. Susan discovered that a word processing job would soon be available in the dressmaking company, so she applied for the job and was hired.

Although her duties were essentially the same, Susan was so happy in her new environment that she had a wonderful attitude and looked forward to going to work every day.

Susan eventually learned how to design and create clothing using a computer. Her new office responsibilities incorporated dress designing with her word processing and other computer skills. Now she had an active role in an industry that she loved.

1.  *What effect did the work environment have on Susan's attitude toward work?*

2.  *If you were Susan, and the building you worked in did not include the dressmaking company, would you continue working at the same job or look for something else?* ■

## Interesting Challenges and Intellectual Stimulation

Suppose that you inherited a large sum of money. Would you continue working? Many people work not because they need the money, but because they find work interesting and stimulating. Work brings meaning and purpose to their lives. Even if money is not an important motivator, they continue going to work every day.

Some jobs and careers are especially fascinating, requiring research, problem solving, invention, product creation, or other intellectual activity. Some people work just because of this intellectual stimulation.

Even if your job is not inherently interesting, you can nearly always make it interesting by being concerned about the people you work with and taking special care to complete the tasks that are assigned to you. Your attitude about what you do can make your work either very dull or very interesting.

# *The Work Ethic*

The United States, through the agricultural age and the industrial revolution, was built on the idea that everyone should do his or her share and make a contribution to society through working. This concept is known as the **work ethic.** Individual contributions need not be huge, but each person should do his or her share to promote the common good.

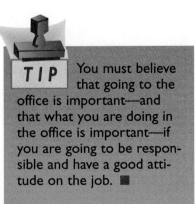

**TIP** You must believe that going to the office is important—and that what you are doing in the office is important—if you are going to be responsible and have a good attitude on the job. ■

The industrial revolution made jobs possible for everyone. Some of these jobs were dangerous, and some employers treated workers cruelly. Labor unions were formed that helped make working reasonable hours under safe conditions possible for everyone.

Some people perform jobs that are clearly designed to promote the common good. Mother Teresa, a nun who spent her life tending the poor in India, is an example. Such people have chosen to work in serving professions that provide the satisfaction of doing something good for someone else.

Many kinds of organizations serve the common good, such as churches, nonprofit community organizations, and social service agencies. These organizations offer diverse and interesting jobs, including office work of all types.

Your job may not directly serve the community, as do those mentioned previously. However, everyone who works makes a contribution by providing the goods and services needed for the economic survival of society.

People work for many different reasons. Different jobs interest different people, and most people work for a combination of reasons.

## Recall Time

*Answer the following questions:*

**1.** What are two definitions of *work*? List and discuss them.

**2.** People are motivated to work because of their own personal needs. What are four reasons people want or need to work?

**3.** Some people work for *creative satisfaction*. What does this phrase mean to you?

**4.** Briefly, what is meant by the term *work ethic*?

# Your Attitude

The reasons you work will affect your attitude toward a job. When people feel they have choices about the type of work they do, they demonstrate a better attitude on the job.

Those who feel obligated to work at dull jobs often feel trapped. Their feelings are reflected in their attitude at work.

Regardless of the job, you can make it interesting by finding new and better ways of doing it, learning to do additional assignments, and helping co-workers to become more efficient.

Having a good attitude about working is an advantage. You will probably work about two thousand hours a year for about forty years, which will mean a total of almost eighty thousand hours. If you do not have a good attitude toward your work, the hours and years will drag by, offering neither creative satisfaction nor any other sort of gratification. Your feelings of self-worth will suffer, and you could feel like a failure.

Do you have a classmate who has a bad attitude about school? How does this student behave? Can you name some of the traits of a bad attitude? See Figure 3.1, page 46, for examples of attitude traits.

This worker resents being interrupted by customers calling to ask questions. Is her attitude positive or negative?

©Corbis/Digital Stock

# Negative Attitude

What is commonly called a bad attitude is usually a negative attitude, and it can take many different forms. Who suffers from one person's bad attitude? Everyone who comes in contact with that person suffers, especially that person herself or himself. Furthermore, the worker with a negative attitude will probably not remain on the job very long.

Workers with a **negative attitude** are unpleasant, are indifferent, and rarely smile. They seldom say good morning to their co-workers, do not often have a good word for their associates, and may never offer to assist others in the office.

A negative attitude is further characterized by constant complaining about nearly everything. Complainers grumble about the boss, about co-workers, about conditions in the office, about the weather, about their salaries, and on and on. In the process of complaining, they are critical of people with whom they work, and they rarely have anything positive to say about their associates. These complainers are tiresome to be around, and other workers will make a point of avoiding them.

People with negative attitudes usually have low self-esteem and blame others for their own mistakes and shortcomings. They constantly make excuses and never admit their own failures. They seem unable to see things from any perspective but their own and are generally concerned only about advancing their own well-being. They often attempt to force their opinions on others.

Do you have any of the qualities that indicate a negative attitude? The wonderful thing about attitude is that it can be changed. You can decide that having a negative attitude will not serve you well, may cause you to lose jobs, and certainly will cause you to lose friends. Then you can set about fixing your attitude.

**FIGURE 3.1 • Examples of Positive and Negative Attitude Traits**

| Positive Attitude Traits | Negative Attitude Traits |
| --- | --- |
| ➕ | ➖ |
| ▪ Shows consideration for others | ▪ Thinks only of self |
| ▪ Respects other opinions | ▪ Forces own opinions on others |
| ▪ Smiles often and with ease | ▪ Almost never smiles |
| ▪ Complains very little | ▪ Complains all the time |
| ▪ Admits making mistakes | ▪ Blames others for own mistakes |
| ▪ Helps solve problems | ▪ Expects everything to go wrong |
| ▪ Looks other people in the eyes during conversations | ▪ Avoids eye contact during conversations |
| ▪ Almost never criticizes others | ▪ Frequently criticizes others |
| ▪ Accepts change or suggestions from others | ▪ Is unwilling to make changes |
| ▪ Has many interests | ▪ Has few interests |

## Positive Attitude

Do you know someone who always seems to have a positive attitude about school? How does this person behave? Can you name some of the traits of a positive attitude?

Generally, people with a **positive attitude** have a high level of self-esteem, are pleasant to be around, and have many friends and numerous interests. They smile easily and go out of their way to greet their co-workers, offer to assist in small ways, and help make life easier and more pleasant for those around them. They are considerate, and they know how to compromise. When appropriate, they willingly change their own ideas and behavior for the good of their associates.

Those people with a positive attitude seem unflappable, and very little appears to trouble them. They rarely complain when things go wrong around them. They willingly take responsibility for the mistakes they make and for their own shortcomings. They do not blame others when things get difficult.

You will seldom hear these people criticize their co-workers or their bosses. They are loyal and able to see things from another person's perspective because they respect other people's views.

Take some time to list your own negative and positive traits. Which word—*negative* or *positive*—do you think more accurately describes you? Check the negative traits that you want to change, and plan how you will go about making them positive traits.

Behavioral scientists believe that our attitudes toward other people, including both positive and negative attitude traits, are based primarily on our genetic makeup. However, they can be, and often are, influenced considerably by cultural aspects, including the attitudes of our parents, other family members, friends, and the larger society. Usually, personality—including our attitudes toward others—is fairly well set by the time we reach our early twenties. So how do you go about changing negative traits into positive ones? Obviously, we cannot change our heredity. But many of our attitudinal traits are habitual. That is, we act and react the same way so often that our actions have become a habit. If the habit is a negative one, then conscious and repeated effort to act or react in a more constructive way can eventually turn the habit into a positive one. This process is similar to behavioral modification, which is a structured approach to changing one's attitudes by first changing behavior.

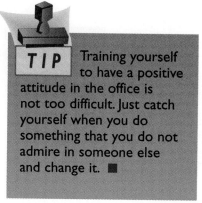

**TIP** Training yourself to have a positive attitude in the office is not too difficult. Just catch yourself when you do something that you do not admire in someone else and change it. ■

## Your Responsibilities

One important aspect of any job is responsibility. Even if your job does not require you to accept total responsibility for the outcome of a project, you will be responsible for your portion of it and for your personal conduct. Your attitude will be reflected in your willingness to meet your responsibilities.

Your employer will have certain expectations of you, and you are responsible for fulfilling these expectations. You may occasionally be unsure what your employer wants you to do. When you feel unsure, ask what he or she expects of you.

©corbisimages.com

Helping out with tasks that might not be part of your job description shows that you have the right attitude.

## Molly Lopez

*Executive Secretary*
*The Clorox Company*

**Q.** Ms. Lopez, how important is a good attitude for an office worker?

**A.** A positive attitude in an office environment is probably one of the most important characteristics you can bring to your job, especially in today's world where the demands are much greater, and employers are much less tolerant than they were just a few years ago.

Today, supporting multiple bosses is generally the rule rather than the exception, and adjusting to the different work styles and personalities can make your job so much more difficult if you do not approach it with a positive attitude. Even the best of jobs will have certain tasks that are not as enjoyable as others; identify them, accept them, and tackle them when you are at your peak.

**Q.** Have you seen any examples of workers being promoted because of a great attitude?

**A.** Yes, two employees were candidates for a promotional opportunity in the Executive Offices. Both had excellent skills. One, however, had the reputation for going the "extra mile" in everything she did. She, of course, received the promotion.

**Q.** Have you seen any examples of workers who have been terminated because of a poor attitude?

**A.** Yes, a man with impeccable technical skills whose work was of the highest quality. However, everyone in the office felt his negative attitude. Within a year of his employment, his "I was looking for a job when I found this one" attitude resulted in his termination.

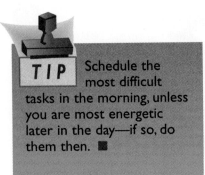

**TIP** Schedule the most difficult tasks in the morning, unless you are most energetic later in the day—if so, do them then. ■

## Cooperation

Your employer will expect you to be cooperative. You will probably not be working alone, and cooperating with other workers will be important. Some people feel their responsibilities are limited to an established set of tasks. Usually, however, the work of different people may overlap from day to day. Sometimes other workers will need your assistance, and you should offer it willingly.

In addition, sometimes you will be given an assignment that you feel is not part of your job—a task that does not fit your job description. Whether you see the request as a regular part of your job or not, you will be expected to take on the assignment willingly, without complaining. You may be asked to do some jobs you just do not like, but your supervisor will think that you are responsible for being cooperative in doing these jobs agreeably and with a positive attitude.

Mary Ann was hired as a front desk clerk in the office at the Young Men's Christian Association (YMCA). She was interested in physical fitness and was delighted to get the job. She was efficient and did all that was required of her, neatly and on time. She liked her job, arrived at work promptly each day, and left at quitting time.

However, Mary Ann rarely smiled and did not seem to have fun with her co-workers and the YMCA members. People got the impression that she was indifferent and did not care about her work. The YMCA is a place where people go to relax and have a pleasant time at their leisure. Even though Mary Ann was good at her job, people complained about her attitude.

Actually, Mary Ann was a conscientious young woman, and she wanted to do her best. She was unaware that she had an unpleasant manner. During her first performance review, her supervisor explained that members were unhappy about her behavior. Mary Ann was eager to know how to improve the situation, and her supervisor gave her some ideas about how to behave more pleasantly.

First, her supervisor suggested that Mary Ann smile more often. Second, she suggested that Mary Ann make sure she understood what the members wanted. Third, she asked Mary Ann to try to meet the members' needs by acting interested in their concerns.

Mary Ann's behavior improved, and her co-workers complimented her on her efforts. Several members spent more time with her and seemed to like her much better. Though she had been unaware of her problem, her willingness to change demonstrated a positive attitude—and she was even happier with her job.

1. **What would have happened if Mary Ann's supervisor had not explained her effect on co-workers and others?**

2. **What if Mary Ann's supervisor had been negative in her criticism?**

3. **What if Mary Ann had not been willing to change?** ■

# Honesty

Businesses lose huge sums of money every year to theft by their employees. You are responsible for understanding what is yours and what belongs to the company. Some people think taking home stationery, copy paper, pens, postage stamps, pencils, or paper clips is acceptable. Some act as if these office supplies are perks (benefits) of the job. In fact, taking such items is usually considered grounds for dismissal. If a policy statement does not clearly state that employees are entitled to help themselves to office supplies, then all supplies should stay in the office to be used for official business.

On full-time jobs, your employer is paying you for a full day's work. Standing around in hallways or in cubicles is not working. Talking on the company telephone to family and friends is not working. Give your employer an honest day's work—you are paid to work a full day.

Your supervisor will expect you to be honest when asked about different aspects of your work. Do not make up stories and excuses for things that are being questioned. Just tell the truth. Your supervisors will appreciate and respect you for it.

Honesty is your responsibility and an obligation you have to your employer.

This young man makes lengthy personal calls from his job. He thinks making local calls is all right. What do you think?

# Dependability

Dependability means that you are on the job every day and that you arrive on time. Continual tardiness can be grounds for dismissal.

If you are ill and cannot go to work, call your employer or supervisor and explain the reason. The earlier you call, the more likely she or he will be able to find someone to take over your responsibilities for the day. Call no later than your usual arrival time.

Missing a day at work without a legitimate reason or not calling is also grounds for dismissal. Some people just decide to sleep in and do not call. This behavior is irresponsible and reflects a negative attitude.

Dependability also means that you can be counted on to complete your work, that you can be expected to do what you are told to do, and that you are reliable. Dependability is an important attribute in any relationship. Your friends and family appreciate knowing that they can count on you to do what you say you will do. Your employer and co-workers will expect it and appreciate it, too.

# Willingness to Learn

When you accept a position with a company, you are responsible for learning what the job entails. You may be learning new things about the job for many months. As you master one aspect, you will find others to learn. Willingness to take direction and to learn all aspects of your job are expected when you accept employment. Show initiative by learning more than your own assigned tasks, and you will increase your probability of being promoted.

You will also be expected to listen to constructive criticism from your supervisor about how you are performing your job. Hearing this criticism may not always be comfortable, but it will be to your advantage. Remember Mary Ann and her job at the YMCA? She willingly accepted suggestions from her supervisor about her behavior. Mary Ann was not aware of her problem. However, when her supervisor pointed it out, she readily listened and made some changes.

# Acceptable Personal Conduct

You will be expected to act in a businesslike manner in the office. That is, you must dress appropriately, be clean and neat, and refrain from cursing, talking loudly, carrying food around, or using other bad manners around customers or co-workers.

Every company and office has rules. For example, some managers do not object if you eat at your desk. In that case, you may bring your lunch or a snack. Most companies have policies that do not allow smoking inside the building, and some have designated smoking areas. If you smoke, do so only where permitted.

Learn the rules of personal conduct and follow them. If things are unclear to you, ask your supervisor so that you will not find yourself doing something you are not supposed to do.

If you have a personal problem, such as alcohol or drug abuse, family dysfunction, or emotional difficulties, you are responsible for seeking help. These problems affect your job sooner or later. Many companies have an industrial nurse or psychologist with whom you may talk. Your discussion will be completely private and confidential. This person will

help you or will make getting the help you need easier. If no such person is available in your company, seek answers from your minister or from your county's department of mental health.

Some positions require special off-the-job conduct. For example, if you work in the office of a public figure, such as a politician, you will be expected to be an upright citizen at all times. If you work for the school system, school officials have certain expectations about your behavior off the job because of your contact with children.

Can you think of any other jobs that would have requirements about how you behave off the job?

Any job brings with it responsibility. Just as you are now responsible and accountable to your teachers through tests and grades, you will also be responsible and accountable to your employers through your duties and behavior on the job.

## Recall Time

*Answer the following questions:*

**1.** What are the characteristics of a negative attitude? What are the characteristics of a positive attitude?

**2.** When you accept a job, you accept responsibility to the job, to your employer, and to your co-workers. What might be included in taking responsibility on the job?

**3.** Employees are responsible for their personal conduct. What does this statement mean?

# Attitudes and Self-Concept

For many years, psychologists have studied human behavior, attempting to determine how and why people behave the way they do. Attitude is demonstrated in behavior, and attitude has roots in how we feel about ourselves, our **self-concept.**

Self-concept is developed through a complex and ill-defined process. An ongoing argument about nature versus nurture is involved. Do we act the way we do because of our genetic inheritance or because of our environments and the way our parents and families cared for us?

Some experts believe that our parents influence our self-concept to a large degree. Some of us were reared by parents whose expectations were difficult for us to live up to. When we did not measure up, and our parents disapproved of what we did, our self-concept suffered. Some people learn early that they are "not okay."

Several years ago, Dr. Thomas Harris explained in his book *I'm Okay, You're Okay* that many of us get the message early in life that we are not at all "okay." Unfortunately, this "not okay" message has far-reaching effects. We carry this belief, this negative baggage, around with us for most of our lives until we actively work to dispel it. Not only do we carry it around, we make it stronger in the ways we talk to ourselves.

Some people are so demanding of themselves that they are never quite satisfied with what they accomplish. These people talk to themselves in a negative manner, saying, "I'll always be stupid," "I'll never be

able to do this," "I'll never succeed," and so on. Some people speak to themselves this way all the time.

**Self-talk** is made up of all the negative and positive thoughts we have about ourselves. These thoughts are stored in our subconscious minds and affect our behavior.

Another concept, related to self-talk, is called a *self-fulfilling prophecy.* This concept means that what you say about your chances of success or failure influences the outcome. When you believe certain things about yourself—about your abilities and personal characteristics—you tend to become the person you believe you are.

How do we change these negative feelings about ourselves? One way is by changing the way we talk to ourselves. In his book *The Self-Talk Solution,* Shad Helmstetter, Ph.D., discusses how we can begin to change negative ideas about ourselves by changing the things we say to ourselves. The idea is that when you feel a negative idea coming on, you quickly change it to a positive one.

For example, suppose that a boy notices a girl at school and is interested in her. He may be telling himself that she would never be interested in him. However, if he can change the message to himself, he may feel that she might like him. He might say to himself something such as, "I'm an interesting person; the girls think I'm cute and appealing."

With this kind of self-talk, your attitude about yourself can change so that your self-confidence is evident. Self-confidence is generally an attractive trait in everybody.

The same kinds of ideas can help you with a positive attitude on the job. If you tell yourself you are likable and capable and competent to do your job, you set yourself up for success.

## Esteem

The need for esteem is one reason people work. **Esteem** can mean how highly you regard others and also how you feel about yourself—part of your self-concept. It is also how people in your environment see you. Esteem implies that you are valued by yourself and by other people. Everyone likes to be liked. Esteem needs are met through accomplishment, good attitude, and values.

**Self-realization** means that you have realized (that is, accomplished) all the important goals and aspirations in your life. It means that you have become the best that you can be. Self-realization is hard to attain, but those who do accomplish it generally do so through their work.

If you go through life without your needs for recognition and esteem being satisfied, your self-concept will suffer.

The process for developing your self-concept is complicated, but the ideas in this section can be helpful when you begin to sort out how you feel about yourself.

## Values

As children grow and develop, they begin to incorporate values into their self-concepts. **Values** are the things that each person believes to be true and important. They could be such things as honesty, integrity, family, friends, industry, and success. Your values are often reflected in your attitude. If working is not important to you, it will show in your attitude and in your work performance. If accepting your share of the responsibility is

not one of your values, that lack will also affect your attitude and performance on the job.

Your self-concept also affects your attitude—in work, in school, and in your social and family relationships. A positive attitude is important for your success on the job and for your happiness in all of life.

If your self-concept is that you are capable of meeting the responsibilities of your job, chances are your attitude will generally be positive.

## Recall Time

*Answer the following questions:*

**1.** Self-concept means how we see ourselves. What are some ways our self-concept is developed?

**2.** Self-talk is a way to undo negative thinking about ourselves. What is self-talk?

**3.** We all have things that are important to us. These things represent our values. What sorts of things come under the heading of values?

**4.** What are some of your values?

# Summary

The way work is viewed and the things that motivate people to work affect attitudes on the job. Ralph Waldo Emerson said that the purpose of life is not to be happy, but to be useful. For many people, work is being useful.

People work for many reasons. For most people, the main reason is to earn a living. People spend money for various things, from necessities, such as food, shelter, and clothing, to leisure-time activities. Most people save some of what they earn for larger expenses such as medical bills and education for their children. Security and independence are probably the biggest motivators behind working to earn money.

People also work for creative satisfaction and the social benefits of being with other people engaged in common goals. Some people work to feel important and strive to earn more money while accepting more responsibility in their work. Others work for the intellectual stimulation.

The work ethic means that everyone should work to do her or his share and make a contribution to society. Almost every job contributes something to society.

Attitudes of different people range from extremely positive to extremely negative. Although most of us fall somewhere between these extremes, nearly everyone could benefit by having a more positive attitude. A positive attitude is characterized by a smile, pleasantness, and willingness to be helpful and to learn on the job. People who have a positive attitude usually relate well to others, make new acquaintances easily, and have many interests. They are loyal, tend not to be critical, and rarely complain. They seem to enjoy life.

A negative attitude is characterized by an unpleasant demeanor, a complaining nature, a practice of blaming others for one's own errors, and a habit of making the job more difficult for everyone. People who have a

A positive attitude in an office environment shows your co-workers that you have a willingness to cooperate.

negative attitude seem unable to see things from any point of view other than their own and generally are not enjoyable to be around. They have fewer friends and a narrower range of interests than positive people.

You will notice, on the job, that the people who tend to have good attitudes are also willing to take on the responsibilities that are part of agreeing to work in an office. These responsibilities include being cooperative, honest, dependable, and willing to learn and take direction.

Acceptable personal conduct is an important responsibility. Good manners, appropriate language, appropriate dress, and general good conduct on and off the job are some areas of personal responsibility.

People's attitudes about work are directly linked with their attitudes about themselves. This attitude is our self-concept, or how we view ourselves. The development of our self-concept is complex and involves both our environments and our genetic inheritance. Sometimes we perceive as young children that we are "not okay" and we carry that knowledge around with us as we grow up. If we feel "not okay," we act "not okay"—thus, we have a negative attitude.

You can change these "not okay" feelings by using positive self-talk and eliminating negative self-talk messages that you might be giving yourself throughout the day.

Our attitudes also reflect our values—the things we consider to be important as we conduct our lives. Some values are honesty, integrity, family, friends, industry, and success.

Your attitude on the job thus develops from many other aspects of your life. Having a better understanding of those areas will help you to be happier and more positive about working.

When you are considering how to improve your attitude on the job, answer the following questions:

- Do I like the job I am doing?
- What are the reasons I want to work?
- Would I work if I did not receive money for it?
- Do I demonstrate a positive attitude?
- Do I demonstrate a negative attitude?
- Am I cooperative, dependable, and willing to learn?
- Do I know and follow company and office rules of conduct?
- How do I talk to myself, with positive or negative messages?
- What do I consider important in my life? What are my values?

# before you leave...

**When you have completed this chapter, answer the following questions:**
1. Why do people who have no need of further income often continue to work?
2. What is the effect of a self-fulfilling prophecy and what is the reason for this effect?
3. How can your thoughts change a negative attitude into a positive one?

# Review & Application

## Check Your Knowledge

1. What is the dictionary definition of *work?*

2. Did our greatest composers and artists work?

3. List several different reasons people are motivated to work.

4. What are considered basic needs?

5. What is creative satisfaction?

6. How does work make people feel important?

7. Define the term *work ethic.*

8. List the attributes of a negative attitude.

9. List the attributes of a positive attitude.

10. List some ways an employer expects an employee to be responsible.

11. What else does honesty mean in addition to simply telling the truth?

12. Describe some ways you are responsible for your personal conduct.

13. List some things you could say to yourself that would enhance your own positive attitude.

14. How do your values relate to your attitude at work?

## Review Your Vocabulary

On a separate piece of paper, write the letter of the vocabulary word that is described below.

_____ 1. realized all important goals and aspirations

_____ 2. mental position or emotional posture resulting in behavior that is unpleasant, indifferent, seldom smiling

_____ 3. all the negative and positive thoughts we have about ourselves

_____ 4. concept implying that you are valued by yourself and others

_____ 5. mental position resulting in behavior that is pleasant, interested in others, and often smiling

_____ 6. what we believe about ourselves

_____ 7. idea that everyone should do his or her share and make a contribution to society through working

_____ 8. things a person believes are important

_____ 9. exertion or effort directed to produce or accomplish something

| | |
|---|---|
| a. esteem | f. self-talk |
| b. negative attitude | g. values |
| c. positive attitude | h. work |
| d. self-concept | i. work ethic |
| e. self-realization | |

## Discuss and Analyze an Office Situation

1. Barry has a job as a computer operator in a busy office. He likes his job and is punctual, honest, willing to learn new things, and responsible in other ways. However, Barry spends weekends drinking with his friends, and some Monday mornings he finds getting to work on time difficult. A nondrinking friend suggests that perhaps Barry's drinking is becoming excessive and a problem, even though Barry is generally functioning well on the job. What should Barry do?

2. Susan is an accountant for a large corporation. She likes her job and generally demonstrates a high level of competency and an excellent attitude. However, problems arise when people speak to her about her work. She becomes defensive and argumentative. Her supervisor has difficulty approaching her with any suggestions.

   Susan's supervisor takes Susan aside to discuss these problems with her. The supervisor discovers that Susan comes from a family where her mother was disapproving and criticized Susan for the smallest mistakes, causing Susan to develop a negative self-concept.

   How might Susan begin to fix her negative self-concept?

## Practice Basic Skills

### Math

Jerry is part of a single-parent family, and he wants to assist with expenses at home. He searches for a job that matches the computer skills he learned while in school. The job he thought he would like doing does not pay as much as some of the others. To help him make his decision, he created a monthly budget to clarify what he needs to earn to help his family the way he wishes.

Create a monthly budget for Jerry with some of the following categories:

- rent
- utilities
- gasoline
- auto insurance
- lunches
- other food
- clothing

What other items will Jerry need to purchase or pay for? If you have a checking account, review your own check register to recall how you have recently spent money. Fill in the figures for Jerry's budget, and add them up.

### English

To maintain a high level of self-esteem and therefore improve your attitude, you must speak and write standard English. Rewrite or key the following paragraph, correcting all examples of nonstandard English.

I can key really good and groove on doing telephone work. If you decides to hire me, I can be an asset to your office because I know how to rap with people real good. I think this job is rad, and I will enjoy be'n a part of this here office. Thank ya a lot.

### Proofreading

In your office job, you may be asked to do some minor editing for your supervisor. You will want to respond to this request with a positive attitude. Rewrite or key the following letter, correcting the misspelled words, nonstandard language, and punctuation errors.

Dear Mr. Brown:

I would like to take this oportunity to speek to you about a business mater in our last shipmat we received several more peaces than we had ordered. We wood hope that you would be willing to adjust our billing of May 3 by deducting the cost of the merchandise, a list of the items we did not order is atached.

Thank you.

Yurs truely,

Mr. John Green

## Apply Your Knowledge

1. Make a list of the kinds of things you might say to yourself if you were practicing positive self-talk. Try saying these to yourself for a few days, then write about the results.

2. Becoming aware of negative ideas and attitudes that you may be demonstrating is important. Make a list of the negative attitudes you suspect you may have. Then ask your friends for honest ideas about how you could improve your negative attitudes. List them and work to put them into practice.

3. One of the first steps in learning to work with people from cultures different than our own is to identify our preconceived ideas about their cultures. Think about the students in your school. Make a list of the various cultures you think they represent. Then, using your word processing program, list both negative and positive ideas you have about each of these cultures. Think about your preconceptions as you attend classes with these students. Compare what you observe about these students with your expectations. Complete your list by comparing your preconceived ideas with your actual observations. What did you learn?

## Using the Reference Manual

Open file ch3ref.doc. Use the punctuation section of the Reference Manual at the back of the book to help you correct the sentences. Save and print.

1. Tina received B grades in the following classes; English, Spanish, and Western Civilization.

2. You may study for this test in three ways, read the chapter, study the summary points, and review your notes.

3. Dear Mr. Scott; etc., etc.

4. The activity began at 5;00 p.m. Mountain Standard Time.

5. The doctor recommended only one third the normal dosage.

6. My post office box number is 3345.

7. The manager insisted on state of the art technology in the offices.

8. The ex President of Babbitt Corporation had no comment.

9. Part of the requirements in computer applications class was to re do the assignment until it was mailable.

10. Can we ignore that twenty five students have not been assigned classes?

# chapter 4

# Getting Along with People

## objectives

**After completing this chapter, you will be able to do the following:**

1. Use human relationship skills in the office to work as a team member.
2. Be supportive of co-workers in the office.
3. Maintain a professional appearance in the office.
4. Acknowledge the good work and ideas of others.
5. Understand and deal with difficult people.
6. Accept criticism gracefully and admit your own mistakes.
7. Rid yourself of unhappy feelings.
8. Be assertive without being aggressive.
9. Accept assignments willingly and set priorities.
10. Keep your boss informed of your progress on assignments.
11. Maintain high ethical standards in office relationships.

### New Office Terms

- aggressive communication
- assertive communication
- assertiveness
- body language
- co-workers

- human relations
- interpersonal relations
- passive communication
- seniority

# before you begin...

**Answer the following questions to the best of your ability:**

**1.** What is the value of taking part in office social activities?

**2.** What is the value of maintaining positive behavior on the job?

**3.** What are some strategies you would use in dealing with difficult people?

**D**uring your adult life, you will spend half your waking hours at work. Few jobs are performed by one person working alone, so you will probably work with other people in a cooperative effort. Cooperation will require good skills, good work habits, and workable strategies for dealing effectively with your co-workers.

**Human relations** and **interpersonal relations** are both terms meaning how people get along with one another. Work is more enjoyable and workers are more productive when they practice good human relations. When they do not, unhappiness on the job and poor performance may result. If you are unable to get along well with your co-workers, you will find career advancement difficult. Some studies show that more than 80 percent of your career success depends on interpersonal skills, or your ability to cooperate effectively with the people in your work environment.

Practicing good human relations skills benefits you in other aspects of your life, too. Begin now to practice some of the strategies and ideas that follow.

Listen to others' requests and comments with an open mind, and they will do the same for you. Listening is an important part of teamwork.

## Technology in the Office    DATA INPUT ALTERNATIVES

For number crunching, the personal computer (PC) is unsurpassed. However, getting data into a PC can be a slow, even annoying, process. Entering data via voice input is a useful alternative. The latest versions of some spreadsheet programs are set up well for voice input. Several voice-input programs now have a read-back mode to help proof documents. Lightweight microphone-headset combinations make voice input easier than ever.

A scanner, especially a scanner with a document feeder, provides an efficient way to enter documents into a computer. Some scanners include optical character recognition (OCR) software. The highest-quality, most complete OCR programs usually must be purchased separately.

Digital photographs may be entered into a computer via camera-to-computer cables. However, a digital film reader is more reliable because it is always connected to a PC.

After data is entered, you must rely on a keyboard and a mouse to manipulate the data. The keyboard that came with your PC may have programmed functions that make it the best choice for your PC. Therefore, you probably will not be looking for a better-quality keyboard. Do look for a better-quality mouse—such as a cordless optical mouse—for smooth cursor manipulation. ■

# Teamwork

Have you participated in team sports, sung in a choir, or worked with others on a committee? You have probably taken part in some group activity and learned that the key to a successful team is cooperation. Each team member must fulfill an assigned role while working in concert with others.

The same sort of teamwork is required in an office. If support and cooperation are missing from daily interactions, little can be accomplished. On the job, you and your team members are usually called *co-workers*. The word **co-workers** means people who work together in a cooperative effort.

Therefore, you should always contribute your share to the overall team effort. Unfortunately on some teams, a few people do most of the work. Many of the advantages of the team approach are lost in this situation. You may find that some of your co-workers are not doing their part. Maybe they are not making any suggestions or carrying out other responsibilities. If you are the team leader, try to encourage them by asking directly for ideas or offering to help plan their part of the work project.

# Expectations

Your co-workers, or *team members*, will have certain implicit expectations. That is, they will expect you to do certain things and to act in certain ways that are implied rather than directly stated.

Your co-workers will expect you to do your share of the work even though they will sometimes be willing to help you. You will be given specific assignments, and you will be expected to complete them within a reasonable time. If you do not, your co-workers will probably resent you.

How would you feel if members of your household left their work for you to do? Imagine that dirty dishes were always left in the sink, no one took out the garbage, and everyone left their belongings lying around the house. Would you become resentful and angry? Your co-workers will be unhappy if they cannot rely on you to complete your assignments. Their success may depend on you finishing your work on time.

## Respect Rules and Territory

Certain rules are established in each office to ensure fair treatment for everyone. If you ignore office rules, your co-workers will be annoyed. They may feel that you think you are somehow better than they are. Always comply with the rules, and you will avoid problems.

People with **seniority** are those who have worked on a job a long time and have gained knowledge and skills through years of experience. They can be helpful to you in your first months on the job. Sometimes, co-workers with seniority have earned some special privileges. If so, observe their rights and treat them with respect. This recognition will help you create good relationships with them.

You will be given a space, or territory, in which to accomplish your assigned tasks. This space may be a desk or an office, and your co-workers will usually respect it.

You, in turn, must respect the territory of others. Do not borrow equipment from a co-worker's space without asking permission. Do not touch someone's personal belongings or behave in ways others do not like. For example, if someone does not like others eating in and around her territory, respect those wishes and do not eat there.

## Be Supportive of Other Team Members

Your job will often be part of a larger operation that depends on your contribution. Thus, the success of your other team members depends on you doing your part. You will need to be conscientious about your part of larger projects and also show an interest in what others in your group are doing. Be aware of how their tasks contribute to the goals that are to be accomplished.

## Be Appreciative and Accepting of Others

Tell your co-workers that you believe what they are doing is important. You may do something as simple as saying, "Great job, Sam." Give co-workers approval as often as possible; it will make both you and them feel good about yourselves.

## Value Cultural Diversity

Americans come in all sizes, shapes, colors, and socioethnic backgrounds. The United States has long been known as a melting pot; its citizens or their ancestors all, except for Native Americans, have come here from other countries, yet they have learned to live and work together.

In the last years of the twentieth century, great changes developed in the American workplace. In the late 1990s, women, minorities, and immigrants made up more than half the workforce. As we begin the new century, 85 percent of all new workers are expected to be women, African Americans, Asian Americans, Latinos, or new immigrants. Some of your

co-workers may have accents to which you are unaccustomed. More Americans with disabilities will look for opportunities in the workplace, too, encouraged by the Americans with Disabilities Act of 1990. Always work toward being tolerant and make those in your business environment feel comfortable no matter how different they are from you. Differences can be interesting, and you can learn from people with divergent life experiences.

A diverse workforce can be an enormous source of vitality and new ideas. You and your co-workers can accomplish more through a cooperative teamwork approach when differences are valued. Prejudice and intolerance waste the talents of those at whom they are directed and create negative energy, hindering progress in getting work done.

An openness to diversity in the workplace often teaches us that we have more in common with others than we thought.

## Be Loyal

Co-workers may sometimes act in ways that you do not approve of, and the company may have policies you do not like. However, do not criticize the company or gossip about your co-workers to others in the office or to outsiders. Engaging in thoughtless conversation will usually catch up with you. Be tactful and monitor what you say. If you would not be willing to say something over the public address system, keeping it to yourself is best. You will encounter exceptions—things you will say in private to your supervisor or to co-workers who have also become close friends. However, what you say in idle chatter can be misinterpreted and cause you problems. Loyalty—the type you expect from your family and friends—is essential to good relationships on the job.

## Be Flexible

Unexpected events often bring rapid changes in the business world, so you must learn to be adaptable. Adjust to changes as quickly as possible, without complaining. Your team members will adapt more easily as well.

## Take Initiative

As you become familiar with your job, perform your tasks without waiting for someone to tell you to get started. After you have finished your own work completely and efficiently, look around to see who may need help finishing theirs and offer your assistance. Helping others gives you the opportunity to learn and grow.

After you have worked at your job for a while, you may think of some new and better ways of doing certain tasks. Make suggestions to your supervisor about how you believe these tasks can be accomplished more efficiently. However, be careful not to sound as if you are telling your boss how to do his or her job.

**TIP** Do not make suggestions for improvements during your first few weeks in the office. Your co-workers may resent a newcomer wanting to make changes too soon. Wait until you understand the workflow and the interrelationships between other jobs in the office. ∎

## Participate in Office Social Activities

As often as possible, attend office social activities even though doing so may sometimes be inconvenient. You may not wish to spend time socially with the people you are with all day at work. However, seeing your co-workers in a more relaxed frame of mind will help you to understand them as individuals.

Office parties are sometimes held for a birthday or to celebrate an important holiday. You may show that you appreciate your co-workers by bringing a gift or a card to commemorate the occasion. You spend half

## James E. Seay

*General Manager, Sales*
*Lucent Technologies*

**Q.** Mr. Seay, is Lucent Technologies concerned with diversity in the workplace? What does diversity mean at Lucent Technologies?

**A.** Diversity in the workplace at Lucent Technologies means to create and sustain an awareness and understanding of the multiethnic, multitalented, most expensive resource available—the resource of people, whose innovative ideas and knowledge are recognized and valued.

**Q.** What advice concerning diversity on the job would you give to a future office worker?

**A.** First, ask what is the company practice and position regarding diversity. Diversity is a fairly new awareness in corporate America. Visible practices and ongoing events far outweigh any policy statements that may sit in someone's desk drawer.

Second, if your company has a diversity program or is interested in developing one, you need to get involved and participate. These programs do not survive solely on good intentions. Finally, focus some aspects of your efforts and resources toward the diverse communities in your area.

your waking hours with your co-workers. Treating them well socially will enhance your working relationships. They will be more likely to see you as a team member if you join these activities and participate with the group.

Information about office politics is often passed along at social functions. You can learn more about your associates as well as about business decisions at these functions. Some of these matters may be important to you and may affect decisions you will make about your career.

## Recall Time

*Answer the following questions:*

1. Julie's supervisor has informed her that the company is providing a weekend workshop on communication skills for the workplace. It is free of charge to all employees; however, attendance is not mandatory. Julie asks whether participants will be paid overtime for attending. On learning that she would not be paid to attend, Julie tells her supervisor she is not interested.

   What conclusions do you think the supervisor will make regarding Julie's level of commitment to her job?

2. Why is gossiping with one's co-workers a harmful and nonproductive activity?

**3.** Carlos, one of your associates in the office, has just received a raise. You know that he deserved it, yet you are very envious. What should you say to Carlos?

**4.** Give an example of flexibility in an employee.

# The Value of Positive Behavior

In your dealings with others, think and act in a positive manner. Negative behavior stops progress, but an "I'll give it my best" approach keeps things moving along. Show enthusiasm in all your work relationships. Keep your mind open to ideas and proposals presented by others. If you feel that disagreeing with a new idea is necessary, offer an alternative.

Do you know someone who always says no to suggestions about how to spend time? Does the following sound familiar?

Rose: Shall we go to a movie?
Anders: Na.
Rose: Shall we go bowling?
Anders: Na.
Rose: How about watching the basketball game on TV?
Anders: Na, not tonight.

This routine can become depressing. After a while, most people choose not to be around a person like Anders. The same thing happens at work. People will seek out your company and your opinion if you have a positive, enthusiastic attitude.

When you arrive at the office, greet people with a smile. A smile on your face will help you have a pleasant attitude—and you feel better when you smile. Keep your emotions under control, do not have temper

Office celebrations are good times to discover the personalities of your co-workers and supervisors.

tantrums; and save tears until you get home. Emotional outbursts in the workplace cause people to be uncomfortable, and they hinder the business at hand.

## Maintain a Sense of Humor

Having a sense of humor does not require you to crack jokes constantly. Making jokes can be disruptive. However, you should be able to see the lighter side of matters, have fun at work, and laugh with your co-workers.

Do not take yourself too seriously. Laugh at yourself and encourage co-workers to laugh with you when you do something awkward or make a minor mistake. No one is perfect. Being able to laugh at your blunders with others will help you cope with stressful situations.

On the other hand, recognize that you are important to the company and to each project on which you work. Do not underestimate the contribution you make or your value as a team member. You are a vital part of whatever project is underway.

In the following example, Ramona is able to maintain her sense of humor at a stressful moment:

Ms. Parkins, the president of the company, is expected in the office any minute. People are scurrying around getting things ready for her visit. Ramona is the receptionist, and her desk is immediately inside the main entrance. She is preparing a bouquet of flowers for the front of the office and goes to get some water. Just as Ramona reenters the office, Ms. Parkins arrives. Ramona bumps into Ms. Parkins, sending water flying. Fortunately, Ms. Parkins is able to avoid most of the water, which lands on the carpet.

"I'm so sorry," Ramona says. "May I help you?" Ramona has never met Ms. Parkins, so she does not realize that the important guest has arrived. Ms. Parkins laughs. "Perhaps you can bring me a paper towel. Then you can tell Mr. Black that Ms. Parkins is here."

"Oh, no, I can't believe it. I wanted things to be so nice," moans Ramona.

"Things are very nice, and the flowers are beautiful. That was quite a greeting." Ms. Parkins laughs again.

Ramona laughs, too.

## Acknowledge the Good Work and Ideas of Others

In the 1989 movie *Working Girl*, a secretary's boss stole one of her ideas and used it as though it were the boss's own. Ultimately, the boss's scheme backfired and the movie had a happy ending, with the secretary receiving the recognition she had earned.

Always give credit where credit is due. You may use someone else's idea if you have her or his permission, but be sure to mention who thought of it.

## Avoid Being a Worrier

Working with people who constantly worry is unsettling. Act with mature assurance that everything will get done on time and correctly and that disaster does not lurk around every corner. Energy spent worrying could be better spent working toward solutions.

## Keep a Businesslike, Professional Attitude

Offices may become hectic with busy telephones, interruptions from supervisors, heavy workloads, and deadlines. You will find times to laugh and have some fun, but remember where you are and act appropriately.

Being businesslike means being calm, courteous, helpful, efficient, and knowledgeable. Being knowledgeable does not mean that you have to know everything but that you know how and where to find the answers to questions you are not sure about.

Your co-workers will have confidence in you if you project a professional attitude. Remember, too, that you are a representative of your company; your presenting a businesslike image gives the public confidence in the company.

Conflicts between people can occur in any setting. Knowing how to manage conflicts and resolve them satisfactorily is vital to good human relationships.

## Maintain a Professional Appearance

People begin to form opinions about you based on your appearance even before you begin your first assignment. Take pride in your personal hygiene, dress, and overall appearance.

Some businesses have dress codes that do not allow mustaches or beards for men, require stockings and high-heeled shoes for women, and so on. Most companies, though, leave style of dress to your discretion. Do not underdress or overdress. Avoid faddish styles; they detract from your professional image. For instance, skirts should not be too short or too long. Wear conservative jewelry; for example, do not wear heavy bracelets that clank and thump.

Keep your workspace neat and clean, too. Clutter in your area detracts from the look of the entire office. Do not have too many personal items—pictures, figurines, stuffed animals—on your desk. You need room to work.

Try to break nervous habits such as humming, whistling, muttering to yourself, drumming your fingers, chewing gum, twirling your hair, or swinging your foot. You will be working closely with many people, so try not to distract them from their work. Avoiding annoying behavior is simply being courteous and considerate of others.

**TIP** Look around you and notice what other people are wearing to work. See what you think looks best—professional, neat, attractive, and so on. Then dress accordingly. The way you dress makes the statement that you take your job seriously (or that you do not!). ■

## Develop a Pleasant Office Voice

The types and sounds of people's voices vary greatly. Television and radio announcers usually have deep, pleasant voices. Some comics have high-pitched, abrasive voices—which are part of their comedy routines.

Listen to your own voice and notice how high or low it sounds. If you are excited, angry, or happy, the pitch of your voice tends to go up—and a higher-pitched voice carries farther.

You may have had the experience of studying in a library when a group with loud voices passed through. Those people may not have been aware that they were disturbing you. However, their voices were unpleasant and out of place in that environment.

## Learn to Be a Listener

Part of showing respect for and interest in your co-workers and your supervisors is listening to what they have to say. Hearing the sound of someone talking is not the same as listening for the precise meaning of what is said. Listening is a special skill, and it is discussed in more detail in Chapter 14.

In one experiment in listening, sixteen people listened to a brief recording. Four hours later, this group was asked to explain, in writing, what they had heard. Three listeners had received the message correctly, nine repeated most of what was said, and four missed the point of the message completely. Receiving a message properly requires some listening skills.

You can teach yourself to be a good listener. Learn to separate the significant parts of a communication from those that are insignificant. You cannot remember every word that is spoken, so you need to be able to distinguish what is important to remember. Ask questions for clarification and for emphasis: "Did you mean . . . ?" or "I'm not sure what you are saying. Can you clarify that for me?"

A busy office contains many distractions—telephones ringing, interruptions, people coming and going. These activities can cause you to miss the main point of a message. In this environment, you will need to make a special effort to concentrate on what you are hearing.

Try to avoid planning your response while the other person is still talking. Your response may be entirely inappropriate if you do not allow the speaker to complete his or her idea.

Developing good listening skills can improve all your interpersonal relationships, and they will be especially important for success on your job.

## Learn Conflict Resolution Skills

Just as conflicts sometimes arise in your personal life, they happen now and then in the workplace, too. Having an occasional conflict is not necessarily bad, but learning how to resolve it in a positive way is important. Effective conflict resolution can build better working relationships and improve teamwork efforts for future projects.

You will manage conflict more successfully if you keep focused on the disagreement. Never bring up another person's supposed "faults." Keep "cool." That is, do not raise your voice or appear excited or frustrated. If emotions heat up, ask for a "time out" to cool down.

When another person is talking, listen carefully. Do *not* spend this time thinking of what you will say next! Listen for the other person's feelings or ideas and try to see what is valid or logical about what he or she is saying. Look for ways to compromise. What are you willing to give up in order to get what is most important to you?

Do not bring up a problem just before lunch or near the end of the working day when people are hungry or tired. However, if you are having a pleasant lunch in a restaurant, after the other person has begun to enjoy his or her meal may be a *good* time to begin a discussion of a problem.

Always settle disagreements with others among yourselves. Do not ask a third party to play the role of peacemaker! Of course, never, ever use physical force against another person.

Some people work at developing peaceful relationships in the office and are able to keep conflicts to a minimum. Unfortunately, others seem to make a habit of being disagreeable.

# Difficult People

Some people are more difficult to get along with than others. They are constantly dissatisfied and have a grouchy, negative outlook. They are not pleasant to be around.

Unfortunately, you may find a few of these difficult people in your work environment. One might even be your supervisor! Consider the following example:

Alan worked with great enthusiasm on a project for his boss, Ms. Escobedo. Alan had been unhappy because he could never satisfy her. He took special care on his project, hoping he might finally please his boss. He even handed the project in before it was due.

Ms. Escobedo called Alan into her office.

"Well, Alan," Ms. Escobedo began, frowning. "Are you certain you covered all important points in this report? We need to be very, very sure it is accurate."

"Yes, Ms. Escobedo," Alan replied, a little timidly. "I was very careful not to leave anything out."

"Do you think it is detailed enough?"

"I believe so, but what do you think, ma'am?"

## Large Office/Small Office

*What's Your Preference?*

### Getting Along with People

A large office usually has many employees with many different personalities. Some co-workers may be easy to get along with, and some not so easy. Consequently, if you work in a large office, you will deal with many types of people. Usually, you will not work with the same one or two individuals all day. Often, you will be able to avoid the individuals with whom you have difficulty.

In a small office with few employees, people usually work closely together. More interaction occurs between the same individuals day in and day out. Therefore, employees who work in a small office must have personalities that enable them to work closely with a small group on a daily basis. No matter where you work, you must maintain good working relationships with your co-workers. Cooperative relationships are especially important in a small office, because you operate so closely with them.

**Would your personality fit best in a large or a small office? Why?** ■

"I suppose it is okay. However, please be a bit neater next time," Ms. Escobedo growled, as she poked at the spotless paper.

Alan was crushed. Not a word of appreciation, not a word of praise, no thank-you for completing the project early.

Some bosses, including Ms. Escobedo, do not understand the importance of positive feedback to their employees. Others think that words of praise will make the employee less motivated and that taking a hard line promotes more and better work.

Difficult bosses pose a particularly troublesome problem because you are more or less at their mercy. Sometimes, a boss is so temperamental that a transfer or change of job is necessary.

You may run into some co-workers who are difficult to get along with, too.

### Types of Difficult People

Some people are chronic *complainers*. They see the negative side of everything and talk about it, loudly and constantly. "I have too much to do. My back hurts. My computer is old and does not work well. I do not get paid enough. It is cold in here. It is hot in here. The food in the cafeteria is awful. The traffic was terrible this morning. My head aches. Rhonda was really bothersome yesterday," and on and on. This type of person's ability to see the negative is endless.

Like Alan's boss, Ms. Escobedo, some people are too *demanding* and are never satisfied. "Can't you do the project faster, neater, more thoroughly? Can't you do more, give more, stay later, or work longer? This change is not what I asked for. I did not say that." Some co-workers act this way, too.

Many offices have *know-it-alls* who tend to be condescending (arrogant). "Oh, I could have done it better. No, that's not what that means. You're wrong again! No, that's not the way to do it. I've done many of these projects, they're very easy to do. Oh, come on, you really do not understand this process? Here, let me show you how." Few people are interested in what this kind of person has to offer.

Then we have the *shirkers*. These people regularly manage to miss out on most of the work. "Oh, I'm sorry, I can't possibly stay late tonight. Here, Chris, can you do this part for me? I'm sorry I missed the meeting. Too bad, I didn't get an assignment. I'll be leaving early today; I have an appointment. Linda, can you get that telephone call for me? David, will you make these copies for me? Tom, will you run this errand for me?" People in an office resent shirkers because they make more work for everybody else by not doing their fair share.

Finally, we have the *criticizers*. They can be bosses or co-workers. "You've done it wrong again. Can't you do anything right? Do you really like that dress? That's some kind of tie. Your handwriting is too hard to read. Your desk is certainly messy. I liked your hair the old way." Few people want to spend time with someone who undermines their confidence by constantly criticizing.

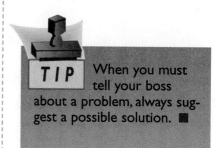

**TIP** When you must tell your boss about a problem, always suggest a possible solution. ■

## Strategies for Dealing with Difficult People

Finding strategies for dealing with both bosses and co-workers whom you find to be unusually demanding and difficult is important. They will require that you extend yourself and that you give a good deal of energy to solving problems. If you improve your working relationships, your work environment will be more tolerable and more pleasant.

### Learn to Be Empathetic

Being empathetic means being sensitive to others' feelings. Try to understand other people's points of view by seeing things through their eyes. You may have heard that you need to "walk a mile in someone else's moccasins" before you make a judgment about her or his behavior. Understanding fosters tolerance. If you understand what the other person is experiencing, tolerating difficult behavior is easier.

Getting to know a person better will help you understand that person. Find out what he or she is interested in: hobbies, studies, and other activities. Then discuss those interests. This information will also help you learn about the person's values—important information to know about co-workers.

### Learn to Read Body Language

You can learn a number of things about people by observing their body language. **Body language** is nonverbal communication through physical action. For example, if you are talking to someone and she is leaning a bit forward and looking intently at you, she is truly involved in the conversation. On the other hand, if your companion is leaning back, looking around the room, or tapping her foot, she is probably not paying attention.

John and Jim worked in the same office. They were at the same pay level but had different job descriptions. John was a clerk; Jim, a mail carrier. John came to work a few minutes early each day, greeted everyone, and set to work on his daily tasks. He acted as assistant to several people, doing small clerical jobs for them. He was interested in what co-workers were doing, enthusiastic, and always willing to do more to be helpful. He saw his job as part of a larger activity and wanted to do his share to ensure the success of the overall project. He liked the people he worked with, and everyone enjoyed his company.

Jim usually arrived at work a few minutes late, often too rushed to greet people. He gave the impression that coming to work was an imposition. For the first hour in the morning, he was grumpy when people asked him to do things. He did not see his work as part of a larger picture. However, he completed the tasks assigned to him efficiently and on time.

One day the president of the company, Ms. Garcia, was coming to town, and the office was in an uproar. Everyone was bustling about because they wanted things to be just right for this important visit.

A co-worker asked Jim to carry some boxes to the back room for storage. Jim promptly replied that his job did not include carrying boxes and that he had his own work to do. John, overhearing the conversation, offered to carry out the boxes even though his own desk was stacked with work.

A few weeks later, a new position with greater responsibility and a higher salary opened up. Both John and Jim were qualified to fill the new position.

**I. Who would you select for advancement? Why? ■**

---

Suppose that your father enters your bedroom and stands with his feet a little apart, firmly planted on the floor, and his arms crossed. What does his body language tell you?

Facial expressions may show a good deal about someone's emotional state. Think about Dad with his planted feet and his crossed arms. How does his face look? Some of the ways we interpret these signals are intuitive, part of what we are born with as human beings. We do not understand quite how we came to know, but without being told, we often sense what people are thinking by looking at their faces. Try it. See if you can tell what a person may be thinking or feeling by the expression on her or his face.

Observing, talking to, and getting to know a difficult person can facilitate your dealing with, tolerating, and being patient with him or her.

### Make Others Feel Important

Sometimes, people's negative behavior stems from their feeling unworthy or inadequate. Challenge yourself to help these people feel better and, therefore, act better. Help them feel important. Be sure you know and use their names correctly. Help them to see that their roles are essential to the overall effectiveness of the work group. Smile and greet them. Invite them to lunch. Show interest in their work, and praise them for a job well done. Chances are that most people in the office will be giving them negative feedback, sometimes causing the difficult behavior to escalate. You can be pleasant to them even if no one else is.

### Accept Criticism and Admit Your Mistakes

If someone constantly criticizes you and if you simply agree with the criticism, it can be very disarming. Epictetus, a Greek philosopher who lived two thousand years ago, suggested, "If someone criticizes you, agree at once. Mention that if only the other person knew you better, he or she

would find much more to criticize!" Keep your sense of humor. It will help you through many difficult times.

Generally, mentioning others' mistakes is inappropriate for you. However, readily admitting your own mistakes will be helpful to your office relationships. Little can be gained by making excuses for what you have done. Excuses are usually transparent. You will gain more respect, and have your co-workers' sympathy as well, if you are straightforward and simply say, "Yes, I did it. I made a mistake. I was wrong."

## Rid Yourself of Unhappy Feelings

You can do things and take attitudes that distract you from difficult encounters, directing your focus and attention elsewhere. These strategies can help you avoid letting someone else's upsetting behavior bother you.

Recognize that the unpleasant behavior has little to do with you or what you are doing. You have not caused it. Remember that the difficult person acts poorly with other people, too, not just with you.

Understand that unpleasant behavior makes a statement about the difficult person, not about your job performance, your personality, or your basic worth as a human being. Accepting this concept is sometimes difficult. If a supervisor acts angrily when dealing with you, you assume that you must have done something wrong, which is not necessarily true.

Even if you have made a serious error, angry behavior has more to do with the other person's state of mind, feelings of worth, or personal stress and strain than it does with what you have done. Good managers rarely display anger, no matter what happens in the workplace.

Remain calm no matter how your associate is acting. Do you remember the attributes that made up the list of professional and businesslike attitudes? They were: calm, courteous, helpful, efficient, and knowledgeable. Remain professional, no matter what others in the work environment are doing.

If you feel that someone is acting inappropriately, take your time when responding to his or her demands. Do not react hastily because you are likely to say or do something you may later regret. Simply say, "I need a few minutes to gather my thoughts. Please excuse me." If you cannot leave the area, tell yourself to slow down, take some time, and not be hasty.

No matter what is going on in the work environment, your first obligation is to the job you were assigned to do. Focus on that. Return to your space. A popular phrase is "Get centered." Getting centered is focusing inward, remembering that you have personal rights and power, that you are a worthy person, and that you choose to continue with the tasks assigned you. Focus on your strengths and duties, away from the bothersome, troublesome person who is causing you discomfort. If you remember who you are, you can sail by unpleasant encounters, continuing to be efficient and effective at your job.

# Recall Time

*Answer the following questions:*

**1.** At a staff meeting, the office manager has just described a new plan of reorganization for the various jobs in your department. You strongly disagree with the proposal. What is the best way to communicate your thinking to the manager? What else could you offer management besides your criticisms?

**2.** Why is maintaining a sense of humor on the job important? Are you sometimes able to chuckle at your own mistakes?

**3.** Norman decides to bring a small radio to the office so that he can listen to the World Series while he works. He does not think anyone else will mind because all the men who work near him also like baseball. Does this attitude show professionalism on Norman's part? Why or why not?

**4.** Name the four types of difficult people described in the "Types of Difficult People" section of this chapter. Choose one type and discuss some strategies for dealing with such a person.

# Assertiveness Versus Aggressiveness

Another interpersonal skill that you can use to deal with difficult people is assertiveness. **Assertiveness** is communicating your needs to others confidently without being aggressive. Do you freely give in to others? Do you shout and bully? Or, do you state your needs clearly and directly? If you do not use an appropriate style of communicating, your needs are probably not going to be met.

In the workplace, where you will spend so much of your life, having your needs met is important. If you usually attack people in a bullying, aggressive way, they will make little attempt to please you or to do what you wish them to do. If you are always passive, giving in to what others request of you, even if doing so is not in your best interest or what you think is right, you will begin to be resentful and feel bad about yourself.

**Aggressive communication** occurs when you overstate what you want, are overbearing, bossy, and pushy, and do not consider the needs of others. People often confuse the terms *aggressive* and *assertive,* but the two styles are clearly different. Aggressiveness can be hurtful and mean, whereas assertiveness usually satisfies the needs of both individuals in an encounter.

**Passive communication** occurs when you do not state what you want, or if you do, you are apologetic and feel guilty. You are likely to let others decide what is best for you and to put their own needs ahead of yours.

**Assertive communication** occurs when you say what you want clearly and directly, without animosity, being firm yet considerate of others' needs.

The three basic methods of communication are aggressive, passive (nonassertive), and assertive. Let's look more closely at these ways of communicating.

Mr. White enters the office of his assistant, Leeann, and shouts, "Leeann, I told you yesterday I needed this report! What have you been doing all day? Why don't I have it?"

Mr. White does not know that the computer malfunctioned, the secretary was ill, and Ms. Doe also asked for a complicated report. Nor does Mr. White bother to ask whether Leeann had any problems with which he could assist her. He just acts like a bully and yells at her.

The hidden side of this encounter is that Mr. White's house is overflowing with out-of-town guests, and he had a flat tire on the way to work. Furthermore, his own supervisor has been overloading him with projects. Mr. White feels that everything in his life is out of control, and all he can do is yell at a subordinate.

How does Leeann respond to this encounter?

"Oh, Mr. White, I'm so sorry. I tried, but you're right. I will do better next time."

Notice that Leeann does not tell Mr. White about her problems with the report. Rather, she dutifully responds that she was wrong and will attempt to be better. Both these people will likely leave the office feeling unhappy or upset.

The encounter would have been more satisfactory for both parties had it gone as follows:

Mr. White raps at Leeann's office door.

"Hi, Leeann. Can you give me the status of the report we talked about yesterday?"

"Hi, Mr. White. I was just going to call you to apologize. Yesterday was a mess; the computer was down, and Adam was ill. Anyway, I'll have it for you by four o'clock. Will that be okay?"

"Sure, that'll be fine. I'm sorry you had problems. Next time, let me know a little sooner. Maybe I can facilitate things for you."

"Thanks for understanding. I'll have it on your desk by four o'clock."

Each person leaves the encounter getting what she or he wants, and each feels good!

In the first example encounter between Mr. White and Leeann, Mr. White behaves in an aggressive way, and Leeann acts in a passive manner. Neither party gets what he or she wants or needs.

In the second example, each acts in an assertive way, letting the other know her or his needs, exactly.

Being assertive is the most effective style of communicating your needs to others. Incorporating assertiveness into all your interpersonal encounters will be helpful to you. Learning to use these skills in the workplace is especially important.

Do you know how to be assertive without becoming aggressive? Why is such knowledge valuable in work situations?

# Bosses as People

The nature of office relationships depends on the structure of the office—how responsibilities are delegated. You will have someone to report to—your boss or supervisor. He or she may have a title such as office manager or administrative assistant. That person, in turn, will also report to someone, and so on up the ladder.

Businesses have a hierarchy of people who are responsible for getting the work done. If you drew a sketch of who reports to whom, it would form a kind of pyramid. An organizational hierarchy looks like a pyramid and is sometimes called an *organizational chart*. See Figure 4.1, page 76.

At the apex, or top, of the pyramid is the owner, the president of the company, or perhaps a board of directors. Along the bottom of the pyramid are people who do the everyday work of the company. In the middle ranges are the middle management people. Notice that those who do the everyday work, the line staff, are the foundation of the pyramid. If these people do not do their jobs, the pyramid will collapse. The company will not be successful unless every level of the pyramid is functioning properly.

Your supervisor or boss is the person responsible for ensuring that you do your job. You, in turn, are responsible to that person. Although you probably have a written job description to cover your general responsibilities, your boss will tell you more precisely what you are supposed to be doing.

**FIGURE 4.1** • **Sample Company Organizational Chart**

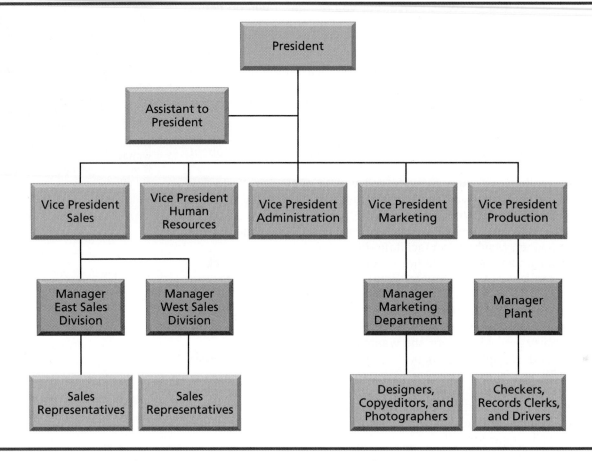

Sometimes we forget that individuals who give us assignments, oversee and supervise our work, and evaluate what we do are people too. Sometimes the boss seems almost "larger than life." She or he has so much power in the office, is able to coordinate so much complicated activity, and seems to remain calm through it all.

In fact, to reach a supervisory position in most offices requires a high level of skill and education, and often years of experience. The boss's working life can be stressful and difficult, just like yours. You can find ways to make your supervisor's life easier, and thus make your own job easier too. Keeping the boss happy is an excellent strategy for success in the office.

## Accept Assignments Willingly

Begin by accepting work assignments pleasantly. You can tell your boss by your tone of voice, by what you say, and by your actions (body language) that you are happy to do the work he or she has assigned you. A supervisor usually is annoyed if you are not interested in additional assignments. Remember, the supervisor's responsibility is to see that the work is done. When your supervisors make requests of you, they are simply doing their

jobs. Make their jobs easier by being cooperative and accepting what they ask you to do.

Sort out, with your supervisor, which of your tasks has priority; that is, if you have more than one job, determine which you should complete first.

# Know Work Priorities

Deadlines help you set priorities. A *deadline* is a specific time when a project must be finished. Keep a list of tasks you need to complete in a given time period—such as today, this week, by the first of the month. Discuss your list regularly with your supervisor. Make sure you know when things need to be done and which are most important to your supervisor.

You may have more than one supervisor. If so, you need to know the order in which you must complete your assignments. Getting this information can be tricky. You will need clear statements from each supervisor about priorities. Managers in some offices adopt a policy that the first work in gets done first. A *first-in, first-out policy* lessens the likelihood that someone will get upset about her or his requests being delayed because of someone else's. Even so, a higher-level supervisor may sometimes rearrange priorities.

# Keep Your Boss Informed

Keep your supervisors informed about the status of matters in the office, especially in their areas of responsibility. For example, if an important telephone call comes in while a supervisor is out of the office, report the telephone call promptly when he or she returns.

Your supervisor will also want to know how you are progressing on projects you have been assigned. If something happens that affects the outcome of a project, report it right away. Do not bother reporting petty matters about interactions among co-workers. However, keep the lines of communication open so that important information is passed along freely. Make getting information your supervisor needs easy.

# Be Understanding

When dealing with supervisors, do not expect them to be superhuman. Supervisors feel the same emotions and frustrations that you do. You hope your supervisor will be fair, competent, pleasant, appreciative, and honest. These qualities are reasonable expectations of someone from whom you are expected to take orders. Unfortunately, supervisors have bad days, too. You may need to be a bit forgiving at times. Perhaps your boss is not feeling well, or perhaps she or he has personal problems. You want your supervisor to be understanding, and sometimes you will have to be forgiving and understanding too.

If you want to have a good working relationship with your supervisor, never criticize him or her in front of co-workers. If you have a complaint that you feel has real merit, take it directly to your supervisor to discuss in private. Do not spread bad news or gossip about your supervisor. Be loyal to your boss, remembering that supervisors are people too.

## Ethics on the Job

You work in the advertising department of the city newspaper as part of a several-member team. Your team has met and established a time schedule to aid the efficient flow of work from one team member to the next.

Your responsibility is to see that the ad copy is complete and on your supervisor's desk each afternoon by 3:00 P.M. Your supervisor then approves the work or sends it back to you for changes before it is forwarded for inclusion in the next morning's paper. You are supposed to receive any copy that needs editing by 4:00 P.M. However, your supervisor often delays returning the ad copy to you until just a few minutes before the time you leave for the day. Then you must decide whether to stay late to complete the work, or to confront your supervisor with the problem.

1. **Team members must learn to be flexible. Does your supervisor have a right to expect you to stay until the work is complete? Why or why not?**

2. **Should you be asked to do this work without overtime compensation?**

3. **What is the best way for you to resolve this problem?** ■

A good way to keep your supervisors happy is to help them look efficient and competent by being efficient and competent yourself. The more effectively you handle your workload, and the more you accomplish, the better your supervisors look. That effect makes them happy, and it will make you happy, too.

## Provide Solutions, Not Problems

Sometimes you will run into a problem when you are attempting to complete a task. Consider possible solutions yourself before you report the problem to your supervisor. For example, if your computer breaks down, you might call the repair service to learn whether you can get a replacement while your machine is being repaired. Or you might be able to use a co-worker's computer. When you take problems to your supervisor, bring solutions too.

## Set Your Own Ethical Standards

Set high ethical and behavioral standards for yourself at work. Think through what you will and will not do to get ahead.

Many situations arise in office politics and interpersonal relations. Everyone in the office knows who is dependable, who is reliable, who is not to be trusted, and who will step on others' toes to get ahead. Secrets about the character of individuals who work together all day are few. Thus, establishing a standard of behavior for yourself that is honest and straightforward will be to your advantage. Your co-workers will appreciate and respect you for it.

Use your best instincts about things that go on in the office. If you feel a situation is not right, ethically or morally, you can always make the choice not to go along. Often, making this choice is difficult because you must face the consequences of being different. Often, employees prefer not to "make waves"; we are often admonished, "Do not rock the boat!"

Be true to yourself, your values, and the things you think are important. Be the best you can be. You can make moral decisions for yourself, and you will be a better employee for doing so.

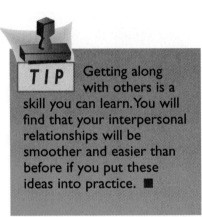

**TIP** Getting along with others is a skill you can learn. You will find that your interpersonal relationships will be smoother and easier than before if you put these ideas into practice. ■

## Recall Time

*Answer the following questions:*

1. You realize that completing all your projects by their deadlines is impossible. Which of the following actions do you take?

    **a.** Go to your supervisor's boss and complain that your supervisor is giving you too much work.

    **b.** Express your anger to your supervisor when others are present.

    **c.** Feel that you have failed and decide another job may be better for you.

    **d.** Sit down with your supervisor to discuss priorities and set realistic goals.

**2.** Kathy is in the middle of copying an important report, which her supervisor is to present at a meeting that day, when the copy machine suddenly breaks down. What steps could Kathy take to remedy the situation? In what order should they be taken?

**3.** Why does an employee with high ethical standards easily command the respect of co-workers?

# Summary

Companies competing in today's business world can achieve great success only when employees are content and fulfilled on the job. When a true spirit of cooperation exists among workers who actively seek to improve their interpersonal skills, they create a pleasant, productive workplace. Cooperation requires that all employees maintain a professional appearance and attitude, be loyal and tolerant of others' differences, and cultivate flexibility and the willingness to initiate projects.

Human relations is an art mastered by few. Most of us have had moments when we did or said things that we would erase if we could. However, dwelling on our negative characteristics and those of others does not make anyone happy and certainly does not increase production. Those individuals who practice positive behavior are enthusiastic, open minded, and confident, and have a sense of humor. The ability to listen to others and read their body language can enable a worker to communicate with even the most difficult people. Likewise, by graciously accepting criticism without making excuses, we invite others to communicate more openly with us.

Assertiveness is the balanced behavior between bullying (aggression) and being a victim (passivity). An assertive person communicates her or his needs to others effectively as well as considerately. In looking at a company's organizational chart, keep in mind that all positions, regardless of rank, are filled by human beings. Not everyone is adept at assertiveness. Furthermore, high rank does not license one to be aggressive, nor does low rank require passive behavior, and vice versa.

As a conscientious worker, practice assertiveness with your supervisor and others, accept assignments willingly, and know how to set priorities and meet deadlines. Always keep your supervisor informed of the status of your work, and if problems arise, try to provide solutions of your own if possible. Never criticize your supervisor in front of others. Be direct and speak to him or her personally. This attitude is also part of having high ethical standards. A trustworthy worker is willing to "swim against the tide," if necessary, to be true to her or his standards of behavior.

As an office employee, be willing to do the following:

- Be a team member and work in cooperation with others.
- Help co-workers with their tasks when you have time.
- Respect office rules and the territory and property of others.
- Be appreciative and supportive of co-workers.
- Participate in office social activities.
- Maintain a positive attitude and sense of humor even when the joke is on you.

- Take pride in a professional appearance and a pleasant voice.
- Have empathy for difficult people and use human relations skills to reach them.
- Practice assertiveness skills in all your office relationships.
- Be honest and straightforward with your supervisor without being disrespectful.
- Learn how to set priorities for your work so that assignments are completed on time.
- Avoid compromising your moral standards even when doing so is difficult and costly.

# before you leave...

**When you have completed this chapter, answer the following questions:**

**1.** What is the value of taking part in office social activities?

**2.** What is the value of maintaining positive behavior on the job?

**3.** What are some strategies you would use in dealing with difficult people?

# Review & Application

## Check Your Knowledge

1. Give two reasons that personal and human relations are important in the workplace.

2. What one word is the key to a successful team of co-workers?

3. Define *expectations*. Give an example of an implicit expectation your co-workers might have of you.

4. How would you regard someone who has seniority?

5. Describe some ways that you could show support for your co-workers.

6. What is the difference between thoughtful conversation and gossip?

7. A worker who is able to adjust to changes rapidly and cheerfully is demonstrating what essential attribute?

8. Why is it valuable to attend office social functions?

9. If you have a consistently positive attitude, your co-workers will want your company and advice. Why is this statement true?

10. Why are temper tantrums inappropriate in the office?

11. A sense of humor can be vital to the office atmosphere. Give an example of humor that might be appropriate at work. Then give another example of humor that might be inappropriate.

12. How would you put together the best possible wardrobe for your position?

13. What are some characteristics of a professional, businesslike attitude?

14. What is the difference between hearing and listening?

15. A co-worker says, "It took you three hours to do that! I could have done it in one." To which category of difficult people does this person belong?

16. Define *empathy*. Why is showing empathy a good strategy for dealing with difficult people?

17. Your boss stares out the window while you are speaking with her. What does her body language tell you?

18. What is gained by being pleasant to someone to whom no one else will speak?

19. Why is making excuses about what you have not done counterproductive?

20. When a boss or co-worker is angry, taking it personally is tempting. What can you do when that temptation arises?

21. Give a simple definition of *assertiveness*. Describe the aggressive and passive forms of communication.

22. What is a hierarchy?

23. If you were a boss, how would you like to be treated by your employees? How should they respond when you give them assignments?

24. What is a first-in, first-out policy?

25. Rather than problems, what do supervisors want from their workers? Phrase your answer in one word.

26. To what are you being true when you have high ethical standards?

## Review Your Vocabulary

On a separate piece of paper, write the letter of the vocabulary word that is described below.

____ 1. nonverbal communication through physical actions

____ 2. term meaning how people get along with one another

____ 3. people who work together in a cooperative effort

____ 4. characteristic of having worked on a job longer than others

____ 5. way of overstating what you want, being bossy, not considering the needs of others

____ 6. way of not saying what you want, or being apologetic and feeling guilty

____ 7. way of saying what you want clearly and directly, without animosity, and being firm yet considerate of others' needs

a. aggressive communication
b. assertive communication
c. body language
d. co-workers
e. interpersonal relations
f. passive communication
g. seniority

## Discuss and Analyze an Office Situation

1. William realizes too late that he left out an important section of a report when he prepared it for mailing to an important client. Not wanting to lose the respect of his co-workers or face his supervisor's criticism, he searches his mind for a logical and believable excuse to give them.

   How could William best gain support and approval from his co-workers?

2. Emily has decided that her boss is a hopelessly difficult person. He is always angry, nothing is ever perfect or on time, and he never thanks her for her work. She avoids speaking with him whenever possible and has begun complaining about him to her co-workers.

   What type of behavior is the boss demonstrating? Is Emily being assertive? What strategies might Emily employ to improve this situation?

## Practice Basic Skills

### Math

Ginger has finally achieved a position of seniority in her office. The company has presented her with a choice of options for more pay. She may choose a simple raise of 15 percent of her present salary, which stands at $1,600 per month, or she may opt for another plan with a base salary plus commissions.

If she chooses the latter plan, she will receive a base salary of $1,700 per month plus 6 percent of her gross sales for the month. Presently, Ginger's monthly gross sales are averaging $4,000. Which plan should Ginger choose?

### English

The following office memo needs revising. Rewrite it, or key it, correcting all examples of nonstandard English, which are inappropriate in the business world.

TO: My boss

FROM: Gloria

RE: dweeby co-workers

Ms. Banks,
I finally have to tell you this story cause I know you are cool and can catch my drift. Like I am so weirded out by these jerks who share my office. Gee, I could really like scream, you know? Please do something before I croak.

### Proofreading

Rekey or rewrite the following paragraphs of a report, correcting all errors.

In anilyzing the profit and loss figures for last quarter ending in august we can see that the shoping center is doing well. Sales have gone stedily up since doors open in january However We have yet to, review which stores are the biggest gainers.

What we can see is is that the biggest gross sales take place on week ends simply because more people are in the mall then; studies show, that people will spend simply because they are their. This situation is called impulse buying. Later is this report' we will address the subject of advertizing aimed at: impulse buyers.

## Apply Your Knowledge

1. Describe an actual experience you have had with another student or co-worker that involved human or interpersonal relations. Based on what you know now, how might you have handled the situation differently?

2. You have developed a great idea for increasing production in your office, and you are eager to share it with your supervisor. When you enter her office, you find that she has just received some bad news. Do you proceed to tell her your idea or do you decide to wait until later? Why?

3. Invite the manager of a local office to speak to your class on the subject of human relations in the workplace. Ask him or her to address the particular problems faced by people of diverse cultures working together. Using a computer, prepare a list of questions you would like the speaker to discuss.

## Using the Reference Manual

Open file ch4ref.doc. Use the punctuation section of the Reference Manual at the back of the book to help you correct the sentences. Save and print.

1. We met in August of 81 at the Golden Gate Bridge.

2. How many Cs did Mario get on his report card?

3. Rudy is very upset because he lost Tonys' coat.

4. Wont we ever be done with this project?

5. The community college drive was launched in April of 89.

6. The two girls father could not be found in the snow storm.

7. The Meatcutters Union meets every third Wednesday of the month.

8. Under the circumstances, we cant do anything.

9. How often are the childrens' play schedules interrupted each day?

10. The neighbors dog is friendly and smart.

# CAREER PORTFOLIO

## PART ONE: Your Place in the Modern Office

### Introduction

The primary purpose of a student career portfolio is to demonstrate what you have learned in a given class or during a certain part of your school career. Your portfolio may include samples of a process or procedure you have mastered, an effort you have made, or specific knowledge or skills you have acquired.

Student portfolios do not have to be limited to classroom experiences. You might also include samples of items that demonstrate learning things on your own, or using your skills outside of school. For instance, you may show how you applied communication skills on the job or how you used ideas from course readings and discussions to better understand people who are different from you.

In the Career Portfolio feature at the end of each of the five parts in this textbook, you will be asked to prepare two or more items for your portfolio showing ways you have used office technology and techniques. How will your portfolio be used? Instead of just showing up with a résumé at a job interview for a position as an executive secretary or administrative assistant, you will arrive with a portfolio showing *evidence* of your skills in the form of spreadsheets and charts prepared in spreadsheet applications; a newsletter you designed; samples of office memos and letters to customers; or procedures you will follow to complete typical office activities.

### General Instructions for Portfolio Projects

1. After you create your student portfolio item, be sure to give it one final proofing for (a) spelling errors, by running the spelling-check program of your word processing program, and (b) grammar errors, by running the grammar program. In addition, refine the content of your document by using the thesaurus feature in the word processing program you are using.

2. Print a clean copy of your document and insert it behind the appropriate tab in your Career Portfolio binder. You will need to purchase an inexpensive but professional-looking binder from an office supply store and set up the sections with the following five tabs:
   - Your Place in the Modern Office
   - Technical Skills and Knowledge
   - Office Support Skills
   - Communication and Problem-Solving Skills
   - Employment Skills

### Specific Activities to Complete

Select at least two of the following items for inclusion in your Career Portfolio, using the information from Chapters 1 through 4.

1. Key a list of at least four reasons you would like to work in a particular office environment such as law, education, medical, or travel. Save and print this list. (Be sure you proof according to the previous instructions.) Insert this list as the first item in your Career Portfolio binder behind the first tab, entitled "Your Place in the Modern Office."

2. Key a list that summarizes the types of attitudes and human relations skills you will need on the job you have chosen. Create the list so that it meets your needs.

3. Describe a situation in which you used the material presented in Chapters 3 and 4 about your attitude and getting along with people. The situation should be one in which you feel you did the right thing and were recognized for it. (Recognize and document the *right* things you do!) Save, print, and insert this list behind the first tab.

# PART II

# Technical Skills and Knowledge

# chapter 5

## Office Computer Systems

## objectives

*After completing this chapter, you will be able to do the following:*

1. Describe the relationship between a management information system and a computer system.
2. List the five classifications of computers and describe the differences between them.
3. Identify the major components of a computer system.
4. Distinguish between the terms *memory* and *storage* and list examples of each.
5. Describe the function of popular computer peripherals such as the pointing devices, digital cameras, and scanners.
6. List several examples of system software and describe a major advantage of using each.
7. List six types of application software and describe the function of each one.

### New Office Terms

- compact disk (CD)
- compact disk–read-only memory (CD-ROM)
- compact disk–recordable (CD-R)
- compact disk–rewritable (CD-RW)
- computer
- computer system
- database management
- data projector
- desktop publishing (DTP)
- digital camera
- floppy disk
- gigabyte

- graphical user interface (GUI)
- graphics
- handheld computer
- hard disk
- high-capacity disk
- integrated software
- mainframe
- management information system (MIS)
- mid-range server
- monitor
- mouse
- operating system (OS)

- personal computer
- personal digital assistant (PDA)
- random-access memory (RAM)
- read-only memory (ROM)
- scanner
- software
- spreadsheet
- supercomputer
- terabyte
- touch pad
- trackball
- word processing

# before you begin...

**Answer the following questions to the best of your ability:**

**1.** What might a computer system in an office look like?

**2.** What is the difference between system software and application software?

**C**omputers are clearly the greatest advancement in technology since the printing press. They provide countless benefits to almost any organization. Industries that have been downsized by global competition can use computers to maximize productivity and ensure superior customer service. A single office worker using a computer can handle most levels of operations, from data entry and document production to complex customer service transactions. Today successful organizations expect employees to be able to use technology, analyze information, and complete routine office activities in the course of their everyday duties.

## Management Information Systems

Organizations use information to manage operations, people, and resources effectively. One of the most effective tools that can help meet these information needs is a **management information system**, also known as an **MIS.** A management information system is an integrated system that is usually computer based and that provides information and aids in decision making critical to an organization's continued profitability and operations.

Though an MIS is typically tailored to each organization's needs, its functions are primarily used for planning and controlling the routine activities that most organizations perform. For example, an MIS can help plan projects and control inventory levels, as well as assist in the performance of such critical functions as monitoring the production, product quality, environment, and budgets of all types of businesses.

What is information? Information is data that has been processed. It helps decision makers by increasing their knowledge and reducing uncertainty. In order for computer-generated information to be trustworthy for decision making, it must possess six characteristics:

- *Accessibility.* Information must be easily obtainable without excessive effort.
- *Relevance.* Information must be meaningful and pertinent.
- *Clarity.* Information must be specific, obvious, and presented in an easily understandable format.
- *Accuracy.* Information must be precise, accurate, and error free.
- *Objectivity.* Information must be unbiased (not slanted by the views of particular parties).
- *Timeliness.* Information must be available when needed and sufficiently up-to-date to aid its users.

©corbisimages.com

Being computer literate is vital for accessing information that organizations make available for decision making.

Computers have been used for many years to perform routine and repetitive operations formerly done by hand; for example, payroll preparation and sales order writing. Today computer systems operate more efficiently if they are customized for the needs of different businesses. Customization is needed because each organization is unique, and the types of information that can be provided by a computer system are as diverse as each organization's use of that information. A management information system is helpful because it ensures that computer-processed information is useful by focusing on the information needs of a particular company.

# Computer Systems

Computer systems should always be purchased with an understanding of how they will be used and what types of components are needed. Buying a computer system is one of the most important decisions an organization makes. It requires thinking about future needs so that existing systems can be updated and adapted to those needs.

## The Computer System

A **computer** is an electronic device that operates under the control of instructions stored in its own memory. Computers can accept data as input in the form of words and numbers, process that data arithmetically and logically, produce usable output from the processing, and store the results for future use.

A **computer system** is a group of computer devices that are connected, coordinated, and linked together in such a way that they work as one to complete a task. Depending on the office setting, you may find relatively small and simple computer systems, composed of only one or two small computers serving an entire office, or large computer systems that store huge amounts of data and information that each person in an organization can access by using a keyboard-type device at his or her desk.

**Ethics on the Job**

You decide to work late one evening to catch up on some work at the office before the state tax auditors arrive the next day. A vice president, to whom you do not report, has asked you to shred a 4-inch pile of papers and to make some monetary changes to five expense claims that have already been paid to him. Your first instinct is to not do it.

*How would you handle this situation?* ■

# Classifications of Computers

Computers are useful because they are fast, accurate, and able to store vast amounts of data. Typically, computer systems are classified according to their physical size, memory capacity, speed, and cost. Although computers may be classified in different ways, five classifications distinctive in the world of computing include: personal computer (PC), handheld computer, mid-range server, mainframe, and supercomputer.

A desktop personal computer.

## Personal Computers

A **personal computer** may be either a desktop or notebook computer that fits on a desk or on your lap. The number of users is usually one, but many may be simultaneously connected, or "networked" together. A personal computer is the type of computer used by most office workers. In general, the price range is a few thousand dollars or less.

## Handheld Computers

A **handheld computer**, sometimes called a *palmtop computer*, is a small computer that fits in your hand. Because of their reduced size, the screens on handheld computers are quite small; however, with most units you can connect the handheld computer to a larger computer to exchange information between the two computers. A business traveler or other mobile user might use a handheld computer if a notebook computer is too large. One of the most popular handheld computers in use today is called a **personal digital assistant (PDA)**. These lightweight handheld computers provide personal organizer functions such as a calendar, appointment book, address book, calculator, and notepad. Handheld computers typically cost several hundred dollars or less.

Among the smallest computers for business use is the palmtop.

## Mid-Range Servers

A **mid-range server** is more powerful and larger in size than a workstation computer. These computer systems can often support up to 4,000 connected users at a time. In the past these types of computers were known as *minicomputers*. Servers of this type cost between $5,000 and $150,000.

## Mainframe Computers

A **mainframe** is a large, expensive, very powerful computer that can handle hundreds or thousands of connected users at the same time. Mainframes can store tremendous amounts of data, instructions, and information and have the ability to process millions of instructions per second. The general price range for this computer is from $300,000 to several million dollars.

## Supercomputers

A **supercomputer** is the fastest, most powerful computer—and the most expensive. Supercomputers are capable of processing more than 12 trillion instructions in a single second. Applications requiring complex, sophisticated mathematical calculations use supercomputers. Supercomputers cost several million dollars.

Table 5.1, page 91, provides a comparative summary describing the users of and applications for each of the five categories of computer systems.

Today machines build machines under the direction of a computer! Some mid-range servers are used in automobile factories to control robots that assemble parts of car bodies.

**TABLE 5.1 • Comparison of Users and Applications for Computer Types**

| Classification | Users and Applications |
|---|---|
| Personal Computer (desktop or notebook) | Used extensively in businesses, homes, and educational institutions for day-to-day document processing and personal information management activities. |
| Handheld Computer | Used by employees whose jobs require them to move from place to place or to travel for business. |
| Mid-Range Server | Used by businesses to provide computing availability to several employees at once and often accessed via a personal computer or a terminal, which consists of only a monitor and keyboard. |
| Mainframe Computer | Used by large businesses and government agencies, such as banks, airlines, and insurance companies for customer and organizational information processing. |
| Supercomputer | Used by organizations that have applications requiring complex, sophisticated mathematical calculations such as those used in weather forecasting and space exploration. |

## Recall Time

*Answer the following questions:*

**1.** Define the term *management information system*.

**2.** What are the five classifications of computers?

Mainframes are the largest computers commonly used in large companies. Banks use mainframes to keep track of the enormous amount of financial information they must store.

Supercomputers are true "number crunchers," with some being able to perform hundreds of mathematical operations every second.

# Components of a Computer System

When purchasing a computer, the first and most important question to ask is, "For what applications or purposes will you use the computer?" With the answer in mind, deciding which processor, keyboard, monitor, and storage devices to buy will be easier. How much memory and what type and size disk drives you need will be the most useful information. To understand how to determine computer needs wisely, study the information that follows.

## Hardware, Memory, and Storage

The basic hardware devices for business computer systems include those items you can physically touch, such as a monitor, a keyboard, a printer, and a computer system unit containing memory chips and storage disk drives.

### Hardware Devices

The following components are considered the essential hardware devices for every computer system.

**Monitor** A **monitor** resembles a television screen that displays information. Monitors range in cost from less than one hundred dollars to several hundred dollars depending on their size and features. The more expensive monitors have additional niceties such as color and high resolution, which produce more attractive and clearer images.

The purpose of a monitor is to allow you to see what you are doing as you use a computer. Your choice of monitor will depend on your preferences as well as your budget. You can choose monochrome or color, screen sizes varying from thirteen inches to seventeen inches or larger, and even two-page monitors with flat screens.

**Keyboard** In the office, the primary input device is the basic keyboard. Different keyboard models are available, with keys located in different places and with varying numbers of keys. Most keyboards consist of three distinct sections: the typewriter (or alphanumeric) keypad with function keys at the top, the cursor movement area, and the numeric keypad. As you enter or key data on a keyboard, it is simultaneously displayed on the monitor screen and stored in the computer's main memory. Ergonomically designed keyboards slant naturally in a soft V-shape and are becoming popular among both office and at-home workers.

**Printer** Printers produce paper output in the form of text and graphics copy. Numerous types of printers are available, with price tags ranging from less than one hundred dollars to many thousands of dollars. Most office printers today are nonimpact, which means they do not print characters by striking the paper. The most-used nonimpact printers in offices today are desk-jet and laser.

Advances in technology have made it possible for monitors to be built as thin as your textbook.

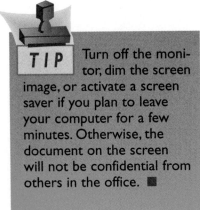

An extended keyboard

An ergonomic keyboard

The printer of choice for most offices is the laser printer. Laser printers can usually produce a number of different typefaces, or fonts, of various designs and sizes. Laser printers today can print in excess of 150 pages per minute. Although companies such as IBM and Apple® manufacture excellent printers, Hewlett-Packard continues to dominate both the low and high ends of the laser printer market.

**Computer System Unit**   The system unit in a typical personal computer usually includes a microprocessor, which is a single silicon chip containing the central processing unit (CPU) and a small amount of special purpose memory. In addition, the system unit contains one or more memory chips mounted on a main circuit board called the motherboard. The microprocessor, with its increasing speed and processing power and continually decreasing prices, has helped revolutionize the way companies do business. Major manufacturers of microprocessors include Intel®, IBM®, and Motorola®.

## Memory and Storage

The capacity of memory chips has been doubling every few years. ROM and RAM chips are the most common memory chips used in computers today. Hard drives, floppy disks, and optical disks, such as compact disk read-only memory (CD-ROM), are the most common computer storage devices. In addition to CD-ROM formats, compact disks are also available in CD-R, CD-RW, and DVD-ROMs. These formats are discussed later in the chapter.

A laser printer can print documents using various fonts.

**Read-Only Memory**   Read-only memory (ROM) chips are used for the permanent storage of certain instructions, most frequently parts of the computer's operating system software that checks the hardware when you turn on your computer. Instructions stored on ROM chips cannot be written over or altered and are not lost when electric current is disrupted or turned off. Some leading manufacturers of memory chips are Motorola, NEC™, Toshiba®, and Texas Instruments™.

**Random-Access Memory**   When users discuss memory in a computer, they usually are referring to RAM. **Random access memory (RAM)** consists of memory chips that can be read from and written to by the processor and other devices. When a computer is on and an operator asks it to do something, certain files are loaded from a storage device, such as a hard disk, into RAM. These files remain in RAM as long as the computer is running. As additional programs and data are requested, they also load from storage into RAM or memory.

The Pentium chip contains more than 3.1 million electronic components on a single slice of silicon.

RAM can hold multiple software programs simultaneously, provided the computer has enough RAM to accommodate all the programs. The program you are working with, however, is the one that usually displays onto the screen. Both memory and storage sizes are typically expressed in these ways: megabyte (MB) or 1 million bytes, **gigabyte** (GB) or 1 billion bytes, and **terabyte** (TB) or 1 trillion bytes. Most business users need a minimum of 128 MB of memory on current computer systems.

**Hard Disks, Floppy and High-Capacity Disks**   In contrast to RAM, a hard disk provides nonvolatile storage. In other words, when the power is off, the software and documents stored on the hard disk remain on the disk. Hard disks are thin, rigid metallic platters coated with a substance that allows data to be recorded in magnetic form.

Most desktop personal computers contain at least one hard disk. Current personal computer hard disks can store from 10 to 75 GB of data, instructions, and information. Data is stored magnetically onto hard disks.

A **floppy disk** is a portable, inexpensive storage medium that consists of a thin, circular, flexible plastic disk. You can remove a floppy and carry it to another computer. A 3.5-inch high-density floppy disk can store 1.44 MB of data.

In contrast to a floppy disk, a **high-capacity disk** has a storage capacity of 100 MB or greater. You can easily transport a large number of files from one computer to another with these disks, as well as store large graphics, audio, or video files. Types of high-capacity disk drives include the SuperDisk™ drive and the Zip® drive.

**Optical Disks**   A **compact disk** (CD), also called an *optical disk*, is a flat, round, portable, metal storage medium. Almost every PC today includes some type of compact disk drive installed into the system unit. These drives read compact disks, including audio CDs.

A **CD-ROM**, or **compact disk–read-only memory**, may contain audio, text, graphics, or video. You can only read the contents of these disks. That is, you cannot erase or modify their contents. A typical CD-ROM holds about 650 MB of data, instructions, and information. This amount is about 450 times more than you can store on a high-density 3.5-inch disk.

Most computers today include either a CD-R or CD-RW drive as a standard feature. Unlike standard CD-ROM drives, you can record, or write, your own data onto a disk with a CD-R or CD-RW drive. A **CD-R (compact disk-recordable)** is a compact disk onto which you can record your own items, writing on one part of the disk one time and another part at a later time. You can write on each part only one time, and you cannot erase the disk's contents.

In comparison, a **CD-RW (compact disk-rewritable)** is an erasable disk you can write on multiple times. A very popular use of CD-RW and CD-R disks is to create audio CDs.

# Other Popular Computer Devices

In addition to the major hardware components, computer operators also use peripheral devices.

When an office computer system is purchased, other devices are required for various purposes. Some of these devices are discussed now.

## Pointing Devices

A pointing device controls the movement of a pointer on a computer screen. A **mouse** is a pointing device that is moved across a flat surface, controls the movement of the pointer on a screen, and is used to make selections from the screen. A mechanical mouse has a rubber or metal ball on its underside, whereas, the newer optical mouse uses devices that emit and sense light to detect the mouse's movement. A cordless or wireless mouse, for instance, relies on battery power and uses infrared light or radio waves to communicate with a receiver.

(a) Apple mouse

(b) Microsoft mouse

(c) Logitech® mouse

Different types of mice are available. (a) Apple, (b) Microsoft's IntelliMouse, (c) Logitech's MouseMan Sensa.

A **trackball** is a stationary pointing device with a ball mechanism on its top. The operator rolls the ball to control the movement of a pointer on a screen. A **touch pad** is a flat, rectangular pointing device that is sensitive to pressure and movement. The operator presses on the pad to control the movement of a pointer on a computer screen.

### Digital Camera
You may use a **digital camera** to take pictures and digitally store the photographed images. You can then download, or transfer, the images into a computer. At that point, pictures may be edited with photo-editing software, printed, faxed, sent via electronic mail, or posted onto a Web site.

### Scanners
A **scanner** is a light-sensing device that reads printed text and graphics and then translates (or saves) the results into a form a computer can use. Scanners can read characters, marks, codes, and graphical images.

### Speakers and Headsets
Computers can also produce music, speech, and other sounds. Because of these capabilities, many PC users add sophisticated speakers to their computers to generate a higher-quality sound that can be heard at a distance. If you are in a quiet environment, speakers might not be practical, so headsets can be used.

### Data Projectors
A **data projector** is a device that takes an image from a computer screen and projects it onto a larger screen so that an audience of people can see the image clearly. For example, many classrooms use data projectors so that all students can easily see an instructor's presentation on a screen.

**TIP** Do not eat food or drink beverages around any computer system. An unexpected spill or food particle could damage the computer, the mouse, or a crucial computer disk. More important, such a mishap could prevent workers from completing an important job on time. ■

A scanner may offer high resolution, color, and grayscale.

## Recall Time

*Answer the following questions:*

**1.** What essential hardware devices should every computer system have?

**2.** What is a major difference between RAM and ROM storage?

**3.** List three examples of other popular computer devices.

## Software

**Software,** also known as a *program,* is a group of instructions executed by a computer. Business and office software used on PCs is categorized as either system software or application software.

### System Software

System software consists of the programs that control the operation of a computer and its devices. It serves as the interface between the user, the application software, and the computer's hardware devices. The most important part of the system software is the **operating system (OS).** The OS is a set of programs containing instructions that coordinate all activities among computer hardware resources. Some of the more popular PC operating systems in use today are Microsoft's Windows® 2000 Professional, Windows® Millennium Edition (ME), and the Mac® OS used on Apple's Macintosh® computers. Today's operating systems, as well as application software programs, are based on graphical user interface, which is discussed next.

**Graphical User Interface**   Graphical user interface (GUI) uses icons, or symbolic pictures, to represent programs, files, and common operations. This approach of using graphics, or pictures, and menus makes working with a computer simpler. Similar functions (save, copy, move, edit) in different programs are executed in the same way. The goal of GUIs is to create a system that a novice computer user can turn on and operate right away without any prior training or the need to refer to manuals or remember commands.

GUIs usually feature information windows or dialog boxes that may be layered on top of one another, similar to file folders on top of a desk. Most windows contain certain elements, including a menu bar along the top of the screen that shows basic command options, scroll bars that move parts of the document into view if the entire document cannot fit within the window, and buttons that will make the window larger or smaller. Typical icons within a window include file folders, alignment buttons, or an artist's color or style palette. Sometimes a dialog box will appear that requests information about the task you are performing or supplies information you might need.

The Windows operating environment is so named because the computer screen is divided into rectangular areas called *windows.* Each application, or program, runs in its own window. At any one time, one window or multiple windows may be open on the screen. Regardless of the number of windows open simultaneously, only one window can be "active" or used at a time.

## Making Office Decisions

Office workers at Company X are excited about the possibility that the firm is purchasing Windows ME. The employees cannot think of a reason not to upgrade all fifty computers to this new operating system, at a cost of less than $100 per computer. From management's viewpoint, however, phasing in Windows ME or any other new operating system is not that easy. Additional expenses include buying new software, retraining employees, and so on.

1. *How should company managers decide when to make a dramatic upgrade in the company's computer system?*

2. *What types of issues should be considered?* ■

**Upgrades to Operating Systems**  To meet the need for an operating system that used GUI, Microsoft developed Windows. Beginning with Windows 3.x as Microsoft's earliest operating system and continuing with upgrades in Windows 95 and 98 operating systems, each upgrade has brought improvements for users. Today the most important upgrades computer operators recognize as improvements to Microsoft's Windows 2000 Professional and the Millennium Edition operating systems are features that make Windows easier to use and more reliable, with fewer "crashes," faster speed, and more integration with the Internet and online user applications.

At the time of this writing, the latest version of the Windows Operating System—Windows® XP—is in limited use. Windows XP Professional integrates the strengths of Windows 2000 Professional, such as standards-based security, manageability, and reliability, with the best business features of Windows® 98 and Windows Millennium Edition, such as Plug and Play, simplified user interface, and innovative support services. According to Microsoft Corporation, this combination creates the best desktop operating system for business whether installed on a single computer or throughout a worldwide network because it increases computing power while lowering cost of ownership for desktop computers.

## Application Software

Application software is productivity software that allows office workers to use a computer to solve a specific problem or perform a certain task. Today numerous application software packages exist for computers of all sizes—from supercomputers to personal computers—with the greatest variety available for PCs. Offices are the largest market for application software, and the uses for personal computers are as varied as the businesses that employ them. However, creating documents, such as correspondence and reports, and managing finances are the two tasks for which computers are most commonly used in an office.

Six types of application software are most often used to process office data and convert it into usable information. These types are: word processing, spreadsheet, database management, graphics, desktop publishing, and integrated software and software suite packages.

**Word Processing**  A word processor makes writing and editing all documents, from a brief memo to a novel, much easier and faster. Using **word processing** software allows you to create, edit, format, print, and save letters, memos, reports, and other text with greater ease and efficiency than using a typewriter.

The real strength of word processors is their ability to edit previously stored material, as well as to format documents and arrange text so that it is presented attractively on a page. Printing features can create headers, footers, and page numbers. In addition, most word processing packages contain a spelling-check feature, a thesaurus, a grammar-check program, and a mail-merge option, as well as features for drawing, creating tables, and helping the operator use the software.

Other than those already mentioned, current versions of word processing software include some additional features: AutoCorrect, AutoFormat, Collaboration Tools for discussions and online meetings, Columns for newspapers and magazines, tracking changes with edits of multiple users, Web page development, and voice recognition activities. Some popular word processing programs are Microsoft Word, Corel WordPerfect, and Lotus Word Pro.

**Spreadsheets**   A **spreadsheet** is a financial planning program that performs mathematical calculations. Spreadsheet programs are used by large and small businesses, as well as by nonprofit organizations, scientists, professors, and private individuals in their homes. Spreadsheet programs have the power to record, organize, analyze, and present all sorts of financial and statistical information.

A spreadsheet program makes calculating depreciation, preparing financial statements, tracking and analyzing financial results, developing a budget, managing cash flow, and examining alternatives easy. When employees need to compute and analyze figures quickly and easily, they use spreadsheet programs such as Excel® by Microsoft, Lotus® 1-2-3 by Lotus Development Corporation, and Quattro Pro® by Corel® Corporation.

**Database Management**   Database management software computerizes and manages recordkeeping and information tasks by helping you store, organize, and retrieve information much more efficiently than you could using paper file folders in cabinet drawers. In fact, this software is often referred to as an electronic file cabinet. Database management involves using a computer rather than a manual system to store, manipulate, retrieve, and create reports from data and information.

*T I P*   Important documents should be proofread two or three times for accuracy. A good technique is to proof a document with a co-worker, especially if large amounts of money are involved. ∎

Data managers allow you to enter information once, perform a complex calculation or sorting routine on that information, and then produce, for example, three different reports based on the results. Databases can store almost any type of information and ensure accurate and up-to-the-minute reports on which to base critical decisions.

Two types of application software have been developed to work with data stored in database files: file managers and database management systems. A file manager enables you to retrieve and work with files, but only one file at a time. For smaller organizations, a file manager may be all that is needed. However, the inability to work with more than one file simultaneously can be a significant limitation as a business grows.

For example, suppose that you want to send a collection letter to customers who are more than thirty days late with their payments. Billing information is collected in an invoice file; customer data is stored in another file. This application is ideal for a database management system (DBMS). DBMS software allows you to construct a database environment for a set of related files and to access and manipulate quickly the information located in several separate files. A DBMS reduces data redundancy and confusion because information can be more easily shared across department and division lines. When information needs to be updated, for example, you need to do so in only one place.

Popular database packages include: Microsoft® Access, Corel Paradox®, Microsoft Visual FoxPro®, and Oracle®.

**Graphics**   Graphics software presents data clearly and quickly in visual form on a computer. Business graphics software is available in two basic forms: analytical graphics software and presentation graphics software. Analytical graphics software allows you to take data from an existing spreadsheet or database file and create, view, and print charts and graphs.

When more professional-looking charts and graphs are needed—for example, to accompany an oral presentation—presentation graphics software is appropriate to use. This type of program allows you to make charts and graphs, diagrams, and other visual aids from scratch.

Business professionals use graphs to define and analyze problems, summarize and condense information, and spot trends or trouble spots. Further, business reports that summarize ideas graphically are more interesting to read, easier to understand, and more persuasive with customers.

Organizations should buy graphics software according to their needs. Simple charting programs are included as part of many popular spreadsheet and database software programs such as Excel and Access. If a company plans to use individualized graphics, however, two good presentation graphics and drawing packages are PowerPoint® by Microsoft and CorelDraw™ by Corel Corporation.

**Desktop Publishing**   Using a microcomputer to assemble words and illustrations on pages and to print them on a high-quality printer, such as a laser printer, is known as **desktop publishing (DTP)**. Desktop publishing software allows you to produce professional-looking newsletters, reports, manuals, brochures, advertisements, and other documents that incorporate text with graphics. Desktop publishing helps businesspeople present ideas powerfully and dramatically.

Using desktop publishing within a company is much less expensive and allows more control than going to an outside printer. With desktop publishing, charts, diagrams, drawings, and even photographs can be

## Computer Software and Equipment

Large offices at one time used mainframe computers extensively. Now, however, with the abilities, speed, and memory of personal computers increasing while prices are decreasing, many large offices use personal computers more than ever before. This increased usage is partly because office productivity software, such as that for word processing, spreadsheet, and database management, is widespread and many more office workers now know how to use a number of computer applications.

The discussion of networked systems in the next chapter will further explain how so much technology is available to most employees in large offices at a fraction of the cost of the personal computer systems that are usually found in small offices (which may have only one or two office workers).

**If you are interested in a computer-related career, will you apply to a large or small company for employment? Why? ■**

## Ethics on the Job

You have just installed the new software package Microsoft Office 2000 Professional onto your office computers. You are tempted to "borrow" a copy over the weekend (because nobody would know) and install it onto the hard drive of your home computer.

***Would you? ■***

easily added to documents to enhance and clarify their messages. Today the technology for producing desktop-published documents is a part of the total integration of information systems in the office.

Even though desktop publishing can be done with high-end word processing packages such as Microsoft Word, the most popular complete desktop publishing software packages sold include Adobe® PageMaker®, Corel VENTURA™, and QuarkXPress®.

**Integrated Software and Software Suites**   Integrated software combines several independent software packages—such as word processing, spreadsheet, graphics, and database—into one package for coordinated use. Integrated packages have several advantages compared with individual software applications purchased separately. They generally cost less, require less RAM and disk storage space, and are easier to use because all modules within the package share the same interface and command structure. The main disadvantage to using integrated software such as Microsoft Works is that the modules within an integrated package offer fewer features and less versatility than their stand-alone versions.

More full-featured versions of each type of software are also on the market. These software programs are similar to integrated packages and are called *software suites*. For example, Microsoft Office 2000, or Office XP, is a collection of full-featured products that perform alike and work together as if they were a single program. They are superior to the usual approach at providing ease of use, integration, and custom solutions.

The Microsoft Office 2000 or XP Professional package includes Microsoft Word, Microsoft Excel, Microsoft PowerPoint, and Microsoft Access, as well as several other applications. These applications have

**TABLE 5.2 • Application Software in the Office**

| Type | Popular Packages | Office Applications |
|---|---|---|
| Word Processing | ▪ Corel WordPerfect<br>▪ Lotus Word Pro®<br>▪ Microsoft Word for Windows | letters, memos, reports, contracts, multipage documents |
| Spreadsheet | ▪ Corel Quattro Pro<br>▪ Lotus 1-2-3<br>▪ Microsoft Excel | budgets, financial statements, what-if analysis, statistical information |
| Database Management | ▪ Corel Paradox<br>▪ Microsoft Access<br>▪ Microsoft Visual FoxPro<br>▪ Oracle | customer listings, personnel listings, inventory items, vendor information |
| Graphics | ▪ Microsoft PowerPoint<br>▪ CorelDraw | graphs, charts, draw and paint projects |
| Desktop Publishing | ▪ Adobe PageMaker<br>▪ Corel Ventura<br>▪ Quark X-Press | brochures, advertisements, newsletters, price lists, catalogs |
| Integrated Software and Software Suites | *Suites:*<br>▪ Corel WordPerfect Office<br>▪ Lotus SmartSuite<br>▪ Microsoft Office | unlimited applications; most of the above |

standardized toolbars and consistent menus, commands, and dialog boxes. Users find that once they learn one application, learning the others is easy. Other popular office software suites are Lotus SmartSuite® and Corel WordPerfect® Office 2002.

Table 5.2 lists some of the most popular software packages in offices today and how they are used to produce specific office documents.

## Recall Time

*Answer the following questions:*

**1.** How does GUI benefit computer users?

**2.** Name some current operating systems.

**3.** List the six types of application software packages.

# Summary

Computers affect the way office professionals work. For that reason, developing computer skills and knowledge is essential to being prepared for jobs today and in the future.

Computer systems are classified into five types: personal computers, handheld computers, mid-range servers, mainframe computers, and super-computers. Personal computers, by far the most used, are available in both desktop and notebook models.

The basic hardware devices for most business computer systems include a monitor, keyboard, a printer, and a computer system unit containing memory chips and storage disk drives. In addition to major hardware components, computer users also employ peripheral devices such as pointing devices, digital cameras, scanners, speakers, headsets, and data projectors.

Software, also known as a program, is a group of instructions executed by a computer. Business and office software used on computers can be categorized as either system software or application software. Examples of system software are: Windows 2000, Windows XP, Windows Millennium Edition, and the Mac OS. The main function of system software is to manage the operations and resources of the computer.

Application software, on the other hand, is specific to a particular problem or task. Although many types of application software are available, the six types used in most offices today include word processing, spreadsheet, database management, graphics, desktop publishing, and integrated software and software suites.

Can you recall the following points mentioned in this chapter?

- Management information systems provide an integrated computerized approach to supply managers with the right information at the right time for appropriate decisions.
- The computer system should match the needs of the individual and organization; decisions must be made regarding how the system is to be used in order to design the best one.
- Two common memory chips used in computers today are the ROM and RAM chips.

# before you leave...

**When you have completed this chapter, answer the following questions:**

**1.** What might a computer system in an office look like?

**2.** What is the difference between system software and application software?

# Review & Application

## Check Your Knowledge

1. Distinguish between the five classifications of computers.

2. Name three types of nonimpact printers often found in computer systems.

3. What is the major difference between RAM and a hard disk drive?

4. Describe three pointing devices.

5. What do a floppy disk and a high-capacity disk have in common?

6. What types of office documents can scanners process?

7. In your opinion, which types of application software are most used in today's business offices and why?

## Review Your Vocabulary

On a separate piece of paper, write the letter of the vocabulary word described below.

___ 1. one of the more popular handheld computers in use today

___ 2. using a personal computer to assemble words and illustrations on a page

___ 3. equal to approximately 1 billion bytes

___ 4. a device used for moving the cursor-like insertion point around the text and for pointing

___ 5. shows you what you are doing as you use a computer

___ 6. a thin, rigid metallic platter that is coated with a substance that allows data to be recorded in magnetic form

___ 7. computerizes and manages recordkeeping and information tasks and is sometimes referred to as an electronic file cabinet

___ 8. an integrated system that is usually computer based and provides information critical for decision making

___ 9. financial planning tools that perform mathematical calculations on financial and statistical information

___ 10. a portable, plastic storage medium

___ 11. allows you to create, edit, format, print, and save office documents such as letters and reports

___ 12. the type of computer used most often by office workers

___ 13. a group of computer devices that are connected, coordinated, and linked together

___ 14. fast and powerful, freestanding, multi-user units that are larger than mid-level servers.

___ 15. the largest, fastest, and most expensive computer systems available

___ 16. prerecorded and can be an optical disk

___ 17. an input device that acts like a miniature photocopy machine connected to a computer

a. compact disk read-only memory
b. computer system
c. database management
d. desktop publishing
e. gigabyte
f. hard disk
g. mainframe computers
h. management information system
i. personal computer
j. personal digital assistant
k. floppy disk
l. monitor
m. mouse
n. scanner
o. spreadsheets
p. supercomputers
q. word processing

## Discuss and Analyze an Office Situation

Conditions in the temporary employment services industry have been changing so rapidly that Benson's Personnel Specialists has had difficulty keeping up with the changes. President J. Michael Benson recently hired an executive assistant, Beth, who has previous experience working on management information systems (MIS). Beth knows and has commented that with

an MIS system in place, Mr. Benson would have information at the right time to make decisions with greater confidence.

Mr. Benson is concerned with the expense of changing the firm's current decentralized computer system, as well as with the best way to approach his twenty-five employees about an MIS system; he hopes to install one within the year.

1. Why do you think employees might feel threatened by the placement of an effective management information system in their organization?

2. What, in your opinion, can management do to calm those fears?

## Practice Basic Skills

### Math

Think like a computer. Do the processing steps necessary to complete the following problems correctly. Remember that a computer will first perform the calculations within parentheses, then any multiplication or division tasks, and finally addition or subtraction tasks. Also, "+" means to add, "−" to subtract, "*" to multiply, and "/" to divide.

a. $37 + 22 - 16 =$    f. $4 + (72/9) =$
b. $45 - 30 - 15 =$    g. $(5*8)*2 =$
c. $10*4 + 12 =$    h. $(100 - 60)*(30 - 20)/2 =$
d. $40/8 + 13 =$    i. $200*(18/6) + 72 + 33 =$
e. $(2 + 2 + 2)*6 =$    j. $(1 + 2)*(4/2) + (55 - 35)/2 =$

### English

*Rule:* When the day follows the month, do not include the ordinal ending *st, nd, rd,* or *th.* When the day precedes the month or stands alone, use the ordinal ending or write the date in words.
*Examples:* We plan to get together before June 15.
The 8th of January is Jimmy's birthday.
*Practice Exercise:* For the following, if a sentence is correct, write OK beside its letter on a separate piece of paper. If a sentence is incorrect, rewrite it correctly.

a. My birthday is on the 11 of December.
b. Spring break begins March 12th.
c. You must buy tickets before Monday, July 23.
d. Tommy is scheduled for his health exam on October 20th.
e. Graduation is scheduled for the 6th of June.
f. Gina will be inducted into the National Honor Society on Monday, April 22.
g. November 5 is my nephew's birthday.
h. Ice skating lessons for Charles Patrick are scheduled to begin on November 26th.

### Proofreading

Rewrite or key the following letter, correcting misspellings and incorrect punctuation.

February 3, 20—

Ms. Midnight Katzen
12 Ricardo Huch Strasse
Poppenweiler-Ludwigsburg
Germany

Dear Ms. Katzen:

Thank you, for your inquiry concernning the World Wide Web (WWW). I hope the folllowing informatin will be helpfull.

The WWW is a vast, groowing collection of online documents and information formated in Hypertext Markup Language and idstributed overr the Internet. The Web incluuds shoping malls filled with virtual retail outlets, private and public repositories of software, libraries, maggazines, news papers; online meeting spotts, and much more. Created in 1989 in Geneva, Switzerland, a scientist developed the Web to faccilitate the sharing of scientiffic documents and data.

Let me know if I can be of futher help.

Truely yours:

Dennis Clinger

## Apply Your Knowledge

1. Part of being comfortable operating a computer comes from understanding its parts. Visualize a computer and indicate on a separate sheet of paper whether each of the following components is located on the outside or inside.

a. RAM
b. Printer
c. Monitor
d. Keyboard
e. Floppy disk
f. Hard disk
g. Control unit
h. Hard copy

2. *Debate the Issue:*

"We live in a society fraught with information overload. Before long, we will become so paralyzed by all this information, we will not be able to sort out what we need from what we don't."

*Instructions:* React to the above statement by quickly jotting down on a piece of paper three or more ideas you have supporting and refuting the statement. Prepare to role-play either point of view in a mock in-class debate.

## Using the Reference Manual

Open file ch5ref.doc. Use the letter styles section of the Reference Manual at the back of the book to help you format correctly. Use block style and open punctuation. Save and print.

(Use Current Date)

Letter Address: Mr. Matthew D. Saikley
Computer Systems Supreme
120 East El Caminito
Pacific Grove, CA 93941

I am interested in a portable computer system that I can use while attending college. Because I will be majoring in business administration, I will also need to purchase appropriate business software.

Please send me any brochures or catalogs you have along with pricing information. I plan to make a buying decision within the month.

Sincerely

(Use Your Name as Sender of Letter)

# chapter  6

# Network Systems and Telecommunications

## objectives

*After completing this chapter, you will be able to do the following:*

1. Explain how local area networks are set up.
2. List several benefits of organizations using local area networks.
3. Describe the role of electronic mail in today's offices.
4. Describe the benefits of using groupware in organizations.
5. Identify five technologies that help workers conduct productive meetings in physically distant locations.
6. Describe the importance of automated workflow in an office that has an effective computer system.
7. Describe the importance of the Internet and the World Wide Web to businesses today.
8. Describe virtual organizations that use virtual workers.

### New Office Terms

- computer network
- computer system
- connectivity
- electronic mail (e-mail)
- groupware
- Internet
- local area network (LAN)
- network operating system (NOS)

- node
- server
- system
- telecommunications
- virtual organizations
- virtual workers
- workflow automation

# before you begin...

**Answer the following questions to the best of your ability:**

1. Describe a networked system in an office.
2. How do businesses use the Internet?

**C**omputers are everywhere—at work, at home, and at school. In the workplace, people use computers to create correspondence such as letters and reports, calculate payrolls, and send e-mail messages with file attachments. Business managers have long sought to improve the ways in which their employees work together, gain access to information, and operate outside the office. Maintaining all the resources its employees might like or need is not financially practical for an organization. When files, devices, and programs are shared among employees through networking, organizations can benefit from time and cost savings.

# Networked Systems in the Office

The trend today toward acquiring technology in the office is to develop networked systems that can be shared rather than to invest in individual personal computers, programs, and printers for each worker. Many types of networked systems are available. Local area networks, electronic mail, groupware, and other long-distance communication systems are discussed later in this chapter. First, let's define the terms *systems* and *networks*.

## Systems and Computer Networks

A **system** implies organization and order of a combination of elements or parts. Office workers no longer use just one office machine to complete a task; their tasks are more complex, and various pieces of office equipment can be connected to others to become part of a system that gets things done. For example, some years ago a typewriter was used as the input device, processor, and output device to produce a three-page report. Today, a computer system can complete the activity with professional-quality results in a fraction of the time.

A **computer system**, such as that shown in Figure 6.1, page 109, is a group of computer devices that are connected, coordinated, and linked together in such a way that they work as one to complete a task. Through the use of a computer system, the three-page report referred to previously would be input with a computer keyboard, processed by editing and other tool features of a word processing software program, and then output to a laser printer.

The future of document processing will not be *paperless*, but it will consist of new documents and document management that can truly capitalize on networked computers. A **computer network** is made up of several devices (computers, terminals, or other hardware devices) connected together by an electronic communications system.

**THE COMPANY INTRANET**

An *intranet* makes use of Internet technology but limits its use to employees within one company or organization. An intranet has access to the Internet, but an intranet is not accessible to outsiders. A company intranet provides fast access to day-to-day information, and it can reduce company costs. It enables users to centralize information resources in a point-and-click environment at any location.

A company intranet can work together with the Internet. An intranet may even be located on a remote site of the Internet, with users accessing data via secure links. Some companies provide customer services online to specific clients or suppliers through a separate network, called an *extranet*. Access via an extranet is restricted by security such as passwords or encryption. ■

Even small organizations that network two or three computers benefit because the costs of operation are reduced significantly when files and resources are shared. Linked computers may be scattered throughout a city, state, country, or the world. Connected computers may be located within a single office building.

To be employable, future office workers should have a working knowledge of the PC and of basic networking concepts. Employers need flexible, creative employees who are able to troubleshoot, solve problems, and find innovative ways to complete tasks using networked technology and systems-oriented procedures.

## Connectivity and Geographic Coverage

**Computer communications** describes a process in which a computer transfer data, instructions, and information to other computers. American businesses are attempting to provide connectivity resources to give people access to the tools they need in order to work better. Connectivity can

**FIGURE 6.1 • Components of a Computer System**

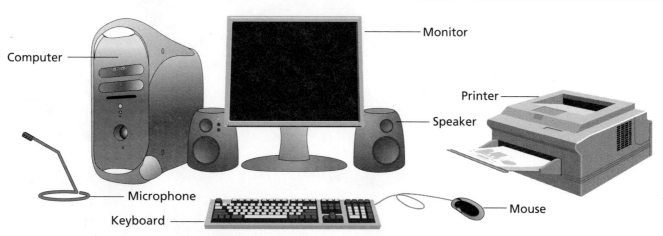

Though comprised of many devices, a computer
system works as one to complete office and business documents.

enhance access to data that are important for completing tasks. **Connectivity** gives equal support to members of a workgroup, a client, or a customer, regardless of geographic location. In other words, connecting people and computers is the key to delivering cost-effective services in today's business environment.

Such new forms of communication and cooperation have inspired various terms, from "virtual networking" and "telecommuting" to "spider-web organizations" and "virtual employees." With the advantages of connectivity and computer networks, such as the Internet and local area network (LAN) systems, more businesses favor work styles that are flexible, less bureaucratic, and more receptive to new ideas.

Networks are categorized based on their geographic coverage and connection lines. A computer network using leased lines from telephone company vendors over a wide geographic distance, for example, is called a *wide area network (WAN)*. A network extending over a few miles or within a city is a *metropolitan area network (MAN)*. LAN systems extend only within a building or group of buildings and use physically wired connection lines. Figure 6.2, page 111, illustrates the three types of networks.

## Local Area Networks

Low costs, versatility, ease of use, and the convenience of thousands of options and application programs make LANs a popular choice in large and small companies as well as in educational institutions and schools. A **local area network** is a computer and communications network that covers a limited geographic area, allows every node to communicate with every other node, and does not require a central node or processor. A **node** is a workstation, terminal, computer, or other device in a computer network. Growing companies can benefit greatly from LANs; even an office with only two or three PCs can enjoy the advantages of local area networking at a relatively low cost.

Networks work well because of a special control program called a **network operating system (NOS)** that usually resides in a server within a

©Anton Vengo/SuperStock International

LANs are used by groups of people who need to work with one another, sharing their resources and data.

**FIGURE 6.2 • Networks in the Office**

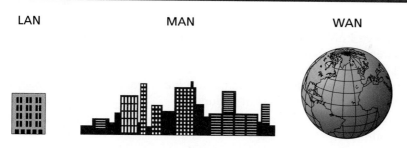

LAN          MAN                    WAN

Networks are described based on
local (LAN), metropolitan (MAN), or world (WAN) access.

LAN. The NOS is critical to LAN operations because it handles the requests for data from all users or workstations on the network. A **server** is a computer device and part of the LAN that allows sharing of other computer devices, such as printers to produce output copies and hard disk units to store files and applications. A server is usually a personal computer with the following characteristics: fast CPU speed, large RAM, large disk storage capacity, fast disk-access speed, plenty of expansion slots available, reliable hardware, and an operating system compatible with standard drivers such as network, disk, and video drivers. Figure 6.3 shows how LANs work between workstations with access to file servers.

**FIGURE 6.3 • Local Area Networks**

### Local Area Network System
### Using Electronic Mail

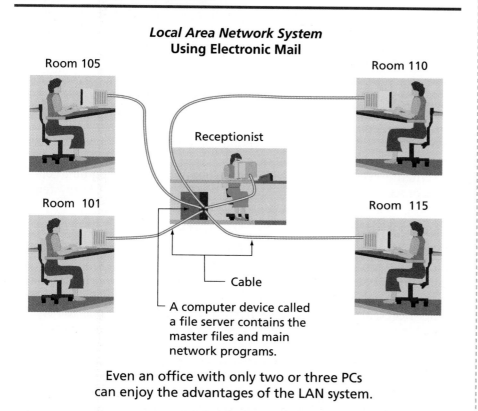

Room 105

Room 110

Receptionist

Room 101

Room 115

Cable

A computer device called
a file server contains the
master files and main
network programs.

Even an office with only two or three PCs
can enjoy the advantages of the LAN system.

### Benefits of LANs

From just about anywhere on earth, you can use a modem-equipped computer and remote-control software modem to dial in to a computer on your office LAN. As you key in data from wherever you are, you can do everything you could do if you were sitting at your desk, and you can see it all on the screen in front of you. Organizations use LAN systems because they offer several benefits and make good business sense. Using LANs has several benefits that include:

1. Improved work-related communications among employees in a workgroup.
2. Easier information sharing with less wasted time.
3. Access to a variety of printers, which eliminates the need to purchase an expensive printer for each group member.
4. Easy, low-cost access to fax facilities.
5. Use of office resources by group members while at home or on the road.
6. Application software sharing for consistency of presentation and ease of editing, upgrading, and maintenance.
7. Common database information available to all members of a group.
8. Methods for scheduling meetings, use of group resources, and employees' time.
9. Equipment connections—for instance, allowing for easy communication between normally noncompatible Macintosh and IBM personal computers.

### Server-Based LANs

Servers can access resources for files, printers, applications, or communications. Many operating systems today have network features built into them. Some of the more popular operating systems that support server-based networks are Novell® NetWare®, Microsoft Windows XP, NT, and 2000, Sun® Solaris™, and UNIX®.

How do you use a server-based LAN office system? Users usually must attach or "login" to the central file server before engaging in any LAN activity. The login command employs the user's name to find the user's profile and authorized privileges in the server; prompts for a password, if needed; and then sets up access rights to the file server resources. Users may be able to use only certain database files or printers during specific times on particular days.

When finished working with the system, users must log out. Log-out is the process of unlinking the user's workstation from the LAN system.

## Electronic Mail

Within today's organizations, little takes place without team effort. Communication tools, such as electronic mail, make cooperation between team members easier. **Electronic mail (e-mail)** is a system used to send messages between or among users of a computer network and the programs necessary to support such message transfers. E-mail or similar messaging systems can facilitate communication among co-workers at different locations or on different shifts.

Suppose that you are administrative assistant to the human resources manager; she asks you to arrange a meeting with seven company employees to discuss an upcoming change in the medical insurance plan. With e-mail, you could send a message scheduling the meeting with all the

### What's Your Attitude?

The marketing department has called a special meeting because of complaints from the three secretaries in the sales department. The secretaries' concern is that staff is not using the e-mail system effectively. They report that only three out of the twelve sales representatives check their e-mail on a regular basis.

Secretaries are to interface by telephone or in person with customers if a sales representative is not available. Then, they are to send an e-mail message to the representative regarding the customer's concern. In the past week, twenty irate customers have called and complained that their sales representatives never contacted them.

1. *Do you think the secretaries are overreacting?*

2. *What are some areas of concern in using e-mail?*

3. *What steps can the management of an organization take to ensure that office and sales staff use e-mail systems properly?* ■

employees simultaneously. You could also send a survey form requesting strategic departmental information at the same time. The human resources manager could then receive those completed surveys (employees could e-mail them back) prior to the meeting. E-mail makes sending, receiving, saving, responding to, deleting, or printing messages easy.

Electronic mail systems are not simply replacements for intraoffice memos. E-mail also provides access to shared fax resources, allows accounting and other software systems to send automatic alerts to appropriate officers, furnishes a means for distributing reports, and allows file transfers among co-workers.

You should, however, keep one warning in mind. Although communication networks offer widespread telecommuting opportunities and personalized media access, they also threaten individual privacy and increase the potential for information discrimination. Ethics should be an important consideration of users and designers of network systems.

## Groupware

Workgroup software, frequently called *groupware*, is one of the fastest-growing computer applications available today. **Groupware** is a combination of electronic technology and group processes that allows individual computer users to be part of a team and share information. Lotus Notes has quickly become the "gold standard" of groupware.

Groupware keeps all documents online and current, serving as a storage area for an organization's vital information. When employees are trained to use groupware effectively, the number of meetings can be reduced and communication between departments easily maintained as a project progresses. Groupware allows co-workers to share, analyze, and use information not only within the same building but also across geographic distances and time zones.

Groupware requires that personal computers be networked in such a way that files may be transmitted on request from one computer to many others. In addition to computers and printers, copiers, fax machines, and telephones may be attached to the network to serve its users' needs.

Groupware may be used for reference, workflow, e-mail, and fax. It has excellent formatting and searching capabilities. Local area networks, wide area networks, and electronic mail together are the backbone of groupware.

**TIP** People who are open to new ideas are "winners" in business. Be the first to respond to a creative strategy by saying, "Let's investigate this further and see if we can make it work!" ■

## Long-Distance Communication Networks

Keeping together a work team that is spread across the company—or even the globe—can be a real challenge to any organization. However, with the right technology, the whole group can stay "in sync." Voice mail, faxes, teleconferences, videoconferences, and collaborative software are all effective ways to gather and share information despite co-workers' divergent schedules and locations.

### Voice Mail and Fax

Voice messaging and faxing are good alternatives for some businesspeople. Most voice-mail systems and fax machines offer a "broadcast" feature, that is, the ability to send the same message to individuals on an established routing list. For example, if your supervisor wants everyone in your department to help brainstorm a new idea, you can arrange for their input through online meetings.

Here's how it works: Your supervisor makes a suggestion and invites a list of people to provide feedback. Participants check their voice mail periodically during their work hours, reviewing progress and adding new comments. For computer-connected teams, broadcast voice mail is an easy way to share information and allow an idea to evolve without a meeting.

### Teleconference and Videoconference

If your supervisor needs frequent status reports from a team, consider using a form of teleconferencing. Telephone-conferencing technology provides audio-only group discussions; it permits dozens of people to call in at the same time.

Videoconferencing is another long-distance communication option. It not only provides two-way audio but two-way video and document exchange as well. (Although videoconferencing is the most costly form of teleconferencing, bringing out-of-state employees to a meeting is a far greater expense.) The picture is always coordinated with the individual talking by the use of voice-activated video cameras. Care must be taken when using this technology because communication ceases when people interrupt, slam down coffee cups, or shuffle papers.

### Collaborative Office Activities

Many software products provide a means to collaborate, or work with other users connected to a server. With Microsoft Office, for example, you can conduct online meetings. An online meeting allows you to share a

## Making Office Decisions

Jethro, a business consultant for a Cleveland firm, was recently injured in an auto accident. Although he is unable to travel to the office, his doctor has given him permission to work at home. He has an idea he would like to suggest to the president of the company.

Jethro would like to see whether one of the other consultants at the firm will agree to help him by "sharing" his consulting workload. He wants the firm to allow him and other consultants to use collaborative software over the next few months until he can physically return to the office. He has asked you to do some research on this new arrangement for him. He would like you to list the advantages and disadvantages of collaborative software for the president's consideration.

1. **What are the advantages of collaborative software in this situation?**

2. **What are some disadvantages of collaborative software for organizations?** ■

document with others in real time. Here's how it works: All participants see the document at the same time. As someone changes the document, everyone can see the changes being made. In addition, during this online meeting, participants can open a separate window and key messages to one another, similar to an online chat room experience.

Instead of interacting in a live meeting, participants may collaborate via e-mail. For example, if you want others to review a report, you can attach a routing slip to the report and send it via e-mail to everyone on the routing slip. When the first person on the routing slip receives the document, he or she can add comments to the report. Once everyone on the routing slip has reviewed the report, it automatically returns to the sender.

### Telephony

Internet telephony enables you to talk to other people over the Internet. Internet telephony uses the Internet (instead of the public telephone network) to connect a calling party and one or more called parties. Here's how it works: With special Internet telephone software loaded onto your computer system, as you speak into a computer microphone, this software and your computer's sound card digitize and compress your conversation and then transmit the digitized audio over the Internet to the called parties. Similarly, software and equipment at the receiving end reverse the process so that the receiving parties can hear what you have just said, just as if you were speaking on a telephone.

Table 6.1, page 116, describes long-distance communication devices.

## Manual and Automated Workflow

As discussed in Chapter 1, workflow is the movement of information from person to person within an organization. As computer systems are expanded, workflow patterns naturally change and should be reexamined. One of the first activities in workflow management is scrutinizing how documents are moved and regulated. It begins by examining how documents, business forms, and other information travel through an organization. This analysis can pinpoint bottlenecks and outdated procedures that impede progress and increase costs.

**TABLE 6.1 • Long-Distance Communication Devices**

| | |
|---|---|
| **Electronic Mail (E-mail)** | A system that enables a user to transmit letters, memos, and other messages directly from one computer to another, where they are stored for later retrieval. |
| **Facsimile (FAX)** | A machine that can send and receive documents over regular telephone lines. The sending machine digitizes and transmits the document (text, graphics, signatures) over the telephone line to the receiving machine, which then reproduces a copy, or facsimile, of the document. |
| **Teleconference** | A telephone conference call that takes place among three or more people in different locations. |
| **Videoconference** | A method of conferencing in which people at different locations can see and hear one another, as well as communicate via computer. |
| **Voice Mail** | A sophisticated, computerized telephone answering system that digitizes incoming spoken messages, stores them in the recipient's voice mailbox, and then reconverts them into spoken form when retrieved. |
| **Telephony** | Technology that allows users to converse over the Internet, just as if they were talking on a telephone. |

# Workflow Arrangements

Various arrangements are used to accomplish efficient office workflow. For example, workstations may be arranged in groups or clusters to make communication and efficient office operations easier. A cluster arrangement may be a Y, an X, or a variation of a circle. Workflow should be promoted and unnecessary traffic patterns eliminated no matter what layout is used. When planning office workflow, be sure to:

- Analyze the interrelationships among equipment, information, and personnel.
- Have work move in as straight a line as possible and revolve workflow around major source documents. Avoid crisscrossing and backtracking, which waste time and energy.
- Avoid requiring an employee to get up and get work to do; work should come to the employee.

# Workflow Automation

One trend toward making information move more efficiently is workflow automation. **Workflow automation** is a type of office software that manages workflow. Once the current workflow system has been analyzed and new routes laid out, workflow software is installed on a firm's computer networks. The function of workflow automation is to convey information—whether a digital image of an invoice or an e-mail query from a customer—instantly to the correct desk and computer.

Substituting a computer network system for a mail cart can be a great help in improving the flow of work in offices. Automation can prevent information from being delayed because it is waiting in an in-basket.

Workflow management can make workers more efficient and productive by sending information more directly and instantly to the correct desk and computer.

Switching from paper to electronic documents, however, is only part of the solution. Procedures for sharing the information must be revised as well. Workflow software can help by making the movement of documents automatic, eliminating the need for someone to decide where the information goes next, collapsing travel time, and avoiding misrouting.

Eventually workflow management may become the backbone of many computer networks, collecting and moving documents, firing up applications programs as needed, and doing other chores as yet undefined. For the present, managers who use workflow software are happy to have an efficient method of improving their productivity with lots of empty in-baskets.

## Telecommunications in Cyberspace

**Telecommunications** is the transfer of data from one place to another over communication lines or channels and includes the dissemination of all forms of information, including voice and video. This concept is often called the *information highway* or *data superhighway*, or simply *cyberspace*.

Transmitting and receiving information is vital to any business. People are most efficient at work when they can say at any time, "I need some information." They do not care whether the information is on a CD-ROM disk, a company file server, or thousands of miles away in some central repository, as long as they can access the needed information to complete their tasks.

Time will not be wasted wondering what program or information source will work. Computer users will simply be "in touch" with data or information whenever and wherever they choose. This ability to exchange documents quickly is crucial to the business office of today and tomorrow.

## Benjamin Lee

*Analyst/Engineer*
*Pacific Gas & Electric*

**Q.** Mr. Lee, what types of technology are becoming commonplace in offices?

**A.** Employees need to know more than how to operate computers, fax machines, printers, and scanners. Employees will be:
- using software such as Microsoft Suite® and Lotus Suite®
- accessing data from the Internet
- utilizing Windows 2000/ME/XP, Windows NT 2000, videoconferencing

**Q.** What advice would you give to a student preparing for a career as an office support person?

**A.** My advice is:
- Learn to communicate—communication skills are exceptionally important; verbal skills rank the highest.
- Be flexible in assignments but work to specialize in one or two areas.
- Have the attitude of **always** being willing to help.
- Learn as many word processing and spreadsheet applications as possible.

The best medium for innovations in telecommunications is the optical fiber. (See Figure 6.4, page 119.) Each fiber, roughly the diameter of a human hair, can transmit as many as one billion bits of information per second in the form of digitized pulses of light. Fiber optics promise superior fidelity, protection from electrical disturbances and security breaches, and a lower cost than copper wire.

Data superhighways, utilizing the power and speed of fiber-optic networks, provide the infrastructure for standardized communication, allowing users to communicate with each other, regardless of the equipment or data type they have. Already in place, for example, are online information and database services. Evolving office procedures and workstyles are introducing to the workplace the virtual organization, the virtual worker, and many more mobile workers.

## The Internet and the World Wide Web

One of the major reasons businesses and home users purchase computers today is for Internet access. Through the Internet, people have access to information from around the globe. The most desirable feature of the Internet is the ability to access it from a computer anywhere: in a restaurant or your car, as well as at home, work, or at school.

The **Internet** is the world's largest network, consisting of a collection of computers and devices connected through modems, cables, telephone lines, and satellites. Each network on the Internet provides up-to-date

**FIGURE 6.4 • Fiber-Optic Cable**

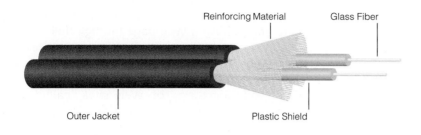

Reinforcing Material    Glass Fiber

Outer Jacket    Plastic Shield

resources for goods, services, and information from every part of the globe. As of this writing, more than 400 million users around the world connect to the Internet for a variety of reasons.

To support users, the Internet provides a variety of services. One of the most widely accessed of these Internet services is the World Wide Web. Other services include electronic mail (e-mail), file transfer, newsgroups and message boards, mailing lists, chat rooms, and instant messaging.

Data sent over the Internet travels via networks and communication channels owned and operated by many companies. These companies, also called Internet Service Providers (ISPs), include both regional and national ISPs. Examples of national ISPs are AT&T®, America Online®, EarthLink™, and WorldCom™.

As stated earlier, the World Wide Web (WWW) is just one of the many services available on the Internet; however, since its emergence in the early 1990s, it has become the most widely used one. The WWW consists of a worldwide collection of electronic documents called *Web pages*. A Web page

**Ethics on the Job**

Your company has recently subscribed to America Online. As you are walking by a colleague's office, you see that he is downloading the most current version of a popular board game from the Net on his office computer.

***Should you let him know that playing computer games could get him into trouble?*** ■

The Internet allows the quick exchange of messages and information across a city—or around the world—without time and distance barriers.

can contain text, graphics, sound, and video, as well as built-in connections (called *links*) to other documents. A word of caution: Do not assume that information on a Web page is correct or accurate, because anyone in the world can easily create and publish a Web page through their ISP.

A Web browser is a software program that allows you to access and view Web pages. Popular Web browsers in use for personal computers today are Netscape® Navigator and Microsoft® Internet Explorer. Several companies maintain organized directories of Web sites, called *search engines*, to help Web users to find or search for information on specific topics. Several search engines are available today; some of the most widely used ones are AltaVista®, Excite℠, Google™, HotBot®, Lycos®, Yahoo!®, and WebCrawler™. Table 6.2 provides a list of terms used by "Net surfers."

## The Virtual Organization and Virtual Workers

New technologies affect how office information systems are used. For example, networking processes present a new and unique challenge to management—the working employee who is absent from view. More and more, companies are becoming virtual organizations with virtual and mobile workers.

**TABLE 6.2 • Internet Terms**

| | |
|---|---|
| **Electronic Commerce** | A financial business transaction that occurs over the Internet—typically investing, banking, or shopping—that eliminates time and distance barriers. Also known as *e-commerce*. |
| **E-mail** | Messages sent to individuals or groups through the electronic highway. |
| **FAQs** | Frequently Asked Questions. FAQ files are always a good place to start learning about a new service or Internet location. |
| **FTP** | File Transfer Protocol. It enables users to make a copy of a file on a remote host and bring it back to his or her computer. |
| **Home Page** | The starting page of a Web site; it is similar to a table of contents. It provides information about the purpose and content of a Web site. |
| **Hyperlink** | A connection to related Web page or part of a Web page. It allows you to obtain information in a nonlinear way. Also called a *link*. |
| **HTTP** | HyperText Transfer Protocol. Protocols are instructions computers understand that tell them how to handle and send hypertext documents from computer to computer. You see *http* at the beginning of URLs. |
| **Internet Address** | An address that identifies each computer or device connected to the Internet. For example, the Internet address for South-Western Publishing is <u>www.swep.com</u>. |
| **URL** | Uniform Resource Locator. A URL is an address or reference code that allows GUI browsers to find specific hypertext documents on any host server in the world. |

## Large Office/Small Office

*What's Your Preference?*

### Networking and Telecommunications

In large companies, you will find a wide array of networks and telecommunications devices available. Most organizations will gladly teach you the proper techniques and procedures to follow when using e-mail and other network devices, but you will benefit by learning as much as you can about these technological advances.

In the small office, your computer may or may not be on a network. Many smaller companies are finding that linking or networking as few as two or three computers into a LAN system is cost efficient. Advanced technology may be available in both large and small offices.

**Would you like to be exposed to a wide range of telecommunications devices and electronic gadgetry, or would you prefer a smaller office environment where you would not be so challenged by change?** ■

Virtual organizations function through collaborative networks that allow users to draw on vital resources as needed, regardless of where they are located physically and whether they belong to the supplier or the customer.

For example, instead of keeping fifty offices with fifty computers open all year long just to accommodate a two-month rush of business, hiring fifty virtual workers makes more sense.

Many employees of medium- to large-size businesses telecommute. Telecommuting is a work arrangement in which employees work away from a company's standard workplace, and they often communicate with the office using communications technology. Telecommuting is done for a variety of reasons: 1) to reduce time and the expense of traveling to the office, 2) to eliminate travel during unsafe weather conditions, 3) to provide a convenient, comfortable work environment for disabled employees, and 4) to allow a flexible work schedule so that employees can combine work and personal responsibilities such as childcare or elderly care.

These workers may be located in Frankfurt, Germany, or Sedona, Arizona; location makes no difference. They dial into the company's database and become an extension of the organization through connection by computers, fax machines, and other innovative means of communication.

Information technologies collapse time and space. Many business organizations are changing rapidly in structure and function and within a few decades will be almost new entities. Virtual organizations are the wave of the future, and you will no doubt find yourself working in this new environment.

### Ethics on the Job

Ursula Barton is a virtual worker responsible for preparing weekly, monthly, and year-end sales reports for a large organization in Boston. Because she lives two hours away from her company, she is required to come in to the office only twice a month for meetings. Ursula feels that under this arrangement, she has time to get a part-time job, and that she can handle both jobs in forty hours or less a week.

*Ursula thinks that "What her managers don't know won't hurt them." Do you agree?* ■

How is the customer served by these new "virtual" businesses? A possible scenario is the following: When a customer calls the company, all information about that customer is displayed on the computer screen of the employee, wherever he or she is located. Customers are unaware of where, how, or by whom they are being served. Widely scattered workers can operate as if they were all located at company headquarters.

The pace of operations is driving businesses toward becoming virtual organizations. As futurist Alvin Toffler predicted more than two decades ago, businesses now run at warp speed. Organizations are under pressure to drastically reduce the time needed to deliver a product from the engineer's workbench to the showroom floor. If they cannot, they stand to lose millions of dollars in investment to competitors who can provide a similar product faster.

## Recall Time

*Answer the following questions:*

**1.** In what ways are fax machines and e-mail different? Both can be used to send messages.

**2.** Define *automated workflow.*

**3.** Define the term *cyberspace.*

# Summary

Through networking, organizations benefit from time and cost savings because files, devices, and programs are shared among employees. Networked office systems can include local area networks, electronic mail, groupware, and other long-distance communication systems such as voice mail, fax, teleconference, videoconference, and collaborative software.

As computer systems evolve, changes occur in the way procedures and documents make their way from desk to desk. Workflow automation software is used to manage the flow of documents by analyzing workflow patterns and developing a more efficient system.

Telecommunications involves transferring data from one place to another over communication lines or channels. With telecommunications, broad access to a wide array of business information is possible through online information and database services such as those available on the Internet.

Because of distance networking, some companies may be described as virtual organizations with virtual and mobile workers. These labels have evolved because workers can now dial into the company's database from anywhere around the world and become an extension of the company, connected by computers, fax machines, and other technological innovations.

Keep in mind these specific ideas from Chapter 6:

■ Networks can be categorized, based on their geographic coverage and connection lines. For example, network systems may be WAN or wide area network, MAN or metropolitan area network, or LAN or local area network.

- On an office LAN system, you must attach or log in to the central file server and give your password in order to gain access to the database, programs, and files.
- Most network systems provide electronic mail capability to facilitate message sending between or among users of a computer network.
- Groupware software, LANs, WANs, and e-mail systems allow employees to share, analyze, and use information across vast distances and different time zones.
- The Internet, a collection of huge supercomputers, telephone cables, and satellite transmission systems, relays data to and from thousands of points across the globe and allows users to have access to millions of computer files.

# before you leave...

**When you have completed this chapter, answer the following questions:**

1. Describe a networked system in an office.
2. How do businesses use the Internet?

# Review & Application

## Check Your Knowledge

1. List two examples of telecommunications in today's office.

2. Discuss the advantages in an office environment of two types of networks described in this chapter.

3. Cite two reasons organizations are installing LANs.

4. What must an operator do before being able to use a server-based LAN?

5. What is the difference between a LAN and a WAN?

6. Why is the Internet described as a "network of networks"?

7. What is the purpose of workflow automation?

## Review Your Vocabulary

On a separate piece of paper, write the letter of the vocabulary word described below.

____ 1. a station, terminal, computer, or other device in a computer network

____ 2. a group of computer devices that are connected, coordinated, and linked together

____ 3. a type of office software that manages workflow

____ 4. the transfer of data from one place to another over communication lines or channels; includes communication of all forms of information including voice and video

____ 5. a computer and communications network that covers a limited geographic area

____ 6. an international "network of networks"

____ 7. collaborative networks that make it possible to draw on vital resources as needed, regardless of where they are physically located

____ 8. devices such as computers, terminals, or other hardware devices connected together by an electronic communications system

____ 9. people who work at home or away from the workplace and have their own computers

____ 10. a computer device and part of the LAN that allows for sharing peripheral devices, such as printers, to produce output copies and hard disk units to store files

____ 11. a system used to send messages between or among users of a computer network and the programs necessary to support such message transfers

____ 12. a combination of electronic technology and group processes that allow individual computer users to be part of a group and share information

____ 13. a concept that gives equal support to members of a workgroup, a client, or a customer, regardless of geographic location

____ 14. a special control program that resides in a file server within a LAN

____ 15. implies organization and order of a combination of elements or parts

a. computer network
b. computer system
c. connectivity
d. electronic mail (e-mail)
e. server
f. groupware
g. Internet
h. local area network
i. network operating system (NOS)
j. node
k. system
l. telecommunications
m. workflow automation
n. virtual organizations
o. virtual workers

## Discuss and Analyze an Office Situation

Northland State University is online with its network system. The problem, however, is that not everyone is connected; only the faculty, top administrators, and a few chosen staff members. When Gail, the administrative assistant to the Dean of Instruction, requested connection so that she could have access to e-mail and the Internet, she was told to write a memo asking her manager to authorize funds to pay for a line drop to her workstation and the purchase of a computer network card at a cost of approximately $100.

Other employees are resentful that Gail is requesting special treatment. They, too, would like to be connected to the network.

1. How should organizations decide who should be on the network initially and who will be phased in later?

2. What can the organization expect if this situation is allowed to continue? Could this problem have been avoided? If so, how?

# Practice Basic Skills

## Math

Help Scotty calculate his summer budget as an electronic spreadsheet would do it. Calculate the totals and savings amounts indicated by the question marks.

|  | June | July | August | Total |
|---|---|---|---|---|
| Revenue |  |  |  |  |
| Park job | 200 | 200 | 200 | ? |
| Allowance | 50 | 50 | 50 | ? |
| Baby-sitting | 100 | 50 | 100 | ? |
| Total revenue | ? | ? | ? | ? |
| Expenses |  |  |  |  |
| Snacks | 75 | 75 | 75 | ? |
| Clothes | 100 | 25 | 75 | ? |
| Movies | 30 | 30 | 30 | ? |
| Vacation | — | 150 | — | ? |
| Gifts, misc. | 50 | 50 | 50 | ? |
| Total expenses | ? | ? | ? | ? |
| Savings | ? | ? | ? | ? |

## English

*Rule:* *Can* implies ability; *may* indicates permission.
*Examples:* Can you prepare a budget using Excel? May I help you proof your term paper?
*Practice Exercise:* Apply the rule to each of the following sentences. If a sentence is correct, write OK by its letter on a separate piece of paper. If a sentence is incorrect, rewrite it correctly.

a. Can I go with you to the computer demonstration?
b. Gina Ann may not be allowed to go to the show because she is grounded for a week.
c. Can you figure the payroll this week?
d. May I put the headings in boldface type?
e. I can run the spelling check using Word software.

f. Can you organize your work in the next five minutes?
g. May we have your name printed legibly on the form?
h. Scanners can be used as an input method.
i. Can I be trained at the same time you are?
j. Can you proofread and edit accurately?

## Proofreading

Rewrite or key the following letter, correcting misspellings and incorrect punctuation.

Ms. Sherol Hines
20543 E. Sunshine Way
Sun City, AZ 85000

Dear Ms. Hines-

Youve asked me what the Internet is and I am happy to to reply. The Internet is too words: information and communication. The Internet is nothing more then a countless number of files stored on comptuers around the world and an agreed methud on how to share them. Every Internet program, from the primative (e-mail) to the addvanced (World Wide Web) began with a few people devicing a protocol for sharing computer files over existing communications net works.

Now on the Web, we can download files (pages) with grafics and bvackgrounds and links to other pages. Let me know if you need more informatoin.

Cordilly yours,

Marion E. Jones

Computers in Cyberspace

# Apply Your Knowledge

1. Brainstorm five examples of e-mail communications that an office worker could send to others in the course of doing his or her job.

2. *Debate the Issue:*

   "The computer and easy access to the Internet are becoming intruders in many homes because they negatively affect the quantity and quality of family communication, in much the same way that television has."

*Instructions:* React to the above statement by quickly jotting down three or more ideas you have supporting *and* refuting the statement on a separate piece of paper. Prepare to role-play either point of view in a mock in-class debate.

## Using the Reference Manual

 Open file ch6ref.doc. Use the punctuation section of the Reference Manual at the back of the book to help you correct the sentences. Save and print.

1. The software had a 'bug' in it.

2. The manager said, "All overtime is cancelled as of this Friday".

3. The child asked, "When will Santa come back"?

4. I will give you ten dollars, $10, if you will teach me the basics of racquetball.

5. "Where will the next workshop on Word Perfect be conducted" asked Angela Johnson.

6. The top scholastic student in senior class—Arlo Riddle—did not get the Kiwanis scholarship.

7. Chapter sixteen was called, "Anne and Her Disappointment".

8. The most difficult-to-use software, and the most fun, was being used by all students.

9. "Do you have any ideas for the newsletter" Habib asked?

10. "Which parcel was lost?" Charelle asked?

# chapter 7

## Computer and Equipment Issues

**After completing this chapter, you will be able to do the following:**

1. List the qualifications computer users need.
2. Cite examples of computer monitoring.
3. Define computer hacking and piracy, relative to ethics.
4. Discuss ways to prevent computer injuries.
5. Describe the relationship between computers and the wise use of energy.
6. Distinguish between centralized and decentralized copying systems.
7. Describe how automated office equipment such as facsimiles, shredders, typewriters, and dictation machines are used in today's businesses.

### New Office Terms

- computer monitoring
- document imaging
- facsimile (fax)
- just-in-time hiring
- shredders

# before you begin...

**Answer the following questions to the best of your ability:**

1. How much energy do computers use?
2. What causes computer-related injuries?

## Computer-Related Employment Issues

Before ending our discussion of computers, we should acknowledge some concerns. Office professionals should have certain qualifications to be competent computer users, be aware that their work performance may be monitored by a computer, and should practice ethical behavior when using a computer.

### Career Opportunities as a Computer User

As permanent jobs become more and more temporary (through downsizing and layoffs), temporary jobs are becoming more and more permanent. Just-in-time hiring is becoming routine for many companies, and qualified computer operators are in high demand. Recent recessions have helped to create **just-in-time hiring** (employing temporary workers to complete only a specific project) because a large pool of experienced, unemployed people who can go to work on a temporary basis on short notice without a training period is available. The growing use of this hiring practice will provide improved future employment opportunities for workers who have many different abilities, including computer skills.

Someone with word processing skills may look for career opportunities as a word processing technician or specialist. Other job titles that involve word processing may include word processing operator, general office clerk, data entry clerk, billing clerk, or records clerk. Job responsibilities may include the following:

- Uses word processing to prepare materials, including correspondence, reports, brochures, and other documents.
- Formats and proofreads materials and makes corrections or changes as directed.
- Maintains records system and document storage based on departmental needs.

Word processing operators may find employment opportunities in a wide variety of office settings that include business, industry, government agencies, and nonprofit agencies. Generally, a high school diploma is the minimum requirement. Entry-level salaries range from $15,000 to $30,000. Microsoft offers the Microsoft Office Users Specialist (MOUS) certification designed to measure and validate users' software skills.

### Employee Monitoring

Employee monitoring involves the use of computers to observe, record, and review an individual's use of a computer, including communications such as e-mail, keyboard activity (used to measure productivity), and

**TIP** Ask questions of others when you receive a new office assignment. Try to determine whether a similar assignment has been completed before. If so, you may save time and effort by using an already proven good plan or idea and adding your own creativity. Remember, work smarter, not harder. ■

## Technology in the Office | KEEPING PERSONAL STUFF PERSONAL

Few people spend every minute in the office on business. Does your computer at work have any game programs on it? Or does it possibly contain a cover letter for an application to work at another company? The company where you work owns the computer you use, but does the company have a right to look through your computer files (hard drive)? Most company executives think so, and many supervisors feel free to search through employees' hard drive files without notifying employees.

The New York Times Company discovered some suspicious activity in one of their departments. The managers decided to scan the hard drives of every employee in that department. They found personal e-mail, pages of jokes, and other personal material. The company fired 10 percent of the employees whose hard drives had been scanned.

Federal judge James M. Rosenbaum suggested in 2001 that company executives warn employees before scanning their computer hard drives. The truth is that employees cannot expect to keep anything that they write on a company computer private. So, if you want to keep personal stuff personal, do not write it on a company computer. ■

Web sites visited. Many software programs that easily allow employers to monitor employees are available. Further, employers may legally use these software programs.

The idea of **computer monitoring** sounds threatening to most office workers, but it can be beneficial and assist them in doing their work. For example, a computer that counts keystrokes and identifies errors might not reprimand the employee and tattle to the boss, but instead suggest that the computer user take a short breather. Other monitors could act as prompters, reminding the office worker of special details when talking with customers, or as coaches, giving tips on improving performance.

Advanced computer systems will be able to make suggestions based on information entered by the employee. Based on this added information, the computer will be able to help employees do their jobs more effectively. Overall, the use of prompts will be positive, for employees will not have to worry as much about remembering countless details.

Monitoring can be done humanely if employees are guaranteed several rights—including access to all information gathered through monitoring. Furthermore, organizations are recognizing that giving employees personal access to this information motivates them. Why? Information given to a supervisor often becomes a weapon; but when it goes directly to a worker, it can improve performance.

## Ethical Use of Computers

Several ethical issues surround the use of information technology. Ethical choices are more complex and difficult when laws do not exist or when their applications to new situations are unclear. Today's office workers are faced with such complications; rapid technological development has left many "gray areas" not yet defined by law.

Specific ethical concerns regarding office computer use include the security and privacy of data, employee loyalty, and the copying of computer software.

### Ethics on the Job

In your opinion, is the increased use of temporary workers by businesses morally right? In forming your opinion, consider that the temporary worker often works for a lower hourly wage, generally has no benefits package, and has no job security. ■

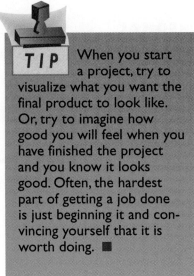

**TIP** When you start a project, try to visualize what you want the final product to look like. Or, try to imagine how good you will feel when you have finished the project and you know it looks good. Often, the hardest part of getting a job done is just beginning it and convincing yourself that it is worth doing. ■

1. *Hacking* is a term used to describe the activity of computer enthusiasts who enjoy the challenge of breaking computer security measures. Hacking is a crime, and gaining unauthorized access to someone's computer files can be as serious as breaking into someone's home.

2. Because the field of information processing is a dynamic environment with a shortage of qualified workers, many job opportunities are available. Although court rulings differ, most employers expect some degree of duty or loyalty on the part of employees. In other words, changing jobs should be done in an ethical fashion. Software packages and company secrets should not be carried to your new job.

3. Software copying, or *piracy*, is the unauthorized copying of a computer program that has been written by someone else. Whether done for personal use or to sell for profit, software piracy is a crime. Most software manufacturers give purchasers authorization to make one copy of a program legally; making additional copies is a violation of copyright law.

4. Practices such as excessive e-mailing, sharing objectionable or illegal material, and theft of intellectual property create ethical questions for everyday computer users at work and at home.

# Health Factors and Energy Issues Related to Computer Use

Computers, by their very nature, create a need for users to exercise caution and have a general awareness of their effects. Practicing good techniques can prevent computer injuries as well as minimize energy usage associated with office and home computing.

## Preventing Computer Injuries

The increased use of personal computers for word processing, data entry, personal organizers, and other business tasks has focused attention on workplace ailments that can reduce employee productivity and increase a company's costs for workers' compensation. Two common maladies resulting from computer use are eyestrain and repetitive stress injury, both of which can be controlled in several ways.

### Eyestrain

The most common computer-related health problem is eyestrain, estimated at 10 million cases a year by vision expert James Sheedy of the VDT Eye Clinic in Berkeley. What causes eyestrain? VDTs (video display terminals) do not emit rays that are harmful to the eyes; however, staring at small letters and numerals on a screen for hours on end can create visual fatigue. Eyestrain can also be caused by the glare of an overly bright or badly placed light that reflects off a VDT screen.

A regular eye examination is important for any computer operator. A number of eye specialists recommend following the "20-20 rule": Keep your face at least 20 inches from the screen, and pause every 20 minutes to look around the room. Exercising your eyes can also help reduce eyestrain.

## Making Office Decisions

Cody Keene, a customer relations specialist at a large hotel in Scottsdale, Arizona, is extremely upset. For the past month, the hotel has been monitoring his activities and performance using a computer. He has just finished reading his computer-generated performance evaluation and disagrees with just about everything in the report.

For example, he feels he was "written up" because when he spoke with five customers about making reservations, the computer showed he forgot to mention promotion packages that could have improved the chances of getting the customers' business. When Cody contacts the administrative office manager about the report, she says that he misunderstands the purpose of computer monitoring. Its purpose is to help employees do their jobs better. In fact, she tells him that, starting next month, prompts will appear on the computer screen to remind employees of promotional offers, along with the details of each.

1. *Do you feel that the information given Cody will reassure him that computer monitoring is intended to be helpful?*

2. *What might be some reasons Cody distrusts this new approach that is intended to "help" him?* ■

## Repetitive Stress Injuries

Pain in the neck, back, shoulders, arms, wrists, and legs can be minimized by movement. Move away from the computer workstation or desk periodically and take regular full-body stretches. Workers often forget how long they have been sitting in one position. As a result, some muscles may tighten and connective tissue may strain.

Shifting the body or changing its relation to the screen and keyboard helps. Repetitive strain injuries, such as carpal tunnel syndrome and tendinitis, are caused by poor keyboarding position, such as elevated elbows or bent wrists, and by excessive pounding of the keyboard.

## Preventing Injuries

In his book entitled, *ZAP! How Your Computer Can Hurt You—and What You Can Do About It,* Don Sellers offers these suggestions for avoiding computer-related injuries.

1. Correct ergonomic problems promptly. The longer stresses continue, the more difficult the damage is to repair.

2. Minimize the strain. If possible, intersperse computer work with other tasks. Key with less force.

3. Move. Every fifty minutes or so, get up. Walk down the hall. Move your hands, wrists, and arms. Bend and stretch. Rotate your shoulders. Turn your head.

4. Rest your eyes periodically. Take a 15-minute rest break every two hours for moderately demanding computer work. During the break, make telephone calls, file records, or do pencil-and-paper planning.

5. Invest in special glasses designed for computer use. Get a prescription that is correct for the distance and angle at which you view the monitor.

6. Balance the lighting. When you look at your computer screen, no "hot spots" of bright light should be behind or around it.

7. Position your monitor 18 to 24 inches from your eyes. Adjust the angle to eliminate reflections, and clean the screen regularly.

8. Sit in a chair that fits you. Have a co-worker check your posture when you are sitting at your computer.

Carpal tunnel syndrome occurs when the lining of tendons passing through the carpal tunnel in the wrist swell, putting pressure on the median nerve and causing pain, tingling, and numbness in the hand.

9. Adjust the surface on which the keyboard sits so that your wrists are not forced into unnatural positions (bent up or down).

10. Work defensively. Sit directly in front of your keyboard.

## Green Computing

Green computing involves reducing the amount of electricity used and environmental waste generated while using a computer. Computers use, and often waste, resources such as electricity and paper. Society has become aware of this waste, and measures are being taken to combat it.

Computers, monitors, and printers should comply with the Energy Star program, which was developed by the U.S. Department of Energy and the U.S. Environmental Protection Agency. This program encourages manufacturers to create energy-efficient devices that require little power when they are not in use.

Each year, more computers are purchased and put into use. The number of computers, however, is not the only thing that drives energy consumption upward. The way people use computers also adds to the increasing energy burden. Research reveals that most desktop personal computers are not being used most of the time they are running. In addition, 30 to 40 percent of personal computers in the United States are left on continuously.

The fundamental technique for saving energy with any type of equipment is to turn it off whenever possible, as stated in the first entry of Table 7.1, page 133, which lists ten strategies for energy-efficient computer use.

## Recall Time

*Answer the following questions:*

**1.** Name one advantage and one disadvantage of computer monitoring.

**2.** List two ways office workers can prevent computer-related injuries.

**3.** Describe three ways computers use energy.

# Other Automated Office Equipment

Because so much is said about computers today, users sometimes forget that other automated systems are just as vital in helping an office run smoothly. You can expect to use equipment other than computers to process office information. On the job, you might use a copier to duplicate information onto paper copies, a fax to send a letter to a customer, a paper shredder to safeguard personnel and financial records, an electronic typewriter to fill in preprinted forms, and a dictation unit to record your thoughts when creating business letters and reports.

## Reprographic (Copier) Systems

Office photocopying needs may be met through a centralized copy center where copier specialists do all the work, or by having several decentralized copiers that employees can use on demand.

**TABLE 7.1 • Strategies for Energy-Efficient Computing**

| |
|---|
| 1. **Turn off your computer and/or peripherals when they are not in use.** A moderate amount of turning computer equipment on and off will not harm it. |
| 2. **Do not run computers continuously (unless they are in constant use).** |
| 3. **Look for ways to reduce the amount of time your computer is on without adversely affecting your productivity.** |
| 4. **Break the habit of turning on all your computer equipment as soon as you enter the office each day.** Turn on each piece of equipment only when you are ready to start using it. |
| 5. **Group your computer activities informally and try to do them during one or two parts of the day, leaving the computer off at other times.** |
| 6. **Do not turn on your printer until you are ready to print.** This suggestion especially applies to laser printers because they consume a large amount of electricity even while idling. |
| 7. **If for some reason you must leave your computer on while you are not working on it, turn off your monitor to reduce energy consumption.** |
| 8. **Turn off your entire computer system (CPU, monitor, and printer) when you go to lunch or will be out of the office for a meeting or errand.** Rebooting when you resume computer work usually takes just a minute. |
| 9. **Do not use the power strip master switch (which simultaneously turns on all equipment plugged into it) if you do not need all your equipment all the time you are working on your computer.** |
| 10. **Be an energy educator and tactfully remind your co-workers and colleagues to save energy by changing their computer habits.** |

Adapted from "Green Computing" by Walter Simpson, *The Secretary*, April 1995, 20–21.

## Centralized Copying

Centralized copy centers can save organizations money by limiting the number of individual copiers needed and by reducing per-copy costs, although upfront costs may be higher because of the price of machines designed to handle high-volume photocopying. Advantages of a centralized system include increased security via access codes and the opportunity to review printing statistics for a specific department or organization. Convenience, storage and workspace requirements, and location are issues to consider when installing a centralized copy center.

## Decentralized Copying

In a decentralized reprographics environment, copiers are strategically and conveniently located throughout a company's offices. With copies becoming less expensive and equipment becoming more sophisticated, many businesses are purchasing additional individual copiers, allowing employees to make copies whenever they need them without having to walk a long way to reach the machines.

This "on-demand" system works well in small offices where the volume of copies does not justify a centralized system. The biggest advantage of the decentralized approach is convenience, while the major disadvantage is lack of control.

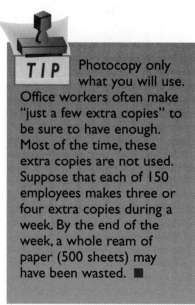

**TIP** Photocopy only what you will use. Office workers often make "just a few extra copies" to be sure to have enough. Most of the time, these extra copies are not used. Suppose that each of 150 employees makes three or four extra copies during a week. By the end of the week, a whole ream of paper (500 sheets) may have been wasted. ∎

In a busy office with a centralized copy center, one or two employees can do most of the copying for everyone in the office.

## Ethics on the Job

How do you feel about workers who take home small amounts (fifty sheets, for example) of copier paper for their personal use, or copy personal documents on the company copier without permission? ■

Whether a copier system is centralized or decentralized, the use of copier controls is growing as companies strive to keep costs down and reduce waste. Approximately 600 billion copies are made annually, and 25 percent of these copies are unnecessary. By using copier controls, a company can determine whether any machines are being used too little or too much.

Several methods of copier control have been developed to help eliminate copier abuse and misuse. One technique is to assign a number to each user so that every time he or she uses the copier this preassigned number is entered and serves to track usage. Another way is to issue each employee a magnetic stripe card that authorizes use and activates the copier.

A new monitoring technique uses telecommunications technology to collect information about all copier activity. A telephone line, personal computer, modem, and software now permit a central computer terminal to generate reports of all copier activity within a company, and costs per copy can be attributed to specific users or departments.

Which features you choose on an office copier depend on the needs of your particular organization. Table 7.2 describes popular copier features.

What does the future hold for reprographic systems? The role of photocopiers is becoming increasingly important with the use of digital technology for document imaging. **Document imaging** is performed with a personal computer that is linked to a copier, scanner, or fax machine. With this setup, the user can scan or create a document and send it to a copier to be duplicated. Additional advances in copier technology include improved copy quality, reliability, and affordability. Many businesses have been hesitant to pay for expensive color copiers, but as new software programs and color printers become available, demand for them will increase and prices will come down.

Using digital copiers is a growing trend. These copiers scan documents, convert them into computer files, and then print copies from those files. Digital copiers offer the economy of a high-speed copier with the quality of digital laser technology. With a host of innovative features and accessories, digital copiers provide high-quality copies and can even be tied into a company's network with optional networking kits.

**TABLE 7.2 • Features of Copier Systems**

| Feature | Examples of Functions |
|---|---|
| Copy Size | Can accommodate from 5.5″ × 8.5″ to 11″ × 17″ |
| Originals | Can be sheets, books, 3-D objects |
| Speed | Can run from 28–801 copies per minute |
| Collating & Stapling | Can assemble copies in order and staple top left corner of set, if desired |
| Duplexing | Can make two-sided copies |
| Reducing & Magnifying | Can make image smaller or larger |
| Other Features: | Front-loading paper drawers, image shift, book copy, automatic paper selection, automatic magnification selection, auto tray switching, large-capacity cassette tray, dual original copying, 20 + bin sorter, color units, energy save, help screens, usage counters, multiple copy countdown system |

# Facsimiles

A **facsimile (fax)** is a machine that translates copies of text or graphics documents into electronic signals, which are then transmitted over telephone lines or by satellite.

## Uses of the Fax

Facsimile machines have changed the way office workers place orders and corporate headquarters staff acquire data from field offices, altering the very nature of business. Today an office without a fax machine is as rare as one without a computer.

The fax is gradually replacing the U.S. Postal Service and overnight express mail services for delivery of business communications. With the convenience of a telephone call, fax machines speed up business interactions in a relatively inexpensive way.

## Concerns Regarding the Fax

Widespread use of fax machines is causing some concern about proliferation and security issues.

**Proliferation**   As businesses and institutions rely more on faxes, questions about product speed and quality, training and usage, and cost containment take on a new urgency. Fax machines provide speed and convenience; however, most offices currently lack the organization or discipline to control this powerful technology by establishing clear, simple guidelines for its use. For example, these guidelines might clarify who is authorized to fax documents, what types of documents are too confidential to fax, and when fax transmission should occur to lower cost.

**Security**   Security is becoming an increasingly worrisome problem. The sheer number of fax machines in use increases the chances of sending confidential information to a wrong number. As more fax machines are connected to networks, unauthorized tapping becomes more possible. Cellular telephones are particularly vulnerable to eavesdropping, making mobile faxing especially risky as well.

Dial carefully when sending a fax, especially if you must send confidential material.

# Shredders

Office paper **shredders** provide document security and, at the same time, help the environment. Many companies use shredders to destroy sensitive material to ensure that it stays confidential. Shredded paper is easier to recycle than unshredded paper and more biodegradable when placed into a landfill.

Paper shredders, the sales of which are increasing each year, vary greatly in productivity and price. Some models fit over waste bins; however, larger machines placed in central locations are generally more powerful and can handle more paper. When buying a paper shredder, consider the materials you will be destroying and the overall capacity in terms of your current and future needs. Paper shredders range in cost from $100 desktop models to heavy-duty ones priced at over $20,000.

Some companies are paying for paper shredders, which used to be considered a luxury, by selling the shreds to recycling centers and to animal farms, where they are used for bedding. Also, enterprising office workers now reuse paper shreds as packing material for fragile items.

Workers in many offices use paper shredders to maintain the confidentiality of information contained in discarded papers.

# Multifunction Devices

A multifunction device is a single piece of equipment that looks like a copy machine, but it provides the functions of a printer, scanner, copy machine, and fax machine. Workers in small offices use multifunction devices because they require less space than a separate printer, scanner, copier machine, and fax machine. Another advantage is that a multifunction device is significantly less expensive than each device purchased separately.

A color printer-copier-scanner delivers color inkjet printing, color copying, and color scanning demanded by small businesses, full-time home-office professionals, and corporate telecommuters.

# Typewriters and Dictation Machines

The increased use of computers by office workers has had a great impact on the use of typewriters and dictation machines. Employees in modern offices seldom use either of these pieces of equipment that were more prevalent a decade ago; nevertheless, they are still found in many offices and used by some workers.

### Typewriters

Using electronic typewriters is often more convenient than using personal computers for tasks such as printing mailing labels and index cards, addressing envelopes, and filling in multipart forms. Modern electronic typewriters are full-featured and can produce error-free copy. They create and correct text copy, and most units also have spell-checking memory, plus an automatic word correction function, Formatting is a simple, one-pass operation with automatic underlining, bold printing, and decimal tabbing. Typewriters range in price from $100 to $700. When selecting a typewriter, you should determine how you will use it and investigate the cost of supplies.

### Dictation Machines

A dictation machine is a device used to capture thoughts quickly on magnetic voice media. The use of dictation machines, however, has decreased in recent years. This decrease can be directly attributed to the advent of portable computers and a lack of trained transcriptionists.

*Answer the following questions:*

**1.** What does "on-demand" copying mean?

**2.** What are two advantages of using the facsimile machine?

**3.** Why do companies shred documents?

**TIP** Using all the electronic wonders on the market today—from special telephones to laptop computers to fax machines—can indeed free your time. Overindulgence or overdependence on machines, however, can waste more of your time than those machines can save. ■

# Summary

Several employment issues related to computers affect how office workers will perform on the job. Office professionals must be qualified computer users, practice good ethics when using the computer, and be aware that in an office setting, their work or even the messages they send using e-mail may be monitored by a computer.

An office worker should also exercise caution when using computers to prevent injuries and know how to minimize energy usage in the office.

Other types of automated office equipment help businesses run smoothly. These pieces of equipment include copier systems, facsimile machines, shredders, multifunctional devices, typewriters, and dictation machines.

Recall the following specific points from this chapter:

■ Ethical considerations that influence office computer use include the security and privacy of data, employee loyalty, and the copying of computer software.

■ Common ailments resulting from computer use are eyestrain and repetitive stress injuries.

■ Computer-purchasing decisions should be made with energy conservation in mind, and computers should be turned off when not in use.

■ Office workers might use a copier to make paper copies, a fax machine to send a letter to a customer, and a paper shredder to safeguard personnel and financial records. In addition, they may have an electronic typewriter and a dictation machine available.

■ Office copier systems may be either centralized centers or decentralized "on-demand" copiers located throughout a company.

■ Fax users should be aware of concerns such as proliferation and security issues.

■ Multifunction devices are multipurpose machines that print, fax, copy, and scan documents.

# before you leave...

**When you have completed this chapter, answer the following questions:**

1. How much energy do computers use?

2. What causes computer-related injuries?

# Review & Application

## Check Your Knowledge

1. How does just-in-time hiring relate to the qualifications of future office workers?

2. If a person does not want to be monitored by a computer, do you think he or she should have a choice in the matter?

3. Why are computer hacking and piracy ethical issues in business?

4. If you know people who suffer from carpal tunnel syndrome or tendinitis, describe their symptoms.

5. List five ways to conserve energy when using or purchasing an office computer.

6. Name the major advantage and disadvantage of the decentralized copier approach.

7. What is the purpose of a facsimile machine?

8. Do you believe the typewriter and dictation machine will totally disappear from the business office in the twenty-first century? Why or why not?

## Review Your Vocabulary

On a separate piece of paper, write the letter of the correct vocabulary word described below.

____ 1. provide document security and, at the same time, help the environment

____ 2. is performed with a personal computer that is linked to a copier, scanner, or fax machine

____ 3. is possible because of the availability of a large pool of experienced, unemployed people who can go to work on a temporary basis on short notice without a training period

____ 4. is the use of computers to help employees do their jobs more effectively

____ 5. is a machine that translates copies of text or graphics documents into electronic signals, which are then transmitted over telephone lines or by satellite

a. computer monitoring
b. document imaging
c. facsimile (fax)
d. just-in-time hiring
e. shredders

## Discuss and Analyze an Office Situation

Tracy Koch has just been hired as a computer operator in an established real estate office in town. She wants to do her best and learn as much as she can on the job. Tracy hopes someday to get her real estate license so that she can sell residential properties. She views the job as a way to learn the business from the ground up.

Almost immediately, Tracy senses something is wrong when she asks the other three office workers questions to clarify her assignments and the office procedures. Two of them, Roxanne and Randy, seem to withhold important information from her intentionally. Tracy thinks that they are telling her only the minimum that is needed. The third person, Denise, is more helpful. Tracy finds herself feeling closer to Denise and uses her as a role model.

1. Why do some office workers have the attitude that they must keep, rather than share, certain knowledge and special procedures?

2. Roxanne and Randy's behavior can lead to human relations problems. What are some other outcomes when employees have negative attitudes?

## Practice Basic Skills

### Math

Calculate the percentages and totals for each question mark in the following table to determine monthly costs and usage.

| Copying Item | Cost/Month | % of Monthly Total |
|---|---|---|
| Toner | $ 250 | ? |
| Paper | 350 | ? |
| Operator time | 1,000 | ? |
| Copier rental | 400 | ? |
| Total | $ ? | 100% |

### English

*Rule:* Whenever possible, avoid dividing a word at the end of a line. When word division is unavoidable, divide at a point that will least disrupt the reader's understanding of the word. Divide words only between syllables. If unsure, consult a dictionary.

*Examples:*   automation   au-to-ma-tion
information   in-for-ma-tion

*Practice Exercise:* Apply the rule to each of the following words. On a separate piece of paper, list the letters for each word. If a word is divided correctly, write OK next to its letter. If it is divided incorrectly, rewrite it correctly.

a. facs-im-ile
b. pho-tocopy
c. busi-ness
d. cal-cu-la-tor
e. off-ice
f. tele-phone
g. in-te-gra-ted
h. gra-phics

### Proofreading

Rewrite or key the following fax transmission, correcting misspellings and incorrect punctuation.

April 27, 20—

TO: Robin Scott, RAS & Co.

FAX # (520) 555-1011

FROM: Raymond at the Youth Hockey Office (520) 555-1122

Thank you for agreing to do the 20 trophies we wil need for the end-of-season ice hockey recognition banquett. A list with the inforrmation you will need to engrav the trofies is attacched. Let me know if you need further information and whether you will have any problm picking them up by May 15.

## Apply Your Knowledge

1. Which office system would you use to process each of the following office tasks? On a separate piece of paper, next to the letter for each description, write the letters EM if you would use electronic mail, FAX if facsimile, or RPG if reprographics.

___ a. pie chart sent from Los Angeles to Chicago

___ b. notice of sales meeting sent to ten sales representatives in the building

___ c. order for ten office chairs sent to a vendor 100 miles away

___ d. memo about business ethics sent through a LAN

___ e. request for six copies of fifty pages to be collated and stapled

___ f. request for six transparencies of a sales presentation

2. *Debate the Issue*

"My rights are being violated as a citizen of the United States when my boss monitors my activities at work using computer monitoring software."

*Instructions:* React to the above statement by quickly jotting down three or more ideas you have supporting *and* refuting the statement. Prepare to role-play either point of view in a mock in-class debate.

## Using the Reference Manual

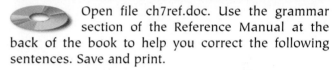

Open file ch7ref.doc. Use the grammar section of the Reference Manual at the back of the book to help you correct the following sentences. Save and print.

1. Class begins at eight fifteen in the morning.

2. Is the glass 1/2 full or 1/2 empty?

3. 3 checks are left in the checkbook.

4. The parade through downtown was over in 45 minutes.

5. The secretary of the Outdoor Club lived at 1151 9th Street.

6. Do you want 2 or 3 5-by-8-inch cards?

7. 44 new students joined the All-City Chorus.

8. Tonya has grown eleven inches in the past two years.

9. Cats are said to have 9 lives.

10. The speed limit sign read fifteen miles per hour.

# CAREER PORTFOLIO

## PART TWO: Technical Skills and Knowledge

**Specific Activities to Complete**

Select at least two of the following items for inclusion in your Career Portfolio, using the information from Chapters 5, 6, and 7.

1. Key descriptions of the types of software packages you might use in your selected office work environment. Beneath each description, briefly list the capabilities of each software package. Save and print this list. (Be sure you proof according to the instructions given previously on page 84.) Insert this document into your Career Portfolio binder as the first item behind the second tab, entitled "Technical Skills and Knowledge."

2. Key descriptions of five situations in which you as an office professional will use networked systems. Save, print, and insert these descriptions behind the second tab as well.

3. List and describe four or five Web site home pages you might use as an office professional to locate up-to-the-minute information needed to perform your job. Save, print, and insert this list behind the second tab.

4. Describe at least three ethical practices office workers should follow when using computers and other office equipment. Save, print, and insert these descriptions behind the second tab.

# PART III
# Office Support Skills

# chapter 8

## Telephone Procedures

### objectives

*After completing this chapter, you will be able to do the following:*

1. List and explain the important qualities of a good telephone voice.
2. List and explain the steps necessary to answer, place on hold, and transfer a business telephone call.
3. List and explain the steps used to screen calls in a business office.
4. List what is needed to record telephone messages for another person.
5. List and explain the types of outgoing telephone calls made in a business office.
6. List and explain the special features of telephone equipment used in a business office.
7. Describe two long-distance services available.
8. Explain other telephonic communication devices.

### New Office Terms

- call screening
- cellular telephone
- conference call
- time zone
- voice mail
- WATS

# before you begin...

**Answer the following questions to the best of your ability:**

1. How important is a telephone in the business world?
2. What are the differences between using a telephone at home and in a business office?

**D**id you know that at this very minute, millions of office workers are using a telephone? Did you know that a telephone is used in approximately 95 percent of all business transactions? More than 100 million business calls are made each day. A customer calls to get information or to place an order. A customer service representative uses a telephone to service accounts and to sell products.

Did you make a business call recently? Maybe you called to get your car repaired, and an office worker made an appointment for you. Perhaps you called to ask what time a store closed. These telephone calls are all business calls. Did you receive polite answers to your questions?

Many people are not hired because they cannot talk properly on a telephone. Sometimes when you answer an advertisement for a job, the preliminary screening is done over the telephone. Individuals may pass all preemployment tests, yet not be hired for the position because of their telephone manners.

Some people lose jobs because they cannot handle business calls on a telephone. A fast keyboard operator might be hired for a job but be terminated if he or she cannot follow proper telephone procedures.

Effective telephone use is crucial to the success of your employer. No company wants to lose business because of an employee's improper telephone techniques. If you appear rude or unconcerned, you will give that impression of your company. However, if you express enthusiasm and confidence in your telephone conversations, callers will view your firm in a positive way.

Potential clients make judgments about your competence and your company's attributes based on how you handle their calls. These potential clients must feel valued and appreciated when you are handling their telephone calls. Do you remember being treated poorly when you made a doctor's appointment or when you called for information about a movie or a restaurant? Do you also remember being treated nicely when you made other calls? How did you react?

In a speech to a group of business students, a human resources manager stated that all office employees frequently use the telephone. Are you prepared to use proper telephone techniques on the job?

The impression you make over the telephone is determined entirely by your voice and good telephone manners.

©Nasi Sakura/SuperStock International

**TIP** Always use generally accepted common courtesies in any business situation. ■

## Proper Procedures

Answering a telephone in a business office is easy if you know the right procedures. The correct methods involve what you say and how you say it.

When a telephone rings, even before picking up the receiver, prepare yourself for the caller. You can prepare as follows:

## Technology in the Office | LIGHTWEIGHT SMARTPHONES

By the end of the 1990s, almost everyone carried a cellular telephone, and they used them on the street, in the market, and while waiting in line anywhere. PDAs (personal digital assistants) became popular, too—especially with men and women in business.

Smartphones are a combination of a cell phone and a PDA operating system. You can use a smartphone to send and receive e-mail and surf the Web. You can also use thousands of software applications available for the Palm PDA.

Early smartphones were too big and too heavy to be easily used. The newer ones are pocket size and weigh only a few ounces. ■

---

■ Stop any work you are doing so that you can concentrate entirely on the caller.

■ Always have a message pad or notepaper and pen or pencil ready.

■ Set aside the problems of the day and have a positive attitude.

Did you know that the way you hold a telephone can affect the sound of your voice? Do not rest the telephone on your shoulder or chin. This position will make your voice sound muffled. The listener may have to ask you to repeat or to speak louder. Hold the telephone about one inch from your lips and speak directly into the mouthpiece.

One important aspect of proper telephone procedures is concentrating on having good voice quality. A caller will not be able to see you smile or see your friendly expressions. You must rely entirely on your voice and good telephone manners to create a positive impression for your company. Here are a few steps to take to have a good telephone voice:

■ Speak distinctly. Use clear, unmistakable words and sentences.

■ Speak with a normal tone. Do not shout at the caller, but speak loud enough to be heard.

■ Speak naturally. Let your pleasing personality show.

■ Speak politely. Be considerate and respectful to the caller.

■ Speak courteously. Talk in a manner that will please the caller.

How you speak on the telephone in an office is quite different from the way you do at home. Talking to a client is not like talking to your friend or neighbor. When you speak on the telephone at work, remember the following:

■ Never use slang. Avoid words such as *ain't* or *huh*.

■ Never have something in your mouth. Avoid chewing gum.

■ Never run words together; for example, not "Whadidya say?" but "What did you say?"

Use standard English when speaking on a telephone in an office. For more information on standard English, refer to Chapter 19.

Receiving and placing calls in an office are also different from receiving and placing calls at home. The following business procedures are recommended for receiving and placing calls.

Taking clearly written notes during a telephone conversation is part of being a good listener.

# Recall Time

*Answer the following questions:*

**1.** What are three ways an office worker can prepare to answer a telephone when it rings?

**2.** What are four important qualities of a good telephone voice?

**3.** Ari, an office worker, receives a call from a new customer who wishes to place an order. Ari has a radio on very softly broadcasting a football game so that the customer cannot hear it.

The customer begins giving the order, but Ari interrupts and puts her on hold because he cannot find anything to write with. Because the customer has a heavy accent, Ari talks very loud and almost shouts at times. He also needs to say "huh" quite frequently during the conversation. Ari concludes the transaction by saying, "Thanks for placing the order."

What would you have done differently if you were Ari?

**4.** Make a telephone call to inquire about clerical job openings at a local business. Ask for the human resources department and request that job descriptions be sent to you. After you place the call, answer the following questions:

**a.** Did the employee in the human resources department appear to be concentrating on your conversation? If not, why not?

**b.** Did he or she have a good business telephone voice—distinct, polite?

**c.** Did he or she not use slang expressions and avoid running words together?

## Incoming Calls

Let's now look at the mechanics of answering a telephone in a business office. The following techniques may be used whether you are answering a telephone system with many lines or a standard business telephone on your own work desk with just a few lines.

The main parts of the telephone that you will encounter on a job are the handset, the hold button, the transfer button, and the incoming and outgoing lines.

Most telephones in a business office have more than one line for incoming and outgoing calls. As this type of telephone rings, the button for the incoming call will begin to flash. To answer the call, pick up the handset and push the button that is flashing.

Most businesses follow certain procedures for answering incoming calls such as the following:

- Answer a call promptly, preferably after the first or second ring.
- Answer by first giving the company name and then identifying yourself.
- Answer by giving the department name and then identifying yourself if the call was first answered by a receptionist.
- Answer your boss's telephone by identifying your boss first, and then yourself.

For example, when customers call Rudy Yee, a receptionist answers the phone, then transfers the call to Rudy. He answers by saying, "Payroll Department, this is Rudy Yee."

When clients call Margo Gonzales, the calls go directly to her desk. She answers by saying, "Good morning; Transworld Company, Margo Gonzales speaking."

Hugh Scott's boss usually answers her own phone. However, when she is away, Hugh answers by saying, "Ms. Lopez's office, Hugh Scott speaking."

Some companies have their own procedures to follow when answering a telephone. Review company telephone policies when beginning a new job.

## Hold or Transfer Calls

Once you have answered an incoming call, the next step may be to hold or transfer the call. If the call is for another person, say to the caller, "One moment, please" or "One moment, please, I will ring her office." Then press firmly on the hold or transfer button and release it.

If the telephone has a hold button, after you press it, the line button for the line or extension you were speaking on will begin to flash on and off. Always remember to push the hold button, or your connection to the caller will be broken.

If you have a transfer button, after you push it, you simply key the extension to which you want the call transferred. The call will ring on that person's telephone. When he or she answers, the light will stop flashing.

Keep these points in mind when holding or transferring calls:

- Ask permission before placing a caller on hold.
- Thank the caller for waiting when you return to a call.
- Never leave a caller on hold for more than thirty or forty seconds before returning to check on the caller.
- When transferring, give the caller the name and number of the person to whom you are transferring the call so that the caller may dial directly to that person if the call fails to transfer properly.

Cora is an administrative assistant for a travel agency. She transfers calls by saying, "Good morning. GO Travel Services, Cora speaking. . . . That item would be handled by our international division. May I transfer you to that department? . . . In case you get disconnected, I am transferring you to Harold Price at 4217."

Have you ever been left on hold for a long time? Leaving someone on hold for an extended period is a common mistake made by many office workers, and it is annoying. Do not make the same error; keep checking back with a caller who is on hold. You can see that a caller is still on hold if the line continues to have a flashing light. Get back to him or her and say, "Do you still wish to hold or may I take a message?"

Many executives want their calls screened before a transfer is made. They want to know who is calling before you put that person through to them. Be sure to screen calls in a polite way so that you do not offend a caller. Some common phrases used for **call screening** include: "May I ask who is calling, please?" and "May I tell Mr. Partel your name?" Check with your employer to see if calls should be screened.

### Ethics on the Job

You have been working in the production department of a large oil company for two years. Part of your job requires that you put the daily mail through the postage meter and take it to the post office. Some days over 200 pieces of mail must be processed.

You are active in a church group that will be holding a fund-raiser at the end of the month. You could easily mail the church flyer from work without anyone knowing.

*Because the flyer is for such a worthy cause, should you use the work postage meter for the mailing?* ■

Use your best telephone manners when screening calls or taking messages.

©Romilly Lockyer/Image Bank

## Messages

Many times, your boss will not be able to take a telephone call. In these situations, politely tell the caller why your boss is unavailable. Then ask whether you can take a message or transfer the caller to voice mail if it is available. For example, say, "I am sorry, she is not at her desk right now. May I take a message or transfer you to her voice mail?" or "I am sorry, Ms. Chavez is out of the office today. May I take a message or transfer you to her voice mail?" You may also want to say when your boss is expected back and to ask whether you or someone else can be of help.

Never say, "She is busy right now." This statement may offend the caller by implying that he or she is not important. Your company does not want to insult any customers.

Sometimes, your boss will be available but will not wish to speak to a particular caller. In that situation, you may use the same phrases you would use if your boss were unable to take the call: "I am sorry, he is not at his desk right now. May I take a message or transfer you to his voice mail?" or "I am sorry, he is out of the office. May I take a message or transfer you to his voice mail?"

One executive secretary in an advertising firm has a special method of screening calls for her boss, Mr. Perkins. Mr. Perkins is particular about which calls he answers. The secretary handles those calls this way:

Caller: May I speak to Mr. Perkins?
Secretary: I am not certain if Mr. Perkins has returned from his meeting. Let me check. May I have your name, please?

In this situation, the secretary can tell Mr. Perkins the name of the caller, and he can decide whether he wishes to speak to the person. If he does not, the caller will be told Mr. Perkins has not returned from the meeting. This method is a good way to avoid offending a caller.

If you need to take a telephone message, you may use a standard form (see Figure 8.1, page 149). This type of form is available as a telephone message pad. The format may vary a little, but you will always need to record who the message is for, the date, the time, who the message is from and the name of that person's company, a return telephone number, the message itself, and your signature or initials.

Recording the correct information on a message form is very important. Here are some helpful hints:

- If you cannot hear, ask the caller to speak louder.
- If you do not understand the message, ask the caller to repeat.
- Always get the caller's telephone number. You will not have to look it up later.
- If you cannot spell the caller's name, ask him or her to spell it for you.
- Before you hang up, read the information back to the caller. Rereading it will ensure that your message is accurate.

Have you ever answered the telephone at home, and the caller said, "Sorry, I dialed the wrong number"? Well, maybe he or she was given the wrong number. Recording the correct telephone number onto the message pad is extremely important. Too many wrong numbers could mean a loss of business for a company. It could also mean the loss of a job for you.

**TIP** If you answer a telephone and the caller gives a first and last name, do not use the caller's first name. Using a personal title and last name is much more businesslike. ■

**FIGURE 8.1** • Telephone Message Form

| To _____ | ☐ URGENT |
| --- | --- |
| | A.M. |
| Date _____ Time _____ | P.M. |

## WHILE YOU WERE OUT

From _____

of _____

Phone _____
      Area Code      Number      Ext.

Fax/E-Mail _____

| Telephoned | | Please return call | |
| --- | --- | --- | --- |
| Stopped by | | Reply by E-mail | |
| Returned your call | | Reply by fax | |

Message _____

_____

_____

_____

_____

_____

Signed _____

Being especially polite when taking messages is good business practice. For example, you can make a caller feel important by using her or his name during the conversation. Assume that you are taking a message for Ms. Huff. The caller is Mr. Carver. To be really polite, say, "I will give Ms. Huff the message, Mr. Carver" or "I will be certain she receives the message, Mr. Carver."

Professional administrative support staff care enough about their jobs to put extra effort into helping callers. They recommend that you try to help a caller receive the correct information or to transfer the caller to the right person who can help. Avoid telling a caller that you cannot be of any help. If necessary, tell him or her that you will find the answer and return the call yourself.

Finally, a good business practice is to let the caller end the conversation and hang up first. The caller may be offended or think you are rude if you seem to be in a hurry to end the call. Practice courtesy and use the caller's name. For example, say, "Thank you for calling, Ms. Harris."

The following list is given to all new employees at a county office in northern California. It is helpful for reviewing tactful telephone phrases.

| Do not say . . . | Do say . . . |
| --- | --- |
| "Who is this?" | "May I ask who's calling, please?" |
| "What's your name?" | "May I have your name, please?" |
| "What is your phone number?" | "May I have your number, please?" |
| "Speak up, please." | "Excuse me, I am having trouble hearing you." |
| "You didn't talk to me." | "I cannot remember talking with you." |
| "What do you want to talk to him about?" | "May I ask what your call is in reference to?" |

## Outgoing Calls

When you work in an office, you will not only receive calls, you will also have to place them. First, prepare yourself for placing the call. To do this:

- Make a checklist of subjects you wish to cover.
- Have all necessary information needed to ask or answer questions. This information may include file folders, notes, and a calendar.
- Be certain to have the correct telephone number. If in doubt, look it up.
- Be aware of the time, especially if you are calling someone in another time zone. Try to call during business hours and avoid lunchtimes.

Now you are ready to make an outgoing call. Remember that when the buttons on a telephone are lighted, someone is talking on those lines. Therefore, when placing an outside call on some telephone systems, you must find an unlighted button on your telephone.

Once you have found an open line (one that is not lighted), pick up the handset, push the button for that line, and key the number you are calling. Give the person enough time to answer—eight or ten rings.

When the party answers, identify yourself before starting the conversation. Also, identifying your company will save time as well. For example,

The caller will have a good impression of you and your employer if you are courteous and helpful.

when the party answers, you could say: "This is Saul Neal calling. May I speak to Ms. Lew?" or "This is Sally Perez from Fresno Travel Service. Is Mr. Allen in, please?"

Sometimes, your boss may want to speak to someone but will ask you to place the call and get the person on the telephone. If you are asked to make such a call, be certain your boss is close by and ready to talk to the person when you have him or her on the line. For example, Mr. Castle asks his executive secretary, Kay, to get Ms. Butler of Invest Savings on the phone for him. Kay keys the telephone number. Ms. Butler answers, and the conversation is as follows:

Kay: Ms. Butler, this is Kay West from Castle & Curl. Bill Castle would like to speak with you. May I put him on the line now?
Ms. Butler: Yes, please do.
Kay [as she signals her boss]: Here he is, Ms. Butler.

Another time-saver when making outgoing calls is to spell uncommon words or names when leaving a message. If your name or your company's name is easily misunderstood, spell it. For example, Orv is an administrative assistant at the law firm of Weinberg and Heller. When people hear the name Weinberg, they may think Wineberg, or Weinburg, or another spelling. When Orv must leave messages, he says the following:

"This is Orv Fletcher from Weinberg and Heller. I would like to leave a message to remind Ms. Reiser of our meeting. . . . Yes, Orv F-l-e-t-c-h-e-r of W-e-i-n-b-e-r-g and Heller. Thank you very much."

Before placing long-distance calls, make sure your company permits them. Also consider the time of day. The time is important because some long-distance service providers charge less for calls made at certain times. Because times differ across the United States, you want to make calls only when you know people are in their offices.

You may want to refer to a **time zone** map before placing long-distance calls. The United States is divided into four time zones: Eastern, Central, Mountain, and Pacific. Time changes by one hour as you move through the zones. Figure 8.2, page 152, is a sample of a time zone map. The map is used to determine time differences in the following way:

| When it is . . . | it is . . . |
|---|---|
| 4 A.M. in Wyoming | 6 A.M. in New York |
| 10 A.M. in most of Kansas | 11 A.M. in New York |
| 7 P.M. in Nevada | 10 P.M. in Massachusetts |
| 9 P.M. in Virginia | 7 P.M. in Arizona |
| 11 A.M. in Texas | 9 A.M. in California |

As you view the map in Figure 8.2, notice that in addition to time differences, it also includes three-digit area codes. This information is handy when you need to place a call to a number outside your area code.

*Directory assistance* is sometimes necessary when you cannot find a number in your telephone directory. To call directory assistance outside your area code, key in the number 1, the area code, and then 555-1212. If you do not know the area code, you can refer to the time zone map:

| For directory assistance in . . . | dial . . . |
|---|---|
| New Mexico | 1-505-555-1212 |
| Maine | 1-207-555-1212 |
| Duluth, Minnesota | 1-218-555-1212 |
| Springfield, Missouri | 1-417-555-1212 |

**FIGURE 8.2 • Time Zone Map**

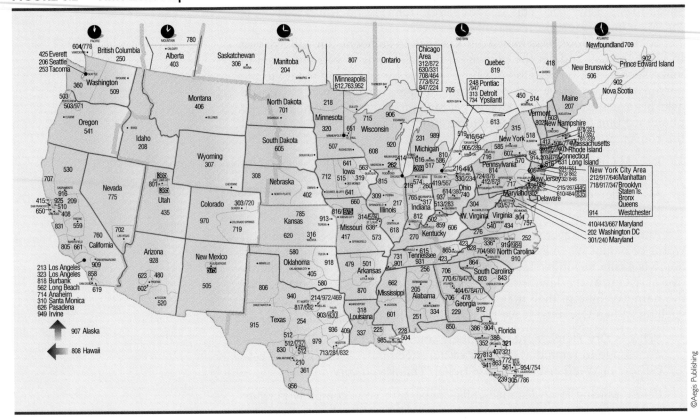

## Other Important Procedures

Workers in most offices follow similar procedures regarding the use of the telephone. These procedures probably include taking and making personal telephone calls, handling disconnected calls, handling wrong-number calls, and arranging telephone coverage when office personnel are away from their desks during breaks or meals, or out of the office due to illness or vacations or other reasons.

### Personal Calls

All companies have a policy on personal telephone calls. Most companies do not allow them, except in an emergency.

Current technology allows companies to identify calls made from all telephone extensions. This technology lets employers charge calls to departments or special accounts. This technology also allows employers to separate business calls from personal calls and to trace each one to the person who made it.

Check company policy on personal calls. Not making personal calls from work is good business ethics.

### Disconnected Calls

Have you ever been disconnected when talking on the telephone? When this accident happens in a business office, the person who made the call usually calls back immediately. If you did not make the call, hang up the telephone to allow the line to be open for the caller to call again.

## Wrong-Number Calls

Reaching a wrong number when making a call is not uncommon. If you call a wrong number on a long-distance call, find out what number you actually reached and hang up immediately. You may then dial the operator and request that the company not be charged for the call. You will have to give the operator the number you reached in error.

## Telephone Coverage

If you are a receptionist or in charge of answering many lines, arranging for telephone coverage when you are away from your desk is crucial. Always ask someone to answer the telephones for you.

## Recall Time

*Answer the following questions:*

1. What are the four major parts of a telephone?

2. You are an employee working for Alex Auto Supplies. When calls come to you, they go directly to your telephone. A receptionist does not answer them first. How should you answer the calls?

3. You are an employee in the accounting department of Garcia Advertising Company. All calls are first answered by a receptionist and then transferred to your desk. How should you answer your calls?

4. Your boss is Ms. Seville. She is not available, so you answer her telephone. What do you say when you answer, and what do you tell the caller?

5. Your boss, Mr. Woo, wants all his calls screened. What does *call screening* mean, and how do you do it?

6. What seven items of information need to be recorded when taking telephone messages?

## Making Office Decisions

Olga works as an administrative assistant for a public relations firm. She enjoys word processing and finds keyboarding proposals for new clients interesting. She works for three bosses and is kept busy most of the day.

In this company, all administrative assistants must take turns relieving the receptionist at lunchtime one day each week. During this period, the telephones are very busy, so no one has time for any other work.

Tuesday is Olga's day to relieve the receptionist. One Tuesday, the receptionist says she has an important lunch date, so she must leave on time. On that same Tuesday, one of Olga's bosses gives her a proposal that must be keyed and sent to a client by 1 P.M. At noon, when the receptionist wants to leave, Olga still has a few pages to complete.

Olga begins to get nervous. She must finish the proposal, yet it is her turn to relieve the receptionist.

**Explain at least three actions that Olga could take in this situation.** ■

# Reference Materials

You will find that telephone books in an office are the same type that you keep in your home. In addition, most offices have several local directories, copies of the Yellow Pages for various geographic areas, and other directories related to their type of business.

When you want to find the telephone number for an individual, a company, or sometimes a government agency, you refer to the White Pages of the telephone book. The names are listed in alphabetic order. Most telephone books also have a separate section for government agencies—divided into the classifications of federal, state, county, and city. For example, to find a telephone number for the Navy, you would look under United States Government, for "Navy" ("Department of").

The local telephone directory Yellow Pages contain an alphabetic listing of businesses only. The businesses are arranged by subject area or according to the service they provide or the product they sell. For example, to find the number of the local Hyatt® Hotel, you would look in the Yellow Pages under hotels.

Company telephone directories list the telephone numbers or just the telephone extensions of employees within a company. They list the various departments and the employees within each department. They also contain an alphabetic listing of all employees. In Figure 8.3, page 155, you will find the telephone number for Randall Adams by looking under Accounting.

# Telephone Equipment

The computer-controlled telephone equipment used in businesses today is very sophisticated. It is set up in various networks and can provide a variety of features for both large and small companies.

Most businesses use equipment that allows incoming calls to go directly to the individual being contacted. However, companies using this system have one general number listed in telephone books in case a caller does not have an individual employee's number. These general calls are usually answered by a receptionist. With this system, employees place outgoing calls directly—they do not need to go through a company operator.

**FIGURE 8.3** • **Portion of a Company Telephone Directory**

*Brimmer & Associates* Employee Directory                    *PAGE 1*

| NAME | MAIL CODE | EXT | NAME | MAIL CODE | EXT |
|------|-----------|-----|------|-----------|-----|
| **ACCOUNTING DEPARTMENT** | | | Darwin, Bette | D1-22E | 8433 |
| Adams, Randell | D2-75 | 8521 | Davis, Vickie | D1-18 | 8036 |
| Arthur, Elaine | D1-13 | 8668 | Easton, Jane | E6-21 | 8771 |
| Balach, Carole | D7-67B | 8621 | Hodsdon, Roger | D7-63 | 8611 |
| Dollison, Lee Anne | D5-18 | 8737 | | | |
| Miller, Jeff | D2-55F | 8780 | **MIS DEPARTMENT** | | |
| Thomas, Joseph | C2-17 | 8071 | Allred, James | D5-19 | 8738 |
| | | | Anderson, Julie | D6-50 | 8710 |
| **ADVERTISING DEPARTMENT** | | | Biggers, Betty | E8-09 | 8009 |
| Aune, Kelly | E1-50 | 8717 | Collins, Danny | B1-22 | 8776 |
| Aws, John | B6-04 | 8028 | Enz, David | C8-19 | 8052 |

Some firms prefer that all calls first go to a receptionist who transfers the caller to the proper employee. This system is used when companies want to screen all callers or when executives believe this method provides better customer service.

When calls are transferred and an employee is not at his or her desk, calls are often answered by the employee's voice mail. Voice mail is similar to an answering machine except that a machine is not needed; computer-controlled telephone equipment provides the service. You will read more about voice mail later in this chapter.

Companies that receive frequent calls from within their own network of telephones may purchase a liquid crystal display (LCD). This piece of equipment is a display terminal that can be connected to telephones. This feature displays the names of callers from within the office.

## Special Features

Once telephone equipment is installed, a company may subscribe to one or more of the following services:

### Automatic Callback

When you call a busy number, the automatic callback feature "remembers" the number and dials it for you automatically after you hang up.

*Example:* You dial a number, and the line is busy. Your preset program will continue to redial until the line is clear.

### Call Forwarding–Busy Line–Do Not Answer

The call forwarding–busy line–do not answer feature automatically reroutes calls to a designated answering station if your line is busy or if you do not answer after a certain number of rings.

*Example:* Your telephone rings five times (the number of rings you have preset); no one answers. The call is automatically transferred to another person's desk.

## Ethics on the Job

Bernice is in charge of supplies for her department. This responsibility includes ordering the supplies, placing them into the storage cabinets, and taking inventory.

Bernice does freelance computer work at home on weekends for small companies that do not have office help.

Bernice takes small supplies—Post-it® notes, paper clips, pens—from her job and uses them at home. Because the supplies are so inexpensive, she thinks that taking these little items is all right.

**Do you agree with Bernice? Why or why not?** ∎

# Edward Gibson

*Senior Clerk, Emergency Registration*
*Merrithew Memorial Hospital*

**Q.** Mr. Gibson, some students think that having good computer skills is all that is needed for a job. Is this belief true? What other skills do you use on your job?

**A.** No; although computer skills are extremely valuable, they are not all that is needed. Critical thinking and the ability to solve problems are just as important. The most important skill to possess is the ability to interact effectively with co-workers and customers—both in person and on the telephone.

**Q.** What advice would you give to a student preparing for a career as a clerk in a hospital setting?

**A.** • Take as many courses as possible in developing good interpersonal skills.
 • Have a genuine concern and compassion for people.
 • Be a volunteer in a hospital and try to get as much overall knowledge of how departments operate and how the office staff interrelate.

Should you need more than a few seconds to get information for a caller, ask if you can put him or her on hold.

©Francisco Cruz/SuperStock International

## Call Hold

The call-hold feature lets you put a caller on hold while you make another call. It also allows you to switch back and forth between on-hold calls. Call hold is different from the hold button because it gives you access to dial tone while a call is being held.

*Example:* You are speaking to a party on the telephone. You need to get some information for the person. You press the hold button to put the person on hold. With the same line, you now place a call to another department to get the information.

## Call Waiting

The call-waiting feature lets a caller reach you even when your line is busy. A gentle signal alerts you to an incoming call.

*Example:* You are speaking on the telephone. You hear a soft beep in your ear. This signal means that another call is coming into your number. You can depress the receiver button to answer the call. The first caller is automatically put on hold, and you can answer the second call.

## Distinctive Ring

The distinctive-ring feature signals the source of an incoming call. One ring means it is an inside call; two rings mean it is an outside call.

*Example:* The telephone rings once. You have a call from inside the company. The telephone rings twice (with two close rings). You have a call from outside the company.

## Speed Dial

The speed-dial feature saves time and prevents wrong numbers by dialing frequently called numbers with a fast one- or two-digit code that you have programmed into the system.

*Example:* You frequently call the same client. The system will dial the number for you after you key the preset code.

## Caller ID

Office workers can identify who is calling from outside a company by using Caller ID. This feature uses a display box to show both local and long-distance numbers. The box can also keep track of a limited number of calls received, even when no one answers the telephone, and the caller does not leave a message.

*Example:* You are expecting a very important call from a client. Your telephone rings, and the number displayed is not your client's number. You do not answer the telephone.

## Conference Calls

A **conference call** allows three or more parties in several locations to participate in the call. The caller first tells the receptionist the names and telephone numbers of those taking part in the conference call and the time of day he or she would like to conduct the call. If the office telephone system has a conferencing feature, a three-way conversation can be arranged in only a few minutes. However, if the system does not have such equipment, the receptionist must call the local telephone service to arrange a conference call. A telephone operator will call all parties to request their availability for a conference call on the preferred day and time. The conference call begins with the person who requested the conference, then each party comes onto the line individually. Conference calls may be local or long distance.

# Long-Distance Services

Executives in companies whose business requires frequent long-distance telephone calls want to reduce the cost of those calls as much as possible. Long-distance telephone service costs may be reduced by two methods: installing a WATS line and adding an 800 or 888 number.

## Wide-Area Telecommunications Service

The Wide-Area Telecommunications Service, or **WATS**, feature provides a way for companies to cut costs if they make frequent long-distance calls to the same area. A company receives a volume discount service for these outgoing calls. In a given office, some telephones may have a WATS line, and some may not.

*Example:* You work for a company that is headquartered in Oregon. The company also has a marketing office in New York. By subscribing to WATS, the Oregon headquarters can call its New York office at reduced rates.

## 800 or 888 Service

The 800 or 888 service feature provides cost-free long-distance service to callers. Calls are automatically charged to the company being called at a volume discount rate.

*Example:* You work for a company that sells computer software. Many of your customers call when they have problems with the software. You install an 800 or 888 number so that your company will pay for the calls.

# Other Telephonic Communication

Advances in telephone technology have improved the service many companies are able to provide their customers and their employees. These services include voice mail, cellular telephones, and pagers.

## Voice Mail

**Voice mail** is a service that functions much like an answering machine, allowing callers to leave a voice message for the called party. Unlike answering machines, however, a computer in the voice mail system converts an analog voice message into digital form. Once digitized, the message is stored in a voice mailbox. A voice mail system usually provides individual voice mailboxes for many users (for example, employees in a company). By accessing his or her voice mail, a called party may listen to messages, add comments to a message, and reply or forward a message to another mailbox in the voice mail system. Some voice mail systems allow mailbox owners to send the same message to a specific group of individuals or to everyone listed in the system's database.

## Cellular Telephones

A **cellular telephone** is a telephone device that uses radio signals to transmit voice and digital data messages. In addition to using it as a telephone, some mobile users connect to the Internet with their cell phones. For example, cell phone users can connect their notebook computer to their cellular telephone to access the Web, send and receive e-mail, enter a chat room, or connect to an office network while they are away from a standard telephone line.

## Pagers (Messaging Devices)

When a worker is often required to attend meetings or check on projects away from his or her usual work area, a **pager** may be the least expensive and most effective way to locate and communicate with that person. Whether you want a traditional pager that can receive numbers or words, or a two-way device that can send as well as receive, companies such as Motorola have messaging devices to fit the needs of the home or business user. The cost of such devices increases depending on whether the devices simply show telephone numbers or serve as sending and receiving messaging devices.

## Recall Time

*Answer the following questions:*

1. How many time zones are in the United States?
2. If it is 4 A.M. in Wyoming, what time is it in New York?
3. If it is 9 P.M. in Virginia, what time is it in Arizona?
4. What is the telephone number for directory assistance?
5. What is found in the Yellow Pages of a telephone book?

# Summary

Employers will continue to give top priority in hiring and keeping workers who are polite, efficient, and cost conscious when handling telephone calls. Using proper telephone procedures for an office requires awareness and preparation. A large corporation in Silicon Valley, California, asks its employees to complete a telephone self-critique on the following points. How would you rate if you worked for this firm? Would you do each of the following?

- Answer on the first or second ring.
- Answer using your full name.
- Answer giving your department name.
- Use the caller's name during a conversation.
- Sound pleasant and agreeable.
- Make a checklist of items to cover before placing a call.
- Have reference material available.
- Take notes on important facts as they are given.
- Ensure accuracy by confirming spelling, numbers, and messages.
- Write complete and legible messages.
- Ask for permission to place a caller on hold.
- Give a caller the name and number of the person to whom you are transferring a call.
- Let the caller say good-bye first.
- Arrange for telephone coverage when you are away from your desk.
- Make long-distance calls during the least expensive time of day.
- Use WATS whenever possible.

# before you leave...

**When you have completed this chapter, answer the following questions:**

**1.** How important is a telephone in the business world?

**2.** What are the differences between using a telephone at home and in a business office?

# Review & Application

## Check Your Knowledge

1. How soon should you answer the telephone after it rings?

2. You receive a call and wish to transfer it to another extension. What happens if you do not press the hold button or the transfer button?

3. Once a person is put on hold, can you forget about him or her? Why or why not?

4. What is good business practice to follow before putting a person on hold in order to transfer a call?

5. When recording telephone messages, what is an extra precaution to take to be certain you wrote down the correct number?

6. Is the time of day important when placing a business call? Why or why not?

7. What is a conference call?

8. What does *LCD* represent?

9. Explain call forwarding.

10. Explain speed calling.

11. Explain WATS.

12. Explain 800 or 888 service.

13. Refer to the company telephone directory in Figure 8.3. List the department and telephone extension for each of the following employees:
    a. Aws, John
    b. Anderson, Julie
    c. Miller, Jeff
    d. Biggers, Betty
    e. Davis, Vickie

14. You are an employee in the customer service department of the Avanti International Travel Association. Your calls are first answered by a receptionist and then transferred to you. How should you answer your calls?

15. You are an employee for Lewis Realty. When calls come to you, they go directly to your telephone; the firm has no receptionist. How should you answer your calls?

16. Your boss is Eric Washington. He is not available, so you answer his telephone. What do you say when you answer the telephone? What do you tell the caller?

17. Refer to the time zone map in Figure 8.2 to answer the following questions:
    a. If your office is in Oregon and you place a call at 10 A.M., what time is it in Minnesota?
    b. If your office is in Ohio and you place a call at 1 P.M., what time is it in Montana?
    c. If your office is in Virginia and you place a call at 4 P.M., what time is it in New York?
    d. If your office is in Texas and you place a call at 9:30 A.M., what time is it in California?

18. Refer to the time zone map in Figure 8.2 to answer the following questions:
    a. What is the area code for Dallas, Texas?
    b. What is the area code for Colorado?
    c. What is the area code for Raleigh, North Carolina?
    d. What is the area code for Oregon?
    e. What number do you dial for directory assistance in Idaho?
    f. What number do you dial for directory assistance in San Antonio, Texas?
    g. What number do you dial for directory assistance in North Dakota?

19. How do workers use voice mail, cellular telephones, and pagers to work more efficiently?

## Review Your Vocabulary

On a separate piece of paper, write the letter of the vocabulary word described below.

1. If you want to know the time difference in another state, you would refer to a _____ map.

2. Three or more people in different locations may all speak together by participating in a _____.

3. The new administrative assistant was asked to use _____ for her boss whenever she answered the telephone.

4. Subscribing to the _____ feature provides a way for companies to cut costs if they make frequent long-distance calls to the same area.

5. A _____ can be used to connect a notebook computer to access the Web.

6. _____ connects analog voice messages into digital form.

    a. call screening    c. time zone
    b. conference call    d. WATS

## Discuss and Analyze an Office Situation

1. Glenda telephones a company to ask about a clerical job. Someone from human resources speaks with her for a few minutes. Glenda is trying to save time, so she is combing her hair while talking on the telephone. To do this, she has to place the handset on her shoulder. Glenda is not worried, though, because the human resources person cannot see her. Glenda also has her television on fairly loud to catch the daily news.

    Glenda is never called for an interview. What may be the reason(s)?

## Practice Basic Skills

### Math

1. Your boss wants you to calculate last year's telephone expenses for your department. To be extra cautious, add both vertical and horizontal figures in the following report and check the totals.

Advertising Department
Yearly Telephone Expense

| MONTH | UNITS | WATS | MESSAGE SERVICE | MONTHLY TOTAL |
|---|---|---|---|---|
| January | $23.78 | $876.90 | $1,876.00 | |
| February | 12.78 | 65.32 | 2,345.78 | |
| March | 18.56 | 643.76 | 2,266.00 | |
| April | 22.00 | 58.21 | 2,177.83 | |
| May | 20.90 | 883.77 | 1,966.45 | |
| June | 19.20 | 78.44 | 2,045.55 | |
| July | 19.60 | 75.45 | 2,099.65 | |
| August | 12.90 | 777.80 | 2,350.88 | |
| September | 23.87 | 768.09 | 1,678.00 | |
| October | 18.60 | 436.45 | 1,880.75 | |
| November | 23.00 | 830.75 | 2,280.55 | |
| December | 19.22 | 80.10 | 1,950.00 | |

Yearly Total

2. Referring to the following report, what is the total cost of telephone calls for extension 6411?

CFEB Company
Telephone Usage Report

| DATE | TIME | DURATION | EXTENSION | COST |
|---|---|---|---|---|
| 06/11 | 08:14A | 1:12 | 6433 | $0.80 |
| 06/11 | 08:30A | 10:00 | 6444 | 2.18 |
| 06/11 | 08:33A | 4:15 | 6411 | 1.24 |
| 06/11 | 10:20A | 2:50 | 6455 | 1.10 |
| 06/11 | 10:55A | 12:56 | 6411 | 4.70 |
| 06/11 | 11:48A | 3:40 | 6444 | 1.90 |
| 06/11 | 01:45P | 4:00 | 6411 | 1.00 |
| 06/11 | 03:30P | 13:40 | 6411 | 5.80 |

### English

*Rule:* Use capital letters when an adjective is derived from a proper name.
*Example:* Japanese art, Mexican food
*Practice Exercise:* Rewrite the following sentences using capitals where necessary.

    a. A special exhibit of american indian art will be in the main gallery.
    b. We always enjoy portuguese food.
    c. I will start a spanish class next month.
    d. The movie has english subtitles.
    e. A new thai restaurant recently opened on the block.

### Proofreading

Rewrite or key the following paragraphs, correcting all errors.

    Any telephone system can conect you from point A to point B. However, todays businesses demand more—more capacity, more capabilities, more flexability. Such demands make our system the logical choice for allmost any company on the move. Wheather you need single station featurers or inhanced software for high-level network control, our system delivers.

    To help your become famliar with these features and learn what they can do for you, heres a brief guide. Making you business better is our aim.

## Apply Your Knowledge

1. Use word processing software to prepare a company telephone directory for the CFEB Company. See Figure 8.3 for an example.

CFEB COMPANY
Company Telephone Directory

| | |
|---|---|
| Accounting | Services |
| Coleman Nancoo 8415 | William Farrell 8413 |
| Bill Johnson 8419 | Maria Garcia 8411 |
| Administration | Darrell Jackson 8436 |
| Lisa Lee 8427 | Steve Jacoby 8418 |
| Chris Walsh 8432 | Systems |
| Marketing | Meghan Gibson 8420 |
| Sean Moore 8412 | Ben Broaddus 8410 |
| Production | Ben Sufi 8434 |
| Suzanne White 8414 | Diane Ochoa 8431 |
| Jason Novak 8433 | |
| Phil Mitchell 8435 | |

2. Refer to Practice Basic Skills, Math Problem 1—Advertising Department Yearly Telephone Expense. Use a spreadsheet software program to input the problem and calculate the answer.

## Using the Reference Manual

Open file ch8ref.doc. Use the punctuation section of the Reference Manual at the back of the book to help you correct the sentences. Save and print.

1. The semicolon is difficult to use correctly, you are required to remember certain rules.

2. We will visit the towns of Aspen, Colorado, Boise, Idaho, and Billings, Montana on our trip.

3. Come to our game, you can expect to have a good time.

4. Remember to push the button first, otherwise, you may cut into someone else's conversation.

5. My sister lives in California: my brother lives in Arizona.

6. You had one good idea, namely, where you said the children will stay.

7. Thank you for the information: it will be very helpful in making our buying decision.

8. The plane will not arrive until 3:00 P.M. therefore, we cannot have lunch with you.

9. I will prefer to change jobs in December, however, the possibility is remote because of the holidays.

10. The rules are very explicit: consequently, you are fired.

# chapter 9

## Filing and Managing Records

*After completing this chapter, you will be able to do the following:*

1. List the purposes for maintaining records.
2. Give examples of classification of records.
3. Give examples of filing methods.
4. List the steps taken to file a record.
5. List types of electronic storage media.
6. List advantages of using electronic storage systems.
7. Give examples of basic indexing rules.
8. Give examples of basic alphabetizing rules.
9. Give examples of a records retention system.

### New Office Terms

- alphabetic filing method
- centralized filing system
- chronological filing method
- cross-reference
- electronic files
- geographic filing method
- hard copy

- indexing
- lateral files
- mobile files
- numeric filing method
- open-shelf files
- rotary files
- subject filing method

# before you begin...

**Answer the following questions to the best of your ability:**

**1.** What are the four basic filing methods? Explain them.

**2.** What are three examples of equipment used for filing records?

**3.** Name types of records storage.

**H**ave you heard of the paperless office? Does one really exist? Will one ever exist?

In the 1980s, personal computers became commonplace in businesses, and employers began to talk about the paperless office. Many people thought that storing information in a computer would eliminate the need for paper.

So far, this belief has not proven true. Individuals still want to see information on a hard copy. **Hard copy** means information printed onto paper, as opposed to saved onto a computer disk.

What are all these pieces of paper that people expected to disappear? Here are some examples:

- a purchase order for a new desk
- the mortgage papers on a building owned by a business
- personnel records of all employees
- all financial papers for tax purposes
- advertisements
- copies of letters
- copies of contracts
- copies of memorandums

©Nasi Sakura/SuperStock International

Missing or misfiled documents can mean hours of wasted, unproductive time searching for them.

A business must maintain records to function effectively. Records are also kept for legal reasons such as for tax reports or to comply with state and federal labor laws. For example, consider a rental agreement between the owner of a small business that rents an office and the owner of the office building. This record will be used for tax purposes, for rent increases, and to prove who is responsible for maintaining the property.

Records should be stored and maintained in an orderly fashion so that information can be located and used when needed. Storing and maintaining records is known as *records management*.

Records management involves developing a filing system that will meet the needs of a particular office. This system must allow you to store records. It must also allow you to retrieve them easily when needed.

Many office workers say that the simpler the filing system, the more efficient it will be. For the rental agreement described previously, the easiest method would be to file the agreement under the address of the property because more than one tenant occupies the building.

# Filing Methods

The basic filing methods used in offices are alphabetic, subject, geographic, numeric, and chronological. Some offices use just one method. Other offices use a combination of two or more.

## Alphabetic

The **alphabetic filing method** is the most conventional and widely used method. It consists of arranging files in order beginning with *A* and ending with *Z*. Files may include records for individuals, businesses, or government agencies.

The following names are listed in alphabetic filing order:

Acme Bread Company
Andrews, Harold
Danford Hauling and Storage
Justine's on the Park
Kirk, Ronald

### Ethics on the Job

Teresa has a brother who is quite ill and who lives in another country. Teresa needs to fax some legal papers to her brother's wife.

Teresa's company has clients in the same country, and employees frequently telephone the clients. Therefore, Teresa sends the papers through the company's fax machine, thinking that "no one will ever know."

*Do you think Teresa should have used the company's fax machine? Why or why not?* ■

## Subject

The **subject filing method** involves arranging files by topics or by subjects. An office worker should be careful when establishing a subject filing system. Choosing meaningful topics or subjects is important for filing and retrieving records accurately.

For example, the human resources department in a hospital may use the following topics for a subject filing system:

Professional
    Doctors
    Nurses
    Administrative Employees
Classified
    Clerical Workers
    Grounds and Maintenance Workers
    Cafeteria Workers

Within each subject area is an alphabetic listing of employees in the company. If you need to locate the personnel file for an office services assistant named Loretta Ramas, for example, you go to the Clerical Workers subject section and then proceed to the *R* section. Arranging files first by subject can simplify and speed the process of retrieving records as compared with using a totally alphabetic system.

An alphabetic listing of subjects used is needed if you use a subject filing system. Consulting this listing will keep you from adding a new subject when one is already on the list. In the previous listing for a hospital, for example, you already have Nurses as a subject, so you would not add that word again to your alphabetic list. The list will also help new employees who need to use the files. You can keep the alphabetic list on sheets of paper, in a card file, or in a computer.

## Geographic

In the **geographic filing method**, records are arranged, or grouped, according to geographic location. The locations are categorized by international, national, or state boundaries. Names within each group are then listed alphabetically.

For example, a trucking firm may use the following geographic system:

East
    Maine
    New York
    Rhode Island

South
    Alabama
    Georgia

Midwest
    Ohio

West
    California
    Oregon
    Washington

©Myrleen Ferguson Cate/PhotoEdit

An alphabetic filing system allows you to find files quickly and accurately.

Within each geographic area is an alphabetic listing of the company's clients. For example, suppose that you need to retrieve the file for Sonic Freight Service of Atlanta, Georgia. You look into the drawer that contains the files for the South. You then look behind the letter *S* for Sonic.

As with other filing systems, users of the geographic method also need some type of cross-reference. *Cross-reference* means identifying related information found in another location. In the previous examples, the client names are cross-referenced alphabetically on a printed list, on cards, or in a computer.

## Numeric

In the **numeric filing method**, records are arranged in numeric order according to numbers assigned to the files. This method is considered an indirect method of filing because you must first consult an alphabetic listing to find the name. The number under which the records for that name are filed is also on the alphabetic list.

The following is an example of a numeric system using consecutive numbers in ascending order:

104358921
105345643
121339564

## Chronological

In the **chronological filing method**, records are arranged in order by date. This method is used in addition to, not in place of, another filing method. For example, a letter from Roger Craig dated June 11 is filed alphabetically under Craig. In addition, a copy of the letter is filed chronologically under the date June 11. Users can easily locate information by date when they have forgotten the contents of a record.

## Recall Time

*Answer the following questions:*

**1.** What is meant by hard copy?

**2.** You are looking at a letter on a computer monitor. Is this letter considered hard copy?

**3.** How will the following names be listed if arranged in alphabetic order?

Lake Street Hardware
Harris, Thomas
Mandel, Laura
Blue Bird Cafe
Harris, Marian

**4.** How will the following numbers be listed if arranged in numeric order?

454213355
219570311
219564133
535892110
134351221

**5.** You have just opened a women's clothing store. You decide to use a subject filing system. What topics could you use?

**6.** An office manager in a new company chooses to use only a chronological filing system. Is this choice a wise decision? Explain.

# Preparation of Records for Filing

Carole is an administrative assistant for a graphics firm located in the South. Carole sets aside time each day for her filing; she uses the following routine to prepare her records. Recall that a record could be a letter, a contract, an invoice, or another document.

## Checking

Carole first inspects a record to see that it has been released for filing. A stamped or handwritten notation on it indicates it is ready to be filed.

## Stapling and Mending

Carole knows that paper clips should not be used for permanent storage of records. So, she removes paper clips and staples the pages together. She also uses tape to repair areas that need mending.

## Deciding

Carole must now decide where to file each record. For example, her company is using the alphabetic filing method. She has a letter from Ana Lewis, a client. She must file the letter where it can most easily be found in the future. Carole decides to file it under Lewis.

## Coding

In a previous job, Carole learned that marking directly on a record where it is to be filed is necessary for accurate filing and retrieval. For this coding process, she underlines the key word to be used for filing. In the letter from Ana Lewis, Carole underlines the word *Lewis*, using a colored pencil. Some office workers write the key word in the upper-right corner of the record.

## Cross-Referencing

Sometimes, you will have material that can be filed under one or more names or subjects. For example, suppose that you receive a letter from

Ms. Simpson, and the subject of the letter relates to Ms. Morgan. You file the letter under Morgan, and file a **cross-reference** sheet under Simpson. Figure 9.1, page 170, shows an example of a cross-reference sheet.

A cross-reference sheet is prepared when a company or a person changes her or his name. For example, Ana Lewis has been a client of Carole's firm for many years. However, her last name became Lewis when she recently married. Carole maintains a folder under the name of *Lewis* with all past and future records. Under *Gable*, Ana Lewis's maiden name, Carole prepares a cross-reference sheet and files it in its alphabetic location with the rest of the *G* folders.

## Arranging

As the last step in preparing to file, Carole arranges the documents so that the filing will go quickly. She places the records in alphabetic order and in groups if the file drawers are in different locations.

# Classification and Retention

Carole was not aware that she needed to know so much about filing until she began working for the graphics company. She soon realized that companies have many different kinds of records. Some are vital to keep, some are important to keep, some are useful to keep, and some need not be kept at all. For example, Carole discovers the following:

■ The graphics firm owns the building in which it is located. The mortgage papers are *vital records* to keep.

■ Businesses must pay taxes, just as individuals do. All files relating to taxes are *important records* to keep.

■ The graphics firm recently purchased a new desk for Carole. The purchase order for the desk is a *useful record* to keep.

■ Carole's boss received an announcement of a luncheon meeting sponsored by a graphics club. He has an appointment that day and cannot attend. Therefore, the announcement should not be kept; it is a *nonessential record*.

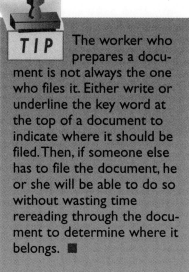

**TIP** The worker who prepares a document is not always the one who files it. Either write or underline the key word at the top of a document to indicate where it should be filed. Then, if someone else has to file the document, he or she will be able to do so without wasting time rereading through the document to determine where it belongs. ■

**FIGURE 9.1 • Cross-Reference Sheet**

## CROSS-REFERENCE SHEET

NAME OR SUBJECT: _____

DATE: _____

REGARDING: _____

_____

SEE: _____

NAME OR SUBJECT: _____

_____

After Carole decides which records are vital and important to keep, her next question to her supervisor is "Do we keep these records permanently? If not, for how long?" This decision is usually made at the time of the first filing and is based on a records retention schedule set up by each company. A records retention schedule is a listing of all the classifications of records and how long each should be retained. Carole's supervisor, Mr. Lloyd, is an active member of the Association of Records Managers and Administrators, Inc. (ARMA International). Thus he is able to give her an accurate answer.

Figure 9.2, page 171, shows a partial listing of the results of a nationwide survey on the subject of records retention. The schedule in this figure was determined by examining the records retention schedules recommended by leading authorities on records storage and by businesses with established procedures.

The information in Figure 9.2 reflects current business thinking. However, the retention periods shown are not offered as a final authority, but

**FIGURE 9.2 • Partial Listing of Nationwide Survey on Records Retention**

| Retenton Schedule | |
|---|---|
| (P = permanent; O = optional; numbers represent suggested years) | |
| Accounts payable ledger | P |
| Accounts receivable ledger | 10 |
| Building permits | 20 |
| Government audit reports | P |
| Annual reports | P |
| Checkbook orders | O |
| Check records | 7 |
| Employee service records | P |
| Pension plan | P |
| Sales invoices | 7 |

as guideposts. State legislatures have established statutes of limitation (laws on how long records must be kept), and federal agencies have regulations that must be followed. Each company makes the final decision on how long to retain records.

# Location of Permanent Records

Carole is concerned about space for all records that must be kept on a permanent basis. She also wonders whether enough room is available for storing records that are not being used but must be kept for long periods. She asks Mr. Lloyd about the space that will be needed.

Mr. Lloyd explains that at their graphics firm, records pass through three stages:

- *Stage 1.* These records are active and should be close at hand. They are referred to frequently, and Mr. Lloyd must have immediate access to them.
- *Stage 2.* These records are only occasionally needed by Mr. Lloyd. They are semiactive and can be placed in storage.
- *Stage 3.* These records are no longer needed by the graphics firm, but they must be kept because of government regulations. They are usually held in permanent storage, often in a separate location.

Carole later learns that these procedures are also followed by many other firms.

# Filing Equipment

Choosing the proper equipment in which to store records is an important part of records management. Choose equipment that will protect the records from damage and that is efficient to use. For example, you may use vertical, lateral, open-shelf, rotary, mobile or portable, or card files.

## Vertical Files

Vertical filing equipment is usually made of metal, sits upright, and has one or more drawers. File folders face the front of the drawer, which makes locating documents easy.

## Lateral Files

Lateral filing equipment is also made of metal, but the drawers rest sideways. File folders are arranged vertically, from side to side, inside the drawers. Cabinets for **lateral files** require less aisle space than vertical cabinets because drawers in lateral file cabinets are not as deep as the drawers in vertical cabinets.

## Open-Shelf Files

Open-shelf filing equipment resembles open bookshelves. File folders are placed onto an uncovered shelf. Equipment for **open-shelf files** saves space. Many employees use color-coded file folders or folder labels to help locate records more quickly.

## Rotary Files

**Rotary files** may be contained in a small unit that sits on a desk or in a large unit that operates on the floor. A small unit may simply be a rotating wheel that holds various business cards. A large floor unit may be electronically operated and contain standard file folders and guides. The files rotate in a circular motion similar to that of a carousel.

## Mobile or Portable Files

When workers must share files on a regular basis, keeping the files in portable cabinets is easier. These portable cabinets are known as **mobile files**. They are usually one-drawer cabinets on wheels, which allows them to be moved from one location to another. The drawer normally has a lid to pull up, rather than the usual pull-out style.

## Card Files

Many office workers keep card files even when other filing equipment is used within the company. A card file is normally a small desktop box or tray that is used for quick reference to frequently needed information. Card files may also be located in a cabinet drawer when more space is needed and quick reference is not important.

# Basic Indexing Rules

When preparing a new folder or card for filing purposes, you must decide in what order to key the name of the person or company. This mental decision is called **indexing**. Once you have keyed the name in indexing order on a folder, then you will file the folder alphabetically with the rest of the folders.

Businesses frequently use vertical filing cabinets. Because these cabinets are taller than they are wide, more cabinets can fit into available floor space.

Businesses also commonly use lateral file cabinets. These cabinets require less floor space for opening the drawers.

## Maintaining Records

A **centralized filing system** is used in most large offices. A company's general files are stored in one central location. Under this system, employees are hired to work exclusively in the central filing area. These employees are responsible for maintaining all centralized files, which includes developing a method to track where the records are located at all times. Lateral or open-shelf storage equipment is usually used in a centralized filing system.

Although small offices may also use a centralized system, they are more likely to use a decentralized filing system. In a decentralized filing system, records are stored in different locations within an office. Each administrative assistant or other clerical employee is responsible for the storage and retrieval of files pertaining to her or his specialized work. Vertical filing cabinets, rather than lateral files, are most often used in small offices.

**Would you like to begin your office career as a records clerk in a large office with a centralized filing system? Why or why not? If you work in a small office, will you remember to set time aside for filing on a regular basis?** ■

## Individual Names

Individual names are indexed by first the surname (last name), next the first name or initial, and then any middle names or initials. For example:

| The name . . . | is indexed as . . . |
| --- | --- |
| Ann E. Delgardo | Delgardo, Ann E. |
| T. C. O'Neil | O'Neil, T. C. |
| J. Linda Singh | Singh, J. Linda |

## Company Names

Company names are indexed in the order that they appear. For example:

| The name . . . | is indexed as . . . |
| --- | --- |
| Westamerica Bank | Westamerica Bank |
| Applied Biosystems | Applied Biosystems |
| C. Martin, Inc. | C. Martin, Inc. |
| Rita Ramos & Sons | Rita Ramos & Sons |

### Ethics on the Job

Lita is scheduled to begin work at 8 A.M. each day. She usually arrives at the office at 7:55 A.M. She turns on her PC and goes to the office kitchen for her morning coffee. She then goes to the rest room and checks her makeup. She is back at her workstation by 8:15.

*Do you agree with Lita's routine? Why or why not?* ■

# Basic Alphabetizing Rules

Lorie started as a temporary office worker six months ago in a large mid-western city. Lorie did not know how to key; therefore, most of her assignments were filing jobs. Lorie began to compare the filing rules she learned in school with the systems she found on various assignments. She noticed many deviations in the filing systems used. Nevertheless, Lorie realized that office workers all followed the same basic filing rules, modeled after ARMA recommendations.

## First Filing Rule

Arrange files in alphabetic order by the first word. The first word is the first one you keyed when you did the indexing. For example:

| Out of Filing Order | In Filing Order |
| --- | --- |
| Erickson, Barbara | Alioto, Martin |
| Clark, Tyler | Clark, Tyler |
| Alioto, Martin | Erickson, Barbara |
| Wiggins, Heloise | Wiggins, Heloise |

## Similar Names of Unequal Length

When two or more names are the same up to a certain letter, the shorter name is filed first. Clark is filed before Clarke. You may remember this rule by thinking "nothing comes before something." For example:

| Out of Filing Order | In Filing Order |
| --- | --- |
| Lowe, Georg | Low, Charles |
| Low, Charles | Lowe, Georg |
| Smithe, Lucy | Smith, Sara |
| Smith, Sara | Smithe, Lucy |

## Hyphenated Names

Hyphenated names are treated as one word. Debbie Wilson-Tobin is filed under Wilson-Tobin. For example:

| Out of Filing Order | In Filing Order |
| --- | --- |
| Lee-Harris, Shelly | Harris, Carol Lee |
| Harris, Carol Lee | Lee-Harris, Shelly |
| Perkins-Millan, Inez | Millan, Flora |
| Millan, Flora | Perkins-Millan, Inez |

## Abbreviations

Abbreviations are considered one unit. For example:

| Out of Filing Order | In Filing Order |
| --- | --- |
| Portillo, Wm. | Burrell, Chas. |
| Burrell, Chas. | Pembroke Rental Co. |
| St. Veronica's School | Portillo, Wm. |
| Pembroke Rental Co. | St. Veronica's School |

**TIP** Schedule fixed blocks of time for group projects. For example, do a batch of filing at one time. Do a batch of photocopying at one time. Key a group of labels or envelopes at one time. This process is more efficient. It also provides longer periods of concentration on one project, which aids accuracy. ■

## Surnames with Prefixes

If an individual surname is compounded with prefixes, it is treated as one word. For example:

| Out of Filing Order | In Filing Order |
|---|---|
| O'Neil, Richard | Del Rosario, Rima |
| Del Rosario, Rima | D'Martini, Christine |
| D'Martini, Christine | Los Robos Lodge |
| Los Robos Lodge | O'Neil, Richard |

## Articles, Prepositions, Conjunctions, and Symbols

Articles, prepositions, conjunctions, and symbols are considered separate filing units. The exception is if the word "the" is the first word of a company name. Symbols such as &, %, $, ¢, and # are spelled out (and; percent; dollar or dollars; cent or cents; pound or number). For example:

| Out of Filing Order | In Filing Order |
|---|---|
| The Fashion Center | Fashion Center The |
| Hospice of Marin | Haswell Group The |
| Top of the Bay Hotel | Hospice of Marin |
| The Haswell Group | Top of the Bay Hotel |
| Anderson & Hartwell | Anderson and Hartwell |

## Names Containing Numbers

When a name contains a number that is spelled out, index the number as a word in alphabetic order. When a name contains a number written as a digit, index the number as a digit in ascending order (from small number to large number). Digit numbers precede all alphabetic words. For example:

| Out of Filing Order | In Filing Order |
|---|---|
| 50 Sutter Place | 9 Months Only |
| One Market Plaza | 50 Sutter Place |
| 9 Months Only | First American News |
| First American News | One Market Plaza |

## Recall Time

*Answer the following questions:*

1. What is the coding process used when preparing records for filing?
2. When is a cross-reference sheet used?
3. What is the difference between indexing and filing?
4. What is the result when you index the following names?

   Donald Hammond
   Stephen Wong
   J. Alice Goldstein
   Sunrise Hill Associates
   Union City Tire & Brake

**5.** What is the result when you arrange the following names in alphabetic order?

Garcia Bakery
Cox, Ben
Day Hour Mini Mart
Apple Annie's
Cox, Chas.
Smith-Hawkins, Paula

**6.** What is the result when you arrange the following names in alphabetic order?

The Kraftsman Group
Del Rose, Teresa
25 Moller Plaza
Society of Brothers

# Preparation of Filing Supplies

Blanche is excited. She has been hired as a receptionist by an architect who has been in business for only a year but who has a good reputation and quite a few clients. Because the architect's business is new, not much work has been done in setting up files for clients. Blanche decides to attack the filing system as one of her first projects. She first purchases a new vertical filing cabinet. She then purchases an office handbook from a local bookstore, reviews the section on records management techniques, and begins to set up the files. Her procedure involves preparing folders and labels, inserting correspondence, and placing folders into a file drawer.

## Preparing Folders and Labels

Blanche prepares a business-size 8.5-by-11–inch folder for each client. She keys a label for each folder, using uppercase letters. After Blanche has worked at the firm a few months, she plans to suggest that the company purchase computer software that will print labels from a template.

While preparing the folders, Blanche is faced with the following problems. She is able to solve them with help from her office handbook.

- She finds two clients with the same name. Her solution is to use labels of different colors for these two clients. In this way, she can more quickly identify the folders.
- She discovers that one client file contains so many reports that they cannot all fit into one folder. Her solution is to prepare two folders for the client and separate them by date headings.

## Inserting Correspondence

Once the folders are prepared, Blanche gathers all correspondence for each client. She arranges the correspondence in the appropriate folder by date, with the latest date on the top. She is extra cautious that the right papers go into the right file folders. She remembers that her boss told her that new business prospects may be lost if the necessary papers are not available when needed for clients.

**FIGURE 9.3 • File Drawer Using File Guides to Separate Folders**

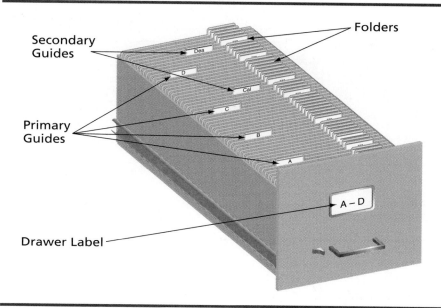

## Placing Folders into a File Drawer

Blanche places the folders in alphabetic order into a drawer of the vertical file cabinet. She then refers to her office handbook and reads the section on file guides. File guides divide file drawers into sections, making locating a folder easier. For example, one guide may be labeled *A*, and all folders behind it begin with the letter *A*. If you have only a few clients, the guide may be labeled *A-D*, and all folders behind it will begin with letters *A, B, C,* and *D*. Both examples are primary guides because they represent major divisions within the drawers.

Blanche completes the project by preparing the primary guides. She also reads about secondary guides, which divide the folders even further into subdivisions. However, she does not think this procedure is necessary for her situation. She does not yet have enough files to make subdivisions useful.

Refer to Figure 9.3 for an example of a file drawer containing both primary and secondary guides. File guides may be purchased at office supply stores.

## Where's the Folder?

No matter how efficient your filing system, it will not work if you cannot find a folder when you need it. One cause of misplaced folders is another employee taking them from the file drawer from time to time. In this case, some notation must be made stating which employee has a particular folder. An out card is used to keep track of records removed from files.

An out card is the same height as the file folders. It may be a different color with the word *OUT* printed in all capital letters on the top tab of the card. Ruled columns on the front of the out card allow an employee to record the date, a description of the file or material removed, when the item is to be returned, the name of the person borrowing the item, and other remarks. See Figure 9.4, page 178, for a sample of an out card.

**FIGURE 9.4 • Out Card**

| DATE | MATERIAL | DATE REMOVED | TO BE RETURNED | REMOVED BY | COMMENTS |
|------|----------|--------------|----------------|------------|----------|
|      |          |              |                |            |          |
|      |          |              |                |            |          |
|      |          |              |                |            |          |
|      |          |              |                |            |          |

An out card is placed in the same location from which a folder or material is removed. An office worker will not use an out card every time a file is removed. An out card is used only when someone outside the immediate office wants a file or if an office assistant or a boss wishes to remove a file for a long period of time.

# Bar Coding Files

Another method of keeping track of files that are checked out from a central location is to use bar coding. This method is similar to that which is used in a library or video store.

Bar codes are placed onto file folders when they are first set up. When an employee checks out a file, the file bar code and the employee's bar code are scanned into the system. When the employee returns the file, the bar code is rescanned.

Bar coding is a fast and efficient method of keeping track of files. Software programs that print bar codes for records management are available.

# Electronic Storage

Although many records are still stored on paper, **electronic files** have replaced many paper files used in the business world. Records may be stored electronically onto hard drives and compact disks.

## Hard Drives

Storing files on the hard drive of a PC is one method of electronic filing. However, when stored on a hard drive, the files may easily be deleted or altered. In addition, the files use up the computer's memory. Therefore, the hard drive is adequate for short-term storage, but it is not recommended for long-term storage.

Electronic records may be created on any computer and stored on hard drives and compact disks.

# High-Capacity Disks

High-capacity disks allow you to easily transport a large number of electronic files from one computer to another. These disks can also store large text, graphics, and audio files. An example of this type of disk is a Zip® disk. A Zip disk is slightly larger than and about twice as thick as a 3.5-inch floppy disk. One disk can store from 100 to 250 megabytes of data.

# Compact Disks

Compact disks, also known as *optical disks*, are used by businesses that want more permanent storage for their files. These disks are flat, round, portable, metal storage media that are usually 4.75 inches in diameter and less than one-twentieth of an inch thick. The best feature about using a compact disk as a storage medium for files is the amount each can hold. A typical CD-ROM (compact disk-read-only memory) holds about 650 megabytes of information. This capacity is about 450 times more than you can store on a high-density, 3.5-inch floppy disk.

Compact disks are available for storage of files in not only CD-ROM format, but also in CD-R and CD-RW. A CD-R (compact disk–recordable) is a compact disk onto which you can record text, graphic, and audio files. With a CD-R, you can record on part of the disk at one time and another part at a later time. Once you have recorded the CD-R, you can read from it as many times as you wish.

A CD-RW (compact disk–rewritable), on the other hand, is an erasable disk you can write on multiple times. To write on a CD-RW disk, you must have CD-RW software and a CD-RW drive. Using these compact disks, you can easily back up large files from your hard disk for temporary or archival (long-term) purposes.

# Other File Storage Media

### Magnetic Tape Storage

Tape is a magnetically coated ribbon of plastic, capable of storing large amounts of data and information at low cost. Tape storage requires sequential access, which refers to reading or writing data consecutively. Magnetic tape mainly is used for long-term storage and backup of files on a computer system.

### Microfilm and Microfiche

Libraries and large organizations use microfilm and microfiche to archive relatively inactive documents and files. These media store microscopic images of documents on roll (microfilm) or sheet (microfiche) film.

# Advantages of Using Electronic Systems

Advantages of using electronic files rather than paper files include:

- *Space.* Filing space requirements are reduced. A larger number of documents can be stored in a smaller amount of space.
- *Retrieval.* An employee can retrieve a document from a computer terminal. This capability provides immediate access to a file.
- *Updating.* Files can be added to an existing disk.
- *Longevity.* Disks provide long-term storage.

Removable electronic storage devices, such as Iomega's Zip disk, can store large quantities of data.

Users can record their electronic records onto CD-R optical disks one time; users can erase and rewrite records onto CD-RW optical disks several times.

Magnetic tape cartridges are often used to back up the contents of a computer's hard disk.

©Verbatim Corporation

Optical disks provide high-capacity storage that is more permanent than storage on a hard drive.

## Recall Time

*Answer the following questions:*

1. You are preparing file folders. How do you solve the following dilemmas?
   a. You need folders for two different clients with the same name.
   b. One client has too many papers to fit into one folder.
2. What purpose do file guides serve?
3. What is the difference between primary and secondary file guides?
4. Why is an out card used?
5. What are two advantages of using an electronic filing system?

## Summary

Filing is a task that all office workers perform. Some do more filing than others, but all workers must maintain files. Most workers use standard filing methods to help make filing tasks efficient.

Most office workers also use basic indexing rules. Once these rules are mastered, filing systems become fairly easy to maintain.

Many companies use electronic filing systems in addition to hardcopy systems. In a few companies, electronic systems replace hard copy systems.

Look at the following list of filing methods and records management processes. Do you understand all of them? If not, which ones do you need to study further?

- alphabetic filing method
- subject filing method
- geographic filing method
- numeric filing method
- chronological filing method
- preparation of records for filing
- records retention
- selection of filing equipment
- basic alphabetizing rules
- electronic filing methods

# before you leave...

**When you have completed this chapter, answer the following questions:**

**1.** What are the four basic filing methods? Explain them.

**2.** What are three examples of equipment used for filing records?

**3.** Name types of records storage.

# Review & Application

## Check Your Knowledge

1. Would you classify each of the following as a vital record?
   a. a letter from your attorney
   b. canceled checks
   c. a copyright
   d. a tax return

2. Arrange the following names in alphabetic order:

   Dearborn Poultry
   Janice's Coffee Shop
   Apple Tree Orchard
   Andrews, Harold
   Kirk, Ronald

3. How does the subject filing method work?

4. Explain the geographic filing method.

5. Arrange the following numbers in numeric order:

   345643501
   075353312
   465493344
   312455352
   129853401

6. Is finding files using the numeric method easy or difficult?

7. Explain how the chronological filing method works.

8. List the steps in the preparation of records for filing.

9. Explain the difference between vertical filing equipment and lateral filing equipment.

10. An office has its files in a one-drawer cabinet that has wheels and is shared by several employees. What is this type of equipment called?

11. Index the following names:

    Amanda C. Parada
    C. F. Del Veccio
    J. Harding Bennett

12. Index the following business names:

    Santos Air Conditioning
    F. H. Daly, Inc.
    Acme Scale Company
    Joe Wong & Associates

13. Arrange the following names in alphabetic order:

    Peter Yu
    William Perry
    Aileen Friedman
    John Fara
    Charles Fara

14. Arrange the following business names in alphabetic order:

    House of Fillmore
    Center for Creative Studies
    Bay Valley Repair
    Sure Clean Carpet
    J. Hall Associates

15. When keying a label for a new file folder, should you use small or large type? Why?

16. Why are file guides used?

17. Give an example of a primary file guide and an example of a secondary guide.

18. When more than one client has the same name, what could you use to distinguish their file folders?

19. List two disadvantages of permanently storing files on the hard drive of a PC.

20. Should each of the following records be stored permanently or for a limited number of years?
    a. accounts payable ledger
    b. accounts receivable ledger
    c. check records
    d. sales invoices
    e. annual reports

21. List types of electronic storage media.

## Review Your Vocabulary

On a separate piece of paper, write the letter of the vocabulary word described below.

1. A document can be filed under more than one name. You file the document under one name and _____ under the other.

2. If information is printed on paper, you have a _____.

3. The _____ method arranges records according to location.

4. The _____ method arranges names by topics.

5. The _____ method arranges records by date.

6. A large company keeps all its files in one central location. This filing system is called a _____ system.

7. When preparing a new folder or card for filing purposes, you must decide in what order to key the name of the person or company onto the folder or card. This mental process is called _____.

8. _____ files are contained on a wheel that rotates in a circular motion.

9. _____ files are portable and shared on a regular basis.

10. _____ files resemble bookshelves.

11. _____ files have drawers that rest sideways with the files arranged from side to side.

12. The _____ method arranges records form A to Z.

13. The _____ method is considered an indirect method of filing.

a. alphabetic filing
b. centralized filing
c. chronological filing
d. cross-reference
e. geographic filing
f. hard copy
g. indexing
h. lateral
i. mobile
j. numeric filing
k. open-shelf
l. rotary
m. subject filing

## Discuss and Analyze an Office Situation

Diane and Ruth are records clerks for a large corporation. Their entire workday is spent in the file room. They are the only two employees doing the filing.

They have little contact with other employees except when someone calls for a lost file. The file room employees have no dress code.

Diane has noticed a strong odor coming from Ruth the past few days. Ruth is a clean person and bathes every day. However, Diane has noticed that Ruth wears the same clothes each day. Diane is guessing the odor is coming from the clothes.

The smell is beginning to bother Diane. Should Diane say something to Ruth? If so, how should she approach Ruth?

## Practice Basic Skills

### Math

1. Your boss asks you to total the following expenses charged to the records management department.

| ITEM | AMOUNT | PRICE |
|---|---|---|
| Hanging folders | 3 boxes | $14.79 per box |
| Hanging folder labels | 5 packages | 4.59 per package |
| Hanging folder frames | 6 boxes | 4.20 per box |
| Tab inserts | 8 packages | 1.05 per package |
| File jackets | 9 packages | 4.19 per package |

2. Your boss receives a discount supply catalog. He asks you to calculate how much would have been saved if the items in exercise 1 had been purchased at the following discount prices:

| ITEM | DISCOUNT PRICE |
|---|---|
| Hanging folders | $6.79 per box |
| Hanging folder labels | 2.49 per package |
| Hanging folder frames | 1.99 per box |
| Tab inserts | 0.69 per package |
| File jackets | 2.29 per package |

3. Compute the total amount that will be charged to the records management department for use of temporary help during the last six months. Use the following information:

Temporary Help
Six-Months Report

| | |
|---|---|
| January | |
| Advertising department | $ 375.00 |
| Records management department | 235.00 |
| Accounting department | 680.00 |
| February | |
| Advertising department | 375.00 |
| Records management department | 460.00 |
| Accounting department | 680.00 |
| March | |
| Advertising department | 235.00 |
| Records management department | 375.00 |
| Accounting department | 680.00 |
| April | |
| Advertising department | 800.00 |
| Records management department | 1,275.00 |
| Accounting department | 1,490.00 |

May
| | | |
|---|---|---|
| Advertising department | | 775.00 |
| Records management department | | 1,030.00 |
| Accounting department | | 1,490.00 |

June
| | | |
|---|---|---|
| Advertising department | | 800.00 |
| Records management department | | 1,490.00 |
| Accounting department | | 1,275.00 |

## English

*Rule:* Use a hyphen when *self* and *ex* are joined with another word.

*Examples:* He was a self-made man. His ex-boss was in the building

*Practice Exercise:* Rewrite the following sentences, placing hyphens where needed.

a. The absence was viewed by all the people as self imposed exile.
b. The woman was self appointed to chair the committee.
c. The meeting was scheduled for 3 P.M. between the attorney and his exwife.
d. He has always been a self supporting person.
e. He furnished a new office for the expresident.

## Proofreading

Rewrite or key the following, correcting all errors.

BOOKS FOR SALE

ACTIVE FILNG FOR PAPER RECORDS by Dr. Ann Bennick, CRM

Active Filing for Paper Records focuses on three bacis topics related to the managemnt of paper records: file systems development, filing equipment, and filing suplies. Implementation and conversion procedures is presented within the context of systems development techniques and ,where appropriate, as the relate to a discussion of spesific procedures, equipment, and supplies.

OPTICAL DISK SYSTEMS FOR RECORDS MANAGEMENT
By William Saffady

Optical Disk Systems for Records Management is divided into two parts. Section One provides an overview of optical disk technology. It defins the various types of storage media and breifly reviews their records management significance. Section Two provides a detailed discusion of optical filing systems, computer-based hardware and software configurations that store digitized document images on opticl disks for on-demand retreival. The discussion emphasises characteristics that influence the evaluation and selection of optical filing systems for records management applications.

## Apply Your Knowledge

1. Using the tables feature of a word processing program, input, save, and print the following words. Use three columns and input in alphabetic order.

| | |
|---|---|
| storage | geographic |
| chronological | numeric |
| lateral | digit |
| vertical | important |
| rotary | reference |
| centralized | business |
| records | retrieval |
| financial | folder |
| paperless | tabs |
| vital | labels |
| alphabetic | supplies |
| index | drawer |

2. The file drawers at CFEB Company contain the following primary guides:

| | | |
|---|---|---|
| A-Cr | Jes-Me | Rx-Th |
| Cs-F | Mf-Pi | Ti-W |
| G-Jer | Pj-Rw | X-Z |

Behind which guide would you file each of the following names?

| | |
|---|---|
| Solano Bakery | Jerrett Pies |
| Yarnell Cheese | Tin Recycled |
| Barnes Culinary | Kraft Dairy |
| Place & Place Products | McMillan Bros. |
| Rennett Corporation | Modems for Less |

## Using the Reference Manual

Open file ch9ref.doc. Use the Manuscripts and Reports section of the Reference Manual at the back of the book to help you supply the correct information. Save and print.

1. Manuscripts may be _____, _____, or space and one-half.

2. The title is keyed _____ and _____ on page 1.

3. For reports bound on the left side, the side margins should be set with the left margin at _____ inch, and the right margin at _____ inch.

4. Subheadings are keyed at the _____ margin in all _____ letters.

5. For reports bound at the top, the first page should have a _____-inch top margin.

6. All other report pages except page 1 are numbered at the top _____ margin, _____ lines down.

7. The title page should contain the _____ and _____ of the report.

8. The table of _____ lists main divisions and page numbers in a report.

9. A _____ is prepared in _____ order to give credit to the sources of information used in the report.

10. The bibliography is usually prepared using _____-spaced lines.

# chapter 10

## Processing Business Documents

**After completing this chapter, you will be able to do the following:**

1. Discuss the major parts of a business letter.
2. Discuss how a block letter is keyed.
3. Discuss how a modified block letter is keyed.
4. Explain the difference between mixed punctuation and open punctuation.
5. List the major parts of a memorandum heading.
6. List three different heading formats used for memorandums.
7. Prepare business envelopes.
8. Describe how templates are used.
9. List the major parts of business reports.
10. List the rules for formatting business reports.
11. Prepare a travel itinerary.
12. Prepare an agenda for a meeting.
13. List the contents of the minutes of a meeting.
14. Make corrections using proofreaders' marks.
15. Explain how to key legal forms.
16. Prepare a tickler file.

### New Office Terms

- agenda
- appendix
- attachment notation
- bibliography
- block letter format
- body
- closing
- default margins
- enclosure notation
- greeting
- itinerary
- leaders
- letter address
- memorandum
- minutes
- mixed punctuation
- modified block letter format
- open punctuation
- proofreaders' marks
- template
- tickler file

# before you begin . . .

**Answer the following questions to the best of your ability:**

1. What are the major parts of a business letter? How should a letter be keyed onto company letterhead?

2. What are the major parts of a business report? What are the rules used for keying a report?

**K**eyboarding is a major part of the job for workers in business offices. What do these workers keyboard?

If you were to survey these workers about the keying tasks most frequently performed, you would find the answer to be envelopes, letters, and memorandums (memos). Records clerks and mailroom personnel do light keyboarding, including keying envelopes and letters. Receptionists perform the same keyboarding duties. Most secretaries and administrative assistants spend many hours keying letters and reports.

Companies want to make a good impression by the appearance of their correspondence. Therefore, office workers need to know the correct format to use when keying correspondence.

## Business Letters

If you key a letter at home, you probably key it and then print it on plain paper. However, when you begin working in an office, your business letters will be keyed and then printed on stationery called *company letterhead*.

©Susan Van Etten/PhotoEdit

Some office workers spend most of their time keying letters, envelopes, memos, reports, and other documents. They understand the importance of using proper formats.

## MAKING TRAVEL ARRANGEMENTS ON THE INTERNET

The traditional method of making travel arrangements through a travel agency is still widely used today. However, more and more people are making their travel arrangements on the Internet. You can make airline, hotel, and car rental reservations very easily on the Internet. Making online arrangements is also much quicker than calling the airlines, hotels, and car companies directly. If you use one of the fast Internet service connections, then you may be able to plan your trip completely in just a few minutes.

If you key the keywords *travel agencies* into a search engine, the results will be a long list of agencies and companies through which you may make travel arrangements. Among the largest and most popular travel Web sites are Expedia.com® and Travelocity.com®. Using these or other travel sites, you can sometimes purchase airline tickets at a reduced price—and charge them on your credit card. You can choose from a wide range of hotels and even see photos of hotel rooms. You can also choose from a variety of car models and sizes from several car rental agencies. Usually, a number of "package deals" that include airline transportation, hotel rooms, and car rental at a special price are available—all with the click of your mouse. ■

Letterhead stationery has the company name, its address (both street and e-mail, and if available, its Web site), and its telephone and fax numbers preprinted on the paper.

When your business letters are finished and printed, they must be properly spaced on the letterhead stationery. They should not be too high on the page, nor should they be too low. They should be evenly placed with equal left and right margins. When clients receive the letters, they must be "pleasing to the eye."

The following section describes procedures used by office workers when formatting letters.

## Major Parts

Figure 10.1, page 191, shows some of the parts of a business letter, which include the date, letter address, greeting, body, closing, sender's name, keyboarder's initials, enclosure notation, attachment notation, and copy notation.

### Date

Key the date two to three lines below the bottom of the letterhead. If you are not using letterhead, begin twelve to fourteen lines from the top of the paper. Key the date using a word for the month followed by numbers for the day and year. An example is June 11, 2002.

### Letter Address

The **letter address** includes the name, title, company, and address of the person receiving the letter. It is keyed four to eight lines below the date. The number of blank lines between the date and the letter address is determined by the length of the letter. Long letters require fewer blank lines; short letters require more.

### Greeting (Also Called Salutation)

Key the **greeting** two spaces after the letter address. The greeting usually begins with the word *Dear* followed by the name of the person receiving the letter. A sample of a greeting is "Dear Mr. Wong:".

### Body

The **body** of the letter begins a double-space after the greeting. The body is the main part of a letter. It contains the reason for the letter, and it is usually at least two paragraphs long.

### Closing

Key the **closing** a double-space after the ending of the body of the letter. The two most common closings used in business are as follows:

> Very truly yours,
> Sincerely,

### Sender's Name

Key the sender's name (the name of the person signing the letter) four lines after the closing. Four lines is enough room for the person to sign the letter. Usually, you will key the person's title on the line after the keyed name.

### Keyboard Operator's Initials

Key your own initials at the left margin a double-space after the sender's name. Your initials are always keyed in lowercase. These initials are also known as *reference initials*.

### Enclosure Notation

The **enclosure notation** is keyed a double-space after the keyboard operator's initials. If this notation appears on the letter, it means something is being enclosed with the letter. You key this notation only if something in addition to the letter is in the envelope. For example, a company may enclose a refund check in an envelope with a letter.

### Attachment Notation

The **attachment notation** is used in place of the enclosure notation when something is stapled or attached to a letter. This notation is keyed in place of the word *enclosure*, a double-space after the keyboarder's initials.

### Copy Notation

Sometimes you may need to send a copy of a letter to another person. If any copies are to be made for other people, a notation is made a double-space after the enclosure notation or, if nothing is enclosed, a double-space after the keyboard operator's initials.

For example, suppose that you are sending a letter to Harry Basset, and you will be sending a copy of the letter to Sylvia Chow. You will key the following notation on the letter:

> c: Sylvia Chow

## Other Parts

An attention line, a subject line, and a second-page heading (information for letters of more than one page) occasionally appear on letters. Although these parts are not always included in a letter, you need to know where to key them.

**FIGURE 10.1 • Parts of a Business Letter**

```
ACME FENCE COMPANY
P.O. Box 795
Daly City, CA 94017
Telephone: 415.555.1329   Fax: 415.555.1333
www.acmefence.com

Date

Name, Title
Company
Street
City, State, ZIP Code

Greeting

_____
                 Body
_____
_____
_____
_____
                 Body
_____
_____
                 Body
_____
_____

Closing

Sender's Name

keyboard operator's initials

enclosure

c:
```

## Attention Line

Key the attention line within the letter address, on the line below the company name. Use an attention line when you address a letter to a company but you want the letter to be directed to a particular department or person. For example:

Angle Hook Company
Attn: Accounts Payable
45 Spooner Street
Boston, MA 02390-1306

ProServ
Attention Harold Gerard
One Spear Street
Oakland, CA 94233-9574

> **TIP** Some important books to always have on hand are a good dictionary, a thesaurus, and one or two office handbooks. These reference books are also available in electronic form either as a separate software package or as part of a complete word processing software package such as Microsoft Word. ■

**Making Office Decisions** You arrive for work one morning and find a letter that you must key to Lee Baxter. Your boss, who has gone on a business trip, left the letter for you to key. The letter must go in that day's mail.

You begin the letter by keying the date and the inside address. You get to the salutation (greeting) and you stop. You do not know whether Lee Baxter is a man or a woman. No one in your office knows.

**What do you do?** ∎

### Subject Line

If you use a subject line, key it a double-space after the greeting. Many people key the subject line in all capital letters. However, a subject line may also be keyed with initial capital and lowercase letters.

A subject line is sometimes called a *reference line*. It is used to alert the reader immediately to the purpose of the letter. The subject line is usually a short phrase referring to the contents of the letter. For example:

Subject: Invoice #345
Subject: Date for Annual Meeting
Re: Your letter of March 18

### Second-Page Heading

If a letter is longer than one page, all pages after page 1 should contain the following information:

- the name of the person to whom the letter is addressed
- the date
- the page number

The placement of this information can be either blocked at the left margin or spaced across the page on one line. It may be keyed in all capital letters or in initial capitals and lowercase letters. For example:

ERIC JOHNSON
SEPTEMBER 17, 2002
PAGE 2

| Eric Johnson | Page 2 | September 17, 2002 |
| --- | --- | --- |

## Letter Formats

Preferred letter formats vary from company to company. The two most commonly used formats, however, are the block letter format and the modified block letter format. Block format has become the most popular because the simple formatting saves keyboarding time. When you start a new job, before you key your first letter, check with your supervisor to see which letter format your boss prefers or which format is used throughout the company.

### Block Letter Format

In **block letter format**, the entire letter is keyed even with the left margin. This is the most commonly used format in industry. You save time by not indenting any parts of the letter.

### Modified Block Letter Format

In **modified block letter format**, the date and closing begin at the center. This format sometimes looks better with certain letterhead designs. Even though the date and closing are indented, paragraphs do not have to be indented.

## Punctuation

Different rules apply for using mixed and open punctuation in the greeting and closing of a business letter.

### Mixed

When using **mixed punctuation**, a colon is keyed after the greeting, and a comma is keyed after the closing. Mixed punctuation is the most popular choice and is preferred by many businesspeople.

### Open

For **open punctuation**, no punctuation is keyed after the greeting or after the closing.

## Margins

When using word processing programs, office support staff typically use **default margins**, or margins that are preset in the program. If margins need to be set, most office workers leave a one-inch margin on both left and right sides of a letter.

## Memorandums

Correspondence that stays within a company is called a **memorandum**, or memo (see Figure 10.2, page 194). The heading section of a memo is formatted in various ways, but it usually contains these headings: To, From, Date, and Subject. The following examples show heading formats office workers may use for memorandums:

TO:
FROM:
DATE:
SUBJECT:

TO:
FROM:
DATE:
SUBJECT:

TO:                   DATE:
FROM:               SUBJECT:

When keying memorandums, keep the following points in mind:

- Memorandums are informal; never use titles. This rule holds true even for the titles Mr., Mrs., Miss, and Ms., which should not be included.
- Do not use a salutation or closing.
- Use the block format.
- Triple-space between the subject line and the body of the memo. The body is the message part of the memo.
- Key the keyboard operator's initials, enclosure notation, and copy notation in the same locations as they are keyed on a letter.

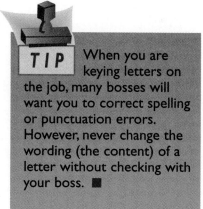

**TIP** When you are keying letters on the job, many bosses will want you to correct spelling or punctuation errors. However, never change the wording (the content) of a letter without checking with your boss. ■

### Ethics on the Job

A large midwestern corporation has a word processing department with five employees. These employees work as a team doing the word processing for all the managers. As long as all the work is completed, no employee is checked for the amount of work he or she has done.

Jason, an employee in this department, attends evening classes at the local community college. Every time he has to study for an exam, he does it during worktime. The word processing still gets done, but the other employees have to work extra hard.

***Do you think Jason should study on the job? How is it affecting the team?*** ■

**FIGURE 10.2 • Parts of a Memorandum**

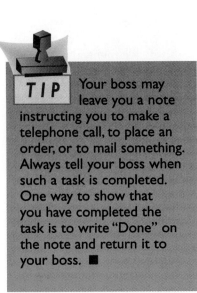

**ACME FENCE COMPANY**
P.O. Box 795
Daly City, CA 94017

M E M O R A N D U M

TO:
FROM:
DATE:
SUBJECT:

_____ Body _____

_____

_____ Body _____

keyboard operator's initials

# Templates

Some companies use a **template** for keying correspondence. A template is a master document or model that contains any text, formats, and styles you want to include in a particular kind of document. Templates enable you to prepare documents more quickly because they supply many of the settings you would otherwise need to create—such as margins, tabs, and alignment.

For example, when you retrieve a letter template the current date appears at the correct location, and the cursor is sitting on the correct line to begin keying the letter address. The margins are also set automatically to fit the company's letterhead.

For memorandums, the headings To, From, Date, and Subject are already on the page. The current date also appears, and the cursor is sitting on the "To" line (see Figure 10.3, page 195).

Word processing software packages supply a wide range of document templates, from letters and faxes to memos, reports, manuals, brochures, newsletters, and special documents such as Web pages.

# Business Envelopes

Business envelopes are known as No. 10 envelopes. They have two major parts, and certain rules are followed when keying them.

**TIP** Your boss may leave you a note instructing you to make a telephone call, to place an order, or to mail something. Always tell your boss when such a task is completed. One way to show that you have completed the task is to write "Done" on the note and return it to your boss. ■

FIGURE 10.3 • Memorandum Template

## Company Name Here

# Memo

**To:**       [Click here and key name]

**From:**    [Click here and key name]

**CC:**       [Click here and key name]

**Date:**    2/19/02

**Subject:**  [Click here and key name]

### How to Use This Memo Template

Select text you would like to replace, and key your memo. Use styles such as Heading 1-3 and Body Text in the Style control on the Formatting toolbar. To save changes to this template for future use, choose Save As from the File menu. In the Save As Type box, choose Document Template. Next time you want to use it, choose New from the File menu, and then double-click your template.

## Parts

The main parts of the information you key onto a business envelope are the return address and the letter address. Sometimes special notations are included (see Figure 10.4).

### Return Address

Most companies have their own envelopes with a printed return address. However, if you must key the return address, begin to key two lines down from the top and three spaces in from the left edge of the envelope.

**FIGURE 10.4 • Business Envelope**

ACME FENCE COMPANY
P.O. Box 795
Daly City, CA 94017

PERSONAL

REGISTERED

MS IRMA LOPEZ
TRANSWORLD EXPORTS
45 FIRST STREET ROOM 203
SAN FRANCISCO CA 94013-3803

### Letter Address

An experienced keyboarder, using an electronic typewriter, puts an envelope into the machine and turns the platen (roller) to the correct spot for keying the letter address. If you have not keyed envelopes before, locating the correct spot can be a problem. Therefore, the rule to remember is to begin about twelve lines down from the top and five spaces left of the center of the envelope. Set a margin or tab at this location.

Keying an envelope using word processing software is quite simple because the word processing program sets the margins. The keyboarder simply clicks on the envelope feature of the program and keys the address. When the envelope is printed, the address will automatically appear at the correct location.

### Special Notations

Common notations for the addressee (person or company that receives the letter) that are keyed onto envelopes include PLEASE FORWARD, HOLD FOR ARRIVAL, and PERSONAL. These notations are keyed a double-space below the return address in capital letters or underlined.

Mailing notations for postal authorities include SPECIAL DELIVERY and REGISTERED. These notations are keyed a double-space below the stamp position in all caps or underlined.

## Formatting Rules—Envelopes

Some points to remember when keying envelopes include:

- Always single-space.
- Abbreviate all state names with two capital letters and no periods.
- Leave at least six lines at the bottom of an envelope. Current Postal Service regulations state that the bottom of an envelope must be free of all notations so that the envelope can pass quickly through the electronic scanners.
- When keying the letter address, the format preferred by the U.S. Postal Service is to use all capital letters and omit all punctuation. All capital letters are read and sorted more quickly by the scanners. However, capitals and lowercase letters may also be used in envelope addresses. Figure 10.5, page 197, shows samples of both methods.

When deciding which method to use, check your boss's preference. If your boss has no preference, use the Postal Service's preferred method.

### Recall Time

*Answer the following questions:*

**1.** What are three keying functions that most office workers perform?

**2.** What are the main parts of a business letter?

**3.** What is the difference between block letter format and modified block letter format?

**4.** What four headings are used in memorandums?

**5.** Where is the word *attention* keyed on an envelope?

**FIGURE 10.5 • Envelope Address Formats**

| Method Preferred by U.S. Postal Service | Method Preferred by Most Companies |
|---|---|
| THE NOODLE CORPORATION<br>ATTN MS SHIRLEY GONZALES<br>2399 PALM AVE<br>BURLINGAME CA 94060-1064 | The Noodle Corporation<br>Attention Ms. Shirley Gonzales<br>2399 Palm Avenue<br>Burlingame, CA 94060-1064 |
| MR PAUL WONG<br>131 BATTERY ST<br>PORTLAND OR 93616-1540 | Mr. Paul Wong<br>131 Battery Street<br>Portland, OR 93616-1540 |
| MS JULIA SINGLETON<br>BUY RITE CO<br>9 ALMOND WAY<br>BOSTON MA 02368-1386 | Ms. Julia Singleton<br>Buy-Rite Company<br>9 Almond Way<br>Boston, MA 02368-1386 |
| MS ROSE MARIE FRAZIER<br>HUMAN RESOURCES DEPARTMENT<br>SAVE NOW BANK<br>23 MONTGOMERY ST<br>SAN FRANCISCO CA 94115-9618 | Ms. Rose Marie Frazier<br>Human Resources Department<br>Save Now Bank<br>23 Montgomery Street<br>San Francisco, CA 94115-9618 |

# Business Reports

At a public relations firm in New York, executives frequently create proposals to present to new clients. As the executives compose their reports, they do all their own keyboarding directly into PCs. The office support staff then makes keying corrections and prints the final copies, which are referred to as *business reports*. Office support staff must know the parts of a business report as well as what keying rules to use in formatting a final copy.

## Parts

The main parts of a business report are the title page, table of contents, body, appendix, and bibliography.

### Title Page
The title page is usually the front cover of the report. It includes the title of the report, the name of the person the report is written for, the author of the report, the company name, and the date.

### Table of Contents
The table of contents includes the titles of the topics in the report and the page number on which each topic begins.

### Body
The body is the main part of the report. It usually includes an introduction, major statements, and a conclusion.

Business reports are often compiled after analyzing spreadsheet printouts.

## Janie Overway

*HR Coordinator, Western Region*
*GMAC Commercial Mortgage™ Corporation*

**Q.** Ms. Overway, employers often speak of the work ethic. What do employers expect of the work ethic in office employees?

**A.** The "work ethic" expected of office employees is no different from that expected of an executive: honesty and integrity. These qualities are demonstrated through punctuality, reliability, taking full responsibility for projects and following through, standing your ground when necessary, and maintaining confidences.

**Q.** What career advice would you give to an entry-level office support employee?

**A.** First, learn about office politics! Office politics is a game, and it has rules. Not knowing the rules only makes you look ignorant. Several good books on the subject are available—buy one of them!

Second, when you have completed Step 1, you will understand the reasons behind the following suggestions:

- Do not go into a company thinking you know it all. Focus on learning to do your job, not on letting everyone know how great you are. People will see your work quality, and you will prove your value to the company by your skills and abilities, even if your skills are not fully honed. Your efforts to listen and learn will be appreciated by management.
- Dress the part! Not "getting" the meaning behind this rule is the number one career gaffe. Even with the acceptance and practice of casual dressing in the business environment, do not fall into this trap.

### Appendix

Some business reports have supplementary information that supports the statements in the body of the reports. This supplementary information is located in the **appendix**, usually following the body of the report. The appendix can be in the form of a chart, a graph, or a table. A report can have more than one appendix.

### Bibliography

The **bibliography** is a listing of all sources used to write the report. It includes books, magazines, newspaper articles, and Web addresses. It usually appears at the end of the report.

## Formatting Rules—Reports

Office workers follow certain procedures when keying the various parts of business reports.

## Title Page

■ Center each line horizontally.

■ Leave several blank lines between each item (title, name of person the report is written for, author, company name, and date). Center the keyed lines vertically on the page.

## Table of Contents

■ Center the titles and page numbers both horizontally and vertically.

■ Double- or single-space, depending on the length.

■ List the topic number, usually as a roman numeral, beginning at the left margin. On the same line, follow with the topic name. On the same line, end with the page number at the right margin.

■ Use **leaders** (periods) between the topic name and the page number.

Note: Word processing software can automatically perform all these functions.

## Body

■ Double-space the body of the report. However, sometimes you will use space-and-a-half spacing in a report, leaving a half-space blank line between keyed lines. You will seldom single-space a report.

■ Use a 2-inch top margin for the first page and a 1-inch top margin for all other pages, a 1-inch bottom margin for all pages, and 1-inch side margins for all pages.

■ Key the headings and subheadings at the left margin, in all capital letters.

■ Key the page number in the center of the page, three lines up from the bottom.

## Bibliography

■ Prepare items in alphabetic order.

■ Include the name of the author, the publication, the publisher, and the publication date for each item.

■ Begin the first line of each item at the left margin, and indent all other lines.

■ Use single-spacing.

■ Use the same margins as in the report.

Employees who must travel for business appreciate having their travel documents prepared neatly and efficiently.

## Ethics on the Job

Roosevelt began a new job as an office assistant for an advertising company. On his second day on the job, he was trained by Carmen to enter information into the company database. He had done similar work at his last job, so he did not bother to take notes during the training.

On the third day Roosevelt was to do the data entry by himself; however, he had to ask Carmen several questions.

*Do you think Roosevelt would have had fewer questions if he had taken notes? Did he waste Carmen's time? Is this behavior fair to the company?* ■

# Travel Arrangement Documents

Angelina is an administrative assistant in the corporate office of a large bank in Chicago. Her boss has to go on a business trip. Planning this trip is Angelina's first experience in making travel arrangements for her boss.

Angelina learns from another employee that business executives within the company either make travel arrangements through a travel agent or make their own arrangements on the Internet using a corporate credit card. The company already has an account established with a local agency.

Before Angelina calls a travel agent or makes travel arrangements online, she writes down the following information:

- where her boss will travel
- date and time of departure and return
- class of air travel
- whether hotel accommodations will be needed
- whether a rental car will be needed

Angelina also looks in her files to learn her boss's preference for seating on the airplane and frequent flyer numbers, if they are used.

Now Angelina is ready to prepare an itinerary for her boss. When her boss returns, she will complete an expense account form for him.

## Itinerary

An **itinerary** is a record of travel plans. It is neatly keyed and includes the date and time of departures and arrivals, location of departures and arrivals, transportation means, and hotel accommodations. It may also include information on car rentals and time and location of business meetings. See Figure 10.6, page 201, for a sample itinerary. Some travel agents will prepare the itinerary for you.

**FIGURE 10.6 • Itinerary**

ITINERARY
LYDIA DELOSARDO
MAY 3, 2002 TO MAY 5, 2002
CHICAGO TO BOSTON

Monday, May 3

| | | | |
|---|---|---|---|
| 8:30 A.M. | Leave Chicago | WA Flight #347 | Breakfast |
| 10:40 A.M. | Arrive Boston | | |
| (Boston Time) | Taxi to Tremont Plaza Hotel | | |
| | (Confirmation #S783012) | | |
| 2:00 P.M. | Meeting with Lum Video, Inc. | | |
| | 678 Boylston Street | | |
| | (617-555-1099) | | |

Tuesday, May 4

| | | |
|---|---|---|
| 9:00 A.M. | Meeting with Lum Video, Inc. | |
| 1:00 P.M. | Meeting with Lacey Disk Company | |
| | 9 Tremont Avenue | |
| | (617-555-1134) | |
| 7:30 P.M. | Dinner meeting One Sutter Place | |
| | Association of Entrepreneurs | |

Wednesday, May 5

| | | | |
|---|---|---|---|
| 10:20 A.M. | Leave Boston | WA Flight #743 | Breakfast |
| 2:00 P.M. | Arrive Chicago | | |
| (Chicago Time) | | | |

## Expense Account Form

When Angelina's boss returns from the business trip, Angelina is asked to complete an expense account form for him. This form is completed when a businessperson wishes to be reimbursed (paid back) for money spent during a business trip.

Most companies reimburse employees for transportation, hotel accommodations, meals, business entertainment, and miscellaneous expenses incurred on a business trip. The employee needs to keep receipts for proof of all expenses.

Angelina must complete a form similar to the one shown in Figure 10.7, page 202, for her boss to be reimbursed for his travel expenses. Once the form is completed, all receipts are attached to the back, it is signed by her boss, and it is sent to the accounting department for processing. In some cases, an additional signature of approval may also be required before the form is processed. Also, some bosses want photocopies kept of the expense form and all attachments.

Some companies will give an employee a cash advance before he or she leaves on a business trip. If the employee receives a cash advance, the cash advance must be subtracted from the amount due on the expense form. Note where the cash advance is deducted on the sample expense account form in Figure 10.7.

## FIGURE 10.7 • Expense Account Form

**EXPENSE REIMBURSEMENT CLAIM**

This section must be TYPED or PRINTED LEGIBLY, or form will be returned.  Submit Original and two copies to Accounting Dept.

SUBMITTED BY: _____ VENDOR NO. _____

DEPT.: _____ (OR) ADDRESS: _____

FOR MEETING HELD:     FROM: _____ , 20 ____     TO: _____ , 20 ____

AT: _____

DEPARTURE DATE: _____ TIME: _____ RETURN DATE: _____ TIME: _____

PURPOSE OF MEETING: _____

REFER TO REGULATIONS on the back of this form BEFORE COMPLETING this section.

| DATE | MEALS | | | TOTAL MEALS | OTHER EXPENSES* Lodging / Transportation / Incidentals (Description/Explanation) | TOTAL OTHER EXPENSES | TOTAL CLAIM |
|---|---|---|---|---|---|---|---|
| | B | L | D | | | | |
| | | | | | | | |
| | | | | | | | |
| | | | | | | | |
| | | | | | | | |
| | | | | | | | |
| | | | | | | | |
| | | | | | | | |
| | | | | | | | |
| | | | | | | | |
| **T O T A L S** | | | | | ///////////////////////////////////////////////////////////////////////////////////// | | |

I HEREBY CERTIFY that the above claim represents a true cost and full accounting of all expenses incurred by me in attending the above-named meeting.

| | LESS: ADVANCED | |
|---|---|---|
| SIGNATURE: _____ | NET CLAIM | |

ADDITIONAL INFORMATION (or) EXPLANATION:

| OTHER EXPENSE(S) PAID BY EMPLOYER: (List PO# and Amount) | ACCOUNT NO. | AMOUNT |
|---|---|---|
| TRANSPTN: _____ | _____ | $_____ |
| HOTEL: _____ | _____ | _____ |
| OTHER: _____ | _____ | _____ |
| _____ | TOTAL | _____ |

SUPERVISOR APPROVAL: _____

*If personal car is used, include mileage reimbursement on this claim form—NOT on Monthly Mileage Reimbursement form.

# Meeting Documents

When Angelina's boss was away on the business trip, she had time to do work for other supervisors. One supervisor asked her to prepare an agenda for the monthly meeting of the company's Computer Software Advisory Committee. Angelina was also asked to attend the meeting and to take the minutes.

## Agenda

The **agenda** is a listing of what is to take place during the meeting. It usually includes the committee name, meeting date and place, call to order, roll call, approval of minutes of last meeting, old business, new business, announcements, date of next meeting, and adjournment (see Figure 10.8).

## Minutes

The **minutes** of a meeting are a record of who attended the meeting and what took place at the meeting. Taking accurate and complete notes of the meeting is important, but recording the meeting word for word is not necessary. You will find reading minutes of previous meetings helpful. Make a seating chart as the meeting begins (unless you know all the members), record the names of persons who make motions, and record the meeting on a tape recorder.

**FIGURE 10.8 • Meeting Agenda**

AGENDA
COMPUTER SOFTWARE ADVISORY COMMITTEE MEETING
ALLSTATE CONFERENCE ROOM C
JULY 15, 2002

   I.   CALL TO ORDER

  II.   ROLL CALL

 III.   MINUTES FROM LAST MEETING

 IV.   OLD BUSINESS
      Final bid on spreadsheet software
      Evaluation results of NetCheck

  V.   NEW BUSINESS
      New word processing software
      State Computer Users' Conference

 VI.   ANNOUNCEMENTS

VII.   DATE OF NEXT MEETING

VIII.   ADJOURNMENT

Formal meetings generally require the participation of the administrative assistant or secretary who will prepare the agenda, key correspondence to individuals who will attend, and record and key the minutes of the meeting.

After the meeting, while it is fresh in your mind, key a rough draft of the minutes from your notes. Then compare the rough draft against the tape recording. From this rough draft, create the final copy by keying the following:

1. The name of the committee and the date of the meeting at the center of the paper.
2. The time and place of the meeting.
3. The name of the person leading the meeting.
4. A list of the names of persons attending the meeting.
5. The body of the minutes, using single-spacing and the same margins as for manuscripts. Set up sections for reading of the minutes and corrections to previous minutes, old business, and new business.
6. The time and place of the next meeting.
7. The time the meeting adjourned.
8. Solid lines at the end of the minutes for the signatures of the chairperson and secretary.

See Figure 10.9, page 205, for an example of minutes of a meeting.

# Rough Drafts and Proofreaders' Marks

Many letters, reports, minutes, and other business documents are revised one or more times before a final copy is printed. When these documents are in rough draft format, **proofreaders' marks** are often used to show the changes to be made.

Proofreaders' marks are standard symbols used by most office workers. They make understanding corrections that need to be made easier. The following is a sample of proofreaders' marks used on a paragraph:

**FIGURE 10.9 • Meeting Minutes**

COMPUTER SOFTWARE ADVISORY COMMITTEE
MINUTES OF MEETING
JULY 15, 2002
ALLSTATE CONFERENCE ROOM C

The meeting was called to order by _____ at 12 noon.

In attendance: _____ _____ _____ _____

_____ _____ _____ _____

_____ _____ _____ _____

_____ _____ _____ _____

Minutes of the June meeting were read by Natalie Smith and approved with the following corrections:

_____

_____

_____

Old Business:

_____

_____

_____

_____

New Business:

_____

_____

_____

_____

_____

_____

Announcements:

_____

_____

_____

The next meeting is scheduled for _____.

The meeting adjourned at 2:30 p.m.

_____      _____
Chairperson                                          Secretary

Customer Service Quality customer service begins with how weell employees understand their role in teh organization and how much they feel they contribute to its success. EMployees with a positive self-image aremore likely to provide quality service to internal and external customers.

Refer to Table 10.1, page 206, to see that you are to do the following:

- Key "Customer Service" in uppercase (all capital letters).
- Delete the extra *e* in "weell."
- Transpose the *e* and *h* in "teh."
- Change the uppercase *M* to a lowercase *m* in "EMployees."
- Leave a space between *are* and *more* in "aremore."

The process for making an insurance claim often involves entering information from a legal document such as a police report.

# Legal Documents

Legal contracts or documents are written agreements between individuals. A legal document may be a printed form such as a rental lease, a sales agreement, or a form to be completed for small claims court.

Electronic typewriters are often used to complete these printed forms. When filling in the information on such a form, the keyboarder uses the same margins as those set by the size of the form. When completing forms with blanks indicated by printed lines, key slightly above the lines. Some law firms repeatedly process many of the same forms, using templates provided on their computer software.

Procedures for keying other legal documents, such as complaints or motions for criminal and civil courts, vary from state to state. In California, for example, the courts require legal documents to be keyed on 8.5-by-11-inch paper, double-spaced, with single-spacing for quotations. Using this size paper saves filing space because legal-size folders or legal-size file cabinets are not required.

Procedures for keying other legal documents, such as wills or right-to-die agreements, are not determined by the courts. The legal profession dictates the format for these documents. They are often keyed on 8.5-by-14-inch paper, double-spaced, with indented paragraphs. In some cases,

**TABLE 10.1 • Proofreaders' Marks**

| MARK | MEANING | EXAMPLE |
|------|---------|---------|
| ℓ | Delete | We will not be on time. |
| ∼ | Transpose | She sent the fax. |
| ¶ | Start a new paragraph | ... at the office. After it ... |
| ◯ | Close up | She was al ready late. |
| # | Insert a space | He arrived;we started. |
| lc | Lowercase | BE on time |
| uc | Uppercase | Call senator Kennedy. |
| ∼∼∼ | Boldface | The meeting is Monday. |
| STET | Leave words in | We will not attend. |
| ...... | Leave words in | We will not attend. |
| ⊙ | Insert a period | Mr Delsalvio is here. |
| ∧ | Insert something | I will be in the hall. |

special legal paper is used. This type of paper is numbered on the left margin and has vertical lines down the sides. However, most of these documents are prepared on 8.5-by-11-inch paper.

## Tickler Files

As you can see from the previous examples, secretaries and administrative assistants, such as Angelina, must keep track of meetings, reports to do, business trip dates, and many other tasks. Some secretaries find using a **tickler file** as a reminder for these tasks helpful.

A tickler file is arranged by dates. Its main purpose is to remind workers of important deadlines. For example, see the file in Figure 10.10. This file contains twelve guides, one for each month of the year. Behind each guide are thirty-one folders representing the days of the month. When a worker wants to be reminded of an important project, deadline, or date, he or she puts a reminder note in the appropriate folder a few days *before* that date. Do you see why the reminder is placed a few days before the due date?

Tickler files may use cards, an accordion pocket file, or a file drawer with file folders. They need not be as elaborate as the system illustrated in Figure 10.10.

A tickler file can also be set up on a computer. You may purchase software that includes a type of tickler file as part of its program, or you may create your own by simply setting up a file for each month. The file can be printed onto hard copy on a monthly basis, or it can be retrieved onto the computer screen when needed.

**FIGURE 10.10 • File Drawer with File Folders Being Used as a Tickler File**

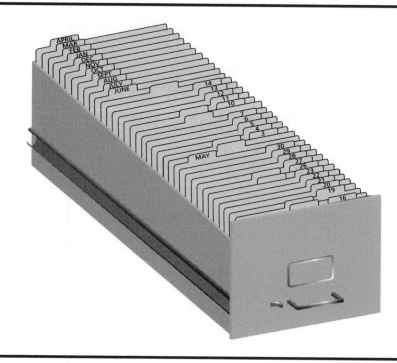

*Answer the following questions:*

**1.** What are the five parts of a business report?

**2.** What four items are usually on a title page?

**3.** What are leaders?

**4.** Are single- or double-spaced business reports preferred?

**5.** What is an itinerary?

**6.** How is an itinerary formatted? Prepare one using the following information:

Amy Nygard, vice president of SaveAll Software, is traveling from Boston to Atlanta and San Francisco. She leaves Boston on United Flight #1127 on May 16 at 8:00 A.M. She arrives in Atlanta at 11:00 A.M. That evening, she stays at the Atlanta Regency Hotel. She leaves on May 17 on United Flight #2217 at 10:00 A.M. and arrives in San Francisco at 1:00 P.M. She stays at the Hotel Union Square that night. She leaves San Francisco on May 18 on United Flight #1130 at 7:30 A.M. and arrives back in Boston at 5:30 P.M.

# Summary

Office workers use certain procedures when keying business documents. Furthermore, they prefer particular forms and styles when formatting business documents.

Just before putting a letter into an envelope, give it one last look and ask yourself the following questions:

- Is the letter keyed too high on the paper?
- Is the letter keyed too low on the paper?
- Are the left and right margins even?
- Is the finished letter "pleasing to the eye"?

After completing a business report, give it one last look and ask yourself the following questions:

- Is a title page included and is it centered?
- Is a table of contents included and is it centered?
- Is the body double-spaced?
- Are the margins set according to the rules for formatting business reports?
- Is an appendix included? If so, is it located directly after the body of the report?
- Is a bibliography included? If so, is it in alphabetic order?

# before you leave...

**When you have completed this chapter, answer the following questions.**

1. What are the major parts of a business letter? How should a letter be keyed onto company letterhead?

2. What are the major parts of a business report? What are the rules used for keying a report?

# Review & Application

## Check Your Knowledge

1. What is the letter address of a business letter?

2. What does the word *attachment* mean when it appears on a letter?

3. Is "4/18/02" acceptable for the date on a business letter?

4. On a business letter, are the keyboard operator's initials in all capital letters?

5. What does "c" mean? Is it always part of a business letter?

6. On a block letter, should you key the date at the left margin and the closing in the center?

7. In a modified block letter, are paragraphs always indented?

8. In mixed punctuation, is a comma allowed in the greeting?

9. If you are keying a letter with a word processing program, what margins do you use?

10. Is using the term *Mr.* acceptable in a memorandum?

11. What are the major parts of a memorandum heading?

12. When keying a memorandum, how many blank lines are left between the subject and the body?

13. Show three heading formats for memorandums.

14. How are templates used in an office?

15. If the word *confidential* is to appear on an envelope, where should it be keyed?

16. What envelope address format does the Postal Service prefer?

17. Does the bibliography appear at the beginning of a business report?

18. In a business report, where do you most often find a table that is supplemental to the report?

19. What person is often contacted when making travel arrangements for a business trip?

20. Does an itinerary usually include the price of an airline ticket?

21. What information is included in a travel itinerary?

22. List the major parts of an agenda for a meeting.

23. What information is included in the minutes of a meeting? Should minutes of meetings be signed?

24. Do all states have use same rules for preparing legal documents for their courts?

25. How many folders are needed for a tickler file? Why?

## Review Your Vocabulary

On a separate piece of paper, supply the missing words by choosing from the new Office Terms listed below.

1. A _____ has all parts of the letter keyed at the left margin.

2. A _____ has the date and closing keyed at the center.

3. In word processing, _____ means to use the margins preset in the program.

4. The main part of a business letter is the _____ of the letter.

5. The word *Sincerely* is used in the _____ of a business letter.

6. The word *Dear* is used in the _____ of a business letter.

7. The word _____ keyed on a business letter means that you are enclosing something with the letter.

8. In a business report, the _____ is a list of the sources used to write the report.

9. In a business report, the _____ contains supplementary information.

10. A _____ contains the words *To, From, Date, Subject.*

11. An _____ is a record of travel plans.

12. Periods used in a table of contents to separate topic names from page numbers are called _____.

13. A _____ is a file arranged by dates.

14. Using _____ in a business letter means to put a colon after the greeting and a comma after the closing.

15. Using _____ in a business letter means to put no punctuation after the greeting or after the closing.

16. What is to take place during a meeting is listed on an _____.

17. What actually takes place at a meeting is recorded in the _____ of the meeting.

18. A _____ is an electronic file that contains the company's standard format for a particular type of correspondence.

| | |
|---|---|
| a. agenda | l. itinerary |
| b. appendix | m. leaders |
| c. attachment notation | n. memorandum |
| d. bibliography | o. minutes |
| e. block letter | p. mixed punctuation |
| f. body | q. modified block letter |
| g. closing | r. open punctuation |
| h. default margins | s. proofreaders' marks |
| i. enclosure | t. template |
| j. greeting | u. tickler file |
| k. letter address | |

## Discuss and Analyze an Office Situation

On Pierre's first day on the job, he is given some letters to key. Pierre wants to impress his employer by not asking questions and just getting the work done. He keys the letters in block letter format because he remembers his teacher in school saying, "All companies use the block format for letters."

At the end of the day, Pierre's supervisor told him that the company does not use block format for letters because of the design of the company letterhead. Pierre is asked to redo the letters.

How could this mistake have been avoided?

## Practice Basic Skills

### Math

Your boss is planning a meeting for all company supervisors that will be held at a local hotel. Refer to the hotel's Conference Price List given below as you answer these questions:

a. How much should you budget for breakfast if you order the following?
2 gallons of coffee
1 gallon of tea
40 whole wheat muffins
3 trays of fresh fruit

b. How much should you budget for the evening meal if you order the following?
25 petits fours
3 dozen Danish cookies
10 mud pies
30 soft drinks

c. You can get 12 slices from the zucchini bread. How much is saved by ordering 4 loaves of zucchini bread instead of 48 whole wheat muffins?

d. A gallon of coffee serves 16 cups. How many gallons would you order to plan for 70 cups?

e. A pitcher of orange juice serves 12 glasses. How many pitchers would you order to plan for 90 glasses?

| Conference Price List | | |
|---|---|---|
| **MORNING COMBINATIONS** | | |
| Item | Quantity | Price |
| Coffee | Gallon | $20.00 |
| Tea | Gallon | 20.00 |
| Orange juice | Pitcher | 16.00 |
| Fresh fruit | Tray | 19.50 |
| Date nut bread | Loaf | 17.50 |
| Zucchini bread | Loaf | 17.50 |
| Whole wheat muffins | Each | 2.25 |
| **EVENING MEAL COMBINATIONS** | | |
| Item | Quantity | Price |
| Fresh fruit | Bowl | $15.00 |
| Petits fours | Each | 1.50 |
| Soft drinks | Each | 1.75 |
| Danish cookies | Dozen | 8.00 |
| Fruit punch | Gallon | 18.00 |
| Mud pies | Each | 1.75 |

### English

*Rule:* Use a comma to separate dependent clauses.

*Examples:* With your help, we will get the task completed by Wednesday. As soon as the machines are repaired, we will return to work.

*Practice Exercise:* Rewrite or key the following sentences, placing commas where needed.

a. For further information call the toll-free number.
b. During the committee meeting a minor earthquake rattled the room.
c. If you need any further help you may call our service representative.
d. In order to get the job done we will need to call a temporary service.
e. As mentioned last week we will need those three reports keyed by 12 noon.

### Proofreading

Correct all errors in the following list, using the proofreaders' marks shown in Table 10.1. Then rekey it, making the corrections.

EARTHQUAKE RECOVERY GUIDELINES

self-help techniques

1. Do not push thoughts and memories of the event away; talking about them is critcial.

2. Do not feeel embarrassed about a repetitious need to talk to people. Try family; friends, co-workers, church and social groups. As what others are doing to cope.

3. Keep your life in balance You can do pracitcal thing to regain a sense of control over your life.

   a. Know what practical things you can do to be prepared for ongoing earthquake strss.

      1. Duck and cover.
      2. Stand under a door way.
      3. Know emergency routes.

4. Sleep in your clothes, put flashlihgts, wallets, shoes, etc., closeby.

5. Follow emergency preparation guidelines in telephone book.

   b. Resume your normal program of activities asquicklyas you can.

   c. Pay careful loving attention to your self—eat nutritional foods, get plenty of rest, drink liquids, and increase other self-nurturing activities.

4. Write about your experiences.

5. Increase physical activity.

6. Practice relaxation, meditation, or prayer activities.

## Apply Your Knowledge

1. Using word processing software, key and print the sample itinerary on page 201 and the agenda on page 203. Use special features of your software—outlines, graphics, fonts, and so on.

2. Using a memo template from your word processing software, key a memo to your instructor in which you describe the parts of a business report.

## Using the Reference Manual

1. Use the addressing envelopes section of the Reference Manual at the back of the book to keyboard envelopes for five of your friends. Be sure to include your return address. (You may make up the addresses if necessary.)

2. Keyboard these envelopes on a sheet of regular 8.5-by-11-inch paper; however, use the size of a business envelope as a guide.

 3. Save as file ch10ref.doc and print a copy.

# chapter  11

# Accounting and Other Financial Activities

## objectives

*After completing this chapter, you will be able to do the following:*

1. Describe the advantages of a computerized accounting system compared with a manual accounting system.
2. List the components of a computerized accounting system.
3. List accounting and other financial activities that are performed by an office worker.
4. Discuss the purpose of a balance sheet.
5. Interpret the accounting equation: Assets = Liabilities + Owner's Equity.
6. Discuss the purpose of an income statement.
7. Interpret the accounting equation: Net Income = Revenue − Expenses.
8. Describe the proper banking procedures to follow in depositing, endorsing, and writing checks.
9. Describe the steps to follow in reconciling a bank statement.
10. Describe how an office petty cash fund is set up and maintained.

### New Office Terms

- accounting cycle
- assets
- balance sheet
- computerized accounting system
- expenses
- file
- income statement

- liabilities
- net income
- owner's equity
- petty cash payments
- reconciliation
- record
- revenues

**Answer the following questions to the best of your ability:**

**1.** What is a computerized accounting system?

**2.** What types of financial activities do office workers perform?

**B**usiness organizations of all types must keep accounting and other financial records. Store sales associates, farmers, factory workers, and owners of businesses must keep records. Regardless of where you work or the position you accept when you graduate, you will probably have to keep some records as part of your job. Why? One reason is that the government requires businesses to keep records so that certain information is reported to the Internal Revenue Service (IRS) on a periodic basis. Another reason is that accurate records are the basis for sound business decisions.

Maintaining accounting records will probably become an important responsibility at some point in your office career. You might be responsible for a range of financial activities, from taking care of the small amounts of cash needed to run an office on a day-to-day basis to helping an accountant prepare the financial statements essential to the success of a business.

The purpose of this chapter is not to teach you accounting procedures, but to describe what types of accounting systems and financial activities you will find in offices today and how related tasks are typically performed.

©David Young-Wolff/PhotoEdit

Using accounting software helps assure that financial records are complete and accurate.

## Technology in the Office | NETWORK FIREWALLS

Many companies have a guarded gate at the entrance of company property that prevents vandals from entering the premises. Firewalls can help keep vandals from logging on to computers in your network. A firewall prevents unauthorized access to your computer when you are on the Internet. It blocks individuals that you (or your company) want to keep out of the computer network, and it permits access to individuals who have approval for access. A firewall performs this blocking function by following rules set up by a company official that specify in advance what types of traffic are to be allowed and what types are to be blocked.

Firewalls provide a "choke point" for security and auditing. This "choke point" can serve as a "phone tap" for tracing those who attempt to get through the firewall. Thus, a firewall can perform the same function for your computer network as the guarded gate does at the company entrance. ■

# Computerized Accounting Systems

Accounting activities may be done by hand and stored on paper. However, most accounting activities are completed with a computer and stored on disk for future updates and revisions. The same financial information is kept in either case. With manual accounting (done by hand), you perform calculations using an electronic calculator. Manual accounting procedures are described later in the chapter.

A **computerized accounting system** is any set of organized procedures used to collect and record accounting data with the use of a computer. Although several accounting software packages are available, Quick-Books by Intuit® and Peachtree® Complete Accounting (PCA) by Peachtree Software, Inc., are among the most popular.

Maintaining accurate business records requires time. Even if the company consists of only one owner-employee, administering all necessary paperwork on schedule is sometimes difficult. Accounting software helps save time and gives a detailed representation of a company's financial picture. A well-designed accounting system produces reliable information that can be used to prepare financial statements for decision making, and it is flexible enough to accommodate additions as the business grows without the need to totally redesign the system.

To some extent, businesses that thrive maintain accurate, up-to-date records in usable form. Competition in business rewards maximum efficiency. Inaccurate accounting records often contribute to business failure and bankruptcy. As business owners and managers strive for economic success, complete, timely, and accurately prepared accounting information is required to make sound decisions and plans.

## The Accounting Cycle

An **accounting cycle** involves recording, classifying, and summarizing financial information for owners, managers, and other interested parties. Completing all stages of the accounting cycle in a consistent, timely, and precise manner is important in all businesses.

The series of procedures in the accounting cycle is repeated for each accounting period. The length of an accounting period depends on the needs

**TIP** When you enter financial information into records, be sure to use the same abbreviations and formats each time. If no established procedures for entering information in a consistent manner are being used, help your organization develop them. ■

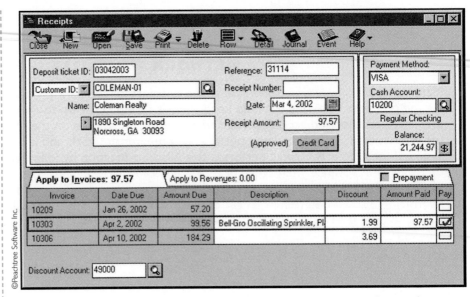

A knowledge of accounting packages, such as Peachtree Accounting for Windows, is useful if your job involves handling financial data.

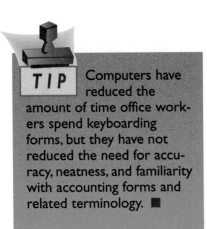

**TIP** Computers have reduced the amount of time office workers spend keyboarding forms, but they have not reduced the need for accuracy, neatness, and familiarity with accounting forms and related terminology. ∎

of a business and how often financial information must be summarized. Typically, a fiscal year consists of twelve monthly accounting cycles, summarized quarterly.

## Computerized and Manual Systems

Computerized accounting systems tend to correspond to manual accounting systems in terms of function and objectives. Both types of systems process transactions, maintain ledger accounts, and produce financial statements and other reports for management to use. When using computers, however, posting is automated. The closing process is often performed by pressing a single key on a computer's keyboard. Furthermore, many computerized systems have built-in controls to examine data validity before transactions are accepted. For example, the system would note a transaction in which debits do not equal credits.

Table 11.1, page 217, is a comparison of the accounting cycle steps in a manual system with the steps of the accounting cycle in a computerized system.

## Advantages of Computerized Accounting Systems

Computerized accounting systems offer many advantages over manual systems, such as speed, error protection, inventory control, and audit trails, as well as automatic posting, report preparation, and document printing.

∎ *Speed.* A computerized system provides information much more quickly than does a manual system. As a result, an individual can handle a large volume of accounting transactions in a fraction of the time required in a manual system. Also, the heavy workload of closing accounts and creating financial statements at the end of each accounting period is greatly reduced because the computer performs these tasks automatically and quickly.

**TABLE 11.1 • Comparison of the Accounting Cycle in Manual and Computerized Systems**

| Accounting Cycle in a Manual Accounting System | Accounting Cycle in a Computerized System |
|---|---|
| 1. Business transactions occur. | 1. Business transactions occur. |
| 2. Any necessary documentation, such as invoices, purchase orders, or checks, is created; the transaction is analyzed and recorded in a journal. | 2. Each transaction is analyzed and entered into a computer, which creates any necessary documents and journalizes the transaction appropriately. |
| 3. Transactions are posted from the journals to the ledgers. | 3. The computer posts transactions from the journals to the ledgers. |
| 4. A trial balance is prepared. | 4. The computer prints a trial balance. |
| 5. Adjusting entries are entered on a worksheet and the worksheet is completed. | 5. Adjusting entries are recorded and the computer journalizes and posts them. (No worksheet is necessary.) |
| 6. Financial statements are prepared and keyed. | 6. The computer generates and prints financial statements requested by the user. |
| 7. Adjusting entries are journalized and posted. | 7. The computer completes the closing process. |
| 8. Closing entries are journalized and posted. | 8. The computer can be used to print a post-closing trial balance or balance sheet. |
| 9. A post-closing trial balance is prepared. | |

■ *Error Protection.* Using a computer decreases the occurrence and posting of careless errors when performing repetitious work such as journalizing transactions. In addition, a good computerized accounting system will have many built-in error-protection features. For instance, in most systems, the computer will not accept any journal entry that does not balance.

■ *Inventory Controls.* For retail businesses, good control over inventory is one of the most vital elements of profitability. Tying up cash by overstocking inventory items can be as disastrous as being understocked on items that sell quickly. Computerized accounting systems generate on-demand, up-to-the-minute reports listing inventory levels and other important information about inventory.

■ *Creation of an Audit Trail.* With a good computerized accounting system, accounting records are well organized with reports documenting each transaction.

■ *Automatic Posting.* In a computerized system, posting is performed automatically by the computer. This feature alone is an enormous time-saver. The repetitive task of posting is extremely time consuming; it is also the source of many errors in a manual accounting system because of mistakes such as double posting, posting to the wrong account or name, or posting the wrong amount. Using a computerized

## Making Office Decisions

Darren Matthew is an office worker at Zero Based Accounting Systems. Because of the professional and competent way in which he completes his work, he is being groomed for a better position. Vi, who also works at Zero Based, is a junior accounting clerk. In a few months, she will be moving to another town, and her position will be open. Darren is hoping to be considered for that position. In fact, he is taking night courses in computerized accounting at the community college and is doing well.

Darren likes Vi and has always admired the efficient and organized way she works. Lately, however, he has noticed that the quality of her work has been lower than before. On two occasions, he has noticed input errors when she entered hourly amounts from time cards into the computerized payroll program. When he tells her about the errors, she seems annoyed with him. Darren does not intend to accuse Vi of knowingly producing inaccurate payroll checks. Nevertheless, he worries about other math errors she might be making of which the company is unaware.

1. **If you were Darren, what would you do about the situation?**

2. **Should Darren just keep a close eye on Vi's work or should he tell his supervisor?**

3. **What other options, if any, does Darren have?** ◼

system ensures that each entry is posted accurately. Because the computer posts immediately, account balances are always up-to-date, which aids in management decisions.

- *Automatic Report Preparation.* A computerized accounting system generates reports automatically. Computerized accounting systems provide printouts of journals and ledgers as well as required financial statements such as balance sheets and income statements. In addition, some computerized systems provide detailed reports about budgets, accounts receivable, accounts payable, and inventory levels.

- *Automatic Document Printing.* In addition to printing reports, a computerized system also provides many of the documents used in day-to-day business operations. With the use of preprinted forms sold in supply stores, the computer can print documents such as monthly statements for accounts receivable customers, checks to pay bills, and payroll checks with year-to-date information on the stubs.

## Components of a Computerized Accounting System

Accounting data are stored in computers by using records and files as shown in Figure 11.1, page 219. A **record**, which is comprised of fields, contains information about one employee, one inventory item, one account, and so forth. A **file**, on the other hand, contains a group of records such as the records for all employees or records for all inventory items.

A great deal of information will need to be entered when a business's accounting records are changed to a computerized system. First, you will need to establish records for each general ledger account; then you can record each customer, each vendor, each employee, and each inventory item. Unless the business is new and has had no transactions yet, you will also need to enter the current balances in each general ledger account, the amount owed by customers and to vendors, inventory amounts on hand, and each employee's payroll history.

FIGURE 11.1 • The Relationship Among a Field, a Record, and a File

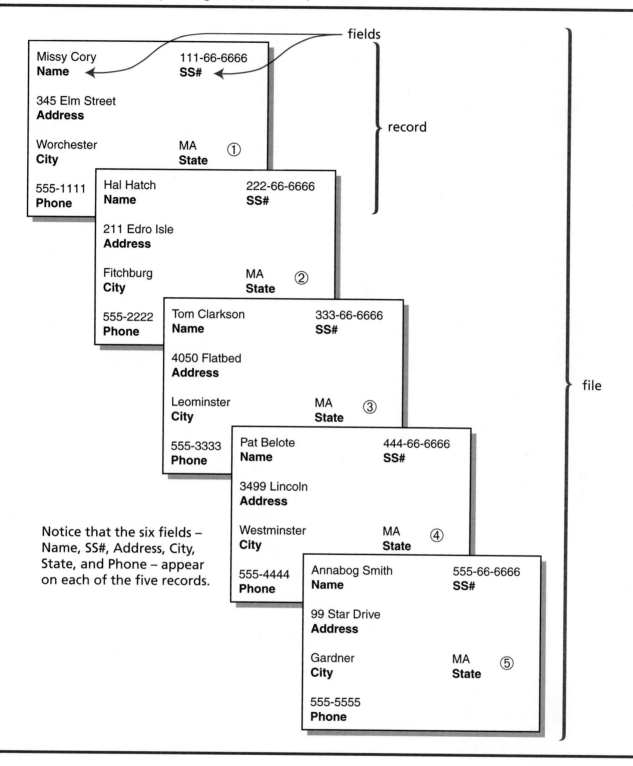

fields

Missy Cory **Name**      111-66-6666 **SS#**

345 Elm Street **Address**

Worchester **City**      MA **State** ①

555-1111 **Phone**

record

Hal Hatch **Name**      222-66-6666 **SS#**

211 Edro Isle **Address**

Fitchburg **City**      MA **State** ②

555-2222 **Phone**

Tom Clarkson **Name**      333-66-6666 **SS#**

4050 Flatbed **Address**

Leominster **City**      MA **State** ③

555-3333 **Phone**

Pat Belote **Name**      444-66-6666 **SS#**

3499 Lincoln **Address**

Westminster **City**      MA **State** ④

555-4444 **Phone**

Annabog Smith **Name**      555-66-6666 **SS#**

99 Star Drive **Address**

Gardner **City**      MA **State** ⑤

555-5555 **Phone**

file

Notice that the six fields –
Name, SS#, Address, City,
State, and Phone – appear
on each of the five records.

Although software programs vary, computerized accounting software packages often include ten or more different modules that work together to protect financial business information and to organize it into an understandable form. Not all the modules have to be installed or used. The most common modules included in computerized accounting software are general ledger, accounts payable, accounts receivable, payroll, inventory, purchase order, job cost, fixed assets, and data query.

### General Ledger

The general ledger (G/L) module is the heart of a computerized accounting software system. The general ledger contains records of current financial transactions that are recorded through journal entries and through the information received from other modules in the system. The general ledger should be activated first. The computer software requires the user to set up the complete chart of accounts because these account numbers are used by the other modules. In other words, normally when another module is activated, you are asked to enter the general ledger account numbers.

The G/L module is the basic module for all computerized accounting systems because it is used to make journal entries, keep track of the company's checkbook, perform end-of-the-financial-period activities, and print journals and financial statements.

### Accounts Payable

The accounts payable (A/P) module keeps track of money owed to vendors by recording purchases and purchase returns. It also helps decide which invoices to pay and then prints the checks. In addition, the A/P tracks year-to-date purchases from each supplier, as well as year-to-date payments that have been made.

### Accounts Receivable

The accounts receivable (A/R) module provides information about money that customers owe. Receipts from customers on account (or those who buy on credit) are entered into the system by using this module.

The A/R module provides detailed information about customers' current balances and then prepares billing statements. Year-to-date sales by customer can be tracked, and sales tax reports can be generated with the accounts receivable program. It will also assess and post finance charges to customers' accounts.

### Payroll

The payroll module keeps a record on each employee, including all payroll information about that employee plus a summary of his or her gross pay and deductions for the entire year. This module not only calculates the payroll, it also prints paychecks and keeps track of the information that must be included on payroll reports required by the government. The payroll module calculates all types of employee wages including hourly, salary, commission, and draw-against-commission.

To make calculations easier, most payroll modules include current tax rates for federal and state taxes, and other payroll deductions. Furthermore, these tax tables are updated regularly by the software manufacturer and are available upon request.

### Inventory

The inventory module is invaluable for keeping track of the products and services sold by the business. It focuses primarily on inventory control and item availability. Computerized inventory tracks item receipts, sales, returns, and any adjustments.

## Large Office/Small Office
*What's Your Preference?*

# Accounting

In a large office, many employees usually share accounting duties. Typically, one department or individual is responsible for one area of the accounting process. For example, one department or individual may be responsible for accounts payable and another for accounts receivable. All work of a department or individual will be merged and made accessible to others within the computerized accounting system.

In a small office, one individual is usually responsible for many areas of the accounting work. Many times, this one person functions as a bookkeeper for the company. Managers in a small office also commonly hire an outside accountant to do the company taxes and other financial reports that are required by law. The bookkeeper will then simply record the day-to-day transactions, accumulating and maintaining the data as needed by company managers and the outside accountant.

*Do you enjoy accounting tasks? If so, should you specialize in this area and work in a large office, or would you prefer to work in a small office where this task is just one part of your total job description?* ■

The numbers of goods on hand are updated, not only by purchase transactions but by sales transactions as well. Putting together purchases and sales permits a business to maintain a perpetual, or continuous, inventory system and to monitor stock levels closely. Following these procedures leads to better inventory control and generally results in companies' experiencing few out-of-stock situations.

## Purchase Order

The purchase order module acts as a bridge between inventory and accounts payable. It allows purchase orders, item receipts, and vendor invoices to be entered.

## Job Cost

The job cost module monitors the cost and profitability of the projects a company performs. Job cost allows estimates of costs to be prepared as well as comparisons of actual expenses to estimated expenses. For example, in a building or construction business, expenses for materials, equipment, labor, and subcontractors can be tracked using this module.

## Fixed Assets

Fixed assets calculates and records tax and accounting data for property, plant, and equipment, including depreciation expenses. It keeps track of the basis and depreciation of assets, investment tax credits (when applicable), and other cost and depreciation information.

## Data Query

The data query module generates custom reports and graphs. This module allows businesses to view, print, and analyze data entered into computerized accounting systems wherever it is needed. Data query supplements the reporting capabilities of each of the other modules.

## Spreadsheets—The Computerized Worksheet

The spreadsheet is, in effect, a computerized worksheet—a series of columns and rows that the user fills with report headings, financial data, and computational formulas. Spreadsheets are used to generate various types of reports in addition to computerized accounting reports such as budgets and depreciation schedules. Spreadsheets are especially helpful in performing "what if" analysis. Popular spreadsheet software used by businesses today includes Excel, Lotus 1-2-3, and Quattro Pro.

Suppose, for example, that a manager is studying an investment opportunity by using a certain set of assumptions in areas such as projected levels of sales, expenses, cash inflows and outflows, and income tax rates. The manager may wish to study the proposal under a different set of conditions. If paper, pencil, and a calculator were the only tools available, revising the computations would take many hours. Using a spreadsheet, however, the essential calculations are automatically refigured with the touch of only a few computer keys. Much of the computational drudgery is therefore removed from the process, allowing more time for analysis and further "what if" scenarios.

In planning future business strategies, companies rely on accurate financial records and reports.

## Recall Time

*Answer the following questions:*

**1.** What are two reasons for maintaining accurate accounting records?

**2.** List five advantages of using a computerized accounting system.

**3.** Why is the general ledger module so important in a computerized accounting system?

# Financial Statements

Changes in financial information are reported for a specific period of time in the form of financial statements. Financial statements permit owners, managers, and accountants to analyze business activities and interpret their effectiveness. Answers to questions such as "How do sales and profits from this year compare with sales and profits from the last two years?" or "What is our cash flow this month?" are provided by analyzing financial statements.

All businesses should prepare financial statements on a regular basis so that they can note any changes or trends immediately. The two most common financial statements used to answer these types of questions are the balance sheet and the income statement.

# Balance Sheet

A **balance sheet** shows the financial condition of a business at a particular time; for example, on December 31, 2002, or June 30, 2003. In reality, the details of a company's financial condition change constantly. Every day, a company pays bills and receives payments. Every day, some inventory is used and must be replaced with new purchases.

Even though the financial picture is in constant motion, every business must take a snapshot of its finances periodically to get some idea of its value or net worth at that particular time. Only an accurate, up-to-date balance sheet can provide this view of a business's finances. The balance sheet shows the assets, liabilities, and owner's equity, or net worth. All balance sheets must satisfy the following accounting equation:

$$\text{Assets} = \text{Liabilities} + \text{Owner's Equity}$$

To understand accounting, you must understand the three basic terms in this equation.

**Assets** are everything of value that a company owns. They can include such items as cash, buildings, and land. As a person, you have assets. Some examples of your personal assets are your clothes, money in your wallet or bank account, and any jewelry that you have purchased or received as gifts.

**Liabilities** are a business's financial obligations or debts. All businesses acquire debts and obligations as they buy goods and services from others. Suppose that you borrow money from a friend and promise to pay it back in a week. This transaction is an example of a liability, or debt, you owe to someone else. Examples of typical business liabilities are mortgages on buildings and charge accounts established with suppliers for materials or services purchased to operate a business.

**Owner's equity** is the claim that an owner has against a firm's assets. To better understand owner's equity, let's look at an example. Suppose that Sharla owns and operates Quick Business Services and wants to sell it. She and her accountant value the assets at $70,000. However, Sharla owes suppliers money; her liabilities amount to $40,000. If Sharla finds a buyer and sells her business for $70,000, she will receive $30,000. This $30,000 represents her owner's equity, because it is the difference between the assets and the liabilities of Quick Business Services.

With reference to this example, remember two things:

- You can use the following variation of the accounting equation to figure owner's equity:

$$\text{Owner's Equity} = \text{Assets} - \text{Liabilities}$$

- In the accounting equation, you must keep the sections before and after the equal sign in balance, or equal at all times. In other words, Sharla's owner's equity is $30,000 because assets of $70,000 minus liabilities of $40,000 equal $30,000.

Let's prepare a balance sheet. Suppose that you and four friends start a business selling baseball caps with your school's name on them. You call your business the Cap Company. On October 1, 2002, the five of you invest a total of $500 into the business. A week later, you enter into an agreement with the Top Cap Manufacturing Company to make the caps for you to your specifications.

In early November, the Top Cap Manufacturing Company sends you an initial shipment of printed caps. A few days later, you receive a bill for $250 payable in thirty days. As a result, your balance sheet as of November 30 contains the following information:

**The Cap Company**
**Balance Sheet**
**November 30, 2002**

Assets
| | | |
|---|---|---|
| Cash | $500.00 | |
| Merchandise | 250.00 | |
| Total Assets | | $750.00 |

Liabilities
| | | |
|---|---|---|
| Top Cap Manufacturing Co. | $250.00 | |
| Owner's Equity | | |
| Paid-in Capital | $500.00 | |
| Total Liabilities and Owner's Equity | | $750.00 |

Business activities, such as buying and selling goods and services, receiving money, and paying bills, cause continual changes in a company's assets, liabilities, and owner's equity accounts. These activities, called *business transactions*, involve the exchange of one item of value for another.

For example, notice that the November 30, 2002, balance sheet shows assets to be greater than the amount of money you and your friends invested. However, the $250 increase is not really all yours. It occurs because you bought $250 worth of caps on credit. This $250 in merchandise is an asset that is "balanced" by the $250 bill from the Top Cap Manufacturing Company.

If you pay for the merchandise the next day, before you sell any hats, you will have $250 less in your cash account and a zero balance in Top Cap Manufacturing Company's account. As a result of this one transaction or exchange, the balance sheet changes considerably in just one day's time, as shown below:

**The Cap Company**
**Balance Sheet**
**December 1, 2002**

Assets
| | | |
|---|---|---|
| Cash | $250.00 | |
| Merchandise | $250.00 | |
| Total Assets | | $500.00 |

Liabilities
| | | |
|---|---|---|
| Top Cap Manufacturing Company | $       0 | |
| Owner's Equity | | |
| Paid-in Capital | $500.00 | |
| Total Liabilities and Owner's Equity | | $500.00 |

Keep in mind that a balance sheet shows the values of certain accounts at a given time. In other words, it shows the status of a company's different accounts. The balance sheet is the source of the term *accounting*.

# Income Statement

An **income statement** is a summary of all income and expenses for a certain time period such as a month or year. It is probably the most frequently studied financial statement. Owners study income statements to determine how much profit they are making. Bankers study income statements to decide whether to approve a business loan.

Unlike a balance sheet, which presents a stationary financial picture, an income statement reflects a business's profitability over a given time period. The accounting formula for income statements is as follows:

$$\text{Net Income} = \text{Revenue} - \text{Expenses}$$

**Revenues,** or income, are all funds an organization raises from the sale of its goods and services. They are generally received in the form of cash payments. Cash, as used in business, may mean currency (bills and coins) or a check drawn on a business or personal checking account.

**Expenses** are the costs a business incurs as it buys the resources it needs to produce and market its goods and services. They are classified as the cost of goods sold (for manufacturing firms) and as operating expenses such as salaries, rent, supplies, and utilities.

**Net income** is the amount of money that remains after expenses are subtracted from revenues. It is commonly called the *bottom line*. If an income statement shows that revenues were greater than expenses, the company made a *net profit*. If expenses were greater than revenues, however, the company suffered a *net loss*.

Businesses detect the reasons for increases or decreases in net income by comparing current and previous income statements. This comparison is helpful in making management decisions about future operations and money management in general.

Suppose that the Cap Company has been in business for one year. Over the past year, it has ordered more caps on three occasions, and sales are continuing to increase at a steady pace.

These transactions are included on the Cap Company's income statement covering the period November 30, 2002, to November 30 of the following year, as shown below.

The Cap Company
Income Statement
For Year Ended November 30, 2002

| | | |
|---|---|---|
| Revenue: | | |
| Sales | | $1,500.00 |
| Expenses: | | |
| Caps Purchased | $450.00 | |
| Advertising Expense | 95.00 | |
| Postage Expense | 37.50 | |
| Miscellaneous Expenses | 96.00 | |
| Less: Total Expenses | | $ 678.50 |
| Net Income | | $ 821.50 |

# Other Financial Activities

As an office worker, you can expect to complete certain types of financial activities. Among those you are likely to perform are banking tasks and petty cash fund maintenance tasks. The tool you will likely use is a ten-key calculator.

## Using a Ten-Key Calculator

Although a computer is used extensively to calculate financial data quickly and accurately, you will find that some workers in business offices still use handheld and desktop ten-key calculators. A ten-key calculator has the capacity to solve numeric problems manually with great speed. Calculators may be either printing or display machines. Printing calculators print numbers onto a paper tape. Display calculators display numbers as illuminated figures on a screen. With a printing-display calculator, users may combine and use both techniques.

When you learn to operate an electronic calculator with the touch system, the technique, speed, and accuracy you develop can easily be transferred to other machines. For example, most personal computer keyboards have a special ten-key section on the right side. If you were a computer data entry clerk at a local bank, you would probably be paid based on the number of keystrokes entered from a ten-key pad.

The basic rule for learning touch operation is to not look at your fingers while depressing the number keys. The ten-key pad is operated with the four fingers of the right hand. The home keys are 4, 5, and 6. These keys are the starting positions for any key from 1 to 9. You make your reaches up or down from the three home keys. Many businesspeople consider being able to touch-operate a ten-key pad as important as being able to keyboard by touch.

Here is a quick lesson on touch operation. Place your fingers onto the home keys, as shown in Figure 11.2, page 227. On most calculators and computers, key 5 has a raised dot or line, which you can easily feel. This elevation makes the starting home row position readily identified by touch.

The finger used to depress home key 4 is used to reach up to key 7 and down to key 1. The second finger is used to depress home key 5 and also to reach up to key 8 and down to key 2. Finally, the finger used to depress home key 6 reaches up to key 9 and down to key 3. On a computer number keypad, the right thumb is used for the zero key.

Your accuracy and speed will naturally improve with practice, if your technique is correct and you keep your eyes on the problem.

If you work with financial records, your ability to operate a ten-key calculator or key pad is as important as your skill with a computer keyboard.

©David Young-Wolff/PhotoEdit

**FIGURE 11.2 • Correct Hand Position at a Calculator**

| Index Finger | Middle Finger | Ring Finger |
|:---:|:---:|:---:|
| 7 | 8 | 9 |
| 4 | 5 | 6 |
| 1 | 2 | 3 |
| 0 | | . |

Thumb

# Banking Tasks

Most businesses put cash receipts into a bank and make cash payments by check. They deposit cash receipts because having money, consisting of bills and coins, readily available in an office is not always a safe choice. Care must be taken in handling money because it can be transferred easily from one person to another with no questions asked. Unfortunately, in most cases, ownership is determined by the person having the money.

For these and other reasons, businesses keep most of their cash-on-hand in a bank and use various banking services. Banking services are safe, convenient, and provide great accuracy in maintaining cash records for businesses. A business depends on banking services to verify accounting records, to compare the business's records of checks written with the bank's records of checks paid, and to transfer cash electronically using *electronic funds transfer* (EFT). With EFT, businesses can make electronic payments and deposits and conduct other banking transactions quickly and in a timely manner with this "paperless" transfer of funds.

Let's review some common banking terms you will encounter while processing banking tasks:

- Placing cash into a bank account is called *making a deposit*.
- A person or business in whose name cash is deposited is called a *depositor*.
- A bank account from which payments are ordered by the depositor is called a *checking account*.

■ A *check* is a business paper used to make payments from a checking account.

■ *Endorsing a check* is signing your name or a company's name on the back of a check in order to transfer the check to a bank or to someone else.

In an office, you may perform three common banking tasks. These tasks are depositing checks that have been properly endorsed, writing checks, and reconciling monthly bank statements.

### Preparing Deposits

To prepare deposits, you follow three steps: (1) endorse all checks to be deposited, (2) fill out the deposit slip, and (3) record the deposit in the check register.

When you deposit a check into a checking account, you must transfer it to your bank by signing your name on the back of the check. This procedure is called *endorsing a check*. You can use three endorsements: blank, restrictive, or full. A *blank endorsement* is a signature-only endorsement. A *restrictive endorsement* restricts the use of the check. Many businesses and individuals write "for deposit only" to ensure that the check amount will only be deposited and not cashed. A *full endorsement* names the party to whom a check is transferred. Figure 11.3, page 229, shows examples of acceptable endorsements.

When you deposit a check, you must list it on a deposit slip along with any bills and coins for deposit, as shown in Figure 11.4, page 230. Be sure to enter the total amount of the deposit in the check register and add it to the old balance to find your new checkbook balance.

**FIGURE 11.3 • (a) Paycheck for Patrick Reynolds (b) Check Endorsements**

a)

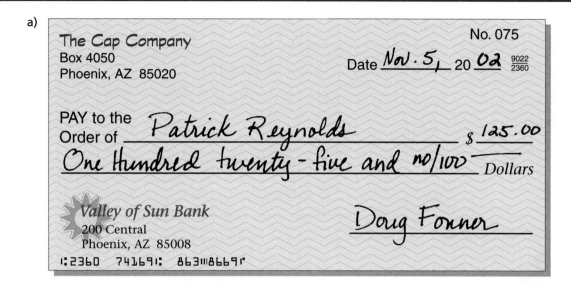

b)

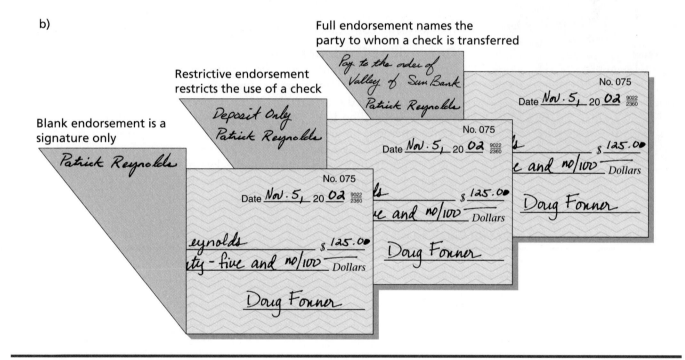

## Writing Checks

Some checks have two parts: the stub or NCR (no carbon required) copy, which remains in the checkbook, and the check itself, which is sent to the person to whom you owe money. The stub or copy provides a record of the important facts about a check. The NCR copy shows all the information; however, if your check has a stub, always fill out the stub first before writing a check so that you will have a clear record of the check. Some checks do not have stubs; you can also keep track of the details of checks you write by using a check register (see Figure 11.5, page 230). A check register contains a listing of each check that was written and each deposit made.

**FIGURE 11.4 • Deposit Slip**

For DEPOSIT to the Account of
Patrick Reynolds
600 E. Oak Drive
Glendale, AZ 85099

Date _Nov. 5,_ 20 _02_

Valley of Sun Bank
200 Central
Phoenix, AZ 85008

⑆2360 741691⑆ 863●5290⑈

9022
2300

|  | Dollars | Coins |
|---|---|---|
| Bills |  |  |
| Coins |  |  |
| Checks: |  |  |
| 9022 | 125.00 |  |
|  |  |  |
|  |  |  |
|  |  |  |
| Total Deposit | 125.00 |  |

**TIP** If you are unable to locate errors while reconciling a bank statement, you may call the bank for assistance. If you find the bank has made an error in entering amounts of money, notify the bank as soon as possible. ■

A business that writes many checks may use a machine known as a check writer or check protector. This machine prints the amount on a check in a way that makes changes to the check amount impossible without being detected. Today businesses are increasingly preparing their checks using computerized systems.

## Reconciling Bank Statements

Even though a computerized accounting package can automatically reconcile a bank statement in only a few minutes, this activity is still one that may be completed manually by office workers from time to time. The purpose of reconciling is to bring your company's checkbook balance and a bank statement balance into agreement.

Usually, a bank sends a monthly statement that summarizes all checking account transactions. It lists all checks processed and paid by the bank, all deposits recorded, and any service fees charged.

**FIGURE 11.5 • (a) Check Register (b) Check Stub**

a)

| Check No. | Date | Check issued to or description of deposit | Amt of check | √ | Amt of deposit | Balance forward 225.00 |  |
|---|---|---|---|---|---|---|---|
| 075 | Nov. 5 | To Patrick Reynolds For paycheck Nov.1-5 | 125.00 |  |  | Check or Deposit | 125.00 |
|  |  |  |  |  |  | Balance | 100.00 |
|  |  | To For |  |  |  | Check or Deposit |  |
|  |  |  |  |  |  | Balance |  |
|  |  | To For |  |  |  | Check or Deposit |  |
|  |  |  |  |  |  | Balance |  |
|  |  | To For |  |  |  | Check or Deposit |  |
|  |  |  |  |  |  | Balance |  |
|  |  | To For |  |  |  | Check or Deposit |  |
|  |  |  |  |  |  | Balance |  |

b)

No. 075                $ 125.00

Date _Nov. 5, 2002_

To _Patrick Reynolds_

For _Paycheck Nov. 1-5_

|  | Dollars | Cents |
|---|---|---|
| Bal Brought Fwd | 225 | 00 |
| Amt Deposited | 0 | 00 |
| Total | 225 | 00 |
| Amt this Check | 125 | 00 |
| Bal Carried Fwd | 100 | 00 |

When you receive a bank statement, compare either your check stubs or your check register entries to the bank's summary. This procedure is called **reconciliation.** Banks usually provide a reconciliation form on the back of the monthly statement. Figure 11.6 shows a sample reconciliation form for the Cap Company. Here are the steps to follow to reconcile a bank statement:

1. Compare the amounts of all deposits shown on the bank statement with the deposit amounts you recorded onto the check stubs or into the check register.

2. Arrange the canceled checks (if they have been returned to you) in numeric order by check number.

3. Compare the amounts of the canceled checks with the amounts entered onto the stubs or into the check register. Make a small check mark on the stub if a canceled check has been returned and the amounts agree. Stubs that are not checked represent checks that were not returned by the bank. These checks are called *outstanding checks.*

4. Prepare the bank reconciliation form (usually on the back of the monthly bank statement). Outstanding checks and any service fees should be deducted from the total and unprocessed deposits added to give a true picture of the amount in the account.

## Petty Cash Fund Maintenance Tasks

Businesses must keep careful records of all money they spend. These records include payments made both by check and with currency. Although businesses prefer to make payments by check, paying with currency is often necessary (and easier). If you buy postage stamps for the office or gas for a company delivery truck, for example, you may have to use currency. Because these payments are in small, or "petty," amounts, they are called **petty cash payments.**

A business normally keeps all its cash in a checking account. Thus, the currency needed for petty cash payments is usually obtained by writing and cashing a check. The amount of the check is an estimate of how much money will be needed for a certain time period such as a week or month. After cashing the check, the office places this currency in a container called a *petty cash box.*

**FIGURE 11.6 • Bank Reconciliation Form**

| The Cap Company Bank Reconciliation Form December 31, 2002 | | | | | | |
|---|---|---|---|---|---|---|
| Checkbook balance | | 525 00 | Bank balance | | | 607 00 |
| | | | Less: o/s checks | | | |
| | | | #129 | | | 525 00 |
| Adjusted chkbk balance | | | Adjusted bank bal | | | 82 00 |

Let's assume that you work for Ms. Larson, and she puts you in charge of the petty cash fund. Ms. Larson starts the petty cash fund by cashing a check for $75. Here are the steps you, as the petty cash clerk, will follow in handling a typical transaction.

Al, your company's delivery person, comes to you and asks for $10 to fix a flat tire on the delivery truck. You first fill out a *petty cash voucher*. This receipt verifies that Al received $10 in cash. When Al returns with a receipt for the tire repair, you staple the petty cash voucher and the tire repair receipt together. At the end of the day, you count the currency, total the petty cash vouchers in the box, and enter the information into the petty cash book. A petty cash book is a record of receipts and disbursements. With Al's transaction, your petty cash balance will look like the following:

| | |
|---|---|
| Total of vouchers in box | $10 |
| Plus cash in box | $65 |
| Equals original fund amount | $75 |

This simple example balances, but sometimes the petty cash fund does not balance. A *cash shortage* occurs when the actual currency in the petty cash box is less than the balance shown in the petty cash book. A *cash overage* occurs when the actual currency in the petty cash box is more than the balance shown in the petty cash book. The goal is to make petty cash balance. If it does not balance, then something is wrong—you have accounted for either too much or too little money. If this situation occurs, you should record any discrepancies in the petty cash book and correct the balances.

When the petty cash fund runs low, you remove all vouchers from the box, add them, and give them to Ms. Larson. She then gives you enough cash to replenish the fund to the regular amount of $75.

## Recall Time

*Answer the following questions:*

**1.** List three common financial activities office workers perform.

**2.** What are the home keys on a ten-key calculator?

**3.** What is the purpose of a petty cash fund?

# Summary

Accounting involves recording, classifying, and summarizing financial information. An office worker assists in the preparation of accounting records. These records ultimately provide the data to prepare financial statements such as balance sheets and income statements. Balance sheets are prepared according to the accounting equation Assets = Liabilities + Owner's Equity. Income statements are concerned with the bottom line, or net profit, which results when total expenses are subtracted from total revenue.

Accounting activities may be performed manually or with a computer. A computerized accounting system is any set of organized procedures used to collect and record accounting data with the use of a computer.

Computerized accounting systems tend to correspond to manual accounting systems in terms of function and objectives. However, with computers, posting is automated, and the closing process is performed very quickly. The major advantages of computerized accounting systems over manual ones are speed, error protection, inventory control, and audit trails, as well as automatic posting, report preparation, and document printing.

Today's office worker will also complete other financial activities. These activities include banking tasks and maintaining a petty cash fund. When you perform office accounting and financial activities, remember the following points:

- The accounting cycle involves recording, classifying, and summarizing financial information.

- Changes in financial information are reported for specific periods of time in the form of financial statements.

- A balance sheet shows the financial condition of a business at a particular time.

- Balance sheets must satisfy the accounting equation:

$$\text{Assets} = \text{Liabilities} + \text{Owner's Equity}$$

- An income statement is a summary of all income and expenses for a certain period of time.

- Income statements must satisfy the accounting equation:

$$\text{Net Income} = \text{Revenue} - \text{Expenses}$$

- Computerized accounting systems may include any or all of the following modules: general ledger, accounts payable, accounts receivable, payroll, inventory, purchase order, job cost, fixed assets, and data query.

- Banking tasks often performed by office workers include preparing deposits, writing checks, and reconciling bank statements.

- A petty cash fund is used to make small payments with currency.

# before you leave...

**When you have completed this chapter, answer the following questions:**

**1.** What is a computerized accounting system?

**2.** What types of financial activities do office workers perform?

# Review & Application

## Check Your Knowledge

1. What advantages does using a computerized accounting system offer over using a manual accounting system?

2. What are records and files in computerized accounting?

3. List the components of a computerized accounting system.

4. What is the purpose of a balance sheet?

5. Describe what *business assets, liabilities,* and *owner's equity* mean in reference to a balance sheet.

6. Why does a business prepare an income statement?

7. Describe what revenue and expense items might be included when preparing an income statement.

8. What financial activities might an office worker use a ten-key calculator to perform?

9. What steps must be followed to deposit and endorse checks properly?

10. Briefly describe the steps involved in reconciling a bank statement.

11. What is the procedure to set up and maintain an office petty cash fund?

## Review Your Vocabulary

On a separate piece of paper, write the letter of each vocabulary word next to the number of its description.

____ 1. The claim an owner has against the firm's assets.

____ 2. Any set of organized procedures used to collect and record accounting data with the use of a computer.

____ 3. Shows the financial condition of a business at a particular time.

____ 4. Involves recording, classifying, and summarizing financial information.

____ 5. A summary of all income and expenses for a certain period of time such as a month or year.

____ 6. The amount of money that remains after expenses are subtracted from revenues.

____ 7. A comparison of either the check stubs or the check register entries to the bank's summary of activity.

____ 8. Cash payments for small amounts made from an office fund.

____ 9. A business's financial obligations or debts.

____ 10. Comprised of fields and stores information about one employee, one inventory item, one account, and so forth.

____ 11. All funds an organization raises from the sale of its goods and services.

____ 12. Everything of value that a company owns.

____ 13. A group of records.

____ 14. Costs a business incurs as it buys the resources it needs to produce and market its goods and services.

a. accounting cycle
b. assets
c. balance sheet
d. owner's equity
e. computerized accounting system
f. expenses
g. file
h. income statement
i. liabilities
j. net income
k. petty cash payments
l. reconciliation
m. record
n. revenues

## Discuss and Analyze an Office Situation

Cecilia is a new secretary in the accounting department at Federated Foods. This job is her third one this year. She is sure this company is a nice place to work because the people here seem to like her.

Cecilia uses a PC to do word processing tasks for the first two weeks on the job. She is looking forward to entering accounting transactions using the general ledger accounting software.

Mr. Ziede is manager of the accounting department. He is concerned because almost one-fourth of the correspondence Cecilia has completed so far has been returned because of spelling or general keyboarding errors. What is most perplexing to Mr.

Ziede is that Cecilia does not see any problems with her skills. She does not seem to care. Cecilia's normal response is that mistakes are easy to fix with a computer, and if she doesn't see an error, someone else will point it out to her.

Mr. Ziede is sure that he will not permit Cecilia to enter accounting data into the computer. However, the immediate problem is whether he should keep her on the job. Cecilia is a nice person, but she is unobservant and fails to recognize errors or problems. Mr. Ziede knows that this attitude cannot be allowed in the accounting department.

1. If you were Mr. Ziede, what actions would you take?

2. If Mr. Ziede decides to counsel Cecilia, what should he say?

## Practice Basic Skills

### Math

1. Complete the bank reconciliation form below on a separate piece of paper. (Follow the instructions on page 231 and refer to Figure 11.6.)

Cookies by Blanche
Bank Reconciliation Form
May 31, 2002

| | |
|---|---|
| Checkbook balance | $592.25 |
| Less: service charge | 5.60 |
| Adjusted checkbook balance | ? |
| Bank balance | $674.25 |
| Add: outstanding deposits | 105.00 |
| Less: outstanding checks | |
| #152 | $ 90.00 |
| #155 | $102.60 |
| Total outstanding checks | ? |
| Adjusted bank balance | ? |

2. Practice the touch method by adding the following columns of figures using a calculator. A good way to check each answer is to add the numbers again in the opposite direction. Write your answers on a separate piece of paper.

| (1) 45 | (2) 55 | (3) 656 | (4) 333 | (5) 444 | (6) 7878 |
|---|---|---|---|---|---|
| 33 | 66 | 333 | 222 | 234 | 5896 |
| 65 | 35 | 456 | 654 | 699 | 4485 |
| 58 | 47 | 699 | 411 | 544 | 8644 |

### English

Abbreviations are often used on purchase orders to save space. Write the meanings of the following abbreviations next to their letters on a separate piece of paper. Refer to an office reference book if you are not sure of a meaning.

(a) c/o
(b) COD
(c) dept
(d) doz
(e) gal
(f) pkg
(g) ea
(h) @
(i) min
(j) max
(k) qty

### Proofreading

Find and correct misspellings and incorrect punctuation in the following letter. Rewrite or key it on a separate piece of paper.

David James
15208 N. 25th Place
Monterey, CA 94039

Dear Mr. James;
I appreciate the information you sent and that I recieved yesterday. In replay to your inquery about activitey tickets, you may contact the following people and they may be able to halp you;; Brooke, Kristy & Daniel.
If I can be of furrther service to you, please call me.

Sincerly yours

Melissa Christine

## Apply Your Knowledge

1. Below are examples of balance sheet items. On a separate piece of paper, write next to the letter of each example the letter *A* if it is an asset account and the letter *L* if it is a liability account.

(a) office supplies

(b) cash

(c) notes payable (City Bank)

(d) accounts payable (Smith's Furniture)

(e) merchandise

(f) office equipment

(g) accounts receivable (May Johnson)

(h) accounts receivable (Della L. Fry)

(i) accounts payable (Republic Supply Company)

(j) FICA tax payable

2. Below are examples of income statement items. On a separate piece of paper, write next to the letter of each example the letter *R* if it is a revenue account and the letter *E* if it is an expense account.

(a) advertising expense

(b) vending machine funds collected

(c) sales of office supplies

(d) salary expense

(e) insurance expense

(f) sale of caps

(g) postage expense

(h) miscellaneous expense

(i) selling expenses

(j) attorney fees collected

## Using the Reference Manual

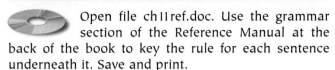 Open file ch11ref.doc. Use the grammar section of the Reference Manual at the back of the book to key the rule for each sentence underneath it. Save and print.

1. Three 3.5″ disks are left over.

2. Pick me up by 7:30 A.M. so that I won't be late.

3. The project took a total of fifteen hours from start to finish.

4. Nine persons were present for the committee meeting on school spirit.

5. Hundreds of spectators will be at the parade.

6. My sister lives on Ninth Street, but my brother lives on 83rd Avenue.

7. Do you see the glass as one-half full or one-half empty?

8. The room measured 16 feet by 24 feet.

9. The deficit is in the billions.

10. The class must have three more students to make full enrollment.

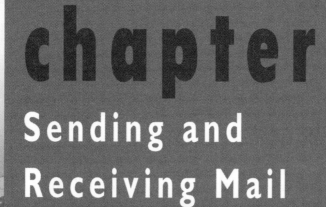

# chapter

## Sending and Receiving Mail

## objectives

***After completing this chapter, you will be able to do the following:***

1. List the procedures used for processing incoming mail in an office.
2. Describe how to arrange mail before presenting it to an employer.
3. List the major classifications of outgoing mail.
4. List other options that office workers may use in addition to the major classifications of mail.
5. List and describe postal equipment used in an office.
6. Discuss how to prepare and pack packages for mailing.
7. Use a ZIP Code directory to locate ZIP Codes.
8. Discuss unauthorized use of postage and supplies.

### New Office Terms

- annotating mail
- bar code sorter (BCS)
- centralized mail department
- confidential mail

- priority mail
- routing mail
- sorting mail

# before you begin...

**Answer the following questions to the best of your ability:**

1. What are at least three classifications of mailing? Explain why each one may be used.

2. In what order should an address be keyed on an envelope? Create a sample.

At 9 A.M. in a city on the East Coast, Vivian starts her day by sorting the mail in the mail services department of a large corporation. At the same time in a town in the South, Maynard begins to sort the mail for his three bosses in the accounting department of a small firm. Vivian is a mail clerk, and Maynard is an administrative assistant. Both know the procedures for processing mail. When you begin to work in a business office, you also must know the procedures for processing incoming and outgoing mail.

In a large company, mail may be processed in a **centralized mail department**. Employees in this department are responsible for all mail that comes into or goes out of the company. At various times during the day, they distribute incoming mail to all company personnel and pick up mail to be sent out. They also distribute interoffice correspondence (mail sent to and from offices within the company).

A small company may not have a centralized mail department. In this case, an office employee receives the mail that is delivered each day by a postal carrier. Once the mail is received, certain procedures are followed for processing it.

## Incoming Mail

The procedures for processing incoming mail include the following:

- sorting the mail
- opening the mail
- date and time stamping the mail
- reading and annotating the mail, if your boss prefers
- performing other helpful procedures
- arranging the mail for your boss

### Sorting the Mail

In office terms, **sorting mail** means arranging or separating mail by type and by receiver names or departments, for example, separating letters from magazines and separating the manager's mail from the supervisor's mail.

Before you begin the process of sorting the mail, clear a work area on your desk. You do not want the mail to be lost or mixed up with other papers. Push all clutter aside and concentrate on this one project.

You may handle the mail for more than one boss or for more than one department. If so, first sort the mail for each person or for each department. Using individually marked folders or trays makes sorting by names or departments easier. Sort the mail within the individual trays by grouping it into piles of correspondence, advertisements and circulars (papers intended for wide distribution), and magazines and newspapers.

## Technology in the Office | HTML (HYPERTEXT MARKUP LANGUAGE)

HTML is the hypertext markup language used on the World Wide Web. It is one of the languages used when creating a Web site. HTML is actually a collection of styles, indicated by markup tags enclosed in brackets that define various parts of a World Wide Web document. HTML was created by Tim Berners-Lee of England while he worked at CERN, the European Laboratory for Particle Physics in Geneva.

HTML documents are plain-text documents (without formatting) and may be written using word processing applications (such as Microsoft Word), if you save the document as "text only with line breaks." HTML documents require four tags for identification:

(1) <HTML> (to tell the browser that the file contains HTML-coded information)
(2) <HEAD> (to indicate that the next element will be the title)
(3) <TITLE> (containing the document title and identifying its content)
(4) <BODY> (containing the actual text, made up of paragraphs, lists, photographs, tables, and other elements)

If you are interested in learning more about HTML and how to create a Web site, a local computer store or bookstore will have a number of books covering the subject. ■

As you are sorting, you may notice mail that has been delivered to your company in error. First, check with your boss to see whether the mail belongs to anyone within the company. If not, cross out the incorrect address, write "Not at this address" on the envelope, and put it into outgoing mail. Only first-class mail will be forwarded without adding extra postage. *First-class mail* is mail that will generally be delivered overnight to locally designated cities and in two days to locally designated states. These areas are selected by the post office.

©Billy Hustacel/Stone

A busy mailroom in a large company demands efficiency and good communication between workers.

# Opening the Mail

Many office workers are asked to open the mail for their bosses. Opening the mail, however, does not necessarily mean they are to read the mail. At some companies, an office worker uses a letter opener to open the mail and then places the mail onto the boss's desk. At other companies, an office worker is required to remove the contents from envelopes. Office workers should always check company policy for the proper procedure.

Before beginning to open the mail, separate all letters that have CONFIDENTIAL or PERSONAL keyed onto them. These letters are **confidential mail** and should be opened only by the person to whom they are addressed. Assume that a letter written in longhand is personal and should be opened only by the person to whom it is addressed. If you open a personal letter in error, be certain to write on the envelope, "Sorry, opened by mistake." Sign your name or initials and tape the letter closed.

Have all necessary supplies ready before opening the mail. You will need a letter opener, a stapler, a pencil, and some paper clips.

Once you have opened the mail, your boss may want you to remove the contents from the envelopes. If so, do the following:

- If the address of the sender is not on a letter, staple or paper clip the envelope to the letter.
- Check the bottom of each letter for the words *enclosure* or *attached*. If you see one of these words, check to see that the material is included. If not, make a pencil notation on the letter that the enclosures were not in the envelope when it was opened.
- Use a paper clip to attach enclosed material to the back of the letters.
- Put all envelopes aside until you have finished sorting the mail. You may have to check for overlooked contents or record new addresses.
- If a letter is undated, write the postmarked date from the envelope onto the letter.

# Date and Time Stamping the Mail

Have you ever received an announcement of an event after it had taken place? Mail may have been delivered late because the letter was temporarily lost during transit, or the announcement may have sat unopened in your house for a few days.

Mail is sometimes received late in a business office. For this reason, companies ask the person who processes the mail to put a date and time on the letters to show when they were received. A rubber stamp is usually used, but the date and time may also be written on a letter with a pen.

Why are companies concerned with the exact date that mail is received? One reason is to verify that a payment is late or that a person has not met a payment deadline. A time difference may exist between the date a letter was received and the date the letter was keyed.

Another reason for knowing when mail arrived is to verify that a person has met the application deadline for a job. Many civil service jobs have deadlines by which applications must be received. If a person does not meet the deadline, she or he will not be considered for the job.

A mailroom in a large company might use mail slots where mail for each department or person is inserted.

©Kwame Zikomo/SuperStock International

# Reading and Annotating the Mail

Chiara Briganti is a busy executive for a management consulting firm. To save time, her administrative assistant reads and annotates the mail each day. **Annotating mail** means underlining important facts and making comments or special notations in the margin of a letter. Examples of facts to underline are model numbers, prices, and meeting dates. An example of a notation you may write in the margin is that you verified that your boss has no other meetings on the date in question.

See Figure 12.1 for a sample of an annotated letter. Note how Ms. Briganti's administrative assistant underlined the date, time, and place of the luncheon meeting. She also made a notation in the margin that no conflicting appointments were scheduled on this date. Can you see how valuable this process could be for a busy executive?

**FIGURE 12.1 • Annotated Letter**

## Stonehill Chamber of Commerce

345 Alpine Terrace
Stonehill, NH  03062-6211
Telephone: (333) 555-1346     Fax: (333) 555-1347     Web site: www.stonehillcofc.org

May 15, 2002

Ms. Chiara Briganti
HiTech Associates
45 Tower Place
Stonehill, NH  03062-3252

*Date O.K.
no conflict*

Dear Ms. Briganti:

Congratulations! You have been selected to receive our annual Woman of the Year Award for your dedication to the business community. All our members agree that you deserve this award.

The award will be presented to you at our annual luncheon awards meeting <u>Tuesday, June 25, 12 Noon at the Pines Conference Center</u>. Please confirm that you will attend by contacting Rose Perez by June 19, 2002.

Sincerely,

*Rosylin Thomas*

Rosylin Thomas
Awards Committee

cb

## Large Office/Small Office

*What's Your Preference?*

### Mail

If you did a survey in your area, you would find that some large offices have their own mailrooms where all mail processing takes place. You would also find that the duties of the mailroom employees include only the processing of incoming and outgoing mail and the distribution of interoffice mail. Because many pieces of mail must be handled daily in these large offices, you would find automatic letter openers and sorting equipment in addition to the standard postage meters and scales.

A survey of small offices would give you a slightly different view of the role of office workers in the handling of mail. In a small office, mail processing is done by a variety of office support staff who handle the mail in addition to their other duties. Your survey would show the receptionist, office support worker, secretary, and other office employees processing the mail for themselves and for their bosses. It would also show that the postal equipment in a small office is usually limited to a postage meter and scale.

**Would you like to begin your office career as a mailroom clerk for a large company? Why or why not? Do you like the idea of having someone else handle your mail for you, or would you prefer making occasional trips to the mailroom to process your own mail?** ■

## Recall Time

*Answer the following questions:*

1. What are three duties of employees in a centralized mail department?

2. What are the procedures for processing incoming mail?

3. Alexandra is an office support person for a small firm. One of her duties is opening her bosses' mail. She opens a letter that is marked CONFIDENTIAL. What should she do?

4. If you were sorting the mail into piles, what three groupings might you use?

5. You open a business letter for your boss. The letter does not have a return address on it. What should you do?

# Other Helpful Procedures

Office workers use many other procedures to help their bosses process the daily mail. Some examples include attaching related materials, using action-requested slips, saving advertisements and circulars, keeping an outgoing mail record, routing mail, and accepting special mail.

## Attaching Related Material

Frequently, before your boss can respond to or take action on a particular piece of correspondence, he or she will need to see other documents. In these cases, you will be helping your boss a great deal if you attach any related material to the letters. You may attach previous correspondence or the file folder that correlates with a letter.

For example, Ken is an insurance clerk for an automobile insurance company. A client writes to his boss concerning an accident. After opening the letter and before giving it to his boss, Ken will attach the client's file folder to the letter.

## Using Action-Requested Slips

If you process and forward a large amount of mail for your boss, using action-requested slips may be helpful. You may either purchase these slips from a stationery store or create them yourself. A sample is shown in Figure 12.2. You simply check the action you wish to be taken.

## Saving Advertisements and Circulars

Saving some of that so-called junk mail is a good way for you and your boss to notice trends in new products. These circulars may be particularly helpful to the advertising department, which is always looking for new ideas and also wants to see what the competition has to offer.

**Ethics on the Job**

Tomeko works as a "floater" in a large law firm. Because of her excellent computer skills, she works in various departments when needed. One day while working in the law library, she deleted a file from the company database by mistake. Because she only occasionally works in this department, no one will know she deleted the file.

*If you were Tomeko, would you tell your supervisor that you made an error and deleted the file? Why or why not?* ■

**FIGURE 12.2 • Action-Requested Slip**

| |
|---|
| ☐ For your approval |
| ☐ For your comments |
| ☐ Please forward |
| ☐ Please return |
| ☐ Note and file |
| ☐ _____ |

If you or your company is concerned about helping to save the environment, you may also put this junk mail into a special box. When the box is full, you can deposit it at a recycling center. You may recycle other items in addition to advertisements. Call your local recycling center for more information.

## Keeping an Outgoing Mail Record

Many companies have found that keeping a daily record of all mail they send out that requires another person outside the company to take action is very helpful. The office support staff can refer to this record on a regular basis and perform any necessary follow-up when action is supposed to occur.

Figure 12.3 shows a sample of an outgoing mail register. In the Description column, you will record the name of the company to which each letter is going, the subject of the letter, and the actual date of the letter. Write the date of the entry (usually the date mailed) into the Date column.

## Routing Mail

Sometimes certain magazines, reports, and special documents need to be seen by more than one person in a company. The most efficient way to handle this situation is by routing the mail. **Routing mail** means attaching a routing slip to correspondence, magazines, reports, and so forth. Each person initials the routing slip after she or he has read the correspondence or other material.

A routing slip is usually a preprinted form commonly used by businesses. See the sample in Figure 12.4 on page 245.

## Accepting Special Mail

Mail is sometimes delivered by express mail, by a messenger, or by a private delivery service. If the mail is delivered to you and your job is to sign the required receipt for it, you should be certain the addressee (person to whom the mail is addressed) works for your company, sign the required mail receipt, and bring the mail immediately to the addressee. This type of mail delivery denotes important information.

**FIGURE 12.3 • Mail Register**

| MAIL REGISTER | | | | |
|---|---|---|---|---|
| DATE | DESCRIPTION | TO WHOM | ACTION TO TAKE | FOLLOW UP |
| 6/25 | Perry Walker Brothers | Perry Walker | Confirm | |
| | | | | |
| | | | | |
| | | | | |
| | | | | |

*Part Three: Office Support Skills*

**FIGURE 12.4 • Routing Slip**

**ROUTING SLIP**

(initial after reading)

Foster, J.          _____

Morales, E.       _____

Prentice, B.       _____

Shapiro, W.       _____

Bala, M. (last)     _____

## Arranging the Mail for Your Boss

Before putting mail on your boss's desk, arrange it according to importance. Check your boss's preference; the following arrangement is acceptable for most executives. The first item listed is on the top of the stack; the last item listed is on the bottom of the stack.

- confidential and personal letters
- correspondence from outside the company
- interoffice correspondence
- advertisements
- newspapers and magazines

The mail is usually placed into the boss's in-basket, and any parcels are put into a separate pile on the desk.

# Outgoing Mail

Office workers use many procedures for processing outgoing mail. A few examples are assembling the mail, selecting classifications for the mail, using the U.S. Postal Service, using private delivery services, using postal equipment, following mailing guidelines, and packing for mailing.

## Ethics on the Job

Leelah's working hours are from 9 A.M. to 5 P.M. She arrives exactly at 9 A.M. each morning and at 4:45 begins closing down her workstation. At exactly 5 P.M., she leaves the office.

*Do you think this behavior is the work ethic expected of employees? Why or why not?* ■

# Assembling the Mail

No letter should be mailed from a business without the proper signature. One of your responsibilities might be to prepare outgoing mail for your boss. Because getting the boss's signature on letters is one of the last steps of the process, you should have the envelopes ready when you present them to him or her. Place the flaps of the envelopes over the front of the letters and attach a paper clip over the flap of each.

Most employers want their mail to go out as quickly as possible, so place any letter needing a signature on your boss's desk in an area where it will easily be seen. Check back on a regular basis to see if the letter has been signed so that you can proceed with the next step.

Once a letter has been signed, bring it back to your desk and prepare it for mailing. However, before you proceed, double-check the following:

- Has the letter been signed?
- Are enclosures included with the letter?
- Is the address on the letter the same as the address on the envelope?
- Make one last check—did you miss any errors or did your boss make any further changes?

Once all this information has been confirmed, fold the letter and insert it into the envelope. Figure 12.5 shows how to fold full-size letterhead (8.5-by-11-inches) into a business envelope.

**FIGURE 12.5 • Steps for Folding and Inserting Outgoing Mail**

**Step: 1**
Lay the letter flat

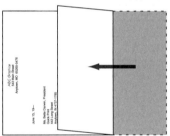

**Step: 2**
Fold one-third of the sheet, from the bottom up

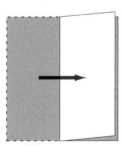

**Step: 3**
Fold the top down to within one-half inch of the fold

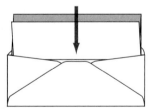

**Step: 4**
Insert the letter into the envelope, with the folded end in first

If enclosures are to be sent with a letter, do the following: If the enclosures are the same size as the letter, fold and insert them with the letter itself. If they are smaller than the letter, staple them behind the letter at the top left of the letter. If they are bigger than the letter, mail them in a large manila envelope with the letter unfolded and inserted as the first page on top of the enclosures.

## Selecting Classifications for the Mail

Melanie has just been employed as a mail clerk for a large law firm. She is quite confused about which classification to use for outgoing mail. Her supervisor explains that the final decision is based upon which way is most efficient. She should make this decision for each particular piece of mail by asking, Should this item be delivered to the destination as quickly as possible, or can money be saved by using a slower, but less expensive, means of delivery? Melanie's supervisor also tells her that she can better understand mailing classifications by reading the U.S. Postal Service's *Consumer's Guide to Postal Services and Products*. In this guide, an office worker may find information on the various classifications of mail: First-Class Mail, Priority Mail, Periodicals, Standard Mail, Package Services Mail, and Express Mail.

### First-Class Mail

Use first-class mail for letters, postcards, and postal cards. First-class mail must weigh 13 ounces or less. If first-class mail is not letter size, make sure it is marked "First Class."

First-class mail will generally be delivered overnight to locally designated cities and in two days to locally designated states. Delivery by the third day can be expected for the remaining outlying areas.

### Priority

**Priority mail** is first-class letter mail and packages weighing more than thirteen ounces. The maximum weight for priority mail is seventy pounds. Free priority mail stickers are available from a local post office.

### Periodicals

Only publishers and registered news agents who have been approved for periodicals mailing privileges may mail at the periodicals postage rates. This classification allows them to send large mailings at a reduced rate.

### Standard Mail

This classification is also referred to as *bulk business mail* or *advertising mail*. It may be sent by anyone, but large mailers use it most often. Non-profit agencies, such as chambers of commerce or religious groups, may also use standard mail. This mail class includes printed material and merchandise weighing less than 16 ounces and requires a minimum of 200 pieces per mailing.

### Package Services Mail

Package services mail is also called *parcel post*. Use this service for packages weighing 1 pound or more. This service may take up to nine days for coast-to-coast delivery, depending upon the availability of transportation.

### Express Mail

Express mail is the fastest mail service. It is also the most expensive one. Express mail guarantees delivery the next day or, in some cases, the same day. Same-day service (when available) is possible only from a large airport mail facility to another large airport mail facility such as LAX (Los

Angeles) to JFK (New York). To send an item by express mail, take it to a post office before the local cutoff time. This time varies by locality, so check with your local post office to find out the cutoff time. You can also drop an express mail item into an express mail collection box. The item will be delivered by noon or by 3 P.M. the next day or the second day—depending on the destination.

## Recall Time

*Answer the following questions:*

**1.** How soon is first-class mail delivered?

**2.** What is another name for standard mail?

**3.** What is package services mail?

**4.** What is the name for the fastest mail service? Explain how it works.

**5.** How do you fold a piece of letter-size paper to be inserted into an envelope?

## Using the U.S. Postal Service

In the *Consumer's Guide to Postal Services and Products,* Melanie reads about other options available through the Postal Service. These options include certificates of mailing, certified mail, collect on delivery, return receipts, delivery confirmation, signature confirmation, insurance, registered mail, international mail, and other services.

### Certificates of Mailing
A certificate of mailing proves that an item was mailed. It does not provide insurance coverage for loss or damage.

### Certified Mail
Certified mail provides a mailing receipt, and a record of delivery is maintained at the recipient's post office. For an additional fee, the sender may also buy a return receipt to provide proof of delivery. Certified mail may be applied only to first-class or priority mail.

### Collect on Delivery
Use collect-on-delivery (COD) service if you are sending merchandise and you want to collect the money owed for its purchase when it is delivered.

### Return Receipts
A return receipt is a sender's proof of delivery. It shows who signed for an item and the date of delivery.

### Delivery Confirmation
Delivery confirmation is available for priority and package services mail. The sender may call an 800 number or go to the U.S. Postal Service Web site (www.usps.com) to find out when an item was delivered.

### Signature Confirmation
Signature confirmation is available for priority and package services mail. The sender may call an 800 number or go to the Postal Service Web site (www.usps.com) to find out when the item was delivered *and* who signed for it.

## Making Office Decisions

Mike is working as an administrative assistant to the vice president of the legal department of a large corporation. In his department are five other workers—an office services assistant, a researcher, and three general office clerks. Mike's status as an administrative assistant is much higher than the status of the other office workers. He has more responsibility and is paid more.

Late Thursday afternoon, Mike has his usual work to finish. He has no urgent work, but he has enough to keep him busy.

A general office clerk is stuffing and sealing envelopes for a large mailing that must be in tonight's mail. The clerk is complaining that the mail may not be finished in time.

*Should Mike help with the envelopes, or should he continue with his own work? Explain your answer.* ■

## Insurance

Insurance may be purchased on registered mail up to a maximum replacement value of $25,000. It is also available up to $5,000 on first-class, priority, and standard mail.

## Registered Mail

Registered mail is the most secure option offered by the Postal Service. It provides added protection for valuable and important mail. Registered articles are controlled from the point of mailing to delivery. First-class or priority mail postage is required on registered mail.

## International Mail

Airmail and surface mail may be sent to virtually all foreign countries. Four, and in some cases five, types of international mail are provided: letter post (for letters, cards, and small parcels under 4 pounds), parcel post, express, and global priority mail. International mail from major metropolitan areas may be sent global express guaranteed. Limited registry service and insurance are available. Information on international mail regulations may be found in the *International Mail Manual* sold by the U.S. Government Printing Office.

## Intelpost

Intelpost (International Electronic Post) is an international facsimile message service available between the United States and more than forty foreign countries. A black-and-white image of a document (text and/or graphics) is printed and delivered in the destination country. The document to be sent may be hand-delivered to the Postal Service or sent by fax or computer. Depending on your choice of delivery option, your facsimile message is delivered either the same day or the next day.

## Easy Stamp Services

The Postal Service has made buying stamps more convenient with EASY STAMP services. Businesses may choose from the following options to purchase stamps: by mail, by telephone, from vending machines, and by computer. Prepackaged stamps are also now sold at the checkout line of many stores, such as pharmacies, grocery stores, gift and card shops, and independent mailing services.

## Other Services

Other services available through the U.S. Postal Service include passport applications, money orders, and postage meters.

## Customer Service

If you have questions that are not answered in the *Consumer's Guide to Postal Services and Products,* you may call the customer service line at the National Postal Center, 1-800-275-8777. With this number you can get ZIP Codes, rates, hours of local post offices, and tracking and ordering information. Certain questions may be answered through their automated telephone system, and customer service representatives handle other questions.

## Information on the Internet

A wealth of information is available at your fingertips when you visit the U.S. Postal Service Web site on the Internet at http://www.usps.com. You may look up ZIP+4 Codes, get information on the latest postal rates, and find answers to frequently asked questions.

# Using Delivery Services

Many office workers have found that using a private delivery service is sometimes more convenient or cost effective. These companies deliver parcels by truck within a city or by airplane to other cities or countries. Firms that specialize in delivery services usually offer the convenience of pickup and delivery. You may locate these firms by looking in the Yellow Pages of your telephone book. Examples of companies that you might find are United Parcel Service® (UPS), FedEx®, Airborne Express®, and DHL Worldwide Express®. The Postal Service has a contract with FedEx to use their planes to transport priority and express mail.

In large cities, private messenger services are used even for short distances—a few buildings or a few blocks. These delivery services often use bicycle messengers. Messenger service is expensive, but the fast delivery is worth the cost to the company. These messenger services can also be found in the Yellow Pages.

A secretary or administrative assistant will keep a file of frequently used private delivery services. The file should be updated regularly. Telephone numbers for those delivery services most frequently used may be coded into a company's system for speed dialing (see Chapter 8 in this text).

Companies that use delivery services usually open a charge account with frequently used services. With a charge account, you only need to telephone the service and request a pickup. The delivery service will ask you for your account number and will bill your company at a later date. You save time by not having to repeat company information whenever you call and by making payments less frequently, which saves on check writing and processing.

Another reason a business may want to use a delivery service is to use the specialized software available from the delivery service. Some delivery services offer free software that allows workers in a business to use its computer to prepare shipments, create labels, maintain an address book of customers, print receipts, track packages, and keep an accurate history of all shipments. The Internet can be used to track packages through the Web sites of some delivery service companies.

Businesses frequently use private delivery services to deliver packages and other mail across the country. Pickup and delivery are part of the service provided.

## Recall Time

*Answer the following questions:*

1. What is the maximum amount of insurance available on registered mail?

**2.** What is the maximum amount of insurance available on standard mail and package services mail?

**3.** Are the following statements true or false?

    **a.** Passports are available through the U.S. Postal Service.

    **b.** The U.S. Postal Service has a contract with Federal Express to use their planes to transport priority and express mail.

    **c.** Money orders may be purchased at a local post office.

## Using Postal Equipment

Special postal equipment used by office workers helps to process mail efficiently. Mailing equipment includes scales, meters, and other items.

### Scale and Meter

Whether you work for a large or small company, you will find that a postage scale and a postage meter are the basic pieces of equipment needed to process outgoing mail. A scale may be purchased at any office supply store. The postage meter must be obtained from a manufacturer that has a product approved by the U.S. Postal Service. The scale and meter may be combined into one piece of equipment.

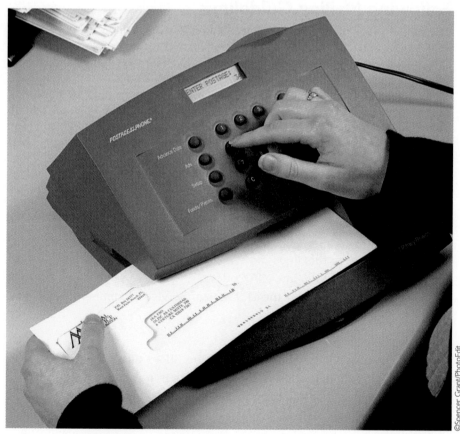

A postage meter and scale are used to process mail, usually at the same time every day so that mail reaches the post office before a business closes for the day.

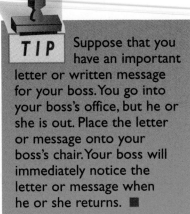

**TIP**  Suppose that you have an important letter or written message for your boss. You go into your boss's office, but he or she is out. Place the letter or message onto your boss's chair. Your boss will immediately notice the letter or message when he or she returns. ∎

A postage scale shows the weight of an item to be mailed. An electronic postage scale will also show the postage required. However, to get this amount, you must first key in information such as the ZIP Code and the class of mail.

A postage meter imprints the amount of postage as well as the cancellation mark for the U.S. Postal Service. This information prints either directly onto standard-size business envelopes, or onto a strip of paper that comes out of the meter and is sealed into place on the envelope. You pay the post office in advance for large sums of postage. Some older meters may need to be taken to a post office to be reset for new postage; however, this type of meter is being phased out. Most postage meters are now set over a telephone line with a modem.

An added feature of a postage meter is that it will dampen and seal envelopes as they pass through it. Many companies do not keep loose stamps in the office; they do all mailing through a meter. Consequently, they avoid loss or waste of stamps.

### Other Items

Companies that process large volumes of mail may use automatic folding and inserting machines as well as collators. Collators automatically assemble items into proper order. Office workers also find sorting trays or racks, mailbags, and mailbag holders helpful. Other useful items include rubber stamps or stickers for special classifications such as priority mail.

## Following Mailing Guidelines

Part of Melanie's mailroom training includes a workshop sponsored by the local post office. At this workshop, she learns that postal sorting centers use special equipment to process mail rapidly. The two main parts of this equipment are the optical character recognition scanner and the bar code sorter. The optical character recognition (OCR) scanner reads an address until it locates the ZIP Code. It then converts the ZIP Code digits into a bar code. The **bar code sorter (BCS)** then sorts or separates the mail into geographic areas. This process continues until the mail is sorted into the final delivery area.

For this equipment to work properly, the Postal Service recommends using the following sequence when addressing mail:

1. recipient's name
2. recipient's street address, post office box number, or rural route number and box number, with any room or apartment number to the right, or at the end, of this line
3. recipient's city, state, and ZIP Code

For even better service, the U.S. Postal Service recommends that you do the following:

- Capitalize everything in the address.
- Use common abbreviations found in the ZIP+4 directories.
- Eliminate all punctuation except the hyphen in the ZIP+4 Code.
- Use two-letter state abbreviations.
- Use ZIP Codes.

When both a post office box number and a street address are used, make sure the place where you want the mail delivered appears on the line immediately above the city, state, and ZIP Code line. For example:

GRAND PRODUCTS INC
475 HOLIDAY PLAZA SW
PO BOX 320 [will be delivered here]
WASHINGTON DC 20260-6320

Your local post office can supply you with free brochures on addressing requirements. Following these requirements will ensure faster processing of mail.

Office workers use both electronic typewriters and personal computers to key and print envelopes. With an electronic typewriter, an envelope is put into the typewriter, and the address is keyed directly onto the envelope. With a computer, the address is keyed into a file, and the output comes through the computer printer. When printing, you may put a single envelope into the printer or use continuous-feed envelopes to print many addresses at one time. For the continuous-feed method, envelopes are attached to each other as they go through the printer.

# Packing for Mailing

When Melanie first begins working in the mailroom, she is quite surprised that at least once a week she has to prepare and package items for mailing. She has binders to mail to attorneys. She has broken merchandise to return to suppliers. She even has personal packages to prepare for the top executives.

Melanie again relies on a brochure from the U.S. Postal Service to obtain information on preparing packages. The brochure contains instructions on how to select the proper container, cushion the contents, close a package, and address and mark a package.

## Select the Proper Container

Fiberboard containers are generally strong enough to ship material of average weight and size. These boxes are readily available at stationery stores. A container should be large enough to hold the contents but not so large as to permit them to shift or joggle. It should contain adequate cushioning to prevent damage.

## Cushion the Contents

Cushioning distributes and absorbs shocks and vibrations while preventing the contents from shifting. Even single items packed alone should be cushioned for safety. Many types of suitable cushioning materials are available, including polystyrene, shredded or rolled newspaper, or bubble plastic. You will want to cushion items especially well if they may break, bend, or otherwise be damaged (for example, a glass figurine).

## Close the Package

Do not use wrapping paper. The box should be strong enough to be an adequate shipping container. Use filament-reinforced tape for closing and reinforcing parcels. Do not use twine, cords, or masking tape.

## Address and Mark the Package

The same mailing guidelines used for addressing letters apply to packages. A parcel should be clearly marked with the address, including the ZIP Code, of both sender and receiver. Any special marking should be placed on the outside of the parcel to alert Postal Service employees to the nature of the contents. Examples are Fragile, Perishable, and Do Not Bend. A post office window clerk has a set of rubber stamps indicating these special instructions and will apply them to your parcel on request.

# Reference Materials

While working in the mailroom of the law firm, Melanie needs to refer to a ZIP Code directory. These directories are available for national and state listings. They are available in hard copy or on CD-ROM. They may also be found in post office lobbies or on the U.S. Postal Service's Web site (www.usps.com). Figure 12.6, on page 255, is a sample page from the California ZIP+4 directory.

The states, cities, towns, and streets within a ZIP Code directory are listed in alphabetic order. To use the directory, first locate the state and city or town at the top of the page. Then look down the columns until you find the street and the number. The ZIP Code is located to the right. Refer to Figure 12.6, a page for the state of California and the city of Cambria.

Find Latham Street. You will notice that house numbers on Latham Street begin at 2100 and end at 2199. The *E* means the even-numbered houses have a ZIP Code of 93428-4206, and the *O* means the odd-numbered houses have a ZIP Code of 93428-4205. Locate Ferrasci Road on the same page. The letter *B* means that both even- and odd-numbered houses have the same ZIP Code, 93428-3517.

No, using all these numbers is not a waste of time. ZIP Codes are necessary for efficient use of optical character recognition scanners. The scanners read the numbers and sort the mail into the right piles by the number locations. Using the 93428-4206 ZIP Code as an example, the first three digits, 934, represent a major geographic area, either a section center (for example a block with many buildings) or a large city. The next two digits, 48, represent the local post office in that area.

The Postal Service encourages businesses to use ZIP+4 for their mailings. This system adds four extra digits at the end of a ZIP Code. An example is 94114-0929. The number 09 represents a group of streets or several blocks, and the number 29 represents a building or floor or department within a building.

# Unauthorized Use of Postage and Supplies

Businesses usually do not allow their employees to use postage or postage supplies for personal mail. Also, employees are usually prohibited from using the postage meter, or taking company envelopes, stationery, labels, or stamps for personal use.

**FIGURE 12.6 • Page from California ZIP+4 Directory**

**CAMBRIA** — **ELLIS AVE**

## CALIFORNIA

**CAMBRIA** — **NEWHALL AVE**

**ELLIS AVE—Con.**
- 1200 1299 E 93428-5956 O 93428-5957
- 1300 1399 E 93428-5958 O 93428-5959
- 1400 1499 E 93428-5960 O 93428-5961

**EMERSON RD**
- 1400 1450 E 93428-4771
- 1401 1499 O 93428-4713
- 1452 1498 E 93428-4714
- 1500 1578 E 93428-4716
- 1501 O 93428-4773
- 1503 1599 O 93428-4715
- 1580 1598 E 93428-4772
- 1600 1699 E 93428-4748 O 93428-4747
- 1700 1799 E 93428-4750 O 93428-4749
- 2200 2299 E 93428-4814 O 93428-4813
- 2300 2399 E 93428-4816 O 93428-4815
- 2400 2499 E 93428-4828 O 93428-4817
- 2500 2599 E 93428-4819 O 93428-4818
- 2600 2699 E 93428-4821 O 93428-4820
- 2700 2799 E 93428-4763 O 93428-4764

**EMMONS RD**
- 200 299 E 93428-4493 O 93428-4494
- 300 399 E 93428-4428 O 93428-4427
- 400 499 E 93428-6404 O 93428-6405
- 1900 1999 E 93428-4552 O 93428-4551
- 2000 2099 E 93428-4510 O 93428-4509
- 2100 2199 E 93428-4512 O 93428-4511

**ERNEST PL**
- 2600 2699 E 93428-5210 O 93428-5209
- 2700 2799 E 93428-5212 O 93428-5211
- 2800 2899 E 93428-5007 O 93428-5006
- 2900 2999 E 93428-5009 O 93428-5008

**ETON RD**
- 2500 2599 E 93428-4104 O 93428-4103
- 2600 2699 E 93428-4102 O 93428-4101
- 2700 2799 E 93428-4106 O 93428-4105
- 2800 2899 B 93428-4100

**EVELYN CT**
- 600 699 B 93428-2017
- 700 799 B 93428-2018

**EVENSONG WAY**
- 2700 2798 E 93428-4326
- 2701 2725 O 93428-4327
- 2727 2799 O 93428-4328

**EXETER LN**
- 400 499 E 93428-1914 O 93428-1913
- 500 599 E 93428-1916 O 93428-1915
- 600 699 B 93428-1917

**EXOTIC GARDEN DR**
- 7400 7499 B 93428-1807

**FALLBROOK ST**
- 300 398 E 93428-4436
- 301 305 O 93428-4497
- 307 399 O 93428-4435

**FERN DR**
- 1700 1799 E 93428-4827 O 93428-4841
- 1800 1899 E 93428-4830 O 93428-4829
- 1900 1999 E 93428-4832 O 93428-4831
- 2000 2099 E 93428-4834 O 93428-4833
- 2100 2199 E 93428-4836 O 93428-4835
- 2200 2299 E 93428-4838 O 93428-4837
- 2500 2599 E 93428-4845 O 93428-4846

**FERRASCI RD**
- 3800 3899 B 93428-3517

**GAINE ST**
- 300 398 E 93428-4457
- 301 323 O 93428-4458
- 325 O 93428-4498
- 327 363 O 93428-4458
- 365 399 O 93428-4498

**GREEN ST**
- 1600 1699 E 93428-5300 O 93428-5302
- 1700 1799 E 93428-5338 O 93428-5339
- 1800 1899 E 93428-5340 O 93428-5341
- 1901 1999 O 93428-5301
- 2000 2099 E 93428-5316 O 93428-5315
- 2100 2199 E 93428-5035 O 93428-5034
- 2201 2299 O 93428-5042

**N GREEN VALLEY RD**
- 500 599 B 93428-6005
- 1100 2099 B 93428-6003

**S GREEN VALLEY RD**
- 6400 6499 B 93428-6004

**GREYSTONE WAY**
- 1100 1199 E 93428-2900 O 93428-2934

**GROVE ST**
- 3900 3999 B 93428-2935
- 4900 4999 E 93428-2902 O 93428-2901
- 5000 5099 E 93428-2904 O 93428-2903

**GUILDFORD DR**
- 5000 5099 E 93428-3204 O 93428-3255
- 5100 5199 E 93428-3206 O 93428-3256
- 5200 5299 E 93428-3208 O 93428-3257
- 5300 5399 E 93428-2709 O 93428-2746

**HADDON DR**
- 1200 1298 E 93428-4610
- 1201 1271 O 93428-4674
- 1273 1299 O 93428-4609
- 1300 1399 E 93428-4612 O 93428-4611
- 1400 1499 E 93428-5126 O 93428-5125
- 2000 2099 E 93428-4612 O 93428-4611
- 2100 2198 E 93428-5126
- 2101 2119 O 93428-5149
- 2121 2199 O 93428-5150

**HARTFORD ST**
- 900 999 E 93428-2814 O 93428-2813
- 1000 1032 E 93428-2906
- 1001 1099 O 93428-2905
- 1034 1098 E 93428-2931
- 1100 1199 E 93428-2908 O 93428-2907

**HARVEY ST**
- 300 348 E 93428-4438
- 301 305 O 93428-6400
- 307 343 O 93428-4437
- 345 399 O 93428-6400
- 350 398 E 93428-4499

**HASTINGS ST**
- 200 299 E 93428-3200 O 93428-3207
- 300 364 E 93428-3266
- 301 399 O 93428-3243
- 368 398 E 93428-3244
- 400 426 E 93428-3267
- 401 425 O 93428-3235
- 427 451 O 93428-3245
- 428 498 E 93428-3246
- 449 93428-3268
  - B 93428-3268
- 453 499 O 93428-3261
- 500 599 E 93428-3210 O 93428-3209

**HEATH LN**
- 5500 5599 B 93428-2708

**HIGHWAY 1**
- 1 199 B 93428-1805
- 200 499 B 93428-1817

**HIGHWAY 46**
- 3100 3599 B 93428-6000
- 4300 4499 B 93428-6007
- 4500 4899 B 93428-6002
- 6000 6299 B 93428-6001
- 6500 8399 B 93428-6006

**HILLCREST DR**
- 800 899 E 93428-2802 O 93428-2801
- 900 999 E 93428-2502 O 93428-2501
- 1000 1099 E 93428-2504 O 93428-2503
- 5100 5199 E 93428-2910 O 93428-2909
- 5200 5222 E 93428-2912
- 5201 5299 O 93428-2911
- 5224 5298 E 93428-2932
- 5300 5399 E 93428-2930 O 93428-2933
- 5400 5499 E 93428-2516 O 93428-2517

**HUDSON AVE**
- 1700 1799 E 93428-5332 O 93428-5333

**HUNTINGTON RD**
- 200 299 E 93428-3600 O 93428-3617
- 300 399 E 93428-3616 O 93428-3615
- 400 499 E 93428-3604 O 93428-3603
- 500 599 E 93428-3606 O 93428-3605
- 600 E 93428-3608
- 601 699 O 93428-3607
- 630 698 E 93428-3608
- 700 799 E 93428-3259 O 93428-3260

**IVA CT**
- 900 999 B 93428-2913

**IVAR ST**
- 300 399 E 93428-4455 O 93428-4456

**JEAN ST**
- 200 299 E 93428-4495 O 93428-4496
- 300 399 E 93428-4459 O 93428-4460

**JORDAN RD**
- 6900 6999 B 93428-2021

**KATHRYN DR**
- 6400 6499 B 93428-2011

**KATHRYN DR—Con.**
- 6500 6599 B 93428-2012
- 6600 6699 B 93428-2013
- 6700 6799 B 93428-2014
- 6800 6899 B 93428-2015
- 6900 6999 B 93428-2016

**KAY ST**
- 2300 2599 E 93428-5970 O 93428-5971

**KENDALL LN**
- 200 299 E 93428-2203 O 93428-2205

**KENNETH DR**
- 700 799 E 93428-4654 O 93428-4655
- 800 899 E 93428-4656 O 93428-4657
- 900 999 E 93428-4658 O 93428-4659
- 1000 1099 E 93428-4660 O 93428-4661
- 1100 1148 E 93428-4681
- 1101 1111 O 93428-4663
- 1113 1151 O 93428-4675
- 1150 1198 E 93428-4662
- 1153 1199 O 93428-4686
- 1200 1299 E 93428-4664 O 93428-4665
- 1300 1399 E 93428-4666 O 93428-4667
- 1400 1499 B 93428-4770
- 1500 1599 E 93428-4769 O 93428-4700

**KENT ST**
- 500 599 E 93428-2436 O 93428-2437

**KERRY AVE**
- 2300 2399 E 93428-5214 O 93428-5213
- 2400 2499 E 93428-4908 O 93428-4907

**KERWIN ST**
- 200 299 E 93428-4425 O 93428-4490
- 300 399 E 93428-4461 O 93428-4462
- 400 499 E 93428-4491 O 93428-4492

**KNOLLWOOD DR**
- 1200 1299 E 93428-3320 O 93428-3322
- 1241 93428-3323
- 1241 93428-3343
  - 101 203 93428-3343
- 1245 93428-3324
- 1247 93428-3330

**LAMPTON ST**
- 200 299 E 93428-4488 O 93428-4400
- 300 399 E 93428-6402 O 93428-6403

**LANCASTER ST**
- 200 299 E 93428-3139 O 93428-3129
- 300 E 93428-3262
- 301 399 O 93428-3247
- 302 366 E 93428-3248
- 368 E 93428-3262
- 378 398 E 93428-3248
- 400 498 E 93428-3212
- 401 411 O 93428-3263
- 413 499 O 93428-3211
- 500 599 E 93428-3214 O 93428-3213

**LANGTON ST**
- 1700 1798 E 93428-5714
- 1701 1773 O 93428-5713
- 1775 1799 O 93428-5752
- 1800 1899 E 93428-5128 O 93428-5127
- 1900 1999 E 93428-5130 O 93428-5129
- 2000 2099 E 93428-5132 O 93428-5131
- 2100 2199 E 93428-5134 O 93428-5133
- 2200 2299 E 93428-4718 O 93428-4717
- 2300 2399 E 93428-4720 O 93428-4719
- 2400 2499 E 93428-4722 O 93428-4721
- 2500 2599 E 93428-4751 O 93428-4762

**LATHAM ST**
- 2100 2199 E 93428-4206 O 93428-4205

**LAUREL PL**
- 1800 1899 B 93428-5500

**LEIGHTON ST**
- 200 240 E 93428-3132
- 201 299 O 93428-3143
- 242 298 E 93428-3142
- 300 344 E 93428-3269
- 301 399 O 93428-3249
- 346 364 E 93428-3264
- 366 398 E 93428-3250
- 400 499 E 93428-3216 O 93428-3215
- 500 599 E 93428-3218 O 93428-3217
- 600 699 E 93428-3254 O 93428-3253

**LEONA DR**
- 2000 2099 E 93428-5216 O 93428-5215
- 2100 2199 E 93428-5218 O 93428-5217
- 2200 2299 E 93428-5220 O 93428-5219
- 2300 2399 E 93428-5222 O 93428-5221
- 2400 2499 E 93428-4910 O 93428-4909
- 2500 2599 E 93428-4912 O 93428-4911

**LEONARD PL**
- 1400 1499 E 93428-5927 O 93428-5928

**LINDEN CT**
- 1600 1699 B 93428-5327

**LONDON LN**
- 1600 1699 E 93428-5343 O 93428-5344
- 1700 1799 E 93428-5323 O 93428-5324
- 1800 1899 E 93428-5325 O 93428-5326

**LONDONDERRY LN**
- 1700 1799 E 93428-5317 O 93428-5318
- 1800 1899 E 93428-5319 O 93428-5320
- 1900 1999 E 93428-5321 O 93428-5322

**LUDLOW AVE**
- 2200 2299 E 93428-4806 O 93428-4805
- 2300 2399 E 93428-4823 O 93428-4822

**LYLE AVE**
- 2800 2899 E 93428-5864 O 93428-5865

**MACLEOD WAY**
- 2500 2599 E 93428-4301 O 93428-4302
- 3000 3099 E 93428-4301 O 93428-4302

**MADISON ST**
- 2100 2298 E 93428-4514
- 2101 2219 O 93428-4513
- 2221 2299 O 93428-4556
- 2300 2399 E 93428-4516 O 93428-4515
- 2400 2499 E 93428-4518 O 93428-4517
- 2500 2599 E 93428-4520 O 93428-4519

**MAIN ST**
  - 1 93428-3436
  - 2 93428-3436
  - 3 93428-3436
  - 4 93428-3436
  - 5 93428-3436
  - 6 93428-3436
- 500 599 E 93428-2345 O 93428-2340
- 600 699 E 93428-2346 O 93428-2341
- 700 746 E 93428-2816
- 701 743 O 93428-2815
- 745 799 O 93428-2825
- 748 798 E 93428-2826
- 775 93428-2830
  - 100 203 93428-2830
- 784 93428-2833
  - A E 93428-2833
- 800 898 E 93428-2818
- 801 93428-2831
  - A D 93428-2831
- 801 813 O 93428-2817
- 815 O 93428-2827
- 815 93428-2832
  - A E 93428-2832
- 816 93428-2824
  - A F 93428-2824
- 817 899 O 93428-2828
- 900 999 E 93428-2820 O 93428-2819
- 1000 1099 E 93428-2822 O 93428-2821
- 1100 1199 E 93428-3316 O 93428-3315
- 1200 1299 E 93428-3302 O 93428-3301
- 1226
  - 1 18 93428-3311
  - 19 36 93428-3312
  - 37 45 93428-3313
- 1226 OAK TERRACE TRL PARK 93428-3317
- 1300 1399 E 93428-3304 O 93428-3303
- 1350 CAMBRIA UNION SCHOOL DIST 93428-3399
- 1400 1499 E 93428-3306 O 93428-3305
- 1437 93428-3333
- 1460
  - 1 16 93428-3314
  - 17 22 93428-3318
- 1460 ROD AND REEL TRL PK 93428-3319
- 1500 1599 E 93428-3308 O 93428-3307
- 1600 1699 E 93428-3310 O 93428-3309
- 1602 93428-3300
  - 1 7 93428-3300
- 1700 1799 E 93428-3008 O 93428-3007
- 1800 1899 E 93428-3010 O 93428-3009
- 1900 1999 E 93428-3012 O 93428-3011
- 2000 2099 E 93428-3014 O 93428-3013
- 2100 2199 E 93428-3016 O 93428-3015
- 2150 93428-3022
  - 2 6 93428-3022
- 2200 2299 E 93428-3018 O 93428-3017
- 2300 2399 E 93428-3404 O 93428-3403
- 2338 93428-3432
- 2380 93428-3431
  - A E 93428-3431
- 2400 2499 E 93428-3406 O 93428-3405
- 2450 93428-3426
  - A F 93428-3426
- 2500 2599 E 93428-3408 O 93428-3407

**MAIN ST—Con.**
- 2580 93428-3429
  - 1 6 93428-3429
- 2600 2698 E 93428-3410
- 2601 93428-3436
  - A F 93428-3436
- 2601 2699 O 93428-3409
- 2650
  - 1 16 93428-3400
- 2650 VENUS ARMS APTS 93428-3400
- 2700 2799 E 93428-3412 O 93428-3411
- 2800 2899 E 93428-3501 O 93428-3502
- 2900 2999 E 93428-3504 O 93428-3503
- 3000 3099 E 93428-3500 O 93428-3507
- 3100 3199 E 93428-3508 O 93428-3509

**MALVERN ST**
- 2200 2299 E 93428-5031 O 93428-5030
- 2300 2398 E 93428-5010
- 2301 2349 O 93428-5039
- 2351 2399 O 93428-5041
- 2400 2499 E 93428-5012 O 93428-5011
- 2500 2599 B 93428-5000
- 2600 2999 B 93428-5046

**MANOR WAY**
- 900 999 E 93428-2929 O 93428-2928

**MARGATE AVE**
- 2800 2999 B 93428-3909

**MARJORIE PL**
- 2300 2399 E 93428-5032 O 93428-5033
- 2900 2999 E 93428-5032 O 93428-5033

**MARLBOROUGH LN**
- 1400 1499 B 93428-4477
- 1500 1599 B 93428-4478
- 1600 1699 B 93428-4479
- 1700 1799 B 93428-4480
- 1800 1899 B 93428-4481
- 1900 1999 B 93428-4482
- 2000 2099 B 93428-4483
- 2100 2199 B 93428-4484
- 2200 2299 B 93428-4485
- 2300 2399 B 93428-4486
- 2400 2499 B 93428-4487
- 2500 2599 E 93428-4447 O 93428-4448
- 2600 2699 E 93428-4449 O 93428-4450
- 2700 2799 E 93428-4451 O 93428-4452

**MARTINDALE RD**
- 2900 2999 E 93428-4006 O 93428-4007
- 3000 3099 E 93428-4008 O 93428-4009
- 3100 3199 E 93428-4010 O 93428-4011

**MCCABE ST**
- 2000 2099 E 93428-5043 O 93428-5044
- 2100 2199 E 93428-5023 O 93428-5038
- 2200 2299 E 93428-5014 O 93428-5013
- 2300 2399 E 93428-5025 O 93428-5024

**MELROSE AVE**
- 1600 1699 E 93428-5716 O 93428-5715
- 1700 1798 E 93428-5718
- 1701 1735 O 93428-5753
- 1737 1799 O 93428-5717

**MERLYN AVE**
- 2700 2799 E 93428-5987 O 93428-5988

**MILLS ST**
- 2900 2999 E 93428-5021 O 93428-5022
- 3000 3099 E 93428-5027 O 93428-5026
- 3100 3199 E 93428-5016 O 93428-5015

**MOONSTONE BEACH DR**
- 5600 5699 E 93428-2210 O 93428-2209
- 5700 5798 E 93428-2212
- 5800 5898 E 93428-2204
- 5900 5998 E 93428-2206
- 6000 6098 E 93428-2208
- 6100 6198 E 93428-1802
- 6200 6298 E 93428-1804
- 6300 6398 E 93428-1806
- 6400 6498 E 93428-1808
- 6500 6598 E 93428-1810
- 6600 6698 E 93428-1812
- 6700 6798 E 93428-1814
- 6800 6898 E 93428-1816
- 6900 6998 E 93428-1818
- 7000 7098 E 93428-1820
- 7100 7198 E 93428-1822
- 7200 7298 E 93428-1824

**NAULT AVE**
- 1400 1499 E 93428-5704 O 93428-5709

**NEWHALL AVE**
- 1500 1599 E 93428-5504 O 93428-5503
- 1600 1699 E 93428-5506 O 93428-5505



603

Over a period of time, a business can lose a large amount of money if employees misuse postage meters or use company postage supplies for private use. Some companies consider this practice to be stealing.

## Recall Time

*Answer the following questions:*

**1.** What information can you get from an electronic postage scale?

**2.** What does a collator do?

**3.** Where can you get an up-to-date brochure on requirements for addressing mail?

**4.** What are three types of materials used for cushioning items in a package?

## Summary

An office worker has to know a large amount of information to process incoming and outgoing mail efficiently. When you begin working in an office, you will need to remember this information in order to follow proper procedures for processing mail.

Use the following list to see whether you are prepared to handle mail processing in an office environment:

■ Once I receive the mail, I know the procedures to follow for processing it.

■ Before putting the mail onto my boss's desk, I know how to arrange it according to level of importance.

■ Before sealing the outgoing mail, I know the procedures for getting signatures, checking for enclosures, and addressing envelopes.

■ Before putting postage on the outgoing mail, I know how to determine which class of mail to use.

■ After determining which class of mail to use, I know how to use postal equipment to determine the cost.

■ If items need to be packed for mailing, I know the most efficient way to pack them.

■ If addresses need ZIP Codes, I know how to use reference materials to locate the proper ZIP Codes.

# before you leave...

**When you have completed this chapter, answer the following questions:**

**1.** What are at least three classifications of mailing? Explain why each one may be used.

**2.** In what order should an address be keyed onto an envelope? Create a sample.

# Review & Application

## Check Your Knowledge

1. List the procedures used for processing incoming mail.

2. Explain the process of annotating the mail.

3. List the column titles commonly used for an outgoing mail record.

4. When is a routing slip used?

5. How are enclosures inserted into an envelope when processing outgoing mail?

6. What is the order in which you would arrange mail for your boss?

7. Name a U.S. Postal Service booklet that will help you better understand mailing classifications.

8. What is the maximum weight for priority mail?

9. Who uses the periodicals rate?

10. If you use package services mail, what is the maximum number of days expected for coast-to-coast delivery?

11. Explain certified mail.

12. List other options that office workers may use in addition to the major classifications mail.

13. Explain the function of the U.S. Postal Service customer service line.

14. Is UPS part of the U.S. Postal Service?

15. Name the two most common pieces of postal equipment used for mail processing in an office.

16. List and explain the two pieces of special equipment used at postal sorting centers.

17. Discuss how to prepare and pack packages for mailing.

18. List the sequence in which to key the letter address on an envelope.

19. If your office does not have a ZIP Code directory, where can you quickly find one?

20. Explain ZIP+4.

21. Create a routing slip for six teachers in your school.

22. List four ways a businessperson may purchase stamps from the U.S. Postal Service.

23. List two reasons workers at a business may want to use computer software to connect with a private delivery service.

24. What is the name of the international facsimile service available through the U.S. Postal Service?

25. What does the Postal Service recommend you do to the following address to bring better service?

    Mr. Brandon Cash
    134 Whipple Drive
    Dallas, TX 75303

26. Rewrite the following address in proper sequence:

    69 Keyport Way
    Ms. Rachelle Mertz
    Huntington, NY
    11745-2325

## Review Your Vocabulary

On a separate piece of paper, write the letter of the New Office Term beside its description.

1. In a large company, mail may be processed in a _____.

2. An office worker may _____ into individual trays for more than one supervisor.

3. _____ is first-class mail weighing more than 13 ounces.

4. The secretary was underlining important facts in a letter; she was _____ the letter.

5. BCS stands for _____.

6. An administrative assistant should not open _____.

7. A routing slip is used for _____ to more than one person in a company.

   a. annotating
   b. bar code sorter (BCS)
   c. centralized mail department
   d. confidential mail
   e. priority mail
   f. routing mail
   g. sort mail

## Discuss and Analyze an Office Situation

Henrico is an office worker for a construction company. He also is the chairperson of a fund-raiser for his church. Henrico has fifty letters to mail for the church; he is trying to decide whether to put them through the company postage meter and not tell anyone. By using the company postage meter, he would save money for the church.

What would you advise Henrico to do? Explain your answer.

## Practice Basic Skills

### Math

1. You go to the post office for your boss. The mail will cost $13.90 to send. How much change do you receive from a $20 bill?

2. At Lucas Advertising, employees must record mail charges for each client. What is the total monthly charge for Levis on the following mail expense register?

MAIL EXPENSE REGISTER FOR APRIL

| Charge To | Amount | Charge To | Amount |
|-----------|--------|-----------|--------|
| Levis | $14.89 | ChevronTexaco | $8.90 |
| HewPac | 7.13 | Levis | 2.90 |
| Levis | 43.90 | Cal Milk | 0.75 |
| Levis | 0.56 | Chevron | 3.78 |
| PacTel | 8.90 | Levis | 0.55 |
| Levis | 0.45 | ChevronTexaco | 8.90 |
| Admin | 6.60 | Levis | 2.67 |

3. You need to reimburse petty cash up to $40. You have used $8.90, $3.45, $15.78, and $0.35 for postage. How much needs to be reimbursed?

4. You mail a package costing $13.50 and a letter at $0.65, and you purchase a sheet of stamps for $12.50. How much change do you receive if you give the postal clerk $30?

### English

*Rule:* For the possessive form of a noun that does not end in *s*, add *'s*.
*Examples:* cat's paw, men's hats, clerk's pay, children's lunch
*Practice Exercises:* Rewrite or key the following sentences on a separate piece of paper, placing apostrophes to form the possessive where needed.

   a. One customers last name was omitted from the mailing list.
   b. Ms. Chins secretary attended the workshop on databases for mailing labels.
   c. Why is the receptionists letter opener sitting on that managers desk?
   d. The mail operators position was eliminated because of all the new PCs.
   e. Invitations were mailed to each members supervisor in order to gain new members.

### Proofreading

Rewrite or rekey the following memo, correcting all errors.

TO: Office Staff
FORM: Orin Martin
DATE: April 5, 20—
SUBJECT: EXPRESS MAIL
Teh following information was recieved from the US Postal Service concerning Espress Mail. Express mail has always been a great value. Now that we have introduced our new overnight letter rate, you can fly with the Eagle for less than ever before.
For a low rate, you can send up to seventy pounds throughout the US overnight. Thanks to our ovrnight reliability, your get guaranteed before-noon delivery between all major markets.
You also have the convenience of 13,5000 Express Mail boxes, 2,6000 Express Mail post offices, and 265,000 letter cariers—more drop-off points than all our competitors combined.
Whether you have an overnight letter or package, why not soar with the Eagle?

## Apply Your Knowledge

1. Using the tables or the columns feature of a word processing program, key the following handwritten names and addresses as they would appear for mailing. Use uppercase and no punctuation. Arrange the list of names into alphabetic order.

a. ms kate roper
tristate
115 montebello rd
jamaica plain ma 02130-6372

b. ms judy wan
aaa hauling
85 whipper lane
stratford, ct 06497-8251

c. mr doro gutierrez
gunn hotel
350 rockingstone ave
larchmont ny 10538-3400

d. mr karl wolfe
us air
1313 gardner blvd
norton oh 44203-2525

e. mr oscar rosa
calistoga water
3607-4th avenue
minneapolis mn 55409-0404

f. ms bette waller
san lorenzo high school
1719 grange circle
longwood fl 32750-3803

g. mr daryl lee
lee catering
115 upper terrace
vicksburg ms 39180-9574

h. mr roger fine
fine word processing
2246 flossmoor rd
flossmoor il 60422-1306

i. ms harriet gandi
calstate
4515 dromedary rd
phoenix az 85018-8432

j. ms mariliee fong
amador appliance
543 sonoma ave.
livermore ca 94525-9618

2. Using a computer software program, input and print the following chart. Use various features of the software program to produce an appealing chart using landscape printing (8.5-by-11-inch paper).

## Using the Reference Manual

Use Table A.1—Post Office Abbreviations in the Reference Manual at the back of the book. Keyboard the two-letter abbreviations for the following twenty states. Save as file ch12ref on your data disk and print a copy.

States:

1. Minnesota
2. Georgia
3. North Carolina
4. Ohio
5. Vermont
6. Washington
7. Arizona
8. Hawaii
9. Alabama
10. California
11. New Mexico
12. New York
13. Florida
14. Nevada
15. Tennessee
16. Texas
17. South Dakota
18. Massachusetts
19. Colorado
20. District of Columbia

| | | | | WORLDPOST | | | |
| | | | (U.S. Postal Service International Services) | | | | |
|---|---|---|---|---|---|---|---|
| KIND OF MAIL | INTELPOST 0 to 1 Days | EXPRESS 2 to 3 Days | PRIORITY 3 to 7 Days | SURFACE AIR LIFT 7 to 14 days | AIRMAIL 4 to 7 Days | SURFACE 4 to 6 weeks | BUSINESS REPLY 4 to 7 days |
| Hand-Delivered Fax | XXX | | | | | | |
| General Correspondence | | XXX | XXX | | XXX | XXX | |
| Business Reply Mail | | | | | XXX | | XXX |
| All Printed Matter | | XXX | XXX | XXX | XXX | XXX | |
| M-Bag Option | | | | XXX | XXX | XXX | |
| Merchandise Shipments | | XXX | | | XXX | XXX | |

# chapter 13

## Managing Office Activities

### objectives

*After completing this chapter, you will be able to do the following:*

1. Describe how to organize your desk and the tools you will use, and determine where to place them.
2. Discuss how and when to plan your day.
3. List different types of calendars and their use.
4. Discuss the use of a calendar and a tickler file to arrange appointments and plan upcoming events.
5. Discuss the differences between formal and informal meetings.
6. List the steps involved in planning a formal meeting.
7. List your responsibilities during and after a formal meeting.
8. Describe how to plan and arrange business trips for executives and other travelers.

### New Office Terms

- agenda
- itinerary
- priorities
- time management

# before you begin...

**Answer the following questions to the best of your ability:**

1. How should you organize your pens and pencils on your work desk?
2. What type of work activity should be planned for the first project in the morning?
3. How would you handle interruptions on the job?
4. What five steps should be followed in planning a business meeting?
5. What are the first several steps in planning a business trip?
6. What should you schedule for an executive on the first day after he or she returns from a business trip?

Someone once said that great minds love chaos and that they love to go about organizing and straightening things to make them work better. This statement may be true for a few people, but most people need order and organization in their lives to be efficient and effective.

You need to be organized in an office environment because you will be receiving, sorting, rearranging, and communicating vast amounts of information. This environment can be overwhelming unless you have systems of classifying and storing details so that nothing gets lost or forgotten.

Several helpful systems that can make your job easier and less chaotic are available. This chapter details many current ideas about how to organize your space, time, and duties in ways that can help you do your job efficiently.

## Organizing Yourself

When you are working in an office, you must organize yourself and your surroundings before you will be able to do your job efficiently. You need to organize your desk and the materials with which you normally work. Additionally, you need to fully understand your duties and what is expected of you.

### Your Desk

You will be spending much of your work time at your desk or work area. You will accomplish more in less time if you have all your work within easy reach. An efficient way to organize your work is to use a desk organizer.

Two types of desk organizers are available. One has horizontal slots in which you may place documents upright so that tabs can easily be read. The other type is made up of several stacked trays. Trays may be different colors, making identifying their contents easier. Label each section or tray with what it will contain. For example, labels that read In Mail, Out Mail, In Work, Out Work, Mr. Jones, and Ms. Wong reflect what you need to process.

Keep tools that you use often on your desk. These tools usually include pens and pencils (in an upright container), a tape dispenser, paper clips, a stapler, a calculator, a pad for telephone messages, and a pad for notes. If

## Technology in the Office  HELP CREATING A WEB PAGE

As you learned earlier, HTML (hypertext markup language) is a language used to format Web pages. However, if you do not know HTML, help is available if you are creating your first Web page. Several programs for creating Web pages use the WYSIWYG (what you see is what you get) approach. These programs make creating Web pages much simpler. As you create your page with one of these programs, you can see what it will look like in a Web browser before you actually publish it on the Internet.

Popular WYSIWYG programs for creating Web pages include Microsoft FrontPage (www.microsoft.com), Netscape Composer (www.netscape.com), included with Netscape Navigator Web browser, and a capable free program, AOLpress (www.aolpress.com.). AOLpress works quite well even if you are not an America Online (AOL) subscriber. ■

you use a computer and store magnetic disks on your desk, do not use magnetic paper clip holders, as they may damage data stored on your disks. You will want your calendar or plan sheet within easy view. Some people also like a few reference items on their desks such as a dictionary, an index containing frequently used telephone numbers and addresses, or a user's manual for the computer or other office machines they regularly use.

You will probably have a telephone. Place it close enough that you can reach it easily and write notes while you talk. If you are right-handed, your telephone might be placed to the upper left so that you can answer it with your left hand, freeing your right hand to write. The opposite would apply if you were left-handed.

Different tasks will require different tools. Before you begin a task, decide which tools you will need and place them on the top of your desk. You may store some of these tools in your desk drawers until you need them. A drawer organizer will keep these items separated so that they are easy to locate when you need them.

You will also keep letterhead stationery, envelopes, and other supplies in your desk drawers. Keep them neat and tidy so that you can easily access the items you need.

If you use a personal computer, you may save desk space by placing it onto a desk extension beside your desk. The processing units of some personal computers are housed in *tower cabinets* (which are vertical rather than horizontal) and have built-in floor supports. You can also place the monitor on a swing-away arm that will allow you to push the monitor out of the way when you need your desk space for other work.

## Your Materials

Your supervisor or office manager will provide small quantities of supplies that you keep on your desk and in the drawers. In addition, most offices have a central storage area for large quantities of supplies such as computer disks, oversized envelopes, printer paper, letterhead stationery, file folders, labels, pens, and pencils.

If you work in a small office, you will probably be expected to keep supplies stocked by reordering them from an office supply store as they run low. Keeping enough company letterhead in stock can be tricky

©Jack Hollingsworth/PhotoDisc

Keep the files that you need close at hand, but try to avoid clutter on your desk.

**TIP** Keep your pens and pencils in an upright container or an attractive coffee mug, with the point ends up. This position enables you to see at once which pencils are sharp and which you will need to sharpen. This position also allows you to select pens according to color of ink without having to take them out one by one to find the color you want. ■

because printing time needs to be considered. So keep track of the materials on hand and reorder early enough so that new stock may be delivered when needed. Put newly received supplies behind or under older supplies so that the older ones are used first.

## Your Responsibilities

To be well organized and efficient, you will need to thoroughly understand what is expected of you and what your duties entail, not only for a day at a time but for the week, subsequent weeks, and coming months. Understanding the function of the company that has hired you is also helpful.

Someone will probably provide some on-the-job training to get you started. The trainer may be the person you are replacing, an office manager, an administrative assistant, or your new boss. You will receive either a verbal or written outline of what is expected of you. You may be given a desk manual outlining many of your duties in detail. If so, refer to it often—and if not, start one of your own, as it will help anyone relieving you when you are on vacation.

Take notes as you receive your training so that you can refer to them in the future. Your boss may have some definite ideas about how certain things should be done. Listen carefully and learn your boss's ideas and preferences about how to perform your work. If you stay in your job but your boss is replaced, ask your new boss for her or his preferences. Become aware of your boss's duties, too, so that you can coordinate your work activities with those of your boss.

Carefully study any materials made available to you. These materials might include an office procedures manual and notes from the person who previously held your job. If you are given instructions for specific jobs, make certain you understand those instructions. Examine the files and determine the status of jobs that are in progress. Become familiar with the different types of stationery and notepads available, and learn which items are customarily used for which tasks.

©Kwame Zikomo/SuperStock International

You will receive some on-the-job training on your new job. Your employer will expect you to listen carefully and ask questions about anything you do not understand.

Learn the names of co-workers and the executives in your office. You will need their assistance in the first few weeks, and they will appreciate it if you call them by name. To help you remember who is who, ask for a written roster of employees and perhaps an organization chart. The organization chart will help you learn who reports to whom within the company.

You may have no one to train you when you arrive at your new job. In that case, you may receive only a procedures manual to guide you. Be resourceful but careful as you sort out what is expected of you and how and when to seek answers. When in doubt, ask your supervisor or a co-worker who is willing to help. Learning everything you are to do may seem overwhelming at first, but you will catch on; and in a few weeks, you will establish a comfortable routine.

# Managing Your Time

In a busy office, some eight-hour workdays seem to be only about three hours long. When you are deeply involved in a complicated project, you may ask yourself, "Where did the time go?" You feel as though you have accomplished only part of what you set out to do during the day. A remedy for this apparent disappearance of time is efficient time management.

**Time management** means the art of knowing what you need to do in a given time frame, setting priorities for projects, and completing projects in the time allotted.

## Set Priorities

**Priorities** are preferences in the order of work activities, usually decided according to levels of importance or deadlines. Setting priorities is the first task in time management, and it is also the most difficult. First, determine exactly what you have to accomplish in a given time frame, then order the tasks in sequence of their importance. Your supervisor will establish some of your day's priorities. If he or she comes to you and says, "This assignment is very important, and I need it before noon," then you have no decision to make about where to begin your work.

After you set your priorities, establish a time during which you will complete each task. You can learn to do this by keeping a log detailing how much time is required to complete different tasks. After a while, you will know how long to allow for specific tasks. For example, after you open and sort the mail for a couple of weeks, you can estimate the average time required. After you key several ten-page reports, you will know how long they take—and you can put a time value on such reports in the future.

You will find that setting priorities for your tasks is not just convenient, but essential. Your boss's effectiveness depends upon whether you complete your tasks in a timely manner. If you do your job well, your boss will be able to do her or his job well, too. Helping the boss often helps the whole company become more productive, which benefits all employees—and your boss will probably be especially appreciative of your efforts.

You may find yourself working for two or even several bosses. This situation occurs more frequently today with the current trend for companies to "downsize," that is, to lay off a number of employees in an effort to become more economically efficient. Setting priorities for your work activities becomes more complicated when several bosses are assigning you tasks. Even so, you will usually be able to determine which project needs

to be completed first and which can wait. Sometimes you will spend part of the day on each of two or more projects because they both need to be completed at about the same time.

You will probably have one person who is your supervisor. If you find that you are being pressured by two or more bosses to complete their work first, ask your supervisor to help you decide what gets highest priority.

## Plan Your Work

Plan your work, then follow your plan. Learn how to create a "things to do" list by noting the tasks you need to accomplish, placing them in order of priority, then allotting them a time for completion. This list will help you dispatch your duties efficiently, but doing so may not always be as easy as it sounds. Although establishing priorities for your workday is important, you must be flexible enough to revise your plan if your supervisor's needs require that you do so.

One of your major responsibilities is to save time for your supervisor by being aware of her or his schedule and doing as much of her or his work as you are capable of doing. To provide this kind of help, you must be flexible with your own time.

When making your plan for the day, leave some fifteen-minute time spaces between scheduled events. You can use these intervals to finish projects that take longer than you expect or to deal with unforeseen matters that arise and rearrange your priorities.

Once you begin to address one task, think it through and plan how you will accomplish it from beginning to end, step by step. Visualize how it will look when completed so that you will have a clear understanding of the desired outcome. If you are unsure about the desired outcome, do not guess. Find out who does know what the end product should look like and ask questions. Do the appropriate research before you begin and have all the necessary tools at hand. You want to do the task correctly the first time. Repeating tasks squanders valuable time; spending time at the beginning of each project to plan properly saves time in the end.

Many people find that making the first task of the day a difficult one helps them manage their time. Some workers take the first half hour after arriving at work to calm down, get centered, and get ready to work. This activity wastes valuable time and will invariably put unwanted pressure on you; you will spend all day trying to catch up, and you might be unable to accomplish all the tasks you need to complete. Do all mental work before you come to the office.

People differ in what time of the day they are most energetic, creative, and efficient. You might hear people say they are "morning persons" or "night persons." Regardless of when you feel you do your best work, try starting your day with a difficult, creative task. Then you can feel that you have already accomplished something early on, setting the pace for the rest of the day.

**TIP** Plan each day's work. Half an hour's planning early can often save several hours' work in the middle of a complicated day. ■

## Manage Details

The endless barrage of details in an office environment is often perplexing. Details about meetings, purchases, scheduling, staffing, marketing, telephone messages, and hundreds of miscellaneous items must be dealt with and stored in the proper place. All these bits of information have a way of sliding away from you if you are not well prepared.

You must not only devise a way of recording details immediately, but you also need to establish methods of storing them so that you can access them easily. You need a system to use consistently.

One helpful way to manage details is to create forms for different types of information. For example, information collected from people walking into the office could be on one form; telephone information on another. However, do not get carried away and design more forms than you need or collect and keep unnecessary information.

You can store the bits of information you have collected in several ways. One method is to place them in the task file to which they are related. Another method is to store them according to accounts; for example, any information coming from Computers Unlimited through the mail would be on your mail form, stored in the Computers Unlimited file. Often, information and details will simply be passed on to the next person and may be stored, temporarily, in that person's mailbox or file.

Devise a system of initials, check marks, or other codes that indicate to you the status of information that comes across your desk. Then the next time you see it, you will know where it has been and where it is supposed to be going.

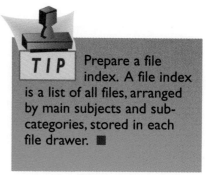

**TIP** Prepare a file index. A file index is a list of all files, arranged by main subjects and sub-categories, stored in each file drawer. ■

## Work on One Task at a Time

When you are planning your day and assigning times and tasks on your "to do" list, allocate blocks of time for individual tasks. You will gain a sense of accomplishment when you are able to complete something. On some jobs, your time is not your own, and you find yourself jumping from task to task, never feeling that you have achieved anything. However, with careful planning, you can usually complete a few tasks each day.

Longer, more complicated tasks take even more planning. For example, if you have a project that will be time consuming but is not due immediately, set aside a reasonable block of time to work on it and find a logical place to stop your work. Make clear notes to yourself about what part has been left undone and exactly where you stopped working on the project.

Whenever possible, work on only one task at a time until you have completed it. This way, you are less likely to omit an important part of the assignment, and your job will be less confusing and more gratifying.

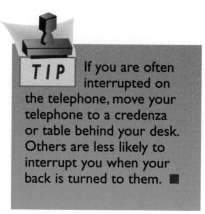

**TIP** If you are often interrupted on the telephone, move your telephone to a credenza or table behind your desk. Others are less likely to interrupt you when your back is turned to them. ■

## Cope with Interruptions

The glitch in your planning will come with interruptions. The first thing to realize is that these interruptions are part of your job. Your attitude in dealing with them will determine how successful you are in returning to the work and the train of thought you were pursuing before the telephone rang or your co-worker asked you a question, for example. Do not become annoyed by interruptions. If you do, your distress will slow you down much more than the interruption does.

For a few days, keep track of how many times you answer the telephone, you assist a co-worker, or your supervisor asks to speak to you. Then you will know how much time to allow for interruptions in your planning. You need not be frustrated by being unable to accomplish all you set out to do. You can plan to do only what you will be able to complete.

**TIP** Schedule time for returning telephone calls when you are between major projects. ■

## Schedule Time to Relax

Your company, by law, must allow a lunch break and two 15-minute rest breaks—one in midmorning, one in midafternoon. Your relaxation needs are to be met during these breaks as well.

However, relaxation periods can be planned in other ways. You will soon discover that some tasks in the office are more difficult, more intense, and more energy consuming than others. For example, sorting mail requires less energy than creating a database in your computer.

You will also recognize your own stamina levels. That is, you may find that after two hours of intense concentration, you need a break.

With this knowledge, you can plan your schedule to include built-in relaxation periods by surrounding a difficult, lengthy task with easier, shorter ones. In this way, you can plan your day so that you are not exhausted before it is over.

## Plan Tomorrow's Work

Before quitting time each day, review the projects you worked on, making notes on what was completed and what was not. Begin to prepare your "to do" list for the next day by estimating how much time each carryover item will require and placing those items into time slots. With this kind of preparation, you can leave the office confident that your work for the next day is well organized.

## Recall Time

*Answer the following questions:*

**1.** Why is getting organized essential in a busy office?

**2.** What are several items you will want to place on your desk? How would you place these items for maximum convenience?

**3.** How would you order and store materials and supplies?

**4.** To organize your work efficiently, you will first need to know your job well. What are some ways you can help yourself become better acquainted with a new job?

**5.** Managing time may seem difficult at first. What are some ways to ensure that you manage your time well?

# Keeping a Calendar

Someone must arrange the order of events for the day in a busy office. Scheduling appointments for one or several people, as well as for yourself, may be part of your job. The best way to keep track of and to schedule appointments, meetings, and events is to use an appointment calendar.

Appointment calendars are available in many formats with different features. If you will not be scheduling many appointments, you may use a simple desk calendar that has space for writing notes and appointments. If your office is especially busy, with many appointments each day, you

will need a calendar with the workday separated into 15-minute intervals. Determine your needs, go to an office supply store, and purchase the one that best suits your requirements.

In many offices, employees use computer programs to keep their calendars electronically. Workers in offices in which a large number of appointments are routinely scheduled are more likely to use computers for scheduling those appointments. Several widely used calendar programs that can satisfy the appointment calendar needs of most offices are available. Some have templates that make the program more useful in specific types of business offices. Updated versions or entirely new electronic calendars are published every year. Check your local computer software store.

Specialized calendar and scheduling programs are available for specific types of businesses such as medical offices, law offices, and others that require unique features. Such programs are available from vendors of software designed for particular businesses.

Using electronic calendars has many advantages, including neatness and readability. If you use an electronic calendar, you may access it by keying in a special code, or password, that ensures the calendar will remain confidential and accessible only by you.

An appointment calendar is an effective management tool for keeping track of and scheduling appointments, meetings, and events.

## Making Appointments

Scheduling is crucial to running an office efficiently. Furthermore, people who come in will judge your business to some extent on how scheduling is conducted.

If you are careful, setting appointments will not be difficult. However, you must follow some guidelines:

- Do not schedule two people at once. This guideline seems obvious, but it does occasionally happen.

- Do not schedule appointments too close together, so as to avoid the possibility of overlapping. Be sure to schedule enough time for each appointment. People expect their appointments to be on time. They consider their time to be of value; they will be unhappy sitting around waiting while your boss finishes with someone else.

- Do not schedule two intense meetings back to back. Give your boss some breathing room.

- Write neatly and clearly on the calendar. If you are unable to read what is scheduled, you do not know what to cancel, if necessary. You also do not know who to call for more information or to change the time or location of the appointment.

- Write the name of the individual your boss is meeting, that person's telephone number, and the type of appointment on the calendar. You will need this information if you must reschedule the meeting.

- Acknowledge that an appointment was kept by making a check mark on the calendar.

- Keep previous years' appointment calendars for reference.

You will devise your own system for keeping your calendar. These guidelines can help you keep track of appointments efficiently.

## Making Office Decisions

Joann is an excellent office worker. She worked for her previous supervisor for several months, and she knew her job well. Because of the good work she did, she was transferred to a new job in a different section.

In her new position, Joann works more closely with her boss than she did in her previous one. She is responsible for making decisions about scheduling appointments and ensuring that her boss's time is well managed. Scheduling appointments is new to her. She has no experience with time management.

Joann is enthusiastic about doing her job well, but she worries that she will be inadequate in her new position.

1. *Which of the following should Joann do?*
   a. *Quit her job and look for something she feels more comfortable doing.*
   b. *Continue in her position, trying to do the best she can on her own.*
   c. *Discuss her problem with her supervisor.*

2. *Would most supervisors understand and appreciate an employee being open about her or his shortcomings?*

3. *If Joann decides to discuss the problem with her supervisor, should she offer to attend a Saturday seminar on time management or ask for time off during the week to attend the seminar?* ■

## Handling Appointment Requests

Before you take over the responsibility of setting appointments, first establish guidelines with your managers so that you fully understand to what extent you have authority to set appointments. The guidelines should answer the following questions: Which kinds of appointments will require an okay from your supervisors? Are certain times of the day to be kept free of appointments? Are certain people always allowed an appointment? Are certain people absolutely not allowed to schedule an appointment?

Some executives set their own appointments, others leave this task to their assistants in the office, and still others share this responsibility with their assistants. These differences usually depend on the type of office. If, for example, you work in a medical office, you will probably set patient appointments without conferring with individual physicians.

Some people will make their appointment requests in person, others will call on the telephone. You will receive some requests in the mail and still others by e-mail. Regardless of how you receive a request, you will need to gather the following information:

■ the name and telephone number of the individual making the request and the company she or he represents

■ the date and time the individual would like to have the appointment and the approximate length of time necessary to complete her or his business

■ the location where the meeting will take place if different from your supervisor's office

■ the purpose of the meeting request, if your supervisor wants you to ask this question

Most appointment requests will be made by telephone. Remember, when you answer the telephone, you are the frontline representative of your business. Always be courteous when dealing with appointment requests. Here is an example of the type of request you might receive and how you should handle it:

Kim [answering the telephone]: Good afternoon, Moon Beam Publications, Kim speaking. May I help you?

Mr. Marquez [speaking on the other end of the line]: Hello, this is Sergio Marquez. I'd like to drop by tomorrow to discuss my contract with Ms. Bradshaw.

Kim: Thank you. One moment, please. Ms. Bradshaw has some free time at three o'clock tomorrow afternoon. Would that be a good time for you? How long do you think you will need with Ms. Bradshaw?

Mr. Marquez: No more than a half hour, I wouldn't think. That will be fine, thank you.

Kim: Good, may I have your telephone number? I'll confirm this time with Ms. Bradshaw and call you right back.

Mr. Marquez: Thank you. My number is 555-2345. Good-bye.

Kim: Good-bye.

This telephone call was handled efficiently and courteously. Kim will verify this meeting with Ms. Bradshaw according to previously established guidelines. Then Kim will call Mr. Marquez to confirm the appointment and enter it into the appointment calendar, blocking off the allotted half hour.

## Entering Recurring Commitments

Some events and meetings in an office will be recurring. For example, regular weekly staff meetings occur in many offices. Block off this special time on the calendar so that unwanted appointments are not inadvertently set (even though everyone already knows this meeting is a regular occurrence).

Perhaps your supervisor or the office manager has a regular Wednesday afternoon manicure or a Thursday afternoon tennis game. In some offices, a special client may have a regular, weekly appointment. Time for all such events that preclude setting outside appointments should be blocked off the calendar, in effect reserving this time weeks in advance.

## Handling Cancellations

Invariably, emergencies arise, people become ill, other activities take precedence, and plans change. Occasionally, you will have to cancel some appointments. If an individual calls to cancel an appointment, cross the name off the calendar and, if the person still wants an appointment, suggest another available time.

If your supervisor directs you to cancel an appointment, call the individual to offer other time options and be as courteous as possible, apologizing for your supervisor. If someone arrives for a canceled appointment because you were unable to contact him or her, apologize and explain that your boss had an emergency. If possible, suggest another person in the office who might be of service, and offer to set another appointment if the individual requests it.

## Coordinating Calendars

Some managers share the responsibility of keeping the calendar with their assistants. In this case, at least once each day the manager and the assistant must meet to check the calendar. At this time, you will make adjustments in time allotments, record new appointments, delete cancellations, and record rescheduled appointments. Coordination must take place each day to avoid confusion and scheduling problems.

**TIP** If you answer the telephone with a smile, your manner will be more pleasant, making a good impression on the caller even though she or he is unable to see your smile. When the telephone rings, take a deep breath, switching gears from whatever task you were doing; smile; and answer the telephone as quickly as possible—preferably after the first ring and always before the third ring. ■

Keeping the calendar for a busy office can be challenging. However, with a good system, you may find it fun and interesting.

## Using a Tickler File

A tickler file is a follow-up file that uses dates to help you remember work that is pending for a week, a month, or longer. You can prepare a tickler file in many different ways. The most common is to use a 3-by-5-inch card file with guides for months (January through December) and dates (1 through 31). The guide for the current month is the first divider in the file, which is followed by the numbered dividers for the dates. At the beginning of each month, the guide for the previous month is moved to the back of the file. (See Figure 10.9 in Chapter 10.)

The purpose of using a tickler file is to remind you of future action that you must take. Suppose that you call your office supply store to order a particular product. The person on the line tells you the item is not in stock but to check with the supply store next week, when it expects a new shipment. You make a note to yourself to call the supply store and place it into the tickler file behind the number that corresponds with the date one week in the future. A week later, you call the supply store to check on the product.

You can also use your tickler file when your boss tells you she or he is expecting out-of-town guests next week and asks you to make dinner reservations for next Thursday. Again, you write a note to yourself, this time to make a call to the restaurant, and file it behind the card for a date early in the week.

Your tickler file will be useful to you only if you make a practice of using it daily. Whenever you plan your day, either the night before or first thing in the morning, remove the notes from your tickler file for that day. Make it a part of your planning process, assigning time for each task you find in the file.

As you complete each task, either throw away the note or write on it the outcome of the task and place the note into the appropriate business job or account file.

Between your tickler file and your calendar, you should be able to handle future events effectively.

## Recall Time

*Answer the following questions:*

1. How and why would you keep a calendar of events and meetings?

2. Managing your boss's or several people's appointments can be complicated. What are four tips that will help you keep everything in order?

3. If you have the responsibility of handling appointment requests, what information will you need from a person wishing to make an appointment?

4. Suppose that you are answering the telephone, and the person on the line requests an appointment with your boss. How should the conversation go?

5. What is a tickler file, and how will you use it?

# Planning and Scheduling Business Meetings

Meetings play an important role in the communication of information in every kind of business. They are held to conduct business, to follow up on a previously discussed activity, or simply to communicate information to an individual or to a group.

The content and style of meetings vary greatly. A worker may meet with his or her supervisor for direction or evaluation. An executive may meet with the board of directors to communicate information and determine the future course of the business. Salespeople meet with outside businesspeople to strike a deal. People in similar positions from different businesses meet to learn how to become more efficient in their jobs.

The one thing common in all kinds of meetings is that they must be run efficiently and effectively to avoid wasting valuable time. Careful planning and preparation are the keys to efficiently run, worthwhile meetings.

## Informal Meetings

Much of the business associated with operating any company is conducted in small, informal meetings. These meetings require little preparation and take place either in someone's office or in a small conference room. In spite of the informal nature of many meetings, everyone who is expected to be in attendance must be notified that meetings are taking place.

Very informal meetings may happen at a moment's notice and take place at any time of day in a busy office. Your supervisor may say, "Lee, will you come into my office? I need to talk to you about something," and thus a meeting takes place.

Small, informal meetings are often used to plan projects and activities in a business office.

Meetings that are more official but still considered informal include staff meetings, committee meetings, and client meetings. These meetings require only that a time and place be set and that everyone who is supposed to be in attendance is notified. The person who calls the meeting will oversee and conduct it.

Staff meetings are the most common type of meeting, and they are usually held in a supervisor's office. Everyone who reports to that supervisor will be in attendance. The purpose of staff meetings is to discuss and plan new projects and directions, solve problems, assess progress, make decisions, and give assignments. Some staff meetings are used to settle disputes and problems between different staff members. You may be asked to make arrangements for such meetings, and you will likely be asked to attend them.

Committees are small groups of people assigned to work on a particular project or task together. These people will meet to plan their approach and make assignments. They may meet once or several times. They will probably set their own meeting times and places by mutual agreement and notify anyone who should be in attendance.

Client meetings are very important even though they are often conducted in a casual atmosphere such as at a restaurant during lunch or dinner. These meetings are scheduled to be convenient for all individuals involved.

## Formal Meetings

Formal meetings have more structure and require more complicated preparation and planning than do informal meetings. These meetings are called to cover a predetermined set of business items. Thus, the discussion follows a preset agenda.

An **agenda** is a list of topics to be covered during a meeting. These topics are usually agreed upon and distributed before the meeting convenes, allowing participants time to prepare for the discussion of them. Sometimes approximate times are listed next to each topic to indicate when the discussion of each one is scheduled. A sample agenda appears in Figure 13.1.

**FIGURE 13.1 • Meeting Agenda**

AGENDA

Board of Directors
Otter Corporation

7 P.M., February 8, 2002

1. Call to order: Ms. Dunlop, chief executive officer
2. Roll call and introductions: Mr. Olson, secretary
3. Minutes of the last meeting: Mr. Olson, secretary
4. Treasurer's report: Ms. Smith, chief financial officer
5. Committee reports
6. Old business
7. New business
8. Date of next meeting
9. Adjournment

You may have responsibilities before, during, and after formal meetings. Your supervisor may ask you to arrange for a meeting room, order food, and prepare materials. You may also be asked to prepare and distribute the documents that announce and describe the meeting to potential participants. Another task might be to make arrangements for travel or accommodations for out-of-town participants.

## Preparation

Because meetings are so important and businesspeople's time is so valuable, preparation for formal meetings must be carefully planned and executed. For example, if participants must make flight arrangements to arrive in time for a meeting, you will need to begin planning earlier than if all the participants live in the same city. The following activities will help you organize and plan these meetings.

**Record Information on the Meeting** As information about an upcoming meeting arrives at your desk, record details in your tickler file according to the dates when action must be taken. Also record on your calendar the dates when you will be doing tasks concerned with planning the meeting such as making room arrangements with a hotel manager.

**Prepare a Meeting Folder** As soon as the meeting is scheduled, create a folder for it. Place into this folder all the bits of information concerning the meeting as they are created. Include information such as names, telephone numbers, and addresses of participants; agenda items; and planning notes.

**Reserve a Meeting Room and Equipment** Your supervisor may give you the responsibility of arranging for a meeting place. As soon as you determine the number of people expected to attend and the time and date of the meeting, begin looking for a room.

Large conferences will often be held in hotels, which usually have meeting rooms for rent. Check the prices before making reservations, as the cost may be prohibitive. Make arrangements for this type of conference well in advance of the conference date.

Some companies have conference rooms, but you must reserve them so that two meetings are not scheduled in one room at the same time. Many restaurants have meeting rooms where groups hold luncheon and dinner meetings. Some banks and churches have rooms you may use for community meetings.

You may also be responsible for arranging for equipment for a meeting. Whoever is organizing the meeting can tell you what equipment is required, such as a public address system, videotape machine, slide projector, overhead projector, liquid crystal display (LCD) for use with presentation software, whiteboard or flip chart for writing, chairs, and tables. Large hotels have many of these items available for use in their conference rooms. Some companies have necessary equipment for use in meetings.

Make arrangements for rooms and equipment as far in advance as possible so that you do not get caught in a crunch as the meeting date nears.

**Notify Participants** You may inform participants of a forthcoming meeting in several ways. The time to notify participants and the type of notification depend on the type of meeting. Some groups and organizations have bylaws that describe procedures for notifying participants of upcoming meetings. You must follow these guidelines to ensure the meeting is official.

In a written notice, give the date, time, and place of the meeting. Describe the purpose of the meeting and request that participants let you know whether they plan to attend. Also provide a date by which participants must notify you of their plans to attend.

For a formal meeting, prepare written notices and send them at least three weeks before the meeting. For a less formal meeting with fewer participants, telephone calls are fine, or you may mail, fax, or e-mail written notices.

Your notices will require follow-up. If the meeting is mandatory, people invited will contact you with valid reasons if they are unable to attend.

If the meeting is voluntary and some people have not let you know whether they will be attending, make follow-up calls to determine how many people will attend. Maintain an accurate roster of who will and will not attend. Keep your roster close to the telephone so that you can easily locate them on your list and write pertinent notes when participants call.

You may wish to make a final follow-up call the day before the meeting to ensure good attendance. If you have arranged for food at the meeting, you need to know how many will be served.

**Prepare the Agenda** Usually the person who will conduct the meeting, the chairperson, or the secretary will prepare the meeting agenda. The agenda will have a format similar to the sample on page 274, and the same format will be followed for subsequent meetings. Participants in the meeting will submit items for the agenda. The chairperson or secretary may also place items on the agenda. You may be responsible for keeping track of these items, keying the agenda, making copies, and distributing it either by mail or at the meeting.

**Prepare the Meeting Room** If you are responsible for preparing the meeting room, arrive early on the day of the meeting to ensure that you have everything needed. For example, make certain you have enough tables and chairs for everyone to sit comfortably.

Be sure the room temperature is appropriate. Also, make sure the lighting is adequate for taking notes and seeing everyone clearly. A room that is too dark or too bright can be unpleasant.

Check to see that the equipment you reserved is in place and functions properly. Do not wait until the participants are arriving before checking the public address system or other equipment. The squeaks and squawks of an errant loudspeaker system can be embarrassing.

If food is being provided, check to be certain arrangements for it are proceeding smoothly. Even if refreshments are not provided, you will probably want to serve coffee, tea, and water. Your meeting will go much more smoothly if the participants are comfortable and feel that you are concerned about their well-being.

**Organize Materials and Handouts** In the days before the meeting, prepare any materials that will be part of it. Design the materials to help communicate information and ensure that the meeting runs efficiently.

These materials might include folders with copies of special information developed by the people planning the meeting. You may distribute pens or pencils and pads for the participants' convenience. In a large meeting where people are not familiar with one another, you will want to provide name tags to make communication easier and help participants avoid the difficulty of having to remember many names.

You may place these materials on the tables where individuals will be seated or distribute them as participants sign in. Other pieces of literature and handouts may be displayed on the table so that participants may examine them and take what they wish.

## Participation

Your role in the meeting should be clearly defined by your supervisor before the meeting. As the person who made the arrangements, you may be responsible for monitoring the meeting to ensure that all goes smoothly. Perhaps you will greet people at the door. If so, greet them with a smile and a pleasant attitude so that they will feel welcome and comfortable. Keep the water and coffee supplies replenished and attend to participants' other needs such as requests for photocopies of specified documents.

**Discuss Ideas** Apart from the role you play as assistant and organizer, you may be asked to share your own ideas or to state your opinion about what others have to say. If so, then participate in that way. However, if your supervisor limits your participation to planning the meeting and taking minutes, do not attempt to join in the discussion.

**Take the Minutes** A role often delegated to secretaries and assistants is recording the events and actions of a meeting by taking minutes. The minutes are the official record of the meeting and concisely document facts about it, though statements and events are not recorded verbatim (word for word). The minutes should provide a clear, accurate accounting of what transpires at a meeting.

A formal meeting requires organizing materials and handouts several days in advance.

Various formats for minutes are acceptable, but minutes will always contain the following information:

- the date, time, and place of the meeting
- the name of the organization or group sponsoring the meeting
- the name of the person conducting the meeting
- a list of the people present—and if others were expected to attend, a list of absentees

In general, if a meeting is conducted according to an agenda, the minutes will take that general form—call to order, roll call and introductions, minutes of the last meeting, treasurer's report, and so on.

Your minutes might begin like the following:

On February 8, 2002, the meeting of the Otter Corporation Board of Directors was convened at 7 P.M. at the Majestic Inn. Ms. Dunlop, the chief executive officer, called the meeting to order. . . .

As you are recording the minutes, recognize that actions are more important than what the participants say. Write the minutes clearly, ensuring that you do not lose any crucial information about business conducted at the meeting.

**Correct the Minutes** Part of the agenda for a meeting will be reading and correcting the minutes of the previous meeting. Someone may disagree with what has been recorded as having taken place. If the correction or addition is small, you may cross out the error and write in the correction. If the correction requires more writing, cross out the mistake and attach another page to record the correct information. Index the correction by placing a reference number next to the crossed-out section, directing the reader to the new page and new information.

After the attending participants have approved the minutes, do not add anything to them.

## Follow-Up

Several tasks will require completion after a meeting. If these tasks are assigned to you, do them as soon as possible, demonstrating efficiency to all parties involved. These tasks may include paying bills, preparing correspondence, or completing reports determined by the business conducted at the meeting. The sooner you do these, the better, while the events of the meeting remain fresh in your mind.

**Prepare and Distribute the Minutes** Sometimes the person who takes the minutes at a meeting is not the person who prepares and distributes them. Therefore, you may have to prepare minutes that someone else has written. You will need to key them neatly according to the format the group has agreed to use. If you are not sure about a word or phrase because of unclear handwriting, question the person who took the minutes to avoid any misunderstandings.

Distribute the minutes according to the group's wishes, either mailing them immediately or mailing them along with the next meeting notice.

**Prepare Related Correspondence** Your supervisor may ask you to prepare correspondence directly related to a meeting. This correspondence might include requests for more information, thank-you notes to participants or speakers, and follow-up information about ideas discussed at the meeting. These tasks should be completed as soon as possible after the meeting is held.

**TIP** Store files according to activity. Store files used daily in a desk file drawer or a small cabinet next to your desk. Store other often-used files in a larger cabinet nearby. Store inactive files in a storeroom. ■

**1.** What are the main differences between formal and informal meetings?

**2.** What is an agenda? How is it prepared and how is it used?

**3.** Several tasks are required when making arrangements for a meeting. What are four of them?

**4.** How are minutes taken? What information must be in them and what format is used?

**5.** Your work is not over when a meeting is over. You may be responsible for many activities after a meeting. What are some of them?

# Handling Travel Arrangements

You may be asked to make arrangements for your managers to travel to a meeting or for participants to attend a meeting at your company. Your supervisor will give you guidelines to follow about company policy regarding travel. As soon as you learn that you will be responsible for making these arrangements, prepare a travel folder.

Consider the following questions when planning travel for someone else:

1. What are the exact destinations, and on what dates does the traveler want to leave and return?

2. How does the traveler wish to travel from one place to another? Some people are uncomfortable flying and would prefer to go by car or train.

3. Does the traveler have special requests, such as a specific time of day to leave and return or, if traveling by plane, a preferred seating assignment? Some people insist on an aisle seat, whereas others want to look out the window. Is a certain airline preferred? Does the traveler have any special food requirements?

4. Will someone at the destination be driving, or will a car rental be required?

5. Does the traveler have a favorite hotel in the destination city or a favorite hotel chain that he or she feels provides good service in most cities? Does the traveler require a specific type of accommodation? Will the traveler require a meeting room at the hotel?

6. Does your manager want you to arrange any other detail of preference or special request?

When you know the answers to these questions, you can plan and complete the travel arrangements.

## Planning

Travel can be complicated and exhausting if not properly planned and orchestrated. You will discover that in any business activity, proper planning in the beginning saves valuable time in the end.

## Early Preparations

Begin your trip folder as early as possible so that you do not have loose papers lying about. Disorganization can cause you to overlook helpful details. Your trip folder will be a file folder that contains all information relevant to a particular trip. Prepare a separate travel folder for each trip.

When you first learn the approximate dates of a trip, make some notes about the time frame for planning: how long do you have to make all the arrangements, and when must you accomplish each task? Make notes about the various aspects of planning the trip and about the tasks and responsibilities assigned to you.

Outline the trip, including the meetings to be attended. If possible, do this initial outlining and planning in consultation with the person who will be traveling. The outline will keep you focused on what you need to accomplish and the status of matters as your plans proceed.

## Final Preparations

Prepare a checklist to use as you make the final preparations. After your outline is complete and the designated tasks are accomplished, prepare your traveler's final itinerary. The **itinerary** is a listing that includes flight numbers, departure and arrival times and places, and information on hotel accommodations and car rentals. If you use the services of a travel agent, you should receive a final itinerary of the travel arrangements from the agent.

**Confirm Appointments** Call each person with whom your supervisor plans to meet and confirm the appointments. Recheck the times, dates, and places of all activities.

**Make Reservations** Make any reservations that have not previously been made. A travel agent may have made most reservations, but with the final setting of the itinerary, some of these reservations might have to be changed.

**Prepare an Itinerary** When you have your outline, your reservations are made, and your meetings are confirmed, you can prepare the final itinerary for your traveler. The itinerary contains a calendar of meetings and hotel and travel reservations with addresses and telephone numbers. Include any instructions about special considerations.

Ask the traveler, who will probably be your boss or supervisor, who else should receive a copy of the itinerary. She or he may need several copies—one to carry, one to stash away in the baggage, and one to leave with the family.

**Assemble Related Items** Place with your boss's itinerary the tickets, travel money, hotel confirmations, and forms for recording expenses.

Early in the planning process, your supervisor began to think about materials to take along. Gather those materials and prepare them in the appropriate manner.

By planning carefully early on, following your checklist, and preparing a detailed itinerary, you can create an easy, well-organized, successful trip. Your boss will be able to accomplish much more on the trip because of your careful work; she or he can spend energy on conducting business instead of tending to other details.

Louise is an administrative assistant in the home office of a large manufacturing company. Louise understands most of the computer programs used in the office quite well. Word processing, spreadsheet, and database programs all seem simple to her. So simple, in fact, that she cannot understand why many of the new workers frequently have difficulty comprehending how to use these programs.

Arnold is a new employee in the office. He spent four hours one morning reading manuals and trying to understand how to use a database program, but he couldn't figure it out. He was feeling frustrated, confused, and angry when he walked into the staff meeting. Although using computer programs was not on the agenda for the day, Arnold announced that he wanted this item added to the agenda. Louise, who was chairing the meeting, agreed and added it as the first item for discussion.

Arnold, still frustrated and angry, began by saying, "This company must use the worst programs on the market—the one for database management is terrible!"

Louise, who not only understood the programs well but had personally selected the database management program, was not sympathetic. She replied, "We have the best programs on the market. The database management program is simple and easy to learn for anyone of average intelligence."

Feeling he had just been insulted, Arnold said, "Excuse me," stood, and walked out of the meeting.

For the past two days Arnold and Louise have not spoken to each other.

1. **What would have been a more effective way for Arnold to share his frustration about the computer program?**

2. **What could Louise have said that would have promoted more effective human relations?**

3. **What should Arnold and Louise say to each other now?** ■

## Using Travel Agents

Your company may not expect you to arrange travel plans. You may be dealing with a travel agency that can make all the arrangements, from booking flights to making hotel and car rental reservations.

Travel agencies are paid a commission for booking hotels and air travel, and they have access, through computers, to arrival times, departure times, and ticket prices for most airlines. Therefore, they can efficiently take care of these details for you. Even if you do work with a travel agency, you will need the information listed previously to ensure a comfortable, enjoyable trip.

Before you begin searching for a travel agent, ask your supervisor whether the company ordinarily uses a particular agency that has provided satisfactory service in the past. If not, you may ask other people for references to a good agency. Using one that specializes in business travel will probably be your best bet.

Before you contact an agency, determine company policy regarding paying for the trip. Is the travel agency to bill the company for expenses, or will you be given a credit card number to give to the agency? When you call the agency, have your trip folder in front of you with all the information the agent requires. You will need to give the agent as many specific details and instructions as possible.

As soon as the agent completes the arrangements, he or she will send you the tickets along with a computer printout of the itinerary and an invoice listing charges. Check this information carefully, then ask your supervisor or the traveler to check it, too. Make necessary corrections with the travel agent without delay to ensure a convenient and pleasant trip.

# Arranging Trips Yourself

Sometimes you may be required to make travel arrangements. For example, if a rush trip comes up suddenly, you may not have time to enlist the aid of a travel agent. Although making arrangements yourself will be less convenient, you should be able to handle the plans adequately.

## Scheduling Air Travel

You will need to do a bit of research when booking airline tickets yourself. If you will be doing a large amount of scheduling, subscribe to one of the many periodicals that help people make travel arrangements. You may find these as well as books about travel in your local library.

If you live in a large city, you will have several airlines from which to choose. Your supervisor might have a preference for one airline. Most airlines provide updated timetables with the following information:

- arrival and departure times
- days each flight is available
- flight numbers
- special services and features of each flight
- toll-free number where more information may be gathered and reservations may be made

Obtain the best price for tickets as well as the most convenient departure and arrival times. You must call airlines and ask questions to accomplish this task. Use the airlines' toll-free numbers so that you can make the calls without paying long-distance fees. Be sure to consider any special programs for frequent flyers or business travelers.

As soon as you decide which airline to use, book the flight. Before you call, place your trip folder in front of you so that you can make the special arrangements requested by your traveler. You will need to know how you will be paying for the tickets. The airline may prefer a credit card number. You may make arrangements to pick up the tickets and pay for them in person, or request that the airline bill your company for the tickets.

You will probably not have time to have the tickets mailed. So, unless you plan to pick up the tickets ahead of time, arrange for your traveler to pick them up at the airport on the day of departure.

## Renting an Automobile

Whether your traveler needs a car at her or his destination or will be making the entire trip by automobile, arrangements have to be made in advance. If you are using a travel agency, it will take care of car rental details as part of its service to you.

If you will be making the arrangements, do some research to secure the best rates. The rates will depend on the size and model of car, destination, and length of time the car will be needed. The cost will include a daily rate plus an additional charge for miles over a certain daily allotment. Most of these details are negotiable and vary from agency to agency.

You may look in the Yellow Pages of your telephone directory to locate the rental agencies in your area. Several car rental agencies are usually located at major airports, and most medium-size towns also have several agencies from which to choose.

### Reserving Hotel and Motel Accommodations

Your traveler may have to spend the night or several nights at her or his destination. A travel agency will be able to book accommodations for you.

Your traveler may have hotel or motel preferences if she or he is acquainted with the town to be visited. Ask before you begin your search. The chamber of commerce in the destination community may help you with finding and arranging accommodations. Most large hotels have toll-free numbers for bookings.

## Using the Internet and Online Services

The Internet and all major online services, such as America Online and MSN, can be very helpful in planning trips. For example, you can check current airline fares and prices of hotel accommodations on your computer. You can even purchase airline tickets, reserve hotel rooms, and rent a car using such Web sites as Expedia.com and Travelocity.com.

Many travel Web sites allow you to view photos of both the hotel room interiors and the outside of the hotel you are considering. You may choose an e-ticket for your airline reservation or pay the delivery cost and receive a paper ticket. If you choose an e-ticket, be sure to print out confirmation of your airline reservation displayed on the Web site.

The Internet, online services, and Web sites are updated constantly. You can use keywords, such as *travel*, to locate a variety of travel sites.

## Continuing Your Work When the Executive Is Away

You may feel that your work will be disrupted while the boss is out of town, but for the most part, you can continue your work as usual. Sometimes you will accomplish more when your boss is away and is therefore unable to create as many interruptions.

Keep careful track of events in the office, visitors, incoming mail, and telephone calls so that you can report them to your boss. Do not set any appointments on the day your boss is due to return to the office. You will be helping your boss catch up.

## Following Up When the Executive Returns

When your boss returns, follow-up work will be necessary. You will need to write thank-you letters to people who provided services or assistance. You will also need to prepare other correspondence associated with the business conducted during the trip.

You may have to prepare detailed reports showing what was accomplished on the trip. You and your boss will have your hands full for several days after she or he returns.

Managing activities and duties in a busy office can appear complex and sometimes nearly impossible, but you can learn some systems that make it easier for you. After you have been working in an office for a while, you may be surprised at how routine all this work will become.

**TIP** When you have the choice, sending some jobs, such as a big photocopying job, to a commercial photocopying company is often better than getting bogged down for days and falling behind on other important work. ■

## Ralph A. Prater

*Team Member, Contributions and Programs*
*ChevronTexaco<sup>SM</sup> Corporation*

**Q.** Mr. Prater, students hear that businesses are becoming more global than in past years. What does global mean?

**A.** Global means that companies are conducting or seeking to conduct business all over the world. In the past, U.S. companies did the majority of their business in this country. That is no longer true for many businesses. Recently I read that because of the global economy, the number of Americans working for international companies has more than doubled since 1980, to nearly 5 million.

**Q.** What advice would you give to a future office worker concerning working in a global economy?

**A.** An office worker in a global economy must be knowledgeable about foreign customs, practices, and nuances of a particular country on any given day in which business is being conducted.

A good starting point for students is to become acquainted with specifics of other countries. For example, learn how to determine currency exchange rates, how to fax or telephone a foreign country, and how to determine the time difference in these countries.

## Recall Time

*Answer the following questions:*

1. Whether you make your supervisor's travel arrangements or leave the details to a travel agency, you need to consider several things before you begin. What are these considerations?
2. Usually, people use travel agencies for their travel needs. How do travel agencies work and what can they do for you?
3. If you schedule your supervisor's air travel, you will have to do some research. What kinds of information will you seek?
4. How do you rent an automobile?
5. How do you arrange hotel or motel accommodations?

## Summary

You may have heard the phrase "Time is money." In a busy office, you may quickly become overwhelmed and waste valuable time if you do not

get organized. Think through every item, from how you will organize the tools on your desk to arranging conferences and planning trips.

The first step in getting organized is to understand your new job. Someone may train you for a few days, or you may be given a procedures manual. After you clearly understand your responsibilities, you can begin to organize matters so that you can handle them.

Managing your time will be crucial to your success. Good time management requires planning your day carefully. Set priorities, assign each task a time for completion, and follow your plans as nearly as possible, while continuing to be flexible.

Design ways of managing details. You will use files and folders, and you may write notes to yourself. Details have a way of disappearing if they are not managed correctly and systematically.

You can often work on just one task at a time until it is completed. However, be prepared for interruptions. They are part of the job, so schedule time for them in your daily work plan. Adjust your schedule so that your work does not remain intense all day. Schedule easier tasks between more difficult ones.

Part of organizing a busy office is keeping a calendar. List all upcoming meetings, events, and appointments. You may be asked to schedule your supervisor's appointments. If so, you will be the "keeper of the calendar." You will block out time for recurring events, handle cancellations, and coordinate your calendar with your boss and others in the office.

A tickler file is a follow-up file that alerts you to tasks you need to do. Using a tickler file in conjunction with your calendar, you should be able to deal with all the events of a busy office.

Much of the business of a company is conducted in formal or informal meetings. You may be responsible for making arrangements for formal meetings. These arrangements will include reserving a room, organizing equipment and refreshments, and preparing materials. Begin your planning by preparing a folder in which to keep details, recording all information that crosses your desk about the meeting, notifying participants, and preparing an agenda.

An agenda is an announcement and listing of what will be discussed at a meeting. Minutes are an accounting of the meeting. You may be asked to take minutes, then prepare and distribute them after a meeting is over. Other follow-up activities will be completing correspondence, such as thank-you notes, and perhaps conducting further research on a project and preparing follow-up reports.

Your boss may attend meetings out of town, and you may make the travel arrangements. If so, make a list of your boss's preferences and special needs before you make any plans. A travel agent can schedule flights, book hotel rooms, reserve rental cars, and take care of other details for you. Most businesses today use travel agencies because of their access to information about arrivals, departures, costs, and so on. If you make the travel arrangements, with a little research you can do the same things the travel agent does.

While the boss is away, take care of business as usual. When the boss returns, you will need a few days to catch up, and you may have follow-up tasks that are generated by the trip.

Plan, plan, plan. Managing office activities is about careful, thoughtful, systematic preparation and planning so that time will be used profitably.

Managing office activities will include some or all of the following tasks:

- Organize the top of your desk and its drawers.
- Organize the purchase and storage of materials and supplies.
- Learn and understand your responsibilities in the office.
- Manage your time.
- Set priorities.
- Plan your work for the day before beginning.
- Create a system for managing details.
- Work on one task at a time whenever possible.
- Learn to cope with interruptions, which are part of any busy office.
- Schedule time to relax.
- Keep a calendar, handling appointments and cancellations.
- Use a tickler file.
- Plan, schedule, and make arrangements for meetings.
- Take minutes and prepare and distribute them.
- Make travel arrangements or make them with the assistance of a travel agent.

# before you leave...

**When you have completed this chapter, answer the following questions:**

1. How should you organize your pens and pencils on your work desk?
2. What type of work activity should be planned for the first project in the morning?
3. How would you handle interruptions on the job?
4. What five steps should be followed in planning a business meeting?
5. What are the first several steps in planning a business trip?
6. What should you schedule for an executive on the first day after he or she returns from a business trip?

# Review & Application

## Check Your Knowledge

1. Describe the importance of getting organized.

2. Describe how you might organize your desk. List the materials and tools and where they would be placed on your desk.

3. Training for a new job may take several different forms. Can you name some of them?

4. Explain how to set priorities for different duties.

5. Discuss various ways to record and store details.

6. When should you plan your day and how do you do it?

7. By law, you are entitled to a lunch break and two 15-minute rest breaks throughout the workday. Describe other ways you can schedule relaxation time into your day.

8. Describe the different types of calendars and their use.

9. Handling appointments can be tricky. What information should you have from your boss if you are expected to set her or his appointments?

10. Describe a tickler file and its use.

11. What are the basic differences between formal and informal meetings?

12. List the steps followed when preparing for a formal meeting.

13. What are minutes and how are they prepared?

14. What is the easiest and most efficient way to deal with travel arrangements?

15. How would you begin making travel arrangements?

16. What things should you know about your traveler before you begin to make her or his arrangements?

17. How would you arrange for airplane tickets? Hotel accommodations? Car rental?

18. What is an itinerary and what information might be on one?

19. What are some last-minute details that may need attention when your boss is leaving on a business trip?

20. How do you deal with the boss's being out of the office?

21. What kinds of activities might take place when the boss returns?

## Review Your Vocabulary

On a separate piece of paper, write the letter of the vocabulary word beside its description.

____ 1. preferences in the order of work activities, usually decided according to levels of importance

____ 2. a list of topics to be covered during a meeting

____ 3. the art of knowing what you need to do in a given time frame, setting priorities for projects, and completing projects in the time allotted

____ 4. a list that includes flight numbers, departure and arrival times and places, hotel accommodations, and car rental information

a. agenda      c. priorities

b. itinerary      d. time management

## Discuss and Analyze an Office Situation

1. Fred has accepted a new job in a new company. The person he is replacing left the job in a hurry because of a health emergency. The boss has given him a little time, but she is busy and training Fred is not her main priority. Other people in the office have similar jobs and are helpful to some extent. Still, Fred is not sure what his duties are and does not clearly understand his responsibilities. If you were Fred, what would you do?

2. Gretchen was in the habit of scheduling her boss's appointments and carefully keeping a calendar of events. One day, Gretchen woke up with a terrible cold and felt she should not go to the office. She called her boss and explained. When she returned to the office, someone else had done the scheduling. That person had set some overlapping appointments and had not blocked out time for a special meeting. How can Gretchen fix the confusing calendar?

## Practice Basic Skills

### Math

You must rent an automobile for your boss's trip. He will be driving to a city 300 miles away and back. He will need the car for three days, and you estimate that he will drive it about 100 miles while in his destination city. He requested that you rent a four-door sedan. You research the matter carefully, asking people what company to use and calling companies in the Yellow Pages. You discover that different companies charge different rates:

- Company 1 charges $34.99 per day for the rental fee and allows 150 free miles per day. Each mile over 150 will cost $0.20.
- Company 2 charges $39.95 per day for the rental fee and allows 100 free miles per day. Each mile over 100 will cost $0.15.
- Company 3 charges $36.95 per day for the rental fee and allows 120 free miles per day. Each mile over 120 will cost $0.25.

Calculate which company offers the best price for renting a car.

### English

You may be called upon to welcome meeting participants as they arrive. Rewrite or key on a separate piece of paper the following greeting, remembering that you are representing your company and correcting words and phrases that are inappropriate because they are rude or simply not standard English.

Hey there, how ya doin'? Where would you like to set it down? This meeting will be a pretty cool meeting, don't ya think? If you want coffee ya gotta get it yourself. Over there on the table below that ugly picture. You'll find it. Hope you dig on the meeting, and have some laughs.

### Proofreading

If one of your responsibilities is to record and prepare the minutes of a meeting, you will want to proofread them carefully to ensure that they contain no spelling or punctuation errors. Rewrite or rekey the following minutes on a separate piece of paper, correcting any errors.

The metting was called to orden at 7:00 PM by the President, Mrs. Brown. Then Mrs. Brwon led the fleg slute. The secretary red the minites from the last meeting and thee wear approvd as red.

The tresurer gave her reprot and a discussion follwoed.

Old buesness include discusion about the water problum.

No newer business was discussed

The meetin was ajourned at 8:00 PM

## Apply Your Knowledge

1. Using your school day as an example, carefully plan your day. Set priorities for events and activities and assign times to each item on your list.

2. Prepare a calendar for yourself, detailing all the activities you have planned for the current month. Give everything a time value. See if this kind of planning helps you keep your activities organized.

3. Plan a business trip. Select a city, an airline, a hotel, and a car rental company, and determine the cost of each service you will require. Refer to maps, airline schedules, American Automobile Association (AAA) books, and any other references you can locate. For guidance, you may discuss your trip with a travel agent, if you wish.

## Using the Reference Manual

Open file ch13ref.doc. Use the proofreaders' marks section of the Reference Manual at the back of the book to help you correct the paragraph. Save and print.

Meetings play an important role in the comunication of informatoin in every kind of business. they are held to conduct business, to followy up on a previously discussed activity, or simply to communicate information to an individual or to a group. Careful planing and prepration are the keys to eficiently run, worth while meeting.

# CAREER PORTFOLIO

## PART THREE: Office Support Skills

**Specific Activities to Complete**

Select at least three of the following items for inclusion in your Career Portfolio, using the information from Chapters 8 through 13.

1. Key a list of the five most important telephone tips you will need to remember on your first job. Save and print this list. (Be sure you proof according to the instructions given previously on page 84.) Insert this list as the first item in your Career Portfolio binder behind the third tab, entitled "Office Support Skills."

2. Key a list of five important rules to remember when you are responsible for filing and managing records in an office. Save, print, and insert this list behind the third tab as well.

3. Key some examples of accepted formats for a letter, a memorandum, and an envelope. Show your documents to a fellow student and incorporate any suggestions that may improve the appearance of the documents. Save, print, and insert these documents behind the third tab.

4. Key a balance sheet and an income statement using the examples in Chapter 11 as a guide. Save, print, and insert these documents behind the third tab.

5. Key five important reminders for office workers when they send and receive mail in the office. Save, print, and insert these reminders behind the third tab.

6. Key a list of how you will go about managing your time while efficiently performing expected office activities on your first job. Save, print, and insert this list behind the third tab.

# PART IV
# Communication and Problem-Solving Skills

# chapter 14

## Essentials of Office Communication

**After completing this chapter, you will be able to do the following:**

1. Describe the communication process.
2. List examples of nonverbal communication.
3. Discuss how filtering negatively affects the communication process.
4. Explain the importance of feedback in the communication process.
5. Describe the difference between upward communication and downward communication.
6. Explain the positive and negative aspects of the grapevine as an informal communication channel.
7. Explain the difference between literacy and workplace literacy.
8. List the five competencies and three-part foundation skills that the SCANS report refers to as basic workplace know-how.
9. Describe techniques and steps workers may use to read, write, and speak more effectively in business activities.
10. Describe several communication behaviors of active listeners.

### New Office Terms

- active listening
- communication
- downward communication
- feedback
- filtering
- grapevine
- lateral communication
- previewing
- Secretary's Commission on Achieving Necessary Skills (SCANS)
- upward communication
- workplace literacy

# before you begin...

**Answer the following questions to the best of your ability:**

**1.** What are some typical office communication networks?

**2.** Which communication skills should office workers be able to demonstrate?

## The Communication Process

Communication is the basis of all relationships. Without it, each of us would live dreary lives in isolation. We need other people, and our connections to others are forged by communication. Yet, because we learned to communicate gradually as we grew up, most of us have never really thought about this valuable skill.

Although most of us take communication for granted, its importance cannot be overestimated. According to experts in this field, we spend about 70 percent of our waking hours communicating—speaking, listening, reading, and writing. Furthermore, in an office setting we can choose the most appropriate communication medium—face to face, telephone, e-mail, written memos, or video.

Simply put, **communication** is the exchange of messages. Messages may be verbal, using spoken or written words; or they may be nonverbal, using symbols, gestures, expressions, and body language. Communication requires a sender (a person who transmits the message) and a receiver (a person who receives the message). The communication process begins when a sender transmits a message and a receiver gets the message. The process is complete when the receiver responds to the message or sends feedback. Whether it is one-way or two-way, effective communication occurs when the sender and the receiver have the same understanding of the message, as shown in Figure 14.1.

**FIGURE 14.1 • The Communication Process**

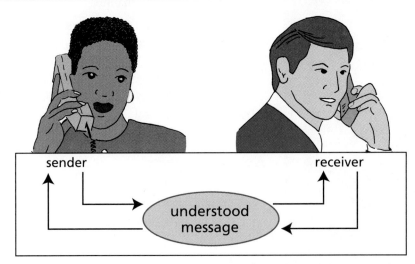

Effective communication has occurred when both the sender and the receiver have the same understanding of the message.

| **Technology in the Office** | **INFORMATION AGE CAREERS—WEBMASTER** |

Many organizations, including most computer and communications companies, educational institutions, the entertainment industry, museums, manufacturing companies, and government agencies operate Web sites. A Webmaster manages an Internet Web site. Some Webmasters design and publish Web sites; however, a Web site designer often creates the Web pages. A Webmaster solves problems when a Web site experiences problems such as failure to respond when users click certain links.

Web audiences expect new and exciting material. New information in the form of text and graphics must be continually added to Web sites to keep them current. Becoming familiar with graphics and multimedia software is important for a Webmaster. Text must be converted to HTML (Hypertext Markup Language). Many Webmasters learn and make extensive use of HTML. However, several excellent Web design software programs now make managing a Web site possible without learning HTML. ■

## One-Way Communication

In one-way communication, the sender transmits a message, the receiver gets it, and the process is complete. For example, an employee calls in to report that she is ill and will be out for the day. The person receiving the call understands the message, makes note of it, and hangs up.

## Two-Way Communication

In two-way communication, the sender transmits a message, the receiver gets it, and subsequently the receiver responds with another message. The process may continue with the sender and receiver alternating roles, giving each other feedback. Office conversations and business correspondence are examples of two-way communication.

## Nonverbal Communication

Most of us think of words as our chief means of communicating. Being clear, concise, and courteous in your choice of words is important. However, studies of face-to-face communication have shown that 80 to 90 percent of the *impact* of a message comes from nonverbal elements such as facial expressions, eye contact, body language, and tone of voice.

Communication experts point out that in face-to-face communication, 55 percent of what we communicate is in our body language, 38 percent in how we speak, and 7 percent in what we say. Further, on a telephone, we have only between 15 and 30 seconds to make a good impression. Only 10 to 20 percent of what we communicate on a telephone is based on what we say; 80 to 90 percent is in how we say it. According to these statistics, nonverbal communication can reveal much more of a message than the words used.

Examples of the four areas of nonverbal communication—facial expressions, eye contact, body language, and voice qualities—are given in Table 14.1, page 296.

**TIP** When communicating, try to control your temper even when faced with unfair resistance. To lose your temper is to lose an opportunity to share your message. ■

Nonverbal communication can have a much greater impact than the words being spoken.

**TABLE 14.1 • Nonverbal Communication**

| Types | Examples |
|---|---|
| Facial Expressions | Smiling, frowning, and raising your eyebrows are facial expressions that communicate feelings. |
| Eye Contact | Making eye contact when speaking with someone is usually desirable. In the United States, for example, people who do not meet your eyes during conversations are thought to be hiding something. The use of eye contact, of course, differs in other cultures. |
| Body Language | Nodding your head, shrugging your shoulders, gesturing with your hands, or shifting your weight from side to side are examples of body language. Body language may indicate a wide range of emotions, from boredom (yawning) to impatience (tapping your fingers or feet). |
| Voice Qualities | A person's voice may be loud or soft, high or low pitched, fast or slow, pleasant or harsh, monotonous or interesting. A voice tells a lot about how a person is feeling physically and psychologically at any moment. |

# Communication Feedback and Filters

Communication and feedback in business are important to reach corporate goals and to maintain good morale. **Feedback** refers to verbal and nonverbal responses that the receiver gives by further communicating with the original sender or another person.

Giving feedback in such a way that the receiver will not feel threatened is not easy. To give feedback successfully requires you to develop sensitivity to other people's needs and to be able to put yourself into the other person's position.

**Filtering** is the tendency for a message to be watered down or halted completely at some point during transmission. Both speakers and listeners have communication filters, or barriers, through which messages must travel. In other words, the speaker sends a message through his or her filters; the listener receives the message through his or her filters. As you can see, total and accurate communication is very difficult to achieve.

Some examples of filters that cause people to misunderstand each other occur when the speaker and/or listener

- do not listen or do not want to listen
- do not understand the "language of feelings"
- do not say enough, or are not given the chance to say enough
- get mixed up in definitions (for example, a speaker often assumes that the listener understands what he or she said)
- fail to indicate to each other that they understand and that continuing the dialogue is not necessary
- give information too fast
- are generally unwilling to ask questions
- experience personality conflicts or differences
- jump to conclusions
- fail to read nonverbal messages

# Office Communication Networks

Communication networks in organizations are unique and reflect, to a large degree, each organization's mission to customers and vision for achieving it. One way to view communication networks is through upward, downward, and lateral communication; another way is through formal and informal communication channels.

Regardless of which network or channel is used, effective communication occurs when the right people receive the right information in a timely manner. If any of these three conditions are not present, communication will be ineffective.

Misunderstandings occur when the message gets blocked or distorted as a result of barriers in either sending or receiving information.

# Upward, Downward, and Lateral Communication Networks

**Upward communication** is feedback of data or information from lower levels in an organization to upper-management levels. This type usually deals with problems, clarifications, attitudes, ideas, and accomplishments. Managers use suggestion systems, attitude surveys, team meetings, complaint procedures, and committees to encourage upward communication from workers.

**Downward communication,** on the other hand, follows an organization's formal chain of command from top to bottom. This type covers procedures, policies, goals, assignments, and directives. A concern with downward communication is that the message decreases in accuracy as it passes through the chain of command. For that reason, managers use written

©Tony Freeman/PhotoEdit

Managers use handbooks, newsletters, bulletin boards, and other clear means of conveying messages downward through the chain of command so that all employees receive accurate information.

materials such as employee handbooks, policy manuals, organizational newsletters, bulletin boards, videos, and meetings to clearly communicate downward within the organization.

**Lateral communication,** also known as *horizontal communication,* occurs between departments or functional units, usually as a coordinating or problem-solving effort. Organizations may set up short-term task forces so that colleagues can discuss unique projects, or they may set up long-term committees so that co-workers can get together and discuss a particular organizational concern or issue on an ongoing basis.

# Formal and Informal Communication Channels

Offices also have communication channels. These channels are different from each other and are usually referred to as formal and informal communication channels.

### Formal Channels

Formal communication channels are the officially prescribed means by which messages normally flow inside organizations, and they are similar to downward communication. Downward communication is also referred to as "following the chain of command." In other words, the correct channel to follow is to discuss issues or concerns with your immediate superior first before going over his or her head to a higher-level manager.

### Informal Channels

The chain of command does not take into account informal communication between members. Informal communication channels convey messages along channels other than those formally designed by organizations. Informal interaction helps people do their jobs more effectively. The best-known types of informal communication within an organization are the grapevine and rumors.

**The Grapevine** The **grapevine** involves transmission of information by word of mouth without regard for organizational levels, and it often provides a great deal of useful information. Unfortunately, however, the grapevine can also distort information, create resentment among workers, and counteract organizational plans and objectives.

Brief, informal meetings help clarify decisions and prevent misunderstandings.

The office grapevine can strengthen bonds between employees; however, it can also distort information and cause discontent because of misunderstandings.

One example of grapevine chatter is talking about an unpopular directive from the boss. Organizational psychologists say such talk is usually harmless. Some feel that the grapevine is an effective way to alleviate the subordinates' sense of helplessness and to strengthen bonds among colleagues.

**Rumors** Generally, a person's best strategy is to let office rumors slide. Trying to refute gossip usually gives it more credence. However, the best approach to follow when clarifying rumors is to attack the source. Private one-on-one conversations with the perpetrators of gossip usually squelch further rumors.

Table 14.2 summarizes the communication networks and channels that operate in businesses.

# Workplace Literacy and SCANS

Do you feel that you are a literate person—a person who can read, write, and do basic math? A major concern for organizations today is the difficulty of locating and hiring a worker who is literate—specifically, one who

**TABLE 14.2 • Communication Networks and Channels**

| Communication Networks | **Upward Communication Is ...** feedback of data or information from the lower levels of an organization to upper-management levels. |
| | *Examples are:* *suggestion systems, surveys, team meetings, complaint procedures, and committees.* |
| | **Downward Communication Is ...** feedback of data or information that follows an organization's formal chain of command from top to bottom. |
| | *Examples are:* *employee handbooks, policy manuals, organizational newsletters, bulletin boards, videos, and meetings.* |
| | **Lateral Communication Is ...** feedback of data or information that occurs between departments or functional units, usually as a coordinating effort. |
| | *Examples are:* *short-term task forces or long-term committees.* |
| Communication Channels | **Formal** Communication that follows the formal chain of command as represented on the company's organizational chart. |
| | **Informal** Communication that allows for informal interaction between workers to help them do their jobs more effectively. |

is able to function in a literate way while performing routine workplace activities. **Workplace literacy** is the aspect of functional literacy related to employability and skill requirements for particular jobs.

The foundation for workplace literacy is a combination of traditional literacy and the ability to pull together information obtained from reading and making calculations and *apply* it in real-life situations. This application of knowledge requires information processing, logical reasoning, and critical thinking capabilities together with basic reading, writing, and mathematics skills.

The need for a high degree of workplace literacy reflects the reality that the basic skill levels that once were sufficient are now inadequate for employees faced with sophisticated quality control systems, team-based work, and participatory management practices. What degree of reading, writing, communication, and personal skills should you have and be prepared to demonstrate on your first job?

Perhaps the most important skill to take to a new job is the ability to read and comprehend well.

## Reading Skills

Today's office professional must be able to read well enough to understand correspondence, reports, records, equipment manuals, directories, charts, and graphs. Reading is the primary method used to locate information needed to make decisions or recommend courses of action. For example, when a new software package or upgrade version is purchased, employees are expected to have the ability to teach themselves through reading and understanding instructions in documentation and other reference material.

## Writing Skills

Composition and grammar skills are becoming critical as more writing responsibilities are assumed by the office professional. Although word processing software can check spelling, word usage, and grammar, it cannot edit for content or proofread completely. Office workers must be able to use a wide variety of reference books to fine-tune their thoughts and produce professional office documents.

## Other Communication Skills

The authors of the book *Workforce 2000* predict that 41 percent of new jobs will require high-level communication and problem-solving skills. The abilities to listen carefully to customers and co-workers and speak well enough to convey one's point of view clearly and effectively are essential. The office professional must be able to communicate with customers both in person and by telephone, understand customer concerns, explain schedules and procedures, relay messages accurately, work as a team player, teach others, reason logically while probing for hidden meanings, and solve problems.

Clearly, the degree of preparedness *expected of all workers* is rising dramatically. Many of the skills expected of a typical worker today were those expected only of managers a decade or so ago.

To be competitive, organizations must either employ literate workers or upgrade the literacy levels of current workers. Table 14.3, on page 302, compares the concepts of literacy and workplace literacy and gives examples of on-the-job workplace skills needed for office-related reading, writing, and problem solving.

**TABLE 14.3   Literacy vs. Workplace Literacy**

| Literacy | In general, the ability to read and understand a wide range of material, as well as the ability to write clearly and coherently. |
|---|---|
| Workplace Literacy | The aspect of literacy related to employability and skill requirements for particular jobs. In general, workplace literacy requires information processing, logical reasoning, and critical thinking capabilities together with basic reading, writing, communication, and mathematics skills. |
| **Examples of On-the-Job Workplace Literacy Skills** | |
| Reading | Locates, understands, and interprets written information in documents well enough to perform tasks. These documents could be manuals, graphs, schedules, reports, or proposals. |
| Writing | Communicates thoughts, ideas, information, and messages in writing. Checks for complete and accurate information and edits for correct information, appropriate emphasis, form, grammar, punctuation, and spelling. |
| Problem Solving | Discovers a rule or principle underlying the relationship between two or more items and applies it in solving a problem. Uses logic to draw appropriate conclusions from available information. |

# Secretary's Commission on Achieving Necessary Skills (SCANS)

"AMERICA 2000: An Education Strategy," initiated by former President George H. W. Bush, is a comprehensive plan to revitalize and reinvent America's schools. One major element of this strategy is the work completed by a commission, appointed by the U.S. Department of Labor, known as the **Secretary's Commission on Achieving Necessary Skills (SCANS).** Advanced by the secretary of labor, SCANS was formed in February 1990 and consisted of thirty-one representatives from business, unions, government, and schools. The commission was charged with the task of defining the know-how needed in the modern workplace and considering how this know-how is best assessed.

The SCANS report, entitled *What Work Requires of Schools,* identifies the eight areas (five competencies and a three-part foundation) considered essential preparation for all workers, whether they are going directly to work after high school or are planning further education. All eight competencies and foundations are highly integrated and require students and workers to be able to draw on *multiple* skills *simultaneously.*

Although the SCANS outcomes are not typically discussed among or even readily familiar to most businesspeople, their impact is enormous for business. In the search for productive employees, these SCANS-identified outcomes are most often required and demanded by employers. As a result of SCANS, the business world has formally directed the schools—kindergarten through university—to teach the needed skills. By the same token, it has indicated that students equipped with these globally competitive skills will be hired.

## SCANS's Five Competencies

The first part of the SCANS guidelines, workplace competencies, states that effective workers are able to productively use resources, demonstrate effective interpersonal and information skills, and work well with systems and technology. Each of the five competencies is described in the following list.

1. *Resources.* All workers know how to identify, organize, plan, and allocate time, money, materials, space, and staff.

2. *Interpersonal Skills.* All workers can work on teams, teach others, serve customers, lead, negotiate, and work well with people from culturally diverse backgrounds.

3. *Information Skills.* All workers can acquire and evaluate data, organize and maintain files, interpret and communicate, and use computers to process information.

4. *Systems.* All workers understand social, organizational, and technological systems; they can monitor and correct performance; and they can design or improve systems.

5. *Technology.* All workers can work with a variety of technologies to select equipment and tools, apply technology to specific tasks, and maintain and troubleshoot equipment.

Table 14.4 provides a clearer understanding of these five competencies by citing typical office tasks performed for each competency.

**TABLE 14.4 • Secretary's Commission on Achieving Necessary Skills (SCANS) Five Competencies**

| Competency | For Example, an Office Worker Effectively Takes the Following Actions: |
|---|---|
| Use Resources Productively | 1. Prioritizes one's own activities according to the manager's preferences, external environment, and target dates by selecting goal-relevant activities, ranking them, allocating time, and preparing and following schedules<br>2. Acquires, stores, allocates, and uses materials or space efficiently |
| Demonstrate Effective Interpersonal Skills | 1. Participates as a member of a team—contributes to group effort by assisting other office professionals in preparing for a board meeting<br>2. Teaches others new skills<br>3. Exercises leadership by communicating ideas to justify position, persuading and convincing others by responsibly challenging existing procedures and policies |
| Demonstrate Effective Information Skills | 1. Acquires and evaluates information from multiple sources<br>2. Organizes and maintains information such as stored computerized information<br>3. Uses computers to process information |
| Work Well with Systems | 1. Understands how social, organizational, and technological systems work and operates effectively with them<br>2. Monitors and corrects performance—distinguishes trends, predicts impacts on system operations, diagnoses deviations in systems' performance, and corrects malfunctions |
| Work Well with Technology | 1. Chooses procedures, tools, or equipment including computers and related technologies to enter and modify final reports in a computer<br>2. Applies technology to tasks and understands overall intent and proper procedures for setup and operation of equipment |

Adapted from "Skills and Tasks for JOBS: A SCANS Report for AMERICA 2000," the Secretary's Commission on Achieving Necessary Skills, U.S. Department of Labor, Washington, D.C., 1992.

## SCANS's Three-Part Foundation

The second part of the SCANS guidelines states that competent workers in the high-performance workplace need the following three foundation skills:

1. *Basic skills*
   - Reading—locates, understands, and interprets written information in documents such as manuals, graphs, and schedules
   - Writing—communicates thoughts, ideas, information, and messages in writing; creates documents such as letters, directions, manuals, reports, graphs, and flow charts
   - Arithmetic/mathematics—performs basic computation and approaches practical problems by choosing appropriately from a variety of mathematical techniques
   - Listening—receives, attends to, interprets, and responds to verbal messages and other cues
   - Speaking—organizes ideas and communicates orally

2. *Thinking skills*
   - Creative thinking—generates new ideas
   - Decision making—specifies goals and constraints, generates alternatives, considers risks, and evaluates and chooses the best alternative
   - Problem solving—recognizes problems and devises and implements plan of action
   - Seeing things in the mind's eye—organizes and processes symbols, pictures, graphs, objects, and other information

3. *Personal qualities*
   - Responsibility—exerts a high level of effort and perseveres toward goal attainment
   - Self-esteem—believes in own self-worth and maintains a positive view of self
   - Sociability—demonstrates understanding, friendliness, adaptability, empathy, and politeness in group settings
   - Self-management—assesses self accurately, sets personal goals, monitors progress, and exhibits self-control
   - Integrity/honesty—chooses ethical courses of action.

## Implications of SCANS for New Workers and Employers

If SCANS recommendations are followed by educators, student assessment in school will be transformed on the theory that multiple-choice, paper-and-pencil tests cannot evaluate students' ability to apply knowledge to real-world problems. SCANS recommends that in its place, every student should establish a student competency portfolio beginning in sixth grade. This portfolio will include several items such as a personal résumé, evidence of competence in specific areas of study, work history, extracurricular experience, and a record of community services.

If completed in a professional manner, your portfolio will tell the story of your progress in a given area. Therefore, when you begin your job search, you can adjust the portfolio to demonstrate that you have the qualities and skills for which the employer is looking. The employer would decide how much weight to give elements in the portfolio, using the company's own needs as a guideline.

*Answer the following questions:*

**1.** Describe three examples of nonverbal communication.

**2.** How does workplace literacy differ from traditional literacy?

**3.** Is the grapevine a formal or informal channel of communication? Explain.

# Effective Reading, Writing, and Speaking Skills in the Office

In your opinion, are good communication skills critical to attaining success in life? Many people feel that how well you communicate can make your daily activities either easy and pleasant or difficult and upsetting. The ability to communicate effectively is a skill that you can acquire just like any other skill. For example, the same practice and awareness of basic principles that are needed to become a good volleyball player are needed to become a good communicator.

To be good communicators in business, workers need to practice effective reading, writing, and speaking skills (as well as listening skills, which are discussed later in the chapter).

## Effective Reading Techniques

You may have discovered in preparing for exams that time spent reading can be either well spent or lost. Whether preparing for an exam or on a job reviewing a business report, you can get more out of your time, energy, and efforts by following a few basic steps. The basic steps in reading for information are previewing, questioning, and reviewing. This method is sometimes called the *PQR system.*

### Previewing
Experienced readers preview the material before they start to read for comprehension. **Previewing** means scanning the selection, looking for main points, and discovering how the material is organized. To preview a report, for example, skim the preface, then turn to the table of contents and examine it to see how the main ideas are related to one another, and finally leaf through the report to get a feel for what is in it. If the report has a summary, read it. If not, read the first and last paragraphs of each major section to get a general idea of what the report is about.

### Questioning
Become an active reader by taking a questioning approach to the material. Ask yourself: Why am I reading this material? How will this material meet my needs? What do I already know about this topic? Asking and answering questions as you read helps you master the material and keeps you focused.

## Reviewing

Most of the time, reading something once is not enough. You review what you read to fix it in your memory. You do this by using three processes—seeing, saying, and writing. First, go back over the material, skimming each section of the article. As you *see* the material, *say* the answers to your questions aloud. Then *write* brief reference notes that summarize the main points. This review method helps you remember by organizing and repeating the material.

## Effective Writing Techniques

The skill of writing business documents is directly related to reading office letters, memos, reports, and other paperwork. Researchers estimate that American businesses generate over 30 billion pieces of original writing each year. Workers on average spend one-third of their time on the job writing letters, memos, and reports.

Much of the writing, however, is unnecessary; most of it is poorly written, and all of it has to be read. A great deal of time is wasted not only by the millions of people who have to write on the job but also by those who have to read all of this writing. Table 14.5 lists ten steps you can take to become a more effective writer.

**TABLE 14.5 • Ten Steps to More Effective Writing**

| Steps | Explanation |
|---|---|
| 1. Determine the purpose of the correspondence. | Ask yourself: What is the reason for writing the letter? What response is required? |
| 2. Decide which type of letter or report is needed. | If you are writing a letter, should it be good news, bad news, or persuasive? If you are writing a report, should it be direct or indirect? |
| 3. Make notes of important points to bring out. | List everything that needs to be said—in no particular order. |
| 4. Organize the notes by topics. | Arrange the points in the order you want to present them. |
| 5. Write freely. | Write as you would talk. In other words, let your writing do the talking. Do not worry about spelling, grammar, and punctuation at this point. These items can be corrected later. |
| 6. Use appropriate sentence structure and length. | Your writing should contain a variety of sentence lengths. Remember, long sentences may be difficult to read, and too many short sentences may make your writing seem choppy. |
| 7. Write several paragraphs. | Short paragraphs permit the reader to identify the facts and points of emphasis. |
| 8. Revise. | Read the document for content. If it is not correct, revise. |
| 9. Edit. | After writing the initial draft, you should take a break from the task of writing. After this break, you should read the draft, correcting the spelling and grammar as you read. |
| 10. Ask for input. | Ask a colleague to read the document for you. Welcome any feedback. |

Source: "Basics for Better Business Writing," by Annette Vincent, Ph.D., *The Secretary*, March 1995, 8.

Using the "five C's" to check your writing is an effective method. The five C's are: complete, clear, concise, coherent, and correct. When you fine-tune your writing effort according to these five criteria, you question your written words and ideas by asking if the writing is

1. *Complete.* Are all the reader's questions answered? Does the reader have enough information to evaluate the message and, if necessary, to act on it?

2. *Clear.* Does the reader get the meaning you intended? Does the reader have to guess what is meant?

3. *Concise.* Do the style, organization, and visual impact of the message help the reader to read, understand, and act on the information as quickly as possible?

4. *Coherent.* Are the ideas presented in a logical, consistent manner that makes it easy for the reader to follow and understand, and if necessary, arrive at a decision or conclusion?

5. *Correct.* Is the information in the message accurate? Is the message free from errors in punctuation, spelling, grammar, word order, and sentence structure?

Some additional business writing suggestions are:

1. *Be specific.* Misunderstandings usually arise when your writing lacks clarity. For example, do not write, "I will get the report to you in a couple of weeks"; write instead, "I will get the report to you by September 15."

2. *Avoid redundancies.* Many writers like to use two words with nearly the same meaning in their sentences, erroneously thinking these words add emphasis to the message. Instead, these redundancies add bulk. Two examples are: pleased and delighted, help and support. Using either word, not both, gets your message across just as effectively.

3. *Be positive, even when the message is negative.* Think about it; don't you find yourself responding more to positive statements rather than to negative ones? For example, instead of writing "The budget will not cover trip expenses over $100," write "The budget will cover trip expenses up to $100."

4. *Turn passive voice into active voice.* Readers can visualize an active statement more easily than they can a passive one. For example, "A meeting will be held on Thursday," is better stated as "We will meet on Thursday."

## Effective Speaking Techniques

From the time you get up in the morning until you go to sleep at night, you use your voice to communicate. At home you converse with your family about the events of the day. With your friends, you chat about whatever concerns you. You use the telephone to talk about business and personal matters. At school, you ask and answer questions in class and speak with other students. If you work, you give directions, explain things, ask and answer questions, participate in meetings, and talk with customers and co-workers. In addition, you may occasionally give oral presentations at school, clubs, church, or work.

**TIP** Stage fright in public speaking can be substantially reduced if you know *what* you want to say, *why* it is a valuable message for your audience, and *how* you will best communicate the importance of the message. ■

When you speak, try to give clear examples, use appropriate language, repeat information, ask questions, and use your voice effectively. Remember, when we speak, our voices reveal information about us. Some facts about your voice that you need to know are:

1. *Your voice has a vital role in confirming another person's first impression of you.* If you sound harsh and abrasive, timid and insecure, or strong and confident, you will likely be viewed that way.

2. *Your voice has a physiological effect upon your listener.* Speak rapidly, and the listener's heart rate and adrenaline level increase. Shout at someone, and his or her blood pressure rises. Speak calmly, and he or she feels a soothing effect.

3. *Your voice is a barometer of your physical and emotional state.* It reveals stress before other physical signs, reflects how tired you are, and gives clues to other emotions. For example, the voice of a person who is upset, tense, angry, or afraid rises.

# Listening and Helping Skills in Business

Good listening habits foster success on the job. Think of the times that someone has asked you a question you just answered. Or, remember the times when someone interrupted when you were trying to communicate a problem and needed someone to listen and help you through it. If interruption is unpleasant in casual conversation, think how annoying it is when conducting business, especially when you are the one trying to communicate to a poor listener.

## Effective Listening Skills

Most of us do not mean to be rude or insensitive to others when we lapse into poor listening practices. Sometimes, roadblocks prevent us from actively listening.

## Roadblocks to Effective Listening

We all experience some realistic and honest roadblocks to effective listening from time to time. These roadblocks are:

1. Our minds will not wait; our thoughts race along four to ten times faster than most people speak.

2. We think we know already, so we listen with "half an ear."

3. We are looking but not listening. Have you ever been introduced to someone and failed to catch the person's name because you were focused on his or her clothes or mannerisms?

4. We are busy listeners; we try to do too many things while we listen.

5. We miss the big ideas; we are listening to words, not concepts.

6. Our emotions make us ignore input when someone offers opposing ideas on matters about which we have strong opinions.

**TIP** When taking a message for someone, besides recording it accurately, the three most important things you can remember to record on the message are the date, the time, and your name. ■

Effective listening is as important to good communication as comprehension is to reading well.

## Active Listening

Good listening skills in the office do not just happen. You must be aware that listening is one of the most essential business skills you can have. One technique you can develop and use is active listening. **Active listening** means restating the sender's total communication (thoughts and feelings) to help the sender understand both of these aspects of his or her communication as you view them.

How do you listen actively? By feeding back the underlying feelings you hear as well as the content of the message, you listen activity. You probably listen actively automatically with friends, but you simply do not realize that you are actively listening.

Specific examples of active listening are: "You sound upset when he uses your equipment," or "You are not pleased with the way the report is coming, are you?" Evaluate your abilities as an active listener by answering the questions in Figure 14.2.

## Effective Helping Skills

Sometimes a friend at school or, if you work, a customer or co-worker, is upset and needs someone just to listen while he or she talks through a problem. When you perceive cues that another person is in this situation,

**FIGURE 14.2 • Are You an Active Listener?**

**Instructions:** Respond to each of the following questions with either a yes or no, and check your score according to the scale at the bottom of the page.

**Do You ...**

1. Limit your talking during conversations: Can you talk and listen at the same time?

2. Think like the customer? Can you understand and appreciate the customer's point of view?

3. Ask questions: If you do not understand something, do you clear it up now so that it does not embarrass you later?

4. Avoid interrupting another speaker? (A pause, even a long one, does not always mean that the sender has finished what he or she wants to say.)

5. Concentrate on what is being said and practice shutting out distractions?

6. Take brief notes to help remember important points?

7. Listen for ideas, not just words?

8. Turn off personal fears, worries, and problems when dealing with others?

9. React to ideas, not the person?

10. Allow the speaker to complete sentences? Or do you jump to conclusions by mentally or verbally completing sentences for the speaker?

| Score Your YES Responses: | | |
|---|---|---|
| | 8–10 | You are a good active listener. |
| | 5–7 | You are making an effort to become an active listener. |
| | 4 & under | Oops, have you wondered why getting a conversation going is difficult? |

and you *choose* to help him or her, you can use a number of communication helping skills. These skills are listed in order of increasing activity and involvement on your part. They are:

1. *Silence.* Simply listening passively with accompanying nonverbal behaviors (posture, eye contact, nodding of the head, and so on) communicates your interest and concern.

2. *Noncommittal acknowledgment.* Brief expressions that encourage the person to continue talking toward an eventual solution communicate your understanding, acceptance, and empathy. Examples: "Oh, I see," "Mmm-hmm."

3. *Door openers.* Gently inviting the speaker to expand or continue his or her expressions of thoughts and feelings shows you are interested and involved. Examples: "Tell me about it." "Would you like to talk about it?"

4. *Content paraphrasing.* Putting the factual portion of the message into your own words and sending it back to check your accuracy in understanding. Examples: "So you really told your boss off"; "You're saying, if your plan works the problem will be solved?"

## Recall Time

*Answer the following questions:*

**1.** What does PQR stand for and when is it used?

**2.** List the five C's for effective writing.

**3.** Cite three examples of roadblocks to effective listening.

# Summary

Communication is the exchange of messages. The messages may be verbal, using spoken or written words, or they may be nonverbal, using symbols, gestures, expressions, and body language. Office communication networks may take on different meanings depending on the way they are viewed—as upward, downward, and lateral communication or as formal and informal communication channels.

Organizations expect and require employees to be literate on the job. In addition to reading and writing skills, office workers need to be able to apply such personal skills as information processing, logical reasoning, and critical thinking. The SCANS report addressed this need and identified eight areas considered essential preparation for all workers, whether they are going directly to work after high school or are planning further education.

To be good communicators in business, workers need to practice effective reading, writing, and speaking skills, as well as listening skills. The basic steps for reading information are known as the PQR system, which stands for previewing, questioning, and reviewing the material you read. When you write, check your writing with the five C's by asking if what you wrote is complete, clear, concise, coherent, and correct. Effective listening skills include recognizing roadblocks to effective listening and becoming an active listener who uses good helping skills.

Key points to recall from this chapter include:

- Communication requires a sender, a person who transmits the message, and a receiver, a person who gets the message.
- Experts point out that 93 percent of what we communicate is in our body language and how we speak, while only 7 percent is communicated by what we say.
- Both the speaker and listeners have communication "filters" or barriers through which messages must pass.
- Although information travels rather quickly through the grapevine, it can become distorted and at times counteract organizational plans and objectives.
- Essential workplace competencies, according to the SCANS report, indicate that effective workers are able to productively use resources, demonstrate effective interpersonal and information skills, and work well with systems and technology.
- The three foundation skills that competent workers need are basic skills, thinking skills, and personal qualities such as responsibility, self-esteem, sociability, self-management, and honesty.
- In office speaking situations, try to give clear examples, use appropriate language, repeat information, ask questions, and use your voice effectively.
- Good listening skills are among the most essential business abilities you can develop to be successful.
- Effective helping skills include silence while listening, noncommittal acknowledgment, door openers, and content paraphrasing.

# before you leave...

**When you have completed this chapter, answer the following questions:**
1. What are some typical office communication networks?
2. Which communication skills should office workers be able to demonstrate?

# Review & Application

## Check Your Knowledge

1. Describe the communication process.

2. Give an example of one-way and two-way communication in which you have participated this week.

3. How do individuals communicate nonverbally?

4. Explain what is meant by the idea that both speakers and listeners have communication filters through which messages must pass. How does filtering negatively affect the communication process?

5. Give some examples of how organizations demonstrate both upward and downward communication.

6. Explain the positive and negative aspects of the grapevine as an informal communication channel.

7. In your own words, define *workplace literacy*. How does it differ from traditional literacy?

8. Why was SCANS formed?

9. List the five competencies and three-part foundation skills referred to as basic workplace know-how.

10. What techniques and steps can workers use to read, write, and speak more effectively on the job?

11. In what ways are active listening and effective helping skills related?

## Review Your Vocabulary

On a separate piece of paper, match the following items by writing the letter of each New Office Term beside its description.

____ 1. the tendency for a message to be watered down or halted completely at some point during transmission

____ 2. feedback of data or information from lower levels in the organization to upper-management levels

____ 3. that aspect of functional literacy related to employability and skill requirements for particular jobs

____ 4. a special commission appointed by the secretary of the U.S. Department of Labor

____ 5. the exchange of messages

____ 6. scanning the selection, looking for main points, and discovering how the material is organized

____ 7. communication that follows the organization's formal chain of command from top to bottom

____ 8. a restatement of the sender's total communication (thoughts and feelings) to help the sender to understand both of these aspects of his or her communication as you view them

____ 9. transmission of information by word of mouth without regard for organizational levels; often provides a great deal of useful information

____ 10. verbal and nonverbal responses that the receiver gives by further communicating with the original sender or another person

____ 11. feedback of data or information between departments or functional units

a. active listening
b. communication
c. downward communication
d. feedback
e. filtering
f. grapevine
g. lateral communication
h. previewing
i. Secretary's Commission on Achieving Necessary Skills
j. upward communication
k. workplace literacy

## Discuss and Analyze an Office Situation

Ling Chu is secretary at Clean Sweep Janitorial Services, a medium-size cleaning service in the Houston metropolitan area. Recently, cleaning supply sales representatives who have spoken to her have told

Ling how other janitorial companies are being sued because their workers have caused medical emergencies due to their inability to read and comprehend directions. Apparently, the workers cannot understand the warnings on labels of chemically based cleaning products.

Ling wonders whether she should discuss this information with the president of the company.

1. Assume that Ling does contact the president. What concerns should they discuss?

2. If you were the president and were apprised of pending litigation for companies similar to Clean Sweep, what steps might you take to deal with the workplace literacy problem?

## Practice Basic Skills

### Math

Using the chart below, answer on a separate piece of paper the following questions about the number of pages prepared during January and February after you have calculated the monthly totals and overall totals for letters, memos, and reports.

a. What percentage of the total number of pages for January is represented by the total number of letter pages for January?

b. What is the total number of pages keyed in both January and February?

c. What percentage of the total number of pages keyed is the total number of letter pages keyed?

d. At a cost of $3.50 per page, what does it cost to key January's reports?

### NUMBER OF PAGES

| Month | Letters | Memos | Reports | Monthly Total |
|---|---|---|---|---|
| January | 622 | 433 | 788 | _____ |
| February | 533 | 401 | 790 | _____ |
| TOTALS | _____ | _____ | _____ | _____ |

### English

Rewrite or key the following sentences on a separate piece of paper, using simpler wording.

a. We will deliver the products in the near future.

b. You should study all of the new innovations in your field.

c. Our office is charged with the task of counting supplies not used in production.

d. This condition can be assumed to be critical.

e. Our goal is to effect a change concerning the overtime pay rate.

f. I will talk to him with regard to the new policy.

g. In accordance with their plans, the company sold the land.

h. Clint is of the conviction that service to the customer has improved.

i. Losses created by the strike went over the amount of eighteen thousand dollars.

j. The consensus of opinion of the parent group is that more money is needed.

### Proofreading

Rewrite or rekey the following memo, correcting misspellings and incorrect punctuation.

| MEMO | |
|---|---|
| TO: | All Staff Members |
| FROM: | John Glenn, Office Manager |
| DATE: | Deccember 23, 20— |
| SUBJECT: | Changes in Corespoondence Preparation |

Please be awarre of the following changes that should be incorporated into outgoing mail begining the first of the year:

1. If you cannot find the name, of the person to whom you are addressing the letter, address it to the postion (Ex., Dear Travel Agent—not Dear Sir or Dear Gentlemen).

2. If the letter is for A. Smith and you do not know if the A is for a man or a woman, you should key *A. Smith* in the letter address. Your salutation should read "Dear A. Smith."

3. Eliminate wornned out phrasess such as:
   • If you have eny questions...

- In answer to your letter datted...
- In as much as...
- Enclosed you will please find...
- I feel . . . I hope . . . sorry . . . glad . . . happy . . . thanks in advance
- Eleminate sexist language

## Apply Your Knowledge

1. Willie Tadano, a new employee at Mountain Pediatric, works with other employees in the general office area. When a new procedure directive arrives in the department, it is sent around to each worker. After reading it, each worker initials the directive and passes it along. A fellow office worker, Persia Gorman, has noticed that Willie puts his initials on the materials without actually reading them. According to other office workers, he then asks them to explain the new procedure to him.
   a. What may contribute to Willie's preference not to read new information?
   b. What can Persia suggest to him?

2. *Debate the Issue:*
   "In today's world, communication is based on speed of the message, not the effectiveness of that message."

   *Instructions:* React to the above statement by quickly jotting down three or more ideas supporting *and* refuting the statement. Prepare to role-play either point of view in a mock in-class debate.

## Using the Reference Manual

Open file ch14ref.doc. Use the proofreaders' marks in the Reference Manual at the back of the book to help you correct the paragraphs. Save and print.

When you plan your written communication, start by definig the purpose and identifying the audience. Then make a outline and revise the outline until it represents your writing objetife.

Geting the ideas down on paper is muh easier if you have done a good job in the first step. The best way to impress your reader is with the clarity and conciseness of your messge, not with the no. of multisyllable words you use.

In the editing process, you might have to keyboard final copy from a rough drft prepared by someone else. In those situations, you should understand the meanings of severla proofreaders marks.

# chapter 15

## Communicating in a Changing Workplace

### objectives

*After completing this chapter, you will be able to do the following:*

1. Describe the role of an office worker in a reengineered and horizontal organization.
2. List some alternatives to the command-and-control hierarchy.
3. Describe the external forces that influence office communication.
4. Describe new attitudes in the workplace about the importance of the customer.
5. Describe the internal forces that influence office communication.
6. Explain how empowerment is a motivational tool and enhances office communication.

### New Office Terms

- alternative work systems
- cross-functional teams
- customer
- empowerment

- horizontal organization
- portable skills
- reengineering
- technology

# before you begin...

***Answer the following questions to the best of your ability:***

1. List some external forces that affect office communication.
2. List some internal forces that affect office communication.

# The Changing Office Environment

Reacting to recent and future economic, political, and social realities—and anticipating future ones—organizations are restructuring around new roles for information and technology. New roles for information will affect an organization's structure and forms of management, and the way office workers do their jobs.

## The Challenge of Change

Successful organizations, managers, and office workers recognize the difficulties presented by change. Figure 15.1 presents several excuses each of us uses from time to time to resist change. However, change is constant. Emerging trends and ideas that will require each of us to occasionally alter our thinking and behavior will always exist.

We have already seen that today's employees have dramatically changed their work expectations, values, and lifestyles. As a result, many organizations are responding with numerous **alternative work systems.** Alternative work systems are nontraditional working arrangements that include office sharing, job sharing, flextime, and telecommuting, which are discussed more fully in Chapter 18.

**FIGURE 15.1 • Common Excuses Not to Change**

It will take too long.
No one asked me. It's hopeless.
I don't have the authority.
It can't be done.
I don't have enough time.
It's too ambitious. It's not my job.
It's just a fad, I'm all for it, but...
It's too expensive.
We don't have the equipment.
We're doing OK as it is.

In the past week, how many of these statements have you used when resisting an idea that required you to change?

## Technology in the Office | VERSATILE STORAGE ON CD/DVD WRITERS

You have many choices in how to store data, ranging from floppy disk to the largest hard disk drives. However, possibly the most versatile storage is provided by combination compact disk/digital video disk (CD/DVD) media writers.

CDs can store about 80 minutes of audio or 700MB of data; DVDs can store 4.7GB of data. You can use inexpensive CDs for storing up to 500 times what you can store on a floppy disk. Or you can use DVDs to store more than six times as much as you can store on a CD. You can record data, photograph files, and video files on either medium—and do it all on one multipurpose writer. A number of reliable brands of CD/DVD writers are available. ■

The familiar management hierarchy depicted on organizational charts as a pyramid was a formal diagram that showed how work was divided. More important, it clarified who in organizations reported to whom. However, that mentality, which worked so beautifully a century ago, has become self-destructive these days. Few business leaders foresaw today's cutthroat competition, as well as the emergence of a more skilled and educated workforce, and the development of advanced technologies that do everything faster and smarter. They have resulted in a change in the way office workers communicate with each other, their supervisors, and customers.

## Business Reengineering, Empowerment, and Work Teams

In 1993 Michael Hammer and James Champy's book *Reengineering the Corporation* informed businesses about the benefits of a new managerial idea called *reengineering*. The authors proposed that when properly applied, reengineering allows companies to do much more with far less—less investment, less time, fewer people. **Reengineering** means the stem-to-stern redesign of the way a company works, from its organizational structure to its corporate culture.

Business reengineering is not about fixing anything. Business reengineering means starting over from scratch. Old job titles and old organizational arrangements—departments, divisions, groups, and so on—cease to matter. What matters is how best to organize work, given the demands of today's markets and the power of today's technologies.

How does reengineering work? Successful reengineering is based on two principal concepts: empowering employees and using cross-functional teams.

**Empowerment** means giving employees closest to the customer the authority and tools required to make many independent decisions. It is founded on the belief that the person doing the job knows better than anyone else the best way to do it and how to improve performance. As a result, empowerment utilizes a worker's abilities and potential to a great extent, while cutting costs and improving customer service. Customers are no longer shifted from one employee to another, decision making is faster, and mistakes are fewer. Worker-empowered organizations are covered in detail later in this chapter.

Another reengineering approach is to use **cross-functional teams** of disparate employees working together in a way that makes them aware of changes that may affect their jobs. These teams, based around task relevance, can propel organizations to new levels of success by increasing employee enthusiasm, involvement, cooperation, and commitment to success.

For example, suppose that you work for an organization that wants to develop a new product line or service. With cross-functional teams, workers from marketing, manufacturing, human resources, and administration will share information and ideas and follow this new concept from start to finish. (See Chapter 17 for a further discussion of teams.)

## Alternatives to the Organizational Hierarchy

A major change occurring in workplaces today involves reorganizing the organizational chart. The pyramid is passé. Wheels, clusters, and inverted pyramids are in style. As a result of these new structures, the manner, methods, and modes of communicating affect the work relationships of not only the president and corporate executive officer (CEO), but also the custodian and receptionist. Figure 15.2, page 321, illustrates some of the imaginative alternatives to the pyramid style of organization that are currently surfacing. These alternatives are discussed next.

1. The *inverted pyramid,* created by Nordstrom™, literally turns the traditional organizational structure upside down. This organizational structure is relatively flat. It has only a few levels, with salespeople and sales support staff on top, making the key decisions. Only one formal rule applies at Nordstrom that employees are expected to honor: Use your own best judgment at all times. The company believes that salespeople should pay more attention to their customers' needs than to those of their bosses.

2. The *cluster* organization brings groups of people from different disciplines together to work on a semipermanent basis. In a cluster organization, groups are arranged like bunches of grapes on a corporate vine; the vine is the corporate vision that connects one group—a bunch of people working together—to another.

3. The *wagon wheel* is another organizational chart redesign—a circular chart, much like a wagon wheel. It has three main parts: the hub of the wheel; a series of spokes, which radiate from the hub; and finally, the outer rim. Customers are the center hub. The spokes could be the business functions, such as finance, marketing, or engineering, or they could be teams dedicated to working on new product development or customer satisfaction. Keeping it all together on the outer rim are the chief executive and board of directors, who are placed there to make sure everybody has, at his or her fingertips, everything needed to serve the customer. In this organizational design, managers are coaches and supporters, not authoritarian whip crackers.

Each of these newfangled designs has its supporters, those who claim that their pet designs are the once-and-for-all cure for everything that ails a company. Not true. Without the right mindset, supporting measures, rewards, and management, even a reengineered organization is doomed.

**FIGURE 15.2 • Nontraditional Organizational Structures**

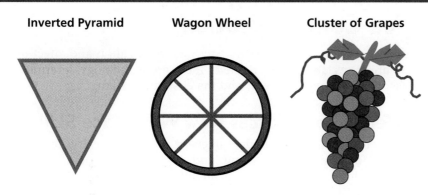

| Inverted Pyramid | Wagon Wheel | Cluster of Grapes |

Three Alternatives to Command-and-Control Hierarchy.

If done right, redesigning an organization can be hugely effective in harnessing the intelligence of its present employees. Reengineering is not the same as reorganizing, delayering, or flattening a company, although reengineering may, in fact, produce a flatter organization.

## The Horizontal Organization

Entrenched bureaucracy is a feature of the typical vertical organization, a company where staffers look up to bosses instead of out to customers. Even after these companies undergo the cutting, downsizing, and delayering designed to streamline their operations, too many layers of management still slow decision making and lead to high coordination costs.

In the quest for greater efficiency and productivity, corporate America's biggest names have redrawn their hierarchical organization charts. The trend is toward flatter, **horizontal organizations** in which managing "across" has become more critical than managing "up and down" as in a top-heavy hierarchy.

In its purest state, the horizontal organization has a skeleton group of senior executives at the top in such traditional support functions as finance and human resources. However, virtually everyone else in the organization works together in cross-functional teams that perform core processes such as product development or sales generation. The result is that the organization might have only three or four layers of management between the chairperson and the staffers in a given process.

## Recall Time

*Answer the following questions:*

**1.** List some excuses that people who do not like to change often use.

**2.** Describe a horizontal corporation.

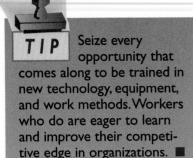
# External Forces Affecting Office Communication

Forces from outside sources that impact the organization and affect office workers are many and varied. Some of them are technology, international business, the quality movement, and the customer as king.

## How Technology Forces New Workplace Skills

The impact of technology is evident in every aspect of society. Technology is a driving force in creating, using, and storing information. In a broad sense, **technology** may be viewed as an aid to make a task easier by using equipment and procedures to create, process, and output information. Technology's impact is also apparent in the changing job market. Employers will hire and pay good wages to employees who demonstrate the ability to use technology effectively.

As pointed out in Chapters 5 and 6, workers must know how to use electronic information technologies to process data with computers and related equipment. These electronic information technologies manipulate text, numerics, graphics, voice, video, and sensory data.

Technology has lowered the skill levels of some jobs or eliminated them altogether, while raising the skill levels of other jobs. Technological advances also allow information and other resources to be transported faster than before. Today's workers most often need to locate, assess, communicate, and apply information as opposed to remembering it. Content changes and new information replaces old information at an alarming rate. Today's workers often lack skills for processing new information and integrating it with what they already know. Those processing, communicating, and integrating skills are vital in a fast-changing business world.

©David Young-Wolff/PhotoEdit

Today's worker must be able to adapt to new situations easily and to apply current skills and experiences to solving new problems.

As a result, employees need new abilities. One important ability is knowing how to learn effectively so that they can quickly apply strategies and tactics for mastering new tasks. They also need to develop portable skills. If you have **portable skills**, you are able to transfer what you already know to slightly new situations. Workers need to recognize when a problem is similar to something they have done before so that they can use skills and previous experience to solve the new problem.

As discussed earlier, literacy at work, unlike in school, is seldom a matter of understanding or writing whole paragraphs. Rather, it involves sets of words that relate in a specific way to the organization and its particular work. Workplace literacy involves the ability to use words clearly and with brevity and accuracy in the context of a given job.

The distinct language of the workplace is not academic in style; over time, workers tend to develop a highly specialized vocabulary, a language apart from the one learned in school. Though writing well is an important communication skill, researchers estimate that the typical U.S. worker spends only about 9 percent of the workday writing and 13 percent of it reading. Another 23 percent of a worker's day is spent in speaking, and a significant 55 percent in listening.

# International Business and Intercultural Communication Skills

Rarely do we meet anyone these days who does not have some connections with another country. The world is indeed becoming a global village in which information and services are transmitted everywhere by fax machine, telephone, modem, and satellite. The ability to transfer information electronically has made information itself a prime export. Most countries do not have good information infrastructures and will buy information properly packaged from the United States. To succeed as employees in this global environment, workers must acquire the tools that will make their organizations internationally competitive.

## International Business Skills

Nothing is mysterious about what knowledge and types of skills today's office workers need to become effective employees in international business. The key is not to wait but to develop these skills in an appropriate international context according to recognizable world standards. Some international business skills include:

1. *Basic understanding of international trade and economics.* Simply put, what a country produces efficiently, it can export; what it does not produce, it will likely import from a more efficient foreign supplier. Organizations realize that improved trade opportunities happen when their employees demonstrate worldwide skills, which include knowing something about religious beliefs, social customs, business philosophy, and family structure in other nations.

2. *Ability to manage information.* One of the driving forces behind our global economy is the revolution in communications. To be competitive, businesses and their employees must be efficient users of information, much of it electronic, whether it is from domestic or foreign sources; familiar with the primary business documents used by nations as they conduct trade with one another; and familiar with the global network communications system that makes possible the instant transmission of business correspondence, news, and vast amounts of business data to virtually any point in the world. The

**TIP** One of the best resources for international business information is the U.S. government. Specifically, information and assistance are available through the Small Business Administration, the Office of International Trade, and the Department of Commerce in Washington, D.C. ∎

sources and types of information are virtually unlimited; the problem is accessing them and processing the acquired data. Being aware that effective information management is at the heart of what most businesses do is critical.

3. *Knowledge of and sensitivity to political and cultural contexts.* Foreign government regulations must be understood and obeyed. Business culture can also vary dramatically from country to country. For example, in Muslim countries the workweek usually begins on Sunday.

## Intercultural Communication

The more international business becomes, the more important recognizing differences among people from different cultures becomes; these differences affect good communication. The more we take advantage of opportunities to interact outside our own cultural boundaries, the better communicators we become. For example, Table 5.1 provides some customs and tips for doing business in European nations relative to greetings, appointments, and social activities.

Successful firms in the international marketplace are companies whose employees not only understand world economics and global competitiveness, but have the ability to communicate effectively with their international counterparts. Employees in the United States need to study intercultural communication issues such as:

- developing techniques that will overcome language barriers, both oral and written

- recognizing the advantages and disadvantages of using interpreters

- studying American negotiation strategies and how they differ from the negotiation patterns of other countries

**TABLE 15.1 • Customs and Tips for Doing Business in European Countries**

| Country | Names and Greetings | Appointments and Punctuality | Socializing and Gifts |
|---------|--------------------|-----------------------------|-----------------------|
| France | Prefer to be addressed by last name; shake hands at beginning and end of meeting | Make appointments in advance; punctuality is a sign of courtesy, but up to fifteen minutes late is still acceptable | Invitation to a home is rare; but if invited, give flowers or chocolates to the host |
| Germany | Use titles and never refer to someone by first name unless asked to do so | Make appointments in advance; punctuality is essential | If invited to a home, bring flowers and follow up with a thank-you note |
| Great Britain | Use first names upon introduction; shake hands only at first meeting | Make appointments in advance; arriving ten to twenty minutes late is expected | Invitation to a home, pub, or restaurant is normal; never smoke until after the toast to Her Majesty's health |
| Italy | Refer to executives by their last names; handshaking and gesturing are common | Make appointments in advance; being late requires an apology | If invited to a home, bring host a bottle of wine, flowers, or chocolates; exchanging business gifts is common |
| Spain | Use of first names occurs quickly; close friends greet with an embrace | Punctuality is not essential | If invited to a home, bring host flowers or chocolates; do not discuss business until after coffee is served |

Adapted from Karen Matthes, "Mind Your Manners When Doing Business in Europe," *HR Focus*, January 1992.

**Making Office Decisions**

Usually Mr. Wong, the president of International Import Agency, prefers to use a work team to deal with problems or issues when they arise rather than to bring in outside consultants. Consistent with this philosophy, he has asked the office manager and two administrative assistants to serve on a work team that is charged with the responsibility of developing an in-house seminar for employees who wish to be able to better adapt to change—especially change that comes from international business relations and services.

1. **How should the three persons proceed in developing this seminar?**

2. **What topics or areas should they include in this training, and why?** ■

■ understanding the impact of one's own culture on personal attitudes and behaviors and recognizing that all global workers are molded by their cultures

■ developing sensitivity to intercultural differences and different value systems

■ learning to feel comfortable using telecommunications technology, such as computer networks, electronic mail, and bulletin boards, to communicate internationally

## Quality and Continuous Improvement

Although the quality movement is over a decade old, its lessons are still considered valid and followed by successful organizations. The basic beliefs held by companies seeking quality and continuous improvement are:

1. Management must demonstrate a long-term commitment to making the improvement process part of the company's values by giving it management focus and leadership.

©CHABRUKEN/FPG International

To be successful in the global marketplace, businesspeople from any culture must be able to communicate effectively with their international counterparts.

2. Improvement must focus on the process, not the people.

3. Preventing problems is better than reacting to them.

4. Acceptance of the customer is the most important reason for doing business honorably and well.

## The Importance of Customers

In organizations, the customer has the influence of a king. As shown in Figure 15.3, a **customer** is an individual inside or outside an organization who depends on the output of its efforts. A customer may be your boss, a co-worker, or another department. In other words, a customer may be anyone who receives the work that you complete. That customer is the one who must be satisfied with the product or service, because in the final analysis, quality is what the customer says it is.

Surveys reveal that although companies lose customers for a variety of reasons, the main reason is that the people they deal with in the company are indifferent to their needs. Many workers' attitudes about the importance of customers are in need of an overhaul.

Personnel Decisions, Inc. recently conducted a four-year survey of customer service employees. The most successful employees, they found, shared four key traits:

1. *Friendliness.* Good employees enthusiastically greeted and made eye contact with customers. They were also able to engage customers in easy and appropriate small talk.

2. *Self-control.* Employees stayed cheerful in tense situations and handled irate customers with ease and respect. In addition, they were patient with indecisive customers.

3. *Dependability and initiative.* The employees showed strong commitment to assigned duties and were highly motivated in their jobs.

4. *Effective problem solving.* Employees showed a willingness to seek help from others when necessary and demonstrated intuition in anticipating a customer's needs.

**FIGURE 15.3 • The Customer Is King**

**REMEMBER**
a customer can be a/an:

- **Client**
- **Boss**
- **Co-worker**
- **Entire Department**

Don't be indifferent to the needs of customers.

The main objective of a worker must be to satisfy the customer, whether that customer is inside or outside the organization.

How do you defuse a customer's anger when it is directed toward you? An article in *The Secretary* offered tips for dealing with customers who are hurt, angry, or both. The following statements may be helpful:

1. *"Let me see if I understand what you are saying."* Listen carefully as the customer vents. Repeat back what you have heard and ask, "Am I getting this right?"

2. *"I'm sorry this problem happened."* Never make the mistake of becoming angry with an irate person. Empathy and sympathy help to calm a person.

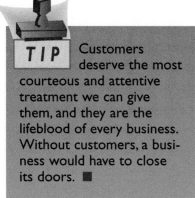

3. *"If I could change it, I would."* You can point out limits, but assure the customer that you will do everything you can.

4. *"We had no way of knowing this problem would happen."* Unpredictable events do happen, and your customer should know that you do not have total control over an outcome. Making such a statement does not mean that you are avoiding responsibilities, but you are just pointing out circumstances that are beyond your control.

5. *"Thank you again for doing business here."* Remind the customer that you still value his or her business.

Customers are the most important people in any business. To use an analogy, customers are not the frosting on the cake—they are the cake. The frosting is an improved reputation and higher profits that result from a top-quality job. The following affirmations are an example of what one successful company believes about customers:

- Customers are not dependent on us; we are dependent on them.
- Customers are not an interruption of our work; they are the purpose of it.
- Customers are doing us a favor when they come in or call; we are not doing them a favor by serving them.

In reality, most customers are easy to please. They simply want us to do what we say we are going to do when we say we are going to do it. They are also pleased, and surprised, when we take the time to follow up and ask if they are satisfied with the product or service they received. The idea of calling to follow up with a customer seems obvious, but its implementation is rare in today's organizations. Imagine how many compliments and good ideas for improvement an organization would receive if follow-up calls were viewed as *opportunities* rather than threats.

## Recall Time

*Answer the following questions:*

**1.** List three ways to improve international communication among workers.

**2.** Who is the customer in businesses today?

# Internal Forces Affecting Office Communication

Two of the most prevalent internal forces affecting office communication are worker motivation and empowerment.

## Motivation on the Job

The major difference between most people and extremely successful people is the gap between what they *know* and what they *do*. Both groups have about the same knowledge base. Extremely successful people are just better at doing what they "should" be doing. Helping workers bridge the gap between what they know and what they do is an important aspect of a manager's job.

Charlotte Bauer and Julie Dodd were at lunch one day and were discussing the new emphasis at work on customers and the importance of pleasing them. Julie said something that surprised Charlotte. Julie said, "Mr. Jacobzak, my boss, pays my salary. For all the talk about serving customers, the real objective is to keep him happy."

As Charlotte drove home that evening from work, she reflected on what Julie said.

1. *If you were Charlotte and agreed with Julie, list two points you would make that would be supportive of Julie's attitude.*

2. *List two points that you would make that would take issue with this attitude.* ■

However, generating genuine and lasting employee motivation is not something management does; rather, it is a process that management fosters and allows to happen. Employees already are motivated. Employees want to do a good job. They want to excel and are naturally motivated to do so. The challenge is to release that motivation. The motivation to work is a complex drive influenced by both external and internal factors.

External motivating factors may be either positive or negative. Punishment, a negative factor, may include the threat of dismissal, refusal of increased salary, or being "called on the carpet." Rewards, a positive factor, may include a salary increase or job promotion.

The problem when organizations motivate office workers exclusively with rewards is that they often run out. The problem with motivating by threat of punishment is that it breeds fear and resentment, which are likely to be expressed in negative behavior that interferes with achieving company goals. Common examples of such behavior are complaints, criticisms, absenteeism, wasted time, forgotten important details, communication of false information, rudeness to customers, and decisions that take the path of least resistance.

Internal motivation most often occurs when an employee's qualities match the requirements of the job. The relationship among motivation, ability, and performance would be simple if productivity were a function of ability alone. If it were, output would correlate with increases in a worker's ability. However, because employees have freedom of choice to perform effectively, ineffectively, or not at all, motivation is necessary to increase output. On-the-job performance and success are related to the type and extent of motivation involved. Although managers can certainly create a climate of positive motivation, in the final analysis, motivation comes from *within* each person.

©Werner Bokelberg/Image Bank

Employees who are motivated from within display positive emotions that foster cooperation.

## Worker-Empowered Organizations

In a world-class organization, everyone in the company has to be empowered to think every day about ways to make the business better in quality, output, costs, sales, and customer satisfaction. In government and other public service organizations as well as in business, demands for high performance will continue to prevail.

## Giselle Martinez

*Administrator*
*Deloitte & Touche*[SM]

**Q.** Ms. Martinez, are oral and written communication skills important for your work? If so, please give an example.

**A.** Both oral and written communication skills are important because an office support person may be given the responsibility of writing memos or letters for the boss. The boss needs to be able to communicate through these memos to all levels of management and to outside businesspeople with professionalism and accuracy.

**Q.** What advice would you give to a student preparing for a career as an office support person?

**A.** To prepare yourself for an office support position, visit and interview professionals within the field. Attend a class or workshop on relevant topics, such as how to organize and prioritize, or how to dress for success.

---

We need to get away from the old workplace adage that bosses think, managers manage, and workers work. Instead, we must commit to a new work style in which bosses, managers, and workers alike will think, manage, and work.

*Empowering* is one of the chief motivational tools used by businesses today. To review, empowerment is a set of practices designed to authorize, drive, and enable day-to-day decision making at lower levels within an organization. In the past, a "one best way" was defined by engineers or professionals charged with that responsibility. Employees were not expected or even *allowed* to join in the decision-making process.

People are empowered when they are allowed and even encouraged to make decisions about the work they do. People are empowered when they feel confident about, in control of, and responsible for their decisions. In a political democracy, people empower leaders; in a business, leaders empower people. Empowerment is a powerful motivational tool. It can be characterized as an emotional and motivational "high" for workers who experience it.

## Recall Time

*Answer the following questions:*

**1.** How are workers motivated on the job?

**2.** What is empowerment?

**3.** How do companies empower people?

# Summary

The office is changing. New roles for information are affecting organizational structure, forms of management, and the way office workers do their jobs. Organizations are becoming more horizontal in the way they are structured. Horizontal organizations demand people who think broadly and thrive on change, who manage process instead of people, and who cherish teamwork as never before.

Outside forces imposed on the organization affect office workers. They include technology, international business, the effects of the quality and continuous improvement process, and the concept of the customer as king.

Two of the most prevalent internal forces affecting office communication are how workers are motivated on the job and the extent to which companies empower workers.

Remember these important points about communicating in a changing office environment:

- Change in the workplace is motivating companies to allow employees to develop alternative work systems such as office sharing, flextime, and telecommuting.

- Empowerment utilizes a worker's abilities and potential to a great extent, while cutting costs and improving customer service.

- As a result of new relationships, the manner, methods, and modes of communicating are providing alternatives to the traditional pyramid style of organization.

- Self-managing, quick-performance teams are the building blocks of a horizontal organization, where performance objectives are linked to customer satisfaction rather than profitability.

- Today's workers most often need to locate, assess, communicate, and apply information (with the help of technology) as opposed to remembering it.

- Office workers must practice and use intercultural communication skills.

## Ethics on the Job

You are the only one Angelina, a co-worker, has told about her recently accepting guardianship of her deceased sister's three children. Over the last few weeks, you have heard other workers saying things behind Angelina's back indicating that she seems to have changed and that her attitude needs adjusting.

*How would you handle this delicate situation? Do you feel an explanation (from you or Angelina) is in order?* ■

# before you leave...

**When you have completed this chapter, answer the following questions:**
1. List some external forces that affect office communication.
2. List some internal forces that affect office communication.

# Review & Application

## Check Your Knowledge

1. In your opinion, will the use of alternative work systems increase or decrease over the next decade?

2. Based on your understanding of them, contrast the key elements of a pyramidal organization to those of a horizontal organization.

3. In what ways are international business skills different from the business skills that are appropriate within the United States?

4. Describe in detail the results when a worker's attitude reflects indifference to a customer's needs.

5. In your own words, describe what worker empowerment means.

## Review Your Vocabulary

On a separate piece of paper, match the following statements by writing the letter of each New Office Term beside its description.

___ 1. nontraditional working arrangements that include job sharing, flextime, and telecommuting

___ 2. abilities you already have that you can transfer to slightly new situations

___ 3. anyone inside or outside an organization who depends on the output of its efforts

___ 4. a company that manages across rather than up and down

___ 5. an aid to make a task easier by using equipment and procedures to create, process, and output information

___ 6. a name for the stem-to-stern redesign of the way a company works

___ 7. giving employees closest to the customer the authority and tools required to make many independent decisions

___ 8. a reengineering approach used to get dissimilar employees working together

a. alternative work systems
b. cross-functional teams
c. customer
d. empowerment
e. horizontal organization
f. portable skills
g. reengineering
h. technology

## Discuss and Analyze an Office Situation

Francisco Grundy, an office worker in Miami's police department, likes the job he's held for ten years, but he isn't crazy about it. His basic attitude is, "I'm just a cog in the wheel. I intend to keep my head down and not make waves. If something goes wrong, I dump the problem onto someone else. I didn't cause the problem, so why should I be identified with trouble?"

1. Does Francisco have an attitude problem? If so, what is it?

2. How does Francisco's attitude affect work within the department?

3. Given the fact that the police department is in the process of reengineering, what issues may Francisco have to deal with in a more horizontal, worker-empowered organization?

## Practice Basic Skills

### Math

Using a ten-key calculator, find the following totals and percentages on this speaker evaluation form and write your answers on a separate piece of paper. A score of 900 points is possible.

**Speech**

| Delivery Elements | Moya | Bart | Oscar |
|---|---|---|---|
| *Nonverbal* | | | |
| Good posture | 80 | 70 | 99 |
| Sufficient movement | 66 | 77 | 96 |
| Appropriate gestures | 76 | 89 | 90 |
| Variety of gestures | 90 | 66 | 79 |
| *Verbal* | | | |
| Pleasing voice quality | 70 | 80 | 90 |
| Adequate loudness | 76 | 74 | 79 |
| Correct pronunciation | 90 | 88 | 93 |
| Businesslike tone | 75 | 95 | 99 |
| Good voice inflection | 81 | 82 | 79 |
| **Total points** | — | — | — |
| **Percentage of total points** | — | — | — |

### English

*Rule:* The subjects (pronouns) each, every, neither, either, somebody, and anybody are singular in meaning, and they require a singular predicate (verb).
*Example:* Each of us has a special beach town.
*Practice Exercise:* Apply the rule to the following sentences. If a sentence is correct, write OK next to its letter on a separate piece of paper. If a sentence is incorrect, rewrite it correctly.

a. Each of the speakers have a message to convey.

b. Every student has to wear a cap and gown on the stage at graduation.

c. Neither of us have our driver's license with us.

d. Either of the proposed suggestions are acceptable to the judge.

e. Somebody is about to speak; please listen carefully.

f. The problem is that anybody has access to the confidential files.

g. Each pair of shoes in my closet have scuff marks on them.

h. Either of the two options are sound courses of action to take.

i. Somebody around here must take responsibility for this computer error.

j. Every one of us are responsible for practicing good listening skills.

### Proofreading

Rewrite or rekey the following reminder list on a separate piece of paper, correcting all misspellings and incorrect punctuation.

**Proper Internet Network Etiquette**

The internet connects networks throughout the world. Below are a list of a few "developed policies, rules, and codes for acceptable behavior as you use the Internet.

■ The servises and resources on the Innernet are generally offered in a spirit of coooperation, or sharing. You may have to limit the amount of time you spend useing a remote sysstem during peek times.

■ Strong support for individual rights, feelings, and opinons may be found on the Internet. Some folks may exprress opinions that aren't to your likeing or may be offensive to you. Before makeing an immediate reply, take some time to consider you response.

■ Generally; laws governing espionage, fraud, harrassment, libel, obscenity, and theft applie to messages carried on electronic networks. A large amount of freedom and openess is espressed on the Internet,but that freedom and openess doesn't mean it's beyond the law.

## Apply Your Knowledge

1. Over the next week as you visit businesses in your community to shop, bank, or do other activities, take note of any slogans or posters on the walls or printed materials on receipts or flyers that advertise the businesses' mission, principles, and/or general attitude toward customers.

   a. List on a sheet of paper at least three observations about different businesses.

   b. Of the three, which business made you feel most like a valued customer? Why?

2. Debate the Issue:

   "Any organization that does not deliver instant customer gratification with a virtual product or service will not be a successful company in the future." (*Definition: A virtual product or service is one that is produced instantaneously and customized in response to customer demand.*)

   *Instructions:* React to the previous statement by quickly jotting down three or more ideas you have supporting *and* refuting the statement. Prepare to role-play either point of view in a mock in-class debate.

## Using the Reference Manual

Open file ch15ref.doc. Use the punctuation section of the Reference Manual at the back of the book to help you insert punctuation marks where needed. Change to single spacing. Save and print.

Organizations need employees with good listening skills to maintain good relationships with co-workers and customers. Good listening skills will help reduce costly accidents and expensive errors and prevent misunderstanding and rumors from developing in an organization

Speaking in business situations conveys instructions information and decisions that help an organization function prosper and grow.

# chapter 16

# Business Math Skills

*After completing this chapter, you will be able to do the following:*

**1.** Name decimal placeholders.

**2.** Add numbers that contain decimals.

**3.** Subtract numbers that contain decimals.

**4.** Multiply numbers that contain decimals.

**5.** Divide numbers that contain decimals.

**6.** Multiply numbers that contain percentages.

**7.** Divide numbers that contain percentages.

**8.** Round off numbers.

**9.** List examples of how basic math is used in business offices.

**10.** Explain why spreadsheet software is used in offices.

### New Office Terms

- decimal placeholders
- dividend
- divisor
- floater

- fraction equivalents
- percentages
- prorated

**Answer the following questions to the best of your ability:**

**1.** What tasks performed by office workers require basic math skills?

**2.** How do you round off numbers? Give some examples.

Ten months after graduating from high school, Tomio enrolls in a basic math class at a local community college. His cousin asks him why. Tomio explains that after only ten months of working as a general office clerk, he realizes how important good basic math skills are in order to advance on the job.

Tomio is a **floater** for a large company. This title means that he works in different departments for various periods of time. After working in these departments, Tomio has recognized the value of good math skills.

When Tomio worked in the advertising department, he had to prepare a report in which amounts of charges were **prorated** to twelve different clients. He used percentages to divide the total amount of expenses for a month among the twelve clients.

While working in the purchasing department, Tomio again had to use percentages, this time to calculate sales tax on items. While working in the payroll department, he had to convert fractions of hours into decimals. In all departments, Tomio had to be fast and accurate when totaling columns of figures to perform tasks such as accounting for petty cash or counting inventory.

Tomio's cousin asks why calculators cannot be used when working in the business world. Tomio responds that calculators are used in most situations. However, math skills are still needed for the following reasons:

- Sometimes, a calculator is not available or it is broken.
- A person with a working knowledge of decimals will know if a decimal point is in the correct place on a calculator.
- The math portion of a software program requires a working knowledge of basic math skills.

Tomio tells his cousin that in his opinion, knowing advanced math, such as algebra or calculus, is not necessary for support office staff. To succeed and advance in an office career, a person must be able work quickly and accurately with decimals and percentages and to know how to round off numbers.

## Decimals

Decimals are used when calculating money amounts. For example, they are used to calculate payroll, purchases, bank accounts, and expenses. Decimals are also frequently used with percentages. For example, they are used with percentages in sales tax, sales commissions, and interest payments.

Decimals are easy to understand, but placing the decimal point in the wrong place causes many mistakes. Decimal places are to the right of the decimal point in a number. They are referred to as **decimal placeholders.**

## Technology in the Office | PORTABLE HARD DRIVE STORAGE

If you transfer files between PCs or need storage for backing up files, a portable hard drive may be the answer. You can use a portable drive to transport presentations or other files to meetings or off-site locations. Current portable drives have as much storage space as many main internal hard drives.

Portable drives are great for system backups, too. If your system goes down, having a mirror copy of your PC's internal hard drive as a backup will help get you back up and running much quicker. If you use a portable drive with an older system, you may need to get one with a parallel port connection. For newer PCs, USB or FireWire connections transfer data much faster. A number of companies manufacture portable hard drives, so you will have a choice. The main differences between models are storage capacity and transfer rate. Those drives with the most storage capacity and the fastest transfer rate, of course, are also the most expensive. ∎

For example, in the number

451.83927

- 8 is in the tenths place,
- 3 is in the hundredths place,
- 9 is in the thousandths place,
- 2 is in the ten thousandths place, and
- 7 is in the hundred thousandths place.

You will need to learn the placeholders of decimals in order to line up the decimals when adding and subtracting. You also need to understand placeholders for rounding off numbers.

## Addition and Subtraction of Decimals

When adding or subtracting decimals, first line up the decimal points and then perform the operation. For example, to add .7, .345, and .92, line up the decimals and add:

$$\begin{array}{r} .7 \\ .345 \\ \underline{.92} \\ 1.965 \end{array}$$

To subtract 5.78 from 28.99, line up the decimals and subtract:

$$\begin{array}{r} 28.99 \\ \underline{5.78} \\ 23.21 \end{array}$$

Nancy works as a secretary for the county health department in an eastern city. She recently encountered two situations that required addition and subtraction of decimals.

In one situation, Nancy's department moved its offices from one location to another. Nancy had several boxes to place onto a forklift that would help move them. The instructions on the forklift stated a maximum amount of weight that it could handle. Nancy had to total the weight of

If your calculator is not working properly, you will be glad that you have developed good math skills.

five boxes—24.7 pounds, 56.25 pounds, 20.40 pounds, 70.1 pounds, and 35 pounds. She lined up the decimals and added:

$$
\begin{array}{r}
24.7 \\
56.25 \\
20.40 \\
70.1 \\
\underline{35.0} \\
206.45
\end{array}
$$

In the other situation, Nancy's boss needed to know the difference between this year's projected budget and the actual amount spent to date. Nancy had to subtract $3 million from $5.8 million. She lined up the decimals and subtracted:

$$
\begin{array}{r}
5.8 \\
\underline{3.0} \\
2.8
\end{array}
$$

## It's Your Turn

Using your knowledge of decimals, copy the following payroll onto a separate piece of paper and compute the weekly net pay.

|     | Weekly Gross | Taxes  | Insurance | Medical Weekly Net |
| --- | ------------ | ------ | --------- | ------------------ |
| 1.  | 806.37       | 190.06 | 18.50     | 1.                 |
| 2.  | 800.52       | 188.36 | 18.50     | 2.                 |
| 3.  | 528.66       | 121.90 | 18.50     | 3.                 |
| 4.  | 780.04       | 180.65 | 18.50     | 4.                 |
| 5.  | 615.64       | 143.20 | 18.50     | 5.                 |
| 6.  | 661.42       | 158.38 | 18.50     | 6.                 |
| 7.  | 934.37       | 240.25 | 18.50     | 7.                 |
| 8.  | 1,098.18     | 290.76 | 18.50     | 8.                 |

## Multiplication of Decimals

You do not line up the decimal points when you multiply. Put the number with the fewest digits on the bottom, and multiply as if the numbers had no decimals. To place the decimal in the answer, do the following:

1. Add the number of decimal places in both numbers you are multiplying.
2. In the answer, count the total number of places you got in step 1 from right to left, and place the decimal at that point.

For example, to calculate $7.53 \times .9$, multiply

$$
\begin{array}{r}
7.53 \\
\underline{\times\ .9} \\
6777
\end{array}
$$

The first number (7.53) has two decimal places and the second (.9) has one decimal place. In the answer, move the decimal three places from right to left. The answer is

6.777    Count 1, 2, 3

Sometimes, you will need to add zeros to an answer to have enough decimal places. For example:

$$.3 \times .2$$

gives you

3 times 2 equals 6

The problem has two decimal places, but you have only one number in your answer. When you have a single-digit result, you must add an extra zero to make the answer:

$$.06$$

For another example:

$$.023 \times .6$$

gives you

23 times 6 equals 138

The problem has four decimal places, so an extra zero must be added to make the answer:

$$.0138$$

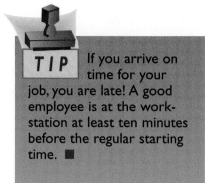

Basic math skills are essential in every kind of business. Every day, workers must calculate orders, weights, measures, payments, mileage, taxes, discounts, and so on.

# Division of Decimals

To divide a decimal by a whole number, you divide as you would with whole numbers and move the decimal directly up from the **dividend** (the number being divided) to the quotient (answer). For example, 2.1 divided by 3 is

$$3\overline{)2.1}$$

$$\overset{7}{3\overline{)2.1}}$$

Move the decimal up into the answer:

$$\overset{.7}{3\overline{)2.1}}$$

To divide a decimal by a decimal, (1) move the decimal in the **divisor** (the number you are dividing by) to the right of all numbers in the divisor; (2) move the decimal in the dividend the same number of places to the right that you moved the decimal in the divisor; and (3) place the decimal in the answer directly above the new location of the decimal in the dividend.

For example, 2.16 divided by .9 is

$$.9\overline{)2.16}$$

$.9\overline{)2.1.6}$  The decimal moves one place to the right in the divisor, so it moves one place to the right in the dividend.

$\overset{2.4}{9.\overline{)21.6}}$  The decimal moves straight up from its new location in the dividend to the same location in the quotient.

For another example, 2.8 divided by .007 is

$$.007\overline{)2.8}$$

$.007.\overline{)2.800.}$  Zeros are added if they are needed as placeholders.

$\overset{400}{7\overline{)2800.}}$

Alberto works in the office of a cattle farm in the Midwest. He is able to apply his knowledge of decimals on a regular basis.

Alberto has to do a weekly estimate on the cost of mileage for the company's trucks. For example, he must take the cost of a gallon of gasoline, $1.199, and multiply it by the number of miles a truck will travel, 163. Alberto multiplies the numbers and puts the decimal in the correct place:

$$\begin{array}{r} 1.199 \\ \times\ \ \ 163 \\ \hline 195.437 \end{array}$$

Alberto must be able to determine the lowest cost of cattle feed. He must take the total cost of the feed listed in the store catalog, $486.72, and divide it by the number of packages to be purchased, 9. Alberto divides and places the decimal in the correct place:

$$\overset{54.08}{9\overline{)486.72}}$$

# It's Your Turn

Using your knowledge of decimals, calculate on a separate piece of paper the value of the items on the following inventory sheet.

|     | Qty | Stock No. | Description | Unit Price | Value |
|-----|-----|-----------|-------------|------------|-------|
| 1.  | 8   | 195982    | Petty Cash Pads | 1.99 | |
| 2.  | 15  | 195909    | Invoice Forms | 4.59 | |
| 3.  | 20  | 205773    | Rollerball Pens | 5.69 | |
| 4.  | 1   | 282509    | Magic Markers | 2.19 | |
| 5.  | 7   | 113407    | Tab Dividers | 2.99 | |
| 6.  | 35  | 277764    | Binders | 6.69 | |
| 7.  | 4   | 472936    | Laser Printer Labels | 18.99 | |
| 8.  | 1   | 481440    | Touch Labeling System | 99.99 | |
| 9.  | 14  | 458844    | Magazine File Storage | 3.49 | |
|     |     |           | TOTAL | | |

# Uses of Decimals in Offices

Inez is an administrative assistant for a management consulting firm. One of her weekly tasks involves the following time sheet:

| Weekly Time Sheet Week Beginning _____ Employee: Elton Beacher | | | | | | |
|---|---|---|---|---|---|---|
| Client | M | T | W | THU | F | Total |
| Levi | 5.2 | 8.0 | 10.0 | 7.5 | 5.0 | |
| Shell | | | | | | |
| First Bank | | | | | | |
| Bay Hospital | 3.0 | 1.5 | | | 2.8 | |
| State Insurance | | | | | | |
| Administrative | 2.6 | | | 3.0 | 4.2 | |

For the weekly time sheet, Inez must total the hours that Elton spent working for each client on a weekly basis. The total hours will then be sent to the accounting department for billing. Let's follow the steps for the client Levi.

1. Inez must total the hours Elton works for Levi:

$$
\begin{array}{r}
5.2 \\
8.0 \\
10.0 \\
7.5 \\
\underline{5.0} \\
35.7
\end{array}
$$

Remember the importance of placeholders. Failure to line up decimals properly may lead to mistakes.

2. The accounting department employees need to understand decimals to calculate the amount to charge the client. The hourly consulting rate is $90. The accounting staff multiplies the hours Elton works for Levi by the hourly consulting rate:

## Ethics on the Job

Carlos works in the human resources department. He recently finished interviewing applicants for an order clerk position for one of the departments. Of the final two applicants interviewed, applicant A scored very high on all written and keyboarding tests. Applicant B barely passed the tests.

When doing reference checks on the applicants, Carlos learned that applicant A was an excellent worker but had a poor attendance record. Applicant B was rated by her former employer as an average worker with a good attitude and good attendance.

*Which applicant should Carlos hire, and why?* ■

$$
\begin{array}{r}
35.7 \\
\times\ 90 \\
\hline
3{,}213.0
\end{array}
$$

The 0 after the decimal has no value; the client will be billed $3,213.

Here is another example of how decimals are used in an office. Greg is an office support worker for a car rental agency. He must prepare the following daily report:

| Mileage on Rented Cars for (Date) _____ | | | |
|---|---|---|---|
| Car Number | Miles Traveled | Gallons Used | Mpg |
| 1345 | 160 | 8.5 | |
| 1489 | 120 | 9.0 | |
| 1690 | 184 | 11.5 | |
| 2078 | 260 | 40.0 | |
| 2090 | 145 | 28.5 | |

For the daily report, Greg must calculate the miles per gallon (mpg) used by each rented car. For example, to determine the miles per gallon of car 1690, he has 184 divided by 11.5:

$11.5\overline{)184}$

$11.5\overline{)184.0}$     The decimal moves one place to the right in the divisor, and it moves one place to the right in the dividend.

$115\overline{)1840.}^{\,16.}$     The decimal moves straight up from its new location in the dividend to the same location in the quotient.

Workers throughout the company clock in and out with a time clock. Periodically, someone from the accounting department must calculate the payroll by using the time cards to total up the hours each employee worked.

*Answer the following questions:*

**1.** Refer to the inventory sheet (It's Your Turn, page 341). Compute the total by adding a sales tax of 6.5 percent.

**2.** Refer to Elton Beacher's time sheet on page 341.
  **a.** How many hours will be billed to Bay Hospital?
  **b.** Using an hourly consulting rate of $65, what would be the charge to Bay Hospital?
  **c.** How many hours will be billed to Administrative?
  **d.** How many hours did Elton work on Friday?

**3.** Refer to Greg's mileage report on page 342.
  **a.** What are the miles per gallon for car 1345?
  **b.** What are the miles per gallon for car 2090?

# Percents

Office workers frequently use math to calculate **percentages**. A percentage is a share of the whole. For example, percentages are used to calculate commissions, to determine sales tax, and to compute interest on loans.

## Changing Percentages to Decimals

To multiply or divide a percentage, you must first change the percentage to a decimal. To change a percentage to a decimal, drop the percent sign and move the decimal point two places to the left. Why two places to the left? Percentage means part of a hundred, and a hundredth is two placeholders.

For example, to change 87.5% to a decimal, do the following:

1. Drop the percent sign: 87.5

2. Move the decimal point two places to the left:

.87.5     Count 1, 2

The result is .875.

More examples are as follows:

| Percentage | Decimal |
|------------|---------|
| 35.8 | .358 |
| 45.25 | .4525 |
| 545.2 | 5.452 |
| 85 | .85 |
| 6 | .06 |

Let's discuss the last two examples, 85 percent and 6 percent. These are whole numbers. We do not usually put decimals in whole numbers, but in a sense they are there, right after the number farthest to the right. You could write 85 as "85." and 6 as "6." When no decimal is shown in the percentage number, you pretend that it is there, at the end to the right.

Once you have changed percentages to decimals, you can multiply or divide them. To multiply or divide percentages, you use the same rules as for decimals. Some examples are as follows:

$$45.3\% \times 870 \text{ becomes } .453 \times 870$$

$$9\% \times 200 \text{ becomes } .09 \times 200$$

Lily works as a secretary for a high school district. Part of her job is to check the accuracy of the sales invoices that are received in her department. For example, she receives a sales invoice for new computers that includes a 6.5 percent sales tax on the $3,200 cost of the equipment. She will check to see if the amount is correct by doing the following:

1. Dropping the percent sign and moving the decimal two places to the left: $6.5\% = .065$

2. Using the rules for multiplication of decimals:

$$\begin{array}{r} 3,200 \\ \times\ \ .065 \\ \hline \$208.00 \end{array}$$

3. Verifying that the amount agrees with the invoice.

## Using Percentages in Offices

Another of Inez's duties at the management consulting firm is to prorate (distribute or divide) expenses to clients. This task involves the following report:

Calculating a fair and accurate invoice for a client requires precise accounting.

| Computer Operator's Billing Time to Clients Month of _____ | | |
|---|---|---|
| Client | Percentage to Be Billed | Amount |
| Levi | 45% | |
| Shell | 10 | |
| First Bank | 30 | |
| Bay Hospital | 12 | |
| State Insurance | 3 | |
| Total | 100% | $3,500.00 |

For the billing report, the computer operator spent 45 percent of her or his work time for the month on the Levi account. The operator spent 10 percent of his or her work time on the Shell account. At this company, clients are billed for the computer operator's time.

To calculate the amount to charge First Bank, Inez will multiply 30% by $3,500:

$$\begin{array}{r} 3,500 \\ \times\ \ \ \ \ .30 \\ \hline \$1,050.00 \end{array}$$

The prorated amount charged to First Bank will be $1,050.

At Greg's car rental agency, the workers at the front counter receive a commission if they go over the rental totals of the previous year. Greg must complete the following monthly report:

| Commission for Front Counter Staff Month _____ | | | |
|---|---|---|---|
| Employee | Amount Over | Rate | Commission |
| Brigg, J. | $300 | 15% | |
| Costello, G. | 600 | 15 | |
| Ramos, H. | 200 | 15 | |
| Patel, T. | 200 | 15 | |
| Rameriz, I. | 400 | 15 | |

To complete the monthly commission report, Greg will multiply the amounts in the Amount Over column by the rate for each person. For example, for Costello, he multiplies 600 by 15%:

$$\begin{array}{r} 600 \\ \times\ .15 \\ \hline \$90.00 \end{array}$$

Greg will write $90.00 in the Commission column.

## Taking Shortcuts in Percentages

Many people seem to remember that 50 percent is the same as $1/2$, and that 25 percent is the same as $1/4$. Using the **fraction equivalents** instead of using percentages may sometimes be a shortcut. A fraction equivalent is a fraction equal to the percent that may be used in its place.

For example, suppose that your boss asks what the estimated telephone expense will be for next month if you cut it by 50 percent of this month's expense. The telephone expense this month is $240.

## Making Office Decisions

Sonia's boss suggests that she attend a professional secretary's conference. Her boss offers to pay expenses, including car mileage. The conference is located 70 miles away.

One of Sonia's friends will attend the same conference and offers to drive. Her company will also pay expenses. Sonia decides to accept her friend's offer.

After the conference, when completing the expense form for reimbursement, Sonia cannot decide whether to put down the mileage. After all, the boss does not know that she did not drive.

**What advice would you give Sonia? Why?** ■

You can change the percentage to a decimal and multiply. This calculation will be 240 × .50.

However, 50 percent is the same as ½. It will be easier to just take ½ of the 240, or, in other words, divide the 240 by 2.

The following are some common fraction equivalents that many people use when calculating percentages:

| Percentage | Decimal | Fraction |
|---|---|---|
| 50% | .50 | ½ |
| 25 | .25 | ¼ |
| 20 | .20 | ⅕ |
| 33⅓ | 33.3 | ⅓ |

Inez needs to give her boss a figure on the number of employees absent on a day the city buses were not operating. The company has 400 employees. Inez learned from the human resources department that 20 percent of the employees were absent on that day. Inez knows that 20 percent is the same as ⅕. She divided 400 by 5 to get 20 percent of 400. She tells her boss that 80 employees were absent on that day.

All employees at Greg's auto rental company have been told to cut expenses for next year by 25 percent. Greg's supervisor asks Greg to complete the following report for his department:

| Expense | Current Amount | 25% Off | Projected Cost |
|---|---|---|---|
| **Projected Expenses for Next Year** <br> **After a 25% Cut** | | | |
| Supplies | $ 80 | | |
| Telephone | 240 | | |
| Copies | 100 | | |
| Travel | 320 | | |

To calculate the first item, supplies, Greg can multiply 80 × .25. However, Greg knows that 25 percent is the same as ¼, so he calculates 80 divided by 4 (25 percent of 80). The 25 percent off for supplies will be $20. Greg still must calculate the projected cost by calculating $80 − $20.

# Rounding Numbers

Recall the earlier example of Alberto, who works in the office of a cattle farm. When Alberto computed the estimated cost of mileage for a company truck,

he arrived at the figure 195.437. Because the amount is to be dollars and cents, Alberto writes $195.44 as the cost. How does he arrive at this number? He rounds the number to two decimal places. His process is to look at the number to the right of the second decimal place (195.437). The number is greater than 5, so he adds 1 to the 3 before dropping the number 7.

The steps for rounding numbers are as follows:

1. Locate the digit in the place to which you want to round.

2. Look at the number to the right of that digit.

3. If the number is 5 or greater, add 1 to the digit and drop all other numbers to the right.

4. If the number is less than 5, just drop all numbers to the right of the digit.

The following examples show numbers rounded to the hundredths place:

| Number | Rounded to Hundredths |
|--------|----------------------|
| 45.62832 | 45.63 |
| 45.62432 | 45.62 |
| 8.125 | 8.13 |
| 8.121 | 8.12 |

Alberto presents the following report to his supervisor. He has to round decimals to whole numbers to complete the report.

| Estimated Mileage Cost Per Driver For Three-Month Period Beginning _____ | | |
|---|---|---|
| Driver | Estimate | To Budget |
| Phair | 181.65 | 182 |
| Evans | 152.30 | 152 |
| Lopes | 168.77 | 169 |
| Ko | 135.25 | 135 |
| Garcia | 180.54 | 181 |

**TIP** Suppose that it is 10 A.M. You look at all the work yet to be done for the day. You are not certain you can complete all of it today. Go to your boss and ask that the tasks be numbered according to priority. Do them in that order. ■

# Recall Time

*Using your knowledge of percents, compute the sales tax payable for the following sales journal. The sales tax is 8.5 percent. Write your answers on a separate piece of paper.*

| | Date | | Sales Slip | Sales Credit | Sales Tax Payable Credit |
|---|---|---|---|---|---|
| 1. | June | 14 | 1645 | 567.90 | |
| 2. | | 16 | 1646 | 325.00 | |
| 3. | | 17 | 1647 | 217.90 | |
| 4. | | 18 | 1648 | 1175.00 | |
| 5. | | 18 | 1649 | 279.95 | |
| 6. | | 18 | 1650 | 299.95 | |
| 7. | | 19 | 1651 | 123.70 | |
| 8. | | 19 | 1652 | 1999.00 | |
| 9. | | 20 | 1653 | 435.90 | |
| 10. | | 21 | 1654 | 555.80 | |

# Math and Spreadsheet Software

Many companies use spreadsheet software with their personal computers to perform office tasks similar to the ones shown in this chapter. The software performs the calculations more quickly and more accurately than an employee. The software will also establish an electronic file for future use. This file is especially useful if changes need to be made.

Although a variety of software programs are available, some of the basic symbols are the same. For example, when entering a formula in a spreadsheet:

+ is used for addition
− is used for subtraction
* is used for multiplication
/ is used for division

An employee can complete many more accounting projects in far less time using a computer with spreadsheet software than he or she can using a calculator, pencil, and ledger pages.

If Greg were to use spreadsheet software for his Mileage on Rented Cars form on page 342, he would use his math knowledge before arriving at a formula for the spreadsheet. His math formula would be:

miles traveled divided by gallons used

A popular spreadsheet program would allow Greg to enter the car number into column A, the miles traveled into column B, and the gallons used into column C. The formula for column D would be:

$$= B/C$$

Using a spreadsheet for Greg's Commissions form on page 345, he would first decide that the situation requires multiplication:

amount times rate

He would enter the employee names in column A, the amount over in column B, and the rate in column C. The commission's formula for column D would be:

$$= B*C$$

In the Projected Expenses chart on page 346, Greg would use his math skills to realize that two operations need to be performed to determine the projected cash. His math calculation is:

current amount minus (current amount times 25% off)

A spreadsheet formula may be:

$$= B - (B*C)$$

In the previous examples Greg does not have to worry about placement of the decimal in the final answer nor about rounding off the answer. The software makes these decisions.

# Summary

All office workers use some form of math in their daily work routines. They may use it in checking a telephone bill, calculating interest, adding columns, or completing a travel expense allowance form.

Most of these calculations are done with electronic calculators. However, sometimes a calculator is not convenient to use. A basic knowledge of math is needed at these times.

Good basic math skills will enable office employees to perform math work quickly and accurately. They are extra skills that will likely help an office worker advance on the job.

The following list may help you decide if you need to improve your basic math skills. For each area listed, decide whether you have a good working knowledge of the skills required or need to improve your ability.

- Decimals
    Add
    Subtract
    Multiply
    Divide

- Percentages
  - Multiply
  - Divide
- Rounding off

# before you leave...

**When you have completed this chapter, answer the following questions:**

**1.** What tasks performed by office workers require basic math skills?

**2.** How do you round off numbers? Give some examples.

# Review & Application

## Check Your Knowledge

1. What basic math skills do office workers use?

2. What are the decimal placeholders in the following number?

   791.45870

3. Give two examples of office tasks that require the use of decimals.

4. In the number 451.93827, what place is the 8 holding?

5. In the number 451.72839, what place is the 7 holding?

6. Add the following:
   a. .8 + .009 + 23
   b. 453 + .08 + 67.9 + .076
   c. 52.3 + 7.27 + 1.968
   d. .63 + .914

7. Subtract the following:
   a. .8 − .5
   b. .7 − .15
   c. 2 − .084
   d. 34.2 − 27.367

8. Multiply the following:
   a. .7 × .8
   b. .03 × .2
   c. 12.3 × .8
   d. .08 × 041

9. Divide the following:
   a. 9.1 ÷ 7
   b. 48 ÷ 1.2
   c. 72 ÷ .09
   d. .345 ÷ .15

10. Change the following percentages to decimals:
    a. 25.9%
    b. 54.35%
    c. 323.6%
    d. 65%
    e. 9%

11. Multiply the following:
    a. 4,500 × 8%
    b. 8,200 × 65%
    c. 890 × 1.2%
    d. 780 × 3.5%

12. What is 25 percent as a fraction?

13. What is 20 percent as a fraction?

14. What is 33.3 percent as a fraction?

15. Show the shortcut operation for finding 25 percent of 400.

16. Show the shortcut operation for finding $33^{1}/_{3}$ percent of 1,800.

17. Round the following numbers to the nearest tenths place:
    a. 1.26
    b. 72.24
    c. .372
    d. 5.339

18. Round the following numbers to the nearest hundredth:
    a. 3.475
    b. 1.279
    c. .3082
    d. .3028

19. Why is spreadsheet software used in offices?

## Review Your Vocabulary

On a separate piece of paper, supply the missing words by choosing from the New Office Terms listed below.

1. _____ are numbers to the right of a decimal point.

2. To _____ means to divide a total expense among more than one client.

3. A _____ works in different departments for various periods of time.

4. One half is the _____ of 50%.

5. A _____ is a portion of the whole.

6. _____ is the term used for the outside number when dividing decimals.

7. _____ is the term used for the inside number when dividing decimals.

   a. decimal place-        d. floater
      holders               e. fraction equivalent
   b. dividend              f. percentage
   c. divisor               g. prorate

## Discuss and Analyze an Office Situation

Juan recently began working as an entry-level office employee. Because it is his first job and he does not have office experience, he accepted a low-paying position.

Juan is trying to stay within a budget, which means he cannot afford to buy his lunch. He must bring it from home.

Most of the other office workers go out for lunch. They ask Juan to join them when they leave for lunch, but he always refuses. He is beginning to think the office workers may not like him if he continues to say no to the luncheon invitations. However, he also realizes that he must stay within his budget.

If you were Juan, would you stop bringing lunches from home? Besides saving money, does bringing lunch from home have any other advantages?

## Practice Basic Skills

### Math

1. Last week, Rosella used the company car to do the following:

| TASK | MILES DRIVEN |
|------|--------------|
| Attend a meeting | 68.3 |
| Deliver a computer | 7.6 |
| Purchase copy paper | 1.7 |
| Drop an employee at the airport | 23 |

What were the total miles driven?

2. A budget was planned for $23.8 million. The amount spent was $25.6 million. How much was overspent?

3. Complete the following report on a separate piece of paper.

| Departmental Report on Hours Worked | | | |
|------|------|------|------|
| Department | Hours Worked Last Month | Hours Worked This Month | Change* |
| Purchasing | 340.5 | 420 | |
| Accounting | 880.6 | 890 | |
| Advertising | 160 | 160 | |
| Human Resources | 340.2 | 350 | |

*Change = Hours worked this month − Hours worked last month.

4. Complete the following sales invoice, writing your answers on a separate piece of paper.

| CFEB Company Sales Invoice | | |
|------|------|------|
| Item | Unit Cost | Amount |
| 3 tape holders | $ 4.78 ea | |
| 25 rolls of masking tape | 6.78 ea | |
| 12 rulers | .90 ea | |
| 20 desk calendars | 7.50 ea | |
| 6 clipboards | 5.94 ea | |
| 2 desk sets | 12.50 ea | |
| | Subtotal | |
| | Plus 6.5% tax | |
| | Total due | |

5. The money for fines at the Hall of Justice is divided between the state, the county, research, and a special judges' fund. One day last week, $8,790 was paid in fines. Prorate that amount for the following report, writing your answers on a separate piece of paper.

| Fines Collected for (Date) _____ | | |
|------|------|------|
| Distribute To | Percentage | Amount |
| State | 30% | |
| County | 40 | |
| Research | 20 | |
| Judges' fund | 10 | |
| Total for the day | | $8,790 |

## English

*Rule:* Use semicolons to separate two independent clauses that are not joined by a conjunction.

*Examples:* The plane flew low; it began to spray the plants. The new machine arrived; it was broken.

*Practice Exercise:* Rewrite or rekey the following sentences on a separate piece of paper, placing semicolons where needed.

   a. My little brother's toy arrived some parts were damaged.
   b. Interest rates fell sales of homes rose.
   c. The fruit ripened early the cooks made jam.
   d. Prices of food in the Philippines had gone up many people began to go hungry.
   e. Personal computers entered the workplace office productivity increased.

## Proofreading

Rekey or rewrite the following report on a separate piece of paper, correcting all errors.

CFEB COMPANY PUNCTUALITY
AND ATTENDANCE POLICY

Five episodes of latness in any three month period will result in a persons being placed on written informal warning, with a copy of the warning sent to Wanda Lambert. Supervisors may, of course, verbally warn an individual before he/she reaches the fifthe latness in a 3-month period. In fact, the supervisor who disscusses the potensial for a written warning before the number of latnesses reaches five is doing the subordinate a favor. Failure to improve after being given a written informal warning will advanced the individual to a formal warning. Formal warning are placed into the individual's permanent personel file and remain there for too years.

Five periods (frequencies) of absense in any twelve months will result in an indeviduals being placed on informal written warning, with a copy of the warning sent to Wanda Lambert. If a supervisor verbaly warns a person prior to doing a written informal warning, she/he has done that employe a favor. With attendence as with punctuality, someone whoe does n't improve adequatly after being given the written informal warning will be placed on formal warning.

1. Using word processing software, key the following invoice, calculating all the figures in the amount column.

| Cheapie Technology Supply Company | | | |
|---|---|---|---|
| 123 East Fargo Street | | | |
| Reston, VA 20191-1596 | | | |
| Sold to | Phase Two 151 8th Street Reston, VA 20191-1596 | | |
| Qty | Description | Unit Price | Amount |
| 6 | Quickwiz software | 525.75 | |
| 3 | Victory computers | 2,200.25 | |
| 2 | Deskjet printers | 375.00 | |
| 3 | 56000 baud modems | 95.50 | |
| 3 | Cables | 8.85 | |
| | Subtotal | | |
| | Sales Tax (7.5%) | | |
| | Amount Due | | |

2. Using spreadsheet software, complete the Projected Expenses chart on page 346.

3. Recalculate the Projected Expenses chart in problem 2 using 20% off instead of 25%.

Open file ch16ref.doc. Use the numbers section from the Reference Manual at the back of the book to help you key a sentence that supplies an example of each rule. Save and print.

A. Spell out numbers one through ten. Use figures for numbers above ten.

B. Use figures for clock time.

C. Spell out fractions.

D. Spell out indefinite numbers.

E. For numbers of street addresses, use the basic rule of "under ten spell out."

F. Spell out numbers that begin a sentence.

# chapter 17

## Communicating in Groups and Problem Solving

355

### objectives

*After completing this chapter, you will be able to do the following:*

1. Identify the types and characteristics of groups in organizations.
2. State reasons people become part of a group.
3. Discuss the impact groupthink issues and hidden agendas have on accomplishing an organization's goals.
4. Describe the concept and application of self-managed teams in organizations.
5. List seven steps in the problem-solving process.
6. List the five conflict management styles.
7. Describe the reasons conflict in organizations may be healthy.
8. Identify the outcomes of win-lose, lose-lose, and win-win negotiating styles.

### New Office Terms

- formal groups
- group
- groupthink
- hidden agendas
- informal groups

- lose-lose negotiating style
- norm
- teambuilding
- win-lose negotiating style
- win-win negotiating style

**Answer the following questions to the best of your ability:**
1. Describe the function of teams in business organizations.
2. What are three negotiating styles?

# The Nature of Groups and Teambuilding Considerations

Effective organizations help their members learn how to work in groups to get results. A **group** is two or more people who interact with each other personally to achieve a common goal. Because much of the work in companies is accomplished through group effort, office workers need to understand how groups function and how they impact both organizational and individual behavior.

## Types and Characteristics of Groups

When individuals associate on a fairly continual basis, groups will form, with or without the approval of management. Individual members receive a great deal of satisfaction from being part of the group. A group may be either informal or formal.

### Types of Groups

**Informal groups** arise spontaneously throughout all levels of a company and evolve out of employees' need for social interaction, friendship, communication, and status. In contrast, **formal groups** are deliberately created by management to attain organizational goals and objectives. Two examples of formal groups are problem-solving committees (that meet on an as-needed basis and are relatively permanent) and task force groups (which usually focus on a specific issue, meet a few times, and then disband).

### Characteristics of Groups

Groups have some common characteristics. For example, groups appear to set norms, instill conformity, and engender cohesiveness. Groups formed with these common characteristics not only in the workplace, but also in other settings such as at school and in the family unit.

**Norms** If being a member of a group is important to an individual, he or she will change personality, beliefs, and behavior to conform to the group. A **norm** is a generally agreed-upon standard of behavior that every member of the group is expected to follow. For example, a norm for a dance group might be the way its members wear their hair at performances and their lively expressions. Human nature compels most of us to gravitate toward groups of like-minded individuals with strong identities, so these norms ordinarily do not offend group members.

**Conformity** Group pressure forces its members to conform, or comply, with the norms established by the group. Because nonconformity threatens the group's standards, stability, and longevity, pressure placed on each

People have a need to interact with others through being part of a group. Most of us belong to several different groups simultaneously.

Our involvement in groups begins when we are very young. We are part of family groups, clubs, classes, church organizations, and various other types of groups.

member to conform is oftentimes intense. Compliance is important to the group because behavior is visible; for the group to succeed, its members must show they are united in their efforts.

**Cohesiveness** Cohesiveness is emotional closeness that exists among group members. It depends on how well the group sticks together and acts as a single unit instead of as individuals.

Everyone has a need for social interaction—a feeling of belonging and identification with one or more groups. Few people like being alone or working in isolation for extended periods of time.

## Technology in the Office — PRESENTATION SOFTWARE

Presenting information using charts and graphs propped on stands in front of an audience is quickly giving way to newer technology. Using presentation software, you can prepare slide shows or multimedia presentations within a single program. Images containing photos, charts, graphs, and text can be combined for attractive presentations for one or several viewers—or for presentation at a large conference. You can even add voice narration so that viewers in another location—perhaps thousands of miles away—will feel as though they are actually at the conference.

Your local computer software store likely has several good presentation software programs. Among the more popular are Microsoft PowerPoint and MetaCreations Office Advantage®. ■

### Ethics on the Job

On a workteam to which you have been assigned, one team member dresses very oddly. You have heard others snicker when he walks into the room.

*What would your personal stand be, given you are all a team and have to work together? What would you do?* ■

### Motivation to Join Groups

Why do we tend to join groups? Research indicates that people do so for the following reasons:

1. *Affiliation.* Group companionship provides feelings of security, belonging, and friendship.

2. *Power.* Strength is built in numbers. The group provides reassurance and support, often giving its members the courage to take a stand on an important issue, an action they might not take on their own.

3. *Identity.* Along with membership in a group comes an increased awareness of personal identity—a sense of being "somebody." Self-esteem is positively reinforced.

4. *Goal accomplishment.* In most situations, a group effort can accomplish goals more effectively than any individual effort, due in part to the variety of skills and knowledge its members collectively provide. The more brain power used to solve a problem, the better the chance for a successful resolution.

## Groupthink and Hidden Agenda Issues

Formal and informal groups are important to organizations and impact their performance in a variety of ways. Groups may have either a positive or negative impact, which often manifests itself in terms of groupthink and hidden agendas of individual group members.

### Groupthink Issues

**Groupthink** is the tendency of members of highly cohesive groups to lose their critical evaluative abilities and, out of a desire for unanimity, to overlook realistic, meaningful alternatives as attitudes are formed and decisions are made. Groupthink can contribute to unethical behavior in the workplace. Symptoms of groupthink are arrogance, overcommitment, and excessive loyalty to the group.

The more cohesive the group, the more likely the individual members tend to "agree not to disagree," especially when challenging the ideas of the group leader. Unfortunately, groupthink can undermine the analytical process, legitimize ignorance, and reinforce biases, because people do tend to be influenced by their peers. Instances of groupthink occur most often at meetings where decisions have been made *before* the meeting even begins. In other words, the other members of the group are there merely to rubber-stamp the leader's choice.

358

While a certain amount of groupthink can be expected in any group situation, certain techniques can minimize its occurrence. For example, the group can diversify its membership to get different perspectives as well as provide opportunities and permission for open debate.

### Hidden Agendas

Another pitfall of group interaction is the possibility that someone will be safeguarding a hidden agenda, or personal goal. **Hidden agendas** are comprised of attitudes and feelings that an individual brings to the group. Although often planned, hidden agendas may also arise spontaneously as a result of a disagreement with some idea expressed by or conflict with a member in the group.

Open communications within a small group can reveal a hidden agenda and keep the decision-making process on track.

When someone has a hidden agenda, goal orientation shifts from the group to the individual; the person with the hidden agenda nearly always, either consciously or subconsciously, places obstacles in the path of the group's planned objective. Hidden agendas represent what an individual, or group, really wants instead of the stated goal.

Although hidden agendas are neither better nor worse than planned agendas, office workers need to understand them. At the very least, their existence must be recognized because they can profoundly interfere with the group's ability to focus and can block its progress.

If not recognized and understood, hidden agendas can waste a great deal of a group's energy and the organization's resources, as shown in Figure 17.1. Three ways a leader can help a group handle hidden agendas are to:

1. Realize that a hidden agenda is a natural part of the group process, because individual members have individual goals and needs.

2. Recognize that a hidden agenda might be present when the group is having difficulty reaching its goals.

3. Decide how to bring the hidden agenda to light.

**FIGURE 17.1 • Hidden Agendas**

Let her wait till the next meeting and she won't be so great when only one or two show up!

Hidden agendas can sometimes be intentionally hurtful.

# Self-Managed Teams and Teambuilding Elements

Today, organizations are transforming into workplace communities in which all members share both gains and pains, and in which the fortunes of each member—employee and investor—rise and fall with performance in the marketplace. The concept of teams is gaining importance as organizations view themselves as interconnected systems with each person accountable for results.

## Self-Managed Teams

A significant trend in current business practice is breaking up the traditional corporate hierarchy and replacing it with self-managed teams.

What exactly is a team? Typically, a team consists of employees grouped together to complete a whole or distinct part of a product or service. Team members make decisions on a wide range of issues, often including such traditional management prerogatives as determining who will perform which tasks, solving quality problems, settling conflicts between members of the team, and selecting team leaders. The team approach seems to be more an overall philosophy than a tightly defined set of rules.

Managers and workers alike participate on teams. Team members need to develop or possess skills in dispute resolution, team building, consensus building, and meeting facilitation. Team members also need personal skills such as the ability to keep agreements, communicate honestly, perform straightforward self-assessment, and give and receive feedback. In the current business environment, teams and self-managed groups at all levels of organizational structure are the most likely basis for fundamental reform in organizations.

What a team might look like is described in Table 17.1. Ideally, an effective team is one that is efficient, productive, and cohesive.

## Teambuilding Elements

Organizations must help build effective teams because teambuilding does not just happen. **Teambuilding** is one of many interventions used to create change in an organization. Its purpose is the creation of a work environment that enables and promotes achievement of organizational and indi-

### TABLE 17.1 • What Does a Team Look Like?

| | |
|---|---|
| Who Are Team Members? | ■ A team is composed of two or more persons in the organization, usually from dissimilar departments. |
| | ■ Its members are competent and knowledgeable in the way they carry out their duties. |
| What Does a Team Do? | ■ The team is constantly learning and growing—adapting to changing requirements and multiple goals. |
| | ■ Its work is consistently superior in both quality and quantity. |
| How Does the Team Concept Work? | ■ Problems and conflicts within the team are addressed quickly and professionally. |
| | ■ The quality of decisions made by the team is high, and members share a sense of satisfaction in work accomplished. |

**Adapted from seminar "Fundamentals of Teambuilding," presented by Jerry Odell, August 1993, Phoenix, Arizona.**

An effective team is one in which every member participates, and all work together toward a clearly stated, agreed-upon goal.

vidual goals. Modern teambuilding efforts usually include concentration on how team members relate with each other and how work is completed.

Here are some ways to help team efforts become more effective:

1. Avoid arguing for your own viewpoint. Instead, state your point as clearly and concisely as you can and listen to others.

2. If the discussion reaches an impasse, do not assume that someone must win and someone must lose. Look for a new option that is the next best alternative for everyone.

3. Never change your mind just to avoid an argument. Encourage differences of opinion among team members.

4. If an agreement comes too quickly, take another look at the issue. Participants in the agreement may have various interpretations of what was agreed to, and differences may be hidden. Make sure that everyone fully understands the intent and content of the agreement.

5. Do not give way to other viewpoints unless you feel they have reasonable merit.

6. Avoid using conflict-reducing tricks to reach agreement such as the majority vote, calculating an average, flipping a coin, or bargaining.

7. Make sure every member of the group contributes.

## Recall Time

*Answer the following questions:*

**1.** What motivates people at work to join groups?

**2.** List two potential problems associated with groupthink.

**3.** Describe a team in a work environment.

## Making Office Decisions

Tandy is the senior office assistant at Southwest Timber Company. She likes her job and has been recognized by management on numerous occasions for her outstanding work. Tandy has enthusiastically taken advantage of the many opportunities to learn and grow at her job since she was first employed four years ago.

Management says that the company is growing and will add more equipment and workers to the office within the year, and will therefore hire a new office manager. Tandy feels she is a natural to get the job and is looking forward to really selling herself during the interview. She knows that as office manager, she could make some changes that would help Southwest run more efficiently.

Tandy and two others inside the company apply for the position. In addition, four people from other companies are interviewed. When the new office manager is announced, Tandy is crushed because she didn't get the job. She is hurt that someone with prior experience as an office manager outside the company was selected. Tandy feels like quitting; she doesn't want to help the new person. She is angry at management for bringing in someone from the outside when she could have done a good job. After all, Tandy knows the company, and this new person has much to learn.

1. **If you were Tandy, would you stay with Southwest Timber Company?**

2. **How would you decide what to do?** ■

# Decision Making and Problem Solving

Decision making is the heart of management, but the need for all office workers to do it and do it well is increasingly becoming critical. Decision making is difficult. One thing is clear, however: Unless you can overcome the fear of making decisions, your career may stall.

## Decision-Making Responsibility

Poor decision makers may be smart and diligent, but when settling on a course of action, they resort to delaying tactics or blame others to avoid responsibility. At work, you are penalized much more harshly for not making a decision at all than for making a poor one. Avoiding this responsibility and failing to make a deadline are cardinal sins that few organizations will tolerate.

### The Decision-Making Process

Decisions are based on facts, intuition, and experience. On paper, decision making is a relatively simple process. The process starts with a need to make a decision; then at least two alternative courses of action are determined, followed by a selection of the best choice from the alternatives.

### Factors to Consider

Keep the following factors in mind when you make decisions:

1. The right person should make the decision.
2. Decisions should contribute to objectives and reflect the organization's vision.
3. Effective decision making takes time and effort but cannot be postponed.

4. Though seldom is only a single acceptable choice available, one direction usually surfaces as the best to take at the time.

5. Decision making improves with practice. The more you do it, the easier it becomes.

6. A decision may not please everyone. The purpose of a decision is not necessarily to please everyone.

7. A decision begins the process that allows other activities to progress.

The following questions may help you make the decision-making task easier and guide you to making effective office and business decisions. When making a decision, ask yourself:

1. What is the basic issue that must be addressed and resolved?

2. Is all the needed information available to make a timely and informed decision?

3. How have similar issues been handled in the past? Should anything be done differently this time?

4. If the stakes appear too high, can a compromise be settled on as a safety net?

Should decisions be made by an individual or by a group? Clearly, the trend is toward empowerment and group decision making; however, to provide some perspective, Table 17.2 lists both advantages and disadvantages of group decision making.

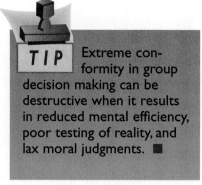

**TIP** Extreme conformity in group decision making can be destructive when it results in reduced mental efficiency, poor testing of reality, and lax moral judgments. ■

## Problem-Solving Steps

People are not born with problem-solving skills; they learn and fine-tune this art over the years. Typically in a work setting, one learns the problem-solving process by observing and emulating others.

A simple technique you can use to speed a solution more quickly is to write a description of the problem you are trying to solve in the form of a question and display it in a prominent place. For example, the question "What is the single most important thing we should do to improve document turnaround time?" displayed on a whiteboard or on a sticky note near a work area can be noticed throughout the workday.

**TABLE 17.2 • Group Decision Making**

| Advantages | Disadvantages |
|---|---|
| Provides the manager with a broad range of information | Holds the manager accountable for the group's decision |
| Lends a more "creative" approach to problem solving | Takes the workgroup's time away from other aspects of their jobs |
| Improves communication in the department | May result in "choosing sides" and cause morale problems |
| Creates high morale in the workgroup | Allows strong personalities to dominate the workgroup |
| Stresses a stronger commitment to decisions made | Requires more supervisory skill |
|  | Is difficult to use if the decision must be made quickly |

Assume that you are interviewing for an executive secretarial position in your city. Surprisingly, you have been offered positions at two good companies on the same day. You feel you could be equally happy working at either one. Answer the following questions to help you decide which offer to accept.

1. **Will you use the decision-making process in deciding which job offer to select? Why or why not?**

2. **What specific criteria would you want the company you work for to meet? Consider managerial style, benefits, salary, size, values of the company, and so on.**

3. **Would your decision-making process be different or affected in any way if your personal circumstances reflected either of the following situations?**
   • **You are a twenty-eight-year-old single mother with an infant child.**
   • **You are a forty-five-year-old married man with two teenage children in high school.** ■

Using the display technique helps to clearly define the problem, which is the first step in the problem-solving process. The following steps represent one approach to problem solving:

1. Define the idea or problem to be acted on.
2. Collect, interpret, and analyze information.
3. Develop possible alternative solutions.
4. Analyze the implications of selected alternatives.
5. Select the preferred alternative.
6. Implement the decision.
7. Follow up, evaluate, and modify the decision, if needed.

# Conflict Resolution

As a student and as a member of a family, you deal with various conflict situations almost routinely. Organizations do, too. Why? Because no two people are exactly alike. This uniqueness guarantees that conflict will always exist.

Because we all have our own personal values, experiences, beliefs, and perceptions, the chance that they will clash with those of someone else from time to time is very real. Conflict is an inevitable part of life, and the workplace is no exception. Because conflict is part of the workplace, effective conflict management is an essential skill for any successful office professional.

Conflict, in itself, is not a bad thing. Disagreement can be a healthy and creative factor in the growth and development of an individual, team, or project. Further, conflict can ultimately strengthen work relationships. Trouble erupts, however, when conflict goes unmanaged and unresolved. Therefore, the goal should not be to eliminate all conflict, but to minimize and redirect dysfunctional discord by seeking and applying constructive solutions.

Whether the outcome of a conflict issue is positive or negative is almost totally determined by the way it is managed. Why not let individual "flash fires" burn themselves out? A thoughtful response is that they can ultimately take a tremendous physical, psychological, emotional, and financial toll on an organization and its employees.

## Understanding and Resolving Conflicts

Until recently, conflict of any sort in the office has been unwelcome—perhaps because many people associate it with a lack of harmony, emotional pain, or destructive behavior.

### Benefits of Conflict

Though it is true that conflicts can have a devastating effect on productivity, morale, teamwork, and ultimately an organization's bottom line, conflicts can sometimes actually be healthy for a business. Here's how:

1. *Conflicts produce change.* Conflict is often the first step in getting rid of outdated procedures, revising regulations, and fostering innovation and creativity.

2. *Conflict leads to unity.* Addressing rather than suppressing conflict opens the lines of communication, gets people talking to each other (instead of about each other), and makes people feel that they are part of a team that cares.

3. *Conflict promotes compromise.* People learn how to work harmoniously, come up with creative solutions, and reach outcomes that benefit everyone involved.

To resolve conflict effectively, you must keep an open mind, listen actively, and realize that a conflict situation is a problem waiting to be solved. In conflict resolution, the objective is to find the best solution for everyone.

### The Conflict Resolution Process

You will find that the steps in the conflict resolution process are similar to the problem-solving procedures discussed earlier. Adhere to these steps when you need to resolve conflicts:

1. *Identify the problem.* Sometimes the problem needs only to be reframed. If you put a new frame on a picture, the picture looks different. If you put a new meaning on a problem, the problem looks different, too. For example, you can look at a glass of water as half full or half empty.

2. *Look for solutions.* Good solutions come most often from random, nonjudgmental brainstorming.

3. *Choose the best solution.* The best solution solves the problem, does not hurt anyone or interfere with his or her rights, and satisfies all parties. The best solution does not create a winner or a loser; both sides should feel as if they have achieved something. When both sides agree, it is called a *win-win solution* (which we discuss more thoroughly later in this chapter).

4. *Act.* Follow through on one of the solutions.

5. *Evaluate.* If your approach turns out to be ineffective, do not look on it as a failure. It just means you have eliminated one approach, and you are ready to try another. We learn by our mistakes. (Go back to step 1.)

Conflict is not necessarily a bad thing if handled well. Through effective communication and negotiation, conflict can lead to needed changes in an organization.

At every step during the conflict-resolution process, communication is important. Communication does not mean just telling someone what you want. It means *listening* to what they want. It means establishing eye contact and being sensitive to body language. It means not making demands or ultimatums, but using suggestions instead.

When conflicts become heated, and they sometimes do, follow these hints to control your impulses:

1. Be aware of your feelings. Although some people are ashamed of their angry, sad, or jealous feelings, these emotions are real, and you are entitled to have them. For example, if you are angry, admit it to yourself and express your anger in a mature way.

2. Take a break if your feelings get too intense to handle. Divert yourself—do something else or go somewhere else.

3. Count to ten slowly. It will give you at least ten seconds to cool off and think about your approach.

4. Consult with someone such as a close friend, relative, or co-worker who has a calming effect on you, and whom you can trust in confidence.

Organizations by their very nature create unique obstacles to problem solving. Be aware that the following workplace realities do at times hamper honest conflict resolution attempts:

1. Employees are afraid to criticize their bosses.

2. People are protective of their positions and power.

3. Technical expertise is intimidating to those with less knowledge.

4. People see problems from their own viewpoints rather than from the broader organizational perspective.

## Managing and Negotiating Effective Solutions

The goal of productive problem solving and conflict resolution is for the parties involved to move from some form of compromise to ultimate collaboration marked by a shared success.

### Conflict Management Styles

According to an article in the *Journal of Business Ethics*, five styles are generally accepted for dealing with conflict. Nothing is inherently right or wrong with any of these styles. In fact, each can be appropriate and effective, depending on the situation, the issues to be resolved, and the personalities involved. In fact, most of us from time to time have used these styles without realizing it—with our families, our friends, or in classroom situations. These conflict management styles are competing, accommodating, avoiding, collaborating, and compromising. Refer to Table 17.3, page 367, for a detailed description and understanding of each conflict management style.

When used appropriately, each style is an effective approach to conflict resolution. Recognize that any one style or a mixture of the five may be used during the course of a dispute to arrive at the collaboration and compromise required for ultimate agreement.

Conflict may be unavoidable in organizations, but the anger, grudges, hurt, and blame that often result from it are not. Although negotiation is defined as conferring, discussing, or bargaining to reach agreements, most workers realize that in practice, negotiations involve conflict and therefore can result in win-lose, lose-lose, or win-win situations.

### Ethics on the Job

Your immediate superior has an attitude of "win at all costs" when negotiating solutions. You realize that if you approach working with others in this way, it will compromise your personal values.

*Do you go along with his negotiating style to keep your job?* ∎

**TABLE 17.3 • Conflict Management Styles**

| Style and Description | Involves |
|---|---|
| **Competing** An aggressive and totally antagonistic style. A "competitor" pursues his or her own views at a colleague's expense. This style is a power-oriented mode in which a group member uses whatever means seem appropriate to win. | Competing could mean "standing up for your rights," defending a position that you believe is correct, or demonstrating a win-at-all-costs attitude. |
| **Accommodating** An unassertive, self-sacrificing, and hospitable style that is in direct opposition to competing. Colleagues who use this approach relinquish their own concerns to satisfy the concerns of another employee. | Accommodating usually takes the form of selfless generosity or blind obedience and yielding completely to another's point of view. |
| **Avoiding** Avoiding is an unassertive, side-stepping, and retreat-oriented conflict management style. An avoider generally chooses to dodge conflict at all costs. | Avoiding takes the form of diplomatically side-stepping an issue, postponing an issue until a better time, or simply withdrawing from a situation either emotionally, physically, or intellectually. |
| **Collaborating** A more cooperative, synergistic, and multi-lateral conflict resolution style. Collaborators find mutually satisfying solutions as they dig into a situation to identify underlying issues. | Collaboration involves agreeing to not compete for resources or not use confrontation, instead to find creative solutions to mutually engaging problems. |
| **Compromising** Compromising means that both parties "split the difference" to settle disagreements. It might mean exchanging concessions or seeking quick, middle-ground solutions. | Compromising involves finding expedient, mutually acceptable solutions that partially satisfy both parties. |

**Adapted from Dawn M. Baskerville, "How Do You Manage Conflict?"** *Black Enterprise,* **May 1993, 63–64.**

## Negotiating Styles

An office professional should expect to spend a good portion of time negotiating with employees and other workgroups as well as with suppliers and customers. When people bargain, they tend to back themselves into corners defending their positions, which results in a number of either win-lose or lose-lose outcomes.

**Win-Lose** The **win-lose negotiating style** is based on the assumption that one side will win by achieving its goals and the other side will lose. When engaging in a win-lose negotiation, the person with the most information is in the most powerful position. A win-lose approach to negotiations is sometimes obvious and appropriate, while at other times it is less apparent and destructive.

# Dan Farley

*Senior Human Resource Representative*
*Silicon Graphics Computer Systems*

**Q.** Mr. Farley, we often hear that decision-making skills are necessary for office support personnel. If these skills are necessary, why?

**A.** Yes, decision-making skills are necessary—for several reasons. One reason is that organizations now are becoming "flatter," meaning that the organization has fewer levels of managerial authority. Individuals are being asked to make more decisions on their own. Someone who has that ability is valuable to an organization.

A second reason is that office support personnel are often the "hub of the wheel" in an office, meaning that they serve many different customers within an organization. Someone who can make logical decisions when multiple demands are being made upon them is going to be successful.

**Q.** What skills do you look for when interviewing for office support positions?

**A.** Referring to my "hub of the wheel" comment, you need someone who is very organized and can handle multiple demands made upon them. Interpersonal communication skills are also very important, because office support personnel interact with so many different people.

Initiative is another characteristic we look for. People in offices are very busy and having office support personnel who do not need to be asked to do everything, who can anticipate demands and make improvements on their own, is invaluable.

---

**TIP** Every time we face up to a problem and resolve it, we grow by learning to get along better with others and by taking responsibility for our own actions. ■

For example, groups often set themselves up for win-lose outcomes by following the principle of majority rule—if 51 percent of the group votes one way, then 49 percent are losers. Another example of the win-lose approach is when the parties start the negotiation process by stating the specific outcomes they want to see.

When the issues involved in a conflict are trivial or when a speedy decision is required, this style may be appropriate. In organizations, it is also appropriate when unpopular courses of action must be implemented—for instance, when implementing the strategies and policies formulated by higher-level managers.

In general, use the win-lose style when:

- you have a clear conflict of interests,
- you are in a much more powerful position, or
- you are not concerned with a long-term relationship.

**Lose-Lose** The **lose-lose negotiating style** comes into play when one party attempts to win at the expense of the other but ultimately creates problems for both parties. Two examples of lose-lose outcomes are when

Often, people who are in the position of negotiating think they must win and others must lose. The best results are achieved when everyone wins.

unreasonable union demands force companies into bankruptcy or when employers destroy the effectiveness of their workers by taking unfair advantage of them.

Mutually destructive outcomes can also arise from personal disputes among employees. For example, feuding co-workers may destroy their own careers by acquiring the reputation of being difficult to work with or of not being team players.

Compromise can sometimes seem better than fighting a win-lose battle and risking a lose-lose outcome. When resources are scarce or limited, compromise may indeed be the best solution.

**Win-Win** The **win-win negotiating style** is based on the assumption that a solution can be reached that will satisfy the needs of *all* parties. Instead of looking at their opponents as adversaries to be defeated, win-win negotiators see others as allies in the search for satisfactory solutions through collaborative means.

In most situations, the needs of the negotiating parties are not incompatible, they are just different. The four basic components of a win-win negotiation are:

1. Separating the people from the problem.
2. Focusing on interests, not positions.
3. Generating a variety of possibilities before deciding what to do.
4. Insisting that the result be based on some objective standard.

As you can see in Figure 17.2, page 370, a vast difference in results exists among the three styles.

By focusing on the end result instead of the means of getting there, you can frequently find win-win solutions. You will want to use the win-win style when:

■  you have common interests,

■  power is approximately equal, or you are in a weak position,

■  a continuing, harmonious relationship is desired.

**FIGURE 17.2 • Negotiating Styles**

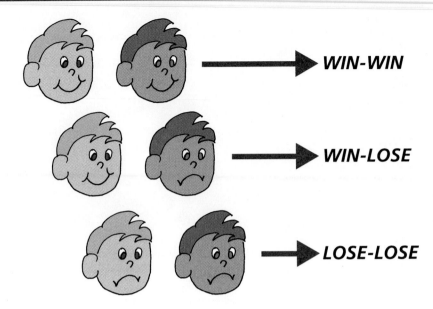

Conflict may be unavoidable in organizations, but its outcome can be positive when the win-win negotiating style is used.

## Recall Time

*Answer the following questions:*

**1.** List five factors to consider when making decisions.

**2.** How is the conflict resolution process similar to the problem-solving steps?

**3.** Briefly describe the three negotiating styles.

## Summary

Because much of the work in companies is accomplished through group effort, office workers must understand how groups function and how they impact both organizational and individual behavior. Whether the group is formal or informal, individuals receive a great deal of satisfaction from being part of a group.

The concept of teams is gaining importance as organizations begin to view themselves as interconnected systems with each person accountable for results. Ideally, an effective team is one that is efficient, productive, and cohesive.

Decision making is becoming critical for all office workers to do and do well. The process starts with a need to make a decision; then at least two alternative courses of action are determined, followed by a selection of the best choice from the alternatives.

In a work environment, decisions must be made when conflicts occur. Whether the outcome of a conflict is positive or negative is almost totally determined by the way it is managed. Conflict, if managed properly, can actually be healthy for a business. The conflict resolution process is similar to the steps in the problem-solving procedures. The goal of productive problem solving and conflict resolution is for parties involved to move from some form of compromise to ultimate collaboration marked by a shared success.

Conflict may be unavoidable in organizations, but the anger, grudges, hurt, and blame that often result from it are not. Most managers realize that in practice, negotiations involve conflict and therefore can result in win-lose, lose-lose, or win-win situations.

Here are a few essential points made in this chapter:

- Informal groups arise spontaneously throughout all levels of a company, whereas management deliberately creates formal groups.

- Groups appear to set norms, instill conformity, and engender cohesiveness.

- People become part of a group for the following reasons: affiliation, power, identity, and goal accomplishment.

- Groupthink and hidden agendas of individual group members can have negative consequences on the overall goals of an organization.

- Self-managed teams make decisions on a wide range of issues, often including determining who will perform which tasks, solving quality problems, settling conflicts between members on the team, and selecting team leaders.

- Conflict is an inevitable part of life, and the workplace is no exception. The goal should not be to eliminate all conflict but to minimize and redirect discord by seeking and applying constructive solutions.

- Five generally accepted styles for dealing with conflict are competing, accommodating, avoiding, collaborating, and compromising.

# before you leave...

**When you have completed this chapter, answer the following questions:**

**1.** Describe the function of teams in business organizations.

**2.** What are three negotiating styles?

# Review & Application

## Check Your Knowledge

1. Identify the types and characteristics of groups in organizations.

2. Why would an office worker want to be identified with an informal group at work?

3. Discuss the impact groupthink issues and hidden agendas have on accomplishing an organization's goals.

4. In your opinion, what is the most effective way for a leader to help a group handle hidden agendas?

5. Describe the concept and application of self-managed teams in organizations.

6. List seven steps in the problem-solving process.

7. What behaviors do you think describe a poor decision maker?

8. List the five conflict management styles.

9. Describe the reasons conflict in organizations may be healthy.

10. Why is letting conflict run its course not a good idea for organizations?

11. Based on your experience, what percentage of the time have you tried to follow most of the five steps when resolving personal conflicts? Were they effective?

12. Identify the outcomes of win-lose, lose-lose, and win-win negotiating styles.

13. Give an example of a win-win and a lose-lose situation you were in recently.

## Review Your Vocabulary

On a separate piece of paper, write the letter of each New Office Term beside the number of its description.

____ 1. attitudes and feelings that an individual brings to a group

____ 2. one of many interventions used to create change in an organization

____ 3. based on the assumption that one side will win by achieving its goals and the other side will lose

____ 4. two or more people who interact personally with each other to achieve a common goal

____ 5. arise spontaneously throughout all levels of a company and evolve out of employees' need for social interaction, friendship, communication, and status

____ 6. one party attempts to win at the expense of the other

____ 7. the tendency of highly cohesive groups to lose their critical evaluative abilities and out of a desire for unanimity, often overlook realistic, meaningful alternatives

____ 8. deliberately created by management for the purpose of attaining organizational goals and objectives

____ 9. based on the assumption that a solution can be reached that will satisfy the needs of all parties

____ 10. a generally agreed-upon standard of behavior every member of the group is expected to follow

a. formal groups
b. group
c. groupthink
d. hidden agendas
e. informal groups
f. lose-lose negotiating style
g. norm
h. teambuilding
i. win-lose negotiating style
j. win-win negotiating style

## Discuss and Analyze an Office Situation

Assume that you are a member of a strategic planning committee and the goal is to review the wording and intent of the organization's mission statement. One individual on the committee exhibits the following behaviors and attitudes during discussions: "I must have everything my way" "Everything has to be perfect."

Using the five steps to resolve conflicts covered in this chapter, describe how you and/or other committee members should deal with this person.

### Math

On a separate piece of paper, write the total amounts for the following purchase order:

|  | Unit Quantity | Description | Price | Total |
|---|---|---|---|---|
| 1. | 12 ea | Yellow pads | 1.55 | |
| 2. | 6 ea | HP toner cartridges | 80.50 | |
| 3. | 12 ea | Dry erase markers (red) | 1.25 | |
| 4. | 24 ea | 3.5″ high-density disks | 1.10 | |
| 5. | 12 ea | Sticky notes (3 × 5) yellow | 2.00 | |
| | | Subtotal | | |
| | | Plus 6.5% tax | | |
| | | TOTAL | | |

### English

*Rule:* When points of the compass are used to designate specific geographic regions, capitalize them. Do not capitalize them when they are used to indicate direction.

*Examples:* Flagstaff is located north of Phoenix. Rapid growth is occurring throughout the Southwest.

*Practice Exercise:* Apply the rule to the following sentences. On a separate piece of paper, if a sentence is correct, write OK. If a sentence is incorrect, rewrite it correctly.

a. Her travels took her to the far east.

b. Sean thought Northerners were very conservative in their thinking on this issue.

c. A second path is located just south of the main trail.

d. Proceed West on Washington Street to reach the Capitol.

e. The weather forecaster reported our area would receive westerly winds over the next few days.

f. The college course dealt with Western civilization.

g. Many people go south for the winter.

h. Is Portugal east or west of Spain?

i. The train was Eastbound toward New York City when the accident occurred.

j. The best restaurant in town is located just south of the public library.

### Proofreading

Rewrite or rekey the following checklist on a separate piece of paper, correcting misspellings and incorrect punctuation.

When you first join a group are you quiet at first? do you keep to yourselv, observing how people interract? You can sharpen your powers of analisis by asking yourself; some questions when you first encounter a group. As you observe, try to answer the follwoing questions;

- What are the objecrtives of the group?
- Are the groups goals cooperative or competetive?
- Does the group function as a team, or do rivalaries exist among members?
- Does the group have a leader? Who is the leader.
- What are the norms of the group? Is it formal or informal?

## Apply Your Knowledge

1. Keep a journal for three days and note examples of decisions you make while at school, at home, at work, and with friends. Evaluate any three of the decisions according to the decision-making process steps.
   a. Did you follow the process?
   b. Identify any decisions that were faulty because you made a snap decision without enough facts, or you wanted more facts and waited too long to decide.

2. Describe two situations where either you or someone you know has successfully used two of the five conflict management styles described in this chapter.

## Using the Reference Manual

 Open file ch17ref.doc. Use the proofreaders' marks section of the Reference Manual at the back of the book to help you correct the paragraphs. Save and print.

# PART FOUR: Communication and Problem-Solving Skills

## Specific Activities to Complete

Select at least three of the following items for inclusion in your Career Portfolio, using the information from Chapters 14 through 17.

1. Key a list of the five ways you will improve your current listening and helping skills. Then, relate each item on this list to on-the-job performance in an office. Save and print this list. (Be sure you proof according to the instructions given previously on page 84.) Insert this list as the first item in your Career Portfolio binder behind the fourth tab, entitled "Communication and Problem-Solving Skills."

2. Describe a situation in which you used the problem-solving process with success. Save, print, and insert this description behind the fourth tab as well.

3. Describe your current international business and intercultural communication skills and areas in which you plan to improve. Save, print, and insert this description and plan of action behind the fourth tab.

4. Evaluate your workplace literacy skills according to the SCANS report. Save, print, and insert the evaluation behind the fourth tab.

5. Create a flyer describing a seminar on conflict resolution, using the desktop publishing features of your word processing package. (Make up appropriate details relative to date, time, place, speaker, cost, and so on.) Save, print, and insert this flyer behind the fourth tab.

# PART V
# Employment Skills

# chapter

## Choosing Your Office Career

*After completing this chapter, you will be able to do the following:*

**1.** Describe in detail the life you dream of having five, ten, and twenty years in the future.

**2.** List the eight steps in career decision making.

**3.** List the work values important to you.

**4.** List four topics on which you will need to gather career information.

**5.** List three sources of career information published by the U.S. Department of Labor.

**6.** Describe your own personal attributes.

**7.** List the types of information you need to include in your plan of action.

**8.** Develop a plan of action to reach your lifestyle and career goals.

### New Office Terms

- aptitude
- benefits
- *Complete Guide for Occupational Exploration*
- *Dictionary of Occupational Titles*
- extrovert
- flextime
- interest survey
- introvert

- job sharing
- just-in-time hiring
- lifestyle goal
- *Occupational Outlook Handbook*
- personality
- values
- virtual organization
- work values

# before you begin...

**Answer the following questions to the best of your ability:**

1. What personal attributes should be considered when choosing a career?
2. What types of career information should be considered when choosing a career?
3. What types of information should be included in a plan of action to reach your lifestyle and career goals?

**A**re you a dreamer? Do you sometimes think about how you would like to live in the future? Daydreaming is often discouraged as a waste of time. Nevertheless, this type of thinking—using your imagination—is the first step in planning anything.

As you consider how you might fit into one type of career or another, keep asking yourself how the work would affect your overall lifestyle. In Chapter 2 you studied which office job classifications will most likely be available through the year 2010 and the types of companies that will provide many of these employment opportunities. You also studied the duties of, qualifications for, and working conditions on jobs such as office clerk, administrative assistant, secretary, receptionist, and customer service representative. Although these job titles represent the majority of office workers, offices provide many other job opportunities as well.

## Career Choice and Lifestyle

You have probably narrowed your ultimate career goal to some type of office work, but you may not have decided on the exact career or job title that you want. Even if you have already decided, you may change your mind. If you are under the age of twenty, you will probably work for about forty years. Planning for and making a career choice is extremely important, because your decision provides a direction for the rest of your life.

Most career choices are tentative, which is good. You should feel free to change your mind about the career you want to pursue if you learn that another career is probably more appropriate for you. Office careers provide a wide variety of work, both for beginning workers and for those with years of experience. Besides differences in the types of skills used, they offer a variety of work environments. For example, suppose that you are a secretary in the racing office at large racetrack. You have a friend who is an administrative assistant in an office at the headquarters of a large computer company. You have another friend who is a secretary in a doctor's office, and yet another friend in a law office. Although your clerical and computer skills may be similar, the different environments provide considerable variation in these jobs.

Whatever your career choice, you must earn enough to pay for your housing, transportation, food, leisure activities, and maybe your children's education. Thus, your work will directly affect all other aspects of your lifestyle.

## Technology in the Office | BIOMETRICS

Biometric identification—such as fingerprint scans, iris scans, and facial scans—has arrived, and it seems a bit scary to some people. However, what could be more fair and accurate than being able to prove that you are you? If you have not already, you may soon see biometrics at your workplace when you log on to a company network or when you want to gain access to a secure area.

Among the most useful scans for identification are those for the finger, hand, iris, face, and voice. Finger scans store a template based on a fingerprint. They are extremely accurate. Finger-scan units for personal computers are available for under $200. Hand scans are not distinct enough for identifying random people, but they are useful for identifying employees. Iris scans are extremely accurate, being able to recognize identical twins. They are used for employee access in some airports. Facial scans can identify people in a crowd without their knowledge, but they have a high false-positive rate. They are used in the business districts of some U.S. cities. A voice scan can verify a person's identity. It has potential for widespread use, as it will work over a telephone. ■

If you can be happy living in a small apartment and using a bus for transportation, then you will not need to earn a high salary. If you dream of a more expensive lifestyle—a house in the suburbs and two cars—then you need to consider future earnings when you look at possible career choices.

You will get more from work than just money. Your work will satisfy, to a greater or lesser extent, your social, psychological, and self-esteem needs. Your work will probably become the central activity around which you plan your daily life.

# Making Career Decisions

Do you feel as though your work will control your life? In many ways, it will, but you may choose the type of work you do. So if you are wondering whether anyone knows the secret to a fulfilling life, perhaps it is choosing the type of work that will provide the lifestyle you want to have in the future. You have a right to do exactly that—and with proper planning, you can take control of your life.

Of course, many people do not take control of their lives. They do not plan for a career. They make a choice, all right, but it is a choice to give up control—to just let things happen to them. You can make a better choice. You will most likely make an intelligent career choice if you follow a decision-making procedure.

Whether you know it or not, you follow certain procedural steps in making any important decision. Some choices are so simple that we do not even recognize the procedure. Choices about which TV show to watch are easy. Choosing which car to buy requires more thought, but you may not follow a step-by-step procedure to do so.

Your career will likely become the central activity around which you plan your daily life, and it will affect every other aspect of your life.

The following eight-step procedure is an adaptation of the decision-making process discussed in Chapter 17. These steps work especially well for making career decisions.

1. *Define your need or want.* What do you want out of life? Think about your daydreams and picture your hoped-for future lifestyle. Consider your values and interests.

2. *Analyze your resources.* Your skills and aptitudes (natural abilities) are the resources you contribute to a career.

3. *Identify your alternatives.* Your alternatives are the careers about which you want to learn more. You have probably already thought about the careers or jobs you believe would be interesting. Select at least three career fields for in-depth research, and you will have some alternatives to compare.

4. *Gather information on your alternatives.* Information on careers includes responsibilities and requirements, working conditions, benefits, and opportunities.

5. *Evaluate your alternatives.* Review all the information you have gathered on alternatives. Compare each alternative with your personal attributes. Would the work activities be interesting? Do the activities, responsibilities, and working relationships match your values? Do you have the skills required? If not, do you have the aptitudes needed to learn the required skills? If you will need further training and education for advancement, how will you complete it? Does this work mesh well with your personality? Can you realistically expect to earn enough to support your long-range lifestyle plans? Is this field likely to have ample opportunities when you begin working?

6. *Make your decision.* Which alternative is best for you? Which is second best? If one alternative is clearly best, then you will probably stick with this decision. Most people, though, need to keep reviewing their career decisions for months or even years (see step 8). Things can and often do happen that make another career alternative more appealing or

appropriate, so think of your initial career decision as a flexible one. No matter how certain you feel about your decision, you may want to change it later.

7. *Plan your action.* Your plan of action is an outline of what you must do to reach your career goal—and thus have your desired lifestyle. This action plan will require setting some planning goals, which are the stepping stones toward bigger goals.

8. *Evaluate your decision.* After making your decision, continue reviewing it to determine whether it is, indeed, the best choice for you. Either you will become even more convinced that it is a wise decision or you will begin to have lingering doubts about whether it is appropriate. If the latter occurs, then review your other alternatives again. If you decide that another choice would have been better, then change your career goal. Before you change it, though, make certain that your new choice matches more closely with your long-range plans for your lifestyle.

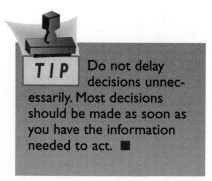

**TIP** Do not delay decisions unnecessarily. Most decisions should be made as soon as you have the information needed to act. ■

# Exploring Personal Attributes

Your personal attributes are your own needs, values, interests, data-people-things preferences, skills and aptitudes, and personality. Once you assess your personal attributes, you can determine which careers will match them.

An easy way to organize the information you discover about your personal attributes (and later, what you learn about career alternatives) is to record all of it in a notebook. Divide your notebook into four sections: Personal Attributes, Career Alternatives, Career Choices, and Plan of Action. As you explore your personal attributes, record this information in the first section. As you gather information about career alternatives, record it in the second section. Use the third section to record information on how your personal attributes match with each of several career alternatives. Finally, use the fourth section to develop a plan of action that will guide you toward your chosen career.

## Needs

When you were younger, you probably began to plan your future by thinking about—daydreaming about—how you would like to live someday. Can you picture now how you would like to live five, ten, even twenty years from now? As you picture your hoped-for future life, you will probably consider the following:

- where you will live
- the type of car you will drive
- how you will spend your leisure time
- your relationships with family and friends
- community, social, and religious activities
- the work you will do to earn a living—your career

Would you like to live the same lifestyle that your parents live? If not, how would you like your lifestyle to be different from theirs?

Your lifestyle is an expression of ideas and feelings that you believe are desirable, important, and worthwhile. These ideas and feelings are called **values**. As you daydream about the future and the lifestyle you want to live, you will picture ways you hope to express your values. Focus

on different parts of your future life, and you will begin to see the whole picture of how you want to live. The way you want to live in the future is your **lifestyle goal.** You must have a clear understanding of your values to visualize your future lifestyle goal clearly. If you are unsure of your own values, this vision of the future will remain blurry.

## Values

If you have a clear set of values, you may find focusing on the future relatively easy. You can set goals and plan how to reach them because you know where you are going.

Your values have been formed throughout your life, beginning soon after birth, and they will continue to change somewhat as you grow older. When you were a child, your values probably mirrored those of your parents or other members of your family. When you were in elementary school, your family was still most likely the primary influence on your values. However, as you have grown older, your teachers and friends have affected them, too. The media, especially TV, have also influenced your values. As a teenager, you probably began to wonder about some of your values.

As young adults, you can easily become confused about what is important. You begin testing reality. We are unsure about a lot of things. Perhaps you are in the process of questioning some of your values now.

Consider what your family, friends, teachers, and others think is important, but decide for yourself what is important to you. As you mature, you will select values that you believe in, and they will become the guideposts in your life.

You may become more confident in your ability to plan for the future by setting and achieving goals as you develop and follow your own set of values. In the beginning, these goals do not have to be especially important ones. Achieving some small goals will build your confidence. In a year, or two or three, this confidence will help you achieve important goals.

We all have general values that define how we live our daily lives. Certain values define needs we expect to fulfill through work; they are sometimes known as **work values.** Your work values may include the following:

- fame
- economic well-being
- creativity
- religious activity
- prestige
- security

- independence
- friendships
- close family life
- humanitarianism

You will be a happier person if your work is compatible with your values than if your work demands opposing values. For example, if fame is important to you, you will likely be happier as a performer than as an accountant. If security is important, you will probably be happier as an accountant than as an aspiring but often unemployed actor.

Sometimes a formal survey is helpful in clarifying values. These surveys are called *values scales* or *values tests*. However, unlike most tests, they have no right or wrong answers. Most surveys simply ask you to respond to a list of statements describing what people like or do not like in their work.

Values surveys are provided by the counseling office in many schools. If you think such a survey would be helpful, ask your school counselor about it.

Your goals for the future are determined in large part by your values. If your values are clearly defined, you will likely have specific goals established.

## Interests

In choosing a career, the first criterion that comes to mind is to find work that is interesting. No job is all fun, but you will be happier doing work you find interesting than doing work you find boring or unpleasant. Try to match the work activities of a career with your own interests. How? Begin by listing all the activities you enjoy doing, starting with what you enjoy most. If you have some hobbies, you may be able to apply the knowledge you learn from one of them to your future work activities.

Your favorite classes in school may indicate interests that can be satisfied through a particular type of work. What in-class activities do you enjoy? Consider, especially, any activities that you might do on the job. You have probably used a computer for word processing and perhaps other applications. Do you like working with a computer? Which applications do you enjoy most?

If you like doing a number of different activities, you will find choosing a satisfying career much easier. If you have not developed a variety of interests, you may have difficulty deciding which career would be absorbing. In that case, take time to explore some new interests that may relate to various work activities.

An interest survey may help you identify work activities that you would enjoy. An **interest survey** lists statements describing a variety of activities. These surveys are called *interest inventories* or *interest tests*. Your response on one of these instruments can help you discover your level of interest in various careers. School counseling offices usually offer interest inventories, so ask your school counselor about them if you would like to take one.

## Data-People-Things Preferences

All jobs require working with data, other people, and things. On some jobs, such as that of an accountant, you would work primarily with data (information). On other jobs, such as that of a receptionist, you would work primarily with people. On yet other jobs, such as that of a copy machine operator, you would work primarily with things (machines).

Have you considered your data-people-things preferences? Do you like reading, writing, or doing math and working alone? Do you prefer

activities involving other people? Are you fascinated when working with things such as building models? Your working relationships with data, people, and things will vary greatly from one type of work to another, and most work involves dealing with all three to some extent. Do not overlook this characteristic when considering careers or individual jobs.

## Skills and Aptitudes

An awareness of your interests and data-people-things preferences will help you choose work that you will enjoy doing. However, simply finding work that sounds interesting is no assurance of success—and you will not enjoy any career or job for long unless you are successful. You have already developed some of the general skills required for all jobs, such as being able to get along well with others. You have probably developed some of the special skills required for office work, too, such as keyboarding (typing) and using a computer for various applications. As you narrow your list of careers, you need to know your aptitude for learning additional skills.

An **aptitude** is the potential for learning a skill. For example, if you found learning to key easy, then you have an aptitude for keyboarding. Learning skills for which you do not have an aptitude will be more difficult; therefore, you need to determine these skills.

You are probably aware of some of your aptitudes. List them in your career planning notebook under Personal Attributes. Your performance in classes at school may indicate certain aptitudes. If you score high on most of your math tests, it is probably because you have an aptitude for math. You will likely be successful in accounting or other careers that require math.

An aptitude test may help you determine how much ability you have in certain areas. Some aptitude tests, such as the General Aptitude Test Battery, indicate levels of aptitude in various areas and list job titles that match your aptitudes. Your school counselor may be able to arrange for you to take one of these tests.

## Personality

Your **personality** is the outward reflection of your inner self. It is apparent in how you look, speak, and act. All employers look for cheerfulness, enthusiasm, honesty, neatness, self-control, tact, and a good sense of humor.

Success in certain careers depends a great deal on specific additional personality traits. Perhaps the simplest way of categorizing personality types is to divide everyone into two groups, extroverts and introverts. An **extrovert** is a person who has an outgoing personality. If you make friends easily and enjoy the company of many people, then you are probably an extrovert. You will most likely want to work where you can interact with a variety of other people. You might enjoy being a receptionist in a busy office where you can greet and talk with numerous clients and co-workers.

An **introvert** is a person with a quiet personality. If you are uncomfortable in a room full of strangers and have difficulty making new friends, then you are probably an introvert. You might enjoy a job as an accountant, where you can work primarily with information and will not be interrupted frequently by other employees.

Neither personality type is better than the other, but each type is more appropriate for certain careers. As you may have guessed, most people fall somewhere between the extrovert and introvert extremes. However, you are probably closer to one personality type than the other.

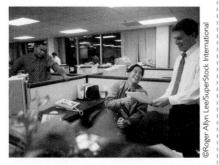

©Roger Allyn Lee/SuperStock International

An extrovert would probably not be annoyed by interruptions in a busy office.

Just as we have measurement instruments for values, interests, and aptitudes, we have tests for personalities, too. They are not tests in the usual sense—they have no right or wrong answers. However, if you would like more information to help you define your own personality, then a personality test may help. Certain of these tests show how similar your personality is to that of most workers in particular careers. If you would like to take one of these tests, ask your school counselor.

## Recall Time

*Answer the following questions:*

1. Sheila has decided on her long-range desired lifestyle. Following the eight-step procedure, what are the next steps she should take toward choosing her career?

2. When you imagine the lifestyle you would like to be living five to ten years from now, what do you see?

3. Raymond is particularly interested in an office job in the travel field. Besides interest, what else is important in evaluating whether a person is "right" for a job?

4. A clerk's job at the library involves categorizing and labeling books while working alone in a back room. As the employer, what personality traits would you look for when hiring someone for this position?

# Exploring Careers

Although your future life is sure to take some unexpected turns, the dreaming and planning for the future that you do now will leave less to happenstance and allow you to take control of your life. If you have yet to settle on a career goal, the following information on exploring careers may help you make that decision. Even if you have decided on a career goal, look again at some other careers—or at some specific jobs within your chosen career field. However, remember that career goals should be kept flexible, and they should be continually evaluated.

Although you can explore careers in many ways, plan to gather information on the following four topics:

- responsibilities and requirements
- working conditions
- opportunities and benefits
- emerging career options

A variety of sources for this information are available.

As you explore career options and job opportunities, consider whether if a particular one is compatible with your skills, values, and personality.

## Responsibilities and Requirements

The most important information you will need about jobs and careers is a description of the daily work activities. These tasks are the ones you will do if you select a particular job or career. As you explore each career and later consider individual jobs, ask yourself, "What are the duties and responsibilities?" Think about whether you would enjoy performing these duties and carrying out these responsibilities.

## Kaycee Hale

*Executive Director*
*FIDM (Fashion Institute of Design & Merchandising)*
*Resource and Research Center*

**Q.** Ms. Hale, do employers look for certain skills when hiring new employees? If so, what are they?

**A.** Today's employers (managers/supervisors) are responsible for assessing "potential" employees as human resource assets—the most valuable capital of any organization. In order to enhance one's organizational competitive edge within the "global village," managers/supervisors must evaluate an interviewee with an eye toward workplace basics, the skills that employers want.

What I look for in a "potential" staff member is:

- computer literacy
- sense of humor
- flexibility
- strong work ethic
- willingness to embrace change
- service orientation
- enthusiasm and energy

**Q.** What advice about the real work world would you give to a student?

**A.** Start making connections. See every encounter as a possible opportunity to make your first impression a positive and a lasting one.

Put your best foot forward in everything you do. Act as if your homework, your class participation, your in-class public speaking presentation, are dress rehearsals for your upcoming interviews and performance evaluations that might result in a promotion.

Show interest, enthusiasm, and personality in class, in meetings, in conversation. You never know who is watching. Maintain a positive attitude with a "can and will do" attitude. Participate in group activities so that you can learn how to work effectively in a team environment.

Expand your horizons. *Soar.* Dare to dream great dreams. Then promise yourself to make them come true!

---

If the duties and responsibilities appeal to you, determine the requirements for success in this career or on this particular job. If you want to earn promotions and pay raises, you will need more than the simple entry-level skills required for a beginning position. How many of these skills have you already developed? Do you have the aptitude to learn high-level skills in this career? What additional training and education are needed for advancement? Where can you get the required training and education?

Some careers are more compatible with your values and your personality type than others. As you investigate each job or career, consider whether the responsibilities and requirements are compatible with your values and personality type.

# Working Conditions

You will probably spend about forty hours each week (two thousand hours each year) on a job, so investigate the working conditions of any job or career you consider. Most office work is done in a pleasant environment, usually indoors and often in air-conditioned, well-lighted offices. Even so, situations can vary considerably. Some offices lack air conditioning and thus are often too hot. Others are noisy or are located in cramped quarters.

The level of stress on a job, whether physical, mental, or emotional, also falls into the category of working conditions. Most office jobs are not physically demanding, but many require more work than you can comfortably complete in eight hours a day—which leads to mental and emotional stress.

Other working conditions worth considering include data-people-things relationships and hours of work.

# Opportunities and Benefits

When you discover several careers in which the work activities and working conditions appeal to you, research their opportunities and benefits to workers.

Check on the usual salary for beginning workers, and find out how much you can earn after working two, three, five, and ten years. Are the benefits appealing? **Benefits**, sometimes called *fringe benefits*, are the extra payments or services, in addition to salary, that the employer provides to employees. They usually include medical and dental insurance, paid sick days, and paid vacations. More and more companies are providing child care, either on the job site or nearby. Some companies provide exercise facilities or health club memberships for employees to use during the lunch hour or other free time.

When you find one or several careers in which you feel you can succeed and that are interesting and rewarding, investigate the expected availability of jobs. You may not want to prepare for work that has limited opportunities or that would require you to move to another city or section of the country.

# Emerging Career Options

Several career options have become more available to office workers in recent years. The most prevalent are temporary work assignments, flex-time, and working at home—telecommuting. These work options primarily affect where and when you work rather than the type of work you do.

## Temporary Work Assignments

Several nationwide companies, such as Manpower® and Kelly Services™, and many smaller companies have for many years provided temporary office workers for businesses. These companies have also, in turn, provided opportunities for many office workers to experience a variety of working environments.

Office workers have more opportunities than ever to work for temporary agencies; doing so has some obvious advantages. If you are a beginning worker with good office skills, your limited experience may disqualify you from some desirable jobs. Your good skills will probably qualify you as a temporary worker, however. Many beginning workers are gaining experience and sharpening their skills as temporary workers.

## Large Office/Small Office
*What's Your Preference?*

### Careers

You will usually find many more career advancement opportunities in a large office than you will find in a small one. The main reason is that more positions are available in a large office. The more employee positions, the more chances for advancement. In a large office, you may find advancement positions such as office assistant I, office assistant II, and office assistant III. These steps up the career ladder often result in higher salaries and more work responsibility. Also, large offices are often part of big companies that have more offices in other locations, which means even more advancement possibilities and more options if you are willing to relocate to a different part of the country.

Career advancement opportunities in small offices are usually limited. Fewer positions are available in small offices or small companies. Once an employee reaches a certain level in a small office, he or she finds little chance for career advancement. In many cases, the only possibility for promotion is to accept a position in a new job category. For example, if you are an office support worker in an insurance office, your only advancement option might be to become a claims adjuster.

**Are you the kind of person who will want to move up the career ladder, or will you be content with a steady job that you know you can do well? To advance, would you prefer to try new and different kinds of jobs, or would you rather continue using your office skills and training at higher levels? ■**

Another reason to consider working for a temporary agency is the opportunity to try a variety of jobs and environments. You can then decide how you want to spend the next forty years.

Most full-time office jobs require working about forty hours per week. Some people—especially parents with small children—may want to work less than full-time. If you want to work a schedule other than eight to five, most temporary agencies will give you work assignments to match your schedule.

### Just-in-Time Hiring

Some companies have begun the practice of **just-in-time hiring,** or not hiring employees until just before they are needed. They may be hired on either a temporary or permanent basis. This hiring practice is an efficient way of utilizing human resources. It is similar to the way manufacturers use material resources by "just-in-time" delivery of parts. Just-in-time hiring occurs most often during periods of high unemployment, when a large pool of experienced workers are ready to start work on short notice.

## Flextime

Some companies allow workers a certain latitude in setting their own hours for arriving to and leaving work. **Flextime** means a system for allowing workers to set their own times for beginning and finishing work within a range of available hours. The concept of flextime has been around for years, and it is accepted by many companies.

## Job Sharing

Some companies have taken the concept of flextime to a new level by allowing employees to share a job. **Job sharing** is seldom a written policy, and it always requires the approval of company management. More organizations today are willing to give it a try when two employees like doing the same job, but neither wants to work full-time. Usually, one full-time job is shared by two people who each work half days. Or, one person may work two days a week and another three days a week. Several combinations are possible, depending on the job and the willingness of company management to allow such flexibility. Some jobs lend themselves to job sharing more than others. Most companies look more favorably on job sharing that involves relatively routine jobs. Jobs that require greater continuity of information throughout the day and from day to day would be more difficult to perform on a job-sharing basis.

## Telecommuting

During the 1990s, as prices of more powerful computers dropped, many people purchased sophisticated desktop computers for home use. These newer machines often are as powerful as those used in most business offices. They allow users not only to write letters and reports but also to prepare complicated documents, databases, and graphics at home as easily

©Reed Kaestner/Corbis

Many companies now allow some employees to work at home, often with computers networked with office computers.

as in an office. Some workers are more productive at home because they have fewer interruptions than in the workplace.

More than ever before, companies are hiring part-time or temporary office workers and allowing them to complete all or most of their tasks at home using desktop or laptop computers. Sometimes the company provides computers, and they may be networked with company computers.

By working at home, you save the time you would spend going to and from an office every day. You also save on gasoline and other car costs, and you eliminate the frustration you would have to endure if you drove through congested traffic. Some companies allow parents of small children to work at home. This policy allows parents to stay home with their children and also save on child care costs.

Many types of work that do not require the use of a computer are done at home, too. However, computers have allowed more office workers to work at home and complete their tasks. An increasing number of people have begun their own office services businesses in their homes, too. You may want to consider this alternative as you think about your career options.

### Virtual Organizations, Virtual Workers

A new form of organization is emerging that uses information technology to collapse space and time. These organizations have the ability to change rapidly in structure and function. They are known as **virtual organizations.** They are defined not by buildings but by collaborative networks that link hundreds or thousands of people together. Why keep a hundred offices open all year to accommodate four or five months of rush business? A virtual business will hire a hundred virtual workers and provide them with laptop computers at a fraction of the cost of maintaining offices for them. Additionally, these virtual workers may be scattered across the country or around the world, yet operate as if they were all in the company home office. The driving force behind this trend is global competition. In business today, "survival of the fastest" is the rule. Collaborative networks can also deliver better products faster, making greater profits for a company.

In virtual organizations, office managers may be not needed. Each worker will likely manage information systems as a team member in a horizontal organization.

# Sources of Career Information

Numerous sources of career information are available. You can find many of them in your school library, a local public library, or elsewhere within your community.

## The Library

Begin your career research in your school library or local public library. Most libraries have career books, magazines, pamphlets, films, and videotapes. Your school library may have a special section devoted to career information. In many schools, this section is called a *career information center*. Many of these centers have computerized career guidance programs that facilitate career research. Previous experience with computers is not required to run most of these programs.

With a laptop computer, cell phone, and briefcase, a worker can set up an "office" almost anywhere and communicate with co-workers.

Most libraries have copies of the following three books published by the U.S. Department of Labor. They provide a wealth of career information.

- *Occupational Outlook Handbook*
- *Complete Guide for Occupational Exploration*
- *Dictionary of Occupational Titles*

The **Occupational Outlook Handbook** includes detailed information on more than 250 occupations (the jobs held by 87 percent of American workers), and it is updated every two years. *The Career Guide to Industries*, a companion to the *Handbook*, provides information on available careers by industry, including the nature of the industry, working conditions, employment, occupations in the industry, training and advancement, earnings and benefits, employment outlook, and lists of organizations that can provide additional information. You may find the *Handbook* and other U.S. Department of Labor publications online at www.bls.gov/oco. The *Occupational Outlook Handbook* is easy to use and provides the following types of information:

- nature of the work
- working conditions
- employment
- training, other qualifications, and advancement
- job outlook
- earnings
- related occupations
- sources of additional information

The *Complete Guide for Occupational Exploration* organizes jobs into twelve interest areas. Each interest area is further divided into work groups and subgroups. The *Guide* provides the following types of information:

- the kind of work done
- skills and abilities needed
- interests and aptitudes
- how to prepare for this kind of work

The **Dictionary of Occupational Titles** includes descriptions of more than twenty thousand jobs. In the main section, "Occupational Group Arrangement," it lists an identification number for and describes in some detail the duties of each job. Copy down the identification number, then turn to the appendix and learn the data-people-things relationships for the job. The *Dictionary of Occupational Titles* is somewhat more complicated to use than the *Occupational Outlook Handbook* or the *Complete Guide for Occupational Exploration*, so read the instructions in the front before you start using it.

## The Community

The business community in your area can also serve as an excellent source of career information. You can benefit from this source in two ways. First, you can gather career information by interviewing several people who earn their living doing the type of work you are considering. Second, you can get some real on-the-job work experience.

### Ethics on the Job

You are employed in the office of a small publishing firm that is just getting started. You are very knowledgeable about the computer graphics programs that your company uses, and your boss has come to rely on your expertise. The stress of meeting publication deadlines is always part of your job. Increasingly, your boss has been asking you to take projects home on the weekend to help with the workload. She has purchased all the necessary software programs and has provided a computer for you to use at home.

You are very happy with your job, but you feel dissatisfied with having to spend all this extra time working on weekends. Your boss trusts you to keep track of the hours you work at home and pays you at your regular rate for them. She then attempts to give you additional time off when the workload is light. You would prefer to be compensated for overtime. Friends suggest that you should simply bill your boss for more hours than you actually work.

1. **Does overbilling seem like an ethical solution to you? Explain your answer.**

2. **What other solutions can you suggest?** ■

Your library research will likely provide an introduction to several careers that interest you and prompt some specific questions. You can probably find answers to these questions by interviewing someone in your local community who has years of experience in the career that interests you. You may know people who work in the careers you are considering. Call them up, explain your interest in their careers, and ask if you may interview them. Most people are flattered by an interest in their work, and they enjoy talking about what they do. If you can, arrange for an interview at the job site so that you can see the equipment and materials used. Before your appointment, prepare a list of questions to guide you during your interview.

If you do not know anyone engaged in a career that interests you, ask your teachers, friends, and parents if they can suggest someone. Or simply look in the Yellow Pages of the telephone book. If you are interested in accounting, for example, look under Accountants.

You will learn more about the duties, responsibilities, and data-people-things relationships of any type of work by actual on-the-job work experience than by any other method. Many high schools have school-to-work programs, mentoring, shadowing, and other work experience activities that allow you to work part-time after school. In many schools, a work experience coordinator will help you find the type of job you would like. Most schools grant credit toward graduation for work completed through the work experience program.

If you are doing productive work, you will be paid at least the minimum wage. However, if you are placed on a job mainly to get some experience and observe other workers, you will not be paid. These nonpaying positions usually provide greater opportunity than do paid positions to explore the many facets of a career. So do not overlook nonpaying work experience.

If your school does not have a work experience program, apply for a part-time job on your own. If you cannot get a paid job in the type of work you would like, consider becoming a volunteer. Volunteers work without pay, usually for nonprofit organizations. Many young people get their first work experience as volunteers in such organizations as the Young Men's Christian Association (YMCA<sup>SM</sup>) or Young Women's Christian Association (YWCA<sup>SM</sup>), the American Red Cross, or a local hospital. Many opportunities are available through volunteer work; however, getting the type of experience you are seeking is sometimes difficult.

## The Internet

Each year, more career information becomes available on the Internet. Many of the sources that formerly required a visit to your local library may now be reached by just clicking your mouse. Try entering keywords, such as *career information,* into a search engine, and you will likely view a listing of dozens of Web sites. Read the titles and brief information provided, then select those that seem to match your interests. Many states, such as Michigan, Minnesota, New Jersey, Oregon, Idaho, and Virginia, have Web sites that provide career information. Also check various online government sources such as the Department of Labor and Bureau of Labor Statistics Web sites.

# *Choosing a Career*

The type of work you do to earn a living will probably become the central activity in your life. It will influence every aspect of your lifestyle. Perhaps no decision in your life will be more important than your choice of career.

Patty has been sure about her future ever since she can remember. "I definitely want to be a model," Patty declares. However, Patty's school counselor advises her to look around a little more before making her final decision. "Patty, I'd like you to take some tests—an interest survey, an aptitude test, and a personality test—just to make sure you are not overlooking other promising careers." To her surprise, Patty discovers a number of career opportunities that appeal to her and that she has never been aware of before. "Wow!" she says. "This information is exciting. I never knew about these other possibilities! I like having these new options."

Renee is also convinced that she wants to become a model. When the school counselor asks Renee to take the tests, Renee refuses. "I already know what I want to do!" she states.

1. **Describe Patty's and Renee's attitudes toward choosing their careers.**

2. **How might Patty's attitude be helpful on the job?**

3. **Based on their attitudes, which student is more likely to succeed?** ■

Unfortunately, many people never get around to making a conscious career decision. Some spend more time planning a wardrobe or deciding which car to buy than they do planning a career. They do not seem to understand that the work they do will control much of their future lives. Unable to make a conscious choice, these people fall into some type of work through happenstance and simply drift through life. They do make a decision, but it is an unconscious decision to give away control of their lives.

Having explored your personal attributes and careers, you need to make your career choice. You may feel reluctant to make such an important decision today, this month, or even this year. However, the sooner you choose a career, the sooner you will have a direction for your life. Remember, no career choice is final; you can always change your mind. Indeed, you *should* change your career choice whenever you determine that another one is better for you.

# Developing Your Plan of Action

Some people with good intentions get as far as choosing a career but never get around to developing a plan to reach their goals. If you have not done so already, plan now how you will reach your career and lifestyle goals. Include the following types of information in your plan:

- training and education
- money for training and education
- jobs leading to your career and lifestyle goals
- major changes that may be required in your personal life

Begin by setting some planning goals. These goals are the relatively minor but important goals you must reach before you can achieve your bigger goals.

Goals must be specific. Saying that you want to be a success or that you want a simple lifestyle is much too general. Describe your lifestyle goal in detail.

Goals must be realistic. Setting goals that are impossible to reach is worse than having no goals at all because such goals will constantly frustrate you.

Write your goals clearly and completely and set a "due date" for each one. Begin with the lifestyle and career goals you want to achieve after five, ten, and twenty years. Then decide what long-range, medium-range, and short-range planning goals will enable you to reach your ultimate goals.

Your ultimate career goal might be to become a certified public accountant (CPA) by the time you are twenty-five years old. You might set a long-range goal to graduate with a bachelor of arts (BA) degree in accounting by the time you are twenty-two. A medium-range goal might be acceptance by a certain college when you graduate from high school. A short-range goal might be to earn an A in this class.

With better planning, most people could have a more satisfying lifestyle than the one they live currently. You can have a satisfying lifestyle because you know how to take control of your life. You know how to explore your personal attributes, investigate careers, and make important decisions. You also know how to develop a plan of action that will guide you toward your ultimate career and lifestyle goals. Your plan of action can do the following four things:

- Organize your activities
- Keep you on schedule
- Help you set priorities
- Give you a feeling of accomplishment when you reach your goals

As you achieve your short-range goals, you will become more confident. You will know that you can achieve your longer-range goals, too.

## Recall Time

*Answer the following questions:*

**1.** Suzy is considering a front-office administrative assistant job for a busy trucking company. What should she find out about her potential working conditions before she makes her final decision?

**2.** What are some advantages to temporary office work through a temporary employment agency?

**3.** Jorge is interested in department store customer service. What sources can he find in the library to research this career?

**4.** If your long-range career goal is to be a bookkeeper, what might be a short-range goal that you can accomplish during high school?

## Summary

Your career choice will be one of the most important decisions of your life. Your work will affect every aspect of your daily life. Such an important decision requires a step-by-step decision-making procedure in which you define your desired future lifestyle; analyze your skills and aptitudes; identify your career alternatives; get information about those alternatives; evaluate the alternatives; make your decision; develop a plan of action to

reach your career goal; and continue to evaluate your decision until you are convinced it is the best for you, or decide to change your career goal to one that suits you better.

Exploring your personal attributes can be helpful in selecting a career that makes you happy. In assessing your own personal characteristics, include a description of the lifestyle you hope to lead; your personal and work values; your interests; your preferences for working with data, people, or things; your skills and aptitudes; and your personality type.

Exploring career characteristics is as important as assessing yourself. The most vital information about jobs and careers concerns their duties and responsibilities. Try to find a match between your own needs, values, interests, and skills and the requirements of a job. Examine the working conditions of a job or career. Are they compatible with your personal preferences? Are the job opportunities and benefits agreeable to you? Investigate the expected availability of jobs in a certain field. Include temporary work, job sharing, and working at home in your list of options.

Use your school and public libraries as valuable sources of information about careers. Many libraries contain extensive resources for your career research. Three books published by the U.S. Department of Labor provide particularly detailed information about jobs and careers: the *Occupational Outlook Handbook,* the *Complete Guide for Occupational Exploration,* and the *Dictionary of Occupational Titles.*

Contact with your local business community can also provide excellent career information. One approach is to interview people who are working in jobs that interest you. Perhaps the best way to find out about a particular job or career is through firsthand experience. Work experience programs or part-time jobs allow you to try out a type of work with on-the-job experience.

Choosing a career goal is truly taking control of your life. It is like sitting in the driver's seat and choosing a destination. To make sure you arrive at the destination, you take along a road map—a plan to reach your journey's end. This plan of action includes setting goals for the training, education, and jobs that will lead to your ultimate career and lifestyle goals.

When preparing for and choosing your office career, you need to:

- Think about how you would like to live in the future
- Ask yourself how different types of work would affect your overall lifestyle
- Believe that career choices should sometimes be changed
- Want to take control of your own life
- Use a decision-making procedure for important decisions
- Record all your career information in a notebook
- Consider what your family and friends think is important but decide for yourself what is important to you
- Know the types of work that would interest you

## Ethics on the Job

You work for a marketing firm as a team member in the animation department. Your supervisor, Luis, is pleased with your work and has offered to spend time teaching you more about the art of animation. You are eager to learn, and you accept his offer. The more time you spend with Luis, the more you both come to realize that you have an aptitude for this kind of work.

During a team meeting, Luis announces that he has been asked to prepare a presentation for a prospective client. It is a big account, and securing the business is very important to your firm's management. Luis requests that you serve as his assistant on this project. You are pleased at the invitation, but you are also dismayed by the fact that the prospective client is a tobacco company. You are even more upset when you realize that this company is looking for a way to market its products to young people. Such a project conflicts strongly with your personal values, but you realize that a successful presentation will help both you and Luis to advance within the marketing firm.

*1. What must you consider before making a decision?*

*2. What solution can you offer?* ■

# before you leave...

# Review & Application

## Check Your Knowledge

1. List the eight steps in career decision making.

2. "Your work will be the central activity of your life." Is this statement true or false? Why?

3. Why is daydreaming about the lifestyle you want to live important?

4. List three things you will probably consider when thinking about your hoped-for future life.

5. List three things that have influenced your values.

6. What are some examples of work values that are important to you?

7. Why would someone take an interest survey?

8. Would a librarian work mostly with data, people, or things?

9. What are some indications of a person's aptitudes?

10. What kinds of work activities would an extrovert enjoy?

11. When you begin to explore careers, on what topics will you need to gather information?

12. List three examples of working conditions.

13. What is it called when a company provides child care?

14. What are the advantages of telecommuting?

15. What are the two best sources of career information?

16. What is the *Dictionary of Occupational Titles?*

17. List the three career information books published by the U.S. Department of Labor.

18. What are the two ways you can use your business community as a source of career information?

19. When choosing a career, what is the importance of developing a plan of action?

20. What are the ingredients in a career plan of action?

21. Why should goals be realistic?

## Review Your Vocabulary

On a separate piece of paper, write the letter of the vocabulary word that is described below.

____ 1. system for allowing workers to set their own work hours

____ 2. outward reflection of your inner self, apparent in how you look, speak, and act

____ 3. person who has an outgoing personality

____ 4. extra payments or services, in addition to salary, that you get from your employer

____ 5. a business organization composed of workers scattered throughout the country or the world and linked electronically rather than being grouped within one building

____ 6. resource that organizes jobs into twelve interest areas

____ 7. person with a quiet personality

____ 8. way you want to live in the future

____ 9. needs we expect to fulfill through work

____ 10. resource that includes descriptions of more than twenty thousand jobs

____ 11. the practice of hiring employees just before they are needed, on either a temporary or a permanent basis

____ 12. ideas and feelings you believe are desirable and important

____ 13. potential for learning a skill

____ 14. list of statements describing a variety of activities

____ 15. resource that includes detailed information on more than 250 occupations and is updated every two years

a. aptitude
b. *Dictionary of Occupational Titles*
c. extrovert
d. flextime
e. benefits
f. *Complete Guide for Occupational Exploration*
g. just-in-time hiring
h. interest survey
i. introvert
j. lifestyle goal
k. *Occupational Outlook Handbook*
l. personality
m. values
n. work values
o. virtual organization

## Discuss and Analyze an Office Situation

1. James has accepted an office job with an accounting firm. The job promises to be a perfect match with James's interests and skills. During the first few weeks of work, however, his employer asks James to change his work hours—to come in later and stay later. This change conflicts with the schedule James has arranged in order to spend time with his family. James's family is very important to him, but he does not want to lose his new job.

   What should James do?

2. Robert enjoys and is skilled at working on cars. He thinks having his own garage someday would be great. However, when a job at McDonald's™ becomes available, Robert takes it for the extra money. After two years, Robert is still at McDonald's—and the idea of having his own garage has become just a dream.

   What was missing in Robert's approach to his career? What could he have done differently?

## Practice Basic Skills

### Math

When considering your lifestyle goals, part of what you must consider is how much money you wish to earn. If you earn $25,000 in one year when the inflation rate is 5 percent, you must earn an extra 5 percent the following year just to stay even.

Suppose that you will earn $25,000 in one year, and the inflation rate remains at 5 percent over the following twenty years. How much will you need to earn in five years to have the same buying power? In ten years? In twenty years? (Note: You will need to calculate each year separately.)

### English

Regardless of what career you choose, you will be required to use standard English on the job. Begin to use standard English now so that it becomes a habit for you. On a separate piece of paper, write or key the correct words to replace the words that are not standard English in the following paragraph.

Jack, I'm kinda' lookin' for a gig. Can you turn me on to something? I dig on music, computers, sports, and cars. Maybe I could get a gig doin' somethin' with those kinda' things. Can you lay any ideas on me about what I might do? I'm a pretty hard worker and a strong dude. What do ya think?

### Proofreading

Whatever your new career entails, you will probably be required to write using correct spelling, punctuation, and grammar. On a separate piece of paper, rewrite or key the following report, correcting all errors.

Report on the Monday Morning Meeting

The mondya morning meeting was tttenned by jane smith, Mary Ann Worsley, George atwood, and mee. The problems with the new action plan was discussed in detale with everyon finally agreein that it filled the needs it was deesigned to fill.

Next we descussed recycling our newspapers. We worked out a methud of picking up the pappers each tuesday to take to the down town center.

The meetin was over by ten oclock.

## Apply Your Knowledge

1. Write or key a description of your desired future lifestyle.

2. What is your long-range career goal (at least twenty years)? If you have not made your decision yet, write down one of the career goals in which

you are most interested. List some short-range (five years) and medium-range (ten years) goals that will help you achieve your long-range goal.

3. Many schools require students to take a foreign language in order to graduate. Think about your future career and decide which foreign language you think would be most helpful in that field. Write a paragraph explaining your choice. Determine how many years you will need to study this language in order to enhance your career prospects. Write a plan for your course of study.

## Using the Reference Manual

Open file ch18ref.doc. Use the proofreaders' marks section of the Reference Manual at the back of the book as well as information learned in this chapter to help you make the corrections. Save and print.

Think about

1. Consider how you would like to live in the future.

2. Ask yourselff how different types of work would affect your overall life/style.

3. Believe that a career choices should sometimes be changed.

4. Want to take con trol of your life.

5. Use a decisionmaking procedure for important decisions.

6. Record all your career information in a notebook.

7. Consider what your family and friends think is important, but decide for yourself what is important to you.

8. Know the types of work areas that would interest you.

# chapter 19

## Finding and Applying for a Job

**Answer the following questions to the best of your ability:**

**1.** How will you go about looking for a job?

**2.** When you hear about a job that you would like, what action will you take?

**3.** What will you do to prepare for a job interview?

You may have chosen your ultimate career goal—or you may at least have some ideas about the job you would like for now. If not, first answer these important questions: What jobs can you do well and what jobs would you enjoy? You will probably think of several related office jobs. Knowing the type of work you would like and the names of one, two, or several jobs for which you wish to apply *before* you start looking will save you time.

You may want an office job to gain experience as a stepping-stone into the career you have chosen. Even if you have not made your career choice, you still may want a part-time job. You may want to earn some money for recreational activities, new clothes, a car, or college expenses.

## Looking for a Job

Whatever your reason for wanting to work, getting the job you want will be a job in itself. You may be well qualified, but so are many others. You will be up against some good competition, and you must convince the employer that *you* are the best candidate. You can convince the employer better than most others if you are motivated, energetic, and prepared.

If you really want to find a job, and you are willing to spend the time required, proven techniques will make your job search more efficient and effective. Begin with the two important hints below that will put you ahead of your competition. Then learn where to look for job leads, how to follow them up with an application, and how to prepare for and conduct yourself in a job interview.

First, most people spend less than five hours a week looking for a job. That amount of time is not enough. Plan to invest as much time per week looking for a job as you will spend working on the job after you are hired.

Second, most people are not well organized for a successful job search. In this chapter, you will learn how to spend your job-search time efficiently, how to go about organizing your job search, how and where to find job leads, how to expand your collection of job leads, and even how to find a job without any job leads.

### Organizing Your Job Search

Remember, job hunting is quite a job itself, and you must be willing to work hard at finding the right one. You will be using a variety of sources to secure job leads. Write down all your job leads so that you will be able to follow up on them.

When applying for a job, arrive on time, be prepared, and dress appropriately.

©James J. Bissell/SuperStock International

## Technology in the Office | JOB VACANCIES ON THE INTERNET

You have probably used the Internet for researching a variety of topics related to school assignments or for your own interests. Several job Web sites that also list jobs by cities, such as Monster.com, may be helpful. Many companies are now listing some of their job vacancies on the Internet. When you begin looking for available jobs, remember the Internet as a source.

You may approach the Internet in several ways when looking for job vacancies. If you know that you want to work for a particular company, you can visit the company's Web site. In many cases, you will then be able to click a topic such as "job openings."

Another way to search for jobs is to simply key "jobs" or "job vacancies" into a search engine. You will likely be presented with a listing of sites. Simply click the ones that seem most promising.

Looking for job vacancies on the Internet has several advantages. You can do it while sitting at your computer. If you are interested in working in another part of the country—or even abroad—making contact with companies many miles away is as simple as clicking your mouse! ■

Before you begin your search, set up a base of operations and collect the supplies you will need. Then be sure you have the necessary legal documents.

### Base of Operations

A good way to organize your job search is to set up a base of operations. The base may be a section of your bedroom or another room in your house or apartment. If you have a study desk, designate one drawer for job-hunting materials. You will need a chair and a telephone nearby—preferably at your desk. These items are the basics. A section of a filing cabinet will help you organize your job search, too. You will need a typewriter or computer with a word processing program when you begin to prepare application documents.

### Supplies

You will also need some supplies. The following items should be enough to get you started:

- *a logbook.* Any loose-leaf notebook will serve this purpose. If you have a computer at home, use the word processing program to keep a log of your progress.
- *one hundred index cards for recording job leads.* Use 4-by-6-inch or 5-by-8-inch cards.
- *an appointment calendar.* Get one that has room for hour-by-hour notations.
- *lined notebook paper.* If you do not have a computer readily available, you will need lined notebook paper for writing rough drafts of application documents. You probably already have this item on hand.
- *one hundred sheets of good-quality bond paper.* Use 20-pound or 24-pound weight and 8.5-by-11-inch paper. This paper will be used for résumés and cover letters. White, cream, or light gray are the preferred colors. About fifty matching envelopes should be enough.

"Ross! Guess what?" hollers Yolanda. "I found a good job lead this morning! When I was waiting for the bus, I spotted an ad in the newspaper for part-time clerical help at Mesa Realty."

"Really? What are the qualifications?" asks Ross.

"Oh, they're all listed in the ad. . . . You know, 'no experience necessary, bilingual desired' and . . . oh, I've got the ad here in my purse."

Yolanda unsuccessfully digs around in her purse for the little ad. In frustration, she dumps her purse contents onto her desk. "I can't find it! I'll just have to find another copy of the newspaper."

1. **Will Yolanda conduct a well-organized job search?**

2. **Is Yolanda likely to be able to keep paperwork organized as an office clerk?**

3. **Is the job at Mesa Realty likely to still be available by the time Yolanda applies for it?** ■

- *stamps.* Use the stamps for mailing application documents.
- *other helpful office supplies.* These supplies include colored pencils or highlighters, scissors, paper clips, a stapler, tape, and a wastebasket.

Finding the right job is difficult even when you are well organized. Good organization allows you to concentrate your time and effort on getting and following up leads, completing application documents, and going to interviews. If you are not well organized, you will waste time waiting in line at the post office for stamps or making repeated trips to an office supply store.

Use your computer or logbook to record everything connected with your job search. Record the calls you have made, the calls you plan to make, names, numbers, and ideas. Write in your logbook every day. Then, each evening, go through your logbook and cross out items you have completed and those items no longer important.

Use your index cards to make job lead cards similar to the one shown in Figure 19.1, page 405. A **job lead card** is an index card on which you record all relevant information about an available job. Index cards provide an efficient system because you can easily rearrange your leads however you want, perhaps placing the most promising ones on the top. You may want to keep a separate set of cards in order by time and date of scheduled interviews.

Write the name of the person you should contact and the company name, address, and telephone number on the front of the card. Write the source of the lead in the lower left corner. If your source is a newspaper want ad, tape the ad to the card as shown in Figure 19.1. Use the back of the card to record whatever you do to follow up the lead. Record the date when you call to request an interview, and the time and date of the interview. Also write down the name of the person you are to see, and, if necessary, directions to the company. Later, write down your impression of the interview and whether you are offered the job.

Use a second card to write down whatever information you can learn about the company such as the product(s) it makes, the service(s) it provides, or other pertinent information. (The "know the company" section later in this chapter explains how to find information about companies.)

**FIGURE 19.1 • Job Lead Card**

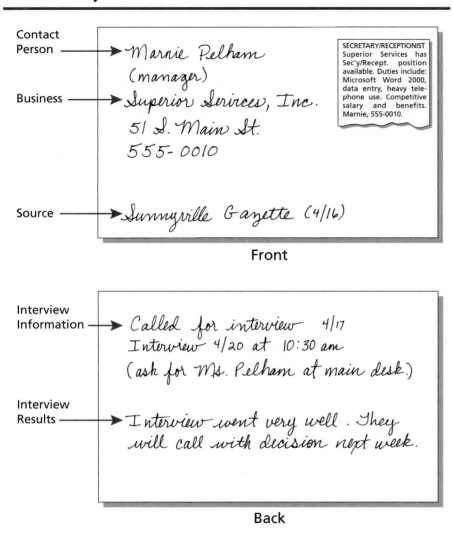

Contact Person →
Business →
Source →

Marnie Pelham
(manager)
Superior Services, Inc.
51 S. Main St.
555-0010

SECRETARY/RECEPTIONIST
Superior Services has
Sec'y/Recept. position
available. Duties include:
Microsoft Word 2000,
data entry, heavy tele-
phone use. Competitive
salary and benefits.
Marnie, 555-0010.

Sunnyville Gazette (4/16)

**Front**

Interview Information →
Interview Results →

Called for interview  4/17
Interview 4/20 at 10:30 am
(ask for Ms. Pelham at main desk.)

Interview went very well. They
will call with decision next week.

**Back**

Then staple this second card, with information about the company, to your job lead card. Just before your interview, review your notes about the company.

If you have a computer that you can use daily in your job search, set up your job lead information using a database program. Record the same information you would if you were using job lead cards. Then print the information you will need before each application or interview.

Use your appointment calendar to keep track of any appointments related to your job search. In fact, put all your appointments in this calendar. Then you will not schedule an interview at the same time you have a dental or other type of appointment.

Many calendar programs are available for personal computers. If you are using a computer for other job search functions, you may want to use a calendar program, too.

Your lined notebook paper, bond paper, stamps, and other office supplies will all come in handy when you start writing letters, filling out application forms, and preparing résumés.

## Legal Documents

The final part of preparing for your job search is to be sure you have all legal documents you will need for employment. These documents include a Social Security card and perhaps a work permit.

**Social Security Card** You probably will not be hired if you do not have a Social Security card. An employer cannot legally pay you until you have provided your Social Security number. Even if you can get someone to hire you, the employer cannot pay you until you have your card.

Every person over the age of one year must have a Social Security number in order to be claimed as a dependent on federal income tax form 1040. Therefore, you probably already have a number. If not, fill out an application and mail it right away. If you do not have one, you may miss out on a job that you would really like.

You can get an application form for a Social Security card at your local Social Security Administration office. Look up the address in your telephone directory. These applications may also be available in your school work experience or job placement office and at your local post office.

**Work Permits** Federal and state labor laws provide for the safety and health of young workers. These laws regulate both conditions and hours of work for students under the age of sixteen or eighteen. Certain jobs are designated as too dangerous for young workers. However, these dangerous jobs usually utilize power-driven machinery or are performed in a hazardous environment. Office jobs do not fall into these categories.

The Fair Labor Standards Act prohibits students under age sixteen from working during school hours. Various state laws limit the number of hours that can be worked in one day or in a week for students under age eighteen. Students are allowed to work more hours per week during summer vacations than during the school year.

If you are under the age of sixteen, you will need a work permit before you can legally begin work. Some states require work permits for all employees under age eighteen. A work permit shows an employer the type and hours of work that are legal. In some states, work permits must specify the exact job duties and hours of work. In this case, a work permit application must be completed by the student worker, a parent, and the employer. A work permit will be issued based on the information in the application.

Ask your counselor if you will need a work permit. These permits are usually issued by a designated school official. Find out about the work permit now, and you can avoid a delay when you do find a job.

## Finding Job Leads

How do you go about finding job leads? The first step is to contact all available sources that might produce one. Sometimes job lead information is incomplete. For example, you may learn that a local insurance company is looking for an office worker. You do not know the job title or the qualifications for the job. You may not even know whom you need to see to apply for it. Follow up even skimpy leads and fill in the missing information yourself. Finding a job you can do well and enjoy requires finding as many job leads as possible and then following up promptly on each one.

Where do you begin looking for job leads? Among the most productive sources of leads are members of your own family and friends, former employers, in-school sources, newspaper advertisements, and employment agencies.

## Ethics on the Job

You work in the human resources office of your local high school district. One of your responsibilities is to mail notices to applicants who are being considered for positions and to arrange interview appointments with them.

Your good friend, Kevin, is being invited to interview for a position in the media services department. When you call to set up his interview appointment, he tells you how eager he is to have this job.

Later that week you see Kevin socially. He asks you if you can tell him any information that will give him an advantage in his interview. You have access to the questions that will be asked of each candidate, and you know that Kevin would make an excellent employee. You would like to help him.

1. **What would you do?**

2. **What are the ethical implications of your decision?** ■

## Family and Friends

Like many young people, you may find your most productive source of job leads right in your own home. Members of your family may hear about job openings where they work. Even if they do not know of any openings, they may have contacts at work and among their adult friends who know that a company is looking for someone with your qualifications.

Job leads often come indirectly through several sources. You probably know one or two people who just recently started new jobs. If you do, they may be able to provide information on jobs from their own job searches.

Write down names of family friends and your own personal friends who might help you find job leads. Consider, especially, adult family friends who work for companies where you would like to work. Give them a call. (This process is often referred to as **networking.**) However, do not ask them if any jobs are available. Instead, ask them either for advice on finding a job or for permission to list them as a reference for a job. Do, though, try to work into the conversation the type of job you are seeking. This approach avoids the usual "Sorry, we don't have anything now, but we'll keep you in mind" answer. This kind of promise is usually forgotten by day's end. Most people are flattered when asked for advice, and being considered important enough to provide a reference is also complimentary. Using this approach, you are not asking for something a person probably cannot deliver—an immediate job. However, you are getting across the point that you are available if the right job comes along.

Some young people wonder whether contacting influential family friends is appropriate when looking for a job. It is, as long as you are qualified to do the work. Many of the best jobs are never advertised because they are filled by friends of company employees.

## Former Employers

Have you previously held a job? Former employers are often good sources of job leads, whether you worked in an office or just held a temporary baby-sitting job. Former employers who were satisfied with your work will most likely want to help you find a job.

For young people looking for their first jobs, a family member is sometimes the best source of job leads.

Friends often are good sources of job leads because some of them may have recently searched for and found jobs.

# Finding and Applying for a Job

Most people find jobs by looking in the employment section of a newspaper and calling or writing to a company. Large businesses often place detailed ads describing a position and starting salary. Some companies use an employment agency to advertise, interview, and find a suitable employee for them. Most large businesses have a human resources department. The people who work in this department place newspaper ads for job openings, review applications, and conduct the initial interviewing and screening. If you pass this screening process, then you will probably interview with the manager or supervisor of the department for which you will be working. You might go through several interviewing steps before you get a job.

Small companies usually do not have a human resources department, but they have someone who deals with personnel issues. The managers or supervisors may place an ad, receive applications, and conduct interviews. You will probably have fewer interview stages than when applying for jobs in large firms. Another difference is that in small companies, employees are more aware of job openings and have more direct access to the person doing the hiring. As a result, they often suggest friends and relatives for job openings before ads are even placed in a newspaper. This type of "word-of-mouth" communication often plays a much bigger part in finding a job in a small office than it does in a large one.

*Would you stand a better chance of getting a job in a large office or a small one? Why?* ■

## In-School Sources

Businesses often call school personnel when they need qualified students for temporary or part-time jobs. Many schools today have school-to-work programs, mentoring, shadowing, and various other work experience education activities. Does your school have a cooperative vocational or work experience program or a school placement office—perhaps combined with a career center? If so, employers might call that office when they have job openings, so check there and make your interests known.

Some employers prefer calling school counselors when they need student employees, as a counselor will know which students are best suited for a particular job. So let your school counselor know when you are looking for a job. He or she may be able to give you a job lead for exactly the job you want.

Business and vocational education teachers usually have contacts in the business community, too. Talk with your teacher about the work you want to do and ask if you may list her or his name as a reference. Teachers are usually proud to recommend their students, and you may get another job lead as well.

School personnel do provide a number of job leads for students, but do not depend on your counselor or someone else in your school to take care of finding the right job for you. Usually the number of students looking for jobs is larger than the number of openings, and several students may be referred for every job. Because of this competition, you might follow up on some good leads and still not get a job through in-school sources.

## Newspaper Advertisements

Many employers place classified ads in the local newspaper when they need to fill office jobs. Make a habit of reading the help-wanted ads. Some papers separate jobs according to type, such as accounting, general office, customer service, and so on. Newspaper ads are a good source of job leads, and you will also learn about the local job market. You may discover how much money is offered for each type of work and the qualifications needed for the jobs that interest you.

Follow up promptly on every ad that might lead to the job you want. If you wait even a day or two, you may be too late.

Avoid ads that require you to make a deposit of money or enroll in a course and pay a fee. Such ads are not offering jobs at all; they are attempts to sell you something.

## Public and Private Employment Agencies

Employment agencies match workers with jobs. When employers call an agency about a job opening, agency representatives write out the qualifications, salary offered, and other details on a job order form, review the records of applicants, and refer several applicants for interviews.

Most cities have both public and private employment agencies. **Public employment agencies** provide free job referral service because they are supported by taxes and operated by the federal or state government. Fill out an application form at the public employment agency near you. You will be interviewed to determine your interests and qualifications. Then, when a job is listed that matches them, the agency will call you. You will be told about the company and the job duties, then referred for an interview if you are still interested.

**Private employment agencies** are not supported by taxes, so they must charge a fee for finding you a job. The fee is either a flat rate or a percentage of the first few months' salary. Employers are often willing to pay the placement fee for higher-level professional jobs; however, if you are a beginning worker, you will probably have to pay the fee yourself. Private employment agencies sometimes have job leads that are not listed with public agencies. If you are not getting all the leads you want, you may want to consider applying at a private agency. However, first exhaust all free services.

## The Internet

Each year, more companies are listing job openings on the Internet. You will probably find job openings near where you live, in other areas of your state, and across the country. The Internet is an especially good place to look for job openings if you are willing to relocate to another part of the country.

©Corbis

Help-wanted ads in the local newspaper usually provide enough information about a job opening to help you decide whether to apply for it.

©Spencer Grant/PhotoEdit

Some companies list job openings on the Internet.

Thousands of Web sites list job openings, so the challenge is sifting through pages and pages of job opportunities to find the one that is right for you. Perhaps the best way to start your search is to simply enter some keywords to describe the job you want into a search engine. You might key *accountant*, *secretary*, or *medical assistant*—titles for jobs that you are seeking.

If you feel that you would like to work for a specific company—or one of several companies—key the company names into the Web browser as keywords. When the company Web site pops onto your screen, you can probably click a link to a list of job openings in that company.

When you locate job openings online for which you would like to apply, send your résumé and cover letter via e-mail. The company may call you or e-mail you to set up a personal interview.

If you want potential employers to look for you, you may post your résumé on one or several general career sites. Two very popular sites are Monster.com℠ and HotJobs.com™, but many others are available. If you do post your résumé, use several descriptive nouns. For example, if you are looking for a clerical job, do not just key *clerk*—be specific. Key *order clerk, adjustment clerk, receptionist*—specific job titles. Using the job title will help employers find you. List your job skills specifically. Do not just write that you are "computer literate." List all your skills and the program applications that you know by name. The old rule about keeping your résumé short no longer applies. Online résumés often run three or four pages.

Online technology now lets you block access to your résumé by individuals or companies such as your current employer. Read the privacy policy for each site before posting your résumé.

## Expanding Your Collection of Job Leads

Get all the leads that you can from firsthand sources. Then expand your collection based on the leads you already have. Every time you follow up a lead that does not result in a job, ask for suggestions about someone else you might contact. From each lead that does not result in a job, try to get at least one or two new leads.

Many other people are looking for work, too. You may not get just exactly the job you want, and you may turn down some jobs offered to you. If you have a number of leads, you can simply follow up the next one. Having several leads will keep you from getting discouraged when you are turned down or if one particular job is not what you want.

## Finding a Job without Leads

The ideal situation is to have numerous job leads. The more leads you have, the better your chances of getting a job you can do well and will enjoy. However, if you do not have many leads, you may need to do some direct calling. *Direct calling* is contacting employers by telephone or in person when you do not know whether they have any job openings. This process is a much less effective way to job hunt than knowing where the jobs are located at the start.

If you decide to try direct calling, you may be successful by contacting the human resources departments of companies where you would like to work. Some companies list jobs available on a bulletin board, and you can check regularly for any new openings that have been listed.

For ideas, company names, and addresses of places you might call directly, refer to the Yellow Pages of the telephone directory. You will probably have better luck going in person than inquiring about a job on

Check job vacancies listed on bulletin boards of companies where you would like to work. Schools and colleges often have bulletin boards in their career centers.

**FIGURE 19.2 • Letter of Inquiry**

120 San Marcos Rd.
Orlando, FL 32802-1822
March 4, 2002

Ms. Carole White
Director, Human Resources
Jensen Computers
710 Chapala Street
Orlando, FL 32802-1723

Dear Ms. White:

My computer teacher, Mr. Reynolds, recently advised me to write to learn whether you expect to hire additional word processing specialists for the summer.

I have completed intermediate and advanced courses in Microsoft Word, and I keyboard 75 words a minute on five-minute speed tests.

If you expect to hire additional word processing specialists for the summer, may I have an application form? If you wish to call me to discuss your summer job openings, my home telephone is 555-1246.

Sincerely,

*Caitlin Justice*

Caitlin Justice

---

the telephone. Either way, direct calling takes time. However, if you contact enough employers, you may find a job this way.

A variation of direct calling is writing a letter of inquiry. A **letter of inquiry** is simply a letter asking whether a specified type of job is available. Suppose that you would like to work in an office of a certain company, but you do not know whether the company has a vacancy. Look up the company's number in the telephone directory and call. Ask the person who answers for the name of the person who hires new employees. If you learn that department heads hire new employees, ask for the name of the head of the department in which you would like to work. Confirm the spelling of any names given to you, write down the address of the company, and then write a letter of inquiry. Be sure to thank the person who gave you the information. Address your letter to the person who does the hiring. An example of a letter of inquiry is shown in Figure 19.2.

## Recall Time

*Answer the following questions:*

1. Fred says that he has been looking for a job for three weeks, but he is always downtown relaxing with his friends after school and on weekends. What suggestions can you give him to help make his search more fruitful?

**2.** What two legal documents should a young person have obtained before beginning to look for work?

**3.** What are seven common sources of job leads?

**4.** How would you use index cards to record job leads and your response to them?

# Applying for a Job

As you continue to seek new job leads, follow up promptly on the ones you have. You should continue to get more leads because the very next one may be the perfect job. However, you must follow up on each lead as soon as you get it. If you do not, someone else may already be working on that job by the time you get around to calling for an interview.

Employers are looking for the person best qualified to fill a job. They will decide whom to hire based generally on their overall impression of each applicant and more specifically on their appraisal of an applicant's ability to do the work.

How do employers get the information they need to choose the best applicant for a job? Applicants provide the information. Before your first interview, prepare a personal data sheet listing all information about yourself that an employer may need.

Most employers will ask you to fill out an application form. This form is used to summarize your job qualifications. Forms are usually short— from one to four pages—and contain the same or similar questions. However, most companies design their own application forms, so each one is a little different from the next.

For many office jobs, employers expect an applicant to present a résumé (pronounced rez-oo-may). A **résumé** organizes, usually on one or two pages, all the facts about you related to the job you want. A résumé should always be accompanied by a cover letter, which is an abbreviated **letter of application.**

A complete letter of application—a sales letter in which you, as the applicant, try to convince an employer that you are the best person for a particular job—includes a description of all your qualifications. However, if you prepare a résumé, your cover letter should not duplicate anything in your résumé. Instead, the cover letter should simply introduce you to the employer and perhaps explain how you learned about the job. The cover letter also provides an opportunity to highlight one particular qualification that makes you appear especially well qualified for the job.

For some jobs, you may be asked to take one or even several **employment tests.** These may include skills and aptitude tests, psychological tests, and general abilities tests. The test most often given to applicants for office jobs is a keyboarding test.

Performing well on employment tests does not guarantee that you will be hired. Almost all employers will require an interview before deciding to hire you.

If you are not qualified for a job, you probably will not get it. Of course, you do not want a job for which you are not qualified, anyway. Taking such a position would be a setup for your failure. If you are qualified for a job, however, the way you present your qualifications may determine whether you are hired.

Fran finds out through her computer club that a member's company is about to expand its local offices. The member, Nick Petersen, suggests that Fran call Ms. Wiley to find out if Coleman Accounting is hiring yet.

The next morning, Fran calls Ms. Wiley and introduces herself. She tells Ms. Wiley she had heard that Coleman Accounting might need some clerical help and that Nick Petersen suggested she call to find out. Ms. Wiley tells her that the company has already started interviewing for two positions, but they are still accepting applications.

"Why don't you come to our office today and fill out an application?" she suggests. "I will be here this afternoon, and I could meet with you."

"That would be great, Ms. Wiley," says Fran.

"All right then, can you come by around four-thirty with your résumé?" asks Ms. Wiley.

"Yes," says Fran. "I'll see you then. Good-bye."

"I'll have to bring my personal data with me to fill out the application efficiently," thinks Fran.

Kofi also finds a good job lead. He locates an ad on the bulletin board at his school for an assistant to the manager of a local insurance company. The ad reads: "Must key 40 WPM. No experience necessary. Will train."

"A management assistant," says Kofi. "Imagine the skills I can sharpen and the new things I can learn in the insurance industry! I need to compose a cover letter and send it with my résumé right away!"

*1. Are Fran and Kofi prepared to put their best efforts into following up job leads?*

*2. What attitudes will guide the way you follow up job leads?* ■

What influences employers most in forming an overall impression of each applicant? A most important factor is the use of standard English. Develop a habit of always using standard English in a business setting.

## Standard English

Usually, an employer will first learn about your qualifications by reading your application, résumé, or letter of application. Later in the interview, you will have a chance to explain why you think you can do the work. Use standard English in everything you write and say to an employer. **Standard English** is the correct style of speaking and writing that you have learned in school. It is the standard way to communicate in business, because the meaning of words used is the same to everyone.

Most people do not use standard English for all their communication. Standard English is not always necessary, or even appropriate. When you write a note to a friend, you probably do not worry much about form. When you are chatting with an acquaintance, you may use slang or other popular words. That communication is informal, and it makes for interesting conversation. However, in business, most communication is formal—which means using standard English.

Standard English means standard grammar, spelling, and usage (vocabulary). "Arleen wants a job interview" is standard English; "Arleen want a job interview" is not. Some people use standard grammar but nonstandard pronunciation, so they are not speaking standard English.

Employers will have several chances to judge your use of language. From the application form, they can see whether you use and spell words correctly. If you submit a résumé or letter of application, they will notice

your ability, or inability, to use standard English. If they see poor grammar or misspelled words, your application will probably be filed in the wastebasket. Employers receive many applications, and they do not usually waste their time interviewing applicants who do not use standard English. Finally, during the interview, they will listen as you speak, and they will take note of your grammar and pronunciation.

## Your Personal Data Sheet

A good way to prepare for the job application process is to complete a *personal data sheet*. This sheet is simply an outline of all the information you may need later when you fill out application forms or prepare résumés.

When you are in an employer's office filling out a form, you may have difficulty remembering the correct spelling of former employers' names, their addresses, and their telephone numbers. Maybe you will forget the exact dates that you attended a former school. You will avoid these problems if you prepare a personal data sheet in advance. An example is shown in Figure 19.3, page 416.

## Application Forms

An application form summarizes information about an applicant's qualifications so that an employer can decide which applicants to interview. The application form is an opportunity for you to show that you are qualified to do a job. Follow these suggestions to improve your chances of being chosen for an interview:

- Complete the application form as neatly as possible. Many forms ask you to print. Make sure all words are spelled correctly by taking a pocket dictionary with you when you expect to fill out an application form.

- Use a pen when completing an application form at an employer's office. However, you can usually take the application form home and fill it out. If so, use a typewriter—unless the form specifically requests that you print. If you key your information onto the form, carefully align the information on the printed lines. Practice on an extra form so that your application will look professional and neat.

- Do not skip over any questions. If a question does not apply to you, write "NA," meaning "Not Applicable," or draw a short line in the space. Let the employer know that you read every question.

- Use your correct name on the form. Include your first name, middle initial, and last name. State your complete address, including the ZIP Code.

- Indicate single or married, only if a question on the application asks for your marital status. Employers cannot legally require you to answer this question. If you answer the question, details are not needed.

- List a specific job title when asked about your job preference. Never use the word *anything*. Employers want a specific answer; several positions may be available.

- Include the names of all schools you have attended, along with the dates of attendance. You may refer to your personal data sheet for this information.

- List your previous work experience in **reverse chronological order**, beginning with your most recent job. If you have not had much experience, include even short-term jobs or volunteer work.

- Provide at least three references. References are the names of people who know you well and will recommend you for the job. Plan ahead

**FIGURE 19.3 • Personal Data Sheet**

## Personal Data Sheet

| Name | Social Security Number |
|---|---|
| Address _____ <br> _____ <br> _____ | Date of Birth _____ <br> Telephone _____ <br> Place of Birth _____ |
| Hobbies/Interests _____ <br> _____ | Awards/Honors/Offices Held _____ <br> _____ |
| Activities/Sports _____ <br> _____ | Other _____ <br> _____ |

**Educational Background:**

| | School Name | Address | Dates Attended <br> From    To |
|---|---|---|---|
| High School _____ | | _____ | _____ |
| Course of Study _____ | | _____ | GPA _____ |
| Favorite Subject(s) _____ | | | |

**Employment History**: (Begin with current or most recent employer.)

| Company | Telephone |
|---|---|
| Address _____ <br> _____ | From To _____ <br> Supervisor _____ |
| Job Titles and Duties | Last Wage/Salary |
| Reason for Leaving | |

| Company | Telephone |
|---|---|
| Address _____ <br> _____ | From To _____ <br> Supervisor _____ |
| Job Titles and Duties | Last Wage/Salary |
| Reason for Leaving | |

**References:** (Names of persons who can provide information about your personal, school, or work background.)

| | Name | Relationship | Address | Home Tele. | Work Tele. |
|---|---|---|---|---|---|
| 1. | _____ | _____ | _____ | _____ | _____ |
| 2. | _____ | _____ | _____ | _____ | _____ |
| 3. | _____ | _____ | _____ | _____ | _____ |

and ask permission to list people's names as references. Good references include teachers or friends established in business. Do not list classmates or your parents.

■ Sign your name at the end. Write—do not print—your name using your first name, middle initial, and last name.

Carefully review the application form shown in Figure 19.4 on page 418.

## Résumés

Employers hiring for office jobs often request that applicants submit a résumé. Your résumé may be keyed on a typewriter or prepared on a computer using a word processing program.

Some typewriters and computer programs offer different type styles, called *fonts*. If you have a choice, choose an easy-to-read style such as Times New Roman or Arial. Avoid italicized and unusual fonts. Word processing programs allow the use of boldface (heavy-faced) type for main headings, which is a nice touch.

Most people use 20-pound bond paper for their résumés. However, 24-pound paper with some cotton content, though slightly more expensive, is more impressive. White, cream, and light gray are probably the best colors. Avoid pink, green, or any dark colors, as they do not photocopy cleanly. Purchase matching envelopes and extra paper for cover letters when you choose your résumé paper.

If you have completed a personal data sheet, then you already have most of the information you will need to prepare your résumé. Many styles of résumés are used. If you want to see a variety of ways to present this information, you may buy an inexpensive book on résumés at your local bookstore. However, if you are a student or a recent graduate, use a chronological résumé format such as the one shown in Figure 19.5 on page 419.

As a young job seeker, you can probably provide all pertinent information on a one-page résumé. Employers are busy, and they prefer résumés that present the facts in as few words as possible. Even applicants with twenty years of experience usually try to limit their résumés to two pages, so be brief. Provide the following types of information on your résumé:

1. *Personal identification*—your name, address, and telephone number.

2. *Career goal*—a brief statement about the career you are working toward. Make sure the goal fits with the specific job you are seeking. For example, if you are applying for a secretarial job, then you might state executive secretary as your career goal.

3. *Educational background*—all schools you have attended, including high school and beyond. Do not list elementary schools, middle schools, or junior high schools. List any colleges or technical schools and your high school. Begin with the school you most recently attended or still attend. List any degrees, diplomas, certificates, or licenses earned. Then add any awards or honors you have received.

4. *Work experience*—jobs you have held beginning with your present or most recent job. If you have had several short-term jobs, list only the four or five that are most related to the one you are seeking. List dates of employment, company name, and your work activities. For brevity and impact, use active verbs to describe your duties. Complete sentences are not necessary here. For example, you might write: "Planned travel arrangements, compiled reports, and prepared weekly

**FIGURE 19.4 · Application Form**

## Application For Employment

All qualified applicants will receive consideration for employment and promotion without regard to race, creed, religion, color, age sex, national origin, disability, marital status or sexual orientation. This application is effective for 90 days. If you wish to be considered for employment therafter, you must complete a new application.

| Name | Date |
|---|---|
| Address _____ | Telephone No. _____ |
| _____ | Length of Time at Current Address _____ |
| _____ | Previous Address _____ |
| _____ | _____ |
| _____ | _____ |
| | _____ |

Position Applying For _____ Expected Rate of Pay _____

Have You Ever Worked for Us? ☐ Yes ☐ No   If Yes, When? _____

| Keyboarding Words Per Minute | Software You Know |
|---|---|
| Machines You Can Operate | Other Skills, Qualifications, or Knowledge |

When Do You Work to Work?

☐ Full-time   ☐ Part-time   ☐ Days        Location Preferred
☐ First Shift   ☐ Second Shift   ☐ Third Shift    ☐ Downtown St. Paul   ☐ Westbury
☐ Any                                            ☐ Eagan

Are You at Least Age 18? ☐ Yes ☐ No        Will You Take a Physical Examination?  ☐ Yes  ☐ No

Do You Know Anyone Who Works for Us? ☐ Yes ☐ No   If Yes, Who? _____

How Did You Learn About Our Company?   ☐ Newspaper   ☐ Television   ☐ Ad   ☐ Radio Ad   ☐ Other

| School | Name and Location | Major | Graduated |
|---|---|---|---|
| High School _____ | | | ☐ Yes   ☐ No |
| College _____ | | | ☐ Yes   ☐ No |
| Business or Trade _____ | | | ☐ Yes   ☐ No |
| Other (Specify) _____ | | | ☐ Yes   ☐ No |

Do You Plan Additional Education? ☐ Yes ☐ No   If Yes, Describe

List In Order All Employers, Begin  with Most Recent Employment

| Name and Location of Company | From/To | Salary | Reason For Leaving |
|---|---|---|---|
| 1. _____ | | | |
| 2. _____ | | | |
| 3. _____ | | | |

Describe the Work You Did with:

1. _____
2. _____
3. _____

May We Contact Previous Employers? ☐ Yes ☐ No   If Yes, Which Company? ☐ #1 ☐ #2 ☐ #3

I hereby certify that the facts set forth in the above employment application are true and complete to the best of my knowledge. I understand that if I am employed, falsified statements on this application shall be considered sufficient cause for dismissal, and that no contractual rights or obligations are created by said employment application.

Signature of Applicant _____       Date _____

**FIGURE 19.5 • Reverse Chronological Résumé**

**Mizuko Matsuoko**
1715 Bliss Street
Winfield, KS 67156-1342
314-555-1265

**Objective**

An entry-level position as a bookkeeper, with opportunities for advancement.

**Education**

1999–2000 Winfield High School.  Graduated in upper 10 percent, Class of 2002.  Courses included:

Accounting, 2 semesters
Office Administration, 2 semesters
Microsoft Office, 2 semesters

**Special Skills**

Keyboarding speed test score: 81 WPM

**Work Experience**

6/00-9/01    BOOKKEEPER (part-time)
Merchandise Mart
Winfield, Kansas

Used Quicken accounting program to record cash receipts and payment to maintain accounts receivable and accounts ledgers. Assisted with payroll records and printing payroll checks.

6/99-9/99    WORD PROCESSING SPECIALIST
Stevenson Junior High School
Winfield, Kansas

Used a computer to write letters and memos. Scanned and updated end-of-school reports.

**References**

Available upon request.

## Ethics on the Job

You have spent several weeks looking for a job as a payroll accounting clerk, and you have just recently accepted a position with a large company. You are happy with your new job. Because of the size of the company, you expect considerable opportunity for advancement in the payroll department.

After you have been on the job for several weeks and have received many hours of training, you are invited to interview for a similar position with one of the other companies where you had applied previously. You are not really interested in changing jobs, but you are flattered by the invitation and curious to know about this other position. You must respond within three days.

1. *Do you owe your current employer your loyalty for the time it has invested into your training?*

2. *If you are not really interested in changing jobs, is accepting the invitation for an interview fair to the prospective employer?*

3. *Do you owe yourself the opportunity to be certain that you have accepted the position that offers you the most?* ■

statements." If your experience is limited, list any part-time or temporary work, as well as volunteer experience.

5. *References*—names of three people who will vouch for your dependability, skills, and good work habits. Include this information only if your résumé is short, and you need to fill space. Otherwise, just state "References available on request." Prepare a separate page for your references that you can give the employer later.

Write, edit, rewrite, and polish your résumé until it is exactly right. Then key it or print it from your computer. Use a good photocopier to make clear copies on your special résumé paper. As you get new job leads, customize your résumé to fit each job. By doing this, you can state your qualifications in ways that seem to fit the job for which you are applying.

Keyboard or print (from your computer) a cover letter. A **cover letter** simply states how you learned about the job and why you are especially

**FIGURE 19.6 • Cover Letter**

1715 Bliss Street
Winfield, KS 67156-1342
April 5, 2002


Ms. Julie Atkins
Kennedy Accounting Services
1700 South Main Street
Arkansas City, KS 67005-1787

Dear Ms. Atkins:

Your job for a bookkeeper, advertised in Sunday's *Courier,* caught my attention immediately. I think you will agree that my qualifications, listed on the enclosed résumé, match your requirements for this job very closely.

Two months ago I participated—along with several hundred top students enrolled in accounting—in the state scholarship examination sponsored by Emporia State University. Today I learned that I placed third in this statewide examination.

After you have reviewed my résumé, I would like very much to make an appointment for an interview. I will call in a few days to schedule a time convenient for you. You may call me at 555-1265 if you prefer.

Sincerely,

*Mizuko Matsuoko*

Mizuko Matsuoko

---

interested in it. You may write why you can do a good job for the company, and you may want to emphasize one or two facts that make you especially qualified for the job. Figure 19.6 shows a sample cover letter.

## Employment Tests

If an employer requires one or more employment tests, you may be asked to complete the testing before your job interview. You are likely to be given the tests before the interview if the testing session will require more than a half hour—or if the employer wants to see the test results before interviewing you. Many employers who require testing will schedule them just before your interview.

In the past, the most commonly used employment test for office workers has been a keyboarding test. Today, almost all offices use word processing programs, and many expect some skill with one or more of the most popular programs. You will probably score higher on a keyboarding test if you know how to use the currently popular word processing programs.

Some companies may simply ask that you take a timed test (usually five minutes) to see how fast and accurately you can keyboard. Other businesses may ask you to complete a more complicated task that is representative of the work done in that office.

You may be applying for a job that allows you to learn while you work—on-the-job training. In this case, an employer may ask you to take

a test to measure your aptitude for learning a particular skill or group of skills. Aptitude tests require more time than the quick five-minute keyboarding test. Employers who use them feel that they are worthwhile, though, because they identify who will be able to learn required job skills.

Some office jobs require good math skills. If you apply for one of these jobs, you will likely be asked to take some type of math test.

Some employers use other general academic tests that measure your ability in English usage, vocabulary, and spelling. The purpose of these tests is to help an employer decide whether you are qualified for a job. If you do not have the qualifications for a job, you will not want it, anyway.

Some employers give personality and psychological tests to job applicants. Other employers give these tests to new employees. These tests are designed to indicate how well you will get along with co-workers or customers.

You may, naturally, be a little nervous when you take these tests, but try not to worry too much about employment tests. Nevertheless, if you know that you will be taking one, do not go to a party the night before, for example. You will perform better on almost any test if you are well rested.

## Drug Testing

In recent years, some employees have used illegal drugs. Drugs can lead to serious problems on the job. In order to prevent this situation, many companies now do both initial and routine drug testing. If you do not use drugs, these tests will not be a problem for you. The real message, of course, is that if you want a job, never even try drugs.

## Recall Time

*Answer the following questions:*

**1.** You are filling out an application for a receptionist's position at a local insurance office. You are having trouble completing the section on prior work experience because you cannot remember the addresses or telephone numbers of your former employers. What could you have prepared that would help you in this situation?

**2.** Why is filling out a job application neatly important? What does misspelling words and writing illegibly tell an employer?

**3.** What are the main areas of information listed on a résumé? How long should your résumé be?

**4.** Violet is applying for a job in the accounting department of an auto parts store. What basic skills should she brush up on before going for her interview and taking employment tests?

# Interviewing for a Job

If your application form or résumé is impressive enough, an employer will want to interview you for a job. An interview is a formal meeting between you and an employer. It is your best chance to convince the employer that you are qualified to do the job. It is also the employer's best chance to evaluate your overall qualifications.

Some interviews are as short as five minutes; others go on for several hours. However, a group of psychologists analyzed job interviews and found that the first minute is the most critical. If you make a good first impression, you will benefit from a *halo effect* that will cause the interviewer to feel positive about you throughout the interview. If you do not impress the interviewer in the first minute, your chances are not very good regardless of how well the rest of the interview goes.

The interview, then, is the most important part of the entire job-seeking process. What can you do to increase your chances of a successful interview? Plan ahead by following these steps:

1. Prepare for the interview.
2. Communicate effectively.
3. Sense when the interview is over.
4. Follow up the interview.

# Prepare for the Interview

Preparing has several advantages. If you know what you want to say ahead of time, you can communicate it more effectively. If you know something about the company, you will have a better idea about how to phrase your questions and answers. Finally, being prepared will boost your confidence and help you to make that critical good first impression.

Your preparation should include learning about the company, selecting the clothing you will wear to the interview, and gathering the materials you will need to take with you. By thinking about these things ahead of time, you will allow enough time to get ready for your interview. You may want to practice interviewing with a family member or a friend, but once you leave your home, you will be on your own.

## Know the Company

During the interview, you will want to show that you are interested in the company, not just the money you can earn from working there. So your first step in preparing for the interview is to do some research on the company. Begin by asking people you know who might have information about the company. Do you know any of the company's current employees, or someone who previously worked there?

Many companies print pamphlets that provide details about their products or services. Others have catalogs that will give you an idea of what the company produces. You may be able to pick up these items from the company well before your interview. Advertisements and press releases may provide additional information. Pay special attention to information that fits with your education, interests, or experiences—and remember to use this information during the interview.

As you research a company, keep in mind the types of questions you may be asked that relate to the company itself. For example, many interviewers ask such questions as "Why do you want to work for this company?" or "What interests you about working here?"

As you learn about the company, write down the questions you will want to ask the interviewer about it. For example, you may want to ask how the job became available, what your working relationship with other employees will be, and what opportunities exist for advancement within the company.

You will probably be a little nervous at the beginning of every interview. However, if you know what to do and say, you may be more self-confident—and you will likely become less nervous as the interview progresses.

Knowing some things about the company helps. The best confidence-builder is to prepare for the interview by practicing your interviewing skills. Perhaps your teacher will allow you and other students in your class to do some role-playing of interviewing situations.

## Dress Appropriately

Generally, avoid extremes and dress appropriately for the office where you hope to work. In the business world, appropriate dress usually means a conservative, dark suit and tie for men. Dresses, skirts and blouses, or pantsuits that are modestly tailored are favored for women. A young woman makes a better impression wearing hose and dress shoes than wearing casual sports shoes.

To most employers, personal cleanliness and neatness are even more important than the clothes you wear. If you need a haircut, get it before your interview. Bathe or shower, wash your hair, clean and trim your fingernails, and brush your teeth. Avoid strong-smelling after-shave lotions or heavy perfume because some people are allergic, and the smell may be overpowering. Use makeup sparingly.

Because only about one-fourth of all adults smoke, the person who interviews you will probably be a nonsmoker. If you smoke, do not do it on the day of your interview, even if you are offered a cigarette. Many companies now prohibit smoking in the office, and more are adopting nonsmoking policies all the time.

Do not wear a large amount of jewelry to a job interview; it may be distracting.

## Take the Things You Need

Assemble the items that you want to take with you to the interview. Include your job lead card and notes on the company, your personal data sheet, your résumé, and your list of questions to ask. Also, take along a listing of the names and addresses of former employers, schools, and references. If you have completed a personal data sheet, you will have your materials in good order. You will probably take some notes during the interview, and you may need to fill out some forms, so take a good pen and a notebook. If you need a work permit form to begin work, take it with you.

## Allow Enough Time

If a week or more has passed since you made your appointment, call to confirm that the interviewer is still expecting you. Then start getting ready early. After you are dressed, read your résumé through carefully several times. It will help you answer questions about your qualifications. Check your job lead card for the address and leave in time to arrive about ten minutes early. Allow some extra time if you have to travel across town—you might be delayed in traffic. On your way to the interview, mentally review what you have prepared.

## Go Alone

Never take anyone with you for a job interview. Some young people take along a friend for support, but employers are not favorably impressed by this behavior. When you arrive, introduce yourself to the receptionist and give the name of the person with whom you have the interview appointment.

# Communicate Effectively

When you meet the person who will interview you, smile. Smiling will help more than anything to create a favorable first impression.

If an interviewer offers to shake hands, clasp his or her hand firmly. However, do not squeeze too hard or pump your hand up and down when you shake hands.

**TIP** Test your handshake with a friend and ask whether it should be firmer, shorter, or gentler. This information is important because people do not usually volunteer to tell you if you have a lousy handshake. Remember, a handshake is often part of your first impression, and you need to perfect a pleasing one. ■

The second thing you can do to create a good impression is to shake hands properly. Wait for the interviewer to offer his or her hand. When he or she does so, grasp the person's hand firmly. Some employers think a wimpy, "limp fish" handshake reveals a weak personality. However, do not squeeze too hard, either. You do not want to begin by hurting the interviewer! Some interviewers do not offer to shake hands. However, the handshake is a traditional business greeting, and you may extend your hand even if the interviewer does not extend his or hers.

Do not sit down until you are invited. If you are not asked to sit, then remain standing—the interview will be a short one. The interviewer will probably suggest that you sit beside or in front of the desk. If you have a choice of where to sit, take a seat beside the desk. With no barrier between the two of you, you have a psychological advantage. As you sit, lean slightly toward the interviewer. This posture indicates that you are interested.

You should have a folder containing your résumé and other papers, and you may have a briefcase or purse. Keep your folder in your lap and place your briefcase or purse on the floor by your chair. Never put anything on the interviewer's desk.

Do not let your eyes roam across papers on the desk—they are none of your business! Look the interviewer in the eye most of the time, shifting your eyes only occasionally so that you do not appear to be staring. Applicants who fail to maintain good eye contact are often considered insecure or are suspected of trying to conceal something.

The interviewer will determine the tone, pace, and style of the interview. Some interviewers will be serious and businesslike, others will be more outgoing and cheerful. Try to respond with the same tone and pace that the interviewer projects. In the usual style of interviewing, you will be asked a series of questions, and eventually you will get a turn to ask your own.

During the interview, speak clearly, listen closely, and show by gestures or facial expressions that you understand and are receptive to the interviewer's thoughts.

Figure 19.7, on page 425, contains a list of questions commonly asked during interviews. When answering questions, pause to give yourself time to compose an answer that is concise but thoughtful. Thinking before answering requires listening very carefully to all of a question before you formulate your answer. Writing down a word or two to help you remember something you want to say in answer to a question is all right. However, never interrupt or talk over another person, especially an interviewer. Good listening skills will help you pick out patterns in the interviewer's questions. You may be able to detect the direction of a line of questioning—organization skills, leadership qualities, or other qualifications. If so, focus your answers on these areas of interest.

When asked about your skills and experience, elaborate somewhat. Answer questions concisely but avoid one-word or one-line answers. Refer to your résumé or other notes to help you with answers. If you think that the interviewer has not understood your answer or that you have not expressed yourself clearly, try again. Stay on the topic until you are sure that your message has been received.

When preparing for an interview, many people overlook specific approaches to interview communication. These aspects include how the interviewer may open the interview and certain questions that are either

**FIGURE 19.7 • Questions Often Asked During an Interview**

1. What type of work are you looking for?
2. Have you done this type of work before?
3. Why are you leaving your present job?
4. How often were you absent from your last (or present) job?
5. How did you get along with your boss and co-workers?
6. What are your greatest strengths?
7. What are your greatest weaknesses?
8. What do you hope to be doing in five years?
9. How do you feel about this position?
10. May we check your references?
11. How does your experience qualify you for this job?
12. How do you take direction?
13. Can you take criticism without feeling hurt or upset?
14. Do you work effectively under pressure?
15. Do you like detail work?
16. Do you prefer working alone or with others?
17. Have you ever been fired or asked to resign?
18. With what type of people do you find working difficult?
19. How well do you work with difficult people?
20. What salary do you expect?
21. What did you like most about your last job?
22. What did you dislike about your last job?
23. What do you know about this company?
24. Do you have any questions?

illegal to ask or difficult to answer. Others aspects include nonverbal communication (body language) and being prepared to ask appropriate questions of the interviewer.

## Some Problem Areas

Some interviewers begin by asking, "Tell me about yourself" or "What can I do for you?" This type of opening is difficult because the question is so broad. Your task is to narrow the focus and direct your answer to support your candidacy for the job.

By preparing for such questions, you can respond appropriately without rambling. State that you are interested in a particular job and explain why you are qualified to do the work. Do not describe your career goals—the interviewer will be interested mainly in what you can do now.

Some personal questions are illegal, but the interviewer may ask them anyway. Questions about marital status, family planning, childcare arrangements, and age are illegal—unless they are real job qualifications. However, if they are asked, you need to deal with them as honestly and tactfully as possible.

Other difficult questions that you should prepare for are probing questions such as "What are your greatest weaknesses?" These questions are variations of "Tell me about yourself." Again, disregard the general question and focus your answer on your strengths—your personal skills and abilities that pertain directly to the job. Try to match the company's needs with your aptitudes. Give examples to support your answers. You

# Priscilla Azcueta

*Director of Professional Services*
*Manpower, Inc./California Peninsula*

**Q.** Ms. Azcueta, what do you look for when interviewing applicants for clerical positions?

**A.** We look for a concise, articulate, and appropriate reply to questions. For example, an applicant should not give too much information about their personal life or interests. The applicant needs to be aware of the interviewer/interviewee boundaries. The applicant should be able to interact with the interviewer.

We look to see if the applicant has personality, is outgoing, and will work as a team player. We look to see if the applicant can work independently.

If the interviewer was off-schedule, we look to see if the applicant is flustered or if the applicant has allowed for the disruption of their interview schedule and time.

**Q.** What recommendation do you have for an applicant to prepare for an interview?

**A.** Be prepared to talk about your strengths and weaknesses and your ability to handle problem-solving situations that may come up in interview questions.

Be prepared for the companies that conduct "behavioral interviews." During these interviews, the interviewer will observe the applicant's body language and look to see if the applicant breaks eye contact to think about the answer before responding to the question. The interviewer will see if the applicant really listens to the question and responds appropriately to the question.

Wear something that makes you feel good, is comfortable, and appropriate for the position for which you are applying. Also, consider your personal hygiene and your overall appearance from top to bottom.

can even use a question on your greatest weakness to your advantage. You might mention a weakness that will enhance your qualifications for this particular job. For example, on a job that requires great organization skills, you might say that your greatest weakness is that you simply cannot stand disorder and tend to overorganize things. Do not reveal a weakness that will disqualify you for the job. Generally, mention work-related weaknesses and avoid personal issues.

You may be asked whether you quit or were fired from your last job. Avoid saying anything negative about former employers. Most interviewers will identify with other employers and will interpret your criticism as incompetence or uncooperativeness on your part. Simply explain, briefly and unemotionally, why you left your last job. Do not make any excuses. If you expect to receive a bad recommendation from an employer, suggest other references who will attest to your qualifications.

## Nonverbal Communication

Two of the first interactions you will have with the interviewer are shaking hands and making eye contact. These interactions are nonverbal ways of communicating. As you learned in Chapter 4, nonverbal communication is usually called *body language*. If this topic interests you, you can find a number of books on body language in your local library.

You will communicate in other nonverbal ways during an interview, and how you communicate will significantly affect your chances of being offered the job. In answering questions, the *manner* in which you speak conveys messages to the interviewer. The tone and volume of voice, rising and falling inflections, and facial expressions are all meaningful. They will impart enthusiasm for the job and the company—or lack of it. Be aware of the mood of the conversation and be ready with either a smile or a serious expression, depending on what is appropriate.

Be aware, too, of your interviewer's body language. You will usually notice some nonverbal clues that will help you understand whether you are coming across effectively. If the interviewer appears disinterested or impatient, you might want to move on to another topic that may elicit more interest and express more enthusiasm yourself to change the mood.

## Appropriate Questions to Ask

The interviewer will expect you to ask some questions. If you are not invited to ask questions and a pause occurs in the conversation after the interview is well under way, inquire if you may ask some questions. Your first questions should show a sincere interest in the company, in the job, and in the employer's needs as related to the job. If the interviewer has not discussed salary and benefits, you may ask about them—but ask these questions last.

Make a list of questions you may want to ask before you go for your interview. Then you will be more likely to remember them and to ask them in an appropriate order. The interviewer will probably cover some of the topics on your list during the interview, so you will not have to ask all your questions. If you think of others as the interview progresses, make a brief note to remind yourself to ask them later. Be sure to ask a few questions to indicate your interest in the job.

Use good judgment about how much time to take up asking questions. If you sense that the interviewer is on a tight schedule, ask only your most important ones.

# Sense When the Interview Is Over

Try to get a feeling for when the interview has run its course. Many interviewers will stand and say something such as "Well, I think I have all the information I need" or "Do you have any other questions?" Unless the interviewer looks rushed, you may ask one or two brief questions at this point—but do not delay your exit more than a minute or two. If the interviewer has not mentioned when a decision will be made on the selection of a candidate for the job, ask when that decision will be made.

In some cases, you may have to take responsibility for closing the interview. If the conversation seems to be drifting, reemphasize your strong points, say that you want the job (if you do), thank the interviewer for her or his time, and leave. On your way out, thank the receptionist or secretary.

It was 4:30 on Friday afternoon. Jack Tuttle entered the human resources department of the Harcourt Accounting Corporation five minutes prior to his scheduled interview with the director. When he introduced himself to the receptionist, Ms. Woodruff, she told Jack that she was very sorry, but the director, Ms. Johnson, would be unable to meet with him that day. Ms. Woodruff said that she would be happy to reschedule the interview for the following week.

Jack was visibly disappointed. He had given up a date with his girlfriend to attend an out-of-town school football game for this interview.

"Why can't Ms. Johnson interview me today?" Jack asked.

"Something unexpected came up, I'm sorry," replied Ms. Woodruff. "Can you come in on Monday afternoon?"

"Then why didn't you call me or leave a message at school? I cancelled an important meeting myself to be here." Jack felt angry toward Ms. Woodruff.

"I would have called you, but she just told me twenty minutes ago that she would be unable to interview any more applicants today. Would you like to come in next week?"

"I guess so." Jack was still unhappy, but he was resigned to returning another day. "I'll check my calendar and call you on Monday."

Based on Jack's conversation with Ms. Woodruff, respond to these questions:

1. *What was Ms. Woodruff's first impression of Jack? If the human resources director asks Ms. Woodruff about the applicants she was unable to interview on Friday, how will Jack's attitude affect his chances of getting the job?*

2. *When Jack does get a job, how well will he get along with other employees?*

3. *What could Jack do to improve his relationships with others on the job?* ■

## Follow Up the Interview

You can profit from every interview, no matter what the outcome, if you take time to evaluate the experience. Ask yourself if a little more planning and preparation would have helped. Did you mention everything about your qualifications that would have helped you get the job? Jot down your notes as soon as possible. Making notes will help you to remember the interview discussion for future reference.

In the evening after the interview, write a thank-you note to your interviewer. It should go into the mail the very next morning. While the interview is still fresh in your mind, you can refer to a particular point discussed. Mention some fact that sets you apart from other applicants. The thank-you letter is an opportunity to add any important information in support of your application that you may have neglected to mention or emphasize during the interview. Figure 19.8, on page 429, shows a sample thank-you letter.

If you have not heard from the company within a week to ten days, give the interviewer a call. State your name and that you were interviewed for a particular job. Then ask, "Have you made a decision on who will be hired for this job?" If you are told that a decision has not been made, say something such as "I would very much like to work for your company, and I know that I can do a really fine job for you." Showing this extra interest may tip the scales in your favor.

**FIGURE 19.8 • Thank-You Letter**

1715 Bliss Street
Winfield, KS 67156-1342
April 23, 2002


Ms. Julie Atkins
Kennedy Accounting Services
1700 South Main Street
Arkansas City, KS 67005-1787

Dear Ms. Atkins:

Thank you for the interview yesterday afternoon regarding the position as bookkeeper. I enjoyed talking with you and learning more about your bookkeeping needs.

Having discussed this position in greater detail, I am more interested in the job than
ever. I also feel even more certain that I have the skills to fulfill your needs.

If I may provide any further information for your consideration, please call me at
home any afternoon after 3:00 P.M. My number is 555-1265.

Sincerely,

*Mizuko Matsuoko*

Mizuko Matsuoko

# Americans with Disabilities

If you are one of the more than 40 million Americans with a disability, do
not be discouraged about finding a job. In fact, the Americans with Disabilities Act of 1990 (ADA) was passed to encourage those with disabilities to pursue careers.

Title I of the ADA prohibits discrimination against any otherwise qualified applicant in any company with fifteen or more employees. It further
requires the employer to make reasonable accommodations for disabled
workers. Reasonable accommodations means that an employer must make
reasonable adjustments in a job or work environment that will enable any
qualified applicant to perform the essential functions of the job.

For example, employers must make existing facilities more readily
accessible and make changes in work schedules or equipment used on the
job. However, employers are not required to lower either the quality or
quantity of the work expected of disabled workers.

## Recall Time

*Answer the following questions:*

**1.** Why is the first minute of an interview important? What do you
need to do in the first minute to improve your chance of being
chosen for the job?

**2.** Joe and Laura are both interviewed for the same keyboarding job at Hayward Lumber. Joe answers all the questions Ms. Hayward asks and is very polite and quiet. Laura asks Ms. Hayward several questions about the company and tells her that she has heard the company is thinking of opening another branch. Even though her keyboarding skills are not as good as Joe's, Laura gets the job. Why does Ms. Hayward choose Laura?

**3.** What will you wear to an interview with Ms. Bailey at the National Bank's main office downtown?

**4.** You are applying for a job as a receptionist in a physician's office. The doctor opens the interview with "Tell me about yourself." How do you best respond?

**5.** What items will you bring with you to an interview to be sure you are well prepared?

---

# Summary

Finding openings and applying for jobs is the last step before entering the world of work. How well you perform this step will determine whether you get the job you would most like or have to settle for something much less interesting. Following certain guidelines will help make your search for a good job successful.

First, when beginning your job search, give plenty of time to the search. You will need to be well organized and have a logical system for keeping track of leads and follow-ups. Before you begin to call prospective employers, be sure that you have a Social Security number and a work permit, if necessary. Also, have a general idea of the jobs for which you qualify.

Make use of as many different sources of job leads as possible, from newspaper ads to employment offices to school and family. Follow up all leads promptly, either calling an employer directly or writing a letter of inquiry if required. When you are asked to fill out an application, be prepared. Have all the information you may need with you on a personal data sheet, and key or print the application clearly. Take time to write a concise résumé; have copies available. Brush up on the math or English skills on which you may be tested, and be sure to use standard English when speaking or writing to prospective employers.

Before you go to be interviewed for a job, be certain you are well groomed and properly dressed. Make sure you have discovered enough about the company to let the employer see that you are interested in more than just the salary. Take your résumé and notes on any questions you may have about the job and company. Be prepared by anticipating the types of question you are likely to be asked and thinking about how you will answer them. Practice describing your qualifications out loud, perhaps in front of a mirror.

Remember that the first minute of an interview is extremely important. Try to make a good impression through a firm handshake, a smile, a pleasant, enthusiastic demeanor, and by responding appropriately to the interviewer's tone and body language. Look the interviewer in the eye and try to overcome any nervousness. Ask pertinent questions but do not be pushy or aggressive. Use common sense and good manners.

Be aware of when the interviewer is trying to conclude the interview. Bring the interview to a close yourself if it begins to move to general conversation, and you sense the interviewer has all the information he or she needs. Follow up the interview with a call or a letter, emphasizing your special qualifications and thanking the interviewer for her or his consideration.

When looking for and applying for a job, do the following:

- Keep records of all your leads and how you followed up on them.
- Use all available sources for job leads.
- Follow up leads promptly.
- Keep a personal data sheet handy for filling out applications.
- Have copies of a résumé ready when needed.
- Recognize the need to use standard English in both speaking and writing.
- Be clean, neat, and well dressed for interviews.
- Find out all you can about the company before an interview.
- Be prepared to explain your qualifications and interest in a job.
- Appear relaxed and competent in an interview.
- Ask questions to show your interest in a company.
- Sense when an interview is over and leave on a high note.
- Evaluate your performance at an interview.
- Write a follow-up letter.

# before you leave...

**When you have completed this chapter, answer the following questions:**

**1.** How will you go about looking for a job?

**2.** When you hear about a job that you would like, what action will you take?

**3.** What will you do to prepare for a job interview?

# Review & Application

## Check Your Knowledge

1. How much time should you ideally spend each week looking for a job?

2. Who needs a Social Security card? A work permit?

3. List all the information you should collect on a job lead card.

4. What office supplies will you need to conduct your job search efficiently?

5. Where should you keep a record of all the actions you have taken in trying to land a job?

6. What are the seven most common sources of job leads?

7. Define direct calling. When should you use it?

8. What information does a résumé contain? How is it arranged?

9. If you need to fill out an application at a company office, how should you prepare yourself to be sure you have all the needed information?

10. What is standard English? Why is using it necessary in business?

11. Should you always apply for a specific job? Would an employer be more likely to hire you if you said you were willing to do anything?

12. Which of your previous jobs do you list first on an application form?

13. What types of people make good references on your application form?

14. What is the purpose of a cover letter?

15. Describe what is meant by the halo effect.

16. What are some steps you can take to prepare yourself for an interview?

17. How can you find information about a company to which you are applying?

18. How can you become more confident about the interview process before actually going to an interview?

19. What things do you need to remember when calling for an interview?

20. What type of clothing is appropriate for an interview at a law office? What types of makeup and jewelry are acceptable?

21. When should you arrive for an interview?

22. What are six things you should take with you to an interview? Which of them should you put on the interviewer's desk?

23. Who should go with you to an interview?

24. What tone should you use in speaking with an interviewer?

25. What should you do if an interviewer's questions are very general, not pertaining to the specific job you've come for?

26. If you had a terrible time with your last employer and felt he was gravely unfair to you, what should you say about him to an interviewer?

27. When should you ask about possible salary and benefits?

28. How can you tell when an interview is over? What are some signs?

29. After an interview, what can you do to make the interviewer remember you well?

## Review Your Vocabulary

On a separate piece of paper, write the letter of the vocabulary word that is described below.

_____ 1. form that organizes all the facts about you related to the job you want

_____ 2. organizations that charge a fee for finding you a job

_____ 3. letter inquiring whether a specific type of job is available

_____ 4. letter that always accompanies a résumé

_____ 5. method in which your most recent job is listed first

_____ 6. correct style of speaking and writing

_____ 7. item on which you record all relevant information about an available job

___ 8. items that may include skills and aptitude tests, psychological tests, and general abilities tests

___ 9. organizations that provide free job referral service

___ 10. written request for work

a. cover letter
b. employment tests
c. job lead card
d. letter of application
e. letter of inquiry
f. private employment agencies
g. public employment agencies
h. résumé
i. reverse chronological order
j. standard English

## Discuss and Analyze an Office Situation

1. Bradley hears about a general office job that has just opened up at a local real estate office. He thinks the job would be perfect for him, especially because he hopes to make his career in real estate. However, he has made a date with his girlfriend for this afternoon, and he is reluctant to change the date. He decides to call the real estate office tomorrow instead.

   What might Bradley have done differently to better his chances of getting the job?

2. Alice is going to an interview with Mr. Beasely of Beasely Electronics. Her friend Judy used to work at the same company. Judy tells Alice that Mr. Beasely is a nice guy, always joking around with employees and buying them coffee on their breaks. When Judy sees that Alice is dressing quite conservatively for her interview, she tells her that conservative dress is not necessary—everyone just wears jeans at work, even Mr. Beasely. She laughs when she sees Alice's résumé, saying that her previous experience at a pizza restaurant will not help her get this job and that she should leave the résumé at home. Alice is confused.

   Should Alice take Judy's advice? Why or why not? How can Alice have the best chance of getting the job?

## Practice Basic Skills

### Math

You think you will like both the jobs you have been offered, but you are trying to decide which will be the best for you financially.

The job at Jones Lumber pays $4.18 per hour for the first forty hours each week and double time ($8.36 per hour) for any hours after the first forty each week. It pays $50 per month toward health insurance and allows full-time workers one paid sick day per month.

The job at Smith's Electrical pays $5.08 per hour, with $1.00 per hour extra on Saturdays. No health insurance is paid for part-time employees.

You plan to work about twenty hours per week during the school year—eight hours on Saturday and a few afternoons after school. Which job gives you the most income per month, including benefits? Assume a four-week month.

### English

Remember that using standard English is important in the business world. On a separate piece of paper, rewrite or key the following passage, underlining examples of non-standard English.

When I start my first job, I'm gonna really do good. I know I will really rip. The boss is a friend of my dad's, and he like me already. If can maintain, I'm sure I will get a raise soon, and I know the guy is gonna be impressed with my performance. I tole him I couldn't wait to get started, cause this job is radical, it's just perfect.

### Proofreading

Rekey or rewrite the following paragraphs of a letter of application on a separate piece of paper, correcting all errors.

Im a student at Roosevelt high school, and I will graduate in june this year. I have been in the business education, porgram all three years, and worked as a aide in the office with the principal and secretery, I also worked for a semester at lawrence radio and TV, where I ansered the telephone on Saturday and wrote some checks as well.

I am going to college at state hoping to earn a degree in accounting, and I have a good undertanding of math and basic accounting. I really think this this job would be good for me, and I no I could do it well. May I call for aninterview? My telephone number is 5551145.

## Apply Your Knowledge

1. Using an electronic typewriter or personal computer, write a letter of inquiry to a local business to learn whether any office positions are open.

2. Using a personal computer and a word processing program, prepare a résumé, including all the parts in the sample résumé shown in Figure 19.5 on page 419.

3. Assume that you are applying for a job with a company that does business in other countries.

Using a word processing program or a typewriter, write a cover letter highlighting the reasons you would like to work for such a company. Emphasize any special skills that would make you valuable to a company doing business internationally.

## Using the Reference Manual

Use the résumé section of the Reference Manual at the back of the book to key your résumé. If you have already prepared a personal data sheet, then you should have most of the information you will need to prepare your résumé.

Save the résumé as file ch19ref.doc and print one copy. (If you have access to a laser printer and it is configured correctly to your hardware and software, print a professional copy for your own use when job hunting.)

# chapter  20

## On the Job:
## What to Expect

### objectives

*After completing this chapter, you will be able to do the following:*

**1.** List the purposes for which an employer usually withholds money from earnings.

**2.** List the topics usually covered by a company's written policies and procedures.

**3.** List and describe what most employers expect of their employees.

**4.** List and describe what you may reasonably expect from your employer.

**5.** Explain how you should behave if you are fired or laid off.

### New Office Terms

- grievance process
- performance evaluation
- probation
- productivity

- severance pay
- termination
- unemployment compensation
- W-4 form

**Answer the following questions to the best of your ability:**

**1.** What policies and procedures do you expect to learn about during your first days on the job?

**2.** What characteristics do most employers expect of their employees?

**3.** As a new employee, what can you reasonably expect of your employer?

You have spent most of your life in a school setting, experiencing only an occasional transition (change), such as going from elementary school to junior high school and from junior high school to high school. During your time as a student, you may have had one or several part-time jobs. Although some people hold formal jobs while also attending school, most of the jobs you have had were probably less structured and less demanding than those you will soon begin to experience.

Soon you will make a major transition into the world of work. Look on your new life as an adventure—a serious one, but an adventure nonetheless. You will have the opportunity to learn new ways of thinking, new methods of doing things, and special styles of organizing new kinds of tasks. You will meet different people in a new kind of setting. You will have much to learn, much to understand, and many new responsibilities.

Millions of people have successfully made this transition. Making a successful transition may be easier if you understand what to expect when you are new on the job. You will likely want to know what the first days will be like, what your employer will expect of you, and what you can expect of your employer. You may even want to know what to expect if your employment is terminated.

## Your First Days on the Job

Before you do any work, you will be required to complete certain paperwork. You have probably already filled out an application for employment, which includes your address and telephone number, education, and prior work experience. You will need to fill out the top section of an employment eligibility verification form. (See Figures 20.1a and 20.1b, pages 437 and 438.) Your employer will use this form to review and verify that you are either a U.S. citizen or an alien who is permitted to work in the United States. You will also need to fill out forms for tax withholding as well as other payroll forms. During your first days on the job, you will likely be introduced to other workers, read certain written policies and procedures, and even learn some unwritten rules.

**FIGURE 20.1A • Employment Eligibility Verification Form**

**U.S. Department of Justice**
Immigration and Naturalization Service

OMB No. 1115-0136

## Employment Eligibility Verification

Please read instructions carefully before completing this form. The instructions must be available during completion of this form. **ANTI-DISCRIMINATION NOTICE:** It is illegal to discriminate against work eligible individuals. Employers **CANNOT** specify which document(s) they will accept from an employee. The refusal to hire an individual because of a future expiration date may also constitute illegal discrimination.

**Section 1. Employee Information and Verification.** To be completed and signed by employee at the time employment begins.

| Print Name:   Last | First | Middle Initial | Maiden Name |
|---|---|---|---|

| Address (Street Name and Number) | | Apt. # | Date of Birth (month/day/year) |
|---|---|---|---|

| City | State | Zip Code | Social Security # |
|---|---|---|---|

**I am aware that federal law provides for imprisonment and/or fines for false statements or use of false documents in connection with the completion of this form.**

I attest, under penalty of perjury, that I am (check one of the following):
☐ A citizen or national of the United States
☐ A Lawful Permanent Resident (Alien # A_____)
☐ An alien authorized to work until ___/___/___
(Alien # or Admission #) _____

| Employee's Signature | Date (month/day/year) |
|---|---|

**Preparer and/or Translator Certification.** *(To be completed and signed if Section 1 is prepared by a person other than the employee.) I attest, under penalty of perjury, that I have assisted in the completion of this form and that to the best of my knowledge the information is true and correct.*

| Preparer's/Translator's Signature | Print Name |
|---|---|

| Address (Street Name and Number, City, State, Zip Code) | Date (month/day/year) |
|---|---|

**Section 2. Employer Review and Verification.** To be completed and signed by employer. Examine one document from List A OR examine one document from List B and one from List C, as listed on the reverse of this form, and record the title, number and expiration date, if any, of the document(s)

| List A | OR | List B | AND | List C |
|---|---|---|---|---|

Document title:_____    _____    _____

Issuing authority:_____    _____    _____

Document #:_____    _____    _____

Expiration Date (if any): ___/___/___    ___/___/___    ___/___/___

Document #: _____

Expiration Date (if any): ___/___/___

**CERTIFICATION - I attest, under penalty of perjury, that I have examined the document(s) presented by the above-named employee, that the above-listed document(s) appear to be genuine and to relate to the employee named, that the employee began employment on** *(month/day/year)* ___/___/___ **and that to the best of my knowledge the employee is eligible to work in the United States. (State employment agencies may omit the date the employee began employment.)**

| Signature of Employer or Authorized Representative | Print Name | Title |
|---|---|---|

| Business or Organization Name | Address (Street Name and Number, City, State, Zip Code) | Date (month/day/year) |
|---|---|---|

**Section 3. Updating and Reverification.** To be completed and signed by employer.

| A. New Name (if applicable) | B. Date of rehire (month/day/year) (if applicable) |
|---|---|

C. If employee's previous grant of work authorization has expired, provide the information below for the document that establishes current employment eligibility.

Document Title:_____    Document #: _____    Expiration Date (if any): ___/___/___

I attest, under penalty of perjury, that to the best of my knowledge, this employee is eligible to work in the United States, and if the employee presented document(s), the document(s) I have examined appear to be genuine and to relate to the individual.

| Signature of Employer or Authorized Representative | Date (month/day/year) |
|---|---|

Form I-9 (Rev. 11-21-91)N Page 2

**FIGURE 20.1B** • Employment Eligibility Verification Form

## LISTS OF ACCEPTABLE DOCUMENTS

| LIST A | LIST B | LIST C |
|---|---|---|
| **Documents that Establish Both Identity and Employment Eligibility** | **Documents that Establish Identity** | **Documents that Establish Employment Eligibility** |

**OR** ... **AND**

### LIST A
**Documents that Establish Both Identity and Employment Eligibility**

1. U.S. Passport (unexpired or expired)

2. Certificate of U.S. Citizenship *(INS Form N-560 or N-561)*

3. Certificate of Naturalization *(INS Form N-550 or N-570)*

4. Unexpired foreign passport, with *I-551 stamp or* attached *INS Form I-94* indicating unexpired employment authorization

5. Alien Registration Receipt Card with photograph *(INS Form I-151 or I-551)*

6. Unexpired Temporary Card *(INS Form I-688)*

7. Unexpired Employment Authorization Card *(INS Form I-688A)*

8. Unexpired Reentry Permit *(INS Form I-327)*

9. Unexpired Refugee Travel Document *(INS Form I-571)*

10. Unexpired Employment Authorization Document issued by the INS which contains a photograph *(INS Form I-688B)*

### LIST B
**Documents that Establish Identity**

1. Driver's license or ID card issued by a state or outlying possession of the United States provided it contains a photograph or information such as name, date of birth, sex, height, eye color and address

2. ID card issued by federal, state or local government agencies or entities, provided it contains a photograph or information such as name, date of birth, sex, height, eye color and address

3. School ID card with a photograph

4. Voter's registration card

5. U.S. Military card or draft record

6. Military dependent's ID card

7. U.S. Coast Guard Merchant Mariner Card

8. Native American tribal document

9. Driver's license issued by a Canadian government authority

**For persons under age 18 who are unable to present a document listed above:**

10. School record or report card

11. Clinic, doctor or hospital record

12. Day-care or nursery school record

### LIST C
**Documents that Establish Employment Eligibility**

1. U.S. social security card issued by the Social Security Administration *(other than a card stating it is not valid for employment)*

2. Certification of Birth Abroad issued by the Department of State *(Form FS-545 or Form DS-1350)*

3. Original or certified copy of a birth certificate issued by a state, county, municipal authority or outlying possession of the United States bearing an official seal

4. Native American tribal document

5. U.S. Citizen ID Card *(INS Form I-197)*

6. ID Card for use of Resident Citizen in the United States *(INS Form I-179)*

7. Unexpired employment authorization document issued by the INS *(other then those listed under List A)*

**Illustrations of many of these documents appear in Part 8 of the Handbook for Employers (M-274)**

Form I-9 (Rev. 11-21-91)N Page 3

## Technology in the Office | MULTIFUNCTIONAL EQUIPMENT

Sometimes additional office equipment is needed to complete tasks efficiently. However, what if space for equipment is already limited? Manufacturers have come to the rescue of small offices that need equipment that will perform several functions. One such product combines a printer, copier, scanner, and a fax.

Multifunctional units are not usually the fastest or best performing in any of their roles. However, for a small office, they can be the best answer to getting the work done without taking up much space or requiring investment in several separate products. One disadvantage is that if you have to send the unit out for repair of any of the functions, you will be without the other functions as well. ■

## Tax Forms, Withholding, and Payroll

The state and federal governments require all workers to pay taxes on the money they earn. The money collected in taxes supports the work of these governments and pays the salaries of government employees.

You are required by law to fill out a **W-4 form**, which provides certain information about the amount of taxes you will be paying (see Figure 20.2). The amount you pay depends on how much money you earn (your gross salary), your marital status, and how many allowances you claim. Each allowance represents one person for whom you provide financial support. Additional allowances are permitted for workers who have dependents (children or elderly parents), are heads of households, or who take a child tax credit. The more allowances you have, the less income tax you will have to pay. A single person usually has one allowance. A family has an allowance for the employee plus allowances for children claimed by this employee.

**FIGURE 20.2 • Form W-4**

---

- - - - - - - - - - - - - - - **Cut here and give Form W-4 to your employer. Keep the top part for your records.** - - - - - - - - - - - - - - -

| Form **W-4** | **Employee's Withholding Allowance Certificate** | OMB No. 1545-0010 |
|---|---|---|
| Department of the Treasury Internal Revenue Service | ▶ For Privacy Act and Paperwork Reduction Act Notice, see page 2. | 2002 |

1  Type or print your first name and middle initial    Last name | 2  Your social security number

Home address (number and street or rural route) | 3  ☐ Single  ☐ Married  ☐ Married, but withhold at higher Single rate.
Note: *If married, but legally separated, or spouse is a nonresident alien, check the "Single" box.*

City or town, state, and ZIP code | 4  If your last name differs from that on your social security card, check here. You must call 1-800-772-1213 for a new card. ▶ ☐

5  Total number of allowances you are claiming (from line **H** above **or** from the applicable worksheet on page 2)    **5**
6  Additional amount, if any, you want withheld from each paycheck . . . . . . . . . . . . . .    **6** $
7  I claim exemption from withholding for 2002, and I certify that I meet **both** of the following conditions for exemption:
  • Last year I had a right to a refund of **all** Federal income tax withheld because I had **no** tax liability **and**
  • This year I expect a refund of **all** Federal income tax withheld because I expect to have **no** tax liability.
  If you meet both conditions, write "Exempt" here . . . . . . . . . . . . . . . . ▶  **7**

Under penalties of perjury, I certify that I am entitled to the number of withholding allowances claimed on this certificate, or I am entitled to claim exempt status.
**Employee's signature**
(Form is not valid
unless you sign it.) ▶                                        Date ▶

8  Employer's name and address (Employer: Complete lines 8 and 10 only if sending to the IRS.) | 9  Office code (optional) | 10  Employer identification number

Cat. No. 10220Q

---

The information requested on the W-4 form includes the following:

- your name with middle initial and your complete address (number and street name, city, state, and ZIP Code)
- your Social Security number
- your marital status
- your total number of allowances
- a notation if you wish to have money withheld from your paycheck for other purposes
- other information concerning a possible exemption (Information on the W-4 form lists reasons that you may not be required to have money withheld, and are thus exempt from withholding.)
- your signature and the date you signed this document

Your employer will keep track of how much money you earn. In addition, on the basis of the information you supplied on your W-4 form, your employer will determine how much money to withhold from each of your paychecks. Charts provide this information, and computer programs do all payroll calculations after the basic information is entered.

Besides state and federal taxes, Social Security tax is withheld according to the percentage currently designated by the federal government. Your employer also pays part of your Social Security contribution. Other deductions may be made for disability insurance, health insurance, or a retirement fund. Your employer also pays into one or two other funds for your benefit. You should receive a complete statement of money withheld with every paycheck (see Figure 20.3, page 441).

You may be required to keep a time card, or you may be instructed to keep track of the time you spend on the job by some other method. You may be asked to write down the time you arrive in the morning, the time you go out for lunch, the time you return from lunch, and the time you leave in the evening. This record enables your employer to determine how much money you have earned. You should have agreed on your rate of pay when you accepted the job. Figure 20.4, page 442, shows a time card.

## Introductions

After you have finished your paperwork, your supervisor will probably take you around to the other employees for introductions. If you have the opportunity before these introductions are made, ask your employer for a list of employee names with their telephone extensions. If not, then ask for this list following the introductions. It will help you remember your co-workers' names. If no one conducts these introductions, your co-workers should come to you and introduce themselves.

Decide to learn your co-workers' names and titles as quickly as possible. If you have a list of employee names, make notes that will help you remember those to whom you are introduced. For example, you might write titles or the office in which each person works. Go over these names several times so that you can commit them to memory. Your new co-workers will be pleased if you are interested enough to call them by name.

Show your good manners by learning how people in the office prefer to be addressed. Different levels of formality are used in different offices. In some offices, people are addressed by their last names such as Ms. Adams, Miss Brown, Mrs. Jones, or Mr. Green. In other offices, everyone is called by his or her first name. Make note of who is called what and how visitors and customers are addressed, and follow these practices. You will fit into the work environment more quickly.

TIP Your employers and the other people who work in your office are only human, and sometimes they make mistakes. Keep track of the hours you spend on the job, separate from your time card. You can jot your hours on the calendar for that day. Then, when you receive your paycheck and the stub that supplies you with all withholding information, you are better able to check it for accuracy. ■

**FIGURE 20.3** • **Paycheck and Pay Stub**

**Restaurants, Inc.**
**Fort Worth, TX 76179-3421**

| Earnings Statement | | Page 001 of 001 |
|---|---|---|
| Period Ending: | | 11/08/02 |
| Check Date: | | 11/14/02 |
| Check Number: | | 311264 |
| Batch Number: | | RI33445502 |

Taxable Martial Status:  S
Social Security Number:  112-22-3344
Exemptions/Allowances
  Federal: 1   0.00 Additional Tax
  State:   0   0.00 Additional Tax
  Local:   0   0.00 Additional Tax

**Ramona Morisot**
**2418 Hadley Street**
**Fort Worth, TX 76179-2415**

| Earnings | rate | hours | this period | year-to-date |
|---|---|---|---|---|
| Reg | 7.000 | 37 | 259.00 | 6216.00 |
| Overtime | | 0 | 0.00 | |
| **Gross Pay** | | | **259.00** | **6216.00** |
| **Tax Deductions** | | | | |
| Federal Withholding Tax | | | 21.17 | 508.08 |
| Social Security Tax | | | 16.06 | 385.54 |
| Medicare Tax | | | 3.76 | 90.24 |
| Dental Coverage | | | 3.00 | 72.00 |
| **Total Tax Deductions** | | | **43.99** | **1055.86** |
| **Total Net Pay** | | | | **215.01** |

| Other Benefits and Information | this period | total to date |
|---|---|---|

Period Beginning:   11/04/02
Period Ending:    11/08/02

The best way to ensure your funds are available
on payday – sign up for direct deposit today.

---

**Restaurants, Inc.**
**Fort Worth, TX 76179-3421**

No. 311264

Date ___11/14/02___

Pay to the Order of ___**Ramona R. Morisot**___   $ ___215.01___

Amount ___**Two hundred fifteen and 01/100**___ Dollars

Texas Federal S&L

Ramona Morisot
2418 Hadley Street
Fort Worth, TX 76179-2415

*Ann Winchell*

# Written Policies and Procedures

Most companies have written policies and procedures. If your new job is with a large company, you may attend a formal orientation meeting for all recently hired employees. At this time, you may be given a policies and procedures manual, sometimes called a *policies and rules manual*. The policies, procedures, and rules will likely be explained to you in detail at the orientation meeting.

If you do not attend an orientation meeting and no one explains the contents of a policies and rules manual, read through the manual very carefully. Policies and rules can be important to your future employment with the company, so ask questions about any items you do not understand.

Policies and rules manuals contain different information in different companies. Some are large documents; others may be just a few pages. In companies that are unionized, you will also receive documents about policies and rules related to the union. The complexity of these documents depend, to some degree, on the complexity of your new company's structure. In some firms, management feels that extensive definition is not necessary and, therefore, provides only a few rules and policies. The topics

The first day at a new job might require a review of the company's written policies.

**FIGURE 20.4 • Time Card**

Week Ending:  September 24, 2002

Employee No.:  54183

Name:  Paul Thornton

| DAY | IN | OUT | IN | OUT | TOTAL |
|-----|------|-------|------|------|-------|
| Mon | 8:02 | 12:02 | 1:01 | 5:03 | 8 |
| Tue | 7:59 | 11:58 | 1:01 | 5:08 | 8 |
| Wed | 8:01 | 12:02 | 1:03 | 5:06 | 8 |
| Thu | 8:01 | 12:06 | 1:00 | 5:08 | 8.25 |
| Fri | 7:59 | 12:02 | 1:02 | 5:01 | 8 |
| Sat |      |       |      |      |   |
| Sun |      |       |      |      |   |

Total time:  40.25 hours

Rate Per Hour:  $10.00

Total Wages:  $403.75 (inc. .25 hr. OT)

addressed in a policies manual often include hiring procedures; work schedules and records; salaries, wages, and benefits; probation periods; performance evaluations; termination of employment; the grievance process; expenses and reimbursement procedures; and other categories such as sexual harassment (this topic is discussed in depth later in the chapter). Every company's manual is unique, created especially for an individual company to meet its own needs.

## Hiring Procedures

One section of a policies and rules manual is usually devoted to explaining procedures the company follows when hiring new employees. Only one interview may be necessary, or a company may use a screening process that requires more than one visit. If a company is hiring a large number of people, several prospects may be interviewed at one time.

Many companies have human resources departments that do all the hiring. If human resources handles hiring, you might not meet your direct supervisor until your first day of work. Companies hire people in many ways, and the hiring procedures section of the policies manual will describe how your company does it.

## Work Schedule and Records

One section of the manual usually describes the work schedule, lunch breaks, coffee breaks, overtime, and so on. It also discusses the necessary records to document the work schedule kept by the employee and employer.

Find out what level of formality is expected on your new job. Your supervisor may feel uneasy hearing you call her Maria if everyone else addresses her as Mrs. Martinez.

## Salaries, Wages, and Benefits

The salaries, wages, and benefits section of the manual describes how salaries are decided and how and when overtime is paid. Overtime refers to any hours worked over forty hours a week, unless other arrangements have been agreed to before an employee starts work at the company. Labor laws govern how many hours each day people may work. This section of the manual also details the availability of special programs that affect the pay schedule such as medical insurance and retirement plans.

## Other Benefits

Other benefits include, for example, vacation time, sick leave, outside training opportunities, and bonus days for good performance. This section of the manual indicates how many vacation days you accrue (earn). Employees commonly earn one week's vacation for every six months worked. Also, employees commonly earn one week's vacation after the first year, then two weeks' vacation after each subsequent year.

The number of paid sick days that an employee may accrue varies greatly from company to company. Some companies give one day of sick leave each month, to be used only if you are ill. Other companies allow a paid sick day when a member of your family is ill and you need to stay home to care for her or him.

## Probation Periods

**Probation** is a period of time usually lasting three to six months after you are hired. During this time, you will accrue no benefits. At the end of the probation period, a formal evaluation should be conducted in a meeting between you and your immediate supervisor. If your job performance is unsatisfactory, you may be terminated. If your job performance is satisfactory, you will become a permanent employee and will be eligible for all available benefits.

**TIP** Read simple documents once and take action. Highlight important points as you read. Reading a document and setting it aside for later rereading can waste time you could use for other projects. Of course, complex documents may need to be reread and studied. ■

### Performance Evaluation

A **performance evaluation** is a written statement outlining the strengths and weaknesses of your job performance. You will probably be evaluated at least once each year. Probation may be reinstated with poor job performance, and again termination is a possibility. You should learn to use the evaluation process to your advantage, discovering which things about your work you need to improve and taking steps to improve them. Your performance evaluation may show that you are doing exceptionally good work. In that case, you might be given a merit pay raise.

### Termination

**Termination** means a request for you to leave a job. In other words, you are fired. One reason for termination is a poor performance review. Other possible reasons are being absent or tardy too often, stealing from the company, coming to work under the influence of alcohol or drugs, and disregarding company rules.

### Grievance Process

Your supervisor may do something you think is unfair. For example, he or she may give you a negative evaluation that you do not think is accurate or justified. The **grievance process** refers to the method a company uses to allow you to state your side in disputes with supervisors or other employees.

### Expenses and Reimbursement

Companies generally reimburse employees for certain expenses. For example, expenses incurred by an employee on business trips are reim-

bursable. Which expenses will be reimbursed are usually identified in a policies manual along with the methods used to document them and methods of reimbursement.

## Other Categories

You may find some other categories in your new company's policies document. The ones listed here are only some of the possibilities. You are responsible for reading the manual completely, making sure that you have a thorough understanding of all topics it covers.

## Unwritten Rules

Throughout this book, discussions are focused on what you might expect and what is expected of you in your office job. Many of these rules are not written but they are, nonetheless, the rules of the job. They are part of the way the business office has been run—probably for a long while. You might refer to these as the *culture* of the office—its system of knowledge, beliefs, and behavior. Usually, the tone and style of an office culture are set by the company's owner or chief executive officer (CEO)—in other words, the main boss.

In some offices behavior is very formal, and workers frown on informal behavior. Some offices are so casual that they have no dress code or expectations of any kind except that you perform the tasks assigned to you, on time and efficiently.

The unwritten rules in your new office must be learned through observing and asking questions. For example, recall the importance of understanding how people in the office are addressed. What are the special ways of getting work done, of passing information, of maintaining a specific attitude that might be part of the office behavior? Is casual dress the order of the day? Is informal English acceptable? You can acquaint yourself with the unwritten rules of your office by watching how other employees act.

## Recall Time

*Answer the following questions:*

1. Before you do any work for your new company, you will be expected to fill out certain papers. One of these will be a W-4 form from the Internal Revenue Service. What information is requested on this form?

2. What do you understand about a policies and procedures manual? What kinds of information will this manual provide a new employee?

3. Every office has unwritten rules. How do you discover what these rules are in your new office?

4. You may have a formal orientation meeting. What sort of information will you expect to receive at such a meeting?

5. Some offices are formal and others are more informal. Who generally sets the style of an office?

# Employer Expectations

Expectations that your new employer will have of you include, for example, a good attitude, cooperation, honesty, willingness to learn, dependability, enthusiasm, and initiative (resourcefulness). These qualities are important components of your successful relationship with your employer. On your first day at work, begin to live up to these expectations.

The expectations listed previously, relate to your attitude. Expectations related to job performance include producing high-quality work, arriving on time, and not being absent frequently. Other performance-related expectations include skillful decision making and problem solving, caring for office equipment, and safety awareness.

## Quality of Work

Your employer will expect high-quality work from you. The success of your company will depend on employees producing quality work. Whether your company provides a service or a product, customers will not return for repeat business if the goods or services provided are of low quality.

A poorly keyed letter or a mistake in an order is an error in quality of work, and it affects the productivity of your company. Pride in your work helps create a sense of ownership in the tasks that you perform and helps you maintain a high standard. If you do quality work, your employer and your co-workers will notice and praise you for it. Likewise, if you do low-quality work, your boss and co-workers will know that, too, and they will not be happy about it.

## Productivity

Quality of work can affect productivity throughout a company. However, what does productivity mean and how is it measured? **Productivity** in the office is the total work accomplished in a given amount of time. If you work next to another office assistant all day long, and she or he keys thirty pages in a day while you key twenty-five, you know that your neighbor's rate of productivity is higher than yours.

Generally, being productive requires working at a steady pace and staying at the job, except for breaks, for all of the eight hours for which you are being paid. If you spend time on the telephone making personal calls, or spend time visiting with other employees while you are supposed to be working, your productivity level will suffer. Bosses do not like to see people standing around chatting or talking on the telephone when they are supposed to be working. This kind of interference with your productivity can cost you your job.

## Tardiness and Absenteeism

You should have signed on to your new position fully understanding what your working hours will be. Some jobs are forty hours each week; some are thirty-seven and one-half hours each week. Whatever your schedule, your employer will expect you to arrive on time and leave at the agreed-on hour.

Some people always arrive a few minutes after starting time. Then, after they arrive, they spend several minutes chatting, fixing their clothing, arranging their personal belongings, and getting set for the day. Just because you are already in the building does not mean you have begun to work. Get all your organizing done before starting time.

**TIP** While applying for a job, Bud was asked how many sick days he might expect to take. His response was "Maybe just one each month," which he believed made perfect sense. The person who was interviewing Bud was appalled. She felt that an employee expecting to take twelve sick days each year was entirely unacceptable. If you are asked this question, simply say that you are very healthy and do not expect to be sick at all. ■

## Large Office/Small Office

*What's Your Preference?*

# What to Expect on the Job

A large company often has an employee manual with written information regarding the company's policies and expectations. Usually, it will list the company's benefits, such as vacation and sick leave, insurance, pensions plans, and severance pay. Other information, such as rules regarding work behavior, is also included. The manual should detail the specific steps for handling grievances and problems, as well as information regarding performance reviews, pay raises, and promotions. Often, a large company has detailed descriptions and salary ranges for each position, with progressive steps, or levels. For example, it may have three levels of administrative assistant positions, such as administrative assistant I, administrative assistant II, and administrative assistant III. Training is sometimes more formal and extensive in a large company than in a small one. Some companies place a great deal of importance on appearance and dressing well, and sometimes this dress code can even affect job advancement. Often, a hierarchy of reporting and procedures exists. Sometimes, getting something accomplished takes longer because a request has to go through many levels of management before it is approved.

A small company may not have an employee manual. Often, information is given informally, usually verbally, and procedures are less formal. You may not have anyone to train you, and you may have to find out how to do things by asking any number of people. More direct interaction and communication occur, and changes or requests are often acted upon quickly without having to go through many people to get approval. Small companies tend to have a more relaxed attitude about dress codes, and people are generally less formal in their communications.

**Which would you prefer—the formal, clearly defined procedures and policies of a large office, or the more loosely structured, informal methods of a small office? Why?** ■

Plan to arrive a few minutes early so that you can greet everyone and not feel rushed. Arriving five minutes earlier takes only a little planning, such as setting your alarm to awaken you five minutes earlier.

Getting into the bad habit of arriving late, or even starting work late, may cause resentment on the part of your co-workers. They have to arrive and begin on time; why shouldn't you?

Absenteeism can be a real problem for employers. It signals loss of productivity and a heavier load for the employees who are at work. Occasionally, you will have reasons that you cannot attend work. Generally,

the only acceptable reason is illness. If you are ill, call your immediate supervisor as early as possible to tell him or her that you have a problem and will not be able to attend work.

Regular attendance and punctuality (being on time) are attributes of dependability. For successful functioning of an office, you must be dependable and reliable, come to work every day, and always arrive on time.

## Decision Making and Problem Solving

Learning when to seek advice on the job and when to make a decision yourself can be a tricky aspect of your new position. You cannot go to your boss every time a small problem requires a decision. You must devise strategies that will help you make some decisions yourself. If you do not, job advancement will be out of the question for you.

If you are puzzled by a problem, take some time to think it through. Avoid being hasty or rash. If the consequences of your decision will not be too dramatic, go ahead and test your decision-making ability. The more initiative you take and the more work you get done on your own without interrupting your supervisor and co-workers with questions, the more successful you will be on the job.

Part of the process of being able to make good judgments is to be able to foresee possible outcomes. If a decision seems to be leading to a very important outcome, perhaps you should get other opinions. However, if the outcome will be more or less inconsequential, make the decision yourself.

At the beginning of your new employment, you will need to ask many questions—and you will be *expected* to ask them. However, after you have become more familiar with your job, you will be expected to make more and more job-related decisions yourself.

## Care of Office Equipment

A major expense in any office is equipment. Fax machines, computer systems, printers, photocopiers, scanners, and calculators all come with a high price tag. Sometimes we do not realize that even the telephone system can be elaborate and expensive. The furnishings—desks, chairs, tables, and storage shelves—are also costly.

You will be expected to take care of the furniture and equipment assigned for your use. Do not eat or drink near your computer keyboard. Dropping food into the works can cause damage. Arrange for regular maintenance and cleaning of your machines if someone else does not have that responsibility.

Treat your machines with respect. Do not drop things onto them or force parts that are supposed to release easily. Learn how to change cartridges and load paper into the fax and printers. Treat your machines as though they were your good friends. The better you care for them, the more they will help you accomplish what you need to do.

## Safety Awareness

Concern for the safety of employees is not as big an issue in an office as it is in a machine shop. Still, your company will probably have some safety rules and procedures, and you should be aware of certain steps that can help ensure the safety of others in your environment.

Most large offices have procedures to follow in the event of a major disaster such as fire or earthquake. A diagram of the building's emergency

Office machines, such as photocopiers, are expensive and require regular servicing to keep them in good working order. Be sure you know how to operate them correctly, as carelessness can cause the need for extra repair and maintenance.

©David Young-Wolff/PhotoEdit

exits should be posted on a wall along with some instructions about what to do in an emergency. Become aware of these directions. Some offices have regular fire drills so that everyone can practice what to do. Your cooperation in these drills may later save you from injury and may even save your life.

Other little details can help ensure safety in an office. For example, do not string electrical wires across floors where people are walking. Be careful about the placement of items on high shelves so that they do not tumble down on people below. Look around your office to check for safety; you may be able to think of other safety tips.

## Office Romances

While you are in school, you see many other people every day. You have opportunities to talk with many young men and women about your own age. You may make friends, date, even meet your life partner at school.

When you no longer attend classes daily, your circle of potential friends, and dates, may become much smaller. One of the places where many people look for friends and possible romantic interests is on the job. Most people do make friends at work; however, going slow and getting to know a co-worker before you decide to spend much time with him or her is best. Sometimes ending a friendship that grew too fast is difficult.

Employees who look for romantic interests on the job need to use at least as much caution as they would in making friends. Go slow. A person who catches your eye may seem like someone with whom you would like to pursue a romantic relationship. Carmen, a young woman in Chicago, got involved too quickly with a young man to whom she was very much attracted. Soon she was thinking, "If only I'd waited a couple of weeks, it would have been obvious that I didn't want to get involved with this man." He became quite upset when Carmen ended the relationship.

Broken relationships in the office are often a problem. Working with someone with whom you have had a close relationship that went sour can be difficult. Also, poor working relationships are a major reason employees are fired. So be cautious. Romance in the office can be risky!

©Jean Luc Fornier/FPG International

Be cautious about becoming romantically involved with a co-worker. If the romance ends, continuing to work together could be difficult.

# Employee Expectations

Your new employer will expect many things of you. You will expect certain things from your employer, too. These expectations include a tour of the office and introductions, training, timely paychecks, communication to keep you informed, evaluation of your work, safe working conditions, and honesty.

## Tour of the Office and Introductions

You can expect that someone in the company will provide you with a tour of the office. This person will show you where materials and supplies are kept, will probably tell you who occupies which offices, and will show you the restroom and lunchroom or breakroom.

At the same time that this tour is being conducted, you will probably be introduced to your co-workers. You can expect that people will be open, friendly, and helpful in welcoming you to your new office.

Your new job could require some extensive training to help you become familiar with specific duties for your position and learn about the company.

## Training

Training you carefully and thoroughly is in the company's best interest. This training will probably include information about company policy and rules, and you should receive a clear statement of what is expected of you. You will likely learn who is your immediate supervisor—the person to whom you will be accountable.

Although you may have learned in school many of the basic skills you need to perform your new job, you will still require some training. For example, you will need to know the details about the job, what precisely your duties will be, and how you should accomplish them. Take advantage of this training, and learn as much as you can now, because in a short while, you will be on your own.

Many companies emphasize cross-training; that is, training employees to perform the tasks usually done by other workers. Cross-training helps employers because when someone is ill or on vacation, another worker can step in and do the work.

If you have an opportunity to learn how to do the work usually done by other workers, take advantage of it. *You* will become more valuable to the company.

## Timely Paychecks

If you come to work each day on time and work all the hours you are assigned, you can expect to get paid for your work. The policies and procedures manual will let you know when you will be paid. For some companies, payday is every Friday; for others, it will be the first and the fifteenth days of the month. Government offices often pay only once a month, usually on the tenth of the month following the month when the money was earned. Every company has established paydays, and you can expect to be paid on those days, and you can plan accordingly.

Along with your paycheck, you can expect an accounting of the money earned and the money withheld for taxes and other items.

# Communication to Keep You Informed

Your employer should keep you informed about changes in company policy, potential changes in your workload or responsibilities, and other changes in the company that might affect you. A good company has a system of communication that allows employees to feel involved and a part of the ongoing business of the company. This communication often takes place in staff meetings, but it can also be accomplished through memos, bulletins, and newsletters. You will receive a large amount of information verbally, from either your supervisor or your co-workers. Pay attention. Some of the things you hear may directly affect your work with the company.

# Evaluation of Your Work

You can expect periodic evaluations that should help you be a better employee. Having careful, thoughtful feedback from your supervisor about the quality and productivity of your work, your attitude, and how you fit into the office environment is a reasonable expectation. The evaluation is also part of the company's communication system.

Part of your evaluation may be criticism of how you work. Do not be defensive. Listen carefully to any criticism. Think about it later, and use this information to become a better worker.

Your employer should also tell you what you are doing exceptionally well. Use both criticism and praise to improve your work skills.

# Safe Working Conditions

On-the-job safety is your new employer's responsibility. Someone should be constantly monitoring the safety of the environment in which you are expected to work.

Although safety is a larger concern in certain kinds of machine shops and factories than in an office, your employer should be vigilant in seeing that safety precautions are taken. Your employer should also have a plan of action for an emergency.

# Honesty

After you work for a few years, you may discover that honesty is probably the most important expectation you will have of your employers. Smart companies invariably have a policy of straight shooting with their employees. *Straight shooting* means direct communication about what you can expect of your employers along the lines of advancement, salary, pay raises, benefits, and so on.

If you think your employer has been unfair, you may want to discuss the problem with her or him. Do not begin the discussion with accusations. Simply say that you are confused about what has happened, and you need to clarify the issues so that you can understand them. Yes, this discussion can be risky, but you do not want to be in a situation where you are being used or manipulated. In such a case, you would be happier leaving this job to seek other employment.

Companies that make promises and do not deliver have serious personnel problems and do not last long in the business world. Be sure you know exactly the sort of business your new company is in before you agree to take the job. Some people have become involved in shady businesses through naiveté (trustfulness) and innocence. If you have any doubts about the nature of the business your company is involved in, find out.

Angela, a word processing specialist, was the newest employee in the office. Her keyboarding skills, however, were better than those of anyone else in the department. When her supervisor, Mr. Bracken, brought work into the department, he would usually give new work to those who were nearly finished with their prior assignments.

Because Angela was the most productive, she was often given big projects near the end of the day and would have to work late to complete them. Angela felt that Mr. Bracken was taking unfair advantage of her because she was a productive worker. She objected to having to work late, but she did not know what to do about it.

Then Angela came up with an idea. She would simply try to avoid Mr. Bracken. Her desk was situated so that she could easily see anyone approaching the department down a long hall. So the next time she saw Mr. Bracken approaching, she quickly left her station and went to the restroom. By leaving her desk several times a week, she avoided several big projects that might have caused her to work late. Instead, Bob and Judy began getting these projects.

Based on what you know about Angela's approach to solving her problem, answer these questions:

1. *How do you think Angela's behavior will affect her chances for promotion?*

2. *How do you think her practice of avoiding Mr. Bracken will affect Angela's relationships with her co-workers?*

3. *What would have been a better way for Angela to solve her problem?* ■

---

Most companies deal honestly with their employees. You need to be able to trust your employers, as they expect to be able to trust you.

## Managing Stress

Stress is anything that triggers your fight-or-flight response. Our distant ancestors found stress very helpful. It motivated them to battle or to run like crazy when confronted by an enemy or a wild and hungry predator. Today stress may be either positive or negative. An example of positive stress is the excitement a musician feels just before going onto the stage for a show. In this case, the fight-or-flight response helps to improve the performance. The excitement a basketball player feels just before a big game can lift the level of play.

Negative stress may be short-term (such as the pressure to make a quick decision when a car swerves into your path). Or it may be long-term (such as the stress you might feel in a high-pressure job). Too much stress, especially over a long period of time, may cause a loss of energy and leave you vulnerable to illness and even premature aging. Photos of U.S. presidents taken before and after four years in one of the most stressful jobs in the world provide a vivid example.

Stress may be categorized into two major types: *physical stress* and *psychological stress*. Physical stress is caused by physical demands on the body (such as illness, accidents, or even prolonged psychological stress). Psychological stress may be simply the result of physical stress. However, psychological stress is usually caused by emotional demands in your personal life (family, friends) or from your work. Psychological, or emotional, stress is often the most damaging type in today's society. Fortunately, we have ways to ease this stress.

Psychological, or emotional, stress may be one of four basic types. The first is *pressure*, which is an internal or external demand to complete a task in a limited time or in a certain way. The second is *frustration*, which is the blocking of your needs or wants. The third is *conflict*, which is the need to make a choice between two or more options. The fourth is *anxiety or fear*, which is one of two basic emotional responses to a perceived threat (the other is anger).

When stress triggers your fight-or-flight response, your body provides you with physical energy not needed to cope with a modern-day situation. This energy generates anxiety. Your body responds to any thought as if it concerns the present, even when you think about the past or the future. A vivid thought (with a strong emotional component) about a past bad experience or a possible future problem may bring on the fight-or-flight response. People who experience prolonged stress usually have attitudes, beliefs, and thinking patterns that perpetuate it.

You cannot totally eliminate stress from your life. Reducing stress through good stress management should be your goal.

The first step in stress management is to treat your body as though it were a machine that needs regular rest, maintenance, and care to work properly. You begin each day with a limited amount of energy. Your energy level varies from day to day, and it is different from that of other people. When you use up your energy supply, you can replace it only by resting and getting proper nourishment. If you do not rest, your body will begin to break down.

Learn to recognize the signs of stress. They include physical, mental, emotional, and relational symptoms such as the ones listed below.

©Corbis/Stock Market

Learning good stress management techniques can help you avoid burnout and health problems related to prolonged stress.

### Physical Symptoms

| | |
|---|---|
| Frequent colds or flu | Fatigue |
| Frequent sighing | Headaches |
| Increased accidents | Insomnia |
| Hyperventilation | Pounding heart |
| Restlessness | Weight change |

### Mental Symptoms

| | |
|---|---|
| Boredom | Confusion |
| Forgetfulness | Negative attitude |
| Reduced ability to concentrate | "Weird" thoughts |

### Emotional Symptoms

| | |
|---|---|
| Anxiety | Bad dreams |
| Crying spells | Depression |
| Frustration | Increased use of profanity |
| Sarcasm | Irritability |
| Mood swings | Short temper |

### Relational Symptoms

| | |
|---|---|
| Avoidance of people | Blaming others for problems |
| Distrusting others | Fewer contacts with friends |
| Increased arguing | Intolerance |
| Lack of intimacy | Resentment |

You probably noticed that some of these symptoms apply to you. Everyone has some of these symptoms. However, if many apply to you, you are probably not managing the stress in your life as well as you should for good health.

Some people have highly reactive bodies. They often experience anxiety-related problems while people around them remain calm. Scientists feel that being highly reactive is often an inherited trait. If you fall into this category, you aren't necessarily doomed to severe anxiety for life. You must understand the symptoms and take care of your needs. These needs may be physical, mental, emotional, or relational.

The following suggestions are ways others have learned to manage stress in their lives. You may find some of them helpful in your own stress management plan.

- **Set Priorities and Reduce Overall Activity.** At certain times in your life, you will face periods of high stress. Everyone does. When this situation happens, reduce your activities. This time is not a time to set new performance records! Set priorities. Do what is most important and cut back on what is not quite as crucial for now. Sometimes stress can lead you to give small details an exaggerated importance. Try to keep a proper perspective on what is vital and what can wait until later. Set some short-term goals. Give your body a rest and you will recover your energy level.

- **Exercise.** Physical exercise can help you work off emotional stress. You probably know that aerobic exercise is vigorous exercise that makes your heart beat faster and requires you to use much more oxygen. Using more oxygen changes your body chemistry. Many people use running, bicycling, aerobic exercises, racquetball, tennis, or other vigorous physical exercise to lower their stress levels. Exercise can even give you an emotional, natural "high" feeling because it causes increased levels of endorphins to be produced in the brain. (*Endorphins* are hormones that have a tranquilizing or pain-killing effect on the body.)

- **Take Time to Relax.** You know that regular rest is necessary to regain energy. One way to assure time for rest and relaxation is to schedule it. Scheduling regular relaxation is as important for your mind and

©V.C.L./Paul Viant/FPG International

Regular exercise, as well as relaxation, is important to your overall well-being and good job performance.

body as scheduling regular maintenance on your car—only a lot more is at stake!

Some proven forms of relaxation include the following. Find a couple you have not used and give them a try.

| Passive Forms of Relaxation | Active Forms of Relaxation |
| --- | --- |
| Biofeedback | Hobbies and crafts |
| Diaphragmatic breathing | Dancing |
| Massage | Tennis, golf |
| Meditation | Jogging, swimming |
| Reading | Team sports |
| Television | Gardening |
| Yoga | Walking |

■ **Talk Out Your Problems.** Talk with someone you trust and respect, perhaps a friend, family member, member of the clergy, or counselor. When you hold a problem inside, you tend to obsess on it (think about it constantly). Most problems are not as big as we think they are when we hold them inside. When you talk about a difficulty, you can usually see that it is solvable, let go of it, and move on with your life. When you talk about a problem, a compromise usually seems more acceptable, too.

■ **Accept What You Cannot Change.** Most people want as much control over their lives as possible, but in the real world, some things we simply cannot change. Worrying about things that are not changeable is self-defeating. When you learn to accept what you cannot change, life gets a lot easier—and the stress level goes down.

■ **Keep a Balanced Lifestyle.** In today's world, both marriage partners often must bring home a paycheck to cover the high cost of living. Many people are even working at two jobs. Caring for young children, arranging for baby-sitters, and driving children to and from school or activities add more responsibilities—and more stress—to the mix. One way to relieve the stress level is to schedule time for regular recreation, to do something that gets your mind off both work and family responsibilities. Sometimes finding time for recreation is not easy. You cannot add any more hours to the day. However, spending some time in a leisure activity or enjoying a favorite hobby almost guarantees that you will be more relaxed. Quitting a second job or reducing your responsibilities elsewhere may well be worth doing. A balanced lifestyle really works!

■ **Eat and Sleep Well.** Of course you would never fall for junk food advertising (at least not on a regular basis). However, eating nutritionally balanced meals every day may be hard to do. Try to make good eating habits a priority in your life. If you do not, your health will likely be compromised. Many nutritionists recommend vitamin and mineral supplements, too.

Sleep needs vary; some people need more sleep than others. However, many people do not get enough sleep and find themselves drowsy in class or on the job. Sleepiness is most common in the early afternoon, following lunch. If you feel tired or drowsy during the day, you probably need more sleep.

An improper diet and insufficient sleep can increase your level of stress from any source. So eat well and get enough sleep!

Stress in your personal life can affect your performance on the job. Personal stress is distracting, causing a lack of concentration on the task at hand, and it may cause you to be less cooperative with your co-workers.

On the job, tasks that you dislike or cannot do well can cause stress. Your employer or certain co-workers may pressure you to perform in a way that makes you uncomfortable. Working on a stressful job for a long period of time may cause burnout. A person with burnout has reached a point where he or she can no longer perform job tasks effectively; he or she should take a rest, perhaps a long vacation, or should move on to other work. Companies lose an estimated $68 billion each year from stress-related disability claims.

Just as personal stress can affect work performance, job stress can carry over into your personal life as well. Both on and off the job, much stress is caused by personal relationships. You do not usually get to choose your co-workers. Even if you are exceptionally cooperative, you will run into people who will cause you stress. Most of us have stressful conflicts with members of our own families, or even friends whom we have chosen.

Some experts say that stress is a bigger problem today than ever before. Some say stress is a twentieth-century phenomenon. Although stress has been recognized as a debilitating problem only in the last few years, it has been around for a long time. (Would you trade your stress for that of the prehistoric man or woman? Every night was an adventure in trying to evade a pack of hungry wolves, a saber-toothed tiger, or some other predator!)

# Freedom from Sexual Harassment

Sexual harassment in the workplace is not a new problem; it has taken place probably since women began working outside the home. Stories of workplace harassment were reported in writings of a hundred years ago. However, harassment has become the focus of increased attention in recent years.

Sexual harassment is any unwanted and offensive sexual look, comment, suggestion, or physical contact that causes discomfort in the workplace.

The Civil Rights Act prohibits sexual harassment in both educational settings and the workplace. Some women do not realize they have been harassed even when the behavior is blatant and severe. Yet harassment often leads to anger, frustration, lowered self-esteem, depression, and physical symptoms such as nausea or headaches. Many women make excuses for such behavior, making statements such as "He didn't mean to do it . . . he didn't think I'd be upset . . . that's just the way he is . . ." Some women blame themselves or accept such behavior without knowing they have a right to complain. Harassment often goes unreported because women are afraid they will not be believed or might be labeled as troublemakers.

Men are also sometimes harassed. However, women are the victims most of the time. Both women and men are responsible for doing whatever they can to prevent sexual harassment from occurring in the workplace.

Sexual harassment often leaves victims feeling powerless and out of control. If it happens to you, what should you do? The following steps have been effective in stopping harassment. You may want to use one or more of these strategies if the need arises.

Sometimes, ignoring unwelcome attention is enough to cause it to stop. If not, more direct or formal action may be necessary.

1.  Say NO to the harasser. Tell the person that you do not approve of his or her behavior. Respond immediately and assertively to let the offender know that such behavior, even if it is just making an offensive remark, is unacceptable. Confront him or her in a safe place, preferably where other workers will witness it. (The harasser's office with the door closed is not safe.)

2.  Ignore or avoid the harassment or harasser. You may feel more comfortable simply ignoring or avoiding the harasser. You might change your own behavior, your hours of work, even your job. This strategy is not always the best, however. Sometimes this strategy works, but usually only temporarily. Additionally, you would be taking on the responsibility of avoiding harassment, which may increase your anxiety. Dealing with the harasser directly, as in number 1 above, is usually more effective.

3.  Keep a written record of the harassment. Write down the time, date, and place along with other relevant circumstances. Keep any pertinent correspondence that could be used as evidence of the harassment, including notes, letters, gifts, memos, and answering machine tapes. Documentation validates your feelings. When all the "little" incidents are listed, you can more easily understand your distress.

4.  Find out if any co-workers witnessed the harassment or your reaction to it. Write down what they heard or saw; ask if they would be willing to put their observations into writing.

5.  Discuss the incident with co-workers. Some of them may have been harassed, too.

6.  Ask for copies of past work evaluations that show the quality of your work. These documents include formal work evaluations and any notes that accompanied a bonus, for example.

7.  Write a letter to the harasser. Confronting the offender in writing may be easier than in person. A four-part letter should include: a statement of the problem; how you feel about it, how it has affected you, and what it has cost you; what you would like to see happen; and what further action you will take if your requests are not met. Mail the letter to the harasser by registered mail with a return receipt requested. Send a copy to a rape crisis center and keep a copy for yourself.

8.  If following these seven steps does not solve the problem, call a rape crisis center. A counselor at the center will provide information and assistance.

9.  File a formal complaint with your supervisor, human resources department, or employer, both verbally and in writing. (Of course, if the harasser *is* your supervisor, you must go over his or her head.) A week or so later, write a follow-up memo about any communication on the matter and ask that it be placed into your personnel file.

10. If a formal complaint does not get results, take your complaint as high up as you have to go until you get an appropriate response.

11. If you still have not received satisfactory action, you may hire a lawyer and sue the harasser. If you choose to file a lawsuit, find a lawyer who has experience with sexual harassment cases. You may want to find one who will take the case on a contingency basis (you pay only if you win the case).

# Termination of Your Employment

On most jobs, if your training and skills match the job description, you will be happy, contented, interested, and successful. Unfortunately, not every job works out so well. What if you are not happy with your work or do not think you will be successful? What if you get another job offer that is just what you wanted all along?

If you are truly unhappy on a job or if you get a much better offer, then you may want to quit. Do not quit without giving the situation much thought, though. Spur-of-the-moment decisions to quit a job are often regretted.

If, after thoughtful consideration, you decide to quit your job, you must give proper notice. This notice is to allow your employer to begin looking for someone to take your place. Usually, if you are paid once a month, a month's notice is considered proper. If you are paid once a week, a week's notice is usually sufficient.

Quitting a job is one form of termination. Sometimes employers terminate workers' employment. Most people have been terminated by being fired from a job at least once.

A termination might make you very unhappy if you do not clearly understand it. At the time of termination, try to get clarification. How, exactly, did your job not work out? What, exactly, should you do differently next time? Spend some time thinking about what went wrong to ensure you do not make the same mistakes again.

In many cases, your job change will be an improvement. If you have a personality conflict with someone, or if you are in a position that is a bit difficult for you, you will be relieved that your employment is over.

If you are fired from your job, ask the reason for the termination. Even good, productive employees are sometimes laid off. If you lose a full-time job, you will probably be eligible for unemployment compensation while you are searching for new employment. An optimistic outlook will be helpful in looking for a new job.

## Layoff

Sometimes, through no fault of your own, you will be laid off. Your company may be going through difficult times, and because you were one of the last people hired, you will be one of the first to receive a layoff notice.

Being laid off is not the same as being fired. People are not laid off because of poor job performance, personality conflicts, or any of the other reasons people are fired. People are laid off either because the company does not have enough work or because an employer is having financial difficulties and cannot afford to pay all the employees.

Generally, your employer will notify you in writing of your layoff, and in some cases, you will be given severance pay. **Severance pay** means money that you get because you were *severed*, or laid off, from a company. Your severance pay may be equal to one, two, or more weeks' salary. No law dictates that an employer must give notice before a layoff, or give severance pay.

## Unemployment Compensation

Your employers must contribute monthly to state unemployment insurance to ensure that you can get compensation when you are dismissed from a company. To be eligible for unemployment compensation, you

must earn a certain amount of money in the weeks and months before your claim.

**Unemployment compensation** is never a large sum of money. It is designed to get the unemployed person through the times when no paycheck is being earned. Generally, if you are terminated from a part-time job that you hold while a student, you will not have earned enough money to qualify for this compensation.

Unemployment compensation is administered by state governments. You are eligible to receive this compensation only if you are seeking new employment at the same time.

## Search for New Employment

For a short time, you will probably want to assess what went wrong with the job. However, you need to begin at once to seek other employment. Remember the old adage that if you fall off a horse, you should get right back on again? This saying applies to employment, too.

If you have had an unhappy experience, go back to all the things you learned about how to get a job in the first place, and put all those strategies in motion so that you are not unemployed for any length of time.

## Optimism

You have had an experience. Now you know more than you did before, and you have actually worked in an office. This experience is to your advantage. Even though the outcome may have been less than desirable, the experience will be helpful as you look for your new job.

Be hopeful, cheerful, and optimistic. Know that you found a job before, you learned a lot, and now you can find another job. Hold the thought that your new job will probably suit you much better, conflicts that were part of the old job will be gone, and your new job may be more fun, more interesting, and more gratifying.

## Recall Time

*Answer the following questions:*

**1.** Employers have many expectations of their employees, including some about attitude. What are some of them? What are some expectations that employers have about the work itself?

**2.** What is the difference between quality of work and productivity?

**3.** What are some things you need to consider when making decisions about problems on the job?

**4.** What are several things you can expect from your employer?

**5.** What are two major types of stress?

**6.** Name the four major ways that signs of stress may be categorized.

**7.** What does being laid off mean? How is it different from being fired?

# Summary

Soon you will be making an important transition from school to regular, full-time work. Look on this change as an adventure, a new learning experience.

As a new employee, you must fill out forms that give your employer certain important information. One will be a W-4 form, required by the Internal Revenue Service. The W-4 form helps your employer know how much to withhold from each of your paychecks for taxes.

You will probably be asked to maintain a time card to determine the amount of your paycheck each pay period.

When you begin a new job, you will receive some sort of orientation to the company and the work you will do. This orientation will help you understand exactly what is expected of you and what the policies and procedures are at this company. In many companies, the policies and procedures are presented in a printed document and will cover such topics as salaries, benefits, paydays, vacation time, overtime, probation, evaluation, termination, sexual harassment, and grievance procedures. Each company has its own policies and procedures to meet its unique needs.

Your orientation will probably also include introductions to other workers, a tour of the office, and some idea of the unwritten rules for the office. Unwritten rules consist of matters such as how people are addressed, what kind of clothing is appropriate, and the kind of speech that you are expected to use.

Your employer will have many expectations of you, some of which will concern attitude, such as being pleasant to other workers, honest, willing to learn, dependable, cooperative, and enthusiastic. Further expectations concern the work itself. These expectations include good quality of work, high productivity, punctuality and good attendance, good judgment, good care of equipment, and awareness of safety.

You can also expect certain things from your employer. You can expect to receive adequate orientation and training, to be paid for the work you do, to be kept informed about ongoing business decisions that might affect you, to have thoughtful feedback about your work in the form of regular evaluations, and to have safe working conditions. Probably the most important expectation you might have of your new employer is honesty in what is said about work, pay, and benefits.

If you have the proper skill and training, chances are you will be successful at your new job. However, unforeseen things sometimes happen on the job. You may be terminated (fired) or you may get laid off. If you are fired, it will be because your work has been evaluated as substandard or because you have a personality conflict with someone on the job. If you are laid off, it will be because the company does not have enough work or because it can no longer afford to pay you.

If you find yourself without a job, evaluate what took place so that it does not happen again. Begin at once to look for a new job, using all the strategies you used in finding this one.

During the first days and weeks on the new job, the following things will occur:

- You will fill out a W-4 form, which has information concerning withholding taxes.
- You will be shown how to keep your time card.
- You will be oriented to the way your office is run.

- You will be given a policies and procedures manual, and you will need to have a clear understanding of its contents.
- You will be given training on how to do your job.
- Your employer will have certain expectations, including that you have a good attitude.
- You will be expected to be at work every day and to arrive on time.
- You will be expected to do quality work with a reasonable rate of productivity.
- You will be expected to observe safety precautions in the office.
- You will be expected to take proper care of office machines and furnishings.
- You can have certain expectations of your employers, such as honesty in their dealings with you.
- You can expect a good system of communication in which your employer keeps you informed about business matters that are important to your job.
- You can expect regular and timely paychecks for the work you do, with a clear statement of money withheld.

# before you leave...

**When you have completed this chapter, answer the following questions:**
1. What policies and procedures do you expect to learn about during your first days on the job?
2. What characteristics do most employers expect of their employees?
3. As a new employee, what can you reasonably expect of your employer?

# Review & Application

## Check Your Knowledge

1. Name several events that you might expect to happen in the first days on your new job.

2. What is the purpose of the W-4 form? Who requires it? What sort of information does it contain?

3. What is the purpose of a time card?

4. How will you discover how to address people in your new office?

5. What kinds of information will you find in a policies and procedures manual?

6. What is a probation period? How long does it usually last?

7. What is a performance evaluation? How can it benefit you?

8. Besides quitting, you might leave your job in two ways. What are they?

9. Describe the grievance process.

10. In an office, things generally happen in a particular way unique to that office. Name some unwritten rules. Who usually sets the style of an office?

11. Name several expectations regarding attitude that your new employer may have of you.

12. Other expectations concern job performance. List and explain several performance expectations that are common to employers.

13. You can also have expectations of your new employers. Name several reasonable things that you can expect.

14. Who is eligible for unemployment compensation? What is its purpose?

15. Discuss the four basic types of psychological stress.

16. Discuss at least three strategies to use to stop sexual harassment.

17. If you are terminated, how will you go about finding another job? How soon should you begin your search?

18. What is the most beneficial attitude for you to have about being in the job market?

## Review Your Vocabulary

On a separate piece of paper, write the letter of the vocabulary word that is described below.

____ 1. money that an employee gets because she or he was laid off

____ 2. method a company uses to allow an employee to state his or her side in a dispute with supervisors or other employees

____ 3. form that provides information about the amount of taxes you will pay

____ 4. total work accomplished in a given amount of time

____ 5. period of time before permanent employment during which an employee receives no benefits

____ 6. small amounts of money paid to unemployed workers to help them through the times when no paycheck is being earned

____ 7. written statement outlining the strengths and weaknesses of an employee's job performance

____ 8. request for an employee to leave a job

a. grievance process
b. performance evaluation
c. probation
d. productivity
e. severance pay
f. termination
g. unemployment compensation
h. W-4 form

## Discuss and Analyze an Office Situation

1. Ernest has been with his new company for three months. When he started the job, he was told he would receive an evaluation and be taken off probation at the end of three months. He would then receive full-time, regular employee status with full benefits. Three months have gone by, and as

time passes, one week, then two, no one has evaluated Ernest's performance. He assumes that he is still on probation.

What should Ernest do to clear up this confusion?

2. Bernardita has been hired on a new job and has been invited to attend an orientation meeting for new employees. She is grateful for the opportunity to learn what, exactly, her job entails. Unfortunately, she finds the orientation to be rather inadequate. In addition, when she reports to work on her first day, no one greets her, introduces her to others, or assists her in any way.

We can expect certain things from new employers. How have Bernardita's new employers fallen short of their responsibility to her? What would you do if you were Bernardita?

## Practice Basic Skills

### Math

Social Security contributions are 15.3 percent of your earned money. Your employer pays 7.65 percent and you pay the rest. If you work forty hours in one week and earn $7.50 per hour, how much will be withheld from that paycheck for your share of the Social Security tax? How much will your employer be paying?

### English

Some offices are formal and some informal. Language reflects the style of an office. If you are working in a very formal office, which parts of the following conversation would not be acceptable to your employer? Assume that you are talking to a customer.

Hi, Eileen. We can fix ya up with a gizmo that will knock your socks off. I've been diggin' on these things for days, and I think you'll think they're pretty super, too. Come on over here and get a load of this. See if you don't think it's just what you've been looking for. It will really do a job for you.

### Proofreading

Part of your new job in the office may be keying and correcting a letter. Different companies use different formats, so you will need to determine exactly how your company wants its letters formatted. Rewrite or key the following letter on a separate piece of paper, correcting misspellings, formatting, and incorrect punctuation.

Mr. Randall Russell, President
Wholesome Produce Company
1345 Class Street
Los Angeles, CA 90024-1355

Dear Mr. Rusel:

I am writing to requesst a corection to the envoice you sent us on May 30. Apparently, we have ben chargd for merchandice we did not perchase, and we do not wunt to pay for it.

I am hopping that you will be abel to cleer up this mater immediately. Thank you.

Yours Truely,
Leah Baker

## Apply Your Knowledge

1. Go to your local Internal Revenue Service office and ask for a W-4 form. Fill it out as you would if you were hired for a new position.

2. Visit your parent's or a friend's business and ask if you might look at the policies and procedures manual. (If you are employed, you could ask your employer if you may bring your company's manual to class.) Become familiar with the types of issues covered in the document. If the business has no such document, interview your parent or friend. Ask how he or she learned about the rules of the company and ask what they are.

## Using the Reference Manual

Open file ch20ref.doc. Use the letter styles section of the Reference Manual at the back of the book to help you arrange the letter using the simplified format. In preparing the letter:

A. Use WHAT TO EXPECT ON THE JOB as the subject of the letter.

B. Use your name as the person writing the letter.

C. Use the current date.

D. Address the letter to your teacher in care of your school's address.

Save and print.

This letter is to clarify our discussion on the telephone last Friday about what new employees can expect on the job. You will want to stress the following ideas in your classroom instruction:

1. New employees can expect to fill out certain paperwork prior to employment. This paperwork will include tax forms, a withholding form, and payroll information.

2. After the paperwork is completed, a new employee will be introduced to other employees and co-workers. New employees need to start remembering names at that time.

3. Most companies will have written policies and procedures. Some companies will share this information in a formal orientation meeting, others will not. All employees need to become familiar with these topics and have access to an employees' policy manual.

I will send additional information as your semester progresses. Have a good school year.

# chapter 21

## Moving Ahead Toward Your Career Goal

**After completing this chapter, you will be able to do the following:**

1. Improve your chances of achieving success by dressing for success.
2. Understand and learn from your work evaluations.
3. Earn pay raises and promotions.
4. Select appropriate programs for further education and training.

### New Office Terms

- constructive criticism
- remuneration
- seminar

**Answer the following questions to the best of your ability:**

1. What is the title of a guide on how men should dress for success?
2. What is the most important status symbol of men's attire?
3. What is the main purpose of an evaluation?
4. What six questions should you ask yourself before you ask for a raise?

After you have worked at your new office job for several weeks, you will likely know all your co-workers and their roles in the office and understand your own job. You should also understand the office rules and procedures and follow them. You will then be on your way toward gaining the reputation of being a good, reliable, competent worker.

What is next? If you are interested in looking ahead to your future, you can do some things to enhance your success and ensure your advancement toward your ultimate career goal.

Dress and appearance, image, attitude, evaluation of progress, assessment of changing career and personal needs, participation in career-related activities, and education are all important considerations in your quest for higher achievement.

When you begin working full-time, you will want to progress toward your ultimate career goal. Doing so will depend greatly on whether you are making progress on your current job. As you learned in Chapter 20, your employer will probably provide a written evaluation of your work on a regular schedule. If you are performing well, you may earn some salary increases and perhaps even a promotion. As you move toward your career goal, you may want to take advantage of some further education and training.

## Your Progress on the Job

You are responsible for completing your work assignments to the best of your ability. Reasonable expectations by your employer include satisfactory quality of work, productivity, punctuality and attendance, and care of office equipment. If you are meeting these expectations and you have a good attitude toward your job and your co-workers, you have a good start toward success on your career path.

Some young people are unsure of what clothing is appropriate to wear to the office. They say they do not want to dress like "an old man" or "an old woman." Usually they are not really talking about old people, but men and women who have worked long enough to establish themselves as productive, responsible employees. People who have achieved success in the business office usually look the part. They dress for success—and their appearance is part of what helps them achieve a certain level of success. Of course, considerable variation exists among offices in how employees are expected to dress. You will have an advantage if you dress similarly to the best-dressed people in your office. You can dress similarly and still dress especially for you and your job.

## Technology in the Office | VIRUS PROTECTION

Computer viruses have been causing serious problems for computer users for more than twenty years, but today's versions are more sophisticated. They are faster moving, and they infect in a variety of ways.

Sharing infected disks spreads many older viruses. Because disks are not used much anymore, most viruses are spread through attachments to e-mail messages. The message itself often tricks the recipient into opening the attachment. Once opened, the virus can infect the e-mail management program and send copies of itself to all users in the address book.

One fast-spreading virus, Nimda, first appeared September 18, 2001. Within a week, the original virus had created about 1.3 million copies of itself worldwide. Computer viruses seem to spread in about as many ways as the common cold. Antivirus software is helpful, but it may not be enough to keep your computer virus free today. Experts recommend a three-layered defense: antivirus software, personal firewall, and software patches downloaded from software makers.

Even if you have what you believe is effective virus protection, be careful. Do not open e-mail attachments from unknown sources. ■

## Dressing for Success

Consider seriously the image you express through your appearance on the job—your grooming and how you dress. How you look makes a statement about how you see yourself, how you see your job, and how you feel about advancement. With the correct information and some effort, everyone can look good.

Dressing for success begins with cleanliness, but it also requires that you be neat and attractive—which is what grooming is all about. Several aspects of grooming of which you should be aware are general health, hairstyles, skin care and makeup, and use of antiperspirant.

### General Health

People who exercise regularly, get sufficient sleep, eat properly, and do not socialize excessively tend to look better. Nothing helps you look your best like the glow of good health and vigor.

Regular exercise means aerobic exercise—running, biking, dancing, walking, or swimming—that is done for at least one-half hour three times or more each week.

Sufficient sleep for most people means six to eight hours of sleep each night. Individual sleep requirements differ, and you may need more or less than the average.

A proper diet consists of daily servings of grains, dairy products, meat, fish, poultry and other proteins, and fruits and vegetables. See Figure 21.1, page 468, for recommended servings of each food group. The healthiest people consume a diet containing many fruits and vegetables. Refined sugar products should not be in your diet at all, and excessive amounts of fats and oils can seriously impair your health and your looks. Avoid eating too many of the wrong foods if you do not want to become overweight and unhealthy.

Sometimes, when you are working forty hours a week, taking time to eat properly is difficult. In our society, we tend to eat on the run, so we often turn to junk foods. However, eating the right foods will give you more energy on the job and help you look your best.

**FIGURE 21.1 • RDA Food Groups**

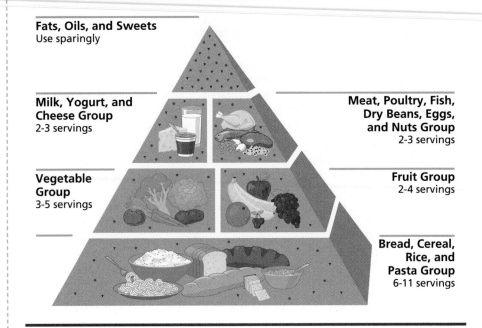

**Fats, Oils, and Sweets**
Use sparingly

**Milk, Yogurt, and Cheese Group**
2-3 servings

**Meat, Poultry, Fish, Dry Beans, Eggs, and Nuts Group**
2-3 servings

**Vegetable Group**
3-5 servings

**Fruit Group**
2-4 servings

**Bread, Cereal, Rice, and Pasta Group**
6-11 servings

Socializing too much on weekends is easy to do after you have worked hard all week. However, returning to work on Monday with a clear head and a healthy glow is difficult if you have socialized excessively. Do not let the way you spend your leisure time adversely affect your health or your work performance.

When you take care of your health, you take a large step toward looking your best on the job.

## Hairstyles

You will find many acceptable ways to wear your hair. The key is to have hair that is neatly trimmed and brushed and never too trendy. Hairstylists can help you determine what best suits your facial features, what will be the most becoming, and what will be easy to manage. Have a hairstyle that you can take care of yourself without having to fuss with it too much. You will be very busy at work, and saving time will be important to you.

Men on the job must carefully consider how they wear their hair. Older men who may be supervising new employees will have set ideas about how men's hair should look. If you expect to get ahead in your business, you will have to cater to the supervisors' opinions. You need to follow good business sense and go along with hairstyle rules. Sometimes, however, long, clean, and well-groomed hairstyles are accepted. Later on, you will have opportunities to take stands on much more important issues than the length or style of your hair.

## Skin Care and Makeup

Some climates are very hard on the skin. You may need to apply a moisturizer each day on your hands, arms, and face to avoid a dry, scaly appearance.

**What's Your Attitude?** Margaret has been on her new office job for about twelve weeks. She likes the job very much and eagerly continues to learn as much as she can about it. Her supervisor considers Margaret an excellent employee because of her enthusiasm and her willingness to take on new responsibilities.

Though Margaret tries to do her best in all areas of her employment, she has a problem with grooming. She does not realize that the clothes she wears are inappropriate in an office setting. She wears trendy skirts that are too short, boots with fringes, blouses with silver decorations and tassels, and other garments that are appropriate for a rock concert but not for an office.

Margaret is called into her supervisor's office for her three-month evaluation. Her supervisor praises her for her excellent working habits, her punctuality, and her dependability.

Then the supervisor asks Margaret about her career goals and her plans for the future. Margaret responds that she eagerly looks forward to advancement and more responsibility. She says that someday she would like to be a supervisor herself.

The supervisor looks surprised. He tells Margaret that he had no idea she had these kinds of ambitions. He thought she was more of a fun-loving girl than a serious career-minded woman. He explains that he arrived at these conclusions strictly from the way she dressed, not from her job performance.

Margaret is very surprised and a little hurt. However, her attitude about the job is so good that she wants to change her image as quickly as possible.

***What would you do if you were Margaret?*** ■

---

Women might want to seek a consultant to help them learn proper makeup application techniques and what colors look best. Makeup that is poorly used can seriously detract from your looks, but carefully applied makeup can enhance your appearance and give you a well-groomed, professional look.

### Shaving
Men have a choice about whether to be clean-shaven. Men who decide they want a beard or mustache should begin growing it at vacation time, because showing up at the office with facial stubble looks careless and unkempt. Be sure to shave your face and neck daily, and trim your mustache or beard regularly if you have one.

### Antiperspirant
Controlling body odor and wetness with a good antiperspirant is important for your grooming. You can begin to perspire immediately after a bath or shower, so apply antiperspirant regularly right after bathing or showering.

## Women's Wardrobes and Work Success
Clearly, business dress has been influenced by a trend toward more casual office attire in many sections of the country. With all the differences in dress codes at different companies, describing what is an appropriate outfit for all employers is impossible. However, research has shown the relationship between how people dress and how successful they are at work. If you want to advance on the job, look around and notice what others are wearing. Do you dress like the highest-paid, most successful women in the office—or like the lowest-paid workers?

©Nathan Michaels/SuperStock International

An appropriate wardrobe reflects your approach to career goals.

The way you dress and groom yourself makes a clear statement about your career goals.

TIP Be aware of your appearance in the office at all times. Take a couple of minutes, two or three times a day, for a *short* grooming break. Sometimes, in a busy office, you forget to touch up your makeup or straighten your hair. Especially when you are expecting a new client or an important guest in the office, take the time to make certain you look fresh.

Remember, you are a representative of your business and your grooming helps assure outsiders that they are doing business with a high-quality company. ■

Many offices have "casual Fridays," when employees dress down somewhat more casually than on other days of the week. In fact, in recent years what is considered *acceptable dress* for women in the office has moved away from the standard navy or gray suit toward more casual wear. Today, you have more opportunities to express your individuality. If you want to advance to better-paying positions, just remember that how you dress makes a clear statement about your career goal. If you hope to advance beyond an office support or administrative assistant position, you must indicate your willingness to do so by dressing like those who hold the positions to which you aspire.

Although research shows that fashions and acceptable dress vary from city to city throughout the United States, some basic rules apply anywhere.

A skirted suit in a dark blue, beige, or gray, with a blouse in a contrasting color, is still the most appropriate office attire for a woman. If you wear a dress, avoid a floral print. Pick a dress—preferably one in a dark color—that shows you are in the office to do business. Knit polyester pantsuits may be comfortable, but they do not show that you are a professional office worker with a promising future.

Wear plain-colored mid-heeled or low-heeled pumps with neutral-colored stockings. Avoid flashy jewelry. Wear simple, small earrings, a simple watch, and only one or two small rings.

*Never* wear a whole row of pierced earrings. Nose, lip, and eyebrow rings are also frowned on by established, successful employees, as well as by most bosses.

## Men's Wardrobes and Work Success

*John T. Molloy's New Dress for Success* (Warner Books) is a guide for men who want to advance in their careers. In many offices, more casual dress is now considered acceptable, but the key to looking the part of a professional on his way up is to dress like the most respected employees who have already been promoted to higher-paying jobs.

When you begin your employment in a new industry, one of the first things you might do is research how people dress in that field. Do this research systematically by observing several male executives and keeping notes on what they wear. The most important observations will come from your own office. After reviewing your notes, eliminate the most conservative as well as the most innovative dress, and you will have an appropriate range of clothing for yourself.

Shades of blue, beige, and gray in different weaves are the colors of choice for men's suits, slacks, and sportcoats. These colors can be combined with contrasting dress shirts in white, blue, yellow, and occasionally other solid colors, the paler the better.

Ties are the most important status symbol of a man's attire. Whether he wears a tie directly affects how he is perceived in terms of social status. In one experiment, men who wore ties to expensive restaurants were allowed to pay by check when they explained to the management that they had left their cash and credit cards at home. Men not wearing ties were refused the same courtesy.

In another experiment conducted in several New York restaurants, men who were not wearing ties were assigned the worst house seating. Men with ties were given the more desirable tables.

In yet another experiment, men who did not wear ties to job interviews were much less likely to get the job.

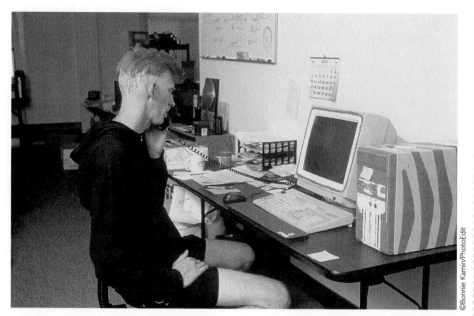

Employers may not be impressed with the way you choose to express your individuality, especially for an office position in which you would have a large amount of customer contact.

The point is, employers and customers alike will take men more seriously if they wear a tie. A tie is a symbol of respectability. Wearing a tie cannot make a man a success in business, but it can help.

Other clothing accessories are important, too. Men should wear only dark shoes and socks. Most leather belts are all right, but be sure the buckle is small; it should not be a large metal decoration. Wear a thin, simple watch—no deep-sea-diving sports watches—and no other jewelry with the exception of a plain wedding band. Many, perhaps most, established office workers do not approve of young men who wear earrings. Why begin with one strike against you? If you want the best shot at a good job, pay raises, and promotions, try for a conservative look. Do not wear tiepins, tie clips, or tie bars—and wear a lapel pin only if it has a significant meaning for you. If you wear cuff links, use only small, simple ones. Only older men tend to wear a handkerchief in the breast pocket, and then only with a conservative suit. Do not wear matching handkerchief-and-tie sets.

You will create your own fashion statement, adopted in part from what you have learned about your industry and what is comfortable and appropriate for you. Choosing clothes for success can be satisfying—and if you are careful about what you purchase, it does not have to be terribly expensive.

## Dressing Especially for You and Your Job

Special jobs have special outfits. Some jobs even require that you wear a uniform, as do those at the front desk of a hotel or in a doctor's office. Wearing a uniform eliminates all questions about what to wear on the job. However, you still have other considerations about your clothing, including taking care of it.

## Take Proper Care of Your Clothes

Whether you wear the latest and most expensive clothing or the same uniform day after day, your clothes should be immaculate—always clean and well pressed. When you undress at the end of the day, hang or fold your clothes neatly to avoid unnecessary and unsightly wrinkling. Most garments have a tag attached that describes their proper care. Follow those instructions, and your clothes will last much longer and look much better.

## Plan Your Wardrobe Carefully

Clothing can be expensive. When you first begin to work, you cannot expect to complete your wardrobe all at once. Choose good-quality, well-made clothing. Use mix-and-match combinations so that you will appear to have a variety of attractive, interesting outfits. For men, gray slacks with navy blazers and two or three good shirts are a good beginning. For women, a couple of dark skirts with several nice blouses or sweaters of different colors will start you off.

Trendy clothing does not belong in a place of business; it is also expensive and goes out of style rapidly. You will do better to spend your wardrobe money on classics that will last you a long while.

## Wear What Looks Good on You

Look around the office to see what other people are wearing. Each of us has a unique look, a style all our own. When you are deciding what to buy and what to wear, be sure the styles you choose are right for you. In other words, wear clothing that is most becoming to you. Someone else may be able to wear a certain style that you admire, but it may not look good on you. Enhance your own looks with clothes that complement your features, hair and skin colors, and personality.

If you incorporate these ideas about dress, image, and grooming into your plan for career advancement, you will probably notice that looking good makes you feel confident and sure of yourself.

©Anton Vengo/SuperStock International

Your grooming and dress reflect the way you see yourself. If you want success, you must dress like those who have already attained it.

**1.** What are several issues you will want to consider as you look toward advancement in your career?

**2.** What are several ideas to consider when thinking about good grooming? Discuss them.

**3.** Caring for your health can be important in how you look. What do you need to do to make sure you remain healthy and vigorous?

**4.** Why do men need to carefully consider what hairstyle they choose?

**5.** Some basic colors are best for clothing for both men and women in the office setting. What are these colors? Discuss several other tips about how to dress on the job.

# Job Evaluations

For as long as you have been a student, you have received regular reports from your teachers about your progress. You are probably not surprised to learn that an important part of your work experience will also be your regular evaluations.

You need to know how your work is being received. Even if you are feeling good about what you have accomplished, you will feel more comfortable when you know what your supervisor thinks. You will learn this information through the process of evaluation—the purpose of which is to inform you about how your supervisor views your work.

## The Process

Someone in your office is responsible for overseeing your work. That person—your boss or direct supervisor—will constantly evaluate your work in an informal way. Your supervisor will notice things about your attitude, your performance, and your work habits nearly every day. Observing workers is your supervisor's job.

In some small offices, job performance evaluations are done informally, at a small meeting or over lunch, with no forms or records of any sort.

Most offices, though, have a formal evaluation process that is standardized for the protection of the employer as well as the employee. If all employees are evaluated with regularity on the same form for the record, no employee can complain about unfair treatment in the evaluation process. Furthermore, a standard format and process help an evaluator to be more precise.

Before your supervisor sets your evaluation meeting, she or he will fill out a form that is designed to record your progress. A sample evaluation form is shown in Figure 21.2, page 474.

Every company designs its own form for evaluation according to its own needs. Generally, a list of categories is on the left side of the page, and ratings are on the right side. Number ratings are often used; higher numbers indicate excellent performance, and lower numbers indicate poor performance. The rating scale might be from 5 to 1 or from 10 to 1. From these numbers, an overall job performance rating can be calculated.

**FIGURE 21.2 • Performance Evaluation Form**

## PERFORMANCE EVALUATION FOR EMPLOYEES

Evaluation Report:    Date Employed            Evaluation Status:

_____ 1st Probationary

_____ Final Probationary    Date Issued _____

_____ Annual

_____ Special Request      Date Due _____

_____ Initial Probationary     _____ Permanent in prob. assign.

_____ Permanent            _____ Temporary

Report for _____ to _____

FULL NAME (LAST NAME FIRST)               SOCIAL SECURITY NO.

POSITION TITLE               DEPARTMENT

### PERFORMANCE RATINGS

Exceeds Work Performance Standards ─┐
Meets Work Performance Standards ─┐ │
Below Work Performance Standards ─┐ │ │

If "Below Work Performance Standards" is checked, please give your reasons for this rating and indicate suggestions made to employee on how to improve.

SUGGESTIONS OR COMMENTS MADE BY IMMEDIATE SUPERVISOR

**1. QUALITY OF WORK**    1. ☐ ☐ ☐
 a. Job knowledge    a. ☐ ☐ ☐
 b. Accuracy    b. ☐ ☐ ☐
 c. Neatness    c. ☐ ☐ ☐
 d. Thoroughness    d. ☐ ☐ ☐

**2. QUANTITY OF WORK**    2. ☐ ☐ ☐
 a. Volume of output    a. ☐ ☐ ☐
 b. Meeting schedules    b. ☐ ☐ ☐

**3. WORK HABITS AND ATTITUDES**    3. ☐ ☐ ☐
 a. Dependability    a. ☐ ☐ ☐
 b. Punctuality    b. ☐ ☐ ☐
 c. Orderliness    c. ☐ ☐ ☐
 d. Compliance with instructions, rules, and regulations    d. ☐ ☐ ☐
 e. Ability to work without immediate supervision    e. ☐ ☐ ☐
 f. Safety practices    f. ☐ ☐ ☐

**4. PERSONAL QUALITIES**    4. ☐ ☐ ☐
 a. Judgment    a. ☐ ☐ ☐
 b. Initiative    b. ☐ ☐ ☐
 c. Adaptability to emergencies and new situations    c. ☐ ☐ ☐

**5. INTERPERSONAL RELATIONS**    5. ☐ ☐ ☐
 a. Employee contacts    a. ☐ ☐ ☐
 b. Public contacts    b. ☐ ☐ ☐

**6. SUPERVISORY ABILITY (if applicable)**    6. ☐ ☐ ☐
 a. Leadership    a. ☐ ☐ ☐
 b. Fairness & impartiality    b. ☐ ☐ ☐
 c. Decision making    c. ☐ ☐ ☐
 d. Training & instructing    d. ☐ ☐ ☐
 e. Planning & assigning    e. ☐ ☐ ☐
 f. Supervisory control    f. ☐ ☐ ☐
 g. Evaluating performance    g. ☐ ☐ ☐
 h. Productivity    h. ☐ ☐ ☐

**7. OVERALL WORK PERFORMANCE**    7. ☐ ☐ ☐

Recommendations by Supervisor:
 ☐ Recommend continued employment
 ☐ Retain in position subject to further evaluation
 ☐ Recommend termination
 ☐ Recommend disciplinary action

Signature of Immediate Supervisor

Title          Date

My signature below is an acknowledgment that I have seen and discussed this evaluation, but it does not necessarily imply agreement with the conclusions of the supervisor.

Signature of Department Head to whom immediate supervisor is responsible

Signature of Employee     Date          Title          Date

When you are evaluated on your work performance, the form will be explained, and your rating will be discussed with you.

Some categories found on these forms are attitude toward job, attitude toward co-workers, attendance, tardiness, ability to follow directions, willingness to take initiative, ability to make good judgments, productivity, quality of work, dependability, personal grooming, ability to get along well with others, and willingness to improve through education and information about the job. Many possible categories exist, and they can be broken down into smaller subcategories if management needs that kind of information about individual employees.

During your evaluation meeting, your supervisor will explain the form to you and carefully discuss your ratings. Generally, you will be asked to sign the evaluation form. Signing the form does not indicate that you agree with the evaluation, only that you received it. Your evaluation will go into your permanent personnel records with your company, and you will be given a copy for your own records.

## The Purpose

The main purpose of the evaluation is to inform both the employer and the employee about the employee's job performance. The information gathered by the job performance evaluation may be utilized in a number of different ways.

You will probably begin your new job on probation, a period during which you can be fired without cause. At the end of three to six months, you will be given an evaluation to ascertain how you are doing and to upgrade your position to that of a full-time, regular employee. Therefore, one use of the evaluation is for advancement.

Another use is to determine whether a pay raise is in order and if so, how much. Most employers understand that good performance should be rewarded. Recognizing workers when they are doing a good job improves morale.

The evaluation may also be used when new positions open up, to discern who among the employees may be best suited to fill them. Especially in the case of advancement, the evaluation plays a big role in the selection process. The evaluation may make clear that an employee would be better suited to work in another department at another type of job. In this case, a transfer may be ordered.

The most important benefit the evaluation offers the employee is the opportunity to discover how well he or she is doing and what can be done to improve performance. Evaluation is part of ongoing education along your path toward your career goal. Sometimes evaluations can be hurtful, but mostly they will be given in the spirit of **constructive criticism**—suggestions that will help you do your job better—and you should receive them as such.

During the evaluation meeting, you will have the opportunity to ask questions or to air any concerns you may be having. Do not bring up petty difficulties with co-workers. Your supervisor will not be impressed if she or he is forced to spend time in that sort of discussion. Rather, bring up issues about work that have been confusing to you. For example, you might want to know how to determine which tasks should take priority, or how to improve some skill with which you are having difficulty. Taking this time to solve troubling, important problems can help raise your level of competence.

Taking the information you learn from your evaluation and immediately putting it to work is in your best interests. If you do that, you will learn to view the evaluation process as a benefit that is important to your development.

# Salary Increases and Promotions

When you began your job with your new company, you agreed on a rate of pay. The final-stage interview is the best time to inquire about procedures for salary increases so that you will know when to expect them. If you are serious about your ultimate career goal, you should also inquire about the possibilities for advancement and promotion. Do you have a future with this company?

No matter how satisfying your job, you will want to know that your employers appreciate you. The most concrete way employers can express appreciation is through a raise in pay.

**Remuneration** (compensation, or pay) comes in many other forms. These forms of remuneration include the benefits that accrue for you during the time you are employed. For example, you could go from earning one week's paid vacation to earning two weeks' paid vacation—a nice benefit, indeed.

As you look to the future, you will set goals that will lead to satisfying your eventual employment needs. These goals will probably include earning increases in pay and may include earning promotions, too. A promotion is another way your employer indicates satisfaction with your work.

You can increase your opportunities for raises and promotions in several ways. Paying attention to appearance and dress is only part of what you can do to further your career.

Davis came to work in the office of a new company just after high school. He is younger than most of the other employees, and he is a little shy. He does his work meticulously. His attitude is excellent because he continually seeks information about how to do his job more effectively. He is eager to advance and to take on more responsibility.

His supervisor, Ms. Jordan, knows Davis is a good worker, but she mistakes his shyness for snobbery and unfriendliness. She is not pleased by what she views as an attitude problem.

Davis's probation has ended, and he will be reviewed. Ms. Jordan calls him into her office for an evaluation. She has filled out an evaluation form, and she explains it carefully to Davis. Davis's ratings are very high on all categories except getting along with co-workers.

Davis is puzzled by this rating and asks Ms. Jordan what it means. As they spend time together chatting, Davis explains to Ms. Jordan that he has a problem with being shy, and she begins to understand that what she has perceived as standoffishness is indeed shyness.

Ms. Jordan is sympathetic to Davis's problem and gives him several ideas to overcome the difficulty. She assures him that with time—and as he feels more secure with his work—his shyness will diminish.

1. *What did Ms. Jordan learn about Davis during his end-of-probation interview?*

2. *Will Davis's evaluation and end-of-probation interview prove helpful to him?* ■

## Types of Compensation

Several forms of compensation are available, depending on the job you have. You may work in the office of a restaurant, in a real estate office, or in some other type of business. Different types of businesses compensate their employees in different ways, including wages, salaries, pay for work accomplished, bonuses, and benefits. Most companies distribute paychecks once a week, every other week, or once a month.

### Wages

People who work in offices often receive a set hourly wage. The amount you will be paid is determined by multiplying the number of hours worked by the agreed-on hourly wage. Generally, your workweek will consist of forty hours. If you work more than forty hours, you are working overtime, and you will be paid one and a half times your hourly wage for each hour of overtime you work.

### Salaries

Many office workers—usually those with supervisory responsibilities—receive a set salary instead of an hourly wage. Thus, no matter how many hours they work, they receive the same salary.

### Pay for Work Accomplished

Some people are paid for each piece of work they do. For example, a word processor may get paid by the number of completed pages. No consideration is made for the amount of time required to do the work, only that the work has been completed. When the work is turned in, the worker is paid. Generally, no benefits of any kind are associated with this pay arrangement.

## Bonuses

A bonus is extra money rewarded or gifted to employees. It might be a special holiday gift, or it might be given because a job was well done. Sometimes, if a company has an especially good season or year, the employer decides to share some of the profits with the employees. Bonuses are an excellent way to boost employee morale.

## Benefits

Recall that benefits are the extra expenses your employer is responsible for, such as various kinds of insurance, Social Security taxes, retirement plans, and so on. Benefits also include vacations and sick leave. Any or all these benefits may be expanded, which increases your total compensation from a company.

# Evaluation of Your Employment Needs: Goal Setting

You will move ahead toward your ultimate career goal faster by setting some career path goals. These goals might include frequency of raises, guidelines for what you want to achieve regarding advancement and promotion, and what you want to accomplish concerning productivity or training on the job.

Have an idea where you want to be in one year and in five years. Often, potential employers will ask, "What do you expect to be doing in five years?" Knowing where you want to go not only helps you answer an employer's question, but it also helps guide you toward your ultimate career and lifestyle goals.

Even if your salary range is adequate for a beginning worker, you may have changing obligations that require you to make more money. For example, you may get married, you may decide you want to save money to further your education, or you may leave the family home, so your expenses may increase. All these changing life situations will require that you upgrade your salary and perhaps your responsibility on the job as well.

From time to time, take a look at your life circumstances. If you are still relatively free of obligations, perhaps you will not need a raise in pay or a promotion for a while. However, things change. Be aware of your own situation so that you can bring about adjustments on the job to meet your changing financial needs.

# Increases in Compensation

In some companies, automatic pay raises are given at certain intervals such as every six months or annually. Often these raises are attached to a good performance evaluation. Salary increases are also related to the kind of job performed. For example, the engineers in a company may get more frequent and higher raises than the office workers. Generally, an industry standard of pay exists for different types of jobs.

Not all companies have a standard procedure for awarding pay increases. In companies that do not, the employer decides when a pay raise should be granted, and in some cases the employer waits for a request for a raise from the employee. If you must request a raise, you will feel more comfortable doing so if you follow the suggestions given next.

## Is Now a Good Time to Request a Pay Raise?

If you think you need to ask for a raise, ask yourself these questions:

1. Have I been on the job a sufficient length of time to warrant asking for a raise?

2. Have I learned my job well and become very efficient, and is my productivity adequate?

3. Do I have good relationships with other employees?

4. Have I been able to make some crucial decisions and judgments that positively affected my work? In other words, have I acted independently when appropriate to do so?

5. Have I had good evaluations and other feedback about my work from my supervisor and co-workers?

6. Does the company seem to be in good condition financially? Can the company afford to pay more now, or would waiting a few weeks until things improve be better?

With the exception of question 6, asking yourself these questions can help you prepare for requesting a raise. If the answer to any of your questions is no, take some time to improve that area before you go to your boss seeking a raise.

## How Do I Ask for a Raise?

If you have decided that the timing is right and that you have, in fact, earned a raise, request an appointment with your supervisor to ask for one. Asking for a raise may be scary, but you will be able to do it. In some companies, if you do not ask, you will stay at the same level of pay for longer than necessary.

First, ask your supervisor what workers must do to get a raise. Your supervisor may then list the requirements for a higher rate of pay. If you have accomplished all of them, say so—and say that you hope to receive your raise soon.

If, on the other hand, your supervisor tells you the company has no set standard to follow, that it has no rules for granting raises, then you must simply state your case. List your good points and talk with confidence about why you deserve a raise. Be respectful—as you always should be—to your boss. Show that you believe you have earned a raise, and you want his or her thoughts on the matter.

If you are denied, accept the decision—and ask what your supervisor wants you to improve in order to earn a raise. Take this direction seriously and begin at once to work on the areas that need improvement so that your raise will be forthcoming at your next request.

# Promotions

By now, you probably know what attributes make a good employee. You have read about a pleasant attitude, the ability to get along with co-workers, good work habits, enthusiasm and desire to learn, and the willingness to take responsibility for your job and decisions related to it. In this chapter you have read about appropriate attire and grooming. If you put into practice all the ideas discussed in this book, you will be a perfect employee. Your bosses will love you and eagerly and regularly promote you along your career path.

**TIP** Office politics are a reality, so try to be aware of how they impact your office. If you are interested in advancing, learn who listens to whom, and which alliances are important. Sometimes in an office, one person will be another employee's mentor, or informal sponsor. Find out about these relationships, because this information may be helpful in aiding your chances for promotion. Do not spy on people or be a busybody, but educate yourself about who relies on whom and how things get done. Your understanding of these things will assist your advancement in the company. ■

# Irene Kinoshita

*CEO*
*Ascolta Training Company*

**Q.** Ms. Kinoshita, what advice would you like to pass on to a group of business students?

**A.** They should understand that downsizing is the result of asking the workforce to redefine itself. Things are changing fast, so those entering the workforce should always be in the learning mode. Your skills are quickly outdated, and you should not expect that the job you are doing now will be the same that you will be doing next week.

The other thing that is really important is not to limit yourself to one job. Instead of saying, for instance, I have a wonderful background in finance and that is all I am going to know, you need to be a whole company person and understand all aspects of a business.

**Q.** What do you look for when you hire people?

**A.** Especially in a small company, we need people who are flexible, people who will say, "That wasn't in my job description but it needed to be done."

I look for communication skills—how well they present themselves, and I expect their writing and speaking skills to be good. I also look for creativity. Are they going to plug along and just do everything I tell them to do, or are they going to create some good ideas, too?

---

Sounds easy, doesn't it? However, you will probably need to consider one more element. You have learned about setting goals to guide you toward your ultimate career and lifestyle. The only missing element is your determination.

As you move along your career path, you will need to demonstrate that you are eager and willing to take on new responsibilities and learn new things. Sometimes, you will need to exercise a degree of assertiveness. Often, you will need to demonstrate initiative, taking on a little more than you are asked to do. Act like you are wearing a sign that reads, "I want to get ahead, I want to succeed, I want to do well." Do not be obnoxious and overdo it, but make clear that you are serious about your job and your career.

Your bosses will be looking for this attitude. They want to advance people who not only have received excellent job performance evaluations, but who are also eager to move up. Be aware of when promotions become available and how to apply for them.

## When Do Promotions Become Available?

Opportunities for promotions become available for two reasons. The first is when an employee who has greater responsibility than you vacates her or his position. The second is when the company creates a new position with greater responsibility than your present one.

In growing companies, new positions are created fairly often. If, in your initial interview, you asked whether promotions would be possible, your boss already knows you are interested. Your good evaluations and your attitude can help your employer make a promotion decision in your favor.

## How Do I Apply for a Promotion?

Your company may make decisions about promotions without input from eligible employees. Some companies, however, advertise that a position is available and that they are seeking someone from within the company to fill it.

If you are seriously interested in promotion, stay alert to changes in the office. Know when someone is vacating a position that might interest you.

Before you actively seek promotion, ask yourself the questions that were outlined earlier about asking for a raise. Make certain you are ready before you ask to be included in the selection process. Then, let your supervisor know that you are interested and that you eagerly seek more responsibility and opportunity.

If a formal selection process is used, prepare your application as carefully as you would when applying for a new job.

# Further Education and Training

You can further enhance the skills that will take you toward your ultimate career and lifestyle goals through formal education and training.

When you initially investigated careers, you determined the types of education and training you would need for an entry-level position and for advancement within each career. After you begin work in the career of your choice, you will probably learn of some additional education and training alternatives that will help you advance in your career. An occasional workshop or **seminar** (meeting in which information is presented and discussed) satisfies the education and training requirements to advance in some careers and in some industries. Other careers and industries require years of formal education for advancement.

In some instances, your company will train you for most of the positions it has available. You will receive the training as you receive the advancements—or when you take a new position in a different department. Willingly participate in all training that your company offers—training will be your ticket to the future.

As you may have already discovered, after you leave high school you may choose from a variety of ways to receive the education and training needed to advance along your career path. These alternatives include on-the-job training programs, vocational schools, community colleges, technical colleges, and four-year colleges and universities.

## On-the-Job Training Programs

On-the-job training is learning by doing. This training is usually provided for jobs that do not require formal education.

## Vocational Schools

The kinds of skills needed to work in an office are often taught as part of the vocational curriculum offered by most high schools.

Many opportunities for further education and training are available. Some companies will reimburse employees for tuition paid to take classes to improve their performance on the job.

If you want more intensive training in office skills, a vocational school in your area can probably provide it. The cost of attending a vocational school varies, but it may be more than the cost of attending your local community college, where you can usually receive similar training.

## Community and Technical Colleges

You can earn up to two years of college-level credit in a community or technical college, and the tuition is relatively inexpensive. Most community colleges offer two types of programs. One program prepares students in general education so that they can transfer to a four-year college or university. The other program provides instruction in vocational skills, such as office skills or computer repair, that requires two years to complete.

Technical colleges also offer programs that run from one to two years. Courses at technical colleges are often similar to those provided at community colleges. However, they are generally designed for very specific careers such as computer repair, licensed practical nursing, medical assistant, medical transcription, diesel engine repair, graphic design, computer programming, computer networking, and so on.

Community colleges and technical colleges often have close ties to the local business establishment and tailor their programs to meet the needs of local businesses.

## Colleges and Universities

Some four-year institutions are less concerned with training students for specific occupations than with providing a general, liberal arts education. However, many four-year colleges and universities offer vocational specialties such as accounting and computer engineering.

Although many colleges and universities are supported by the state, a college education can still be very expensive. Give as much thought as possible to what you want to do in the future. If your chosen profession does not require the expense and rigors of a four-year college program, choosing another type of educational setting may be advantageous.

Whatever your decision about further education and training, you know what is expected of you, and you know what you can expect of the people for whom you work. You are well on your way to succeeding in your new office career. You can look on your new life as an adventure, with limitless possibilities. You can be and do whatever you choose. With the right information and effort, you will be successful in your new career.

## Recall Time

*Answer the following questions:*

**1.** What are the main purposes for conducting a job performance evaluation? List the categories that might be rated on an evaluation form.

**2.** What does your employer provide that can be considered benefits?

**3.** What are several questions you might want to ask yourself before you ask your boss for a raise or for a promotion?

**4.** Several different types of training and educational programs are available to you. What are some of them? Describe why you would choose one or another.

## Summary

After you have become successful on your first real job, what is next?

One way you tell your employer that you are ready to do more is by your appearance, which signals many things about you. Look like the person you want to become.

Attending to your health is a major step toward looking well. Exercise, proper eating habits, sufficient sleep, and a reasonable social life are the keys to that healthy, attractive glow.

You also want to be clean, neat, and businesslike. Though trendy clothes are fun for leisure time, if worn to work they imply that you do not take your job seriously.

Much research has demonstrated which clothing helps one to achieve a successful career. For women, appropriate dress includes skirted suits of blue, gray, or beige, with a contrasting blouse, neutral-colored hose, and plain-colored pumps.

Men should wear suits or slacks and sportcoats of blue, gray, or beige, with shirts in solid, pale, contrasting colors. Research shows that when men wear a necktie, others perceive them as respectable and responsible.

When planning your wardrobe, select clothing that is not too expensive and that will hold up well. Taking care of your clothes helps them last so that over time you can increase the variety of things you have to wear, and you will always look good.

As you seek advancement, you will find that your regular job performance evaluations provide valuable information. These evaluations are conducted by your supervisor, and generally he or she will use a standardized form and procedures so that every employee is treated the same.

At the time of your employment, you may have discussed salary increases. After you have been on the job for a while and you have been doing a good job, you may want to ask for a raise. In some companies, raises are connected with the performance evaluation and are given on a regular basis without a request from the employee. In other companies, you may have to ask your supervisor for a raise.

Setting employment goals will help you determine when you need a pay raise, how rapidly you wish to advance, and what additional training you will need.

When positions become available in your company, check your career goals to see if the new positions advance you in the direction you want to take. You may have to apply formally for a new job, or your bosses may select someone on the basis of her or his job performance evaluations.

When you determine what direction you want to take, you may need to investigate the educational and training requirements for that job.

When you begin to think about your career path and how best to achieve your goals, you will want to consider the following:

- Do everything you know how to do to be successful in the position you now hold.
- Meet the expectations of your employers regarding attitude, productivity, and good work habits.
- Be careful about your grooming. Keep yourself clean and neat, with your hair properly combed. If you are a woman, make sure your makeup is right.
- Choose your wardrobe carefully to reflect how you feel about advancement and taking on more responsibility. Avoid trendy clothes.
- If you are a man, always wear a necktie to important meetings and every day to work if it is appropriate.
- Understand the purpose of your job evaluations and use them effectively.
- Know how and when to ask for a raise.
- Know how to ask for a promotion.
- Research what your chosen position will require in terms of education and training. Know the types of training that are available.

# before you leave...

**When you have completed this chapter, answer the following questions:**

1. What is the title of a guide on how to dress for success?

2. What is the most important status symbol of men's attire?

3. What is the main purpose of an evaluation?

4. What are six questions you should ask yourself before you ask for a raise?

# Review & Application

## Check Your Knowledge

1. How can you assess how well you are progressing on your job?

2. You should keep in mind several things about grooming. Name them.

3. Good health plays an important role in how you look. Discuss several ways you can help take good care of your health.

4. What should women wear to work?

5. What does the way we dress say about us?

6. What does the research tell us about men wearing neckties?

7. What are the best colors for men's clothing?

8. Describe the purposes of a job performance evaluation.

9. How can a job performance evaluation be helpful to you?

10. What should you consider when thinking about asking for an increase in salary?

11. What should you consider when thinking about asking for a promotion?

12. How do positions in a company become available?

13. Name three types of training and education.

14. Discuss the advantages of attending a community college.

15. What is on-the-job training? What kinds of jobs require this type of training?

16. How are vocational schools different from training programs in other kinds of educational settings?

## Review Your Vocabulary

On a separate piece of paper, write the letter of the vocabulary word that is described below.

_____ 1. a meeting in which information is presented and discussed

_____ 2. suggestions that will help you do your job better

_____ 3. compensation, or pay

a. constructive criticism

b. remuneration

c. seminar

## Discuss and Analyze an Office Situation

1. Garth has done a fine job in his new position. He is respected as a man who has a good attitude, is always willing to take on more responsibility, is reliable, and is capable. A new position has opened up in his department that requires more responsibility and offers a better salary. Garth's supervisor has offered him the position. Garth does not know whether to accept the offer because he has not really thought through what he wants to accomplish in the long run.

   Garth has not taken a fundamental planning step. What is it? What would you do if you were Garth?

2. Rosemary has been on the job for several months, and she has never had an evaluation. She approaches her supervisor and asks to have an evaluation and, hopefully, a salary increase. At the evaluation meeting, Rosemary's supervisor gives her an evaluation that is not too favorable and denies her request for a pay raise. Rosemary is surprised and hurt by her supervisor's evaluation. She thought she was doing whatever was requested of her.

   How can Rosemary use this evaluation to her advantage?

## Practice Basic Skills

### Math

A person may be remunerated in several ways for the work she or he does. When agreeing to a certain type of pay, you should be aware of what you might be making if you were employed under another type of pay structure. For example, compare the following:

- *Job 1.* You work forty hours per week at $6 per hour, and you expect to work five overtime hours each week at $9 per hour.

- *Job 2.* You work the same number of regular and overtime hours as in Job 1, but you are offered a flat salary of $300 per week.

Assuming that the two jobs are exactly alike except for the method of payment, which job should you take?

## English

When your supervisor evaluates your work, he or she will notice whether you use formal or informal language. In business settings, informal language is not appropriate. Read the following paragraph, then rewrite or rekey it in standard English on a separate piece of paper.

I do not really know what I wanna do with myself. I like this job well enough, I mean, it's pretty groovy, and it gives me some dough to buy tapes and stuff. Maybe what I need is to go to college for a while. College might be radical. Lots of cool people to meet and swinging parties to go to. This work stuff is for the birds, anyway.

## Proofreading

In your office job, you may have occasion to proofread a letter or report that a supervisor hands you to keyboard. See if you can find the mistakes in the following paragraph, and rewrite or rekey it correctly on a separate paper.

We are hapy to anounse that our knew line of clothing is out. We hope you wil join us at our fall sho where our new lien will be shown. The springe fashions will be off particular interst to you becaus the stiles are fresh, cool, and exciting.

The shwo will be heald on Mondy, Juli 23rd at 3:00 P.M. at the Coral Room of the Blue Lagoon Hotel. Please let us know if you entend to atend. make your resergvations by callin 714-555-1109.

## Apply Your Knowledge

1. Think about what you want to accomplish in the next five years. Write a comprehensive goal statement that includes specific steps to accomplish in a specific time frame.

2. Visit a clothing store. Keep in mind the kinds of statements you want to make with what you wear. Take a notebook and make notes about things you see that you would like to buy. If you bought all the garments that you feel would make up an appropriate wardrobe, what would the clothing items be? How much would the items cost?

## Using the Reference Manual

Open file ch21ref.doc. Use the interoffice memorandums section of the Reference Manual at the back of the book to help you follow an acceptable format using the current date. Assume that you are the writer and that you are sending this memo to the office staff. Save and print.

Because your appearance on the job affects your progress in our company, I feel we need to cover some "unwritten" norms about dressing for success.

1. Dressing for success begins with cleanliness and being neat and attractive in your appearance. People who exercise regularly, get sufficient sleep, eat properly, and do not have excessive social lives also tend to look better.

2. The key to an appropriate office hairstyle is that it be neatly trimmed, brushed, and never too faddish. Women might want to seek a consultant to help them decide what colors and amount of makeup to wear. Men who choose not to be clean-shaven must be sure to trim a mustache or beard regularly.

3. An overall guideline to follow in dress is to dress like the people who hold the positions to which you aspire. Basically, for women, a skirted suit in a dark blue, beige, or gray—with a contrasting blouse—is the most appropriate office attire. For men, blues, browns, and grays in different weaves are the colors of choice for suits, slacks, and sportcoats. These colors may be combined with contrasting dress shirts in white, blue, yellow, and occasionally other colors.

If you have any questions about these items, please feel free to address them at our next staff meeting on Monday morning.

# CAREER PORTFOLIO

## PART FIVE: Employment Skills

### Specific Activities to Complete

Select at least two of the following items for inclusion in your Career Portfolio, using the information from Chapters 18 through 21.

1. Key the procedure you will follow to locate possible office jobs in the community. Save and print this list. (Be sure you proof according to the instructions given previously on page 84.) Insert this list as the first item in your Career Portfolio binder behind the fifth tab, entitled "Employment Skills."

2. Key a sample letter of application. Save, print, and insert this letter behind the fifth tab also.

3. Key a current résumé. Show a draft of the résumé to a fellow student and incorporate any suggestions that may improve its appearance. Save, print, and insert your résumé behind the fifth tab.

4. Key a listing of where in your town you can go to receive additional training after this course. Consider programs in which people prepare to be office workers by taking courses in business schools, by working on office and computer application certificates at a community college, and by enrolling in business administration courses at a local university. Save, print, and insert the list behind the fifth tab.

# LETTER STYLES

This section will expose you to different letter styles. All rules given here are up-to-date with current business standards. However, when beginning a new office job, always check first with your boss to see if the company has its own rules and preferences.

## Major Parts of a Letter

**Date**—The date is keyed two to three lines below the bottom of the letterhead. If you are not using letterhead paper, begin 12 to 14 lines from the top of the paper.

**Letter Address**—The letter address is keyed four lines below the date.

**Greeting**—The greeting is keyed a double-space after the inside address. Also called the *salutation*.

**Body**—The body of the letter begins a double-space after the greeting.

**Closing**—The closing is keyed a double-space after the ending of the body of the letter. Also called the *complimentary close.*

**Sender's Name**—The name of the person who signs the letter is keyed four lines below the closing.

**Keyboard Operator's Initials**—Your initials as keyboarder are keyed in small letters a double-space after the sender's name.

**Enclosure Notation**—The enclosure notation is keyed a double-space after the keyboard operator's initials.

**Copies Notation**—The copies notation is keyed a double-space after the enclosure notation or a double-space after the keyboard operator's initials if the letter does not have an enclosure notation.

## Format

Letter formats will vary from company to company; however, the following are the three most common formats used by business today.

**Block Letter Format**—The entire letter is keyed even with the left margin (see Figure A.1).

**Modified Block Letter Format**—The date and closing begin at the center (see Figure A.2, page R-2).

**Simplified Block Letter Format**—The simplified block letter format has no greeting or closing, has a subject line, uses the block arrangement (see Figure A.3, page R-2).

## Punctuation

Two different rules dominate letter punctuation for the greeting and closing. These rules are as follows:

**Mixed Punctuation**—For the mixed punctuation rule, a colon is used after the greeting, and a comma is used after the closing (see Figure A.1).

**Open Punctuation**—For the open punctuation rule, no punctuation is used after the greeting or after the closing (see Figure A.2, page R-2).

### FIGURE A.1 • Block Letter Format

February 2, 20—
(4 returns)

Mr. Jessie Johnson
44 Warren Avenue
San Antonio, TX 76435-4422

Dear Mr. Johnson:

The next meeting of the Southwestern Association of CPAs will be held at the Newport Hyatt in San Antonio on April 8 at 7 p.m. This meeting will be a joint venture of the SACPA and the Future Accountants Association. The topic of the meeting will be "Automating the Accounting Office."

The main speaker of the evening will be Katherine Cornell, president of the National Association of CPAs. Cornell has just completed designing and installing fully automated facilities for her firm's new location in Atlanta. The office of the future has arrived for this company.

I know you will not want to miss the meeting. Your registration form, which must be returned to me by March 1, is enclosed.

Sincerely,


Harriet Yatamoto
Meeting Coordinator

ak

Enclosure

January 4, 20—

(4 returns)

Robert Alvarez
46 Market Avenue
Plymouth, MA 02360-4653

Dear Mr. Alvarez

Because styles and popular tastes change, we make a point of see-ing that our magazine stays ahead of the times. Apparently we have succeeded. The American Society of Styles recently presented our magazine with a national award.

Readers of such a magazine are also ahead of the times, and we invite you to extend your subscription now before it expires. We have made renewing your subscription easy with the enclosed reply envelope.

Thank you for your continued support. I look forward to your reply.

Sincerely

Diane Eastbrook

mk

Enclosure

## Letter Placement

Before beginning to key a letter, decide where to set your margins. For some keyboarders, margin settings depend on the size of the letter. If you are not sure where to set your margins, use the following informa-tion as a guide:

| Size of Letter (Estimated) | Side Margins | Dateline Position |
|---|---|---|
| Short (fewer than 100 words in body) | 2 inches | line 18 |
| Average (101–200 words in body) | 1.5 inches | line 16 |
| Long (more than 200 words in body) | 1 inch | line 14 |
| Two-page | 1 inch | line 14 |

Many progressive keyboard operators leave their margins at one setting for all work.

December 12, 20—

(4 returns)

Mrs. Julia Chung
CRANCO
P.O. Box 139
Lowell, MA 02660-0139

(3 returns)

Simplified Block Letter Format

(3 returns)

This letter is written in the time-saving simplified block letter for-mat. To key this format, follow these steps:

1. Use the extreme block format with blocked paragraphs.

2. Key the letter address four lines below the date.

3. Omit the formal salutation and complimentary close.

4. Use a subject line and key it in capital letters or capital and low-ercase letters a triple-space below the address; triple-space from the subject line to the first line of the letter body.

5. Key enumerated items flush at the left margin; indent unnum-bered listed items five spaces.

6. Key the sender's name and title in capital letters or capital and lowercase letters four spaces below the letter body.

7. Key the keyboard operator's initials a double-space below the sender's name.

Correspondents in your company will like the simplified block let-ter format not only for the distinctive "eye appeal" it gives letters, but also because it reduces letter-writing costs.

F. James Lucey
President

kc

c: Sue Rodeo

# ENVELOPE ADDRESSING

Many people blame the Postal Service for lost or delayed mail. However, many times mail is lost or delayed because of errors in the address. This section presents good business practice for keying addresses on envelopes.

## Return Address

Most companies have their own envelopes with a printed return address. However, if these envelopes are not available, begin to key the return address two lines down and three spaces from the left edge.

## Letter Address

An experienced keyboarder who uses a typewriter to address envelopes inserts an envelope and positions it into the correct place without counting lines from the top. If you have not keyed envelopes before, a good rule to remember for business envelopes is to key the address near the center—about 2 inches from the top edge and 4 inches from the left edge.

An address must contain at least three lines; avoid addresses of more than six lines. The last line of an address must contain only three items: the city, the state, and the ZIP Code, preferably ZIP+4.

## Things to Remember

Envelope addresses may be keyed in caps and lower case or in all caps/no punctuation. All caps with no punctuation is recommended so that mail may be sorted by electronic scanners. (1) Always single-space; (2) key all states with two capital letters and no periods; (3) current Postal Service regulations state that the bottom of the envelope (about six lines up) must be free of all notations so that the envelope can go through the electronic scanning equipment.

## Notations

1. Attention—keyed in the letter address
2. Personal or Confidential—keyed a double-space below the return address

The following address formats are recommended for envelopes. Table A.1 shows the postal abbreviations for the United States and Canada.

The Noodle Corporation
Attention: Mrs. Shirley Gonzales
2399 Palm Avenue
Burlingame, CA 94010-2388

Mr. Paul Wong
131 Battery Street
Portland, OR 93616-1244

Ms. Julia Singleton
Buy-Rite Company
9 Almond Way
Boston, MA 02368-1900

Miss Rose Marie Frazier
Human Resources Department
Save Now Bank
34 Montgomery Street
San Francisco, CA 94115-3456

Note: The Postal Service prefers all capital letters and no punctuation.

THE NOODLE CORPORATION
ATTENTION MRS SHIRLEY GONZALES
2399 PALM AVENUE
BURLINGAME CA 94010-2388

MR PAUL WONG
131 BATTERY STREET
PORTLAND OR 93616-1244

MS JULIA SINGLETON
BUY RITE COMPANY
9 ALMOND WAY
BOSTON MA 02368-1900

MISS ROSE MARIE FRAZIER
HUMAN RESOURCES DEPARTMENT
SAVE NOW BANK
34 MONTGOMERY STREET
SAN FRANCISCO CA 94115-3456

**TABLE A.1 • Postal Abbreviations**

| US State, District, or Territory | Two-Letter Abbreviation | US State, District, or Territory | Two-Letter Abbreviation |
|---|---|---|---|
| Alabama | AL | North Dakota | ND |
| Alaska | AK | Ohio | OH |
| Arizona | AZ | Oklahoma | OK |
| Arkansas | AR | Oregon | OR |
| California | CA | Pennsylvania | PA |
| Canal Zone | CZ | Puerto Rico | PR |
| Colorado | CO | South Carolina | SC |
| Connecticut | CT | South Dakota | SD |
| Delaware | DE | Tennessee | TN |
| District of Columbia | DC | Texas | TX |
| Florida | FL | Utah | UT |
| Georgia | GA | Vermont | VT |
| Guam | GU | Virgin Islands | VI |
| Hawaii | HI | Virginia | VA |
| Idaho | ID | Washington | WA |
| Illinois | IL | West Virginia | WV |
| Indiana | IN | Wisconsin | WI |
| Iowa | IA | Wyoming | WY |
| Kansas | KS | | |
| Kentucky | KY | | |
| Louisiana | LA | **Canada** | **Two-Letter Abbreviation** |
| Maine | ME | | |
| Maryland | MD | Alberta | AB |
| Massachusetts | MA | British Columbia | BC |
| Michigan | MI | Labrador | LB |
| Minnesota | MN | Manitoba | MB |
| Mississippi | MS | New Brunswick | NB |
| Montana | MT | Newfoundland | NF |
| Nebraska | NE | Northwest Territories | NT |
| Nevada | NV | Nova Scotia | NS |
| New Hampshire | NH | Ontario | ON |
| New Jersey | NJ | Prince Edward Island | PE |
| New Mexico | NM | Quebec | PQ |
| New York | NY | Saskatchewan | SK |
| North Carolina | NC | Yukon Territory | YT |

# INTEROFFICE MEMORANDUMS

Correspondence that stays within a company is keyed using interoffice memorandum format. This format is arranged in various ways, but it always contains these headings: To, From, Date, and Subject. When keying memorandums, keep the following points in mind:

- Memorandums are informal and should never contain titles. This rule also holds true for the terms Mr., Mrs., Miss, Ms. Use no salutation or complimentary close.
- Use block format.
- Triple-space from the subject to the body of the memo.
- Key keyboard operator's initials, enclosure notation, and copies notation in the usual locations.

You will find the following formats used for memorandum headings:

1. TO:
   FROM:
   DATE:
   SUBJECT:

2.      TO:
     FROM:
      DATE:
   SUBJECT:

3. TO:                          DATE:
   FROM:                        SUBJECT:

# PUNCTUATION

Punctuation is a means of making written communication easier to read and comprehend. The following rules will provide you with an easy guide to the most common punctuation questions, but it should not be considered a final authority.

## Comma

An often-used form of punctuation, the comma is also the source of much confusion and many errors. It should be used as follows:

*Rule:* Before conjunctions that join independent clauses.

*Examples:* The meeting is at three o'clock, and we will be on time.

The keyboarder finished the project, but he did not get it mailed before the deadline.

*Rule:* To set off a subordinate clause preceding a main clause.

*Example:* If you finish your exam on time, you will be given an extra reward.

*Rule:* To separate words and phrases in a series.

*Examples:* The company sold tires, batteries, spark plugs, and mirrors.

The secretaries in the office, the clerks in the plant, and the managers in the factory are all willing to change to flexible schedules.

*Rule:* To separate dependent clauses.

*Examples:* With your help, we will complete the task by Wednesday.

As soon as the machines are repaired, we will return to work.

*Rule:* To set off nonrestrictive clauses.

*Examples:* Juanita, who is in the other room, unlocked the office this morning.

The Fifth Avenue bus, which is usually late, is the one for Clover City.

*Rule:* To set off introductory words or phrases.

*Examples:* Incidentally, I left the lights on.

By the way, I saw George yesterday.

*Rule:* To separate two or more adjectives when each modifies the same noun. Do not use a comma between the two adjectives if one modifies a combination of the noun and the other adjective.

*Examples:* The blue-eyed, blond young woman walked down the street.

Mr. Jones was an important American diplomat.

*Rule:* Before *Inc.* in a company name or according to the company's preference. After *Inc.* in a sentence if a comma is used before *Inc.*

*Example:* Lewis & Wong, *Inc.,* would like an answer to its letter.

*Rule:* Before *Jr.* and *Sr.* in a person's name or according to the person's preference. After *Jr./Sr.* in a sentence if a comma is used before *Jr./Sr.*

*Example:* Samuel Adams, Jr. was elected to the board of directors.

*Rule:* To set off words in direct address.

*Examples:* Thank you for the offer, Mr. Pate.

Your services were most appreciated, Madam President.

*Rule:* To separate the day of the month from the year, and the year when used with the month.

*Example:* On July 20, 2001, Susan graduated from college.

*Rule:* To set off unrelated numbers.

*Example:* In the World Series of 1990, 45 runs were scored.

## Semicolon

Use the semicolon as follows:

*Rule:* To separate two independent clauses that are not joined by a conjunction.

*Examples:* The plane flew low; it began to spray the tomato plants.

The new machine arrived; it was broken.

*Rule:* To avoid confusion when two independent clauses contain other commas.

*Example:* The word processing machine, which was broken, was purchased at Ames & Harris, Inc.; they will replace it today.

*Rule:* To avoid confusion when a sentence contains words in a series.

*Example:* We have offices in San Francisco, California; Portland, Oregon; Seattle, Washington; Reno, Nevada; and Ogden, Utah.

*Rule:* To introduce an illustration composed of an independent clause.

*Examples:* Be sure to ask good questions; for example, what is my future with the company, when will I be evaluated, and when will I receive a promotion.

Manuel is the coordinator; that is, he schedules all classes.

## Colon

Use the colon as follows:

*Rule:* To introduce a list or a quotation. Capitalize the first word after a colon if it begins a complete sentence.

*Examples:* You may now purchase the following items: shoes, dresses, shirts, and ties.

Patrick Henry said: "Give me liberty or give me death."

*Rule:* To separate hours and minutes.

*Example:* It is now 10:15 P.M. in New York City.

*Rule:* After the salutation in a formal business letter.

*Example:* Dear Mr. Jones: I am writing in response . . .

## Hyphen

Use the hyphen as follows:

*Rule:* To join compound numbers when they are spelled out.

*Examples:* We have twenty-nine calculators in the office.

We began the employment office with forty-three job orders.

*Rule:* To write fractions when they are used as words.

*Examples:* Only one-half of the workers attended the party.

Exactly three-fourths of the work was done on time.

*Rule:* To join compound adjectives modifying the same word.

*Examples:* We decided to send the package by third-class mail.

She was the most hard-to-reach executive in the whole building.

He received an award for the best-kept plants within the complex.

*Rule:* To join *self* and *ex* to another word.

*Examples:* He was known as a self-made man.

His ex-boss was in the audience.

*Rule:* To be certain your meaning is clear.

*Examples:* The workers began to re-cover the office sofa.

He was quite angry because he was told to re-lay the carpet.

## Apostrophe

Use the apostrophe as follows:

*Rule:* To indicate the plural form of lowercase letters, symbols, and words.

*Examples:* Your keyboarding exercise contained three *b*'s keyed as *v*'s.

For line 3, use *#*'s and not *#*s.

Six misspelled *and*'s appeared in the sentence.

*Rule:* To indicate the omission of numbers and to indicate the omission of letters in contractions.

*Examples:* She is from the class of '02.

I'll be at the office by 3 P.M.

## Apostrophe in Possessive

*Rule:* For the possessive form of a noun that does not end in *s*, add *'s*.

*Examples:* cat's paw, clerk's pay, men's hats, children's milk

*Rule:* For the possessive form of a noun that ends in *s*, if the word is singular, add *'s* unless the word is awkward to pronounce; if the word is plural, add the apostrophe only.

*Examples:* singular—class's pet, press's ink, dress's sleeves

plural—clerks' union, streets' lights, trucks' tires, houses' numbers

*Rule:* For the possessive form of proper names; if the name is singular and has one syllable, add *'s*; if the name is singular and has more than one syllable, add the apostrophe only; if the name is plural and ends in *s*, add the apostrophe only.

*Examples:* Ross's, Dennis', Charles's, Adams', Andersons', plaster of Paris' reputation

*Rule:* For the possessive form of compound nouns, add the apostrophe to the last word. (If the compound is plural, reword the sentence and avoid using the possessive form.)

*Examples:* mother-in-law's house

passer-by's reaction

(Instead of writing *my sister-in-laws' children*, write *the children of my sisters-in law*.)

## Quotation Marks

Use quotation marks as follows:

*Rule:* To enclose direct quotations.

*Example:* Mary asked, "Will you please repeat the assignment?"

*Rule:* To set off titles of book chapters, short stories, articles, speeches, songs, and poems.

*Example:* The story was titled "The Boy and His Dog."

*Rule:* To set off slang words, definitions, and words intended to show irony, and to emphasize words.

*Examples:* The girl wore a "rad" outfit.

Recessions cannot be gauged solely by the "gross domestic product."

It's such a "beautiful" day here in the rain.

## Quotation Marks with Other Forms of Punctuation

*Rule:* Periods and commas are always placed inside closing quotation marks.

*Examples:* Julia said, "I would like to go home now."

"I would like to go home now," said Julia.

*Rule:* Exclamation points and question marks go inside or outside a quotation mark, depending on whether they are part of the whole sentence or part of the quoted material.

*Examples:* Mary asked, "Did I miss dinner?"

Did Mary say, "I must have missed dinner"?

## Parentheses

Use parentheses as follows:

*Rule:* To set off clauses, phrases, or words that clarify or explain part of a sentence but are not essential to the meaning of the sentence.

*Examples:* The nicest car (the Lexus™) was not chosen.

The larger (20' × 20') rooms were much nicer.

The merchandise was damaged (as were all the parcels in the lot), and we returned it unopened.

*Rule:* To clarify dollar amounts.

*Example:* The cost to you will be thirty dollars ($30).

# GRAMMAR

## Abbreviations

*Rule:* Spell out titles of persons when they precede last names. Exceptions to this rule would be Mr., Mrs., Ms., and Messrs.

*Examples:* Captain Poldark

Doctor Singh

Professor Rosario

*Rule:* Abbreviate Jr., Sr., Esq. when they follow a name.

*Examples:* Victor Worg, Jr.

Francis Borghi, Esq.

*Rule:* Abbreviate academic titles when they follow a name.

*Example:* Patricia Frazier, Ph.D.

*Rule:* Do not abbreviate days, months, or addresses.

*Examples:* The interview will be Thursday, June 11.

The company is located at 246 Corbett Avenue in San Ramon.

## Spacing of Abbreviations

*Rule:* Abbreviations that consist of all capital letters usually do not have periods or spaces between the letters.

*Examples:* YMCA    FBI

*Rule:* The trend is to use no periods and no spaces in abbreviated academic degrees and geographic names.

*Examples:* BS degree    USA    MD    CPA

*Rule:* For time, use periods but no spaces.

*Examples:* a.m.    p.m.

## Plurals

*Rule:* The basic rule is to add *s* to form the plural of most words.

*Example:* pencil, pencils

*Rule:* If a noun ends in *y* and is preceded by a vowel, add *s* to form the plural.

*Example:* key, keys

*Rule:* If a noun ends in *y* and is preceded by a consonant, form the plural by changing the *y* to *i* and adding *es*.

*Example:* deputy, deputies

*Rule:* If a noun ends in *o* and is preceded by a vowel, add *s* to form the plural.

*Example:* trio, trios

*Rule:* If a noun ends in *o* and is preceded by a consonant, add *es* to form the plural.

*Example:* cargo, cargoes

*Rule:* Some nouns form their plurals in irregular ways.

*Examples:* child, children; mouse, mice; woman, women; ox, oxen

*Rule:* If a compound noun is a solid word, form the plural by treating the last part of the word as if it were alone.

*Examples:* doghouse, doghouses; guidebook, guidebooks

*Rule:* If compound words are spaced or hyphenated, form the plural by changing the main part of the word.

*Example:* mother-in-law, mothers-in-law

Note: The English language has many exceptions, so consult a dictionary when in doubt.

## Numbers

*Rule:* Spell out numbers one through ten. Use figures for numbers above ten.

*Examples:* We will eliminate five positions because of the contract loss.

The hotel served 352 guests last year.

*Rule:* Spell out indefinite numbers.

*Example:* Thousands of people were at the concert.

*Rule:* Use both words and figures for large numbers.

*Examples:* 23 billion, 9 million

*Rule:* Spell out fractions.

*Example:* Nearly one-half of the workers were absent.

*Rule:* Spell out numbers that begin a sentence.

*Example:* Eleven new restaurants opened in the area.

*Rule:* Use both words and figures when two numbers appear together. Spell out the shorter number.

*Example:* Please order four 22-inch tapes.

*Rule:* For measurements, use figures.

*Example:* She gained 12 pounds last month.

*Rule:* Use figures for clock time.

*Example:* We begin work at 8:30 A.M.

*Rule:* Use words for periods of time.

*Example:* The project took thirty hours to complete.

*Rule:* For numbers in street addresses, use the basic rule of spelling out numbers ten and under. For house numbers, the number one is the only number that must be written as a word.

*Examples:* We moved to Seventh Avenue.

The meeting will be held at 340 East 27th Street.

I live at One Westwood Drive.

## Capitalization

Capitalize words as follows:

*Rule:* The first word in a sentence.

*Example:* The secretarial position is advertised as that of an administrative assistant.

*Rule:* Proper names of persons, places, and things.

*Examples:* My uncle is Walter Gonzales.

We will be visiting Plymouth, Massachusetts.

They had a picnic on Angel Island in San Francisco.

*Rule:* The title of a person preceding his or her name.

*Example:* Tell Uncle Harry to call Senator Wong.

*Rule:* Names of organizations and companies.

*Examples:* Girl Scouts, Chamber of Commerce, Elks Club, General Motors™

*Rule:* Periods of time—months, days, holidays.

*Examples:* We will visit on the fourth Tuesday of July.

The parade will be on Memorial Day.

*Rule:* Adjectives derived from proper names.

*Examples:* Japanese art, Mexican food, Oriental rugs

*Rule:* Titles of books, magazines, and newspapers.

*Examples:* A popular book in 1990 was *All I Really Need to Know I Learned in Kindergarten.*

Many people read *The New York Times.*

We have a subscription to *Sunset* magazine.

*Rule:* Directions when they refer to specific sections of the country.

*Examples:* The office will move to the South for cheaper labor.

The job is offered on the East Side of town.

*Rule:* Personal titles when they refer to specific persons.

*Example:* The President of General Motors will be at the meeting.

*Rule:* The first word of the salutation of a letter and the first word of the closing.

*Examples:* Dear Ms. Jones

Yours truly

*Rule:* The first word of a direct quotation.

*Example:* Mary Jane said, "Please wait for me."

*Rule:* In hyphenated words, the words you would ordinarily capitalize.

*Example:* We plan to leave in mid-April.

# WORD DIVISION

Maintaining a consistent right margin is very important for the overall appearance of all keyed work. Word processing software will make word division decisions automatically. However, if you must decide where to divide a word at the right margin, remember that words can be divided only between syllables. The following rules are preferred:

1. Never divide words of one syllable:

   curl, halves, raze

2. Divide compound words where the two words join:

   hair/line, house/coat, land/lady, over/power

3. Divide hyphenated words at the point of hyphenation; keep the hyphen at the end of the right margin:

   self-esteem, one-half

4. Do not divide names, dates, or addresses:

   Senator Alvin Wong, January 23, 2002, 239 Lincoln Avenue

5. Do not divide abbreviations or contractions:

   PT&T, PG&E, can't, didn't, wouldn't

6. Divide after a prefix and before a suffix:

   intra/state, post/script, regi/ment, wordi/ness

7. When a single-letter syllable comes within a word, divide between the letters:

   chari/oteer, concili/ation, evalu/ation, extenu/ation

Although word processing and other software have changed line-division rules, good business practice requires the following:

- Bring at least 3 letters to the second line.
- Avoid leaving fewer than 3 letters on the first line.
- Avoid having several hyphenated lines in the same paragraph. Only one hyphen to a paragraph is a good rule to follow.
- Avoid dividing the last word of a paragraph or of a page.

Remember, you, the keyboarder, may be concerned about keeping the right margin even. However, reading several divided lines is much more difficult for the reader. Think of your clients!

# RÉSUMÉS

Many times, the first step in landing a job is submitting a résumé. An ad in the newspaper, a telephone call, or an inquiry may provide the impetus to put yourself on paper. Your résumé must be neatly keyed and provide the right information.

The information in the résumé must fit the job for which you are applying; however, you need to follow some basic rules. All résumés should contain at least the following:

▪ identification
▪ education
▪ experience
▪ references

Résumés will vary according to the person and according to the position available. However, some good general guidelines are:

▪ Provide a brief description of current and previous job duties. Explain in detail, but use brief phrases. Do not be repetitive.

▪ Use action verbs when describing past duties. Examples are *managed, produced, sold, trained, handled.*

▪ Include any special skills or knowledge, such as a foreign language.

▪ Be neat. Be sure the copy is free of errors. Place the information evenly on the paper.

▪ Try to keep the résumé to one page and definitely no more than two.

▪ If you photocopy your résumé, be sure the copy is top grade.

Figures A.4 and A.5 show samples of résumés.

## FIGURE A.4 • Résumé 1

Elvira Lopez
115 Tanglewood Drive
Eastmont, MA 02365-1155
(213) 555-1252

**EDUCATION**
2002        Eastmont Business College, Associate Arts Degree, Office Administration
            Eastmont, Massachusetts

1997        Eastmont High School, Eastmont, Massachusetts
            Graduated with a major in business.

**EXPERIENCE**
1999 to     Boston Insurance, Boston, Massachusetts
present
            Word Processor
            Keyed correspondence from transcription machines.

1997 to     Action Realty, Brookline, Massachusetts
1999
            General Office Clerk
            Answered telephones, keyed letters, keyed forms, sorted mail, made bank deposits.

**REFERENCES**
Ms. Joyce Wong        Mr. Walter Alverez        Dr. Sheila Wakem
963 Eighth Avenue     67 Warren Avenue          26 Second Avenue
Eastmont, MA 02365    Eastmont, MA 02365        Eastmont, MA 02365

## FIGURE A.5 • Résumé 2

Robert Mar
96 Ocean Avenue
Green Valley, CA 95261-1196
(707) 555-1050

OBJECTIVE      An entry-level keyboard operator position where I am able to use my skills and achieve growth and advancement.

SKILLS         Keyboarding—60 wpm
               Personal computer
               10-Key Calculator by Touch
               Machine Transcription
               Basic Filing
               Software: Microsoft Word, Excel, Access, WordPerfect, PowerPoint

TRAINING       Regional Occupational Program
               Office Occupations Class
               Green Valley, California

EDUCATION      Green Valley High School
               Second and Downey
               Green Valley, California

WORK           Federal Records Center
EXPERIENCE     San Bruno, California
               Duties: Filing and retrieving income tax forms
               2000 to 2002

               J. Gorman Warehouse
               Brisbane, California
               Duties: Inventory, stock, and labeling
               1999 to 2000

REFERENCES     Available upon request.

# MANUSCRIPTS AND REPORTS

Many times on your job, you will be asked to key a business report. Sometimes, you may have a manuscript to prepare for a publisher or a college class. Following are instructions for preparing these reports and manuscripts.

## Spacing and Margins

Manuscripts may be single-space, double-space, or space-and-a-half. Double-spacing is the easiest to read; however, many businesses presently tend to use the space-and-a-half.

Setting margins will depend on whether your report will be bound or unbound. For reports to be bound at the top, use the following guidelines:

- First page has 2.5-inch top margin.
- All other pages have 1.5-inch top margin.
- All pages have 1-inch bottom margin.
- Side margins are 1 inch.

For reports to be bound on the left side, use these guidelines:

- First page has 2-inch top margin.
- All other pages have 1-inch top margin.
- All pages have 1-inch bottom margin.
- Left-side margin is 1.5-inches, right is 1 inch.

## Titles, Headings, Subheadings

Key the title centered and capitalized on page 1 (see "Spacing and Margins" section above for how far down). Triple-space after the title.

Key subheadings at the left margin in all-capital letters. For spacing after subheadings, (1) if you indent, use the same spacing as in a report; (2) if you use block style, leave one extra line.

## Page Numbers

The number on page 1 can be centered and keyed ½ inch from the bottom of the page. However, if the title is on the first page, many people omit the page number.

All other pages are numbered at the top right margin, 3 lines down.

Note: Key the number only. Do not use the word *page* or the hyphen.

## Title Page

Depending on the size and formality of a report, you may want to prepare a title page. The title page will always contain the following:

- title of the report (centered)
- author of the report (centered)

The title may contain the following:

- name of the business
- date

## Bibliography

Credit is given at the end of a report to the sources of information used in the report. The bibliography is usually the last page of the report. Use the following rules for the bibliography:

- List the sources in alphabetic order.
- Include the names of the author, publication, and publisher and the date.
- Key the first line of each item at the left margin, with all other lines indented.
- Single-space lines.
- Use the same margins as in the rest of the report.

## Table of Contents

Depending on the size and formality of a report, you may want to prepare a table of contents. If so, do the following:

- List the main divisions and page numbers.
- Use the same margins as in the rest of the report.
- Use leaders between headings and page numbers.

# PROOFREADER'S MARKS

| Mark | Meaning | Example | Correction |
|------|---------|---------|------------|
| ≡ | uppercase | in the united states | in the United States |
| ⌒ | close up | mix the e ggs and milk | mix the eggs and milk |
| ∽ | transpose | run to cath up | run to catch up |
| ∧ | insert something | ask the big question | ask the big question |
| ℰ | delete (take out) | a large gaudy box | a large box |
| # | space | now is thetime | now is the time |
| / | lowercase | try not to Worry | try not to worry |
| ◯ | spell out | ask Dr. Shay | ask Doctor Shay |
| ∿ | boldface | We have five guests. | We have **five** guests. |
| ¶ | paragraph | Buy it now. If you wait . . . | Buy it now.<br>If you wait . . . |
| stet | leave words in | Do not stop on the way. | Do not stop on the way. |
| ⊙ | insert a period | Come in today⊙ | Come in today. |
| ∧∨ | insert punctuation | If they go we stay.<br>Johns sweater | If they go, we stay.<br>John's sweater |
| ⌐ | move left | ⌐Use this one. | Use this one. |
| ⌐⌐ | move right | Never stop reading.⌐⌐ |          Never stop reading. |

# Glossary

## A

**Accounting cycle** The process of recording, classifying, and summarizing financial information for owners, managers, and other interested parties for a specified period of time (monthly, quarterly, yearly).

**Active listening** A restatement of the sender's total communication to help the sender understand the message as the receiver views it.

**Agenda** A listing of events—reports and discussions—to take place during a meeting and the topics to be covered.

**Aggressive communication** An exchange of information that occurs when a person overstates what he or she wants and is overbearing, bossy, and pushy, and fails to consider the needs of others.

**Alphabetic filing method** The method of arranging files in order beginning with *A* and ending with *Z*. The most conventional and widely used filing method.

**Alternative work systems** Nontraditional working arrangements that include office sharing, job sharing, flextime, and telecommuting.

**Annotating mail** The process of underlining important facts and making comments or special notations in the margin of a letter.

**Appendix** A section of a report that contains supplementary information, such as charts, graphs, or tables, and that usually follows the body of a business report.

**Aptitude** The potential for learning a skill.

**Assertive communication** An exchange of information that occurs when a person states what she or he wants clearly and directly, without animosity, being firm yet considerate of others' needs.

**Assertiveness** The ability to communicate one's needs to others confidently without being aggressive.

**Assets** Everything of value that a company owns.

**Attachment notation** A notation used in place of the enclosure notation when something is stapled or attached to a letter or memorandum.

## B

**Back-office jobs** Positions that involve little or no contact with the public.

**Balance sheet** A financial statement that shows the assets, liabilities, and capital—or net worth—of a business at a particular time.

**Bar code sorter (BCS)** A special piece of equipment used by postal centers to sort or separate mail into geographic areas after the ZIP Codes have been converted to bar codes.

**Benefits** The extra payments or services, in addition to a salary or wage, that people receive from their employers. Also called *fringe benefits*.

**Bibliography** A listing of all sources used to write a business report; usually appears at the end of the report.

**Block letter format** The format in which an entire letter is keyed even with the left margin. The letter format most commonly used in industry.

**Body** In a business letter, the major part, consisting of paragraphs that provide the reason for the letter.

**Body language** Nonverbal communication through physical action.

## C

**Call screening** The process of determining who is calling to allow the person being called to accept or decline the call.

**Centralized filing system** A system in which a company's general files are stored in one central location.

**Centralized mail department** An area where all the mail in a large company is processed.

**Chronological filing method** The method of arranging files in order by date.

**Civil service jobs** Government positions with federal, state, county, and city agencies.

**Closing** In a business letter, the part that follows the body. The two most common *closings* in a business letter are "Very truly yours" and "Sincerely."

**Communication** The sending and receiving of information. The communication process includes a sender and a receiver.

**Compact disk (CD)** A flat, round, portable, metal storage medium. Also called an *optical disk*.

**Compact disk–read-only memory (CD-ROM)**
A prerecorded optical disk with high storage capacity, suitable for storing both sound and images. Used for storing large, infrequently updated information, such as encyclopedias, and for storing multimedia files.

**Compact disk–recordable (CD-R)** A compact disk onto which data may be recorded by writing on one part of the disk or all of it at one time. Data may be recorded on each part only one time, and cannot be erased.

**Compact disk–rewritable (CD-RW)** An erasable disk to which data may be written multiple times.

**Complete Guide for Occupational Exploration** A U.S. Department of Labor publication that organizes jobs into twelve interest areas and further divides those areas into work groups and subgroups.

**Computer** An electronic device, operating under the control of instructions stored in its own memory, that accepts data as input, processes that data arithmetically and logically, produces usable output, and stores the results for future use.

**Computer monitoring** The use of computers to observe an employee's work habits to help find ways to make the employee more efficient.

**Computer network** A combination of computer devices—computers, terminals, or other hardware devices—connected by an electronic communications system.

**Computer system** A group of computer devices that are connected, coordinated, and linked in such a way that they work as one to complete a task.

**Computerized accounting system** A set of organized procedures used to collect and record accounting data with the use of a computer.

**Conference call** A telephone feature or special service that allows three or more parties in several locations to participate in a call.

**Confidential mail** Letters that should be opened only by the person to whom they are addressed.

**Connectivity** The concept of connecting the people and computers of a work group electronically over a network, regardless of geographic location, giving equal support to all members.

**Constructive criticism** Suggestions that will help employees do their jobs better.

**Cover letter** A letter that always accompanies a résumé and that simply states how an applicant learned about a particular job and why she or he is especially interested in that job.

**Co-workers** People who work together in a cooperative effort.

**Cross-functional teams** The reengineering approach of using disparate employees working together in a way that makes them aware of changes that may affect their jobs.

**Cross-reference** A notation filed in one place to refer searchers to look in another place for a document.

**Customer** An individual inside or outside an organization who depends on the output of its efforts; anyone who receives the work completed.

# D

**Data projector** A device that projects an image from a computer screen onto a larger screen so that an audience can see the image clearly.

**Database management** The use of a computer rather than a manual system to store, manipulate, retrieve, and create reports from data and information.

**Database management software** Computer programs that perform recordkeeping and information tasks. Often called an *electronic file cabinet*.

**Decimal placeholders** Numbers to the right of a decimal point.

**Default margins** Preset margins in a word processing program.

**Desktop publishing (DTP)** A process of assembling words and illustrations onto pages, often in a columnar format. The documents are usually printed on a high-quality printer. Used for newsletters, reports, manuals, brochures, ads, and other documents that incorporate text with graphics.

**Dictionary of Occupational Titles** A U.S. Department of Labor publication that contains descriptions of more than twenty thousand jobs.

**Digital camera** A camera used to take photographs that are stored digitally. The digital images may be downloaded or transferred to a computer. The photographs may be edited with photoediting software, printed, faxed, sent via electronic mail, or posted onto a Web site.

**Digital versatile disk (DVD)** An optical storage medium with improved capacity and bandwidth compared with the compact disk. Also know as *digital videodisk*.

**Dividend** A number that is divided.

**Divisor** A number by which another number is divided.

**Document imaging** A process of scanning or creating a document with a personal computer linked with a scanner or fax, and then sending it to a linked copier to be duplicated.

**Downward communication** Communication that follows the organization's formal chain of command from top to bottom.

# E

**Electronic files** Information stored on a computer hard drive or on more permanent disks.

**Electronic mail (e-mail)** A system used to exchange messages among users of a computer network and the programs that support such message transfers.

**Employment Development Department (EDD)** A state department that handles unemployment job placement.

**Employment tests** Instruments used to determine an applicant's qualifications for a particular job. Examples include skills and aptitude tests, psychological tests, and general abilities tests.

**Empowerment** The act of giving employees closest to the customer the authority and tools required to make many independent decisions.

**Enclosure notation** The word *enclosure* keyed at the bottom of a business letter to indicate that something is being enclosed or included with the letter.

**Encryption** Any procedure used to convert plain text into a mathematical code to prevent anyone but the intended recipient from reading it. Encoding or writing in code.

**Ergonomics** The study of the relationship between people and their work environment.

**Esteem** The degree to which people value themselves and others. Part of a person's self-concept.

**E-ticket** An electronic airline ticket stored in an airline's computer system.

**Expenses** The costs a business incurs as it buys the resources it needs to produce and market its goods and services.

**Extrovert** A person who has an outgoing personality.

# F

**Facsimile (fax)** A machine that translates copies of text or graphics documents into electronic signals and transmits them over telephone lines or via satellite to another such machine that translates them back into visual images and prints the document.

**Feedback** Verbal and nonverbal responses that the receiver gives by further communicating with the original sender or another person.

**Field** A unit of information in a database system.

**File** A collection of records that share the same format, or have the same fields, in a database management system.

**Filtering** The tendency for a message to be watered down or halted completely at some point during transmission.

**Flextime** A system for allowing workers to set their own times for beginning and finishing work within a range of available hours.

**Floater** An employee who works in different departments of a company for various periods of time.

**Floppy disk** A portable, inexpensive storage medium consisting of a thin, circular, flexible plastic disk.

**Formal groups** Groups that are deliberately created and set up by management to obtain organizational goals and objectives.

**Fraction equivalents** Fractions that are equal to given percentages.

**Fringe benefits** See *Benefits*.

**Full-time work schedule** A plan under which employees work a standard forty-hour week.

# G

**Geographic filing method** The method of arranging, or grouping, files according to geographic location.

**Gigabyte (GB)** A measure of computer storage capacity equal to approximately 1 billion bytes.

**Grapevine** The transmission of information by word of mouth without regard for organizational levels.

**Graphical user interface (GUI)** An operating system that instructs a computer through visual methods rather than text-based commands. The operator uses icons to represent programs, files, and menus in a windows environment.

**Graphics software** Computer programs that present numeric data clearly and quickly in visual form.

**Greeting** In a business letter, the part that follows the letter address and usually consists of the word *dear* followed by the name of the person receiving the letter. Also called the *salutation*.

**Grievance process** The method a company uses to allow employees to state their side in disputes with supervisors or other employees.

**Group** Two or more people who interact with each other personally in order to achieve a common goal.

**Groupthink** The tendency of members of highly cohesive groups to lose their critical individual evaluative abilities and, out of a desire for unanimity, to overlook realistic, meaningful alternatives as attitudes are formed and decisions are made.

**Groupware** A combination of electronic technology and group processes that allows individual computer users to be part of a team and to share information.

# H

**Handheld computer** A small computer, sometimes called a *palmtop computer,* because it will fit into a user's hand.

**Hard copy** Computer output created at a printer that is a permanent printed copy of processed information.

**Hard disk** A thin, rigid metallic platter that records data in magnetic form, providing nonvolatile, or permanent, storage, usually within the system unit.

**Hidden agenda** A personal goal based on attitudes and feelings that an individual brings to a group.

**High-capacity disk** A disk that has a storage capacity of 100 MB or greater.

**Horizontal organization** A company that has a skeleton group of senior executives at the top in traditional support functions such as finance and human resources, with everyone else working together in cross-functional teams that perform the core processes such as production and sales.

**Human relations** How people get along with one another. Also called *interpersonal relations*.

**Hypertext markup language (HTML)** A language used for describing how pages of text, graphics, and other information are organized, formatted, and linked on the World Wide Web.

# I

**Image editing** A skill used to manipulate photographs and graphic art so that images are more pleasing or have greater impact.

**Income statement** A summary of all income and expenses for a certain time period such as a month or a year.

**Indexing** The process of keying the name of a person or company in its proper order on a file folder or card.

**Informal groups** Groups that arise spontaneously at all levels of a company.

**Integrated software** The combination of several independent software packages, such as word processing, spreadsheet, graphics, and database, for coordinated use in one package.

**Interest survey** An instrument containing a list of statements describing a variety of activities. Sometimes called an *interest inventory* or *interest test*.

**Internet** The world's largest network, consisting of a collection of computers and devices connected through modems, cables, telephone lines, and satellites.

**Interpersonal relations** See **Human relations**.

**Introvert** A person with a quiet personality.

**Itinerary** A listing of travel plans that includes flight numbers, departure and arrival times and places, hotel accommodation information, and car rental information.

# J

**Job lead card** An index card on which a job seeker records all relevant information about an available job.

**Job sharing** An arrangement in which two people divide responsibility for a single job.

**Just-in-time hiring** The practice of employing temporary workers to complete only a specific project, on short notice, and without a training period.

## K

**Keyboard** The input device usually used to enter data and instructions into a computer. Most keyboards consist of the typewriter keypad, the cursor movement keys, the numeric keypad, and the function keypad. Also called a *terminal* when connected with a monitor.

## L

**Lateral communication** Horizontal communication that occurs between departments or functional units, usually as a coordinating or problem-solving effort.

**Lateral files** Storage cabinets in which drawers rest sideways.

**Leaders** Periods used across the space between a topic name and its page number in a table of contents.

**Letter address** In a business letter, the part that follows the date and includes the name, title, company name, and address of the person receiving the letter.

**Letter of application** A sales letter in which an applicant describes all of his or her qualifications and tries to convince an employer that he or she is the best person for a particular job.

**Letter of inquiry** A letter inquiring whether a specified type of job is available.

**Liabilities** A business's financial obligations or debts.

**Lifestyle goal** The way a person wants to live in the future.

**Local area network (LAN)** A computer and communications network covering a limited geographic area. Does not require a central node or processor.

**Lose-lose negotiating style** A bargaining method used by one party who attempts to win at the expense of the other but ultimately creates problems for both parties.

## M

**Mainframe** A large, powerful computer that can handle many users at the same time, process large volumes of data at incredibly high speeds, and in many cases store millions of characters in primary memory.

**Management information system (MIS)** An integrated computer system that provides information critical for decision making.

**Memorandum** A written document that is less formal than a letter and is sent to other employees within a company; it contains the headings To, From, Date, and Subject. Also called a *memo*.

**Microsoft Office user specialist (MOUS)** Certification for desktop proficiency on Microsoft Office applications.

**Mid-range server** A larger and more powerful computer than a workstation computer. These computer systems often can support up to 4,000 connected users at a time.

**Minutes** A record of who attended a meeting and what actually took place.

**Mixed punctuation** The punctuation rule that in a letter, a colon is used after the greeting and a comma is used after the closing. The preferred punctuation rule in the business world.

**Mobile files** Portable cabinets containing file folders that may be moved from one location to another.

**Modified block letter format** The format in which the date and closing of a letter begin at the center of the page.

**Modular design** A plan in which a structure is made of pieces that can easily be taken apart, rearranged, and put back together.

**Monitor** A computer display device that allows users to see what they have entered into a computer. It resembles a television screen and may be monochrome or color.

**Mouse** A hardware device attached to a keyboard and used for pointing and for moving the cursor-like insertion point around the text.

**Multifunctional equipment** A combination of several types of office equipment such as printer, copier, scanner, and fax.

## N

**Negative attitude** A bad mental position characterized by low self-esteem and a tendency to blame others for one's own shortcomings. Workers with a *negative attitude* are unpleasant and indifferent; they rarely smile, and they constantly complain.

**Net income** The amount of money that remains after expenses are subtracted from revenues. Commonly called the *bottom line.*

**Network operating system (NOS)** A special control program in the server within a LAN that handles the requests for data from all users on the network.

**Networking** The process of contacting people who might be able to help a job hunter find job leads.

**Node** A workstation, terminal, computer, or other device in a computer network.

**Numeric filing method** The method of arranging files in numeric order, according to numbers assigned to the files.

## O

**Occupational Outlook Handbook** A U.S. Department of Labor publication that contains detailed information on the skills required for more than 250 occupations. Updated every two years.

**Office workflow** The activity that revolves around the processing of information in an office.

**Open punctuation** The punctuation rule stating that in a business letter no punctuation is used after the greeting, and no punctuation is used after the closing.

**Open-shelf files** File containers that resemble open bookshelves.

**Operating system (OS)** A set of programs containing instructions that coordinate all activities among computer hardware resources.

**Organizational chart** The way in which the levels of authority are determined.

**Owner's equity** The claim that an owner has against a firm's assets.

## P

**Partitions** Panels used to separate areas or divide a large area into smaller work spaces.

**Passive communication** The exchange of information that occurs when people do not say what they want or, if they do, are apologetic and feel guilty.

**Percentage** A share of a whole.

**Performance evaluation** A written statement outlining the strengths and weaknesses of an employee's job performance.

**Personal computer** A computer unit containing memory, a keyboard for entering data, a monitor for displaying the data entered through the keyboard, one or two disk drives for storing files on disks, and a printer for producing final copy.

**Personal digital assistant (PDA)** A lightweight handheld computer that provides personal organizer functions such as a calendar, an appointment book, an address book, a calculator, and a notepad.

**Personality** The outward reflection of a person's inner self, apparent in how that person looks, speaks, and acts.

**Petty cash payments** Small payments made with currency from an office fund, rather than with checks.

**Portable skills** Abilities that can be used in new situations.

**Positive attitude** A good mental position characterized by a high level of self-esteem and respect for other people's views. Workers with a *positive attitude* are pleasant to be around, have many interests, smile easily, and rarely complain.

**Previewing** In effective reading, the practice of scanning the selection, looking for main points, and discovering how the material is organized.

**Priorities** Preferences in the order of work activities, usually decided according to levels of importance or deadlines.

**Priority mail** First-class mail weighing more than 13 ounces.

**Private employment agencies** Organizations that are not supported by taxes and that charge a fee for finding people jobs.

**Probation** A period of time usually lasting three to six months after a person is hired, during which the employee does not accrue benefits.

**Productivity** The total work accomplished in a given period of time.

**Program** See **Software**.

**Proofreaders' marks** Standard symbols that most office workers use on rough drafts of documents to show changes and corrections that need to be made to those documents.

**Prorated** An amount that is divided by percentages among two or more entities.

**Public employment agencies** Organizations that provide job referral service free of charge because they are supported by taxes and operated by the federal or state government.

# R

**Random-access memory (RAM)** The temporary, high-speed memory area in a computer system unit, active only when the computer is on, where programs and documents are stored while in use. Also called *main memory* or *primary storage*.

**Read-only memory (ROM)** Permanently stored instructions, most frequently parts of an operating system's software that checks the hardware when the computer is turned on.

**Reconciliation** The procedure of comparing check stubs or check register entries against a bank's statement or summary of all checking account transactions.

**Record** A unit of information, comprised of fields, about one employee, one inventory item, etc. In a database management system, a set of fields that describes one logical unit of information.

**Reengineering** The stem-to-stern redesign of the way a company works.

**Remuneration** Compensation, or pay, for doing a job. *Remuneration* may include benefits as well as a salary, a wage, or a payment for work accomplished.

**Replacement needs** Needs to fill job openings because people leave occupations.

**Résumé** A form, usually one or two pages in length, that organizes all the facts about an applicant related to the job he or she is seeking.

**Revenues** All funds an organization raises from the sale of its goods and services. Also called *income*.

**Reverse chronological order** The order in which work experience is listed on a résumé. The most recent job is listed first.

**Rotary files** A wheel that contains records and that rotates in a circular motion. The wheel may be a small unit that sits on a desk or a large unit that operates on the floor.

**Routing mail** The process of attaching a routing slip to correspondence and then having each person identified on the routing slip initial the slip after reading the correspondence.

# S

**Safety hazard** Any object or situation that poses a danger or a chance of being injured.

**Scanner** An input device that copies graphic images into a computer and allows text to be entered without rekeying.

**Secretary's Commission on Achieving Necessary Skills (SCANS)** A commission formed in 1990 for the purpose of defining the know-how needed in the modern workplace and considering how this know-how is best assessed. The commission was made up of representatives from business, unions, government, and schools.

**Self-concept** How people feel about themselves.

**Self-realization** Esteem at its highest level; the point at which a person has accomplished all the important goals and aspirations in his or her life and has become the best that he or she can be.

**Self-talk** All the negative and positive thoughts people have about themselves.

**Seminar** A meeting in which information is presented and discussed.

**Seniority** The status of having worked on a job a long time and having gained knowledge and skills through years of experience.

**Server** A computer device and part of a LAN that allows sharing of peripheral devices such as printers and hard-disk units.

**Service-producing industries** Businesses that exist to provide an intangible product, or service, to the public. Examples include the banking, insurance, health care, and education industries.

**Severance pay** Money that a person gets because she or he was severed, or laid off, from a company.

**Shredder** A machine that destroys documents by cutting them into small strips that can then be recycled.

**Software** Sequenced instructions that direct computer hardware in performing assorted tasks. Also called a *program*.

**Sorting mail** The process of arranging or separating mail according to the kind it is and who is to receive it.

**Spreadsheet** A financial planning program that performs mathematical calculations and can record, organize, analyze, and present all sorts of financial and statistical information.

**Standard English** The correct style of speaking and writing that people learn in school and use to communicate in business.

**Subject filing method** The method of arranging files by topics or subjects.

**Supercomputer** The largest, fastest, most expensive computer system available, used primarily for scientific applications requiring complex and lengthy calculations.

**System** The organization and order of a combination of elements or parts.

## T

**Teambuilding** The creation of a work environment that enables and promotes achievement of organizational and individual goals.

**Technology** An aid to make a task easier by the use of equipment and procedures to create, process, and output information.

**Telecommunications** The transfer of data from one place to another over communication lines or channels, including the dissemination of all forms of information, including voice and video.

**Template** A preprogrammed software format for documents such as letters, memorandums, reports, brochures, etc.

**Temporary office workers** Employees who work for a few days or a few weeks at one company until a job is completed.

**Terabyte (TB)** A measure of computer storage capacity equal to approximately 1 trillion bytes.

**Termination** A request for an employee to leave a job.

**Tickler file** A follow-up file that is arranged by dates and used to remind a person of important deadlines and work that is pending for a week, a month, or longer.

**Time management** The art of knowing what needs to be done in a given time frame, setting priorities for projects, and completing projects in the time allotted.

**Time zone** One of four areas of the United States—Eastern, Central, Mountain, and Pacific—in which the same standard time is used. The time changes by one hour as a person moves from one zone to another.

**Touch pad** A flat, rectangular pointing device that is sensitive to pressure and movement. The operator presses on the pad to control the movement of a pointer on a computer screen.

**Track ball** A stationary pointing device with a ball mechanism on its top. The operator rolls the ball to control the movement of a pointer on a screen.

## U

**Unemployment compensation** A small amount of money, administered by the state, that is paid to unemployed workers to help them during the times when no paycheck is being earned.

**Upward communication** Feedback of data or information from lower levels in an organization to upper management levels.

## V

**Values** The things a person believes to be true, important, desirable, and worthwhile such as honesty, integrity, family, friends, industry, and success.

**Virtual organization** An organization defined by its ability to accomplish business goals through collaborative networks. Known for its ability to change rapidly in structure and function. May have little or even no space devoted to production.

**Virtual worker** An employee who works at home or at other locations away from the office, through computer connection with the company's database, fax, telephones, and other innovations.

## W

**W-4 form** A document that all workers in the United States are legally required to fill out and that provides certain information about the amount of taxes a worker will pay through payroll deductions.

**WATS** Wide-Area Telecommunications Service. A telephone feature that provides a volume discount for outbound calls from a given office.

**Win-lose negotiating style** A bargaining method that assumes one side will win by achieving its goals and the other side will lose.

**Win-win negotiating style** The bargaining method that assumes that a solution can be reached that will satisfy the needs of all parties.

**Word processing** The efficient processing of words or text. Also known as *text processing*.

**Word processing software** Computer programs that allow the user to create, edit, format, print, and save text material with greater ease and efficiency than by using a typewriter.

**Work** Any useful activity or purposeful, creative endeavor.

**Work ethic** The idea that everyone should do her or his share and make a contribution to society through working.

**Work values** Values that define needs people expect to fulfill through work.

**Workflow automation** A type of software designed to manage office workflow on a firm's computer network.

**Workplace literacy** A condition in which workers have the basic skills, such as reading and writing skills, to perform assigned tasks satisfactorily.

**Workstations** Areas that are similar to desks except that they are larger and contain more electronic equipment.

# Index